Introduction to
Cross-Cultural Psychology

Critical Thinking and Contemporary Applications

Eric Shiraev

Northern Virginia Community College

David Levy

Pepperdine University

Allyn and Bacon

Boston   London   Toronto   Sydney   Tokyo   Singapore

We dedicate this book to our immediate and extended families, both here and abroad—with deepest respect, eternal gratitude, and boundless love.

Executive Editor: Rebecca Pascal
Series Editorial Assistant: Whitney Brown
Marketing Manager: Caroline Croley
Editorial Production Supervisor: Susan McIntyre
Editorial Production Service: Nesbitt Graphics, Inc.
Composition Buyer: Linda Cox
Manufacturing Buyer: Megan Cochran
Cover Administrator: Kristina Mose-Libon
Electronic Composition: Nesbitt Graphics, Inc.

Copyright © 2001 by Allyn & Bacon
A Pearson Education Company
160 Gould Street
Needham Heights, MA 02494
Internet: www.abacon.com

Library of Congress Cataloging-in-Publication Data

Shiraev, Eric.
    Introduction to cross-cultural psychology: critical thinking and contemporary application/Eric Shiraev, David Levy.
    p. cm.
Includes bibliographical references and index.
    ISBN 0-205-29566-5
    1. Ethnopsychology—Methodology. 2. Cognition and culture. I. Levy, David A., 1954-II. Title.
GN502. S475 2000   00-044756
155.8—dc21

Printed in the United States of America

10 9 8 7 6 5 4 3 2 1   05 04 03 02 01 00

Contents

3 CRITICAL THINKING IN CROSS-CULTURAL PSYCHOLOGY 55

4 COGNITION: SENSATION, PERCEPTION, AND STATES OF CONSCIOUSNESS 99

5 INTELLIGENCE   130

6 EMOTION   164

7 MOTIVATION AND BEHAVIOR 191

8 HUMAN DEVELOPMENT AND SOCIALIZATION 219

9 MENTAL DISORDERS 247

10 SOCIAL PERCEPTION AND SOCIAL COGNITION 277

11 SOCIAL INTERACTION 303

12 APPLIED CROSS-CULTURAL PSYCHOLOGY: SOME HIGHLIGHTS 327

Preface

Welcome to cross-cultural psychology. The field is new and exciting, fascinating in its content, important in its applications, challenging in its goals and aspirations, yet sometimes scarcely able to keep pace with the rapidly changing conditions of modern times.

Look at the world around us. Previously invincible barriers—both literal and metaphoric—that have separated people for hundreds, even thousands of years are increasingly cracking, crumbling, and finally collapsing before our eyes. Within a relatively brief period of history, the telephone, radio, television, motion pictures, and, more recently, computers, e-mail, and the worldwide web are drastically altering our perceptions of time, space, and each other. One key click and, in an instant, you are virtually on the opposite side of the planet. Or even on a different planet.

We travel and migrate from one place to another on a scale previously unknown—even unimaginable—in human history. The United States alone naturalizes almost one million new citizens and hosts nearly a half million international students every year. More than 20 European countries are moving toward their economic and political unification. After more than 40 years of East versus West antagonism, a wall in Berlin came tumbling down and Germany once again was whole. Hong Kong has been reunited with China. From Northern Ireland to the Middle East, centuries of bloody ethnic and religious conflicts seem to be closer than ever to some kind of peaceful resolution. People of widely different cultures appear to be getting closer and closer to one another. The world is indeed becoming a smaller place.

Or is it? Are such beliefs devoid of factual foundation, resting more on wishful thinking and naive optimism than empirical evidence? Are we guilty of committing the Naturalistic Fallacy, confusing what "is" with what "ought" to be? Some people contend that the basic differences between cultural groups are, and always will be, irreconcilable. Pundits argue that what appears to be "civilization," "cultural enlightenment," and "social evolution" are largely illusory. Beneath this perilously thin veneer lurks raw human nature: selfish, greedy, even violent. To be sure, some progress has occurred. But more and more countries are becoming split along ethnic and religious lines. Minority groups around the world continue to be ostracized, threatened, assaulted, and the target of both systematic and random acts of discrimination. Some politicians question the universality of human rights, sociologists point out that ethnic groups do not naturally "blend" together, and the number of intercultural marriages is still low. There is also an undeniable increase in international tensions and ethnic conflicts.

Consider Bosnia, Rwanda, Sierra Leone, Timor, Kosovo, Punjab, and Cyprus; is there any valid reason to believe that the list will not continue to grow?

Even if the world is becoming smaller, what does this mean? To some individuals, "smaller" implies a sense of community, connectedness, and camaraderie. But to others, it is tantamount to cramped, crowded, and confining. Where does that leave us and where are we headed?

In searching for answers to questions such as these, we discovered an enormous body of theories, research, books, journal articles, and websites. On closer examination, however, what emerged was not particularly encouraging or even useful: lots of unsupported theories, lots of contradictory findings, lots of defensiveness and emotionally charged posturing, and lots of thinking that was a great deal less than clear. How do we even begin to sort through all of it? Is there a way to separate the proverbial wheat from the chaff? By what means can we thereby make informed decisions? These are some of the questions that we (the authors) have been struggling with for some time. And, in a nutshell, they are largely what prompted us to write this book.

The background leading to our collaboration is briefly worth noting. Although we are of a similar age and share a number of common characteristics (from career choice to taste in music), we grew up in very different worlds. Eric Shiraev was born and raised in the city of Leningrad in the former Soviet Union, where he obtained his first academic degrees and published his first book. David Levy is from southern California, where he received his formal education and training, and where he currently works as a psychology professor, psychotherapist, and researcher. Thus, each of us brings a distinctly unique set of experiences and perceptions to this project. We were struck by both the similarities and differences in our respective backgrounds, and we sought to utilize these complementary contributions to maximum effect.

In discussing our past, we discovered that as we were entering college, neither of us knew very much about cross-cultural psychology. By the time we started graduate school (at Leningrad State University and at UCLA), our interest had begun to grow. But the real fascination with cross-cultural psychology emerged much later, specifically when each of us spent an extended period of time teaching in the other's home country. The appeal has never waned, and continues to this day.

Goals of This Book

We have endeavored to distill and synthesize the knowledge gained from our own respective educational, research, training, and life experiences into a manageable set of four primary goals.

- To introduce the field of cross-cultural psychology to undergraduate college students.
- To understand contemporary theories and research in cross-cultural psychology.

- To provide the reader—both instructors and students—with a useful set of critical thinking tools with which to examine, analyze, and evaluate the field of cross-cultural psychology in particular, and education in general.
- To assist current and future practitioners from a wide variety of fields and services.

Intended Audiences

This book was designed with the following readers in mind:

1. As a primary or supplementary text for undergraduate college students from a diverse array of majors (including but not limited to psychology, sociology, anthropology, education, philosophy, journalism, political science, etc.).
2. As a supplementary text for graduate students in areas such as psychology, social work, education, law, journalism, nursing, business, and public administration.
3. Clinical psychologists, counselors, and social workers.
4. Educators and other practitioners who work in contemporary multicultural environments.

Brief Overview

The book consists of 12 chapters. Chapters 1 and 2 review the key theories, approaches, and research methods of cross-cultural psychology. Chapter 3 introduces principles of critical thinking and applies these tools directly to topics in cross-cultural psychology by identifying common errors and providing useful antidotes. Chapter 4 focuses on cross-cultural aspects of sensation, perception, and states of consciousness. The fifth chapter is devoted to the interface of cross-cultural psychology and intelligence. Chapters 6 and 7 are comprised of cross-cultural analyses of motivation and emotion, respectively. Issues related to human development and socialization are examined in Chapter 8. Chapter 9 focuses on the diagnosis, treatment, and explanation of mental disorders from cross-cultural perspectives. The topics in Chapters 10 and 11 concern cross-cultural accounts of social perception and interaction. Last, Chapter 12 identifies several applied problems of cross-cultural psychology in contemporary American society.

What Makes This Book Different?

Emphasis on Critical Thinking

We firmly believe that critical thinking is perhaps the most vital and indispensable component of higher education and learning. Despite widespread consensus about this assertion throughout the educational community, however, it has been our experience that specific tools for critical thinking are rarely, if ever, provided to students during the course of their schooling. In other words, people may be convinced of the value of critical thinking, but they are left not knowing quite what to do about it. This book seeks to remedy that dilemma.

We view critical thinking as a series of skills that can be successfully taught and learned. As such, we provide the reader with specific strategies, methods, and techniques (along with lots of practice) to achieve this goal. For purposes of this book, each critical thinking principle ("Metathought") is illustrated primarily from the theory and application of contemporary cross-cultural psychology. Keep in mind, however, that these principles transcend the confines of any particular topic and can be utilized in a diverse array of fields.

In one sense, we use critical thinking to teach cross-cultural psychology; in another, we use cross-cultural psychology to teach critical thinking. This bidirectional relationship underscores the interdependence between the "content" and the "process" of thinking and learning.

Pedagogical Features to Enhance Learning

We have included a variety of pedagogical devices throughout the text.

- **Exercises and Activities.** There are more than 30 exercises strategically placed throughout the book. These can be used in any number of ways, including classroom discussions, demonstrations, debates, individual or group take-home assignments, term papers, and oral presentations. Boxes entitled "Critical Thinking" were designed explicitly to provide practice in developing critical thinking skills as they relate to cross-cultural psychology.
- **Chapter Summaries and list of Key Terms with definitions** appear at the conclusion of every chapter.
- **List of Suggested Readings:** These features appear on the book's website.
- **"A Case in Point"** boxes: In some instances, vivid examples or stories are best able to speak for themselves. In each chapter these boxes review and illustrate a number of controversial issues in cross-cultural psychology, display cases and research findings, and introduce various opinions about human behavior in different cultural contexts.
- **"Cross-Cultural Sensitivity"** boxes: These boxes present some controversial remarks, statements, and actions that underscore the importance of empathy in interpersonal communications.
- **Quotations:** Scores of quotations appear throughout the text. These are intended to serve a number of functions: to provide divergent points of view, to pique the reader's interest and curiosity, to utilize humor as a means of facilitating learning, and to induce critical thinking. Sources include Dr. Martin Luther King, Jr., Omar Khayyam, Confucius, Mohandas Gandhi, Laotse,

Albert Einstein, P. T. Barnum, Vladimir Nabokov, R. D. Laing, Jackie Mason, Miguel de Cervantes, the Bible, and common folk proverbs from a variety of cultures (Chinese, Russian, Yiddish).

- **Vignettes:** Each chapter begins with a vignette, a description of a real-life case, situation, or problem related to the chapter's subject.

Additional support for the text can be found on our Website at www.abacon.com/shiraev.

Focus on Applied Contemporary Problems in American Society

We have dedicated ourselves to making this text as useful, practical, and relevant as possible. As a result, we made it a point to address a variety of applied contemporary themes and to present cross-cultural analyses for a series of complex problems that American society faces today, or is likely to face in both the near and distant future. Throughout, we attempted to strike a balance between not making the book too theoretical (and, therefore, not particularly useful in the real world) or too concrete (which would not cultivate independent thinking).

Last, we wish to make our own values clear and not to present them as if they were "facts" or "truths." We believe that despite all the ethnic, cultural, religious, racial, and national differences, people can (and in fact should) learn to become more understanding, respectful, and tolerant of each other. Without appearing unduly optimistic, we do have faith in the enormous potential power of knowledge, reason, and compassion to help realize these goals.

It is true that cross-cultural psychology alone cannot solve the profound problems facing the human race. However, knowledge coupled with good will certainly can create a positive psychological climate that might eventually generate useful solutions. We hope that our enthusiasm about cross-cultural psychology and critical thinking is contagious and will serve to enhance your own academic, professional, and personal growth.

Acknowledgments

No project of this magnitude could have been realized without the invaluable contributions, assistance, and support of scores of individuals. We have benefited from the insightful feedback and advice of colleagues, from the diligent efforts of research assistants, and from the patience and understanding of family members and friends. In particular we wish to acknowledge Maykami L. McClure, Kristen N. Dial, Elizabeth Laugeson, Beth Levy, Jacob Levy, Lucy Levy, Dmitry Shiraev, Dennis Shiraev, Thomas Szasz, Fuji Collins, Evangeline Wheeler, Alex Main, Susan Siaw, Sergei V. Tsytsarev, Cheryl Koopman, Richard Sobel, Gerald Boyd, Vlad Zubok, Diana Smith, Joseph Morris, Judith A. Farrell, William M. Lamers, and Vinnie DeStefano. We can never thank them enough.

We would also like to thank reviewers G. William Hill, Kennesaw State University; Jill Norvilitis, Buffalo State University; Yvonne Wells, Suffolk University; and Evangeline Wheeler, Towson State University for their insightful comments.

A special word of appreciation is due to the administrations, faculty, staff, and students at our respective academic institutions (Pepperdine University, George Mason University, and Northern Virginia Community College), where we have consistently been provided with an abundance of encouragement, assistance, and validation. We also would like to take this opportunity to acknowledge the tremendous support we received at every stage of this project's development from the team at Allyn and Bacon, in particular, Rebecca Pascal, Carolyn Merrill, Joyce Nilsen, Amy Goldmacher, Susan McIntyre, and Bridgett Dougherty at Nesbitt Graphics. Last, on a more personal note, we wish to express our mutual feelings of thankfulness for our relationship to each other as collaborators, as colleagues, as comrades, and as friends.

Eric Shiraev
David Levy

CHAPTER 1

Understanding Cross-Cultural Psychology

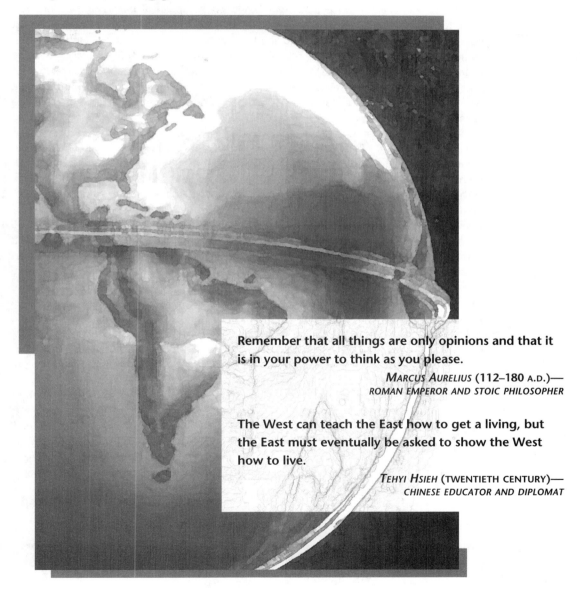

Remember that all things are only opinions and that it is in your power to think as you please.

MARCUS AURELIUS (112–180 A.D.)—
ROMAN EMPEROR AND STOIC PHILOSOPHER

The West can teach the East how to get a living, but the East must eventually be asked to show the West how to live.

TEHYI HSIEH (TWENTIETH CENTURY)—
CHINESE EDUCATOR AND DIPLOMAT

Any person who fears persecution because of his or her race, nationality, ethnicity, orientation, political values, or religious beliefs may seek asylum in the United States. Maria Gonzalez, a schoolteacher, was a native of Nicaragua. She and her minor daughter fled their country and sought political asylum in the United States. However, immigration officials denied her claim for asylum. As a last legal resort, Maria asked the court not to deport her from the United States because she feared she and her daughter would be killed as soon as they got back in Nicaragua. Her fear of persecution was based on her political beliefs and actions she undertook under the Sandinistas—a political regime in the 1980s. She stated in her court papers that she feared for her "life and liberties" because of her "counterrevolutionary" activities in her home country in the past. A judge, however, argued that Nicaragua became a democratic country and the new government should grant amnesty to all people for past civil and criminal misdeeds. Therefore, according to the judge, Maria did not have a well-founded fear of persecution and should be deported from the United States back to Nicaragua.

There won't be any dramatic escapes, sudden turns, and bizarre revelations. This is the end of the story. What we have here is a simple decision. Judge A decided that person B should not be afraid to get back to her home country because—from Judge A's standpoint—everything is all right there now. But please, hold on! Can a judge, sitting in a comfortable chair in the United States Court of Appeals, know and understand what people do, need, want, and feel in a small country wounded by many years of a civil war? Can people of different cultures understand each other's fears? Can people who were born and raised in free societies sense this crippling feeling of being a small cog under a colossal, omnipotent, and frightening machine of the authoritarian government? Can outsiders understand that even though democracy may be formally declared in any place on earth, people's customs, prejudice, hatred, and fears stay? Maria argued in her case that no matter what kind of government exists in the capital city of Nicaragua, the real power in the provinces remains in the same hands that it was 5 or 10 years ago. People still remember who this woman was 10 years ago and why she was their enemy. . . . Alas, her arguments were not persuasive enough for the court. The judge saw the case from one particular point of view: if a country is democratic, people should be safe there. Maria and her daughter were probably deported.

We all see things the way we see them. We are different because we had different upbringings and resources available to us, learned from different textbooks, ate different foods, and pledged allegiance to different flags. Or maybe we are more similar to each other than one thinks? Maybe we speak the same language of understanding and care? And maybe the judge, after a pause, stood up and said, "Let me reconsider my decision. I looked at this case from a different perspective and now I understand it better. Maria Gonzalez and her daughter may stay."

Source: Gonzalez v. I.N.S., 77 F.3d 1015 (7th Cir. 1996). In the United States Court of Appeals for the Seventh Circuit No. 95–1451 MARIA NELLY GONZALEZ and KAREN JORDANA GONZALEZ, Petitioners, v. IMMIGRATION AND NATURALIZATION SERVICE, Respondent. Petition to Review an Order of the Board of Immigration Appeals. Nos. A29-769-888 and A29-769-889

Cross-cultural psychology is about seeing seemingly obvious things from a different perspective. This discipline does not attempt to influence judges' decisions. Cross-cultural psychology attempts to teach people how to understand and connect with each other a little bit better.

What Is Cross-Cultural Psychology?

Before reaching adulthood, most of us do not choose a place to live or a language to speak. Growing up in cities, towns, and villages, no matter where—near a snowy Oslo or in a humid Kinshasa—people learn how to take action, feel, and understand events around them according to the wishes of their parents, societal requirements, and traditions of their ancestors. The way people learn to relate to the world through feelings and ideas affects what these individuals do. Their actions, in turn, have a bearing on their thoughts, needs, and emotions.

Conditions in which people live vary from place to place. Human actions and mental sets—formed and developed in various environments—may also fluctuate from group to group. These kinds of differences—and of course, similarities—are studied by cross-cultural psychology (Gudykunst & Bond, 1997). **Cross-cultural psychology** is the critical and comparative study of cultural effects on human psychology. Please notice two important elements of the definition. This is a *comparative* field. Any study in cross-cultural psychology draws its conclusions from at least two samples that represent at least two cultural groups. Because cross-cultural psychology is all about comparisons, and the act of comparison requires a particular set of critical skills, this study is inseparable from *critical thinking*.

Cross-cultural psychology examines psychological diversity and the underlying reasons for such diversity. In particular, cross-cultural psychology studies—again, from a comparative perspective—the linkages between cultural norms and behavior and the ways in which particular human activities are influenced by different, sometimes dissimilar social and cultural forces (Segall et al., 1990). For example, do victims of torture, rape, and genocide experience similar painful symptoms across cultures? If they do (Koopman, 1997) can a psychologist select a therapy aimed to treat posttraumatic symptoms in the United States and use it in other cultural environments, as in Vietnam or Bosnia?

Cross-cultural psychology studies cross-cultural interactions. For instance, during several centuries, southern and central Spain was under Arab control. How did Islam and Arab culture, in general, influence the culture and subsequent behavior, tradition, and values of predominantly Christian Spaniards? Can we find any traces of Arab influence in individual behavior in Spain and Hispanic cultures today? Is it possible to measure such traces at all?

Cross-cultural psychology cares not only about differences between cultural groups. It also establishes psychological universals, that is, phenomena common for people in several, many, or perhaps all cultures (Berry et al., 1992; Lonner, 1980). The structure of human personality—relatively enduring patterns of thinking, feeling, and acting—is, perhaps, one of such universals. For example, it was found that the same composition of personality is common in people in various countries (such as Germany, Portugal, Israel, China, Korea, and Japan). These universal traits include neuroticism, extraversion, openness to experience, agreeableness, and conscientiousness (Costa & Crae, 1995).

Cross-cultural psychological examination is not just a single observation made by a researcher, psychotherapist, or social worker. Listening to an anecdote or witnessing a vivid event cannot substitute for systematic comparisons of behavior and experience measured under different cultural conditions (Triandis et al., 1980).

Is cross-cultural psychology different from cultural psychology? First and above all, **cultural psychology** seeks to discover meaningful linkages between a culture and the psychology of individuals living in this culture. The main message of cultural psychology is that human behavior is meaningful only when viewed in the sociocultural context in which it occurs (Segall, 1979). For instance, a cultural psychologist may be interested in describing how particular religious views on divorce affect both behavior and attitudes of young parents in a country. Or a scientist may be interested in investigating how fundamental principles of Islam are incorporated into an individual's consciousness and personality traits (Monroe & Kreide, 1997). Overall, the main focus of cultural psychology is to study whether, when, and how individuals growing up in a particular culture tend to internalize this culture's qualities. Cultural psychology advocates the idea that mental processes are essentially the products of an interaction between culture and the individual (Piker 1998).

Culture is simply how one lives and is connected to history by habit.
LE ROI JONES—CONTEMPORARY AMERICAN WRITER AND CIVIL RIGHTS ADVOCATE

Culture is not just an ornament; it is the expression of the nation's character, and at the same time it is a powerful instrument to mould character. The end of culture is right living.
W. SOMERSET MAUGHAM (1874–1965)—ENGLISH PLAYWRIGHT AND NOVELIST

Basic Definitions

Culture

There are perhaps hundreds of definitions of culture. Some of them are elegant and brief, like one proposed by Herskovits (1948), who considered culture as the human-made part of the environment. Other definitions are more specific and state that culture is a wide range of settings in which human behavior occurs. Culture is manifested through particular behaviors and values—typically transmitted from generation to generation—and held by individuals of a society. Culture may function as a moderator of the relationship between experience and social behavior. Culture may also be a label for a set of contextual variables (political, social, historical, ecological, etc.) that is thought by the researcher to be theoretically linked to individual behavior. In brief, most existing definitions of culture focus on ideas, values, practices, norms, roles, and self-definitions (Hermans & Kempen, 1998; Segall et al., 1999; Triandis, 1996).

For the purposes of this book, we define **culture** as a set of attitudes, behaviors, and symbols shared by a large group of people and usually communicated from one generation to the next. Attitudes include beliefs (political, ideological, religious, moral, etc.), values, general knowledge (empirical and theoretical), opinions, superstitions, and stereotypes. Behaviors include a wide variety of norms, roles, customs, traditions, habits, practices, and fashions. Symbols represent things or ideas, the meaning of which is bestowed on them by people. A symbol may have the form of a material object, a color, a sound, a slogan, a building, or anything else. People attach specific meaning to specific symbols and pass them to the next generation, thus producing cultural symbols. For example, a piece of land may mean little for a group of people living a few miles away. The same land, nevertheless, may be a symbol of unity and glory for the people living on this land.

Cultures can be described as having both explicit and implicit characteristics. Explicit characteristics of culture are the set of observable acts regularly found in this culture. These are overt customs, observable practices, and typical behavioral responses, such as saying "hello" to a stranger. Implicit characteristics refer to the organizing principles that are inferred to lie behind these regularities on the basis of consistent patterns of explicit culture. For example, grammar that controls speech, rules of address, hidden norms of bargaining, or particular behavioral expectations in a standard situation may be viewed as examples of implicit culture.

No society is culturally homogeneous. There are no two cultures that are either entirely similar or entirely different. Within the same cultural cluster there can be significant variations and dissimilarities. For instance, any capitalist society is diverse and stratified. However, some Western countries are more stratified than others, and others achieve relative equality among their citizens. The simple comparison between the United States and Western Europe shows that despite some existing beliefs, Western Europe is more stratified than the United States because the distance—in terms of their income—between the elite and lower class in Europe is more significant than the distance between the American rich and poor. We will get back to critical thinking principles of comparisons in Chapter 3.

Society, Race, and Ethnicity

We commonly use terms such as society, culture, nationality, race, and ethnicity interchangeably. However, they are different. A society is composed of people, whereas a culture is a shared way of interaction that these people practice. How does the term culture differ from race, ethnicity, and nationality?

Race is defined by most specialists as a group of people distinguished by certain similar and genetically transmitted physical characteristics. For example, Rushton (1995) looks at a race as a more or less distinct combination of heritable traits, morphological, behavioral, and physiological characteristics. As an illustration, narrow nasal passages and a short distance between eye sockets mark the Caucasian. Distinct cheekbones identify a Mongoloid. Nasal openings shaped like an upside-down heart typify a Negroid. Levin (1995) suggests that the differences among the races are also evolutionary. The Negroid race, according to this view, occurred first in sub-Saharan Africa approximately 110,000 years ago and later evolved in Mongoloid and Caucasian races. It is essential to mention, however, the high or low frequency of occurrence of such physical—related to body—characteristics because most physical traits appear in all populations. For example, some Germans have frizzy hair and some Africans have red hair. There are many dark-skinned European Americans and light-skinned African Americans.

Some experts suggest that race is rather a social category. Why? Because, from these researchers' viewpoint, race indicates—first and foremost—particular experiences shared by many people who happen to belong to a category that is called "race" (Gould, 1994, 1997; Langaney, 1988). Arthur Dole (1995), for example, recommends abandoning the term "race" altogether and instead using terms such as "continental origin" (African), "anthropological designation" (Caucasian), or "colonial history" (Latino) to describe large categories of people. Brace (1995) suggests that because race is a social construct, a product of social assignation, all racial differences really reflect only the difference between arbitrarily established categories.

Despite some scholars' objections, race is considered an important element of people's identification. For instance, in contemporary United States, the government, as well many private organizations and agencies, may ask anybody who applies for a job in those organizations to identify their race or origin and there are formal guidelines for race identification (Table 1.1).

The Hispanic category incorporates, as you see, people of any racial group. How many people of each race or group of origin live in the United States? Table 1.2 provides some estimates made by the U.S. Bureau of the Census—a government organization that provides statistical analysis of the American population—of the distribution of races in the United States by 2005.

In the United States, the term **ethnicity** usually indicates your cultural heritage, the experience shared by you and other people who have a common ancestral origin, language, traditions, and often religion and geographic territory. A **nation** is defined as a people who share common geographical origin, history, and language, and are unified as a political entity—an independent state recognized by other countries. For example, those who acquire the status of a national of the United States, that is, be-

TABLE 1.1	Racial Categories in the United States

White (includes people of European, Arab, and Central Asian origin)

Black (includes people of African origin)

Native American (includes people of American Indian, Eskimo, and Aleut origin)

Asian (includes people of East Asian and Pacific Islander origin)

Hispanic (includes people of South and Central American origin)

TABLE 1.2	U.S. Population by 2005 (Estimates)
Race/Origin	**People by 2005**
All Races	285,981,000
White (including Hispanic)	232,463,000
Hispanic origin (of any race)	36,057,000
Black	37,734,000
American Indian, Eskimo, and Aleut	2,572,000
Asian and Pacific Islander	13,212,000

Source: The U.S. Bureau of the Census, Current Population Reports, Series P25-1130, Population Projections of the United States by Age, Sex, Race, and Hispanic Origin: 1995 to 2005.

come citizens, are either born in the United States or obtain their national status through a naturalization process.

There is a lot of confusion in the way people across countries use the words race, ethnicity, and nationality. What is often labeled as race or ethnicity in the United States is termed nationality in some other countries. For example, if Ron, who refers to himself as being an African American, marries Lilia, who refers to herself as a Latina (a popular referral to one's Hispanic origin), their marriage would be labeled an interracial marriage in the United States. The same marriage would be labeled either cross-ethnic or international in Russia and some other countries. In addition, there are

A CASE IN POINT

Ethnicity and Nationality: How They Are Understood in the United States (an excerpt from Shiraev & Boyd, 2001)

There are different ethnic groups within most nations and the United States is not an exception. Similarly, there could be different national groups within an ethnic group.

Same nationality, different ethnic groups: Martha and Martin are both U.S. citizens. Nationally, they are both Americans. However, ethnically, Martha is Brazilian, because her parents emigrated from Brazil when she was a little girl and she received her U.S. citizenship a few years ago. Martin is a seventh-generation New Yorker. His ethnic roots are mixed: Irish, French, German, and Russian.

Same ethnic groups, different nationality: Hamed and Aziza are both Palestinian exchange students living in New Jersey. Hamed's parents live in Tel-Aviv and both he and his parents are Israeli citizens. Aziza is a Jordanian national and holds a Jordanian passport.

CROSS-CULTURAL SENSITIVITY

Fairfax hospital emergency room was busy as usual on a typical Saturday afternoon. Perhaps in every emergency room the patient has little privacy and whatever one says is heard by anyone who happens to be around. A young doctor was examining newly arrived patients—a usual routine to determine the seriousness of their symptoms. He just finished questioning a woman—she was apparently fine—and was about to leave to take care of another patient waiting nearby. "Doctor, where did you go to school?" the woman asked. "Wake Forest," the doctor replied. "And what's your nationality?" The curious woman continued. "I am American," replied the doctor with a smile. "No, no, what is your nationality?" insisted the lady putting an emphasis on the last word. "You look Chinese or Vietnamese to me." "Ma-am, I am American, I was born here. My parents came from China, but they are U.S. nationals too. You can call me Chinese American." "Oh, I see," concluded the lady loudly. "I knew I was right: You are Chinese."

Some people still associate the word "American" with a particular "European" look and "tv-anchor" accent. For some it is hard to comprehend that the United States has always been and will continue to be a multiethnic community. Skin color, name, and hair texture do not automatically determine a person's nationality or religion. "It is not big deal," said the doctor to one of the authors who witnessed this conversation and asked the doctor if he was offended by the woman's comments. "So long as I live I correct people's remarks about my ethnicity. Some people do not get it. It will never change." Doctors are not supposed to make wrong predictions. However, our hope is that this prediction was incorrect.

racial categories common in the United States that are not recognized in many other countries, for example, in Panama, Brazil, or South Africa.

We should not forget that human groups are constantly moving and mixing with others. In the United States, perhaps more frequently than in other countries, people have freedom to choose their cultural identity and the group with which they want to be identified. Such phenomena as ethnic or national identity are becoming increasingly dynamic and based on different interests, ideas, and the choices of the individual.

Empirical Examination of Culture

We often refer to people by saying, "she is from a different culture," or "let us think about his unique cultural background." Are there different types of cultures? Many academic psychologists have been working and continue to work on the premise that cultural differences can be conceptualized in terms of cultural dichotomies. Among such dichotomies are high versus low power distance, high versus low uncertainly avoidance, masculinity versus femininity, and collectivism versus individualism. Let us examine them.

Power distance is the extent to which the members of a society accept that power in institutions and organizations is distributed unequally (Hofstede, 1980). It is assumed that there are cultures high and low on power distance. Most people in "high-power-distance" cultures generally accept inequality between the leaders and the led, the elite and the commons, the managers and the subordinates, and breadwinners and other family members.

 The higher the soar the smaller look to those who cannot fly.
FRIEDRICH NIETZSCHE (1844–1900)—GERMAN PHILOSOPHER

 Ask advice of your equals, help of your supervisors.
DANISH PROVERB

A classic caste-based Indian society is one of high-power distance. Expectedly, there are also cultures low on power distance, in which equality is a preferred value in relationships. For example, in the United States many young people may address older adults by their first names. This practice is unacceptable in many other countries.

People in more **masculine** cultures compared with more **feminine** cultures pursue such behavioral patterns as responsibility, decisiveness, liveliness, and high ambitions. Caring for others, consensus-seeking behavior, and gentleness are more often seen as feminine characteristics. Masculinity emphasizes work goals, such as earning and advancement. Femininity, as an opposing attribute, is based on values of modesty and caring for the weak. There were several attempts of masculinity-femininity assessments in various countries. For instance, Hofstede (1996) placed the following countries together according to their citizens' high scores on masculinity: Japan, Germany, Britain, Mexico, and the Philippines. Among countries scoring low were the Netherlands, France, Portugal, Costa Rica, and Thailand.

If life were eternal all interest and anticipation would vanish. It is uncertainty, which lends its fascination.
YOSHIDA KENKO (1283–1350)—JAPANESE OFFICIAL AND BUDDHIST MONK

If you forsake a certainty and depend on an uncertainty, you will lose both the certainty in the uncertainty.
SANSKRIT PROVERB

Uncertainty avoidance is the degree to which the members of a society feel uncomfortable with uncertainty and ambiguity. People in cultures high on uncertainty avoidance tend to support beliefs promising certainty, and to maintain institutions protecting conformity. Likewise, people in cultures low on uncertainty avoidance are apt to maintain nonconformist attitudes, unpredictability, creativity, and new forms of thinking and behavior.

Collectivism and **individualism** are perhaps the most frequently mentioned and examined cultural characteristics (Triandis, 1989). Individualism is typically interpreted as complex behavior based on concern for oneself and one's immediate family or primary group as opposed to concern for other groups or society to which one belongs. Collectivism, on the other hand, is typically interpreted as behavior based on concerns for others and care for traditions and values. Group norms in collectivist cultures—above anything else—are likely to direct individual behavior. People in collectivist cultures, in general, tend to prefer harmony-enhancing strategies of conflict resolution. People in individualistic cultures prefer more competitive strategies.

A CASE IN POINT

Expectations May Create Stereotypes

In many publications, China is identified as a collectivist culture. Expectedly, some should anticipate that in survey answers, Chinese residents would always be giving "collectivist" replies. That was not the case in one study reported by Pei (1998). For example, 77 percent of Chinese respondents (5,455 respondents in six provinces) disagreed with the statement: "In a lawsuit involving an individual and a collective entity, the judgment should favor the latter" (76–77). When asked, "Should police officers detain a person for the sake of public safety even though they were unable to determine his guilt?" 47 percent opposed detention, and only 28 percent supported it (77). As you see, the answers were somewhat "individualist."

Collectivism is expected to be high in the Asian countries, in the traditional societies, and in the former communist countries. Individualism is high in Western countries (Triandis, 1996).

 What man wants is simply independent choice, whatever that independence may cost and wherever it may lead.
FYODOR DOSTOEVSKY (1821–1881)—RUSSIAN NOVELIST

Collectivism and Individualism: Further Research

Harry Triandis (1996) offered a more detailed and sophisticated understanding of the individualism-collectivism phenomenon. He suggested examining it from two dimensions: vertical and horizontal. In the vertical cultural syndrome people refer to each other from power and achievement standpoints. They communicate with each other as employees and employers, and leaders and the led. People are also engaged in various activities as friends, family members, and co-workers. Thus, benevolence and equality may represent the horizontal cultural syndrome. Totalitarian regimes, for example, are likely to emphasize equality (horizontal level) but not emphasize freedom. Western democracies tend to emphasize freedom (vertical level) but not necessarily equality.

People in traditional societies such as India tend to be vertical collectivists. People in the United States may be viewed as vertical individualists. People in Sweden may be seen as horizontal collectivists. Why? Americans tolerate inequality to a greater extent than people in Sweden do; Swedes are willing—at least many of them—to be taxed at higher rates so that the income inequality is reduced. Indeed, economic inequality between the top and bottom 10 percent of the population is three times lower in Sweden than it is in the United States (Triandis, 1996).

National examples of collectivism and individualism vary. For instance, American collectivism is expected to be different from Asian collectivism. The Asian form of collectivism puts pressures on individuals to avoid disagreements with others because in Asian cultures, a concern about harmony with and happiness of others may be seen as more important than your own personal comfort (Barnlund 1989, 1975). In Latino collectivist cultures—Mexico as an example—people desire to maintain balanced relationships with others. This may be accompanied by the hidden pursuit of personal goals. In other words, it may look like they avoid confrontation during the process of negotiations, however, they remain competitive against each other in indirect ways.

Fijeman and colleagues (1996) conducted an interesting study in Hong Kong, Turkey, Greece, the Netherlands, and the United States. All the subjects were college students who were asked to express their opinions regarding eight hypothetical situations of psychological and economic need. In particular, the participants were asked to indicate their readiness to help others with money, goods, or personal hospitality. This study challenges some simplifications in the traditional understanding of collectivism and individualism. The main point is that people in collectivist cultures not only expect to contribute to others, they expect others to support them back! On the other hand, people in individualist cultures not only expect to contribute less to others, but also tend not to expect others to help or support them, thus reducing their own expectations of entitlement.

Independence and interdependence also became frequently used terms in cross-cultural psychology. In some cultures, most people seek to maintain their independence from others by attending to their individual selves and by expressing their unique inner attributes. In other cultures, people are interdependent and accentuate attention to others, fitting in and maintaining harmonious relationship with people of higher, lower, or the same status levels (Markus & Kitayama, 1991).

Cultural Syndromes

Every category displayed earlier is a label, which tends to describe one or several characteristics of a culture. Harry Triandis (1996) introduced the concept "cultural syndrome" as the pattern, or combination of shared attitudes, beliefs, categorizations, definitions, norms, and values that is organized around a theme that can be identified among those who speak a particular language, during a specific historic period, in a definable geographic region. Examples of such syndromes include tightness—particular rules and norms applied to social situations and sanctions applied to those who violate these norms; cultural complexity—a number of different cultural elements; activity and passivity (for instance, action versus thought); honor—a combination of attitudes and related to them practices that support aggressive actions in the name of self-protection; collectivism and individualism; vertical and horizontal relationships, or egalitarian.

Cross-cultural psychologists use several approaches to examine human activities in various cultural settings. Let us now consider several of them.

Sociobiological Approach

Sociobiology is a theoretical model that explores the ways in which biological factors affect human behavior and thus lay a natural foundation for human culture. This theoretical paradigm claims that general biological laws of behavior are perfectly suited as a fundamental explanation of human behavior. Culture is just a form of existence that provides for fundamental human needs and subsequent goals. According to this approach, the prime goal of human beings is survival. To endure, humans need food and resources. People look for mates, conceive, give birth, and then protect their offspring until children mature. Humans of all cultures, like animals, try to avoid unnecessary pain and eliminate anything that threatens their well-being.

One of sociobiology's strongholds is Social Darwinism. According to the natural selection principle, described by Charles Darwin, some organisms—due to various, primarily biological, reasons—are more likely to survive than others. Typically, healthy, strong, and adaptive individuals have better chances of survival than weak, unhealthy, and slow-adapting human beings. According to the "survival of the fittest" principle (Spenser, 1954), if members of a particular group are better fit to live in an environment than members of other groups, the first group has more of a chance to survive and, consequently, develops a social infrastructure. Therefore, its members have a chance to live in improved social conditions that will make people more competitive. Natural selection also removes practices, norms, and beliefs that have outlived their usefulness.

Competition steadily develops society by favoring its best-fit members. Survivors pass on their advantageous genes to their offspring. Over generations, genetic patterns that promote survival—such as aggressiveness, initiative, curiosity, or obedience—become dominant and then form foundations for a culture. Biological differences between men and women, like size, strength, bodily hormones, and reproductive behavior, laid foundation for cultural customs that reinforce inequality between the sexes.

All in all, as you will see further in the text, proponents of this approach offer natural and evolutionary explanations for a diverse array of human behaviors, including cooperation, aggression, intelligence, morality, prejudice, sexual preference, and infidelity.

Sociological Approach

This is a general view of human behavior that focuses on broad social structures that influence society as a whole, and subsequently its individuals. Several prominent sociological theories have had a profound impact on scientific and comparative understanding of human behavior in cultural contexts. On the whole, these theories imply that society exists objectively, apart from our individual experience. There are particular social forces that shape the behavior of large social groups and human beings develop and adjust their individual responses in accordance to the demands and pressures of larger social groups and institutions. Thus culture is both a product of human activity and its major forming factor.

There were several views confined within this approach. One of them, the structural-functional view was developed in the works of Emile Durkheim (1924), Talcott Parsons (1951), and other prominent social scientists. According to this view, society, as a complex system, functions to guarantee stability and solidarity among its members. Once created by people, society turns and confronts its creators, demanding subordination and obedience. Cultural norms and values become extremely important regulators of human behavior. Society provides a moral education for restraining the needs and desires of its members.

This system worked perfectly, according to Durkheim, in traditional societies prior to the industrial revolution in the 1800s. However, with the improved living conditions and growth of personal freedom, many individuals in industrialized societies free themselves from moral obligations. As a result, people receive little moral guidance in their lives. Lack of moral mutual support results in violence, crime, suicide, and other anomalies.

In societies with simple technologies, strong tradition becomes a powerful moral regulator demanding conformity from the society's members. Sharing the same collective conscience, members of such societies penalize those who are different. Everyone is expected to act and think in the same way. This coercive "solidarity" provides people with a powerful sense of belonging. In modern, wealthy societies, on the other hand, discarded traditions break psychological ties among the individuals—like pieces in a broken vase. A huge variety of specializations in the society should make people bond back together. They are interested in relying on one another, but this confidence is based on specialization and diversity and not on tradition or survival needs.

The views of another prominent social scientist, Max Weber, are represented in the symbolic-interactionist approach to understanding society and the individual within it. According to Weber (1922), preindustrial societies develop traditions. Passing traditions on from generation to generation, these societies evaluate particular actions of individuals as ether appropriate or inappropriate. Capitalist societies, on the contrary, endorse rationality. Rationality is a deliberate assessment of the most efficient ways of accomplishing a particular goal. Reason defeats emotions, calculation replaces intuition, and scientific analysis eliminates speculation.

The circle of life goes this way: individuals develop their ideas; the ideas transform the society in which these individuals live; and transformations in the society, again, affect human ideas. The Protestant church, for example, became the moral guide for the rapid development of European and North American capitalism. Modern success-oriented societies promote values of efficiency and achievement. Members of such societies see each other on the basis of "what they are," not "who they are," as happens in traditional societies.

According to the conflict view developed by Karl Marx, economic factors are the prime causes of human behavior and beliefs. Each society is divided roughly into two large and antagonistic social classes. The owners of the resources are members of the most powerful social class. Those who own neither resources nor technologies (the majority) become a social class without access to power. In an attempt to preserve power, the ruling class creates government, ideology, education, law, values, religion, and arts. Thus, each society contains at least two subsystems or cultures: the culture of the ruling class and the culture of the oppressed. The oppressed classes create their own beliefs, values, norms, and traditions. These norms and traditions reflect the class' need for social and political equality.

 In class society everyone lives as a member of the particular class, and every kind of thinking, without exception, stamped the brand of a class.
MAO TSE TUNG (1883–1975)—CHINESE COMMUNIST LEADER

According to Marx, people of the same social class, but of different ethnic groups, have much more in common than people of the same ethnic or national group, but of antagonistic social classes. When people are equal, when there are no differences among social classes regarding their access to resources and technologies—all national, ethnic, and racial differences will eventually disappear.

Ecocultural Approach

According to this crossdisciplinary comprehensive approach, the individual cannot be separated from his or her environmental context. People constantly exchange messages with the environment, thus transforming it and themselves. In other words, these interactions are reciprocal (Goodnow, 1990). The individual is seen not as a passive and static entity influenced by the environment, but as a dynamic human being who interacts with and changes the environment (Harkness, 1992). For example, parents educate their children and at the same time their children educate them.

According to Bronfenbrenner (1979), cross-cultural psychologists ought to do their investigation beyond the direct experience of the individual in laboratory conditions. The specialist should pay serious attention to the variety of settings in which the individual develops and understand the culture in its entirety. Bronfenbrenner divides the ecological environment into four interdependent categories: Microsystem, Mesosystem, Exosystem, and Macrosystem. The Microsystem involves immediate family members, schoolteachers, friends, and others who can have face-to-face interaction with the individual. The Mesosystem comprises the linkages between two or more environmental settings. For example, a child may attend a religious school on Sundays and the teacher from this school and the child's parents may work together, improving the child's understanding of religion. The Exosystem includes the media, extended family, legal and social organizations, and other influencing agents who may have an indirect impact on the individual. Finally, the Macrosystem consists of customs and beliefs most valued in a particular society.

According to the ecocultural approach, human environment is a part of a larger cultural system. Both the environment and the individual are seen as open and interchanging systems. Each individual's development takes place within a particular "developmental niche" that can be viewed as a combination of various settings (Harkness & Super, 1992). First, there are physical and social settings in which the individual lives: the people, the available products, and services. Second, there are collections of

A CASE IN POINT

An Ecocultural Approach: Culture and Availability of Space

As Jordan and Sullivan report (1998), lack of space has a huge impact on Japanese lifestyle and culture. Crowding has become one of the most significant elements of Japanese society. You are squeezed and squashed on the train, elbowed on the crowded street, and kicked in the swimming pool with 10 other people in the same lap lane. Almost all of its 126 million people live in huge urban conglomerates, where space is extremely tight and expensive. The average Tokyo dwelling is about 620 square feet. Most Japanese houses do not have basements, the number of bathrooms is usually one, and front doors in many dwellings open directly into the road because many streets have no sidewalks. Many large companies own guesthouses for entertaining by their top executives, who often don't have a home large enough to accommodate dinner guests.

customary practices that convey messages to and from the individual. Finally, there are caretakers' beliefs and expectations about children and their rearing. These three types of settings mediate the individual's development within the larger culture.

The ecocultural model in contemporary cross-cultural psychology was further developed by John Berry, who implies that among the major environmental factors influencing individual psychology are (1) ecological and (2) sociopolitical settings (Berry, 1971, Berry et al., 1992). The natural setting in which human organisms and the environment interact is called the **ecological context,** which includes the economic activity of the population. Factors such as presence or absence of food, quality of nutrition, heat or cold, and population density have a tremendous impact on the individual. **Sociopolitical context** is the extent to which people participate in both global and local decisions. This context includes various ideological values, organization of the government, and presence or lack of political freedoms. Through (1) genetic transmission, (2) cultural transmission, and (3) acculturation, people adjust to the existing realities and acquire roles as members of a specific culture. When ecological, biological, cultural, and acculturation factors are identified and taken into consideration, the specialist ought to be able to explain how, why, and to what extent people differ from one another.

The Cultural Mixtures Approach: A New Cross-Cultural Psychology in the Twenty-First Century?

Dutch psychologists Hubert Hermans and Harry Kempen (1998) introduced a concept about a principally new direction of research in cross-cultural psychology. Instead of studying psychological phenomena in cultures confined in their geographic locations—Japan, France, Mexico, and so forth—researchers should switch their attention to new cultural mixtures, contact zones, interconnected systems, and multiple cultural identities. The "old" cross-cultural psychology, as the authors argue, is still captivated by an illusion that cultures are generally static and confined within particular geographic locations. However, the ongoing social, economic, technological and political realities have already transformed contemporary cultures, which have become heterogeneous and extremely complex (Appadurai, 1990). Cultures are moving and mixing. No doubt, people keep and will retain their cultural knowledge. However, because of travel, migration, new communication links, and globalization of the world economic ties, cultural knowledge is already shared at varying degrees. Some subgroups have more access to specific cultural messages than others. People have more freedom to choose what cultural messages they want to receive. Phenomena such as culture identity are becoming increasingly dynamic, absorbing the commingling of different backgrounds, interests, ideas, and choices in one individual self. What is the contemporary cultural identity of New York City or Paris residents, for example? They perhaps represent today's examples of cultural mixtures. All in all, the authors call for the fundamental revision of the subject of contemporary cross-cultural psychology, one that should change with the changing cultures.

Some studies support the idea about the importance of a new approaches to cultural dichotomies. For instance, Matsumoto and colleagues (1997) measured collectivism and individualism in four countries, including Japan and the United States. They asked people to assess 25 items that indicated various behaviors—related to respecting of traditions, compromising one's wishes for the sake of the group, acting together with the group, being similar to members of the group, and so on. One of the findings was that the Japanese sample was not more collectivist than the U.S. sample. The authors explain such results by suggesting that contemporary Japan is changing. The subjects of this study were college students, a group that has to express some form of individualism as a necessary trait in their future professional careers in an industrial and democratic society. A second possibility is that the American sample consisted of a large number of Latino, Asian, and African American subjects who scored more collectivist than other groups in the United States.

The Integrative Approach: A Summary

To combine and critically apply these—and possibly other approaches to cross-cultural psychology—let us introduce two general concepts that will be used throughout this book: **activity** and **availability of resources.**

For the cross-cultural psychologist, human behavior is not only a "result" or "product" of cultural influences. People are also free, active, and rational individuals who are capable of exercising their own will. **Activity** is a process of the individual's goal-directed interaction with the environment. Human motivation, emotion, thought, and reactions cannot be separated from human activity, which is (1) determined by individual, socioeconomic, environmental, political, and cultural conditions and also (2) changes these conditions. In fact, human psychology develops within human activity and manifests through it (Vygotsky, 1932). Imagine, for example, a child who grows up in a zone of an ethnic conflict and for whom survival becomes a primary activity. He or she develops emotions, motivation, and cognitive processes quite different from those children who grew up in safe conditions. At the same time, because this child can also engage in activities similar for children in most environments—like playing, learning arithmetic, thinking about the future, helping parents, to name a few—the child will be likely to share many common psychological characteristics with his or her counterparts around the world. Cultures may be similar and different in terms of the most common activities of their members.

Presence of and access to resources essential for the individual's well-being largely determine type, scope, and direction of human activities. There are societies with plenty of resources available and there are regions in which resources are extremely scarce. Geographic location, climate, natural disasters, or absence of such may determine how much resources are available to individuals.

Quality of environment and access to resources may become crucial factors determining many cultural characteristics. They may directly or indirectly affect human activities and individual psychological developments. For example, rapidly worsening economic conditions may also directly affect individual behavior. When the economic crisis hit Japan in 1997, the number of violent crimes went up dramatically, especially among teenagers (up 40 percent compared to 1996, Ministry of Health and Welfare of Japan, 1998).

Poverty, for instance, is clearly linked to a shorter life span and poorer health. The poor tend to live in more harmful environments and are more likely to be exposed to diseases and other risks than those who are not poor. Malnutrition in childhood, particularly during the first year of life, childhood infections, and exposure to accidents and injuries all make chronic and sometimes disabling diseases more likely in adult life, causing substantial changes in individual activities. According to estimations, more than 840 million people in the world are still below the nutrition threshold—representing the minimum dietary requirements (WHO, 1999). Overall, would a condition such as poverty affect the way people make decisions, see themselves, others, and their environment? We will be addressing this question everywhere throughout the text.

Presence of resources does not mean equal availability to all members of that society. **Access to resources** is another important factor that unifies and separates people and cultures from one another. People's access to resources—and this will be a focus of our attention as well—affects many aspects of culture and individual behavior. Geographic isolation, inequality within a country or region, and the extent of such inequality may influence people's activities and their well-being. Most psychological studies that examine ethnic and cultural minorities point at inequality and oppression as major causes of psychological differences between minorities and mainstream cultural groups (see, for example, Jenkins, 1995). As an example, oppression is often defined as an unequal distribution of resources that causes a sense of psychological inferiority among the oppressed (Fowers & Richardson, 1996).

However, not only material resources and access to them determine major characteristics of culture and culture-linked behavior. Ideas and practices that implement these ideas are inseparable from individual psychology. As we mentioned earlier, Weber revolutionized scientific views on the role of ideas in human life. Take, for example, the role that people assign to their families and ancestors. Since ancient times in Chinese society, contrary to European countries, the family—not the individual— has been regarded as the basic social unit. The human being, therefore, is valued primarily as part of a larger community and not as a self-contained individual.

A CASE IN POINT

Wealth and Individualism

There is a positive correlation between wealth and individualism (see McClelland, 1961); however, a society can accumulate wealth but remain collectivist, such as Kuwait or Singapore. One might argue that capitalism should promote individualism. Capitalism is based on the principle of competition that is protected by democratic political freedoms, which guarantee power for the majority—if the majority establishes its power through elections. Such free competition requires a surplus of available resources. Others, however, may also successfully argue that collectivism is based on cooperation and it does not exclude competition: people may compete among themselves while still basing their relationship on principles of cooperation.

 To forget one's ancestors is to be a brook without a source, a tree without a root.
CHINESE PROVERB

Such understanding of the nature of Chinese interconnectedness may, in fact, explain tremendous achievements of the Chinese society (Ho, 1998). At the same time, such "collectivist" views on the individual may have allowed Chinese leaders in the past to disregard human individuality and see people as sheer numbers and a means for the achievement of particular political goals. Chinese Communists, for example, during their numerous political campaigns in the 1950s and 1960s, physically eliminated thousands and thousands of dissidents—those who dared to speak up against the dictatorship and ideological oppression.

The ecocultural approach significantly enriched the scientific understanding of human activity around cultures. Cross-cultural psychologists inevitably empower themselves with knowledge from anthropology, history, and sociology. This knowledge will certainly be helpful in data interpretation. For example, human ecological systems may be influenced by particular societal practices and human activities. To illustrate, a Japanese worker is likely to spend his or her entire life in the same place in the same company, whereas an Indian migrant worker in Kuwait is likely to change places of work and living. All in all, any knowledge in cross-cultural psychology would be incomplete without comprehending basic economic, political, and ideological processes taking place in the world.

The analysis of collectivism and individualism should also take into consideration many economic, political, and situational factors. In societies with scarce resources, the collectivist type of relationship is perhaps more effective than the individualist because collectivism stands for help and mutual support and guarantees the individual some access to scarce resources in exchange for personal cooperation with and contribution to society. Think, for example, about the distribution of resources in any community. Individualism may be high in those communities in which people do not have to make collective decisions about how to distribute resources and in cases when the government has little power over people's lives. Collectivism is supposed to be significant in societies in which collective decisions are necessary to decide how to distribute resources (Triandis, 1996). Overall, totalitarian empires facilitate collectivist values, and collectivist values reinforce totalitarian empires. The government exercises complete control over the mass media, schools, and colleges. Finally, the state keeps centralized control over the economy and resources.

What Is Indigenous Psychology?

One of the assumptions in contemporary cross-cultural psychology is that it is not possible to fully understand the psychology of the people in a particular ethnic or any other social group without a complete understanding of the social, historic, political, ideological, and religious premises that have shaped people of this group. Indigenous theories, including indigenous psychology, are characterized by the use of conceptions and methodologies associated exclusively with the cultural group under investigation (Ho, 1998). Kim and Berry (1993) define indigenous psychologies (plural is a suitable form because apparently any group of people can develop its own psychology) as the scientific study of human behavior, or the mind, that is designed for a people and native, not transported from other regions. Maybe because of disappointing beliefs that contemporary psychologists cannot really comprehend all other cultures, a growing interest in indigenous psychologies has emerged in the 1990s.

What Is Ethnocentrism?

Please consider an example. College students in several countries were asked to draw a map of the world in 10 minutes, putting in as much detail as possible. In almost all cases, the students' own country was drawn disproportionately large (Whittaker & Whittaker, 1972). Perhaps what is most familiar to us tends to be exaggerated.

Ethnocentrism, in a way, is an exaggeration. This is the view that supports judgment about other ethnic, national, and cultural groups and events from the observer's own ethnic, national, or cultural group's outlook. In psychology, for example, various theories that rely on concepts alien in the studied culture are subject to the pitfalls of ethnocentrism. For those who grew up in one place and have never been exposed to other countries, the differences between Chile and Argentina, France and England, and blacks and Hispanics in the United States would appear insignificant. Ethnocentrism narrows our perception of other countries and social groups. Ethnocentrism is also a distortion of reality.

In most cases, being ethnocentric is also judging from the position of a cultural majority. Values and norms accepted by any majority have great power because of the sheer size of the majority and because of the fact that its members hold most positions of power.

What Is Multiculturalism?

Seeking equality in treatment for all social and cultural groups has become a standard in contemporary psychology (Fowers & Richardson 1996; Sears, 1996). **Multiculturalism** is an individual psychological and theoretical view that not only encourages recognition of equality for all cultural and national groups, but also promotes the idea that various cultural groups have the right to follow their own unique paths of development and have their own unique activities, values, and norms.

The multicultural view does not allow considering one culture as higher than another or one culturally approved activity as better than another activity, from a different culture. Moreover, multiculturalism suggests that cultural groups should be free from the imposition of other groups' norms and standards. Cross-cultural psychology, using a multicultural approach, strengthens national schools of psychology by providing evidence about behavior, motivation, and emotion of people who live in other national, ethnic, and cultural contexts.

A Brief History of the Field

Cross-cultural psychology, a relatively new field, descended from scientific general psychology. It is also part of an intellectual tradition, rooted mainly in Europe but developed primarily in the United States. However, the old roots of cross-cultural psychology spread back in the history of contemporary science. Beyond its historical links with general psychology, cross-cultural psychology has diverse influences, including some that originate in disciplines such as anthropology, physiology, sociology, history, and political science. Please note that many specific views that contributed to modern cross-cultural psychology will be described in every chapter. Therefore, only a few important trends will be mentioned here.

Despite our scarce and incomplete knowledge about ancient philosophers and their scientific creations, it is possible to suggest that the scientists were aware of human diversity and emphasized the existence of some group and social differences in human behavior. After a relatively stagnant period in the Middle Ages, some essential changes in human scientific interest of diversity started to emerge, especially after the fifteenth century (Jahoda & Krewer, 1997). Among some of the contributing factors to such a trend were advances in science, growing number of contacts with other people, geographic expeditions, and trade. Perhaps the most radical changes in human thought on diversity occurred during the Enlightenment era, between the seventeenth and nineteenth centuries. Via books and systematic education, many argumentative debates on the nature of human beings began to reach the minds of thousands of educated people. Works and publications of René Descartes in the Netherlands, Francis Bacon and David Hume in England, Immanuel Kant in Prussia, Denis Diderot and Jean Jacques Rousseau in France, and other prominent thinkers have shaped many contemporary views on reason, emotion, values, and behavior.

By the end of the nineteenth and the beginning of the twentieth century, the interest in the comparative subject in social sciences continued to grow. Anthropologists, psychologists, and social scientists, such as Emile Durkheim or Gabriel Tarde in France, Vladimir Bekhterev in Russia, and some others tried to offer an attractive theory or simple analogy (i.e., "social instinct" or "imitation") as explanations for cross-cultural human behavior. Gradually, the focus of research was changing from speculative to empirical. Francis Galton conducted his comparative research on intelligence. William Rivers undertook data-gathering expeditions to New Guinea and Richard Thurnwald went to Melanesia to study people's cognitive functions. Psychological studies and anthropological observations in the middle of the twentieth century led many scientists to believe the key to the understanding of human behavior was the interaction between the individual and his or her cultural environment. By the 1960s, cross-cultural psychology began to establish itself as an independent discipline.

Among many notable developments, the 1960s were marked by the publication of an international study of cultural influences on visual perception (Segall et al., 1966) and the launch of the *International Journal of Psychology* (1966). At this time, cross-cultural psychology was informally established by the publication of the *Journal of Cross-Cultural Psychology* in 1970. Today, the editors of the journal focus on studies that describe the relationships between culture and psychological processes. They believe that all psychology is cultural and all cultures are psychological. They seek to publish papers that present culture as a mediating and moderating variable or antecedent to all behaviors. The journal encourages comparisons between two or among more cultures. It also includes studies of some cultural comparisons between minority or ethnic groups in one country (Editors of Cross-Cultural Psychology, 1997).

In 1972 the International Association for Cross-Cultural Psychology and the Society for Cross-Cultural Research were established. By the 1980s, two major pathbreaking handbooks were published, one in cross-cultural psychology (Triandis et al., 1980) and the other in human development (Munroe et al., 1981). Among recent remarkable developments is the publication of the second edition of the *Handbook of Cross-Cultural Psychology* in 1997. Today, cross-cultural psychology is an international discipline. Many specialists represent this field from virtually every country in the world.

 EXERCISE 1.1

Global Unification or Global Clash?

At least two contrasting views on the contemporary world, both valuable for cross-cultural psychology, can be presented.

On one hand, in an increasingly interconnected world society, the concept of independent, coherent, and stable cultures becomes irrelevant. People from different cultural origins are drawn into close relationships. It is seen, for example, in the unprecedented expansion of tourism, the flourishing of multinational corporations, and the emergence of new geographic entities. The European Community has been created and the International Monetary Fund continues to rescue many troubled national economies. Many trade barriers have been eliminated and travel restrictions are eased. The dissemination of pop culture, the increasing flow of migrants, the growth of ethnic diasporas, and the emergence of Internet communications are signs of the globalization of human culture.

On the other hand, there is tremendous evidence in support of "global separation" of cultures and ethnic groups. So many countries have fallen apart along ethnic and religious lines. Czechoslovakia, Yugoslavia, and the Soviet Union have collapsed into 21 separate states. Ethnic and religious conflicts continue to tear apart Cyprus, Israel, India, Rwanda, South Africa, and many other countries. Ethnic groups continue to demand independence in Canada, Russia, Turkey, Iraq, and Serbia. Religious and ethnic minorities are attacked in Germany and Indonesia, France and Sri Lanka, Pakistan and Afghanistan. Rapid growth of religious fundamentalism marked the recent social developments in many countries.

Assignment:

Please compare these two opposite trends: the separation and globalization of cultures. Which trend do you consider more powerful and compelling? Eventually, will cultures merge or become more separated from one another? Support your view with facts and reasoning.

CHAPTER SUMMARY

- Cross-cultural psychology is the critical and comparative study of cultural effects on human psychology. As a comparative field, cross-cultural psychology draws its conclusions from at least two samples that represent at least two cultural groups. The act of comparison requires a particular set of critical thinking skills.
- Cross-cultural psychology examines psychological diversity and the underlying reasons for such diversity. Using a comparative approach, cross-cultural psychology examines the linkages between cultural norms and behavior and the ways in which particular human activities are influenced by various cultural forces. Cross-cultural psychology establishes psychological universals, that is, phenomena common for people in several, many, or perhaps all cultures.
- Cultural psychology seeks to discover meaningful linkages between culture and psychology of individuals living in this culture. Overall, the main focus of cultural psychology is to study whether, when, and how individuals growing up in a particular culture tend to internalize this culture's qualities.
- No society is culturally homogeneous. There are no cultures that are either entirely similar or completely different. Within the same cultural cluster there can be significant variations, inconsistencies, and dissimilarities.
- Cross-cultural psychologists establish and conceptualize main culture's features in terms of cultural dichotomies. Among such dichotomies are high- versus low-power distance, high- versus low-uncertainly avoidance, masculinity versus femininity, and collectivism versus individualism.
- Cross-cultural psychology uses several approaches to examine human activities in various cultural settings. Sociobiology is a theoretical model that explores the ways in which biological factors affect human behavior and thus lay a natural foundation for human culture. The sociological approach focuses on broad social structures that influence society as a whole, and subsequently its individuals.

There are particular social forces that shape the behavior of large social groups and human beings develop and adjust their individual responses in accordance to the demands and pressures of larger social groups and institutions.

- According to an ecocultural approach to cross-cultural psychology, the individual cannot be separated from his or her environmental context. People constantly exchange messages with the environment, thus transforming it and themselves.

- According to a "culture mixtures" approach, researchers should switch their attention form traditional views on culture to new cultural mixtures, contact zones, interconnected systems, and multiple cultural identities.

- An "integrative" approach to cross-cultural psychology emphasizes human activity, a process of the individual's goal-directed interaction with the environment. Human motivation, emotion, thought, and reactions cannot be separated from human activity, which is (1) determined by individual, socioeconomic, environmental, political, and cultural conditions and also (2) changes these

conditions. Two factors, presence of and access to resources, largely determine type, scope, and direction of human activities.

- Indigenous theories are characterized by the use of conceptions and methodologies associated exclusively with the cultural group under investigation. Indigenous psychology is the scientific study of human behavior or the mind, that is designed for a people and native, not transported from other regions.

- Ethnocentrism is the view that supports judgment about other ethnic, national, and cultural groups and events from the observer's own ethnic, national, or cultural group's outlook. Multiculturalism is a view that encourages recognition of equality for all cultural and national groups and promotes the idea that various cultural groups have the right to follow their own unique paths of development and have their own unique activities, values, and norms. Cultural relativism eliminates specific moral and cultural values from research and offers the opinion that any value is good so long as this value exists in a particular culture.

KEY TERMS

Activity A process of the individual's goal-directed interaction with the environment.

Availability of Resources A measure indicating the presence of and access to resources essential for the individual's well-being.

Collectivism Behavior based on concerns for other people, traditions, and values they share together.

Cross-Cultural Psychology The critical and comparative study of cultural effects on human psychology.

Cultural Psychology The study that seeks to discover systematic relationships between culture and psychological variables.

Cultural Relativism The view that eliminates particular moral and cultural values from re-

search and offers the opinion that any value is good so long as this value is a norm in a particular culture.

Culture A set of attitudes, behaviors, and symbols shared by a group of people and usually communicated from one generation to the next.

Ecological Context The natural setting in which human organisms and the environment interact.

Ethnicity A cultural heritage shared by a category of people who also share a common ancestral origin, language, and religion.

Ethnocentrism The view that supports judgment about other ethnic, national, and cultural groups and events from the observer's own ethnic, national, or cultural group's outlook.

Femininity The extent of emphasis on interpersonal goals, friendly atmosphere, consensus, modesty, caring for the weak, and quality of life.

Individualism Complex behavior based on concern for oneself and one's immediate family or primary group as opposed to concern for other groups to which one belongs.

Masculinity Complex behavior that promotes values such as heroism, achievement, assertiveness, and material success.

Multiculturalism The view that encourages recognition of equality for all cultural and national groups and promotes the idea that various cultural groups have the right to follow their own paths of development and have their own unique activities, values, and norms.

Nation A large group of people who constitute a legitimate, independent state, and share a common geographic origin, history, and frequently language.

Power Distance The extent to which the members of a society accept that power in institutions and organizations is distributed unequally.

Race A large group of people distinguished by certain similar and genetically transmitted physical characteristics.

Sociopolitical Context The setting in which people participate in both global and local decisions; it includes various ideological issues, political structures, and presence or absence of political and social freedoms.

Uncertainty Avoidance The degree to which the members of a society feel uncomfortable with uncertainty and ambiguity.

CHAPTER 2

Methodology of Cross-Cultural Research

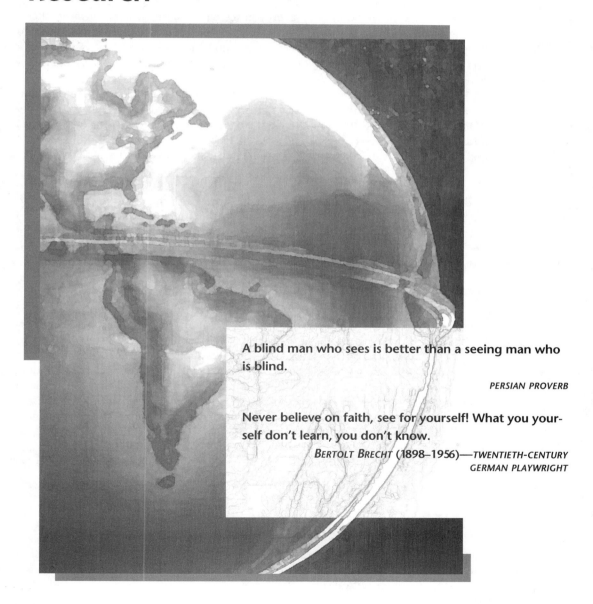

A blind man who sees is better than a seeing man who is blind.

PERSIAN PROVERB

Never believe on faith, see for yourself! What you yourself don't learn, you don't know.

BERTOLT BRECHT (1898–1956)—TWENTIETH-CENTURY GERMAN PLAYWRIGHT

In the early 1990s one of our friends, then a graduate student at UCLA, asked us to help conduct a comparative Soviet-American study on the perception of obedience. After we translated the survey questions from English to Russian, made a thousand copies of the questionnaire, and videotaped testing materials, we flew to the Soviet Union to gather our research data. We studied a wide variety of samples, from school children to construction workers, from engineers to psychology majors. There was only one problem. We needed to get access to Soviet cops, but couldn't get permission from a county police chief. To our elation, however, after a few days of delays we finally were allowed to interview 100 police officers. We rushed to the police station, met with a local police chief, and handed him cash for "using" his officers as research subjects. (For the money he received from us he probably could have bought a new color TV for the recreation room.)

The procedure went well and when the last policeman had filled out the questionnaire, we went back to the chief's office to thank him for his assistance. "Oh, you are very welcome," he replied with a smile. "I really wanted to help you to get the best results. I told my lads—he referred to policemen—to be serious and give you their best answers. I told them that it is a Soviet-American study and that they should have given you the most decent answers."

We couldn't believe what he was saying to us! Did he really instruct his policemen to give us only "decent," that is, socially desirable answers? If that was the case, we could not have used the results of the study because all other American and Soviet subjects did not receive any instructions from their bosses about how to answer the questionnaire. And now, an officer tries to create a better image of the Soviet cops and instructs his subordinates about how to answer questions!

This is perhaps one of the most common methodological problems of any comparative research: the subjects' attempts to present themselves as better than they usually are, assuming that their answers will be compared with their counterparts' surveys overseas. How could we have prevented such a situation? Perhaps we should have better hidden the fact that we were conducting a comparative research study. However, the next day one of our colleagues clarified the situation for us. He asked whether we knew why it took the police chief several days to give us the "green light" to conduct this research. When we said we didn't, he enlightened us. "The chief was making phone calls and gathering information about you and your research project. You did not have a chance to hide that this was a comparative Soviet-American study. Please don't blame yourself. That's the Soviet environment: you have to second guess and verify everything. The police chief did everything that he was supposed to do and any other cop in his place would have done the same. In a way, you had a representative sample."

To better understand the diversity of human activity, psychologists have to gather reliable evidence—verifiable facts and consistent data interpreted in the most unbiased way. This chapter deals with research methodology in cross-cultural psychological studies. It gives an overview of the most popular methods used by cross-cultural psychologists and offers critical suggestions about the process of gathering facts and interpreting data in comparative studies.

Goals of Cross-Cultural Research

Imagine, a researcher wants to find out what psychological factors influence the relative stability of arranged marriages of Indian Americans, whose family unions last longer than marriages among European Americans and other ethnic groups. To find the answer, the researcher should conduct a scientific investigation and choose appropriate methods. What does the psychologist aim to pursue in this particular project?

First, the researcher wants do *describe* some major differences between the arranged and nonarranged marriage. Suppose one of the most important differences is so-called conflict-avoiding behavior of both spouses in the arranged-marriage family: they seldom escalate tensions and try to resolve every minor problem in their relationship before the problem grows unsolvable.

Then, when some differences between ethnic groups are found, the researcher tries to *explain* whether these factors affect marital stability. If they do, then why and how does this influence take place? After an explanation is offered, the psychologist tries to disseminate the received data and their interpretations. He or she may attend a conference, share the data with colleagues and students, or publish an article in a scholarly journal.

The practical value of the received data may be high if they not only explain but also *predict* the factors that determine successful marital relationships identified by the research. For example, the psychologist could suggest that conflict-avoiding behavior is effective primarily in arranged-marital relationships, but not in other types of marriages in which conflict-resolution behavior is more efficient than conflict-avoiding activities. If this is the case, practitioners could use these research data to help other people to better understand and manage—that is, effectively *control*—their family relationships.

By and large, research methodology in cross-cultural psychology can be divided into two categories: quantitative and qualitative.

Quantitative Research in Cross-Cultural Psychology

Quantitative research in cross-cultural psychology—and in psychology in general—involves measurement of certain aspects of human activity from a comparative perspective. The variables chosen for examination have to be studied empirically, primarily through observation as opposed to other forms of reflection, such as intuition, beliefs, or superstitions. Because cross-cultural psychologists are interested in establishing similarities, differences, and other statistical relationships that occur between two or among several variables, the most common data are **measures of central tendency.** The measure of central tendency indicates the location of a score distribution on a variable, that is, describes where most of the distribution is located. There are three measures of central tendency: the mode, the median, and the mean.

The most frequently occurring score is called **the mode.** For example, you compare the test performances of two groups of people: *A* and *B*. Then you find out that most people in group *A* received 10 points for the test and most people in group *B* received 7 points for the test; you can compare 10 and 7 as the groups' modes. Mode, as you see, in most cases does not provide you with accurate accounts of the scores in the studied groups. Therefore, a better measure of central tendency can be used—**the median.** When 50 percent of all scores are the score X or a score less than X, the median will be X. For example, if you have the scores 1, 2, 2, 2, 3, 4, 5, 5 5, the median would be 3 because half of the distribution—scores 1, 2, 2, 2—is before the 3 and half of the distribution—scores 4, 5, 5, 5—is after the 3. The numerical value of the scores is not what determines the median. In brief, the median is the score at the 50th percentile. For example, you want to know the socioeconomic status of the population in the country in which you conduct research. You will have to find a point on the country's income distribution scale that indicates a 50 percent level. Suppose this point is $12,000. This measure will indicate that $12,000 is the median income in this country. The median, however, does not adequately describe some data. Imagine a child is taking a test on cognitive development and receives the following scores: 2, 3, 3, 4, 9, 9, 9. The median in this case will be 4; however, this description virtually ignores the high scores received on the last three tests. The student could have gotten scores 6, 6, and 6 instead of 9, 9, and 9; however, the median will be still be 4.

Now look at Table 2.1. It displays the median scores of income per years among major groups of origin (racial groups). Median scores in this table indicate that 50 percent of the families in each category make more than the median score and 50 percent of the families make less than the median score.

The most convenient and frequently used measure of central tendency in cross-cultural psychology is **the mean.** The mean indicates the mathematical central point of a distribution of scores. It is determined by adding up all the scores and dividing by the number of scores you just added. For example, by adding the scores 2, 3, 7, 8, 15, and dividing the sum (35) by 5, which is the number of scores, you would have a mean of 7. However, this measure does not always accurately describe highly skewed distributions. Imagine, for example, that you examine aggressive reactions in people's behavior during an experiment. In four experimental conditions the score of angry reactions is 10. The mean will be 10. Then on the fifth condition the score is 0. That will bring the mean down to 8, which could be somewhat misleading because any observer unfa-

TABLE 2.1	Median Income per Household in 1998
All races	$38,885
White	$40,912
Non-Hispanic white	$42,439
Black	$25,351
Asian and Pacific Islander	$46,637
Hispanic origin	$28,330

Source: U.S. Census Bureau, Current Population Survey, March 1998.

miliar with this research would assume that all the scores were distributed around 8. Therefore, when you collect statistical data you always have to be aware of the distance between the two most extreme scores in your set of data (the range) and deviations of the scores around the mean (the variance).

Quantitative Approach: Measurement Scales

When you measure distance, weight, volume, motion, or temperature, the results represent quantity, magnitude, or degree. Human activities can be measured along these dimensions too. Choosing a correct measurement scale becomes a crucial factor for the overall success of any psychological research. There are four types of measurement scales: nominal, ordinal, interval, and ratio. With a nominal scale, each score does not indicate an amount. This scale does not measure any rank, or order and is used mostly for identification purposes. For example, in the question: "What languages do you speak?" the scale: *English–Spanish–Mandarin–Arabic–Other* is a nominal scale. Remember the description of the mode? In fact, the mode is usually used to describe central tendency when the scores reflect a nominal scale of measurement (Heiman, 1996).

In an ordinal scale the scores designate rank order. A rank order may indicate the subject's preference, attitude, or opinion. For example, you may ask your subjects from two countries to pick and rank the most valuable traits in a personal friend: assertiveness, honesty, intelligence, creativity, confidence, sense of humor, and so on. This procedure will require usage of an ordinal scale. This scale, however, as you see, does not measure the distance between the ranks.

In an interval scale, each score indicates some amount. There is presumably an equal unit of measurement separating each score. In the question: "Do you support or oppose sexual relations between any two unmarried individuals?" the scale *Definitely support* $(+2)$, *Conditionally support* $(+1)$, *Do not know* (0), *Conditionally oppose* (-1), *Definitely oppose* (-2) is a rank scale. The scores here could be either positive or negative (for example, the Fahrenheit scale) and zero does not indicate a zero amount. In other words, there is no true zero point.

With a ratio scale the scores reflect the true amount of the present variable, and zero truly means that zero amount of the variable is present. Ratio scales cannot include negative numbers and are used to measure quantitative variables, such as the amount of time spent in front of television, the number of errors made on the test, or number of hits on a website.

Quantitative Approach: Looking for Linkages and Differences

A specialist or student conducting research in cross-cultural psychology often needs to establish **correlations,** or the relationships between two or among several variables. If in one set of data, when variable X is low variable Y is also low; and when variable X is high variable Y is also high, we have a positive correlation between the variables. If, according to another data set, when variable A is low, variable B is high; and when variable A is high, variable B is low, we have a negative correlation. For example, the relationship between frequency of picture exposure and picture liking is positively correlated. In a study conducted by Zajonc (1968), different people were shown photographs of different faces and the number of times each face was shown was varied. The more often the subjects saw a particular photograph, the more they reported liking the face pictured on it. An example of negative correlation is a cross-cultural correspondence between income and violent crime: the higher income per capita in a region, the lower the rates of violent crime in that area.

A measure of correlation—**correlation coefficient**—contains two components. The first is the sign that indicates either positive or negative linear relationship. The second is the value. The larger the absolute value, the stronger the relationship. For example, the intelligence scores of identical twins raised either together or apart are highly correlated: $+0.88$. The intelligence scores of nonrelatives raised together are relatively low: $+0.20$ (Bouchard et al., 1990).

Does correlation establish a cause-and-effect relationship between the variables? For example, children with lower IQ scores are likely to have lower grades and enjoy school less than children with higher IQ scores (Moffit et al., 1981). Does the performance on IQ tests affect deviant behavior, or is deviant behavior a cause of the low grades and poor test performance? From introductory psychology classes you perhaps remember that correlational studies often leave the question of cause and effect unanswered. A psychologist who, for example, finds a positive cross-cultural correlation between (1) violent crime and (2) level of poverty in a particular country, in most cases would not be able to make a conclusion about which, if either, factor was the cause, and which, if either, was the effect or result. In other words poverty may cause crime, crime can contribute to poverty, or a third—unknown to the psychologist—variable may contribute to both. For a more detailed critical analysis of correlation see Chapter 3.

One of the most important statistical methods used in cross-cultural psychology is the *t*-**test** for independent samples. If the researcher has independent pools of subjects, for example, schoolteachers in Israel and Egypt, he or she can try to test how significant the differences in attitudes between these two samples are. (Two samples are considered independent when the subjects are randomly selected and the selection of subjects for sample A is done independently of the selection of subjects for sample B). The *t*-test procedure aims to estimate whether the difference between two samples occurred by chance. If it is not accrued by chance, the difference between two samples is considered to be statistically significant.

To what extent should two scores be different from each other to provide the researcher with confidence that there is a significant difference between the samples? There is not one universal formula for this. Factors such as the size and type of the sample, its representativeness, distribution of individual scores, measurement scale used in research, and many other conditions can affect the outcome of the comparative procedure. Some researchers, nevertheless, offer statistical guidelines for interpreting differences in comparative research (Cohen, 1977). For instance, in differences considered small the distribution of scores should be 15 percent nonoverlapping and 85 percent overlapping. It happens when, for example, 85 percent of the members of two ethnic groups score within the same range on a test. For medium differences their distributions should be 33 percent nonoverlapping and 67 percent overlapping. And for large differences the distributions are 47 percent nonoverlapping and 53 percent overlapping. If we translate from the language of statistics to behavioral terms, the large differences are clearly present and therefore easily observable, medium differences are present but only somewhat observable, and small differences can be detected only by statistical methods.

 Nothing in the world can one imagine beforehand, not the least thing. Everything is made up of so many unique particulars that cannot be foreseen.
RAINER MARIA RILKE (1875–1926)—AN AUSTRIAN POET

Qualitative Approach in Cross-Cultural Psychology

Qualitative research is conducted primarily in the natural setting, where the research participants carry out their daily activities in a nonresearch atmosphere. Psychologists try to detect and describe some illicit or unspoken aspects of culture, hidden rules, innuendo—the so-called contexts that are often difficult to measure by standard quantitative procedures (Marcella, 1998). It is obvious that the usage of these methods can bring the element of subjectivity to cross-cultural research, which can produce both positive and negative outcomes. In what other instances might you use qualitative over quantitative research? You may try qualitative procedures when dealing with topics that are difficult to measure (such as dreams, pictures, drawings, songs), subjects or topics for which standardized measures are not suited or not available (subjects who are illiterate or unable to use answer scales; see Tutti et al., 1996), and variables that are not completely conceptualized or operationally defined (in many cultures, sexual harassment or mental illness; see Chapter 9).

Researchers often have to combine both qualitative and quantitative methods. Let us go back to the opening vignette. In this example, the sample participants and their answers were influenced by the police chief. We might choose a qualitative design for this study—in addition to quantitative procedures—because it is difficult to measure the extent to which the survey answers were influenced by the police chief's actions.

One form of qualitative research is **psychobiographical research,** or a longitudinal analysis of particular individuals—usually outstanding persons, celebrities, and leaders—representing different countries or cultures. Most of the time, specialists try to collect empirical evidence in order to compose a personal profile of the individuals under study. To collect such evidence, diaries, speeches, comments, letters, memoirs, interviews, and witnesses' accounts are examined. Psychobiographical research provides an in-depth picture of how behavior is formed and transformed under certain cultural conditions.

Major Steps for Preparation of a Cross-Cultural Study

A solid cross-cultural study should address all basic requirements applied to an empirical study in general psychology (see A Case in Point, below).

Ultimately, the researcher attempts to explore both the significance and meaning of cross-cultural differences or similarities. Because research in cross-cultural psychology is comparative, investigative strategies may pursue at least two goals.

Choosing an **application-oriented strategy,** researchers attempt to establish the applicability of research findings obtained in one country or culture to other countries or cultures. In this type of research, a methodology or procedure tested in a particular cultural context (for example, in Japanese collectivist society) is tested in a different cultural setting (for instance, in Finnish individualist society). To illustrate, an Argentinean psychologist who created a unique form of behavioral therapy may conduct an examination of the therapy's effectiveness in neighboring Chile.

Comparativist strategy focuses primarily on similarities and differences in certain statistical measures in a sample of cultures. For example, a Canadian researcher

A CASE IN POINT

A Sample of a Multistep Approach to Cross-Cultural Research Design

Step 1. Describe a problem (an issue) you have to investigate. Review the scholarly literature on the topic. You may use popular journals, magazines, and newspapers for additional references. Check available sources in the language of the country or countries you examine, if necessary.

Step 2. Identify your research goal, that is, explain what you want to achieve as a result. Then introduce one or several hypotheses for your study. You can use at least two strategies: (1) inductive: you collect data first, and then make a conclusion about the studied samples; (2) deductive: you select a theoretical concept first; then you collect data to demonstrate or reject the selected hypothesis.

Step 3. Identify and describe the research sample of your study: groups of people, newspaper reports, children's drawings, texts, etc.

Step 4. Choose or design a methodology for your project. Make sure that your method does not violate research ethics. Refer to your local Human Subjects Review Board for approval. Put together a schedule (timetable) for your project.

Step 5. Conduct a pilot study, a preliminary exploration of the method to see how your methodology works and whether there are any obstacles to data collection.

Step 6. Collect research data.

Step 7. Interpret your data using statistical procedures.

Step 8. Present the results and analyze them critically in a report.

Step 9. In your report, suggest where and how your data should be or could be used (i.e., in education, therapy, conflict-resolution, etc.).

establishes that educational level and size of the family are negatively correlated on the national level. Then she would use a comparativist strategy to identify similarities or differences in the relationships between education and family size in a sample of other countries.

A crucial element for a successful comparative study is the selection of methodology. Often, the same method can be used in different countries without any modifications other than translation. One example of such direct application of the same method is a study conducted by Hofstede (1980), when the original questionnaire was translated into 10 languages in 53 countries. In other cases, an adaptation of the original method is necessary, which usually includes the rephrasing of questions or statements, adding or deleting some words to clarify meaning, breaking up sentences, and so on. Some authors believe that many psychological tests from one culture can be effectively applied—after adaptation, of course—in other countries (Butcher et al., 1998). Others suggest that on some occasions, an entirely new method should be designed for a comparative study. As an example, Cheung and colleagues (1996), arguing that Western personality inventories were inadequate to measure the main elements of Chinese personality, put together a new personality questionnaire specifically for Chinese people.

One of the major concerns of any cross-cultural study is **equivalence.** For example, if an investigator tries to make cross-cultural comparisons of anxiety disorders, he or she should show evidence that the methods selected for the study measure the same phenomenon across other countries chosen for the study. In addition, the methods should be of the common origin. For this purpose, investigators should not collect data in Brazil or Japan using one particular questionnaire on anxiety and then compare the results with an Argentinean or French sample in which another questionnaire was used.

Sample Selection

What types of cultural, ethnic, or national samples should the psychologist select for a cross-cultural study? There are at least three strategies for sample selection (van de Vijver & Leung, 1997). One strategy is availability or convenience sampling, in which the researcher chooses a culture by chance or, most likely, because of the researcher's professional or personal contacts in the country in which the samples are selected. For instance, if you have a former classmate and good friend working as a professional psychologist in India, will you hesitate to collaborate with her in a comparative study?

A second type of sampling is called systematic. The psychologist selects national or ethnic samples according to a theory or some theoretical assumption. The samples may be selected because they represent people who practice different customs. For example, a psychologist who studies marital satisfaction in arranged families may choose countries with and without the arranged-marriage tradition. In the first category will be included Germany, Spain, Chile, and Australia. In the other category, countries such as India, Pakistan, and Somalia can be selected.

A third sampling strategy, random sampling, is when a large sample of countries or groups is randomly chosen, that is, any country or group has an equal change of being selected in the research sample. As an illustration, this method was used by Schwartz (1994), who, in one of the most fascinating comparative projects in psychology, examined human values in 36 randomly selected countries.

In a **representative sample,** the characteristics of a sample accurately reflect the characteristics of the population. The determination of the size of a representative is the chief problem of practically all studies in cross-cultural psychology. There are some statistical methods that determine more or less accurately the size and type of the sample (Heiman, 1996). In general, the smaller the sample, the greater the sampling error, and the greater the result of chance factors. (The sampling error indicates the extent to which the sample is different from the population it represents.) Conversely, the larger the sample, the lower the sampling error. For example, a study that establishes a cross-cultural negative correlation between power distance on one hand, and leader communication and psychological approachability on the other, is likely to contain very small sampling error because it was conducted on a sample of 39 countries of different cultures (Offermann & Hellmann 1997).

One of the most reliable methods of designing a representative sample is random sampling. A random sample is expected to be representative. The mean score received for a representative sample is likely to be a good estimation of the entire population. However, this is just a general assumption. Even random sampling may produce an unrepresentative sample, the one that was perhaps described in the opening vignette.

A sampling error may occur when a researcher tries to establish samples based on assumptions. For example, a psychologist studying behavioral differences between representatives of collectivist and individualist cultures may choose France and Germany as the rich, West European, and industrialized countries and compare them to Bangladesh and Pakistan, two Asian, predominantly rural, Muslim, and developing countries. Such a strategy may have certain disadvantages because of potentially significant differences between the national samples.

Research has shown, time and time again, that estimates derived from large samples are more **reliable** than estimates derived from small samples. Nevertheless, when forming judgments, we typically do not take this principle into account. As a consequence, despite the fact that data collected from small samples cannot be counted on as trustworthy predictors of a population's characteristics, we are prone to commit the error of overgeneralizing from too small a sample. Let us illustrate this concept mathematically. What do you think: does "7 out of 10" look like better odds than "60 out of 100"? Yes, it looks like the first one is better. However, which of these indicators is more reliable? The more reliable indicator is the "60 out of 100" because it is drawn from a larger, that is, more reliable sample!

The sample should be representative of a larger ethnic, national, or other social group. Two national samples cannot be claimed if they are comprised, for example, of French suburban middle-class professionals and Uruguayan college students from Montevideo. In this case it will be unclear what differences are measured: either between two national groups or between students and suburban residents? Even the re-

CRITICAL THINKING

Sampling and the Interpretation of Results

Buda and Elsayed-Elkhouli (1998) paired samples from the United States, Egypt, and Persian Gulf states (namely, Kuwait, Saudi Arabia, and United Arab Emirates). The U.S. sample displayed significantly higher scores on individualism than the Arab sample did. In addition, a difference was detected between the Egyptian and Gulf samples; Egyptians scored lower on collectivism than their counterparts. The authors attribute these differences to Egyptian exposure to Western influence. Many Egyptian citizens travel to other countries and are influenced by Western culture, especially in the capital city of Cairo.

However, looking critically at the samples selected, a point of concern may be raised. The overall sample of this study was 400 subjects, which included approximately 130 women. The Egyptian sample included 224 men and 75 women; of the 102 American subjects, 55 were women; the Gulf sample contained exclusively men. Overall, did this study measure differences among three national groups, or did it actually display the differences between male subjects from the Gulf countries, mostly men from Egypt, and a mixed sample from the United States?

sults of the famous Hofstede study (1980) that were based on a large sample of 88,000 IBM employees in more than 60 countries should be accepted with caution. Because all the studied individuals were employees of a large international corporation, the sample could only conditionally represent the diverse populations of respective countries.

All in all, when selecting and analyzing samples for cross-cultural research please beware of substantial differences in the demographic and social characteristics of the chosen subjects.

 You cannot create experience. You must undergo it.
ALBERT CAMUS (TWENTIETH CENTURY)—FRENCH NOVELIST, PHILOSOPHER, AND JOURNALIST

Observation in Cross-Cultural Psychology

If you are recording people's behavior in their natural environments (for instance, on the streets of Madrid and Bombay) with little or no personal intervention, this procedure is called **naturalistic observation.** A scientific, cross-cultural observation should use identifiable and measurable variables. An example of cross-cultural observation could be a study of different walking patterns in several countries (see Chapter 10) in which the researcher had no impact on how fast the individuals walked on the street. Most of the time, spontaneous observation is biased and the observer's attitudes can have an impact on the results of observation. For a Chinese observer, for example, most American elementary schoolchildren may seem "unrestrained" and "hyperactive." By contrast, to an American psychologist, Chinese pupils in the classroom may appear "restrained" and "hesitant."

In the **laboratory observation,** on the other hand, the subjects are brought in, and you—as a psychologist—design specific situations or prepare a set of stimuli and then ask the participants to respond.

The use of this method requires the researcher to display two important virtues: patience and skepticism. One question should be persistently asked: "Did I observe everything about the studied issue, or is there anything else hidden from me?" An interesting illustration of observation is a study of the Utku Inuit culture (Briggs, 1970). The researcher initially found—as a result of observation—a virtual absence of anger reactions among members of this ethnic group. Does this observation mean that these individuals do not experience anger at all? Not at all. A more patient observation provided a new set of data. Even though there were no displays of anger in interpersonal relationships of the Utku Inuit, anger could still be vented in at least two ways: against dogs and against those persons who were expelled from the community.

Let us beware of other potential biases of observation. In particular, consider how our own motivational biases, personal wishes, or desires for something to fit (or not fit) a particular category may distort our perceptions and subsequent judgments. For example, a specialist may believe that a particular therapeutic method does not work for certain ethnic groups. A reporter may create a theory that achievement on cognitive tests has something to do with gender. Thus, even though there may be a match (or absence of such) between two variables, if you do not want it to exist, you would not be likely to perceive it. Similarly, if you want there to be a match, you would be more inclined to "see" one, whether or not it actually exists. Could you come up with an example of this practice from your personal experience?

Survey Methods

Surveys are, perhaps, the most common technique of data collection in cross-cultural psychology. In a typical survey, the researcher asks the subject to express his or her opinion regarding a particular topic, issue, or issues. There could be open-ended and, more commonly, multiple-choice questions. Open-ended questions give subjects some freedom to express themselves, to explain many nuances of their thoughts and feelings. However, such answers are difficult to interpret quantitatively. Moreover, some subjects—small children or people with little language proficiency, or those who are afraid to give away information about themselves—have difficulty articulating their ideas. Multiple-choice questions, although easier to analyze, also limit the choice of an answer for the respondent. Moreover, in Chapter 5 we will argue that, in some instances, lack of familiarity with formal response scales may affect individual test scores. Keep in mind that standard, paper-and-pencil tests are not com-

CROSS-CULTURAL SENSITIVITY

What kind of obstacles should a Western researcher anticipate when he or she decides to conduct a survey in a country located thousands of miles away from home? Can a telephone survey be used? There are not many phone lines around. Can people be asked at random and in person? This might create a problem. Imagine, a foreign researcher in a small town asking people questions and writing their answers down on a piece of paper. Do we expect people to be open with the researcher? Perhaps some alternative survey methods should be used in such situations. For example, Ho (1998) describes a procedure that is used in psychological research in the Philippines. This is a special unobtrusive survey procedure called *pagtatanung-tanong* that can be used in relatively small, stable, and homogeneous communities. One of the advantages of this method is that the researcher avoids making the interviewees feel that they serve as "subjects" and their answers are used as research information. Using this method the researcher may ask questions in natural, nondisruptive contexts. The researcher is conversing with people, "asking around." The questions may be asked in sequence and they may lead to the formulation of new questions and further clarifications if needed. Inconsistency in the answers would indicate that there is a diversity of opinions among interviewees. If the answers are consistent, this might indicate a particular trend in people's opinions. Conducting this type of research does not disturb people and allows some sensitive issues to be addressed that—in the case of a "standard" opinion poll—would have been unanswered.

mon in all countries. In many communities, for example, the use of such imported questionnaire techniques is constrained by higher rates of illiteracy and people's reluctance to deal with the unfamiliar.

Experimental Studies

To conduct an **experiment,** you put randomly assigned subjects in particular experimental conditions. By varying these conditions, you try to detect specific changes in the subjects' behavior, attitudes, emotions, etc. In an experiment, the condition(s) that are controlled, that is, can be changed by you, are called **the independent variable(s).** The aspect of human activity that is studied and expected to change under influence of the independent variable is called **the dependent variable.** As an experimenter, you control the independent variable: you change the conditions of the experiment.

In a typical cross-cultural experiment, two or several groups are put in preferably identical experimental conditions. Ethnicity, nationality, or other cultural identification of the members of studied groups will typically represent the independent variable. If the experiment is designed properly, any differences in subjects' activity measured by the experiment could be explained, hopefully, as caused by the subjects' cultural background. Please remember that the ultimate goal of any experiment in cross-cultural psychology is to show that there are or there are not any changes in the dependent variable associated with the ethnicity, nationality, religion, culture, or other identities of the subjects.

A simple illustration of an experimental procedure can be drawn from Lawson (1975), who studied flag preference in two groups of schoolchildren: Arabs and Jews. The researcher measured how often children of the two groups, both living in Israel, would chose symbols representing their national identity: either Israeli or Palestinian flags. In this study, the decision to choose a picture with a particular flag on it was the dependent variable. Pictures containing depictions of various flags were the independent variable—and that variable was manipulated by the experimenter. In this experiment, after responses of the participating children were recorded, it was found that the Arab and Jewish schoolchildren in Israel were significantly different in their flag preference, clearly divided along their Arab–Jewish origins (Lawson, 1975).

Let us consider another example. Steffensen and Calker (1982) tested two groups, U.S. and Australian Aboriginal women, by asking them to listen to and then recall two test stories about a child getting sick. In one story, the child was treated by Western medicine (a situation—independent variable—familiar to American women) and in the other by native medicine (a situation familiar to Australian women). The stories were recalled better—and the quality of recall was the dependent variable—when they were consistent with subjects' knowledge. American women remembered better the stories with medical treatment; Australian women recalled better the stories with traditional treatment.

Content-Analysis

Content-Analysis is a research method that systematically organizes and summarizes both the manifest (what was actually said or written) and latent (the meaning of what was said and written) content of communication. The researcher usually examines transcripts of conversations or interviews, television or radio programs, letters, newspaper articles, and other forms of communication. The main investigative procedure in content-analysis consists of two steps. Initially, the researcher identifies coding categories. These can be particular nouns, concepts, names, or topics. First-level coding is predominantly concrete, and involves identifying properties of data that are clearly evident in the text. Second-level coding is more abstract and involves interpreting what the first-level categories mean.

Content-analysis of responses is especially valuable when researchers—for various reasons—cannot use standard questionnaires. For example, a study of undocumented aliens in the United States (Shiraev & Danilov, 2001) revealed that the vast majority of the subjects selected for this research did not want to give written answers because of their fear of being detained by immigration authorities. The subjects preferred verbal communication with the interviewer who could use a tape-recorder. For this reason, a quantitative version of the basic interview that contained numerical scales could not

A CASE IN POINT

A Modification of an Interview Question

Question 14 from the "standard" interview:

"In the past, have you ever had bad dreams (nightmares) about being forced to leave (or deported from) the United States?"

Measurement scale:

Constantly   Frequently   Occasionally   Seldom   Never   Cannot tell

Modified question 14 for a new version of the interview:

"Now tell me please, in the past, have you ever had bad dreams (nightmares) about being forced to leave (or deported from) the United States?"

Additional questions to be asked in the new version of the interview:

"If yes, do you remember them?" "Could you please describe (one) some of them?" "Do you have such dreams often?" "How often?"

have been used in many occasions. Instead, a special qualitative version of the interview was prepared to fit the new requirements of a "verbal" interview (see A Case in Point box, above).

Because content-analysis allows psychologists to use quantitative categories of assessment, this may increase the reliability of this investigative procedure.

Focus-Group Methodology

Focus-group methodology is used intensively both in academic and marketing research. The principal advantage of this method is the opportunity to analyze social, gender, and ethnic discourse on some issues in depth: for example, whether a particular fashion product would have any success among a certain ethnic group, or whether a psychotherapeutic procedure would be "working" for several cultural groups.

The most common usage of this method is a procedure in which a group responds to specific social, political, or marketing messages. The typical focus group contains 7–10 participants. Based on the goal of specific research, the group could be either homogeneous or heterogeneous (ethnically, nationally, professionally, etc.). However, the use of focus-group methodology presents a number of problems for cross-cultural psychologists because these groups do not usually represent randomly selected samples. Also, due to the lack of external validity of any particular focus group outcome, specialists agree that the validity of the focus-group method in general—and in cross-cultural psychology in particular—rests on the repetition of findings across different groups (Kern & Just, 1995).

Meta-Analysis: Research of Research

You know that the same psychological problem or issue is usually studied independently by several researchers or research teams. Indeed, an element or aspect of human activity may be examined from many different angles. Imagine that you study the relationship between family climate and mood disorders in various countries and find that there are more than 30 studies available on this subject and they were all published between 1970 and 2000. How can a scientific generalization be made from all these studies? Is it possible to analyze these data and make a conclusion about the linkages—or absence of—between the quality of family relationships and incidents of mood disorders in the family members? You might realize that a standard comparative review is not a solution. These studies are difficult to compare because they appear to be extremely diverse. Some of them are based on interviews with a few dozen families, whereas others included hundreds of participants from different countries at different times.

There is a special statistical method that allows cross-cultural psychologists to do quantitative analysis of a large collection of scientific results and integrate the findings. It is called **meta-analysis.** In brief, meta-analysis refers to the analysis of analyses—usually called "combined tests"—of a large collection of individual results in an attempt to make sense of a diverse selection of data (Wolf, 1986). One of the attractive features of this method is reliance on statistical formulas, and an imperative to include a large selection of studies, and not only those that appear to be "good" and "interesting."

Meta-analysis has some disadvantages, however. The method attempts to compare studies that deal with variables that are defined differently. For example, if two researchers identify collectivism in their own dissimilar ways, any comparisons of the two would produce invalid and unreliable results. Moreover, many studies use unlike measuring techniques, and are often based on results obtained from dissimilar subject pools. And finally, meta-analysis pays attention to largely published studies that represent significant findings. Therefore, nonsignificant findings are either overlooked or ignored and this may add to some bias in the process of sample selection.

A Hidden Obstacle of Cross-Cultural Studies: Test Translation

The majority of cross-cultural projects—especially of the survey type—require translation from the researcher's language to other language or languages. In such cases, one of the most difficult tasks appears before the investigator: to make sure that the translated version of the method is as close to the original version as possible. However, even a well-translated version of a test is always different from the original one. Languages have dissimilar grammar rules and sentence structures. Sometimes one sentence in the English language requires two sentences in other languages to convey the meaning of the original. At first glance some identical words may have different meanings, such as the words "friend" in English and "amigo" in Spanish. Some words require additional clarifications. Take, for example, the word "cousin." In Arabic and Russian languages this word is translated in a particular way so that it always indicates the cousin's sex. An English version, however, does not typically specify who this person is: "he" or "she." The researcher should, if possible, use short sentences, avoid the passive voice in verbs used, and try to repeat nouns (instead of using "it," "former," or "latter"). Metaphors (such as "pie in the sky") and vague words (such as "probably" or "frequently") should also be routinely avoided because they are difficult to translate (Brislin, 1970).

Some words and phrases, common in the vocabulary of the average American, may have no equivalents in other languages. As an example, the phrase "sexual harassment" requires additional detailed explanations when it is translated in some other languages. If you have trouble believing that this is possible, ask anyone—a Spanish, Arabic, Urdu, Vietnamese, or Hebrew-speaking person—to translate the phrase "sexual harassment" into their language. They will perhaps come up with a phrase in their native tongue. Then ask another person from the same country to translate this phrase back to English. You will likely receive anything but "sexual harassment" as a result of this translation.

All in all, there are some generic rules that can be used for successful translation in cross-cultural studies.

A CASE IN POINT

Test Translation

For illustration, we will use a brief description of the procedure conducted by H. Kassinove, D. Sukhodolsky, C. Eckhardt, and S. Tsytsarev (1997) for a translated version of a State-Trait Anger Expression Inventory. To examine the possible universality of a theoretical model of anger created by Spielberger, a special Russian State-Trait Anger Expression Inventory was created. In this questionnaire, a subject had to indicate his or her agreement with several statements that stand for different manifestations and experiences of anger. The statements—taken from the original American version of the inventory—were translated from the English language to Russian by a native Russian-speaking psychologist with assistance from a Russian psychiatrist. The new translated items were then back-translated by an advanced clinical psychology doctoral candidate at Hofstra University, New York. This person and an assistant were born and educated in the former Soviet Union. Because of the presence of some unique idioms used in English to describe anger, for example, "harboring grudges," "keeping cool," or "feeling burned up," several items did not receive an exact Russian translation. To overcome this obstacle, adjustments were made to recreate several items in the Russian version. Another Russian-speaking American assistant back-translated these items from Russian to English. The complete research team then held special discussion sessions to reach a consensus about the most disputed translations. Such careful translation and back-translation procedures with the help of several researchers create an internally consistent and theoretically sound assessment device for the psychometric measurement of anger in Russian-speaking individuals.

- First, the translation process from the beginning ought to be conducted by bilinguals, that is, by people proficient in both languages. They should conduct the so-called back-translation: initially, they translate the original version of the method and then transfer this version back into the original language. Then both versions are compared.

- Second, it is quite beneficial to have several people do the translation so that there will be several versions of it. These versions can then be compared and converted into one.

- Third, both versions of a questionnaire can be administered on the same bilingual individuals. If the investigator gets similar results on both versions, this is a good indicator that the translation was conducted successfully (Sechrest et al., 1972).

Comparing Two Phenomena: Some Important Principles

How similar are people in Tokyo and New York in terms of thoughts, emotions, and reasoning? Theoretically, there are two answers to this question, each one reflecting a distinct approach to cross-cultural psychology (Berry et al., 1992). Psychologists supporting **the absolutist approach** will argue that psychological phenomena are basically the same in all cultures: honesty is honesty, sexual abuse is abuse, and depression is depression, no matter where, when, or how the researcher studies these and other psychological phenomena. Within this approach, there is a tendency to use the standards of one group as the norms for viewing other groups. From the absolutist perspective, psychological processes are expected to be fairly consistent across different cultures. However, the occurrences of certain processes and behaviors may vary from culture to culture. The scientist, therefore, can study human activity from a position "outside," comparing different cultures and using similar criteria for such comparisons. Assessments of such characteristics are likely to be made using standard—for one country—psychological instruments and their translated versions. Evaluative comparisons can be frequently made from these assessments (Segall et al., 1998).

The second, **the relativist approach,** implies that human behavior in its full complexity can be understood only within the context of the culture in which it occurs. Therefore, the scientist should study an individual's psychology from within his or her culture. For relativists, there is typically little or no interest in similarities and parallels across cultures. Since there are no context-free psychological processes or behaviors, valid comparisons cannot be made among cultures. In other words, from the relativist view practically any cross-cultural comparison is biased.

Quite often in cross-cultural literature, the reader will find the expressions "etic" and "emic." The term *emic* refers to the absolutist position, whereas *etic* stands for the relativist approach. As expected, it is difficult to find a psychologist who is a die-hard absolutist or relativist. Most cross-cultural psychologists today accept a view that combines these two approaches. There are some phenomena in psychology that are universal for all social groups, both large and small, including cultures and subcultures. On the other hand, there are psychological phenomena that are unique for only particular social and cultural conditions. Therefore, psychological comparative measures should be developed in culturally meaningful terms, and comparisons and interpretations of findings have to be made cautiously. This approach does not separate the etic and emic concepts. Instead, it somewhat interconnects them. One of the tasks of cross-cultural psychology then is to determine the balance between both universal and culturally specific characteristics of human behavior, emotion, motivation, and thought.

Even though the absolutist and relativist approaches seem to be dissimilar, they both make sense. Take, for example, the relativist standpoint on phenomenon such as greeting procedures. For anyone examining human communication across countries, it will soon become obvious that the rules of contact are quite unlike. In some cultures, such as the United States or Canada, a handshake is appropriate for both men and women. In Slavic countries, most women do not normally shake hands when they meet another person. In Northern Europe, men rarely kiss each other when they meet, whereas in the Arab Middle East this type of greeting is appropriate. Direct eye contact is considered appropriate in many countries, with the exception of some East Asian cultures, where people, in most cases, greet each other with a bow, without eye contact. Even the distance of conversation varies substantially across countries and regions (see Chapter 11 for more detail on this issue). Therefore, it is very difficult to study greeting styles in different cultures because in these cases, according to an American expression, we would be comparing "apples to oranges."

The absolutist approach is defendable too. Imagine yourself for a minute as a professional psychologist who studies physical and sexual abuse against women in a particular country. By studying cases, and conducting individual interviews, you uncover evidence that women in this country are abused to a significantly greater extent than American women are. Some critics, that is, supporters of the relativist view, might suggest that your data are invalid because "American" views on abuse cannot be applied to other national samples. You, however, could argue that there is no such thing as "cultural" justification for abuse, as there should not be a "cultural" justification for violence and murder.

 Resemblances are the shadows of differences. Different people see different similarities and similar differences.
VLADIMIR NABOKOV (TWENTIETH CENTURY)—RUSSIAN AMERICAN WRITER

On Similarities and Differences: Some Critical Thinking Applications

Without comparisons, there is no cross-cultural psychology. When we compare—take, for example, emotional expressions in two countries or test scores in two national or ethnic groups—we look for either similarities or differences between two variables. When comparing any two phenomena, initially they may "match" with respect to their mutual similarities. But no matter how many features they might share in common, there is no escaping the inevitable fact that at some point there will be a "conceptual fork" in the road, where the phenomena will differ. We may refer to this juncture as the point of critical distinction (PCD), before which the phenomena are similar, and after which they are different. When we are attempting to define, com-

CRITICAL THINKING

Inseparable Differences?

With respect to specific cross-cultural topics and themes, what, for instance, is the meaning of diversity without uniformity? Minority without majority? Atheism without theism? Monotheism without polytheism? Liberal without conservative? Democratic without autocratic? Traditionalist without reformist? Integrationist without segregationist? Prejudiced without unprejudiced? Tolerance without intolerance? Slavery without liberty? Western without Eastern? "Us" without "them"? "I" without "you"?

pare, and contrast any two phenomena, it is imperative that we identify and examine the PCDs that are relevant to the particular events under examination. If, for instance, we are interested in exploring the similarities between the events, we should examine the variables that appear before the PCD; if, by contrast, we wish to analyze the differences between the same two events, we should focus on the variables that appear at and after the PCD. Of course, to gain a full and comprehensive understanding of their relationship, we should examine the variables that appear both before and after the PCD, with particular attention to the PCD itself.

When a difference is found, we often contrast the samples and the larger populations they represent. However, when we contrast individualism and collectivism, for example, we should realize that these two opposites depend on each other for their very conceptual existence! Without one, its opposite ceases to exist. How can we possibly define the concept of "collectivism," for example, without also addressing what we mean by "individualism"? How can we define "biased" in the absence of defining "unbiased"? Can we ever truly understand "conformity" without also understanding "dissent"? This same principle holds true for scores of other opposites: feminine and masculine, subjective and objective, low-power distance and high-power distance, altruism and selfishness, high context and low context, coercion and consent, ability and disability, hunting culture and gathering culture, adaptive and maladaptive, functional and dysfunctional. Remember, to define or understand any phenomenon or issue, its theoretical opposite should also, whenever possible, be addressed and explored.

As these examples illustrate, to contrast a phenomenon with its polar opposite is to give definition to both terms.

Cultural Dichotomies

There Are Fewer Differences Than One Might Think

As was mentioned earlier, mainstream cross-cultural psychology operates in a tradition of cultural dichotomies reflecting a classificatory approach to culture. Typically, these dichotomies have been formulated as contrasts between Western and non-Western cultures. The Westerners (mostly citizens of the richest European and American nations, including some other countries who share major Judeo-Christian values) are commonly associated with individualism, independence, and "egocentrism" (i.e., the individual is a paramount value). The non-Westerners are associated with collectivism, interdependence, and "sociocentrism" (i.e., community and society are supreme values). However, some experts consider such generalizations as simplistic and inaccurate (Hermans & Kempen, 1998). They argue that cultural dichotomies do not and cannot meet challenges raised by the process of global technological and demographic changes. But most importantly, such stereotypical distinction between the "West" and "non-West" often turns labels and symbols into "things," a typical reasoning error (see Chapter 3 for a more detailed discussion). As a result, entire nations that are diverse and heterogeneous may be endowed and labeled with the qualities of homogeneous and distinctive objects. Using such assumptions, people may not only *think* that Americans are individualists, but also *communicate* with them as if all Americans were selfish. Likewise, they may not only think that Japanese are collectivists, but also interact with them as if they all were unselfish.

Any given group (or individual), in reality, falls somewhere between the two hypothetical extremes. Moreover, these orientations are relative to different social contexts. For instance, a person may be individualistic within his or her own culture, yet much more collectivistic as compared with other cultural groups. Similarly, a person might strongly favor collectivism, but the culture in which he or she lives may be somewhat more individualistic than other cultures.

There Are More Differences Than One Might Expect

When the researcher works with samples in Western, technologically developed nations, he or she should understand that most of these countries enjoy considerable cultural and social diversity. For example, imagine a psychologist conducting a three-country study of first-year students' attitudes toward verbal abuse. The research samples are carefully selected. They contain students of the same age, with an equal proportion of men and women. However, what can remain undetected in the study are (1) national differences in higher education and (2) the ways in which people in the studied countries become students. In this hypothetical case, researchers should be aware of a highly competitive system of higher education in Germany and Japan: to become a student, it is necessary to take and pass difficult qualifying exams on different subjects. Many young men and women fail in the process. Critical evaluation of the subject pool of this hypothetical study, therefore, could reveal the fact that this project does not measure the difference among three compatible representative samples. Instead it attempts to uncover differences between (1) highly educated, motivated, and relatively successful Japanese and German men and women and (2) a randomly selected "average" group of American college students who did not go through as difficult a process of precollege selection as their counterparts overseas. We will get back to this example again in Chapters 8 and 11.

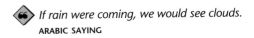 *If rain were coming, we would see clouds.*
ARABIC SAYING

Avoiding Bias of Generalizations

In general, we do formulate conclusions about particular groups of people. We may base our impressions on certain research studies of cross-cultural comparisons. But what kinds of comparisons are we looking for? By and large, our attention is drawn to the studies that demonstrate the most conspicuous, prominent, or salient differences. We then are prone to overgeneralize from these few extreme examples to the group as a whole, the result of which is an inaccurate generalization.

Consider an interesting research finding. It was established that in Chinese romantic-love songs topics of negative or pessimistic expectations are more prevalent than they are in American love songs. This conclusion was made after an analysis of 80 Chinese and Americans songs was conducted (Rothbaum & Tsang, 1998). Do these findings indicate that people in China are more pessimistic than Americans? Maybe they are. Maybe they are not. Pessimism in songs does not necessarily and accurately reflect people's pessimistic attitudes in real life.

To avoid making quick generalizations from research findings, we advise you to use the following recommendations for critical evaluation of cross-cultural research data.

- What were the size and representation of the chosen samples in this project? If the study included just 50 subjects from two countries who answered several-question surveys regarding attitudes toward religion, it is not possible to make reliable conclusions about religious differences between the studied nations.

- Was the method chosen for the study adequate in different cultural settings? Was it translated properly? When it could be demonstrated that the instrument, produced in one setting, was nonetheless applicable in many other settings, differences obtained with that instrument could be taken as reflections of some cultural variables.

- Are the data convincing? To make sure that the results of the study reflect a particular trend and are not due to chance alone, the researcher should repeat the same study to accept the data with confidence or find out about other, similar studies.

- Are there any factors that could have affected the outcome that were not taken into consideration during the study? For instance, psychophysiological events are believed to be the same across cultures. In fact, they largely do not belong to the sphere of interest of cross-cultural researchers. However, such physiological factors can produce unexpected effects (Berry et al., 1992). As an example, studies on alcohol consumption and smoking (see Chapter 9) show the significance of physiological factors in cross-cultural studies.

Overall, be cautious about generalizations. One of the most crucial items of your critical evaluation of the results is an analytical look at the research samples available

TABLE 2.2	The Nonresponse Rate for Individual Households
Population	**Nonresponse Rate**
White non-Hispanic	22.0%
Black	43.4%
Hispanic	36.6%
Asian or Pacific Islander	33.9%
American Indian, Eskimo, or Aleut	36.9%
House/apartment owner	17.7%
Renter	38.7%
Spousal household	19.4%
Nonspousal household	38.1%

Source: The U.S. Bureau of the Census. Population Division Working Paper No. 19, July 1997.

for analysis. Searching for reliable data, the researcher may have good intentions and collect his or her research data from a random sample that accurately represents the population under examination. For example, a psychologist conducts a comparative survey in a culturally diverse area and mails questionnaires to different households at random. Is this specialist aware of nonresponse rates—the percentage of households that does not return questionnaires mailed to them? The U.S. Bureau of the Census published interesting data on nonresponse rates among various groups in the United States (see Table 2.2)

What do these numbers suggest? According to the Bureau estimations, among all ethnic groups, the most "responsive," that is, those groups that are likely to send a questionnaire mailed to them back to the sender, are those who live with a spouse and own property! This means that the researcher will be likely to get the responses not from the random sample of households, but rather from married individuals with relatively high income (because they can afford to buy property) and, predictably, higher educational level. The samples, in fact, that will be compared in this study are predominantly middle-class married individuals.

When comparing large groups such as American whites, blacks, Latinos, Asians, or any other ethnic or religious groups, do not forget that these groups are far from being homogeneous. Among them are individuals who are educated and those who are not, who are wealthy and poor, live in cities or small towns. In cross-cultural research it is always useful to request additional information about the countries in which you do research. For example, the diversity or homogeneity of the population and people's experience of such diversity may affect observation procedures. According to Matsumoto (1992), individuals from homogeneous societies (Japan, for example) may detect and identify other people's emotions less accurately than people from heterogeneous societies do (the United States, for example).

Furthermore, people may have either strong or weak psychological attachment to their cultural heritage, norms, customs, and values compared to other people who belong to the same group. Every social group has individuals with very high intellectual skills as well as individuals with very low IQ scores. Some people have scores of ancestors who lived and are buried in this land; others, from the same group, came recently. Among immigrants, there are scientists and engineers who emigrated from their home countries for economic reasons and political refugees who escaped political persecution. Taiwan and China may represent one culture in someone's view; however, these nations are different ideologically, politically, and even philosophically. The citizens of these political entities may have quite different life-styles, attitudes to various issues, and values.

We should not criticize others, however, for making generalizations. Cross-cultural psychology requires a great deal of imagination and abstraction. Concrete human activities take place in diverse and unique contexts, with a huge variety of underlying factors. To understand and compare psychological phenomena, the researcher should assume that the number of such factors is limited. This inevitably leads to generalizations.

Herein lies the tragedy of the age: not that men are poor—all men know something of poverty; not that men are wicked—who is good? Not that men are ignorant — what is truth? Nay, but that men know so little of men.
W.E.B. Du Bois—AMERICAN SOCIOLOGIST, WRITER, AND TEACHER

Know More about Cultures You Examine!

There are few things as important for cross-cultural psychologists as overall knowledge about countries and people that they study. Travel, collaboration, and exchange of ideas may shed some light on issues and problems that appeared to be familiar and could escape perception (Dogan, 1990).

Gabrielidis et al. (1997) studied cultural differences in preferences for conflict-resolution styles using a poll of 200 students from state-funded universities in the United States and Mexico. The students were asked to answer 20 questions regarding individual choices of conflict resolution: competition, collaboration, avoidance, and accommodation. According to the results, Mexican students preferred conflict-resolution styles that emphasized concern for the outcomes of others—such as accommodation and cooperation—to a greater degree than did the students from the United States. From one opinion, Mexicans, as members of a collectivist culture, can negotiate things, reach compromises, and care about each other. From another opinion, however, Mexico, as a nation, and its government fail to resolve the country's own internal ethnic conflicts and these paper-and-pencil tests cannot produce any reliable evidence about typical "Mexican" conflict-resolution styles.

Grieve not that men do not know you; grieve that you do not know men.
Confucius (551–479 b.c.)—CHINESE PHILOSOPHER

Overall, watch, analyze, raise doubts, and watch again! It is quite possible that the differences among examined samples in a comparative study may be explained in several ways. Take, for example, a study conducted by George Domno in 1986. In this study, he compared the dreams of 562 Hispanic individuals from Mexico, Spain, and Venezuela who were asked to make assessments of their dreams. These data then were contrasted with the data obtained from a non-Hispanic American sample. The results revealed some cultural differences. For example, the number of recalled dreams reported by American respondents was significantly higher than in all three Hispanic groups. Moreover, both Mexican and Venezuelan participants had greater negative emotions associated with their dreams than Spanish and U.S. participants. The author explained the difference in the number of reported dreams by suggesting that Hispanic groups are more passive in their coping styles. Moreover, they consider unpleasant dreams a bad omen, and, therefore, simply do not want to reveal them as often as non-Hispanics do.

A CASE IN POINT

A Sample Study of Collectivism–Individualism

Marshall (1997) examined two samples in New Zealand and Indonesia, both including garbage collectors, bus drivers, and senior college professors. Each social category contained 25 respondents, for a total sample of 150 people. Each group was given a questionnaire that contained 14 statements: seven characteristics of an individualistic orientation and seven representing a collectivist orientation. The respondents had to suggest their agreement with the statements on a 5-point scale.

Collectivist statements: I cannot be happy if any of my friends are unhappy. I feel good to work as a part of a large organization. I like to share my problems with my friends. It is wiser to choose your friends from people with similar social and family backgrounds as yourself. The people at work depend on me, so I should not let them down no matter how badly the organization cheats me. Most of my decisions are made together with relatives and friends. My first duty is to ensure the well-being of my relatives.

Individualistic statements: If the organization I work for suffered financial difficulties and asked me to accept a substantial drop in pay, then I would look for another job. I usually do what I feel is best for me, no matter what others say. Happiness lies in maximizing my personal pleasure. Ideally, I would like to work for myself or own my own company. I deeply resent any invasion of my personal privacy. My happiness depends on my state of mind, regardless of how those around me feel.

The results revealed a trend: Indonesian participants were more collectivistic and less individualistic than their counterparts from New Zealand. Because this study examined the same professional groups, the differences between samples may be explained, from the author's point of view, by cultural differences, that is, collectivism and individualism.

Question. What other explanations can you offer for the differences found in this project? Please consider that New Zealand is more advanced economically than Indonesia and there is—contrary to Indonesia—a large middle class in New Zealand.

However, these differences may be attributed to other features—if one looks carefully at some subtle factors. Even though the subjects of this study were people of the same occupational status, they could be significantly different in terms of their living conditions and sleeping arrangements. American and European families typically have fewer children and more individual privacy in their homes and apartments than do families in many other countries. Sleep patterns may affect how well dreams are retrieved from memory.

In addition, factors such as recent political developments in the countries studied, sporting events, weather changes, and stock market numbers may affect the way people evaluate their own lives. Cultural differences may be detected in the relative importance assigned to certain events. For example, in the United States, a 4 percent level of unemployment is considered "normal" and is therefore unlikely to be the subject of most people's concerns. In South Korea, on the contrary, the same unemployment level in 1998 was considered tragic, because for many years people considered a zero level of unemployment as the only acceptable level. As a result, many individuals in the late 1990s were preoccupied with frustrating thoughts and gloomy predictions about the future (Jordan & Sullivan, 1998).

You should also anticipate that research participants from collectivist countries might present themselves as more collectivist than they usually are because of the social desirability of collected behavior in the society under examination. In other words, people can reply and act in a certain way, not necessarily because this is their typical behavior, but because they want to impress the researcher and give him or her a socially desirable answer. Some studies of the mental health in East Asian countries (China, Japan, and Korea, for instance) revealed that people were giving different information when they wrote about their feelings on a piece of paper and when they told about their experiences in the presence of a professional psychologist (Park, 1988).

EXERCISE 2.1

1. Please identify several potential sampling errors in the cases below:

    Case 1. A professor studies students' ethnic stereotypes. There are 55 people in his class. On Monday morning, 25 showed up for class. The professor asks these students to fill out questionnaires, assuming that a group of 25 is a representative sample for this particular class.

    Case 2. A student union conducts a poll among ESL students by collecting 300 responses from 150 men and 150 women. The interviews took place in the college library where patrons are approached at random and asked to answer a few questions.

    Case 3. A radio talk show host decides to study people's opinions about affirmative action and asks listeners to send their E-mails to the station.

2. It is crucial to know that your question is understood correctly by participants. People typically do not answer what you ask but what they think you

mean by asking (Zaller, 1992). Below are some rules that might be useful in any survey research.

- Don't ask persuasive questions ("People condemn this initiative; do you?").
- Don't put two questions in one ("How often do you feel anxiety and frustration?").
- Don't ask questions that are difficult to comprehend ("Which paradigm can become the explanatory model for these phenomena?").
- Don't ask rhetorical questions ("When will the world start living without violence?").
- Don't ask questions that already have "ready" answers ("Do you think that people can discriminate against each other?").

Using these tips, could you detect what is wrong with the questions below? Please correct and rewrite them.

1. Do you think that people migrate from place to place because they look for better lives?
2. How often do you discuss ethnic or social problems with your parents?
3. What is your favorite TV or radio talk show?
4. How often do you feel depressed, frustrated, or angry watching the evening news?
5. If prejudice is caused by unconscious factors, to what extent do these variables overlap with the previously established contextual conditions?
6. What is your parents' ethnic background?

 EXERCISE 2.2

Here is a description of a cross-cultural survey (Levine, 1991). Please analyze and write down variables that were chosen for testing. Critically examine the procedure. Do you notice any bias in sample selection? Do you see any potential problems with the way the reports about dreams were collected? Do you see any problems with the interpretation of the results? If you had the time and resources, what would you add to the research procedure?

General Characteristics of the Studied Samples

This study investigated the role of culture and social environment in the representation of conflict in the dreams of Bedouin, Irish, and Israeli children, groups of different social and religious backgrounds. Bedouins are seminomadic groups (most of the time, they move from place to place) living according to ancient Muslim customs. They have neither running water nor electricity. Their life depends almost entirely on the health of their livestock. Bedouins live in large extended families and maintain a highly supportive social system. Children of religious settlers represented the Israeli sample; they are known as "kibbutzniks." They have large homes, electricity, television, and swimming pools. The social philosophy of the Israelis emphasizes individuality and interdependence, as well as self-achievement and cooperation among the members of their community. The Irish sample was taken from a village in which people are physically separated from each other, residing on small farms. Contrary to the Irish sample, which was not exposed to any violent conflict or confrontation, both Israeli and Bedouin children were exposed to the ongoing ethnic and political conflict in the region.

Method

Children were asked to record their dreams in their logs. They were supposed to do this on awakening for 7 consecutive days. Each child was asked to give as complete a narrative as possible of the previous night's dream. A special measure was designed to rate (1) the presence or absence of conflict in the dream; (2) the style of conflict representation (i.e., self-representation or depiction of the others in conflict, and the realistic quality of the conflict); and (3) the content of the conflict (i.e., threats to physical integrity, social responsibility, threats to the dreamer's independence, conflict over affection or rejection, material resources, and status). Conflict was defined as the frustration of a motive, presence of a threat, or the result of two or more incompatible response tendencies. Three assistants, one from each studied country, were trained to use the assessment method. Each assistant worked with the sample from his or her native country.

Results and Discussion

This study analyzed the dreams of only 77 children. This limitation allowed the researcher to pay attention to only the most significant differences. Among the samples, altogether, 63 percent of the dreams were rated as containing conflict. It was expected that both Israeli and Bedouin children, because of the ethnic conflict between Arabs and Jews, should have more conflict-revealing dreams than Irish children. In all three samples, the conflict-revealing dreams were reported about twice as often as nonconflict ones. However, the number of conflict-revealing dreams was almost equal in the studied samples. Perhaps interpersonal relationships within both Middle Eastern groups, despite the ongoing ethnic conflict, could provide some sense of protection and care for the children. There was also a difference between Bedouin children on the one hand, and Irish and Jewish groups, on the other, in terms of the frequency in appearance of nonhuman opponents in the dreams. Indeed, the Bedouin sample, which demonstrated a higher frequency of nonhuman opponents, lives in absolute dependence on the physical environment. Bedouin's survival is more dependent on the forces of nature. In contrast, Jewish and Irish children live in an environment in which they can exercise some control over it. Unlike Bedouin and Irish children, one of the most frequent dream conflicts reported by kibbutz children involved threats to their independence. Compared with the other groups, the Irish children's dreams reflected their withdrawal from interpersonal relationships. This observation may reflect the geographic isolation of their rural community.

CHAPTER SUMMARY

- There are four basic goals of research in cross-cultural psychology: description, interpretation, prediction, and management. After identifying the goals, the researcher has to choose a methodological approach that is most appropriate for the implementation of these goals. In general, research methodology in cross-cultural psychology can be divided into two categories: quantitative and qualitative.

- Quantitative research in cross-cultural psychology involves the measurement of certain aspects of human activity from a comparative perspective. The variables chosen for examination have to be studied empirically, primarily through observation, as opposed to other forms of reflection, such as intuition, beliefs, or superstitions. The most common data are measures of central tendency: the mode, the median, and the mean. There are four types of measurement scales: nominal, ordinal, interval, and ratio.

- Among the most important statistical methods used in cross-cultural psychology are correlational methods that establish relationships between two variables and the *t*-test for independent samples, which aims to estimate whether the difference between two samples occurred by chance.

- Qualitative research is conducted primarily in the natural setting, where the research participants carry out their daily activities in a nonresearch atmosphere. Qualitative studies are also conducted when there are difficulties in measuring variables, in situations when the subjects cannot read or use answer scales, or when there are no standardized measurement instruments available. Qualitative research is also useful in situations in which variables are not completely conceptualized or operationally defined. The qualitative method can be useful when the experiences and priorities of the research participants heavily influence the research.

- Choosing an application-oriented strategy, researchers attempt to establish the applicability of research findings obtained in one country or culture to other countries or cultures. The comparativist strategy, on the contrary, focuses primarily on similarities and differences in certain statistical measures in a sample of cultures.

- There are several strategies for sample selection. One strategy is availability or convenience sampling. Another type of sampling, called systematic, involves the psychologist selecting national or ethnic samples according to a theory or some theoretical assumption. A third sampling strategy is random sampling. In this case, a large sample of countries or groups is randomly chosen, that is, any country or group has an equal chance of being selected in the research sample.

- Cross-cultural psychologists use all of the typical psychological methods of investigation: observation, survey, experiment, content-analysis, psychobiography, meta-analysis, focus-group methods, and other procedures.

- The majority of cross-cultural projects—especially of the survey type—require translation from the researcher's language to other language or languages. In such cases, one of the most difficult tasks that appears before the investigator is to make sure that the translated version of the method is as close to the original version as possible.

- There are at least two approaches to the analysis of cross-cultural data. Psychologists supporting the absolutist approach argue that psychological phenomena are basically the same across cultures. However, the occurrences of certain processes and behaviors may vary from culture to culture. The relativist approach implies that human behavior in its full complexity can be understood only within the context of the culture in which it occurs.

- Cross-cultural psychologists should see similarities in different phenomena; likewise, similarities should not overshadow potential differences between samples. The specialist should be aware that to contrast a phenomenon with its polar opposite is to give definition to both terms. All polar opposites are dependent on each other for their very conceptual existence.

- Cross-cultural psychologists should avoid biases of generalization. At the same time, it should be understood that cross-cultural

psychology requires a great deal of imagination and abstraction. Concrete human activities take place in diverse and unique contexts with a huge variety of underlying factors. To understand and compare psychological phenomena the researcher should assume that the number of such factors is relatively limited.

 # KEY TERMS

Absolutist Approach   A view in cross-cultural psychology that psychological phenomena are basically the same in all cultures.

Application-Oriented Strategy   An attempt to establish the applicability of research findings obtained in one country or culture to other countries or cultures.

Comparativist Strategy   An attempt to find similarities and differences in certain statistical measures in a sample of cultures.

Content-Analysis   A research method that systematically organizes and summarizes both the manifest and latent content of communication.

Correlation Coefficient   A number that summarizes and describes the type of relationship present and the strength of the relationship between variables X and Y.

Dependent Variable   The aspect of human activity that is studied and expected to change under the influence of an independent variable(s).

Equivalence   Evidence that the methods selected for the study measure the same phenomenon across other countries chosen for the study.

Experiment   The investigative method in which researchers alter some variables to detect specific changes in the subjects' behavior, attitudes, or emotions.

Independent Variable   The condition(s) that are controlled by the researcher.

Laboratory Observation   Recording people's behavior in an environment created by the researcher.

Mean   The mathematical central point of a distribution of scores.

Measure of Central Tendency   The measure that indicates the location of a score distribution on a variable, that is, describes where most of the distribution is located.

Median   The score in a distribution located at the 50th percentile.

Meta-Analysis   The quantitative analysis of a large collection of scientific results in an attempt to make sense of a diverse selection of data.

Mode   The most frequently occurring score in a distribution.

Naturalistic Observation   Recording people's behavior in their natural environments with little or no personal intervention.

Psychobiographical Research   A longitudinal analysis of particular individuals, usually outstanding persons, celebrities, and leaders, representing different countries or cultures.

Relativist Approach   A view in cross-cultural psychology that psychological phenomena should be studied only from "within" a culture where these phenomena occur.

Representative Sample   A sample having characteristics that accurately reflect the characteristics of the population.

Survey   The investigative method in which groups of people answer questions about their opinions or their behavior.

t-Test   The procedure that aims to estimate whether the difference between two samples occurred by chance.

CHAPTER 3

Critical Thinking in Cross-Cultural Psychology

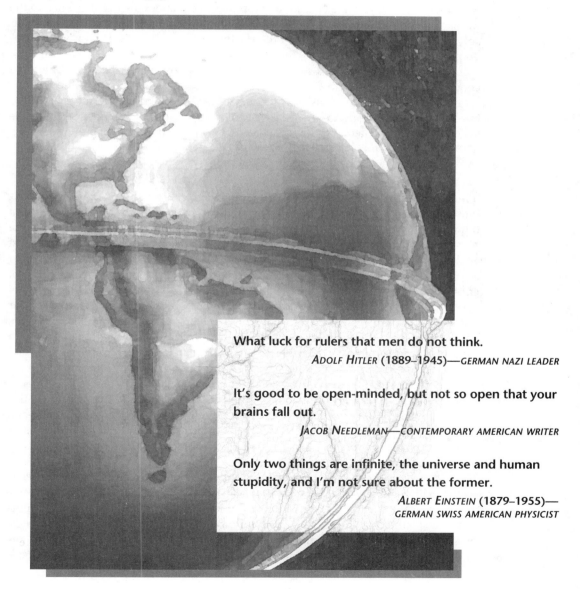

What luck for rulers that men do not think.

ADOLF HITLER (1889–1945)—*GERMAN NAZI LEADER*

It's good to be open-minded, but not so open that your brains fall out.

JACOB NEEDLEMAN—*CONTEMPORARY AMERICAN WRITER*

Only two things are infinite, the universe and human stupidity, and I'm not sure about the former.

ALBERT EINSTEIN (1879–1955)— *GERMAN SWISS AMERICAN PHYSICIST*

This story could have been told in New Orleans. Or maybe in New York. Or perhaps in Tokyo, Cape Town, or Buenos Aires. A woman walks into a doctor's office complaining that she's a zombie. The doctor, trying his best to convince her otherwise, says, "You're walking and talking, aren't you?" "Zombies walk and talk," replies the patient. "Well, you're breathing, too." "Yes, but zombies breathe." "Okay, what *don't* zombies do? Do they bleed?" "No, *of course not,*" says the patient. The doctor replies, "Good. Then I'm going to stick this needle into your arm and we'll see if your idea is right or wrong." So he plunges the needle deep into the woman's arm, and, sure enough, blood starts to pour out of the wound. The woman is aghast. In utter dismay, she turns to the doctor and says, "My God, I was wrong . . . Zombies *do* bleed."

What is the moral of this story? Compelling facts are quite often not compelling enough. What matters more is our interpretation of these facts. One of the most significant characteristics of our thinking is the way in which we become personally invested in—and then tightly cling to— our beliefs and interpretations. This tendency, called the belief perseverance effect, can frequently lead us to freely distort, minimize, or even ignore any facts that run contrary to our reality.

Thinking is one of the most essential of all human characteristics. It is intrinsic to almost everything we do. But do we ever think about thinking? How often do we subject our thinking process to critical analysis?

Educators rightfully profess that learning how to think critically is one of the most vital and indispensable components of learning; yet, specific tools for **critical thinking** are rarely, if ever, provided to us. Thus, although we may be convinced of the value of critical thinking, we are left not knowing quite what to do about it.

Herein lies the theme of this chapter, whose express purpose is to improve your thinking skills, to teach you to think critically, to help you think about thinking—in a word, to promote **metathinking** in cross-cultural psychology. Metathinking is not a magical, mystical, or mysterious abstraction. It is not an unattainable gift that is miraculously bestowed on the intellectual elite. Rather, it is a skill (or more accurately, a series of skills) that can be successfully taught and learned (see Levy, 1997). The thought principles or **metathoughts** (literally, "thoughts about thought") contained in this chapter are cognitive tools that provide the user with specific strategies for inquiry and problem solving in cross-cultural psychology. In this way, they serve as potent **antidotes** to thinking, which is often prone to be biased, simplistic, rigid, lazy, or just plain sloppy.

For the purposes of this book (portions of which were adapted from Levy, 1997), each metathought is illustrated primarily from the theory and application of contemporary cross-cultural psychology. Keep in mind, however, that these principles transcend the confines of any specific topic and can be utilized in a diverse array of fields, ranging from philosophy and theology to law, political science, history, sociology, anthropology, journalism, business, medicine, sports, the arts—in fact, in all areas of education and learning.

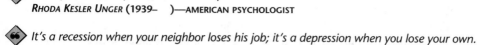

Description is always from someone's point of view.
RHODA KESLER UNGER (1939–   )—AMERICAN PSYCHOLOGIST

It's a recession when your neighbor loses his job; it's a depression when you lose your own.
HARRY S. TRUMAN (1884–1972)—THIRTY-THIRD U.S. PRESIDENT

The Evaluative Bias of Language: To Describe Is to Prescribe

Language serves many functions. Certainly one of its most common and most important purposes is to help us describe various phenomena, such as events, situations, and people: "What is it?" Another purpose is to evaluate these same phenomena: "Is it good or bad?" Typically, we consider descriptions to be objective, whereas we consider evaluations to be subjective.

However, is the distinction between objective description and subjective evaluation a clear one? The answer, in the vast majority of cases, is no. Why? Because words both describe *and* evaluate. Whenever we attempt to describe something or someone,

TABLE 3.1	The Same Person as Described from Two Different Perspectives
From Jenny's Value System	**From Lee's Value System**
old	mature
naïve	idealistic
reckless	brave
manipulative	persuasive
spineless	cooperative
childish	childlike
weird	interesting
obsessed	committed
anal retentive	tidy
dependent	loyal
codependent	empathic
narcissistic	high self-esteem
lunatic	visionary
psychotic	creative
bum	vocationally disadvantaged
sociopath	morally challenged
dead	ontologically impaired

the words we use are almost invariably value laden, in that they reflect our own personal likes and dislikes. Thus, our use of any particular term serves not only to describe, but also to *prescribe* what is desirable or undesirable to us.

This problem is not so prevalent in describing objects as compared with people. Let us take, as an illustration, the terms *cold* and *hot*. For material substances, both terms refer literally to temperature: "That liquid is very cold," or "That liquid is very hot." When we use these same terms to describe an individual, however, they take on a distinctly evaluative connotation: "That person is very cold," or "That person is very hot."

Our best attempts to remain neutral are constrained by the limits of language. When it comes to describing people (for example, in conducting research) it is nearly impossible to find words that are devoid of evaluative connotation. Incredible as it may seem, we simply do not have neutral adjectives to describe personality characteristics, whether of an individual or an entire group. And even if such words did exist, we still would be very likely to utilize the ones that reflect our own personal preferences.

The evaluative bias of language is illustrated in Table 3.1 and the accompanying exercise. Let us say that two different observers (Jenny and Lee), each with a different set of values, are asked to describe the same person, event, or group. Notice how the words they use reveal their own subjective points of view.

EXERCISE 3.1

The Interdependence of Values, Perceptions, and Language

Ready to try some on your own? Remember that you are to select words that reveal Lee's personal attitudes and values, that are consistently more "positive" than Jenny's. (Some suggestions appear in Appendix 1 on page 352.)

Jenny	Lee	Jenny	Lee
problem	_____	abnormal	_____
failure	_____	ethnocentrism	_____
terrorist	_____	chauvinism	_____
hostage	_____	cultural impurity	_____
murder	_____	discrimination	_____
genocide	_____	reverse discrimination	_____
brainwashed	_____	child abuse	_____
handicapped	_____	child neglect	_____
disabled	_____	handout	_____
primitive	_____	kleptomaniac	_____

This metathought also undersores the reciprocal influence of attitudes and language. That is, not only do our beliefs, values, and perceptions affect our use of language, but our use of language in turn influences our beliefs, values, and perceptions (see *bidirectional causation*). For example, by referring to a person or group as *sick*, we are more inclined to perceive them as sick, which in turn leads us to label them sick, which prompts us to assume that they are sick, and so forth.

The bidirectional relationship between attitudes and language has direct relevance to the use (and misuse) of "politically correct" terminology. Consider the ways in which names applied to various ethnic groups have changed as a function of different social and historical contexts. What values might be related to, for example, the use of *Indian* versus *Native American*? *Iranian* versus *Persian*? *Oriental* versus *Asian*? *Colored* versus *Black* versus *Negro* versus *Afro-American* versus *African American*? Why is *person of color* "in," while *colored person* is "out"? Similarly, what do the terms *pro-choice* and *pro-life* not so subtly imply about the moral stance of anybody who happens to have a different point of view? In these cases and countless more, we see how values both shape and are shaped by our use of language.

Antidotes

1. Remember that descriptions, especially concerning personality characteristics, can never be entirely objective, impartial, or neutral.

2. Become aware of your own personal values and biases, and how these influence the language that you use.

3. Avoid presenting your value judgments as objective reflections of truth.

4. Recognize how other people's use of language reveals their own values and biases.

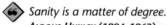

He that is not with me is against me: and he that gathereth not with me scattereth.
[THE] BIBLE

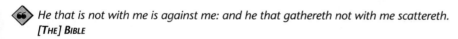

Sanity is a matter of degree.
ALDOUS HUXLEY (1894–1963)—TWENTIETH-CENTURY ENGLISH AUTHOR

Differentiating Dichotomous Variables and Continuous Variables: Black and White, or Shades of Gray?

Some phenomena in the world may be divided (or *bifurcated*) into two mutually exclusive or contradictory categories. These types of phenomena are **dichotomous variables.** For example, when you flip a coin, it must turn up either heads or tails—there is no middle ground. Similary, a woman cannot be "a little bit," "somewhat," or "moderately" pregnant—she is either pregnant or not pregnant. Here are some other examples:

- A light switch is either on or off.
- An individual was born in Rwanda or he wasn't.
- A person is either male or female (with some rare exceptions).

Other phenomena, by contrast, consist of a theoretically infinite number of points lying between two polar opposites. These types of phenomena are **continuous variables**. For example, between the extremes of black and white there exists a middle ground comprised of innumerable shades of gray.

The problem is that we often confuse these two types of variables. Specifically, people have a natural tendency to dichotomize variables that, more accurately, should be conceptualized as continuous. In particular, most person-related phenomena are frequently presumed to fit into one of two discrete types (either category A or category B), rather than as lying along a continuum (somewhere between end point A and end point B). In the vast majority of cases, however, continuous variables are more accurate and therefore more meaningful representations of the phenomena we are attempting to describe and explain.

With particular respect to cross-cultural psychology, the potential pitfall of false dichotomization is illustrated by the concepts of *individualism* and *collectivism* (see Chapter 1). What are some examples of continuous variables that frequently are assumed to be, or treated as if they were, dichotomous?

> *normal–abnormal*
>
> *mental health–mental illness*
>
> *introverted–extroverted*
>
> *biased–unbiased*
>
> *competitive–cooperative*
>
> *autonomous–dependent*
>
> *functional–dysfunctional*
>
> *adaptive–maladaptive*

 EXERCISE 3.2

Identifying Dichotomous Versus Continuous Variables

The following exercise will give you some practice at differentiating dichotomous and continuous phenomena. For each of the terms below, indicate those that refer to dichotomous phenomena (D) and those that refer to continuous phenomena (C). (Answers appear in Appendix 2 on page 352.)

feminine–masculine: _____	perfect–imperfect: _____
married–single: _____	young–old: _____
conscious–unconscious: _____	present–absent: _____
prejudiced–unprejudiced: _____	rich–poor: _____
slavery–freedom: _____	liberal–conservative: _____
racist–nonracist: _____	airborne–grounded: _____

homosexual–heterosexual: ____	responsible–not responsible: ____
licensed–unlicensed: ____	acculturated–unacculturated: ____
integration–segregation: ____	mailed–unmailed: ____
alcoholic beverage– nonalcoholic beverage: ____	democracy–dictatorship: ____
sexist–nonsexist: ____	guilty verdict–not guilty verdict: ____
heterogeneous– homogeneous: ____	tolerance–intolerance: ____
materialistic–spiritualistic: ____	successful basketball shot– unsuccessful shot ____
traditionalist–reformist: ____	power on–power off: ____
addicted–not addicted: ____	subjective–objective: ____
similar–different: ____	politically correct– politically incorrect: ____
dead–alive: ____	

Antidotes

1. Learn to differentiate between variables that are dichotomous and those that are continuous.

2. Remember that most person-related phenomena—such as traits, attitudes, and beliefs—lie along a continuum.

3. When making cross-cultural comparisons, try to avoid artificial or false dichotomies (Hermans & Kempen, 1998).

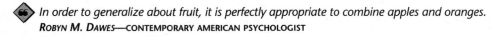

In order to generalize about fruit, it is perfectly appropriate to combine apples and oranges.
ROBYN M. DAWES—CONTEMPORARY AMERICAN PSYCHOLOGIST

Everyone and anyone is much more simply human than otherwise, more like everyone else than different.
HARRY STACK SULLIVAN (1892–1949) AMERICAN PSYCHIATRIST

The Similarity–Uniqueness Paradox: All Phenomena Are Both Similar and Different

By way of introducing this metathought, let us examine the following problem: Which of the following four words does not belong with the other three?

    A. Canadian   *B.* Italian   *C.* Cuban   *D.* Hindu

The correct answer to this question is *D*, because *Hindu* is the only term that represents a religion rather than a nationality. But wait, the correct answer is *B*, because none of the others is European. Then again, the correct answer is *C*, because this is the only group with a communist government. Is that it? Not quite. The correct answer is *A*, because Canadian is the only word on the list that contains an even number of letters.

So which is it? Can it be that all four answers are correct? If so, how can every term be both similar to and different from the others? The solution to this apparent paradox lies in the cognitive schema or perceptual set with which one initially approaches the problem. More specifically, it is a function of the particular dimensions or variables on which one has evaluated the response options.

As you can see, determining the similarities and differences between any set of events—two cultures, for example—is dependent on the perspectives from which you choose to view them. In this way, phenomena can be seen as both unique from and, at the same time, similar to other phenomena.

Let us examine briefly the interlocking processes of comparing and contrasting phenomena. First, how do we determine the degree to which phenomena are similar? To begin with, any two phenomena in the cosmos share at least one fundamental commonality: namely, they are both phenomena. With this as a starting point, they may subsequently be compared along a virtually infinite array of dimensions, ranging from the broadest of universal properties to the minutest of mundane details.

For instance, when you compare two groups of people you can focus on physical features (height, weight, hair and eye color, health, strength, attractiveness), demographic characteristics (age, ethnicity, nationality, culture, religion, income, occupation), social context (competitive, cooperative, structured, ambiguous, restrictive, permissive), personality attributes (intelligence, motivation, maturity, creativity, psychological problems, attitudes, values, beliefs, goals), personal tastes (in art, music, food, clothing, wallpaper), and so on.

 EXERCISE 3.3

Exploring Similarities and Differences

The following exercise will give you some practice at comparing, contrasting, and identifying points of distinction from a diverse array of sociocultural phenomena. First, browse through the list below and select three word pairs that, for whatever reason, capture your interest. Then, utilizing any dimensions or sorting variables that might be helpful, for each pair answer the questions: (1) "How are they similar?" and (2) "How are they different?"

God and Satan
heaven and hell
religion and art
religion and science
religion and mythology
religion and psychotherapy
religion and slavery
religion and freedom
Judaism and Christianity
Catholicism and Protestantism
Buddhism and Hinduism

the Bible and the Koran
the Bible and the Constitution
religious leaders and political leaders
religious conversion and cult indoctrination
television evangelists and infomerical salesman
men and women
homosexuality and heterosexuality
Western philosophy and Eastern philosophy

Jewish Americans and African Americans

Native American tribes and African tribes

Spanish culture and Mexican culture

Japanese art and Chinese art

Israeli music and Arabic music

Italian food and French food

racism and sexism

ignorance-based racism and hostility-based racism

racial inequality in 1950 and racial inequality in 2000

White supremacists and Black nationalists

prejudice against women and prejudice against teenagers

affirmative action and discrimination

discrimination and reverse discrimination

government and parents

nations and families

patriotism and nationalism

customs and laws

Democrats and Republicans

Capitalism and Socialism

Communism and Nazism

infancy and old age

the Olympics and war

your cultural background and the President's cultural background

your cultural background and your best friend's cultural background

your cultural background and an adversary's cultural background

What is the purpose of this exercise? First, it illustrates that any two phenomena, no matter how seemingly disparate at first glance, always share at least some similarities. Second, phenomena invariably are differentiated by various points of critical distinction, which, in essence, define the boundaries delineating one phenomenon from another. Third, by utilizing this method of comparing and contrasting phenomena, you probably gained new insights and discovered some fresh perspectives into these relationships that you heretofore might not have considered. Fourth, given the fact that any two events are similar *and* different, it is crucial to take them *both* into account in your assessment of the phenomena.

Keep these principles in mind whenever you are faced with the task of comparing and contrasting sociocultural phenomena. You are likely to be more than just a little surprised each time you realize that the dimensions or variables you select for purposes of evaluation ultimately will determine just how "similar" or "unique" the phenomena turn out to be.

Antidotes

1. When comparing and contrasting any two phenomena ask yourself, "In what ways are they similar?" *and* "In what ways are they different?"

2. Before beginning your evaluation, ask yourself, "What is the purpose of this analysis?" Asking this question will help you to choose the most appropriate and relevant dimensions and sorting variables.

3. Carefully and judiciously select the dimensions on which you will evaluate various phenomena. Recognize that the dimensions you select will ultimately determine the degree of "similarity" or "uniqueness" displayed between the two phenomena.

4. Despite what may appear to be an overwhelming number of similarities between two events, always search for and take into account their differences; conversely, regardless of what may seem to be a total absence of commonalities between two events, search for and take into account their similarities.

5. Do not allow yourself to be swayed by individuals who maintain that "These events are exactly the same," or "You can't compare these events because they have absolutely nothing in common."

 A good circus should have a little something for everybody.
ATTRIBUTED TO P.T. BARNUM

 There's a sucker born every minute.
P.T. BARNUM (1810–1891)—AMERICAN SHOWMAN

The Barnum Effect: "One-Size-Fits-All" Descriptions

A **Barnum statement** is a personality description about a particular individual or group that is true of practically all human beings; in other words, it is a general statement that has "a little something for everybody." The **Barnum effect** refers to people's willingness to accept the validity of such overly inclusive and generic appraisals.

Barnum statements pervade the popular media, from broadcast to print, in the form of self-help primers, astrological forecasts, psychic hotlines, biorhythm and numerology readings, and interpretations of dreams, palms, or favorite colors. To find them, you need look no further than the contents of your most recent fortune cookie. (See Levy, 1993, for a satirical essay on this topic, "The One-Size-Fits-All Psychological Profile.")

These statements are frequently used in our everyday descriptions of both individuals and specific sociocultural groups with whom we interact. For instance, we may confidently announce, "Immigrants have self-esteem issues." (Who *doesn't*?) Or "Chinese are sensitive to criticism." (Who *isn't*?) Or "Women do not want to be rejected." (Who *does*?)

The variations on this theme are virtually infinite. To list but a few: "He has a streak of prejudice in him." "She has some sensitive spots about her cultural background." "Hindus search for meaning of life." "Caucasians favor members of their own group." "Italians enjoy food." "Minorities just want their rights." "Republicans care about family values." "Homosexuals are concerned with sex." (See Appendix 3 on page 353 for an extended list of Barnum statements related to sociocultural groups.)

A CASE IN POINT

"Your Personality"

A number of researchers have presented subjects with Barnum-like personality descriptions, such as those below (Forer, 1949).

"You have a strong need for other people to like and admire you. You have a tendency to be critical of yourself. . . . At times you have serious doubts as to whether you have made the right decision or done the right thing. You prefer a certain amount of change and variety and become dissatisfied when hemmed in by restrictions and limitations. You pride yourself on being an independent thinker and do not accept other opinions without satisfactory proof. You have found it unwise to be too frank in revealing yourself to others. At times you are extraverted, affable, sociable; at other times you are introverted, wary, and reserved. Some of your aspirations tend to be pretty unrealistic."

When subjects in the experiments were led to believe that the bogus personality description was prepared especially for them, and when it was generally favorable, they nearly always rated the description as either "good" or "excellent" (Dickson & Kelly, 1985). In fact, when given a choice between a fake Barnum description and an authentic personality description based on an established test, people tended to choose the phony description as being more accurate (see Snyder, et al., 1977, for a review of research in this area).

EXERCISE 3.4

"De-Barnumizing" Barnum Statements

Begin this exercise by selecting a few Barnum descriptions. Then, "de-Barnumize" each statement by incorporating any potentially useful qualifiers, modifiers, or adverbs. To get you started, here are two examples:

> Barnum statement: *Roberto is sensitive to criticism.*
> De-Barnumized statement: *Roberto is particularly sensitive to criticism.*
> Barnum statement: *Native Americans have an appreciation for nature.*
> De-Barnumized statement: *Compared to modern, industrialized societies, Native Americans display a greater appreciation for nature.*

Now try one of your own:

> Barnum statement: _____
> De-Barnumized statement: _____
>
> _____

Antidotes

1. Learn to differentiate Barnum statements from person- and group-specific descriptions and interpretations.

2. Be aware of the limited utility inherent in Barnum statements. Specifically, remember that although Barnum statements have validity about people in general, they fail to reveal anything distinctive about any given individual or sociocultural group.

3. Whenever feasible and appropriate, make it a point to reduce the Barnum effect by qualifying personality descriptions and interpretations in terms of their magnitude or degree.

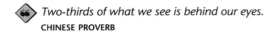 *No two people look at one individual from the same point of view. For instance, I have a girlfriend. To me, she's the most remarkable, the most wonderful person in the world. That's to me. But to my wife. . .*
JACKIE MASON (1937–   )—AMERICAN COMEDIAN

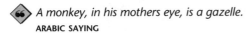 *A monkey, in his mothers eye, is a gazelle.*
ARABIC SAYING

Two-thirds of what we see is behind our eyes.
CHINESE PROVERB

The Assimilation Bias: Viewing the World through Schema-Colored Glasses

One of the most fundamental and pervasive of all human psychological activities is the propensity to categorize. People appear to possess an innate drive to classify, organize, systematize, group, subgroup, and otherwise structure the world around them.

We categorize everything from persons, objects, places, and events, to concepts, experiences, feelings, and memories. The phenomenon is omnipresent, the breadth is enormous, and almost nothing is immune: gender and race, religions and occupations, cultures and nations, subatomic particles and celestial constellations, time and space.

We can conceptualize all such categories as mental representations, or **schemas**. A schema is a cognitive structure that organizes our knowledge, beliefs, and past experiences, thereby providing a framework for understanding new events and future experiences (see Cantor & Mischel, 1979; Fiske & Taylor, 1991; Levy et al., 1988; Piaget, 1952; Taylor et al., 1994). Put another way, schemas (or *schemata*) are general expectations or preconceptions about a wide range of phenomena. In the cross-cultural domain, these include perceptual sets about people based on their age, gender, race, religion, vocation, socioeconomic status, political affiliation, social role, or any other characteristic. In fact, we may view stereotypes as equivalent to group schemas (Hamilton, 1979, 1981). (See Chapter 10 on Social Cognition.)

What function do schemas serve? First and foremost, they enable us to process the plethora of stimuli we continually encounter in a relatively rapid, efficient, and effortless manner. In other words, schemata reduce our cognitive processing load.

Whenever we are faced with new information, we quickly and automatically compare it to our preexisting schemas, which greatly simplifies the task of organizing and understanding our experiences.

What happens when we come across information that is discrepant from our preconceptions? Put another way, what do we do when there is a clash between the data and our schemas? The Swiss psychologist Jean Piaget (1954, 1970) identified two complementary processes that we utilize in such situations: *accommodation* and *assimilation*. According to Piaget, both of these responses are integral components of cognitive development, and constitute the means by which we adapt to our environment and construct our reality (see Chapter 8 on development).

Accommodation refers to the process wherein we modify our schema to fit the data. In other words, we change our preexisting beliefs so that they make room for (that is, "accommodate") new information. Assimilation, by contrast, means to modify the data to fit our schema. Here, we incorporate new information into our preexisting beliefs—even if it means distorting the information itself.

The conduct of scientific investigation involves the processes of both assimilation and accommodation. Specifically, psychologists use theories to help them make sense out of an overwhelming array of seemingly disjointed, frequently bewildering, sometimes incoherent, and all-too-often ambiguous events. In other words, they assimilate observed phenomena into their conceptual schemas. And so long as the data and the theory "fit" each other, assimilation effectively and successfully serves its purpose. Suppose, however, that a particular observation disconfirms or contradicts the scientist's expectations; that is to say, the new datum does not fit the old theory. Now what? In the pursuit of knowledge, good scientists put aside their pride, their stubbornness, and their egos and they alter their theory to accommodate the facts.

Do people in general make appropriate use of assimilation and accommodation? The answer, by and large, is no. Time and time again the discrepancies between data and schemas typically are resolved more in the direction of assimilation than accommodation. In other words, we are inclined to make the data fit the schema, rather than the other way around.

Because schematic processing occurs automatically and relatively unconsciously, it is very resistant to change—even when it is fraught with errors. We tend to overlook, misconstrue, or outright reject valid information when it is not consistent with our schemas. In a word, a fundamental and pervasive liability of schematic processing can be seen as a problem of assimilation.

This bias manifests itself in a wide variety of forms and contexts. Specifically, it leads us to rely excessively on vivid but not necessarily appropriate information, to fill in gaps in our knowledge with schema-consistent but erroneous information, to conduct biased searches for evidence, to recall or misinterpret information about past events so that it validates our schemas, to unwittingly elicit the very events that we expect to find, and to engage in and perpetuate sociocultural stereotyping.

In sum, schemas bias our perceptions of reality to make them consistent with what we already believe. As such, the **assimilation bias** represents a significant obstacle to clear thinking and effective problem solving. In viewing the world through "schema-colored glasses," we subject virtually all the incoming information to varying degrees of distortion, misinterpretation, and invalidation.

A vivid case in point is provided by Robyn Dawes (1994), who tells of an incident involving flagrant gender bias in decision making. The dean of a major medical school, perplexed as to why his institution was unsuccessful in its attempts to recruit female students, asked a colleague of Dawes to investigate the problem. What emerged was striking. One of the interviewers had been rating applicants with respect to their "emotional maturity," "seriousness of interest in medicine," and "neuroticism." As it turned out, the vast majority of females did not receive positive evaluations on any of his criteria. Specifically, whenever the woman was not married, he judged her to be "immature." When she was married, he concluded that she was "not sufficiently interested in medicine." And when she was divorced? "Neurotic," of course. No win. No escape. No admittance.

 EXERCISE 3.5

Changing the View with Different Lenses

The following exercise will give you some practice at viewing the same phenomenon through different sociocultural lenses. Select one of the perspectives from the list below (or of your own choosing) and write a few statements as to how that individual might perceive, explain, or react to a teenager from Oregon who engages in body piercing. Then, "switch lenses" by viewing the same teenager from a different perspective.

parental figure(s) • Zulu tribal chief • midwestern farmer • Hollywood casting agent • Marine drill sergeant • Holocaust survivor • New Age philosopher • inner-city gang member • psychiatrist • cultural anthropologist • vocational counselor • fashion designer • rap artist • priest • shaman • underground photographer • pimp • yuppie • sexual sadomasochist

Antidotes

1. Do not underestimate the extent to which your prior beliefs, knowledge, and expectancies (schemata) can affect your current experience, impressions, and perceptions.

2. Try to become as aware as possible of schemata that are important to you; awareness of schemata increases your ability to modify them.

3. Experiment with temporarily lowering or altering your "perceptual filters" or "schema-colored glasses" by attempting to understand someone else's subjective (phenomenological) perceptions and experience.

4. Learn to differentiate your use of assimilation versus accommodation, particularly when you are faced with a discrepancy between your beliefs (schemas) and the information (data). Beware of the general tendency to assimilate rather than to accommodate.

5. Prod yourself to accommodate when, out of habit, reflex, or just sheer laziness, you would typically be inclined to automatically assimilate.

All that glitters is not gold.
ANONYMOUS

 If my theory of relativity is proven successful, Germany will claim me as a German and France will declare that I am a citizen of the world. Should my theory prove untrue, France will say that I am a German and Germany will declare that I am a Jew.
ALBERT EINSTEIN (1879–1955)—GERMAN SWISS AMERICAN PHYSICIST

The Representativeness Bias: Fits and Misfits of Categorization

In everyday life, we are frequently called on to make rapid judgments in circumstances that do not lend themselves to thoroughness or accuracy. Consider the following scenarios:

- At a job interview, you have a limited amount of time to figure out how to create the right impression.
- In a counseling setting, you might be assigned the task of expeditiously evaluating an individual from a cultural group about which you know very little.
- While traveling in a foreign country, you are approached by a group of strangers, and you need to quickly determine their intentions.

An ideal strategy for making decisions in these situations (and countless others like them) would involve the opportunity to conduct a comprehensive and systematic analysis of the problem, collect relevant data, test various hypotheses, draw appropriate inferences, thoroughly evaluate the pluses and minuses of all possible outcomes, and arrive at the optimum conclusions before having to take final action.

Well, so much for the ideal. For obvious reasons, such a strategy is impractical in most real-life circumstances. We simply do not have the time, information, or resources (not to mention incentive) that would enable us to solve most problems in this manner. Nevertheless, we proceed to make decisions and give answers in the face of varying degrees of uncertainty.

Cognitive psychologists Amos Tversky and Daniel Kahneman (1974) theorized that people use a variety of mental shortcuts, or **heuristics**, that reduce complex and time-consuming tasks to more simple, manageable, practical, and efficient problem-solving strategies. We all have a repertoire of such shortcuts that we tend to use automatically, without necessarily considering their accuracy or validity in each situation.

Unfortunately, these shortcuts are double-edged swords. On one hand, they permit highly efficient information processing and rapid solutions to the problem. In other words, they help us to make quick "seat-of-the-pants" decisions. However, they do so at the expense of thoroughness and precision. In essence, we trade off accuracy for speed. Thus, the price we pay for their efficiency can be bad judgments.

Tversky and Kahneman (1973, 1982) identified a number of such shortcuts, the most basic of which they termed the **representativeness heuristic.** Essentially, this involves judging the likelihood that something belongs to (that is, "represents") a particular category. Stated slightly more formally, representativeness is a method of estimating the probability that Instance *A* is a member of Category *B*.

We use the representativeness heuristic to identify phenomena in our environment by intuitively comparing the phenomenon (be it people, objects, events, research data, or ideologies) to our mental representation, prototype, or schema of the relevant category. In so doing, we are attempting to ascertain if there is a "match" on the basis of whether the phenomenon's features are similar to the essential features of the category. If there is a match, we conclude that we have successfully identified the phenomenon; if not, we continue our cognitive search.

One of the most common uses of the representativeness heuristic involves judging whether a person belongs to a specific group based on how similar he or she is to "typical" member of that group. In this way, we may conclude, for example, that Ted (*A*) is Jewish because he looks like your prototype of a Jewish person (*B*). Or that Jane (*A*) is a lesbian because she behaves like your stereotype of a lesbian (*B*). In like manner, we use the representativeness heuristic for identifying everything from ideological categories (religious, philosophical, political) to causal explanations (random, unintentional, malevolent). As you can readily see, this simple act is fundamental to all subsequent inferences and behaviors: Before any other cognitive task can be addressed, we first must answer the question, "What is it?"

Although in most instances the representativeness heuristic yields quick and relatively accurate results, it sometimes produces systematic errors in information processing. This effect, which we refer to as the **representativeness bias,** can occur as a result of numerous factors. Some of these include our reliance on inaccurate or faulty prototypes, our failure to take into account pertinent statistical data (such as base rates, sample size, and chance probability), or our inclination to allow our motivational needs to bias our cognitive search and subsequent evaluations.

EXERCISE 3.6

Examining Sociocultural Schemas and Stereotypes

As an exercise in identifying and exploring the nature and content of your own cognitive schemata, select three specific instances drawn from various sociocultural categories (such as ethnic background, occupation, religion, socioeconomic status, or political affiliation). You can choose from the following list or come up with any other examples that might be more relevant to your own life experience.

Russian • Italian • German • French • Mexican • Arab • Chinese • Native American • South African • Iranian • New Yorker • lawyer • soldier • actor • therapist • rock musician • police officer • taxicab driver • corporate executive • professional athlete • politician • nurse • nun • insurance salesperson • truck driver • convenience store clerk • mortician • Buddhist • Jehovah's Witness • Jews for Jesus • Scientologist • Republican • environmentalist • welfare recipient • yuppie • gay activist • vegetarian • heroin addict • alcoholic • single parent • senior citizen • AIDS patient

First, note the initial thoughts, impressions, or images that come to mind regarding the category. Next, rate (on a scale from 1 to 5) the degree to which your schema for that category is *specific* (well defined, vivid, clear) versus *broad* (diverse, loose, vague). Then describe in detail the particular content (i.e., your personal perceptions) of each schema. Now try to determine and describe the schema's etiology (origin) and development. Last, try to recall (or imagine) an occasion where you came across an instance that clearly was inconsistent with (i.e., did not "fit") your schema. How did (might) you respond? What happened (might happen) to the schema itself?

Social Schema #1: _____

Distinctness of Schema: *Specific*   1   2   3   4   5   *Broad*

Content: _____

_____

Etiology and development: _____

_____

Your response to schema-inconsistent event: _____

_____

Before concluding this metathought, two final points deserve mention. Despite the problems, pitfalls, and liabilities associated with the use of cognitive heuristics, we persist in relying on them as an integral component of our decision-making processes. Why? One of the main reasons is that, on the whole, they provide us with more right answers than wrong ones. Moreover, even in those circumstances in which they are incorrect, the results typically are inconsequential.

One significant exception, however, can occur in relation to our usage of prototype categories about particular groups of people, based on, for example, their race, gender, culture, nationality, religion, sexual orientation, or even psychological diagnosis. When viewed in this context, such group-related schemata are equivalent to stereotypes. Thus, when heuristics such as representativeness are utilized with respect to these categories, extreme caution is advised. As history has repeatedly demonstrated, stereotyping can have far-reaching and potentially harmful social consequences, not the least of which include prejudice, bigotry, and discrimination—outcomes that are far from inconsequential.

Antidotes

1. In situations in which you are likely to utilize the representativeness heuristic, make a conscious effort to consider the possibility that the prototype in question might be inaccurate, biased, or incomplete.

2. Take into account relevant statistical information, such as base rates, samples sizes, and chance probability.

3. Beware of the natural tendency to overestimate the degree of similarity between phenomena and categories.

4. Recognize that your personal attitudes about people and group prototypes can bias your comparisons and subsequent judgments.

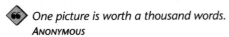 *When a dog bites a man, that is not news. But when a man bites a dog, that is news.*
JOHN B. BOGART (1836–1920)—AMERICAN JOURNALIST

One picture is worth a thousand words.
ANONYMOUS

The Availability Bias: The Persuasive Power of Vivid Events

As a means of introducing this metathought, let us begin with a brief quiz. Give your best estimates for the following questions:

1. What are the odds of sustaining a fatal accident traveling by car as compared with traveling by commercial airplane?

2. Which racial group comprises the largest proportion of Americans living in poverty: blacks, whites, or Hispanics?

3. Which age group is at highest risk for committing suicide: teens, middle age, or elderly?

4. Which country has a higher suicide rate: Sri Lanka or the United States?

Setting aside for the moment the actual answers to these questions, spend a few moments considering the cognitive processes you utilized in reaching your conclusions. How, specifically, did you go about arriving at your estimates for each question? Did you notice any similarities in the mental strategies you employed?

If you are like most people in this way, your estimates probably were determined primarily on the basis of how easily or quickly specific instances of each question came to mind. And what types of instances are likely to stand out in memory? In general, the most powerful impressions are created by events that are particularly vivid, dramatic, important, personally relevant, or otherwise salient to us. We also are prone to more quickly think of instances that are simply easy to imagine.

Unfortunately, however, the problem in relying on the ease with which events can be retrieved from memory for determining their likelihood is that our perceptions cannot necessarily be counted on as an accurate reflection of reality. Specifically, this strategy leads us to overestimate their actual occurrence, frequency, or distribution in the world.

Did you inadvertently succumb to this bias in answering any of the questions posed above? Let us examine each one in turn.

1. Few events are more disturbing than the graphic sights and sounds of a catastrophic airplane crash. Even a mere glimpse of these horrific images on the eleven o'clock news is likely to stamp in our minds a potent and indelible impression. Such tragic accidents, therefore, become easily accessible and readily available in our memory. As a consequence, many people erroneously jump to the conclusion that they are at greater risk when traveling by commercial airplane than by car. Yet, mile for mile, Americans are nearly 100 times more likely to die in an automobile accident than in a commercial plane accident (Greenwald, 1986).

2. Nearly *half* of all poor individuals in the United States are white, approximately one-quarter are black, and just under one-quarter are Hispanic. Why might people be inclined to overestimate the proportions of racial minorities? In addition to the salience of their skin color, these groups do, in fact, display disproportionately higher rates of economic hardship. Specifically, almost 30 percent of Hispanics and blacks in the United States are living below the poverty level, whereas less than 10 percent of white Americans are poor (U.S. Bureau of the Census, 1997).

3. Although the overall national suicide rate in the elderly (65 and over) has dropped significantly over the past 60 years, this group still displays the highest proportion of self-inflicted deaths in the United States (McIntosh, 1992). This fact is likely to come as a surprise to many people who would identify teens as the age group at greatest risk. What might account for this misperception? There are at least three possible factors. First, whenever a teenager takes his or her own life, the event is particularly salient to us. We find it shocking, disturbing, and especially tragic that a young person, full of future potential, would choose irrevocably to end it all. Second, when it comes to suicide *attempts*, at least two-thirds of individuals who try (but fail) to kill themselves are under the age of 35 (Hawton, 1992). Here again, the salience even of "unsuccessful" suicide attempts by younger people can exert a disproportionate impact on our impressions and distort our perceptions. Third, the actual rate of "successul" suicides among teenagers (and even children) has, in fact, risen dramatically over the past several decades (Berman & Jobes, 1992). Looking across cultures, the increase in adolescent suicide is not unique to the United States, but appears in 23 out of 29 countries that have been studied (Lester, 1988). This trend also may lead us to overestimate the occurrence of suicide in younger age groups. Now consider suicides committed by the elderly. In general, they do not draw as much attention. They do not capture our focus. They do not startle us as particularly newsworthy. The net effect? "Out of sight, out of mind."

4. The suicide rate in the United States is 15 cases per 100,000 people. The suicide rate in Sri Lanka is 47 per 100,000—more than three times the U.S.

rate. Still, many people believe that suicide rates are substantially higher in the United States than in other countries. What is the reason for this misperception? Among several reasons is the attention paid by the American media to various stories involving suicide, especially among celebrities. It is also assumed by some people that Western industrial countries "should" have higher suicide rates than the rest of the world because of factors such as high stress and lack of emotional support systems. Although these assumptions are not illogical, they are only assumptions. They cannot explain the complicated picture of suicide and its causes across the world.

The specific cognitive strategy demonstrated in the above examples has been termed the **availability heuristic** (Tversky & Kahneman, 1973) because it refers to the process of drawing on instances that are easily accessible or "available" from our memory. This heuristic helps us to answer questions concerning the frequency ("How many are there?"), incidence ("How often does something happen?"), or likelihood ("What are the odds that something will occur?") of particular events.

If examples are readily available in memory, we tend to assume that such events occur rather frequently. For instance, if you have no trouble bringing to mind examples of X (Southern hospitality, for instance), you are likely to judge that it is common. By contrast, if it takes you awhile to think of illustrations of Y (Germans sense of humor, for example), you are prone to conclude that it is uncommon. In sum, when an event has easily retrieved instances, it will seem more prevalent than an equally frequent category that has less easily retrieved instances.

As is the case with the representativeness heuristic, very little cognitive work is needed to utilize the availability heuristic. Further, under many circumstances, the availability heuristic provides us with accurate and dependable estimates. After all, if examples easily come to mind, it usually is because there are many of them.

Unfortunately, however, there are many biasing factors that can affect the availability of events in our memory without reflecting their actual occurrence. Problems arise when this strategy is used, for instance, to estimate the frequency or likelihood of rare, though highly vivid, events as compared with those that are more typical, commonplace, or mundane in nature. When our use of the availability heuristic results in systematic errors in making such judgments, we may refer to this as the **availability bias**.

Perhaps the single most important factor underlying the availability bias is our propensity to underuse, discount, or even ignore relevant base-rate information (that is, data about the actual frequency of events in a particular group) and other abstract statistical facts in favor of more salient and concrete, but usually less reliable, anecdotal evidence. As a consequence, personal testimonials, graphic case studies, dramatic stories, colorful tales, intriguing narratives, eye-catching illustrations, vibrant images, extraordinary occurrences, and bizarre events all are liable to slant, skew, or otherwise distort our judgments.

With respect to sociocultural issues, a significant problem resulting from the availability bias concerns our proclivity to overgeneralize from a few vivid examples, or sometimes even just a single vivid instance. This error is responsible, at least in part, for the phenomenon of stereotyping (see Chapter 10).

In general, how do we formulate our beliefs about particular groups of people, whether racial, cultural, national, religious, political, occupational, or any other category? We typically base our impressions on observations of specific members of the group. But which members? By and large, our attention is drawn to the most conspicuous, prominent, or salient individuals. We then are prone to overgeneralize from these few extreme examples to the group as a whole, the result of which is a role schema or stereotype. In this way, the availability bias leads us to perpetuate vivid but false beliefs about the characteristics of a wide variety of groups in our society.

The moral? We tend to be more persuaded by an ounce of anecdotal evidence than by a pound of reliable statistics. Although vivid and dramatic events can make for appetizing fiction, they are ultimately unsatisfying to those with a taste for reality.

Antidotes

1. When estimating the frequency or probability of an event, remind yourself not to reach a conclusion based solely on the ease or speed with which relevant instances can be retrieved from your memory.

2. Take anecdotal evidence not with a grain but with several large shakers of salt. Although personal testimonies and vivid cases may be very persuasive, they are not inherently trustworthy indicators of fact.

3. Make a conscious effort, whenever feasible, to seek out and utilize base-rate information and other pertinent statistical data.

4. Remember that the best basis for drawing valid generalizations is from a representative sample of relevant cases.

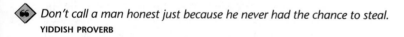 *Don't call a man honest just because he never had the chance to steal.*
YIDDISH PROVERB

You never see a Rolls Royce with a bumper sticker that reads, "Shit Happens."
GEORGE CARLIN (1937–   )—AMERICAN COMEDIAN

The Fundamental Attribution Error: Underestimating the Impact of External Influences

How do we explain the causes of people's behavior? We typically attribute their actions either to their personality or to their circumstances. Put another way, we make dispositional attributions or situational attributions. Dispositional attributions involve assigning the causes of behavior to people's personality traits, characteristics, or attitudes, that is, to "internal" influences. Situational attributions, in contrast, involve assigning the causes of behavior to people's circumstances, surroundings, or environment, that is, to "external" influences (see Chapter 10).

In reality, of course, behavior is due to combinations of many factors, both internal and external, that vary in the degree to which they are responsible for causing a person's actions. However, in arriving at causal attributions, we have a tendency to overestimate people's dispositions and to underestimate their situations. In other words, we are prone to weigh internal determinants too heavily, and external determinants too lightly. We are thus likely to explain the behavior of others as resulting predominantly from their personality, whereas we often minimize (or even ignore) the importance of the particular context or situation. This mistake is so prevalent, in fact, that the social psychologist Lee Ross (1977) termed it the **fundamental attribution error**.

What are some illustrations of this attributional bias? If a person does not make eye contact when talking to you, you might presume that the individual is "untrustworthy," "shy," or "sneaky." If someone brings you a gift for no apparent reason, you might conclude that the person is "thoughtful," "generous," or perhaps even "manipulative." Notice how these attributions essentially disregard any external or situational factors that might be responsible for producing these behaviors. Consider, for instance, the potential influence of their cultural traditions and societal rules of interpersonal communication.

To take another example, consider the dilemma of the homeless. Some people are prone to explain a homeless person's condition in terms of personality factors, such as laziness, moral weakness, drug abuse, or mental illness. These attributions, however, fail to take into account the situational factors that can (and do) perpetuate homelessness, such as a lack of affordable housing, job scarcity, discrimination, and an unstable economy.

This same principle applies to our attributions about a diverse array of other specific subgroups within our society. How do we explain differences between, for instance, men and women? We explain them, by and large, in terms of inherent dispositions. We may thus conclude that men are "innately" more competitive, or "it's in their nature" for women to be more cooperative, while overlooking societal expectations, constraints, and sanctions that shape gender-role behavior. Along these same lines, can you think of situational factors that might have led one particular group toward athletic achievement and another toward academic achievement? Small business ownership? Underground crime? Overrepresentation in positions of upper management? Underrepresentation in the military? Having many children? Poor test performance? Eating disorders? Violence? Apathy? All told, we are liable to ignore such sources of external influence that could account for intergroup differences in behavior.

 EXERCISE 3.7

Exploring the Effects of Social Context

This exercise serves to underscore the enormous, yet typically unnoticed, power of the social situation in influencing our feelings, attitudes, and behavior. Imagine yourself in the following scenarios and how you might respond to the simple question, "So, how are you doing?" For each situation, indicate not only what you might

say, but also provide a brief description of your probable thoughts, demeanor, and the emotional tone of your response.

At a job interview: _____

At a class reunion: _____

At a funeral: _____

With your parents: _____

With your best friend: _____

With a total stranger: _____

With someone who is hearing impaired: _____

With someone who is wheelchair bound: _____

With someone who is physically very attractive: _____

With someone who is physically very unattractive: _____

In a group of nuns: _____

In a group of rabbis: _____

In a group of white supremacists: _____

In a group of black supremacists: _____

In a foreign country where you do not speak the language: _____

When approached by a homeless child: _____

When approached by a homeless adult: _____

When approached by a police officer: _____

When approached by a prostitute: _____

When approached by a group of Hispanic youths: _____

When approached by a group of Hispanic tourists: _____

When approached by a group of Japanese tourists: _____

When approached by a group of people singing and dancing in orange robes and offering you free incense: _____

In looking over your answers, observe that *all* the variability in your responses is attributable to the situations themselves, since both you and the initial question were fixed and held constant. One final point deserves mention. Can you determine which of these responses reflects the "real" you? Notice that this question is, in itself, virtually unanswerable without also taking into account the context of the situation.

What is responsible for this attributional error? Social psychologists have identified two principal sources: **cognitive biases** and **motivational biases.**

Cognitive biases refer to systematic mistakes that derive from limits that are inherent in our capacity to process information. Because we are not capable of perceiving everything in our environment, our focus is automatically drawn to the most prominent or "eye catching"—that is, perceptually salient—stimuli. This can lead us to formulate biased and inaccurate causal attributions (Taylor & Fiske, 1975). Specifically, we are prone to equate the most perceptually salient stimuli with the most causally influential stimuli.

In contrast, motivational biases refer to systematic mistakes that derive from our efforts to satisfy our own personal needs, such as the desire for self-esteem, power, or control. Simply put, motivational biases serve the function of making us feel better, even if they do so at the expense of distorting, obscuring, or falsifying reality.

Are we motivated to prefer one type of causal attribution over another? It would appear so. In the case of Western cultures in particular, we are socialized from early childhood to believe that people can control their destiny and are the masters of their fate. As such, society generally condones dispositional attributions, while it discourages situational attributions. In this way, we can fool ourselves into overestimating the degree of control that we actually do have, while underestimating the impact of external factors that lie beyond our control. We are prone, therefore, to exaggerate our perceptions of controllability.

One very unfortunate consequence of this motivational bias is that people who are harmed by forces that are truly out of their control may be held more responsible for their circumstances than they should be. In other words, our illusion of control may lead us to blame people for the bad things that happen to them.

Why does this occur? Melvin Lerner (1970) theorized that we have great difficulty accepting the unfairness and injustices of life. Further, we have a strong need to believe that we live in a "just world" in which good is rewarded and bad is punished. This belief leads us to conclude that people get what they deserve and deserve what they get: "What goes around, comes around."

Instances of such attributions abound:

- *Rape victims must have behaved seductively.*
- *Homosexuals must have brought AIDS on themselves.*
- *People with physical disabilities must have done something wrong.*
- *People in poor countries must have been responsible for what is happening to them economically.*
- *Victims of persecution must be guilty of something, or they wouldn't be persecuted.*

What compels people to make such attributions? Once again, we do it, in all likelihood, to preserve our illusion of control. It is psychologically more comforting to blame others for the disasters that befall them, rather than face the cold reality that we live in an unjust world in which such events can happen at random. After all, if negative events are uncontrollable, they could just as easily happen to *us*. In other words, by assigning dispositional attributions, we hope to experience a greater sense of control over our destiny. Further, it provides a justification for our indifference to (or even oppression of) society's victims: If people themselves are responsible for their own plight, there is no need for the rest of us to help them. (In fact, they probably *deserve* it.)

Antidotes

1. Do not underestimate the power of external, situational determinants of behavior.

2. Remember that at any given time, how people behave depends both on what they bring to the situation ("who" they are) as well as on the situation itself ("where" they are).

3. Keep in mind that this attributional error can become reversed, depending on the perceiver's point of view. Specifically, although people are prone to underestimate the impact of others' situations, they tend to overestimate the impact of their own situations.

4. Be sure to take into account both cognitive and motivational biases that are responsible for producing these attributional errors.

 Respect a man, and he will do the more.
ANONYMOUS

To believe a thing impossible is to make it so.
FRENCH PROVERB

The Self-Fulfilling Prophecy: When Expectations Create Reality

The attitudes and beliefs that we hold toward other people can—with or without our intent—actually produce the very behaviors that we expect to find. In other words, a perceiver's assumptions about another person may lead that person to adopt those expected attributes. This phenomenon is known as the **self-fulfilling prophecy.**

In what is probably the most famous—and still controversial—study of the self-fulfilling prophecy, Robert Rosenthal and Lenore Jacobson (1968) informed teachers at a San Francisco elementary school that on the basis of a reliable psychological test, some of the pupils in their classroom would show dramatic spurts in academic performance during the upcoming school year. In reality, there was no such test, and the children designated as "intellectual bloomers" were chosen at random. Nevertheless, when the children's performance was assessed several months later, those students who had been earmarked as "bloomers" did, indeed, show an improvement in their schoolwork; even more remarkably, their IQ scores had increased. The teachers thus unwittingly created the very behaviors that they expected.

The self-fulfilling prophecy has been demonstrated with a diverse array of both positive and negative perceiver expectancies, including hostility (Snyder & Swann, 1978), extraversion (see Snyder, 1984), gender stereotypes (Skrypnek & Snyder, 1982), racial stereotypes (Word et al., 1974), and even stereotypes concerning physical attractiveness (Snyder et al., 1977). These studies underscore how prejudice of any kind can set in motion a self-perpetuating and ever-escalating vicious cycle of adverse repercussions, (see Bidirectional Causation), in which the self-fulfilling prophecy serves to influence not only how the prejudiced person behaves toward the victim, but also how the victim may then behave in a way that confirms the person's initial prejudices.

Not only are we seldom aware of the extent to which our expectations can influence the behavior of others, but we probably are even less aware of how the expectations of others are capable of influencing *our* behavior. It is thus important to remember that our actions are shaped not only by our own attitudes, but also by the expectations of those with whom we interact. Put another way, we are continually cultivating the constructions of each other's social realities.

Given the ubiquity of the self-fulfilling prophecy, we would do well to consider its potential impact in all of our social interactions. In an ethnic minority community, for instance, what do you suppose might occur if a police officer were to expect neighborhood residents to be hostile and dishonest? Resistant? Helpless? Paranoid?

In like manner, what if a resident expects police officers to be hostile and dishonest? Unfair? Callous? Abusive? The police and community can ultimately end up creating a reciprocally reinforcing projection system that supports their respective initial expectations, much of which may be occurring outside of their direct awareness.

EXERCISE 3.8

Exploring Manifestations of the Self-Fulfilling Prophecy

As an exercise, select two scenarios—either hypothetical or factual—involving the self-fulfilling prophecy. In making your selections, consider a variety of topics (e.g., stereotyping, prejudice, child rearing, testing, competition), settings (e.g., research, classroom, workplace, religious), and societal or governmental policies, programs, and laws (e.g., welfare, unemployment, affirmative action, desegregation, immigration, bilingual education, sexual harrassment, mandatory retirement). Then for each scenario, present your thoughts as to how Person *A's* expectations might influence his or her behavior toward Person *B*. Last, discuss how Person *A's* actions could cause Person *B* to behave in accordance with Person *A's* prior expectations. In other words, identify some of the specific factors or events that you believe are capable of transforming Person *A's* initial expectations into the reality of Person *B's* subsequent attitudes and behavior.

Scenario: _____

Effects of Person *A's* expectations on behavior toward Person *B*:

_____

_____

Effects of Person *A's* behavior on Person *B's* subsequent actions:

_____

_____

Antidotes

1. In all of your social interactions, remember that expectations can, in themselves, create their own reality.

2. Make a conscious effort to become aware of your own expectancies and the ways in which they may lead you to induce those very behaviors in others.

3. Do not forget that your own behavior is not immune to the influence of the self-fulfilling prophecy. Specifically, keep in mind that your behavior can be shaped by the expectations other people have of you.

4. In conducting research, initiate safeguards to reduce the potential impact of expectancy effects. This may be accomplished by, for example, keeping the experimenters unaware of (i.e., "blind" to) the specific purpose, goals, or hypotheses of the study.

 President Bush taking credit for the collapse of Communism is like a rooster taking credit for the arrival of the dawn.
SOURCE UNKNOWN

 ROGERS' LAW: As soon as the stewardess serves the coffee, the airliner encounters turbulence.

DAVIS' EXPLANATION OF ROGERS' LAW: Serving coffee on aircraft causes turbulence.
ARTHUR BLOCH (1948–)—AUTHOR

Correlation Does Not Prove Causation: Confusing "What" with "Why"

A correlation is a statement about the relationship or association between two (or more) variables. Correlations thus enable us to make predictions from one variable or event to another. That is, if two events are correlated (or "coappear"), then the presence of one event provides us with information about the other event. A correlation does not, however, necessarily establish a causal relationship between the variables. In other words, causation cannot be proven simply by virtue of a correlation or coappearance.

As an example, let us consider the correlation between creativity and psychological disorders (see, for example, Andreason & Canter, 1974; Andreason & Powers, 1975; Jamison, 1993). Great painter Vincent Van Gough, Russian novelist Fyodor Dostoevski, and American writer Ernest Hemingway all suffered from emotional disorders that seriously disrupted their lives. More recently, popular American comedians John Belushi and Chris Farley developed serious (and ultimately fatal) drug addictions. Based on these observations, what may we conclude? That psychological disorders cause creativity? Perhaps. But maybe creativity causes psychological disorders. Then again, isn't it possible that creativity and psychological disorders reciprocally affect each other? To complicate matters further, what about the possibility that some other variable, such as a genetic predisposition, causes both creativity and psychological disorders?

Put another way, given a correlation between *A* and *B:* Does *A* cause *B*? Does *B* cause *A*? Do *A* and *B* cause each other? Does *C* cause *A* and *B*? Could there be some combination of these causal relationships? Unfortunately, a correlation alone does not (in fact, cannot) provide us with the definitive answers to these questions. The following are some examples of correlated variables about which people frequently (but erroneously) may infer causality.

Example 1: Research indicates that watching violent television programs appears to be mildly but positively correlated with aggressive behavior (see Huesmann, 1982). This correlation does not, however, prove that TV violence causes aggressiveness. Perhaps aggressive people prefer to watch violent TV programs. Maybe aggressiveness and TV violence, in a "vicious cycle," feed off each other (see Bidirectional Causation). Or consider the possibility that family conflict causes both aggressive behavior and the watching of TV violence.

Example 2: Do you know that there is more aggression in hot meteorological conditions than in cold ones? For example, rates of homicide and rape are generally higher in warmer than in colder climates (Anderson, 1987). Why? It would be absurd, of course, to propose that the weather is affected by violent crimes. It certainly is much more likely that meteorological conditions somehow affect violent behavior. However, we do not know if other factors, such as poverty, density of population, or government policies affect incidents of homicide and rape.

Example 3: Suppose that certain ethnic minority groups display disproportionately higher rates of delinquency, academic failure, teenage pregnancy, drug abuse, criminality, or psychopathology. In other words, let us assume a relationship exists between group membership (e.g., Hispanic Americans) and the incidence and severity of these problems. What could account for this trend? One of the most commonly overlooked but critical factors is socioeconomic status. Specifically, poverty appears to be a much stronger predictor for such behaviors than is ethnicity itself. Now, what if (as happens to be the case) such groups are, on average, located at a lower rung on the socioeconomic ladder? We could be inclined erroneously to focus on skin color and ethnic identity, while underestimating the effect of economic circumstances (see the Fundamental Attribution Error).

Example 4: Similarly, let us examine the debate regarding racial (specifically black versus white) differences in IQ scores. In their controversial book, *The Bell Curve* (1994), Richard Herrnstein and Charles Murray propose that such correlations can be explained primarily in terms of differential genetic inheritance (see also Jensen, 1973; Rushton, 1994, 1995). Needless to say, this conclusion cannot be accepted without taking into account factors such as the roles of socioeconomic status, access to quality schooling, parental role modeling, family structure, peer influence, cultural norms, as well as both personal and societal expectations (see the Self-Fulfilling Prophecy).

Consider also correlations between incidents of homelessness and mental illness, teen pregnancy and welfare benefits, poor grades in school and legal troubles, ethnicity and alcohol consumption, gender roles and mass media. In all of these instances (and countless more), beware of concluding causation based solely on correlation or coappearance. Further, when a correlation is observed, be sure to examine all plausible pathways and directions of causation.

One particular type of faulty reasoning, the **post hoc error**, refers to the mistaken logic that because Event B follows Event A, then B must have been caused by A. This error, also known as **parataxic reasoning** (Sullivan, 1954), may be seen as a kind of "magical thinking," because events that occur close together in time are construed as causally linked. As it turns out, most superstitions are based on parataxic reasoning. For example, if a football coach does not shave before a game, and his team then wins, he might assume that not shaving somehow caused the success. As a result, he may adopt this superstitious behavior for future games.

 ## EXERCISE 3.9

Exploring Correlation and Causation

To give you some practice at applying these principles, try to identify some of the possible causal relationships, pathways, and explanations that could account for each of the correlations presented below.

Example

"Eveningness" and optimism appear to be negatively correlated (Levy, 1985); that is, people who are "evening types" tend to be more pessimistic than "morning types." Why might this be true?

1. Optimism may cause "morningness."
2. Morningness may cause optimism.
3. Optimism and morningness may affect each other.
4. Satisfying job may cause both optimism and morningness.

Exercise A

Many societies believe that the most effective way to control or deter aggression is through the use of punishment, including the death penalty. The preponderance of research evidence, however, shows a positive correlation between murder rates and the number of executions, rather than the negative relationship predicted by deterrence theories (see Segall et al., 1997). Assuming this correlation is valid, how might it be explained?

1. _____

2. _____

3. _____

4. _____

Exercise B

Suppose you read an article reporting a negative correlation between religiosity and depression (that is, the less religious, the more depressed). What factors could account for this relationship?

1. _____

2. _____

3. _____

4. _____

As these examples illustrate, although correlations may provide us with accurate—and frequently very useful—information regarding "what" relationships exist, they cannot be counted on to answer the question "why?" Even in those circumstances in which a correlation strongly *implies* causation, it does not *prove* causation.

Antidotes

1. Remember that a correlation or coappearance is not, in itself, proof of causation.

2. Keep in mind that correlations enable us to make predictions from one event to another; they do not, however, provide explanations as to why the events are related.

3. When a correlation is observed, consider all possible pathways and directions of causation. For example, if Event A and Event B are correlated, does A cause B? Does B cause A? Do A and B cause each other? Does C cause A and B?

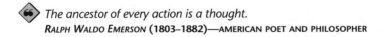 *The ancestor of every action is a thought.*
RALPH WALDO EMERSON **(1803–1882)—AMERICAN POET AND PHILOSOPHER**

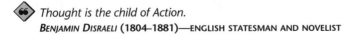 *Thought is the child of Action.*
BENJAMIN DISRAELI **(1804–1881)—ENGLISH STATESMAN AND NOVELIST**

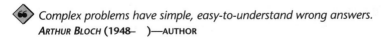 *Complex problems have simple, easy-to-understand wrong answers.*
ARTHUR BLOCH **(1948–)—AUTHOR**

Bidirectional Causation and Multiple Causation: Causal Loops and Compound Pathways

Bidirectional Causation

Although we typically tend to think of causal relationships as being **unidirectional** (Event A causes Event B), frequently they are **bidirectional** (Event A causes Event B and Event B causes Event A). In other words, variables can, and frequently do, affect each other. This relationship also may be referred to as a causal loop or, depending on our subjective evaluation of the particular situation, either a "healthy spiral" (if we happen to like it) or a "vicious cycle" (if we do not). (In this regard, see in this chapter the Evaluative Bias of Language.)

As an illustration of this principle, let us look at the widely debated psychological question, "Does thought cause emotion, or does emotion cause thought? Which comes first? Which is the cause and which is the effect?" (see Berscheid, 1982; Mandler, 1975; Weiner, 1980; Zajonc, 1980). When viewed as a bidirectional relationship, however, the argument may be moot: clearly, thoughts and feelings affect each other.

Consider also the bidirectional relationship between psychological disturbance and one's social environment. Specifically, it is probable that cold, rejecting, and hostile parents can cause emotional and behavioral problems in their children. At the same time, do not ignore the possibility (even the likelihood) that children with emotional and behavioral problems also might cause their parents to become cold, rejecting, and hostile.

Bidirectional relationships are as interesting as they are plentiful:

- self-esteem and popularity
- motivation and encouragement
- curiosity and knowledge
- respect and responsibility
- frustration and helplessness
- apathy and powerlessness
- criticism and defensiveness
- paranoia and secrecy
- education and opportunity
- opportunity and success
- understanding and communication
- money and power
- poverty and failure
- race relations and news coverage
- alienation and segregation
- discrimination and defiance
- violence and prejudice
- war and defeat
- war and victory

 EXERCISE 3.10

Identifying and Disentangling Causal Loops

As an exercise, consider the bidirectional relationship between unemployment (Event *A*) and delinquency (Event *B*).

- First, describe some ways that unemployment (*A*) might result in delinquency (*B*).
- Next, describe some ways that delinquency (*B*) can lead to unemployment (*A*).
- Is it possible to determine which is (or was) the "initial" cause? If so, how?
- Under what circumstances might it be important to identify which was the initial cause?
- Under what circumstances might it be *unimportant* to identify which was the initial cause?

For some more practice, select another bidirectional relationship (either from the list above or an original example from your own experience).

As you can see, "cause" and "effect" are relative terms: a cause in one instance becomes an effect in another. From this perspective, asking the question, "Which comes first?" although interesting, may be unnecessary, irrelevant, or even unanswerable. Thus, when faced with such chicken-and-egg questions, remember that your answer may depend entirely on where you happen to enter the causal loop.

Multiple Causation

Immigrants to the United States and Canada from the Indian subcontinent display higher rates of coronary heart disease than the population of the countries to which they moved (WHO, 1999). What is the cause?

Actually, the form of this question is somewhat misleading in its implication that there is a *single* cause. In point of fact, any effect may be, and usually is, the result of not just one but several causes, which are operating concurrently. Virtually every significant behavior has many determinants, and any single explanation is inevitably an oversimplification. Thus, in this case, we would need to consider a wide range of possible factors (e.g., genetic, dietary, stress, family norms, and cultural traditions), all of which could, to varying degrees, be involved.

To take another example, what causes depression? Is it caused by early childhood trauma? Or a vital loss? Or a perceived failure? Or unrealistic expectations? Or a faulty belief system? Or internalized anger? Or learned helplessness? Or a biochemical predisposition? Or lack of opportunity?

Now, try replacing each *or* with *and*. Depression thus may be seen as caused by a variety of factors, including early childhood trauma, *and* a vital loss, *and* a perceived failure, *and* unrealistic expectations, *and* a faulty belief system, *and* internalized anger, *and* learned helplessness, *and* a biochemical predisposition, *and* a lack of opportunity.

EXERCISE 3.11

Exploring Compound Pathways

Applying the same principle, consider the multiple determinants of *homophobia*. List as many possible factors as you can think of (suggested answers appear in Appendix 4 on page 354). Do the same with some other topic related to cross-cultural psychology. (You might browse through the index of this book for some ideas.)

In sum, every time you are faced with a question, issue, or problem that is presented in terms of "*either/or*," stop for a moment. Now, try replacing *either/or* with *both/and*. For example, the statement, "Prejudice is caused by either ignorance or hatred," becomes "Prejudice is caused by both ignorance and hatred" (and probably many other factors as well). Then ask yourself, "Is this new formulation *useful*?" In a great number of situations, you are very likely to find that it is.

Antidotes

1. Do not assume a priori that the causal link between two variables is a unidirectional "one-way street."

2. When investigating directions of causation, consider the possibility that the variables are linked in a causal loop, that is, each might be both a cause and an effect of the other.

3. Remember that in a case of bidirectional causation, which variable appears to be the "cause" and which variable appears to be the "effect" may depend entirely on the point at which you happen to enter the causal loop.

4. In attempting to explain why an event occurred, do not limit your search to one cause. Instead, explore multiple plausible causes, all of which may be responsible for producing the effect.

5. When faced with an *either/or* question, always consider the possibility that the answer might be *both/and*.

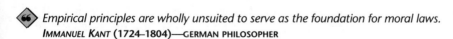

Empirical principles are wholly unsuited to serve as the foundation for moral laws.
IMMANUEL KANT (1724–1804)—GERMAN PHILOSOPHER

It is of fundamental importance not to make the positivist mistake of assuming that, because a group are "in formation," this means they are necessarily "on course."
R.D. LAING (1927–1989)—SCOTTISH PSYCHIATRIST

The Naturalistic Fallacy: Blurring the Line between "Is" and "Should"

One very important way in which our personal values can bias our thinking is when we equate our description of what *is* with our prescription of what *ought* to be. This occurs, for instance, whenever we define what is good in terms of what is observable. This error in thinking is called the **naturalistic fallacy.**

Examine the following statements: "What's typical is normal; what's normal is good. What's not typical is abnormal; what's abnormal is bad." Notice how, in each case, a description of what exists becomes converted into a prescription of what we like or dislike.

As the Scottish philosopher David Hume pointed out over 200 years ago, values, ethics, and morality are based not on logic or reason, but on the sentiments and public opinions of a particular society. Thus, no description of human behavior, however accurate, can ever ordain what is "right" or "wrong" behavior. It makes no difference whether we are studying cultural customs, religious convictions, political beliefs, educational practices, recreational activities, sexual proclivities, or table manners. If most people do something, that does not make it right; if most people do not, that does not make it wrong.

Of course, the converse is also true: If most people do something, that does not make it wrong; if most people do not, that does not make it right. In other words, there is no need to idealize someone just because he or she is different from the crowd. Likewise, we need not condemn someone solely for doing what others do. The point is that, in any case, we must be careful not to confuse objective description with subjective value judgment.

Let us briefly elaborate on these four variants of the naturalistic fallacy.

1. *common = good* The error here is to equate what is average, conventional, or popular with what is right. What are some of the assumptions underlying this perspective? "Everybody does it, so it must be okay." "The majority knows best." "All those people just can't be wrong." To take a concrete example: "Because the vast majority of people in a particular country approve of physical punishment of children, this opinion must be the right one."

2. *uncommon = bad* On the flip side of the same coin, that which departs from the norm is presumed to be wrong. Whether judging deviant behavior, unpopular beliefs, unusual customs, or unconventional appearances, the verdict is inevitable—if it's different, it's condemned. Example: "Since only a small minority of the world's population is homosexual, homosexuality must be wrong."

3. *common = bad* In this scenario, an individual rejects something solely because the majority accepts it, separate and apart from its own merits or drawbacks. On what basis? "The masses are always wrong." "If most people do it, it can't be good." "Since society is a flock of mindless sheep, anything they stand for is bound to be immoral." Example: "The establishment believes in marriage, therefore I certainly do not."

4. *uncommon = good* Along the same lines, any deviation from what is normal is deemed, per se, to be desirable, irrespective of its inherent value. Why? "Anything that's different is better than what's average." "If it's unusual, it's

good." "Anybody who has the courage to rebel against conventional thinking must have something important to contribute." Example: "I would rather have people look at me as strange than not notice me at all."

To view this phenomenon in a cross-cultural perspective, consider some of the practices that, in the past, have been widely accepted as correct: human sacrifice, slavery, child labor, public execution, denial of religious freedom, involuntary medical treatment, and the burning of books, heretics, and witches. By today's standards, it may seem painfully clear to most of us that these practices were morally wrong. Yet what are the chances that future generations will dismiss—perhaps even mock—much of what we currently take for granted as right? (Can you foresee any in particular?)

 EXERCISE 3.12

Exploring Manifestations of the Naturalistic Fallacy

As an exercise, try to think of specific examples that represent each of the categories below. (To help get you started, look through the following list of topics: gender roles, racial segregation, civil disobedience, affirmative action, birth control, child rearing, war, psychopathology, artistic expression, fashion, music, advertising, illegal immigration, personal hygiene.)

Common, therefore good: _____

Uncommon, therefore bad: _____

Common, therefore bad: _____

Uncommon, therefore good: _____

T. H. Huxley once noted that "the cosmic process has no sort of relation to moral ends" (cited in Miner & Rawson, 1994). His assertion notwithstanding, our view of nature itself is subject to the naturalistic fallacy. This happens when we equate what is "natural" with what is "right." Or when we proclaim that "things are as they should be." Or presume that whatever occurs in nature is good because nature is, in itself, good. How could it not be good? After all, just consider snow-capped mountains, golden sunsets, fragrant flowers, the miracle of birth, the instinct to survive, indeed life itself. From herbal remedies to organic pesticides, if it is from nature, then it is inherently good.

There is only one small wrinkle. Perhaps, not surprisingly, we are less inclined to cite examples from nature that we do not happen to like. What about birth defects and leprosy? Or drought and famine? Earthquakes and monsoons? Strychnine and oleander? Are these phenomena any less a part of nature? Are they somehow "unnatural"?

CROSS-CULTURAL SENSITIVITY

What does it mean to follow the principles of "multiculturalism"? Does it imply that we should accept anything and everything that happens in other cultures, whether in different countries or even within our own country? Does it mean that cross-cultural psychologists should set aside their own values and tolerate, for instance, the sexism and discrimination against women that are widely practiced, particularly in many developing countries? Would a multiculturalist perspective dictate the acceptance of polygamy in other countries, even though it is a federal offense in the United States? Should we cease condemning certain groups for their religious intolerance? Are we obliged—on the grounds of multiculturalism—to approve sexual harassment in Russia, for example, as a "celebration of their unique culture"? Do we remain silent about forceful female circumcision in Africa, a practice considered body mutilation by officials in Europe and the United States? After all, who are we to judge? "This is what they do in her culture." Consider the fact that from their perspective, many of *our* practices may seem immoral.

The school of thought that attempts to reduce (or even eliminate) particular moral and cultural values from study and research and maintains that any value is good, so long as it exists in a particular culture context, is called *cultural relativism*. Taken to its logical conclusion, the societal norms even of Nazi Germany, communist North Korea, and the former totalitarian Soviet Union should not be judged and criticized from an outside perspective because this act would be considered an "intervention of cultural imperialism."

What do you think about cultural relativism? Are there any limits to this perspective? Do you believe that everything truly is relative, and that there are not more universal standards by which to evaluate different cultural practices? Is it possible to reconcile the dilemma between respecting the beliefs of others without sacrificing one's own? Is there a point at which values such as tolerance and acceptance become potentially harmful? Can you draw a line between relativism and multiculturalism?

In essence, nature is held to a double standard: we embrace the "good" parts and ignore, dismiss, or rationalize away the "bad" parts. But we cannot have it both ways. Nature is, morally speaking, just nature. The values we impart to it are a different matter.

Even social scientists are not immune to committing this error. A case in point is the field of evolutionary psychology, which asserts that behavior, like anatomy and physiology, is largely the product of genetic inheritance. Proponents of this approach, basing their theories on the Darwinian principles of natural selection and adaptation for reproductive success, offer evolutionary explanations for a diverse array of human behaviors, including aggression, intelligence, morality, prejudice, territoriality, xenophobia, mating, sexual preference, and infidelity (see Barkow et al., 1992; Futuyma, 1979; Symons, 1979; Wright, 1994).

For instance, according to these theorists, men are genetically predisposed to seek out a variety of nubile young females as sex partners. Women, in contrast, natually prefer fewer, monogamous relationships with wealthy and powerful men. Further, evolution determines that men, compared with women, inherit a greater proclivity to kill their spouses over sexual infidelity.

For the sake of argument, let us set aside the numerous criticisms of evolutionary psychology (e.g., Holcomb, 1996; Schlinger, 1996) and assume that these theories are valid. Where does that leave us? What are the implications? That sexual double standards are "natural" and therefore acceptable? Would this justify promoscuity, adultery, deceit, and betrayal? Are greed, materialism, racial segregation, and war to be sanctioned? Could we really criticize or condemn someone for infidelity? How can we hold people accountable for spousal abuse, statutory rape, or murder? After all, it's "in their nature."

Clearly, even if evolution does influence what we do, that does not inherently make it morally good, desirable, or correct. Put another way, what is "true" isn't necessarily "right." It would be erroneous, for example, to condone acts of violence solely on the grounds that aggression is an intrinsic product of our genetic inheritance. It is one thing to *explain* human conduct; it is quite another to *excuse* it. Maybe our behavior is, in part, attributable to the process of natural selection. Then again, perhaps, to borrow a line from the movie *The African Queen*, "nature is what we were put on earth to overcome."

Antidotes

1. Do not make the mistake of equating statistical frequency with moral value. Thus, if most people do something, that does not intrinsically make it right; if most people do not, that does not therefore make it wrong. In like manner, if most people do something, that does not make it wrong; if they do not, that does not make it right.

2. Learn to differentiate objective descriptions from subjective prescriptions. Specifically, do not confuse one's description of what "is" or "isn't" with one's prescription of what "should" or "shouldn't" be.

To be positive: To be mistaken at the top of one's voice.
AMBROSE BIERCE (1842–1914)—AMERICAN JOURNALIST AND POET

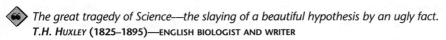

The great tragedy of Science—the slaying of a beautiful hypothesis by an ugly fact.
T.H. HUXLEY (1825–1895)—ENGLISH BIOLOGIST AND WRITER

The Belief Perseverance Effect: "Don't Confuse Me with the Facts!"

In our attempts to understand the world around us and to navigate our way through life, we adopt a wide variety of beliefs, the content of which ranges from the mundane (the best brand of detergent, the most flattering hairstyle) to the profound (the meaning of life, the existence of God). One of the most significant characteristics of our beliefs is the degree to which we become personally invested in them. The attachment may be so strong that our beliefs feel as if they are a vital and indispensable component of our very identity.

What happens, then, when our beliefs are challenged by new facts (such as research data)? Particularly those beliefs that we happen to like? Or those that we regard as important? Or those that we have come to accept as truths?

If we were to respond to such challenges in a purely rational manner, we would simply detach our personal feelings from the dispute, evaluate the substance of the challenge as objectively and dispassionately as possible, and then, if appropriate, modify our beliefs accordingly. We would, in other words, accommodate the new information by modifying our preexisting schemas (see the Assimilation Bias).

But we are not always so rational. In fact, sometimes we are not rational at all. Specifically, when our beliefs are being challenged, we are prone to feel that we personally are being challenged. When our beliefs are criticized, we feel criticized. When our beliefs are attacked, we feel attacked. Our first impulse, therefore, typically is to protect our beliefs, as if to protect ourselves. As such, we tend to cling to our beliefs, sometimes even in the face of contrary evidence. This bias in thinking is called the **belief perseverance effect** (see Lord et al., 1979).

When we engage in belief perseverance, we usually respond to such challenges by discounting, denying, or simply ignoring any information that runs counter to our beliefs. That is, we treat potentially disconfirming evidence or arguments as if they did not really exist. For example, suppose a friend of yours adamantly maintains that "rape is an act of violence, not of sex." In response, you point out that it isn't an "either/or" question; rape can be, and is, an act of both violence and sex. You explain further that the particular means of the assault differentiates rape from other types of violent acts (see the Similarity–Uniqueness Paradox). We would not call it "rape" if, for instance, a person were knifed in the back. Rape, in contrast, is a violent act specifically involving the sex organs. As such, it need not necessarily even entail the assailant's sexual pleasure or sexual gratification to be considered a sexual act. "In other words," you conclude, "rape is an act of sexual violence." Your friend pauses a moment, apparently mulling it over, and then replies, "Oh, I see what you mean. That makes a lot of sense. But I *still* think that rape is an act of violence, not of sex."

Our beliefs can be so intractable, in fact, that they stubbornly persevere even when we acknowledge that the evidence supporting them is erroneous. This was evidenced in a research study in which subjects were administered a personality test that purportedly showed them to be especially "socially sensitive" (Ross et al., 1975). Subjects were subsequently informed that the test actually was *fake*, and therefore provided invalid results. Even with this knowledge, however, subjects still persisted in believing that they were socially sensitive. Other studies have corroborated the general conclusion that it requires much more compelling evidence to change our beliefs than it did to create them in the first place (Ross & Lepper, 1980).

Can we engage in belief perseverance without rejecting contradictory information? What if we are not able, or even choose not, to discount, deny, or ignore potentially disconfirming evidence? Is there any way that we can continue to cling to our cherished beliefs and still emerge victorious? The answer, as you probably have already anticipated, is yes. Like the martial arts expert who masterfully redirects and transforms his opponent's force to his own advantage, in a brilliant feat of logical contortionism, we simply find a way to bend, twist, or reframe the information so that it actually *supports* our original belief.

Let us now turn to a sampling of variations on this very robust theme (Table 3.2). Of particular interest, note how the participants in these brief scenarios are able to support their positions by employing a creative assortment of flaws in thinking, including tautologous logic, misattributions of intentionality based on consequences, confusing feelings with truth, and errors in deductive and inductive reasoning. (These examples were drawn directly from our own experiences in a variety of settings, including classrooms, workshops, therapy sessions, media broadcasts, and waiting in line at a movie theater.)

| TABLE 3.2 | Illustrations of the Belief Perseverance Effect |

Employer: New Yorkers always do a better job. I've known it since my youth.

Employee: But our new sales rep from Los Angeles outsold every New Yorker in the department.

Employer: Yeah, but if we had given the same region to a New Yorker, we would have made *twice* the profit.

Minority Group Leader: I am absolutely certain that there's a government plot against us.

Interviewer: Now, hold on. Do you have any *evidence* that there's a plot against you?

Minority Group Leader: No, but do you have any evidence that there *isn't*?

Crusader: All atheists, at their core, are profoundly depressed due to a lack of belief in God.

Atheist: I don't believe in God, and I am not depressed.

Crusader: Then you might not realize it, but you actually *do* believe in God. Or maybe you are depressed but just aren't aware of it.

Sociopolitical Theorist: Jews control the media.

Reporter: But the vast majority of people who head the networks and newspapers aren't Jewish.

Sociopolitical Theorist: Exactly my point. All that proves is how *clever* they are in creating the *appearance* that they do not have any power. They have *so much* control that they've been able to dupe you into believing that they do not have *any* control.

Female Group Therapy Member: All men really want is sex and nothing else.

Male Group Therapy Member: I'm a man, and that's not all *I* want.

Female Group Therapy Member: Well, then either you're lying to me, or you're lying to yourself, or you're not *really* a man.

EXERCISE 3.13

The Perseverance of Sociocultural Beliefs

As an exercise in further examining the various manifestations of belief persever-ance, try completing the following scenarios on your own:

Person A: All Scots are cheap.
Person B: My parents are from Scotland, and they're not cheap.
Person A: _____.

Person A: Aryans are the master race.
Person B: Then how come they *lost* World War II? Especially to "inferior" races?
Person A: _____.

Person A: I'm antiabortion because I believe in the ultimate sanctity of life.
Person B: But you're in favor of the death penalty.
Person A: _____.

Person A: The terrorist is insane.
Person B: But he claims to be completely responsible for his actions.
Person A: _____.

Person A: You're a racist.
Person B: No, I'm not.
Person A: _____.

Person A: The only reason she got the job is because she's an ethnic minority.
Person B: _____.
Person A: _____.

Person A: The only reason she *didn't* get the job is because she's an ethnic mi-nority.
Person B: _____.
Person A: _____.

Person A: Racial discrimination in America is no better now than it was 50 years ago.
Person B: _____.
Person A: _____.

Person A: Immigrants coming to this country are just looking for a "free ride."
Person B: _____.
Person A: _____.

Person A: Homosexuality is a mental illness, just like any other mental illness.
Person B: _____.
Person A: _____.

Person A: The Holocaust didn't really happen.
Person B: _____.
Person A: _____.

Person A: God is on our side.
Person B: _____.
Person A: _____.

Antidotes

1. Keep an open mind to different, and especially challenging, points of view.

2. Remind yourself (and others as well) to think carefully about how you evaluate evidence and to closely monitor your biases as you formulate your conclusions.

3. Make it a point to actively *counterargue* your preexisting beliefs. That is, ask yourself directly in what ways your beliefs might be wrong. One specific method of doing so is to *consider the opposite*.

4. When faced with a discrepancy between your beliefs and the facts, resist the natural tendency to assume that your beliefs are right, and the facts must somehow be wrong.

Conclusions: "To Metathink or Not to Metathink?"

Last, let us turn to an evaluation of this chapter's principal content: the metathoughts themselves. In a sense, metathoughts may be seen as cognitive schemas. As such, they provide the same benefits—and, of course, are subject to the same liabilities—inherent in all schematic processing (see the Assimilation Bias). More specifically, in terms of advantages, they can

- significantly reduce or eliminate a wide variety of systematic biases, errors, and mistakes in thinking related to cultural and cross-cultural phenomena;
- improve the clarity of thinking and the accuracy of solutions;
- open pathways to new perspectives and alternative points of view;
- promote and facilitate innovative and creative approaches to problem solving;
- serve as a foundation for identifying other as-yet-unidentified cognitive errors (that is, new metathoughts), as well as their antidotes.

As for disadvantages, their use

- requires more time and effort (particularly at first) to analyze theories and facts;
- involves greater complexity at the cost of simplicity;
- is likely to result in increased ambiguity;
- can sometimes leave you feeling frustrated or confused;
- may be impractical or inappropriate in some situations.

In sum, like all other choices, the acceptance or rejection of these ideas entails costs as well as benefits. Thus, once you have made the effort to study, understand, and apply these metathought principles in cross-cultural psychology and your own life, take stock of their pluses and minuses. By weighing them out in this manner, you will be able to make much more informed choices as to your particular course of action. Either way, the decisions ultimately are yours.

Thomas Szasz once remarked, "I do not have the answer to every one of life's problems. I only know a stupid answer when I see one" (quoted in Miller, J., 1983). In like manner, the metathoughts will not necessarily provide you with the best solutions to all of the questions that you will ask or that will be asked of you. Nevertheless, cultivating your skills of critical thinking in cross-cultural psychology certainly will, at the very least, enable you more easily and consistently to identify and discard "the stupid ones," thereby freeing your time, energy, and resources for more productive endeavors.

 ## CHAPTER SUMMARY

- Critical thinking is one of the most vital and indispensable components of learning. The thought principles or metathoughts (literally, "thoughts about thought") presented in this chapter are cognitive tools that provide the user with specific strategies for inquiry and problem solving. In this way, they serve as potent antidotes to thinking that is often prone to be biased, simplistic, rigid, lazy, or just plain sloppy.

- In describing phenomena, particularly social phenomena, the language that people use invariably reflects their own personal values, biases, likes, and dislikes. In this way, their words can reveal at least as much about themselves as the events, individuals, and groups they are attempting to describe.

- Dichotomous variables are a matter of classification (*quality*), whereas continuous variables are a matter of degree (*quantity*). The problem is that people have a tendency to dichotomize variables that, more accurately, should be conceptualized as continuous.

- All phenomena are both similar to and different from each other, depending on the dimensions or sorting variables that have been selected for purposes of evaluation, comparison, and contrast. No phenomenon is totally identical or totally unique in relation to other phenomena.

- Barnum statements are "one-size-fits-all" descriptions that are true of practically all human beings, but that do not provide distinctive information about a particular group or person. Thus, the problem with Barnum statements is not that they are wrong; rather, because they are so generic, universal, and elastic, they are of little value.

- The *assimilation bias* represents a significant obstacle to clear thinking and effective problem solving. In viewing the world through "schema-colored glasses," we subject virtually all the incoming information to varying degrees of distortion, misinterpretation, and invalidation.

- To identify any given phenomenon, we automatically and intuitively compare it with our mental representation, prototype, or schema of the relevant category. Errors due to the *representativeness bias* can occur as a result of faulty prototypes, failure to consider relevant statistical data, or motivational biases.

- We utilize the availability heuristic whenever we attempt to assess the frequency or likelihood of an event on the basis of how quickly or easily instances come to mind. Thus, vivid examples, dramatic events, graphic case studies, and personal testimonies, in contrast to statistical information, are likely to exert a disproportionate impact on our judgments.

In this way, anecdotes may be more persuasive than factual data.

- In arriving at causal attributions to explain people's behavior, we have a tendency to overestimate the impact of their internal personality traits (dispositions) and to underestimate the impact of their environmental circumstances (situations). This *fundamental attribution error* appears to be due to cognitive biases and motivational biases.

- The assumptions, attitudes, and beliefs that we hold toward other people can, with or without our intent, actually produce the very behaviors that we expect to find. Similarly, our own behavior may inadvertently be shaped by other people's expectancies of us. In sum, with the *self-fulfilling prophecy*, expectations can generate their own reality.

- Correlations may provide us with accurate and useful information regarding "what" relationships exist, but they cannot be counted on to answer the question, "why?" Even in those circumstances in which a correlation strongly implies causation, it does not prove causation.

- In contrast to unidirectional causation, when Event *A* causes Event *B*, in bidirectional causation Event *A* and Event *B* are linked in a circular or causal loop, in which each is both a cause and an effect of the other. In such instances, the pathway of causation is a "two-way street." Further, any given event can be, and typically is, the result of numerous causes.

- The frequency of an event does not inherently determine its moral value or worth. What is common, typical, or normal is not necessarily good; what is uncommon, atypical, or abnormal is not necessarily bad. Conversely, what is common is not necessarily bad, and what is uncommon is not necessarily good.

- We have a tendency to stubbornly cling to our beliefs, sometimes even in the face of disconfirming evidence. Thus, when these beliefs are challenged, we feel impelled to protect them, almost as if we were protecting ourselves. One consequence of this *belief perseverance effect* is that it generally requires much more compelling evidence to change our beliefs than it did to create them in the first place.

 ## KEY TERMS

Antidote   A remedy to prevent or counteract an adverse effect.

Assimilation Bias   The propensity to resolve discrepancies between preexisting schemas and new information in the direction of assimilation rather than accommodation, even at the expense of distorting the information itself.

Availability Bias   Any condition in which the availability heuristic produces systematic errors in thinking or information processing, typically due to highly vivid although rare events.

Availability Heuristic   A cognitive strategy for quickly estimating the frequency, incidence, or probability of a given event based on the ease with which such instances are retrievable from memory.

Barnum Effect   A phenomenon that refers to people's willingness to accept uncritically the validity of Barnum statements.

Barnum Statement   Any generic "one-size-fits-all" description or interpretation about a particular individual that is true of practically all human beings.

Belief Perseverance Effect   The tendency to cling stubbornly to one's beliefs, even in the face of contradictory or disconfirming evidence.

Bias   A prejudicial inclination or predisposition that inhibits, deters, or prevents impartial judgment.

Bidirectional Causation   A mutual, reciprocal relationship between two variables wherein each is both a cause and an effect of the other.

Cognitive Bias   Any systematic error in attribution that derives from limits that are inherent in people's cognitive abilities to process information.

Continuous Variable   Any variable that lies along a dimension, range, or spectrum, rather than in a discrete category, that can theoretically take on an infinite number of values and is expressed in terms of quantity, magnitude, or degree.

Critical Thinking   An active and systematic cognitive strategy to examine, evaluate, and understand events, solve problems, and make decisions on the basis of sound reasoning and valid evidence. More specifically, critical thinking involves maintaining an attitude that is both open minded and skeptical; recognizing the distinction between facts and theories; striving for factual accuracy and logical consistency; objectively gathering, weighing, and synthesizing information; forming reasonable inferences, judgments, and conclusions; identifying and questioning underlying assumptions and beliefs; discerning hidden or implicit values; perceiving similarities and differences between phenomena; understanding causal relationships; reducing logical flaws and personal biases, such as avoiding oversimplifications and overgeneralizations; developing a tolerance for uncertainty and ambiguity; exploring alternative perspectives and explanations; and searching for creative solutions.

Dichotomous Variable   Any variable that can be placed into either of two discrete and mutually exclusive categories.

Fundamental Attribution Error   A bias in attempting to determine the causes of people's behavior that involves overestimating the influence of their personality traits, while underestimating the influence of their particular situations, that is, overutilizing internal attributions and underutilizing external attributions.

Heuristic   A mental shortcut or rule-of-thumb strategy for problem solving that reduces complex information and time-consuming tasks to more simple, rapid, and efficient judgmental operations, particularly in reaching decisions under conditions of uncertainty.

Metathinking   The act of thinking about thinking; engaging in a critical analysis and evaluation of the thinking process.

Metathoughts   Literally, thoughts about thought, which involve principles of critical thinking.

Motivational Bias   Any systematic error in attribution that derives from people's efforts to satisfy their own personal needs, such as the desire for self-esteem, power, or prestige.

Naturalistic Fallacy   An error in thinking whereby the individual confuses or equates objective descriptions with subjective value judgments, in particular, by defining what is morally good or bad solely in terms of what is statistically frequent or infrequent.

Parataxic Reasoning   A kind of "magical thinking," frequently responsible for superstitious behaviors, in which events that occur close together in time are erroneously construed to be causally linked.

Post Hoc Error   A shortened form of *post hoc, ergo propter hoc* ("after this, therefore because of this"), referring to the logical error that because Event *B* follows Event *A*, then *B* must have been caused by *A*.

Representativeness Bias   Any condition in which the representativeness heuristic produces systematic errors in thinking or information processing.

Representativeness Heuristic   A cognitive strategy for quickly estimating the probability that a given instance is a member of a particular category.

Schema   A cognitive structure or representation that organizes one's knowledge, beliefs, and past experiences, thereby providing a framework for understanding new events and future experiences; a general expectation or preconception about a wide range of phenomena.

Self-Fulfilling Prophecy   A phenomenon wherein people's attitudes, beliefs, or assumptions about another person (or persons) can, with or without their intent, actually produce the very behaviors that they had initially expected to find.

Unidirectional Causation   A relationship between two variables wherein one is the cause and the other is the effect.

CHAPTER 4

Cognition: Sensation, Perception, and States of Consciousness

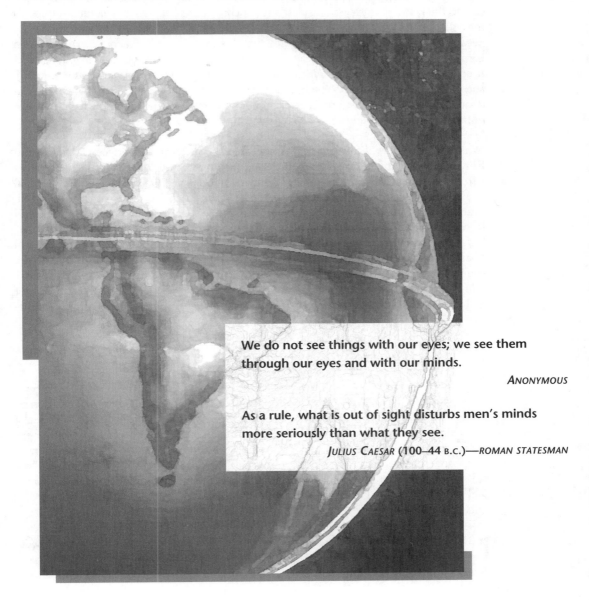

We do not see things with our eyes; we see them through our eyes and with our minds.

ANONYMOUS

As a rule, what is out of sight disturbs men's minds more seriously than what they see.

JULIUS CAESAR (100–44 B.C.)—ROMAN STATESMAN

At the end of class Albert raised his hand and asked a question: "Do cross-cultural psychologists acknowledge important differences between Europeans and non-Europeans in America?" He then contended that for centuries, the ancestors of the former group relied mostly on visual perception. Europeans, he said, must see, verify, measure, and then rationalize their impressions. They do not feel or believe a priori; they must experience everything before their own eyes. Africans, he said, referring to his own ancestors, were different because of environmental conditions that caused them to rely mostly on hearing and touch. They felt objects and vibrations through their skin, could masterfully express themselves through their voices, and did not always need visual verifications. Albert concluded that due to such perceptual differences between European and African ancestors, white Americans are more likely to succeed in engineering, science, and writing, whereas African Americans tend to excel at playing music, singing, and other nonvisual arts. "Do you have any evidence to support your idea?" One of the students replied. "You see, you need verifications. I do not have them. I simply feel this way," responded Albert laughing at his own answer.

Was Albert right when he daringly suggested the differences between Africans and Europeans? Are there any significant visual, auditory, and other sensory differences among people of various cultures? Or maybe people see, hear, and feel the physical world in the same way? If not, what particular characteristics of vision, smell, touch, or taste have the strongest cultural roots? On a more "practical" side, should fashion designers pay attention to certain colors either liked or disliked by particular ethnic or national groups? Do pilots in all countries prefer to scan the control board in front of them from left to right? Can people in southern Brazil enjoy the sound of music liked by people in Western China? Do people see the same dreams? We will try to address these and other questions throughout this chapter. First let us begin with a brief review of the most basic principles underlying human cognitive processes.

Sensation and Perception: Basic Principles

The process by which receptor cells are stimulated and transmit their information to higher brain centers is called **sensation.** You see a blue star in the evening sky or feel a dull pain in your arm—all sensations begin from an environmental stimulus, either external or internal, in the form of energy capable of exciting the nervous system. Sensation converts external energy into an internal neurophysiological process, which "results" in a particular psychological experience: we see the star and feel the pain. Do we feel all environmental stimuli? Obviously not, because certain stimuli are not experienced at all.

The minimum amount of physical energy needed for an individual to notice a stimulus is called an **absolute threshold.** The **difference threshold** is the lowest level of stimulation required to sense that a change in the stimulation has occurred. **Sensory adaptation** is the tendency of the sensory system to respond less to stimuli that continue without change. We can adapt, for example, to particular conditions, such as heat or cold, the presence or absence of air pollution, and spicy food. Residents of a small resort town in Spain are less likely to attend to the air they breathe, whereas a tourist visiting this town from a polluted Mexico city or Los Angeles is likely to notice the incredible freshness of the air.

For each of the five senses, vision, hearing, smell, touch, and taste, discrete neural pathays normally carry sensory information, a signal, to specific regions in the brain. The nature of sensation depends on the location of the brain that is activated by a signal. For example, electrical stimulation of the primary visual cortex, which is located in the occipital lobes of the brain, produces visual sensations, whereas stimulation of the auditory complex in the temporal lobes is experienced as sound. Color sensation is a process based on the functioning of three different types of cones in the eye's retina. Each cone responds to wavelights, but fires most persistently at a particular point on the spectrum. Thus short-wavelight cones are responsible for the sensation of blue, middle-wavelight cones produce the sensation of green, and long-wavelight cones produce red sensations. Mixing these three primary colors together, most individuals detect as many as one thousand color shades (Brown & Wald, 1964). When a person detects a smell, information from the receptors travels directly to the primary olfactory complex in the frontal lobes. Taste receptors consist of two paths. The first path is connected to the primary gustatory cortex in the brain, which allows people to detect tastes. The second path is connected to the brain's limbic system, which can generate immediate emotional and behavioral responses to tastes. Several receptors in the skin feed into a single sensory neuron that is connected to the spinal cord. This allows for immediate reflexive action, such as the quick movement after touching something hot.

The process that organizes various sensations into meaningful patterns is called **perception.** Physiologists assert that perception involves activation of association areas in the cortex, thus integrating prior knowledge with current sensation. Three colored vertical stripes displayed in sequence on a piece of material—blue, white, and red—will have little meaning for a boy from Bangladesh or Northern Ireland. However, for a French adult, this sequence of colors would be associated with the French national flag. When one of us takes a guitar and plays the first cords of the song "Stairway to Heaven," many American or British students identify it as a classic-rock ballad written by Led Zeppelin. On the other hand, those who grew up outside the Western tradition of rock music interpret these notes as nothing more than a "melody."

Sensation and perception are two basic processes first studied in psychological laboratories more than one hundred years ago in Germany, France, Russia, Great Britain, and the United States. Comparative analysis of the data obtained by these laboratories shows remarkable quantitative and qualitative similarities in both sensory and perceptual processes in people of different countries (Yaroshevski, 1975). However, in most experiments, psychologists studied sensation using a "standard"— for psychological research in the 1800s—sample of subjects: the researchers themselves, their academic assistants, and, of course, the students. Therefore, the data in such studies were obtained mainly from highly educated, white male subjects. Cross-cultural investigation of sensation began with the research conducted by Rivers (1901) and associates, who selected their subjects in Europe and Torres Strait Islands, a territory near Australia. Rivers examined a popular assumption about the extraordinary visual sharpness of non-Europeans. The assumption was disproved: the vision of the Torres Strait Islanders was not found to be outstanding. Will further studies reveal similarities among cultural groups?

How Culture Influences What We Perceive

Our experience with the environment shapes our perception by creating perceptual expectations. These expectations, known as a **perceptual set,** make particular interpretations more likely to occur and increase both the speed and efficiency of the perceptual process. Perceptual sets common in people of a particular culture—and most relevant to their experience—are not necessarily developed in individuals from other cultures. For example, we can turn our heads toward potentially meaningful sounds because of our previous experience with them. Most people who live in big metropolitan areas in the United States will be almost indifferent to the sound of a siren from a passing ambulance or fire truck. Some foreign tourists, however, would stop and stare at such a scene on the streets of Washington D.C. or Chicago. An American tourist in Russia may be annoyed by the sound of a single mosquito flying in the hotel room, whereas a resident of a northern Russian village will pay no attention whatsoever to these flying insects.

Personal experience influences one's sensation and perception. If many individuals from a particular group share such experiences, there should be some common group-related sensory or perceptual patterns. For example, we are usually aware of the aroma outside a restaurant when we are hungry, yet we are much less sensitive to it when our stomach is full. In general, if we need something we pay attention to the stimuli that are linked to the gratification of the need. But what if a person is constantly deprived of food or water, like millions of people on earth are? In one study researchers examined the effects of food and water deprivation on word identification (Wispe & Drambarean, 1993). The deprived participants perceived the need-related words (words standing for food and drinks) at shorter exposure times than the nondeprived subjects. In another classic study, researchers compared the perceptual experiences of children from poor and wealthy families (Bruner & Goodman, 1947). They asked children to adjust the size of a circle of light to match the sizes of various coins, a penny, a nickel, a dime, and a quarter. Children from wealthier families tended to see the coins as smaller than they actually were, whereas children from poor families overestimated the size of the coins. The investigators argued that the need for money among children from poor homes influenced their perception of the coins. This interesting finding has been reproduced in Hong Kong with similar results (Dawson, 1975).

Environmental conditions affect our sensation and perception in many ways. For example, an individual can live in a crowded city and have only limited access to open landscapes. This will probably influence, as we will see later, the person's perception

CRITICAL THINKING

Origin and Sensory Preferences

This chapter opened with an episode in which Albert raised a question about basic cultural and psychological differences between African Americans and European Americans. His hypothesis resembles the so-called compensation hypothesis: Africans are likely to excel in auditory (hearing) tasks, whereas Europeans deal more effectively with visual (seeing) stimuli. In other words, Africans may prefer to communicate through the auditory modality whereas white Europeans might favor written communications. If Africans, compared to Europeans, appear to have difficulty with the study of mathematics, this can be "compensated" by a high facility for learning languages and a good sense for rhythm and music (McLuhan, 1971). According to Shade (1991), one of the important features in African American perceptual style is the preference of auditory, aural, and tactile perceptions, as compared with predominantly visual perceptions common in European Americans. African Americans are trained to concentrate on people rather than abstract ideas and nonhuman objects. A similar suggestion was extended to the field of art. Auditory and tactile sensations and perceptions were proposed as being specifically African and quite different from the visual culture of the Europeans. Some authors propose the existence of *verve*, a special element of African psychology. This is an energetic, intense mental set or preference to be simultaneously attuned to several sensory stimuli rather than singular events or a linear set of stimuli (Boykin, 1994).

These hypotheses are intriguing; however, there is very little empirical data to support assumptions about substantial sensory differences between Africans and Europeans. Empirical studies have also come up short in supporting the hypothesis of physiological differences between visual and auditory transmission of information among different cultures. No evidence was found to back a hypothesis about the superiority of black students in auditory judgments and white students in visual judgments. Empirical evidence on the prominence of auditory, tactile, or kinesthetic cues for Africans is also very limited. However, these findings should not discourage anyone from conducting further research in this fascinating area of cross-cultural psychology.

of depth. Studies have shown that hunter and gatherer cultures have a lower rate of color blindness among their members than societies practicing agriculture. Indeed, from an evolutionary standpoint, not many colorblind hunters could have survived because of their inability to distinguish details, colors, and contours, a skill critical in hunting or gathering activities (Pollack, 1963). Another example refers to the level of noise in the surrounding environments. People who live in deserts do not suffer hearing loss to the extent that city dwellers do (Reuning & Wortley, 1973). In deserts the level of noise is significantly lower than it is in urban areas and this could explain the difference in hearing problems.

The absence of experience can become a significant factor that affects perception. For example, researchers raised kittens in complete darkness except for several hours each day. During these brief periods, the kittens were placed in a cylinder with either horizontal or vertical stripes (Blakemore & Cooper, 1970). The animals could not observe their own bodies and the only object they saw were the stripes. Five months after the beginning of the experiment, the kittens reared in "horizontal" environments were unable to perceive vertical lines. Their brains lacked detectors responsive to vertical lines. Similarly, the kittens reared in "vertical" environments were unable to perceive horizontal lines. The animals' brains adapted to either "horizontal" or "vertical" worlds by developing specialized neuronal pathways. Similar results were obtained in studies of individuals who were born blind but obtained sight after a surgical procedure later in life (Gregory, 1978). Most of these people could tell figure from ground, detect colors, and observe moving objects. However, many of them could not recognize objects they previously knew by touch. The absence of a visual experience affected these people's cognition after sight was gained!

Stressful situations also affect the way we see and hear. It was suggested, for instance, that our perceptual system could defend us against perceiving anxiety-evoking stimuli. To prove this suggestion, researchers compared the time subjects took to identify emotionally neutral words, such as *house or tree*, with comparable time for presumably anxiety-provoking words, such as *bitch and rape*. As predicted, the emotionally threatening words required longer exposure times than the neutral words before they were recognized (McGinnis, 1949). This study, however, was not replicated in other cultures and psychologists can only guess how an individual's perception is affected when one continuously lives in a stressful environment.

On the whole, environmental conditions, as well as socialization and acculturation practices, determine culture-related differences and similarities in sensation and perception. Children learn to pay attention to certain stimuli, reject others, and develop particular cognitive preferences for some culture-related images, smells, tastes, and sounds (Shiraev & Boyd, 2001).

How People Perceive Depictions

Draw a person on a piece of paper. Make sure you draw the head, the body, the hands, and the legs. Do not skip the ears and the mouth. No matter how well or how poorly you draw, the immense majority of people around the world should identify what you drew as a picture of a person. Even though most will identify your drawing as a person, they should quickly correct their answer after you ask them: "Is this person real, or is it just a picture?" The answer most likely will be, "It's a picture."

Perception of depictions, however, is linked to a person's educational and socialization experience or the lack thereof. In a study conducted among the Mekan—a remote group in Ethiopia with limited access to formal schooling and little exposure to pictures—scientists used detailed drawings of animals. With few exceptions the subjects identified the animals, but only after some time and with obvious mental effort (Derwgowski et al., 1972). Hudson (1962) who studied how South Africans perceived and interpreted safety posters and signs provided another demonstration of the linkages between educational experience and perception. The number of misinterpretations of the posters was much lower for urban and more educated subjects than for rural and less educated individuals.

A CASE IN POINT

Picture Interpretation and Access to Media

Liddell (1997) reported that children in South Africa were less skilled interpreters of pictures than their white European counterparts, and this tendency was first noticed as early as in the 1960s. The differences between the samples were larger for African children from rural areas. The mistakes in picture interpretation included making mistakes in depth perception, identification of face blemishes, and interpretation of motion markers. Also, South African children had more difficulties than children in the European sample in creating narrative—short descriptive—interpretations of the pictures. Do these results suggest that because pictures may be a relatively poor source of organizing the South African children's knowledge, the authors of school textbooks should limit the usage of pictures?

We want you to think about the results from a different perspective. The children in the examined samples, despite recent progress in communications, still face a tremendous lack of opportunities compared with their European or North American peers. Limited access to television and movies, inability to use personal computers at home, limited access to computers at school, lack of pictorial materials at home, and many other poverty-related problems can contribute to the significant limitations in the child's usage of pictures. Make your call now. What do you think, should you suggest limiting the number of pictures in South African textbooks or should you rather insist that the child have better access to pictorial materials outside the classroom?

How People Scan Pictures

There is evidence that scanning patterns are subject to some cultural variations. The most significant finding is that the direction we examine pictures—from left to right, from right to left, or from top to bottom—is linked to our reading habits (Goodnow, J., & Levine, R., 1973). For example, it is likely that people in England, Argentina, or Canada, who read from left to right, also have a left–right scanning pattern; Arab and Hebrew readers, who read from right to left, should demonstrate a right–left scanning pattern; and Japanese readers, who read from top to bottom, should have a top–bottom pattern of picture scanning. However, some studies challenge this reading–scanning link. For example, in a test on the copying of geometric figures, Hebrew subjects showed a left–right preference. How did the researchers explain this finding? Both Hebrew and English scripts require mainly left-to-right strokes for single letters. In comparison, in the Arab language, the right-to-left direction is required for the writing of individual letters. Therefore, from a practical standpoint, it is always useful to examine not only reading but also writing patterns of a particular culture. These findings can raise interesting questions about how some professionals (i.e., pilots, operators, etc.) of different cultural backgrounds scan signals from monitors and other visual indicators displayed in front of them.

Visual scanning is perhaps related to drawing. Take, for instance, the drawing of circles. The differences between cultural groups are perhaps based on the way people learn to write in their native language. If writing requires more clockwise movement, then the child is more likely to make his or her circles in the same manner. In a comparative Japanese American study the direction of circle drawing for American students and Japanese students was compared. Results showed that with advancing grade, Americans increasingly drew circles in a counter-clockwise direction whereas the Japanese increasingly drew them in a clockwise direction (Amenomori et al., 1997). Another study showed that children who speak Hebrew tend to draw circles in a clockwise direction more often than the other two groups studied, whose language was French or English (Zendal et al., 1987).

Perception of Depth

Depth perception refers to the organization of sensations in three dimensions, even though the image on the eye's retina is two dimensional. Look at the drawing of the famous Devil's tuning fork (below). Now we challenge you to draw the fork by memory, without looking at the picture. Why is it difficult? The picture is two dimensional with several confusing depth cues. However, the brain, because of our experience with depth cues, interprets this object as three dimensional. It is interesting that many people without formal schooling or previous exposure to three-dimensional pictures do not find this particular picture confusing (Hudson, 1960; Deregowski, 1972). Those who are not familiar with how to interpret depth cues—usually due to environmental conditions, extreme poverty, and lack of formal schooling—will perceive them as two dimensional. Some non-Western subjects experience difficulty with pictorially presented depth stimuli. However, according to several studies, education and training can significantly improve depth perception (Leach, 1975; Nicholson et al., 1977).

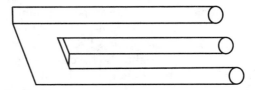

Altogether, picture perception may be considered a combination of cognitive skills. Some national, regional, or culture-specific conditions determine which skills will improve in individuals and which skills will remain underdeveloped.

 Beware in case you lose the substance by grasping at the shadow.
AESOP (SIXTH CENTURY B.C.)—GREEK FABULIST

Are People Equally Misled by Visual Illusions?

Look at the pictures on page 107. They represent famous visual illusions. In the Müller–Lyer illusion, the line on the left appears shorter than the line on the right. In the Ponzo illusion, the upper line appears larger than the one on the bottom. In the horizontal–vertical illusion, the vertical line appears to be larger than the horizontal one. The vast majority of us are susceptible to these illusions; even though we know that the lines are equal in length, they appear unequal to us. However, such susceptibility is not common in all individuals and there are some cultural variations in how people perceive visual illusions.

For example, a study of receptiveness to the Ponzo illusion in the United States and Guam suggested that non-Western and rural subjects showed less susceptibility to the illusion than the individuals from either Western or urban areas (Brislin, 1993). Likewise, on both the Müller–Lyer and horizontal–vertical illusions, the Western samples, living primarily in industrial urban environments, were more illusion prone than any of the non-Western samples. Subjects from regions with open landscapes were more susceptible to the horizontal–vertical illusion than subjects from regions in which such views are rare (Segall et al., 1966).

How can we interpret such perceptual differences? As suggested earlier in the chapter, if certain groups differ in their visual perception, such differences may be influenced by the different experiences of the members of these groups. According to a popular "carpentered world" hypothesis (Segall et al., 1966), people who are raised in an environment shaped by carpenters—most of us live in rectangular houses with rectangular furniture and similar street patterns—tend to interpret nonrectangular figures as representations of rectangular figures seen in perspective. They also have a tendency to interpret the lines in the horizontal plane that look as if they are moving away from an observer as appearing to be shorter than the lines that cross the viewer's line of vision (the horizontal–vertical illusion).

Virtually all people who had formal schooling got used to converting two-dimensional pictures into three-dimensional images even though pictures on computer screens and photographs in magazines are displayed on a flat surface. Certain perceptual sets (see the beginning of the chapter) allow people to see "flat" objects as if they actually exist in "volume" (Segall et al., 1990).

Some Cultural Patterns of Drawing Pictures

Individuals with no formal schooling, young children, and early artists did not acquire the ability to convert three-dimensional perceptions into two-dimensional paintings or sketches. In some cultural groups, their paintings often display objects, details, and surroundings independently of one another. For instance, Australian Aborigines usually depict the trunk of a crocodile as seen from above, while the head and the tail are drawn as being seen from the side (Dziurawiec & Deregowski, 1992). Beveridge (1940) and Thouless (1932) found that African drawings available to them were less affected by visual cues than European drawings were. With the lack of perspective in African pictures, objects were depicted as they were in reality rather than how they actually appear to the observer.

Perceptual distortions are easily found in various forms of drawings. For instance, in many national art traditions a linear perspective does not occur. Numerous perceptual distortions are found in modern art, as well as in ancient Egyptian, and medieval Spanish art (Parker & Deregowski, 1990). The polydimensional representation of space has been used at some period in most cultures. In much of ancient Egyptian and Cretan painting, for instance, the head and legs of a figure were shown in profile, but the eye and torso of a figure were drawn frontally. In Indian and early European paintings, created before the seventeenth century, figures and other vertical forms were represented as if seen from ground level, whereas the horizontal planes that figures and objects stood on were shown as if viewed from above. Paul Sezanne, a famous French artist, represented things on his paintings as if seen from different directions and at varying eye levels. Cubism, one of the prominent schools in modern art, aimed to give the viewer the time experience of moving around static forms in order to examine their volume and structure. In cubist pictures, the viewer is specifically encouraged to examine the surfaces of depicted objects from every possible angle.

All in all, we see that environmental conditions and cultural traditions can affect some mechanisms of human perception. However, the differences among cultures are repeatedly found not to be profound.

Perception of Color

Color has three universal psychological dimensions, hue, brightness, and saturation. Hue is what people mean by color, brightness refers to a color's intensity, and saturation indicates a color's purity. If there are similar underlying physiological mechanisms of color perception, does this mean that perception of color has very little cultural variation? Are culturally sanctioned activities able to influence color perception?

According to so-called language-related theories of color perception—that emphasize the role of language in the identification and labeling of colors in each and every language—there are words that are linked to various units of the visible spectrum (Berry et al., 1992). The developing child learns these words and starts to use them in order to identify colors. It is interesting that even though the vast majority of healthy individuals are able to detect the same range of colors, there are languages that lack certain words for particular colors. For example, the color red is always represented by a separate word, whereas the colors green and blue are sometimes not distinguished linguistically. An explanation for this finding is based on an assumption that due to environmental conditions the less vivid colors were less salient to non-Europeans and for that reason less likely be identified and labeled with a separate word (Ray, 1952).

There were other attempts to explain such a perceptual confusion between the colors green and blue. Some studies stress physiological differences between racial groups in terms of their color perception. For instance, Pollack (1963) demonstrated that certain visual perceptual skills might be related to factors such as retinal pigmentation. He found that persons with denser retinal pigmentation had more difficulty detecting contours and showed relative difficulties in perceiving the color blue. However, physiological models of cultural differences in the detection of color did not gain as much popularity as the theories that emphasize the importance of learning experiences and linguistic norms of perception.

The subjective social and individual psychological meaning of color can be crucial to our understanding of color perception. There are strong universal trends in people's feelings about colors. In one prominent study, data from 23 cultures revealed stable cross-cultural similarities. The concept "red" was perceived as being quite salient and active. "Black" and "gray" were considered bad, whereas "white," "blue," and "green" were considered good. "Yellow," "white," and "gray" were persistently seen as passive (Adams & Osgood, 1973).

The history of human civilization gives many examples about other trends in color interpretation. Take, for example, the color red. In many nations it became a political symbol of violence, revolution, and revolt. In totalitarian China and the Soviet Union government officials made red banners the country's official flags. The official flag of Nazi Germany was also red. Rebellious students in Europe waved red flags during mass violent demonstrations in the 1960s. A red flag was also raised by radical guerrilla fighters in South and Central America, in Southeast Asia, and in South Africa. In the 1970s, one of the most notorious left-wing terrorist groups in Italy carried the name Red Brigades.

Another interesting set of facts is related to human perception of black and white. More than two decades ago researchers found that preschool children in the United States from various racial groups tended to prefer light- to dark-skinned people on pictures and photographs and to favor the color white over black. European children also displayed a tendency toward the positive evaluation of light-skinned figures relative to dark-skinned ones (Best et al., 1975). Moreover, cross-cultural research has established that people all over the world associate the color white with more positive feelings than black and that this bias seems to emerge by the preschool years in the countries of Japan, France, Italy, Germany, and Great Britain. Subsequent research has shown that native African children share the same color bias (Williams & Best, 1990). The association of the color white with something "good," "pure," and "familiar," and black as primarily "negative," "unclean," and "unknown" is common in many cultures. The investigators speculate the pan-cultural preference for light over dark may reflect a generalization from light and dark cycles of the day. Light is generally associated with certainty and safety, whereas darkness is more likely to represent danger and uncertainty. Carl Jung believed that the color black carries an inborn meaning of uncertainty and unpredictability for humans and our ancestors: enemies and predators were ready to attack at night when detecting them was difficult. A dark cave is full of unpleasant surprises: who is hiding there? A child cries and asks his parents to leave the lights on because he is afraid to stay alone in the dark room. Nature may have endowed humans with a tendency to dislike the dark, just as it has endowed them with a susceptibility to a fear of snakes and spiders. Sea pirates raised black banners over their

A CASE IN POINT

A Cultural Interpretation of the Color Black

The prominent trend in interpretation of the color black can be further demonstrated in the following joke known across many countries. A little boy asks his mother about why brides always wear white dresses and prefer bright colors. His mother answers that every bride wants her wedding day to be the prettiest, the happiest day in her life. That is why every woman who is getting married wants to emphasize the significance of her wedding by wearing white and bright colors. "Oh, I know now," her son replies. "I understand why grooms are always wearing black." Most of us will get this joke because there is a particular cross-cultural pattern in our interpretation of colors. The punchline here is covert: the boy actually didn't say anything definite about the color black. However, the listener is likely to follow (this is the point of the joke!) the boy's reasoning. The color black is associated with something negative, sad, and undesirable. Therefore a wedding is not the happiest day in the groom's life. (Of course another popular stereotype about men's negative attitudes toward marriage is also likely to be evoked).

Questions: If these and other observations suggest that the color black is likely to be associated with predominantly negative feelings does this trend mean people in many cultures are prejudiced against the black color? If yes, what can we do about it? What do you think, is it possible to change culture-based perceptions of color?

ships as a symbol of intimidation. In Christianity, angels are white and demons are black. In addition, people from various religious backgrounds wear black clothes when they are mourning. In the English language definitions of the word "black" include "without any moral light or goodness," "evil," "wicked," "indicating disgrace," and "sinful." Definitions of "white" include "morally pure," "spotless," "innocent," and "free from evil intent." In 1993, one of the most difficult years in recent Russian history, when a newspaper asked Russians what color they associated with their lives, 42 percent said gray and 21 percent said black. Most of them felt as though they entered into "darkness" when things were extremely difficult (Kelley, 1994).

In summary, it appears that there is a significant degree of similarity in the way color terms are used in different cultures. Verbal labels, if they are not available in the lexicon of a language, can be readily learned. Perhaps systematic formal schooling and the availability of various informational sources, such as books, television, and computers, can play a significant role in such learning.

Other Senses

So far in this chapter, our attention has been directed at vision, the most systematically studied modality in cross-cultural psychology. There is significantly less information concerning other types of sensation or perceptual cross-cultural processes. Let us consider some relevant data and hypotheses.

Hearing

A Hungarian scientist, Georg von Bekesy, won the Nobel Prize, the most prestigious scientific award, for his empirical study of the neural mechanisms of hearing. Psychology textbooks emphasize the universal nature of human auditory sensation and perception processes. Most variations in hearing are based on individual physiological differences, which are related to age, education, professional training, environmental conditions, and general experience. The most important differences are related to the meanings attached to particular sounds in different cultures. During childhood and the following periods of socialization, individuals get used to particular voices, sounds, and even noises, and subsequently interpret them according to the norms established in their culture. For more information on speech perception, see Chapter 10.

Taste

People across the world respond to four basic tastes—sweet, sour, bitter, and salty. It has been shown that individuals of different cultures vary only insignificantly in their ability to detect these four primary tastes. However, as might be expected, there are tremendous cross-cultural variations in taste preferences and beliefs about basic flavors (Laing et al., 1993). For example, people in the regions closer to the equator generally prefer spicier foods, compared with their counterparts living farther to the north or south. Therefore, Italians will be likely to consider Scandinavian cuisine as dull, whereas some people in Sweden or Denmark will refer to Italian food as spicy. We will get back to the topic of taste perception when we analyze hunger motivation in Chapter 7.

Smell

Even though researchers today understand the physiology of the olfactory sense, our knowledge about how smell affects behavior is very limited. There are data suggesting that exposure to a substance (underarm secretion) may affect the menstrual cycle in women (Cutler et al., 1986). In another study, investigators examined the positive impact on safe driving of having a pleasant odor in the car (Baron & Kalsher, 1996). However data on cross-cultural variations in olfactory perception are mostly anecdotal and focus mainly on cross-cultural differences in odor preferences and prevailing odors.

Touch

The sense of touch is a combination of at least three qualities: pressure, temperature, and pain. The last one has received the most attention from cross-cultural psychologists. Many individual and situational characteristics, for example, skin texture, age, social status, presence or absence of other people, and level of individual motivation, can determine perception of pain. Passively experienced anxiety can increase pain. Fear, anger, or stress can inhibit it. Love and pride can cause some people to hide even the most excruciating pain.

CROSS-CULTURAL SENSITIVITY

You perhaps know that police—in order to subdue the most violent suspects—regularly use pepper spray. It causes some eye and skin irritation and is considered to be a quite effective preventive force. Now read how stereotypes may affect professional judgment. A Massachusetts training police officer in an interview with a local newspaper, the *Cambridge Chronicle,* suggested that members of ethnic groups accustomed to eating spicy foods are less susceptible to the use of pepper spray against them. Members of ethnic groups who have consumed cayenne peppers from the time they were small children, the officer explained, might have a greater resistance to the spray. Among these "high-resistance-to-pepper-spray" groups are Mexican Americans, Pakistanis, and members of Louisiana's Cajun population. Fortunately, the Cambridge Police Commissioner later corrected his subordinate and said that there is no scientific evidence to support any statements about the pepper spray susceptibility of certain ethnic groups (Police Apologize for Spice Remark. *Reuters,* August 16, 1999).

Some specific cultural norms and expectations influence people's experience of pain (Morse & Park, 1988). For example, subjective reports of labor pain are lower in societies where childbirth is not considered to be a defiling event and where little help or comfort is offered to women in labor. Differences in the ability to endure pain are often a function of the circumstances in which the perception of pain is occurring. People exposed to harsh living and working conditions may become more stoical and less susceptible to pain than those who live and work in comfortable conditions (Clark & Clark, 1980). People without adequate access to health care may use a higher threshold to define unbearable pain, compared with those with guaranteed medical care (Halonen & Santrock, 1995).

Proprioceptive sense helps people register body position and movement. Individual variations in our ability to detect and then coordinate body position can be significant. The evidence of cultural differences and similarities is mostly anecdotal. Some well-known facts about a few Romanians who are good in gymnastics, some Russians who are superb in ballet, and certain East Asians who are excellent in martial arts should not encourage anyone to make any valid generalizations. Further studies, of course, are necessary.

 Nothing really belongs to us but time, which even he has who has nothing else.
BALTASAR GRACIAN (1601–1658)—SPANISH WRITER AND JESUIT PRIEST

Perception of Time

Talk to several people who have traveled or lived abroad. They could tell you how people in different cultures perceive and treat time guidelines. One of our colleagues from the Caribbean recently said that on his island people are generally not in a hurry compared with Americans, who usually are. Indeed, it is believed that Westerners tend to define punctuality using precise measures of time: 1 minute, 15 minutes, an hour, and so forth. In other cultures time can be treated differently. According to Hall (1959), before the informational revolution, in the Mediterranean Arab culture there were only three standard sets of time: *no time at all*, *now* (which is of varying duration), and *forever* (too long).

Akbar (1991), who compared perceptions of time in European American and African cultures, acknowledged the Westerners' emphasis on precise measurement of time. He suggested that time in the European and North American cultures is treated as a commodity or product that can be bought and sold as any other item for consumption, whereas in the African system, time is not viewed as a commodity.

The African time concept is very elastic and includes events that had already taken place, those that are taking place right now, and even those that will happen. Time can be experienced through one's own individual life and through the life of the tribe to which each individual belongs (Nobles, 1991). In Swahili—the language widely used in Eastern and Central Africa—there are two words that indicate time: *sasa* and *zamani*. The first one stands for the present and generates a sense of immediacy. The second word indicates the past, but not merely as a "warehouse" of time. It is also a connector of individual souls. Most African peoples perceived human history in the natural rhythm of moving from *sasa* to *zamani*. The life cycle is renewable. After physical death, as long as a person is remembered by relatives and friends who knew him or her, this person would continue to exist in the *sasa* dimension. When the last person who knew the deceased also dies, that means the end for that individual.

Different culture-related patterns of time perception may affect interpersonal communications. Take, for example, the idea of "being late." Ninety-one students at the Federal University in Niteroi (Brazil) and 107 students at California State University at Fresno were asked about their perception of time in several situations. The average Brazilian student defined *lateness* for lunch as 33 minutes after the scheduled time, compared with 19 minutes for the American students. Brazilians also allowed an average of about 54 minutes before they would consider someone early, whereas the Fresno students drew the line at 24 minutes. Unlike their American counterparts, the Brazilian students believed that a person who is consistently late is probably more successful than one who is consistently on time.

 EXERCISE 4.1

You can easily replicate a small survey, which we conducted recently at two colleges on the U.S. East Coast. We asked 129 students the same question: "Imagine the following situation. You are hosting an afternoon meeting with four student delegations from four countries: Japan, Italy, Russia, and Germany. They all arrived yesterday and now are staying in different hotels downtown. Please hypothesize which of the delegations will arrive on time and which will be more likely to arrive late for the meeting?" Of the answers we received, in 97 replies, students suggested that both German and Japanese delegations should to be on time. One hundred and three answers indicated that both Russians and Italians could be late. You may conduct a similar survey in class. Understand, however, that these popular stereotypes provide little evidence about the actual perception of time in various cultures.

People who experience time pressure—they realize that their time very limited—usually move faster than people who do not feel that they are limited by time constraints. In one study researchers measured how long it would take pedestrians to walk 100 feet along a main downtown street during business hours on sunny days. In Japan (Tokyo and Sendai) the time was 20.7 seconds. In England (London and Bristol) it was 21.6 seconds. In the United States (New York, Rochester) it was 22.5 seconds. In Indonesia (Jakarta and Solo) it was 27.2 seconds (Levine & Wolff, 1992).

Empirical research provides some evidence about cultural differences in time perception. Yet one can argue that many contemporary technological developments, including rapidly increasing access to television and the Internet, as well as the growing complexity of modern life should make and do make cultural differences in time perception relatively insignificant. If two people develop two different culture-related patterns of time perception, one should learn how to predict some potential difficulties in their communication. For example, two people may have a different understanding of time intervals and what it means to be "late" for an appointment. However, these difficulties may be eased as soon as they share with others what they mean by expressions such as "I will do it later," "I will see you soon," or " please wait a little."

Did you know that age and aging might be related to an individual's perspective of time, at least in people of the industrial world? In turn, this changing individual time perspective may impact many other personal attitudes (Cutler, 1975). Perhaps for most people, in early childhood, the dominant perception is that time is limitless. Early adulthood brings the realization that time is a scarce resource. Middle age and later stages lead to the perception that time becomes seriously limited. As Gergen and Black (1965) pointed out, orientations toward problem solving in international politics are substantially related to one's psychological perception of personal future time: older politicians may be in a "hurry" to resolve conflicts. Renshon (1989) also argued that in the arts, the phenomenon of late-age creativity and boldness occurs relatively often. The last works of Shakespeare, Rembrandt, Verdi, Beethoven, Tolstoy, and Picasso all suggest that the final stages of the life cycle often bring release from conventional concerns and free the artist to make major creative statements that represent a culmination of his or her vision.

 Culture opens the sense of beauty.
RALPH WALDO EMERSON (1803–1882)—AMERICAN POET AND PHILOSOPHER

 Beauty is nothing other than the promise of happiness.
STENDAHL (1783–1842)—FRENCH NOVELIST

Perception of the Beautiful

The song *Let It Be* performed by the Beatles or a Mexican folk song, a dress designed by Versace or a Peruvian picturesque poncho, a Persian rug or a Nigerian ivory statuette, the Taj Mahal palace or a Chinese porcelain vase—these creations can be enjoyed by anyone and everyone on the planet. The term **aesthetic experience,** or perception of the beautiful, is used to identify the feeling of pleasure evoked by stimuli that are perceived as nice, attractive, or rewarding. Some researchers suggest that aesthetic responses are underpinned by the amount of cortical arousal produced by some stimuli in the brain (Berlyne, 1974, 1960). People seek certain stimuli because the activity of dealing with them is pleasant. Others consider aesthetic appreciation as curiosity and stimulus-seeking activities (see Chapter 7 on intrinsic motivation). Berlyne (1971) mentioned that the characteristics of a stimulus that generally evoke curiosity, joy, and appreciation are those such as novelty, ambiguity, incongruity, and complexity.

There are perhaps several common perceptual mechanisms that lead to similarities across cultures in aesthetic appreciation. For example, there are empirical studies in which subjects from different cultures displayed similarities in their evaluation of different works of art, primarily paintings (Child, 1969). Many similarities in perception and appreciation of beauty were found in different cultural groups despite socioeconomic differences among them (Ross, 1997; Berlyne, 1974). For instance, in a survey conducted by Nasar (1984), both Japanese and American subjects were asked to evaluate videotapes and slides of urban street scenes in each country. An examination of preference scores revealed that both Japanese and U.S. subjects preferred foreign scenes to native ones. In both groups, the scenes of orderly and clean streets with very few vehicles on them were more often preferred.

Beware though. There are tremendous inconsistencies in how people see and interpret both beautiful and ugly creations. For instance, in the history of Western painting, impressionism as a new artistic genre was publicly ridiculed and rejected. Many years later it became an internationally acclaimed style and collectors began to pay huge sums of money for impressionist paintings. When the Eiffel tower was first erected in Paris, most people condemned this grandiose landmark. Today, who can imagine Paris without the Eiffel tower?

CRITICAL THINKING

As Beautiful as . . . Your Money Can Buy

Beautiful things sell. Art collectors and art dealers around the world know this well. Today many classical paintings change hands, not for thousands, but millions of dollars! However, does the price tag on a painting or sculpture determine how beautiful the creation is? Why are the smallest paintings by Cezanne or pencil sketches by Leonardo almost priceless, whereas a beautiful original colorful landscape could be purchased for $20 from a street artist in Rome? Do you agree with the supposition that sometimes people first assign and attach value to particular pieces of art and only then do they begin to evaluate this object from the standpoint of aesthetic perception? If a sculpture is considered "famous" or a song "popular" by most members of our society, are we likely to consider the sculpture as "beautiful" and the song as "nice"? Do you think that our evaluation of a song, painting, fashion style, or dance changes according to how well or how poorly it is advertised or promoted?

Each culture has its own standards of beauty and they influence individual perceptions. What is considered novel and beautiful in one culture may be viewed as ugly or antiquated in another. We often change our perceptions with time. Do not forget that we also have unique individual tastes and perceptions of what should be considered beautiful. Consider clothing fashion, for example. Most of us do not wear shirts, pants, and skirts that were in style and looked "nice" 10, 5, or sometimes even 3 years ago.

Cultural aesthetic standards can be numerous and widely defined; they can also be limited in appearance and narrowly defined. For example, in the countries in which governments or ideological institutions control the media, and therefore restrain the free flow of information, such standards of beauty and ugliness are typically precisely defined. Because of the lack of available information, scarcity of products, and ideological pressures, people's choices are limited and certain items—clothing, music, or even hairstyle, for example—quickly become dominant in a particular country (Shiraev & Danilov, 1999; Shiraev & Bastrykin, 1988).

Perception of Music

The traditional music of different cultures may fluctuate in notion and harmony. For instance, conventional Western harmony is different from Japanese and Indian styles (Sadie, 1980). In many non-Western traditions the idea of the note, as a stable, sustained pitch, is foreign. Some Indian and Japanese musical intervals—or tonal dyads differing only slightly in frequency ratio—are perceived as extreme dissonance in the West and are usually avoided by composers and musicians. However, these intervals appear to be beautiful and are used freely in the classic music of these two countries (Maher, 1976).

Contemporary Western music notation reflects the underlying general perception of beauty developed in Western culture. Perceptual problems that can cause displeasure in the Western listener—born and raised in Sweden, Italy, or Ukraine—may occur because of the different scales, intervals, and rhythmic patterns used in Western and non-Western music. In non-Western cultures—for example, in Middle Eastern Islamic countries—classical music for the most part is not written down in advance, as is the practice in Europe and America. Notwithstanding the fact that written notations are found in many cultures around the world, in many non-Western countries, classical music is usually improvised on framework-like patterns. In fact, in these societies many types of music exist mostly in performance. One should not exaggerate, nevertheless, cultural differences in musical perception. Contemporary mass media, global trade, and frequent interpersonal contacts provide unique opportunity for many people to learn, understand, and appreciate different musical styles.

Let us make some preliminary conclusions. As we have learned, most psychologists share the contemporary belief that sensory differences among cultures are insignificant and their impact on human behavior is minimal. In general, the universal similarity in the anatomy and physiology of human sensory organs and the nervous system seems to suggest that sensory impressions and their transmission through the perceptual system are basically the same across cultures. Despite similarities, however, people may see beautiful and ugly things differently, and there is a substantial weight of cultural factors in our aesthetic perception.

Most of the time, healthy adults are aware of their sensations and perceptions. A street vendor in Spain or a teacher in Pakistan can describe what they see or hear and are able to separate the "objective" reality from thoughts about it. No matter what we do, either paying careful attention to some events or **daydreaming** about others, we are aware of our subjective experiences.

The ultimate gift of conscious life is a sense of mystery that encompasses it.
LEWIS MUMFORD—TWENTIETH-CENTURY AMERICAN HISTORIAN AND CRITIC

Suffering is the sole origin of consciousness.
FYODOR DOSTOEVSKY (1821–1881)—RUSSIAN NOVELIST

Consciousness and Culture

Imagine the following science fiction scenario. Earlier today all adults have left the earth. Only 1-year-old children remain on the planet. They have plenty of food and water. The children are immunized against all known and unknown diseases. They will possess all the technologies and machines created by their parents and ancestors. Smart robots will take total care of the children and protect them day and night. Remember, no adults are left with the children. No one will teach them how to speak, read, or write. Here is the question. In 20 years, will these physically healthy children be able to reflect their own existence and be aware of their own sensations, feelings, and thoughts? It is difficult to make predictions. Nevertheless, psychologists and anthropologists suggest that without adults and other material and symbolic carriers of culture, such as media, books, values, and traditions, these children's self-awareness will be significantly different from the consciousness of their parents.

Culture is an inseparable attribute of human **consciousness**—the subjective awareness of one's own sensations, perceptions, and other mental events. It is a process that has several stages or states. The "normal" flow of consciousness may consist of periods of full attention and concentration or relative detachment from the outside events. Periods of wakefulness are altered by periods of sleep. Under various circumstances, the normal flow of consciousness can be altered by meditation, psychoactive substances, trance, or hypnotic suggestion. However, the very concept of consciousness is elusive, thus making its cross-cultural examination particularly difficult.

From the dawn of scientific exploration of mental life, ancient thinkers were aware of consciousness. Major ideas about human consciousness were developed within the Christian, Moslem, Jewish, Hindu, Buddhist, and other theological schools of thought (Smith, 1991). They developed fundamental ideas about the soul as immortal, divine, and separable from the body. With further development of philosophy and science, two types of fundamental views on consciousness were established. One view was held by the monists, who believed in the inseparability of the body and soul. The second view was held by the dualists, who recognized an independent existence of body and soul. Both of these philosophical platforms still affect many people's personal views on consciousness.

The idea of individual consciousness as dependent on socialization experiences and other cultural factors was developed throughout the twentieth century by a number of psychologists (Wundt, 1913; Vygotsky, 1932; and Piaget, 1963). According to psychological anthropologist Hallowell (1955), people live within a **behavioral environment,** a mental representation of time, space, and the interpersonal world. Specific cultural beliefs and practices shape the individual's behavioral environment. For example, among the Ojibwa Indians studied by Hallowell, their behavioral environment included the self, other people, their gods, existing relatives, and deceased ancestors. Thus, when considering an action with moral consequences, the Ojibwa take into account possible impacts of the action on spirits and relatives.

Consciousness directs human behavior in ways that are adaptive in particular physical and social environments. Living in a noisy city or mountain village, people often respond automatically to their environment and can process information without continuous conscious awareness. Important choices, however, require more complex responses. Therefore, people tend to focus on things that are important for survival or the accomplishment of a goal. A motorist in New York will definitely pay attention to traffic reports on the car radio, whereas his guest from South Africa may not attend to them at all. Consciousness devotes extra cognitive resources to information that may be particularly meaningful for individual adaptation. For instance, the contents of the consciousness of Ifaluk, a people of Micronesia in the Pacific Ocean, reflect the way their culture structures reality: people are aware of their immediate location at all times because life depends on successful navigation of the surrounding ocean (Lutz, 1982). It can be expected that important environmental and social conditions would be prime areas of interest for people. For example, a devastating famine or civil war in a country is likely to occupy people's minds and be a prime concern of the population regardless of where the disaster takes place.

It is not uncommon to come across opinions about the main attributes of Western consciousness as being linear, pragmatic, and rational (Jackson, 1991). If this is the case, these elements of consciousness should be overwhelmingly present in various forms of Western art. If consciousness is rational, it should be reflected in "rational" forms of artistic expression. However, the history of Western art (literature and painting, for example) shows numerous examples of nonlinear, mystical, multidimensional, and irrational views reflected by the writer's pen or the artist's paintbrush. Existentialism and symbolism in literature, cubism and primitivism in painting, and modernism in music are all examples of irrational and nonlinear perception and reflection of reality by Western artists. Perhaps one of the best illustrations of a nonlinear perception of life is the literary world of Gabriel Garcia Marquez, one of the most significant writers of the twentieth century. A Colombian native, he spent most of his life in Mexico and Europe as a journalist and writer. Take, for example, his most famous novel *One Hundred Years of Solitude.* The main characters in the book live within several time dimensions. It seems that they are not concerned with time at all. Occasionally, the past is diminished into a single moment, and then the future becomes present and twisted in a mysterious way. The dead return home and those who are alive disappear in the skies without a trace. Consciousness becomes circular and brings back memories and transfers individuals in time and space. Analyzing Marquez' work, one can find elements of the Catholic religious doctrine, Spanish cultural tradition, and Native Indian beliefs. Perhaps such a mixture of different influences reflected in the author's mind and in his literary works reveals many fascinating aspects of human consciousness. Please read *One Hundred Years of Solitude* by Marquez. Will you find it difficult to confine human consciousness within the boundaries of Western or non-Western labels?

Sleeping is no mean art: For its sake one must stay awake all day.
FRIEDRICH NIETZSCHE (1844–1900)—GERMAN PHILOSOPHER

In the drowsy dark cave of the mind dreams build their nest with fragments dropped from day's caravan.
RABINDRANATH TAGORE (1861–1941)—BENGALI POET AND NOVELIST

Sleep and Cultural Significance of Dreams

At this moment, about a third of the world population is sleeping! **Sleep** is a nonwaking state of consciousness characterized by general unresponsiveness to the environment and general physical immobility.

During sleep, responsiveness to external, and particularly visual, stimulation is diminished, but it is not entirely absent (Antrobus, 1991). There are tremendous individual variations in how "wakeful" we are when sleeping. In addition, cultural practices, sleeping arrangements, and general environmental conditions can influence people's responsiveness to external stimulation during sleep. There are also significant individual variations in terms of duration of sleep. In every country around the world some individuals sleep for 5 or 6 hours, whereas others need 9 or 10 hours. There is evidence that the amount of sleep each of us needs is physiologically determined (Horne, 1988). However, duration and patterns of sleep may vary from culture to culture. As an illustration, in a study of the sleep–wakefulness cycle in Mexican adults, Taub (1971) found that the average duration of sleep in Mexican subjects was longer than in other Western countries.

Since the dawn of our existence, humans have wondered and persistently speculated about both the nature and significance of **dreams,** story-like sequences of images occurring during sleep. McManus and co-authors (1993) make a distinction between two types of cultures in terms of their interpretation of dreams. *Monophasic* cultures value cognitive experiences that take place only during normal waking phases and do not incorporate dreams into the process of social perception and cognition. Dreams are regarded as indirect indications of the dreamer's concerns, fears, and desires (Bourgignon, 1954). *Polyphasic* cultures value dreams and treat them as part of reality. The first type of culture is typically associated with a materialistic worldview on psychological experience. The second type of culture is associated with the spiritual or traditional view.

For many years, people considered dreams as experiences accumulated by the dreamer's traveling soul or revelations conveyed to the dreaming individual from the spiritual world. This polyphasic view on dreams can be found in contemporary cultural

A CASE IN POINT

Culture and Napping

It is afternoon in Barcelona. You think it could be a good time to do some shopping. No, you are wrong, most stores are closed at this hour. Primarily in Hispanic and some other cultures, there is a tradition of having an afternoon nap (siesta). At this time, most small businesses are closed. This practice is not common and even considered impossible in most European countries and North America. Of course, thousands of people in Finland or Austria do take afternoon naps, but this habit is considered to be a matter of necessity or individual preference rather than a custom. Nevertheless, here we should avoid making generalizations regarding cultural traditions of sleep and their long-term influence on business. It is true that in most North European countries there is no such thing as a siesta break, so stores stay open during afternoon hours. However, in Germany, Finland, and some other European countries, most small stores and shops are closed for the day by 5 or 6 P.M. Hence, when you are visiting Dusseldorf or Helsinki, do not plan your shopping after dinner.

groups. Robert Moss (1996) describes several core elements in the traditional dream practice of Iroquois, a Native American tribe. Dreams are perceived as flights of the soul, which leaves the body and travels in space and time. Therefore, dreams are real events and should be taken literally. Dreams demand action because they indicate something that the person has failed to perform while awake. For Iroquois, dreams also yield information about future events. Similarly, Araucanos in Chile believe that dreams help to communicate with other people and are related to future events (Krippner, 1996). Among many native peoples in Australia, it is believed that one can travel in his or her dreams for particular purposes. Among some African tribes there is a conviction that both the living and deceased relatives can communicate with the dreamer. Dreams can be transmitted from one person to another and some people can do so with malicious purposes. Some Zambian shamans imply they can diagnose a patient's illness through information contained in this person's dreams (Bynum, 1993).

Contemporary science develops several views on the nature of human dreams. Some physiologists, for example, suggest that dreams are pure biological phenomena with no psychological meaning (Crick & Mitchison, 1983). One of the most prominent contemporary views on dreaming (Hobson, 1988) implies that during this altered state of consciousness, the brain stem is activating itself internally. This activation does not contain any ideas, emotions, wishes, or fears. The forebrain produces dream imagery from "noisy" signals sent up to it from the brain stem. As this activation is transmitted through the thalamus to the visual and association zones of the cerebral cortex, the individual tries to make sense of it. Because the initial signals are essentially random in nature, the interpretations proposed by the cortex rarely make complete logical sense. However, the issues most relevant to the individual enter his or her dreams in some way because the incoming signals are compared with the dreamer's existing knowledge and attitudes (Foulkes, 1985; Cartwright, 1992). In other words, culture-based experiences should influence our dreams.

Certainly, Christians do not usually see Prince Buddha in their dreams, and a Muslim is very unlikely to dream about the Virgin Mary. For an Arab boy, his fear may manifest in the image of an Israeli soldier, whereas for an Israeli boy, his fear may manifest in the form of an Arab terrorist. Victims of the Holocaust may have nightmares involving Nazi camp guards, a theme totally unknown to those who know nothing about the history of World War II (Koopman, 1997).

Despite significant differences in the manifest content of dreams (i.e., the actual content of the recalled dream), the latent content (the dream's meaning) is believed to be cross-culturally comparable. The similarities in the way people describe the content of their dreams were demonstrated in a Japanese American study (Griffith et al., 1958). Students in both groups reported having dreams about falling, eating, swimming, death, snakes, finding money, examinations, being unable to move, and various sexual experiences. Clarissa P. Estes, a best-selling author, suggests: "We all dream the same dreams worldwide. . . . Dreams are compensatory, they provide a mirror into the deep unconscious most often reflecting what is lost, and what is yet needed for correction and balance" (Estes, 1992, p. 458).

Dream scenarios are personal, but they are enacted within the stage set by the dreamer's sociocultural reality (Roll et al., 1976). Take, for example, a study in which the dreams of more than 200 Finnish and Palestinian children were compared (Punamaki & Joustie, 1998). Half of the subjects were selected from working-class and middle-class Finnish suburbia and half were taken from two areas in the Middle East. One represented the Gaza strip, an extremely violent area with frequent military confrontations. The other area was not known for any violent outbursts. Children in both groups were asked to report their dreams daily over a 7-day period. The recorded dreams were content analyzed. It was found that life in a violent environment was linked to a greater extent to dream content than the culture and other personal factors. The Palestinian children who lived in the violent social environment reported having predominantly intensive and vivid dreams, which incorporated aggression and persecution as main themes, more often than the other children studied did. It was also found that in Arab children's dreams there were predominantly external scenes of anxiety that typically involved fear. In Finnish children, dreams contained anxiety scenes that involved mostly guilt and shame. The authors interpreted the results by referring to social and cultural conditions in the studied samples. The Finnish society is considered to be more individualistic than the Palestinian society and therefore more oriented toward the experiences directed into individuals themselves. The Finnish children are less interdependent than Arab children. Also, according to the established cultural traditions, the Finnish understanding of dreaming is based predominantly on Freudian influences that emphasize the importance of individual psychological reality. According to the Arab tradition, dreaming is mainly understood as an external message from forces to guide the dreamer.

Keep in mind one important difference between these two cultures. Finland is an economically advanced and democratic European country with one of the highest incomes per capita in the world. Palestinian people for many years experienced poverty, injustice, and authoritarianism, and suffered from constant struggles between various political groups for influence and power. It is plausible to propose that everyday stressful experiences can contribute to dream content.

In another study, hundreds of dreams reported by U.S. and Indian students were evaluated (Grey & Kalsched, 1971). As expected, traditional Indian gender roles and practices were reflected in the reported dreams, including greater sex segregation. Substantial gender differences were also found in other cross-cultural studies of dreams, according to which women are likely to experience dreams in which the dream character is abused and attacked (Cartwright, 1992). One finding reported by Munroe and Munroe (1972) in an East African sample showed that both males and females express roughly equal amounts of aggression in the reported dreams. Subsequent analysis revealed that a high proportion of aggression in female dreams was linked to situations in which the women were victims of attack and abuse, a concern that reflects reality.

It was found that the theme of death was present considerably more often in the dreams of Mexican American women compared with European American women (Roll & Brenneis, 1975). Do you think that this difference between two samples was caused by the fact that Mexican Americans have larger extended families, therefore statistically, they witness the death of relatives more often than individuals from other ethnic groups do?

Specialists in Turkish folklore identify a typical theme in dreams reported by males: the quest, both physical and spiritual, for the most gorgeous and beautiful woman in the world. According to one explanation (Walker, 1993) this preoccupation may be linked to

CRITICAL THINKING

Can Dreams Predict Anything?

There are popular stories about famous discoveries taking place during sleep. The famous benzene ring and the periodic system of chemical elements were allegedly "discovered" by their authors when they were dreaming. In many famous fairy tales, literary works, and film creations, heroes and heroines read important life forecasts in their sleep. We all know that in every country, there are people who believe that dreams can predict the future or may be considered an omen of something to come. It is a belief in Turkey that if one discloses a dream about receiving a favor before the favor is offered, then the event foretold in the dream may end in disaster (Walker & Uysal, 1990). A 1999 Russian calendar of dreams predicted that a tooth lost in one's dream will mean a misfortune for this person in the future. Around the world, there are books written and manuals published on how to interpret each particular dream. Why do so many people maintain such an attitude toward dreams? We have to take into consideration how powerful people's superstitions are as regulators of behavior. We follow them often without a conscious attempt to think critically. Meanwhile, some dreams may be rationalized. Imagine a person has a dream about a car accident. When the dream content does not coincide with an actual car accident the day after the dream, the content of the dream can be easily forgotten. If an accident really happens, he or she is likely to refer to the dream: "I knew this was going to happen." Similarly, when dream content coincides with a conscious attitude, we tend to hold an opinion about the possible motivational power of dreams. In general, knowledge about dreams and critical thinking abilities can diminish an individual's dependency on dreams as predictors of the future.

the tradition of arranged marriage. According to this practice, many Turkish men cannot see their brides before the time of the wedding. This emotional deprivation creates a state of secret admiration and fascination of the future wife. Another explanation, however, can be offered. Because the relatives of the bride and groom commonly arrange many Turkish marriages, most men's relationships with women lack the important elements of romanticism and adventure. As a result, men "compensate" in their dreams for this missing romantic activity and experience.

Tedlock (1987) suggested that people's reports about their dreams include more than the dream report. She implied that what one tells about a dream is based on a particular cultural concept of the dream and culturally sanctioned ways of sharing dream content. Using particular rules of communication, we may report some elements of our dream and delete others. In short, our culture may change our experience of dreams and therefore our dreams are loaded with cultural elements that include not only dream content but also the ways in which dreams are communicated (Ullman & Zimmerman, 1979).

Imagine now somebody from a different country is sharing with you his or her recent dream. Can you interpret its contents? There are some people who claim that they can interpret any dream right after you share one with them. We seriously doubt such propositions. Besides hidden psychological factors, there are numerous contextual influences that affect not only the dream but also the way it is recalled, shared, and interpreted. These are some questions that you perhaps have to ask when you listen to someone's dream. What motivates the person to recall and tell his or her **dream**? (Is it a teacher's assignment, your request, or a spontaneous conversation?) Under what circumstances is the dream recalled? Who is present during the dream recollection? What is the relationship between the dream teller and the listener? How is dreaming understood in the teller's culture? How is dreaming understood in the listener's culture? What meaning do certain dream symbols carry in the studied culture?

No matter how psychologists explain dreams, researchers can provide plenty of interesting facts about the interaction between culture and the psychological experiences of dreams (Roll, 1987). Dreams not only reflect our private world of hopes, fears, and concerns, but also mirror the environment in which people live. This environment is shaped by cultural norms, according to which the dreaming individual's brain organizes and retrieves various images in a "culturally ascribed" manner (Levine, 1991, p. 472).

 The supernatural is the natural not yet understood.
ELBERT HUBBARD (1856–1915)—AMERICAN AUTHOR

Beyond Altered States of Consciousness

Altered states of consciousness (ASC) is the general name for phenomena that are different than normal waking consciousness and include mystic perceptual and sensory experiences, including meditation, hypnosis, trance, and possession (Ward, 1994). Like Cinderella in the famous fairy tale—a neglected outcast daughter in her stepmother's family—ASC are not highly regarded by Western academic psychologists. The rapid development of empirical research based on the pragmatism and positivism of European science coupled with the skepticism encouraged by the Enlightenment era contributed to the lack of scholarly attention to ASC. Under the influence of the Protestant tradition and in Western Europe, altered states of consciousness were considered mostly as abnormal phenomena. Similarly, many mental disorders, especially incurable ones, were commonly interpreted as supernatural developments (Warner, 1983).

Meanwhile, ASC is a widely reported phenomenon across the globe. The different forms of ASC are identified in the majority of societies and may be viewed as a special form of human experience (Laughlin et al., 1992; Ward, 1994). Let us consider several ASC.

Trance is a sleeplike state marked by reduced sensitivity to stimuli, loss or alteration of knowledge, and automatic motor activity. Trances are often induced by external sources, such as music, singing, and direct suggestion from another person. Trances may provide a sense of protection, wisdom, and greatness. For the group, it can provide a sense of togetherness and unity. Mass religious ceremonies, collective prayers, rock concerts, political gatherings, and other collective actions can induce a trance in the participants. There is a difference between a visionary trance, when a person is experiencing hallucinations, and a possession trance, when a person reports that his or her body is invaded or captured by a spirit or several spirits. The possession experience is usually, but not always, recalled with fear and hesitation because of its traumatic significance. Trance-like and possession experiences are described as parts of religious practices in many cultures (Bourguignon, 1976; Rosen, 1969). According to one survey, visionary or possession trance states were reported in 90 percent of the countries in a large world sample (Bourguignon, 1994).

Several religious groups, like born-again Christians, consider trances as part of their regular religious experience (Griffith et al., 1984). Incidences of visionary trances are more common among men than in women and in hunter–gatherer societies. Pos-

A CASE IN POINT

Mass Hysteria and Possession as Altered States of Consciousness

Lee and Ackerman (1980) documented and analyzed an interesting case of mass possession at a small college in West Malaysia. The incident involved several mostly female students who manifested various physical symptoms and bizarre behaviors, such as difficulty breathing, convulsive muscular contractions, and screaming. The victims were oblivious of their surroundings, went through dance frenzies, reported demonic possessions, and complained about seeing strange creatures. The possessed claimed that they became other beings, because of the spirits that had taken over the body. *Bomohs* or traditional Malai healers were called to help. They treated the possessed individuals by sprinkling them with holy water, sacrificing a small animal in an attempt to pacify the offended spirits, and giving victims talismans to protect them from evil spirits. Notably, when the healers confirmed the existence of spirits in the victims' bodies, it provoked further incidents of possession. Moreover, most people in the area believed that the symptoms of this altered state of consciousness were contagious.

session trance is more typical among women and those who are not from hunter–gatherer cultures (Lee & Ackerman, 1980; Bourguignon, 1976; Gussler, 1973).

Possession is explained better when it is evaluated simultaneously from the observer's standpoint, the victim's point of view, and from the perspective of the community at large (Lee & Ackerman, 1980). In this context, there are several scientific explanations related to the previous case and other similar episodes of "demonic possession." One explanation appeals to the stress accumulated by victims from job dissatisfaction, work conflicts, and economic hardship. Individuals who claim possession are provided with socially acceptable outlets for their previously restrained frustration. In other words, possession is a form of catharsis that prevents further frustration.

Moreover, the outbreak of mass hysteria can be considered the result of conflict within the group of students, intense competition for prestige and leadership, and hostility from the local community. For victims, their bizarre behavior can be viewed as a bargaining tactic to resolve some campus-related problems. Claming possession, they were able to shift the balance of power in their college by disrupting order and creating chaos. Moreover, the students found a way to violate a powerful taboo against their own violent behavior. Victims could vent their frustration without having to be fully responsible for their actions: by attributing undesirable actions to the spirit world, they were able to deal with the problematic situation without being embarrassed. Others also pursued their self-interests. Some wanted to assert their professional status as healers. Some wanted to help to demonstrate their altruistic traits. Finally, the townspeople regarded possession as a just punishment delivered by supernatural forces against the college for what they believed to be moral corruption of the students.

> *Nowhere can man find a quieter or more untroubled retreat than his own soul.*
> *MARCUS AURELIUS* (112–180)—ROMAN EMPEROR AND STOIC PHILOSOPHER

Meditation is a quiet and relaxed state of tranquility in which a person achieves an integration of thoughts, perceptions, and attitudes. Usually, this state is attained with the cooperation of a special principle or belief. People who meditate often describe their experience as leading to liberation from the self or an expansion of conscious awareness. In Buddhism, for example, it is believed that meditation leads to a deepened and clearer understanding of reality (Ornstein, 1986). During meditation, a special state of consciousness can be achieved in which obstacles of private desire are completely consumed.

Meditation can be highly therapeutic because it might reduce stress (Collings, 1989). Contrary to contemporary scientific principles of psychotherapy, which require control over the outcome of one's actions, in many types of meditation principles of detachment from others are valued. A meditating person withdraws the senses from objects of pleasure or hardship. If the complete state of detachment is reached, then the individual is able to feel tranquility, serenity, and love. Those trained in detachment are far less subject to the stresses and strains of life, compared with people who do not practice meditation.

Do we sense or feel after we die? Will death mean the ultimate end of conscious reflection of reality, or a beginning of a new psychological experience? One of the most fundamental and puzzling questions that almost every person on earth asks with anxiety and hope is about experience after death. Skeptics insist that there is no credible evidence about after-death experiences. It is known, for example, that some people during meditation or under hypnosis may report about their "previous lives." Nicholas Spanos (1987–1988) reports that people who are not fantasy prone or who do not believe in reincarnation rarely produce experiences about the "other" life under hypnotic suggestion. On the other hand, when they are hypnotized, fantasy-inclined people who believe in reincarnation could offer vivid details of "past lives." It has been reported in other studies that fantasy-prone persons are especially susceptible to near-death and other out-of-body experiences (Ring, 1992). Of particular interest to cross-cultural psychologists is that in nearly all reports about reincarnation, people say that in their previous lives they were of their current ethnic or religious background. In other words, a Chinese person will be extremely unlikely to claim having been an Ethiopian farmer in his previous life. Moreover, people typically report being someone famous, as opposed to being a layperson (Reveen, 1987–1988). Skeptics also point out that most people who claim reincarnation typically lack the knowledge about the historical time when they used to live. They cannot say, for example, the emperor's name, identify major events, or name the main currency.

The contemporary psychological evidence suggests that the most fundamental mechanisms of sensation, perception, and the main states of consciousness, including both the normal flow of consciousness and its altered states, are universal across cultures. In all, the important differences are primarily concerned with the specific content of these experiences and the ways people process information according to both overt rules and covert practices of their countries and communities. With the development of technologies and human interaction, different human experiences are rapidly learned by various cultural groups through television, movies, art, the Internet, interpersonal contacts, and many other forms of communication. People learn more about each other by revealing their dreams and religious experiences, and through understanding different mental realities. Still, we know little about our diverse cognitive world and the cultural backgrounds underlying it. There are many pages in the book of human psychology that remain unturned.

 EXERCISE 4.2

A Cross-Cultural Psychoanalytic Interpretation of Dream Content

Clarissa P. Estes (1992) rightfully suggests that there are many dreams that reflect both immense and extensive feelings that the dreamer, in real life, is unable to cry about. In short, dreams release our suppressed concerns. Please read some of the author's interpretations of several common dreams. They, as Dr. Estes believes, are typical in women of all cultural and social backgrounds.

In this dream, a woman is helping an old person to cross the street. Suddenly, the old person smiles diabolically and "melts" on her arm, burning her deeply (or harms her in some other way). The dream sends a message that malevolent things are disguised as benevolent things. The woman tries to avoid threatening facts, but the dream shouts a warning to her: stay away from somebody and be careful in your current relationships (p. 54).

In the "scary dark man" dream, a frightful intruder appears in the woman's apartment or house. She can feel his presence, his breath. The woman experiences horror and helplessness. She cannot scream for help or dial an emergency number. This dark man may appear as a thief, Nazi, rapist, terrorist, and so forth. The meaning of the dream is that the woman should awaken and reconsider her life again: something frightening is going on inside her. This is a dream of a woman who is "drying out" who is deprived of her creative function, and so far makes no effort to help herself (p. 66).

In the "injured animal" dream, a woman sees an injured or wounded animal. This dream could represent a serious violation of the woman's freedom and other basic rights. Being unable—due to cultural censorship—to understand why her rights are violated, the woman accepts this safe way of symbolic expression of her concerns. An injured animal dream appears especially often in women in cultures in which they are deprived or their rights, abused, and discriminated against (p. 276).

If a disembodied voice is heard in the dream (the voice that does not belong to a particular person or creature), this could mean that the woman's life is coming to an extreme. It could be a sign that she has "too much positive stimulation" or "too many responsibilities," and so forth. The woman is either "overloved" or "underloved," either "overworked" or "underworked." Bottom line, she must reevaluate her current life (p. 278).

Assignment: Write your critical comments regarding each of these interpretations. Could you agree with some of these explanations? What interpretations do you disagree with? Explain why.

 ## EXERCISE 4.3

Watch the classic movie *The Exorcist*, which you can rent in any video store. Answer the following questions.

What kind of altered states of consciousness can we recognize in the main character of the movie: visionary trance or possession trance?

There is a tradition found in many tribes around the world, such as in Mission Indians in California, to assign special duties of communicating with the spirit world to a medicine man (Caprio, 1943). In the movie, who was given the duty to negotiate and eventually expel the spirit from the girl's body?

Please summarize and generalize the diagnoses given to the girl by various doctors. What other cultures were mentioned in the conversations or can be seen in the movie? Try to give your opinion of why the theme of possession is still very popular among educated people.

CHAPTER SUMMARY

- Our experience with the environment shapes our perception by creating perceptual expectations. These expectations, known as a perceptual set, make particular interpretations more likely to occur. They allow people to anticipate what they will encounter and, therefore, increase both the speed and efficiency of the perceptual process.

- There are several factors that may contribute to differences in people's sensation and perception. There are physical and environmental conditions, genetic factors, socialization norms, and acculturation practices.

- Studies on cross-cultural differences in the perception of simple patterns showed only small variations. Cross-cultural similarities in the drawing of visual patterns suggest the presence of a common mechanism for perceptual processes. Shape constancy of perception is significantly influenced by learning experiences. Culturally specific conditions determine which skills will improve in individuals in a particular culture and which skills will remain underdeveloped.

- Psychologists offer several hypotheses that explain cultural differences in illusion susceptibility. The carpentered world hypothesis postulates a learned tendency among people raised in an environment shaped by carpenters to interpret nonrectangular figures as representations of rectangular figures seen in perspective.

- There is a strong degree of similarity in the way color terms are used in different cultures. Moreover, verbal labels, if they are not available in the lexicon of a language, can be readily learned. Education, travel, interpersonal contacts, and the media can play a significant role in the development of color recognition and labeling.

- There are perhaps common perceptual mechanisms that lead to similarities across cultures in the perception of time and in aesthetic appreciation. Many similarities in perception of the beautiful were found in different cultural groups despite apparent socioeconomic differences among them. Because the traditional music of different cultures may differ in notion and harmony, there are some cultural differences in the perception of musical harmony.

- The universal similarity in the anatomy and physiology of human sensory organs and the nervous system seems to make it likely that sensory impressions and their transmission through the perceptual system are comparable across cultures.

- Consciousness is a process, which has several stages or states. The "normal" flow of consciousness may consist of periods of full attention and concentration or relative detachment from the outside events. Periods of wakefulness are altered by periods of sleep. Under various circumstances, meditation, psychoactive substances, trances, or hypnotic suggestion can alter consciousness. The understanding of consciousness is based on general cultural views of mental life and the relationship between body and soul.

- From a cultural standpoint, the normal flow of consciousness directs our behavior in ways that are adaptive in particular physical and social environments. Individual consciousness is dependent on socialization experiences, which, in turn are based on cultural factors, collective forms of existence, or shared collective experiences. Human consciousness develops together with the development of both physical and social environments. Increasing knowledge of the world at the same time broadens consciousness.

- Both duration and patterns of sleep may vary individually and from culture to culture. Despite significant differences in the manifest content of dreams, the latent dream content is believed to be generally similar in people living in different cultures. Dreams not only reflect our private world, but also mirror the environment in which we live. The dreaming individual's brain organizes and retrieves various images in a "culturally ascribed" manner.

- Phenomena such as meditation, trance, hypnosis, supernatural beliefs, and near-death experiences during coma are very common in practically every culture. Analyzing them, a specialist should take into consideration personal characteristics of the studied individuals, their educational level, and position within the society. Specialist should also notice that certain life circumstances can influence individual experiences. Another set of conditions is a predominant cultural attitude toward altered states of consciousness expressed in the media, people's everyday conversations, or public opinion (if data are available).

 ## KEY TERMS

Absolute Threshold   The minimum amount of physical energy needed for the observer to notice a stimulus.

Aesthetic Experience   A term used to identify the feeling of pleasure evoked by stimuli that are perceived as beautiful, attractive, and rewarding. The term also refers to displeasure evoked by stimuli that are perceived as ugly, unattractive, and unrewarding.

Altered State of Consciousness (ASC)   The general name for phenomena that are different than normal waking consciousness and include mystic experiences, meditation, hypnosis, trance, and possession.

Behavioral Environment   A mental representation that orients people to dimensions such as time, space, and the interpersonal world.

Consciousness   The subjective awareness of one's own sensations, perceptions, and other mental events.

Daydreaming   Turning attention away from external stimuli to internal thoughts and imagined scenarios.

Depth Perception   The organization of sensations in three dimensions, even though the image on the eye's retina is two dimensional.

Dreams   Storylike sequences of images occurring during sleep.

Difference Threshold   The lowest level of stimulation required to sense that a change in the stimulation has occurred.

Meditation   A quiet and relaxed state of tranquility in which a person achieves an integration of emotions, attitudes, and thoughts.

Perception   The process that organizes various sensations into meaningful patterns.

Perceptual Set   Perceptual expectations based on experience.

Sensation   The process by which receptor cells are stimulated and transmit their information to higher brain centers.

Sensory Adaptation   The tendency of the sensory system to respond less to stimuli that continue without change.

Sleep   A nonwaking state of consciousness characterized by general unresponsiveness to the environment and general physical immobility.

Trance   A sleeplike state marked by reduced sensitivity to stimuli, loss or alteration of knowledge, and the substitution of automatic for voluntary motor activity.

CHAPTER 5

Intelligence

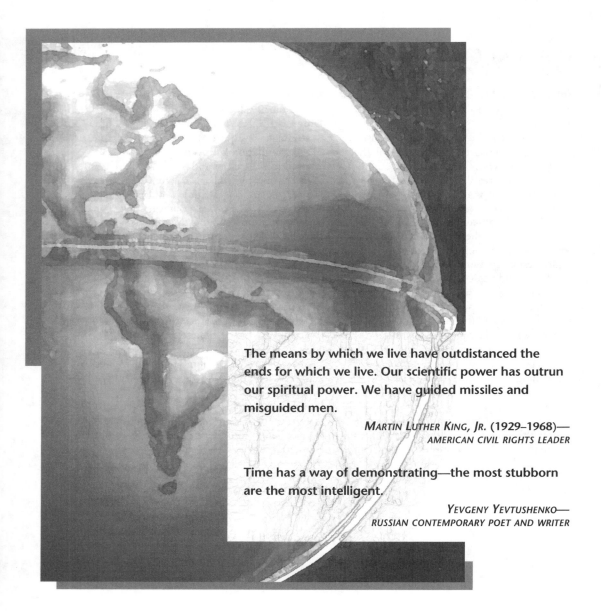

The means by which we live have outdistanced the ends for which we live. Our scientific power has outrun our spiritual power. We have guided missiles and misguided men.

MARTIN LUTHER KING, JR. (1929–1968)—
AMERICAN CIVIL RIGHTS LEADER

Time has a way of demonstrating—the most stubborn are the most intelligent.

YEVGENY YEVTUSHENKO—
RUSSIAN CONTEMPORARY POET AND WRITER

Our friend Charles Wiley—a journalist who has visited almost every country in the world—showed us a recent photo that he took in the People's Republic of China. We were at Charles' house and his guests took turns staring at the photo. On the picture, there was an entrance to Jinan University in Guangzhou. The large sign at the entrance read (as Charles translated to us): "Be loyal to the country, be faithful to your friends, persevere with your mission, be respectful to your parents and teachers." "You see," said one of the guests. "This is why the Chinese have such great test scores. They learn about discipline and hard work from early childhood. Look at their IQ numbers. They are ahead of everybody and it's no wonder. I wish I could send my two teenagers to China. Maybe there they would learn something useful." Everybody laughed and the conversation quickly switched to football. Two months later, one of us—who got a copy of the photo—showed it to a colleague who was born in Beijing. "You know," he replied, "You are asking me whether loyalty and respect are prime educational and cultural values in China. I do not want to disappoint you. It looks fine on the paper but in reality things are different. Do you think that *all* people there are just puppets who do whatever the government tells them to do? Do you think that *all* people there are loyal to their friends?" "No, but we're talking about the overall relationship between self-discipline and high test scores." "Oh, self-discipline. . . . It's family pressure," the friend replied with a mysterious smile. "You have to understand the Chinese family. Intelligence is a result of family influence."

Defining Intelligence

First of all, what is **intelligence**? Ask psychology professors at your college or university. If you ask ten of them, then you will receive nine different definitions. Just nine? What about the tenth teacher? (If you are asking this question now you are already revealing curiosity, an important feature of your intelligence.) The tenth professor will simply refer you to the introductory psychology textbook currently in use.

A quick glance through several introductory psychology textbooks published in the 1990s would reveal the same diverse picture: intelligence is defined in a variety of ways. For example intelligence may be described as a set of mental abilities; the capacity to acquire and use knowledge; problem-solving skills and knowledge about the world; the ability to excel at a variety of tasks; or as a skill that allows us to understand, adapt, learn, reason, and overcome obstacles. Which point of view should we choose? First, most definitions include the word knowledge. Intelligence is knowing and understanding the reality. Then, most definitions draw attention to problem solving, which leads to an assumption that intelligence is a set of mental skills that helps individuals to reach a goal. Intelligence is also an ability to use knowledge and skills in order to overcome obstacles. And finally, intelligence helps in the adaptation to changing environments.

Such an inclusive understanding of intelligence can be useful for cross-cultural psychologists because it allows them to incorporate the cultural factor in the discussion of intelligence. Indeed, people live in different environments and acquire knowledge and skills necessary to pursue goals and adapt to different cultural settings.

A CASE IN POINT

Are Successful People Always Successful?

Maria's parents brought her to the United States when she was 9. Back in Brazil, she was an excellent student and had particular success in music and math. In her new school in Virginia, she achieved English language proficiency within one year. By age 14, her test scores on science and math were among the best in class. She was successful in almost every academic activity in which she participated. A school psychologist said to Maria's parents that her IQ, according to a test, was 125. The girl continued to play music and became the top goal scorer in a spring soccer tournament. Now imagine you are a teacher in a new middle school that Maria has to attend this year. Will you expect this girl to have high test scores and good grades? What circumstances could prevent Maria from pursuing excellence in everything that she does? Explain your opinion.

Intelligence is also inseparable from **cognition,** a diversified process by which the individual acquires and applies knowledge. It usually includes processes such as recognition, categorization, thinking, and memory.

From an introductory psychology classes you may remember that there are several scientific approaches to intelligence. Let us consider them briefly, using the previous vignette as a starting point for discussion.

Some researchers, especially during the earlier stages of intelligence testing at the beginning of the twentieth century, suggested the existence of a general factor—or central cognitive function—that determines a certain level of performance on a variety of cognitive tasks (Spearman, 1927). The existence of this central cognitive function was evidenced by a set of positive correlations among performances on verbal, spatial, numerical, and other assessment problems. People with high academic ranking tended to score well on measures such as general knowledge, arithmetic ability, and vocabulary. On the contrary, people with low scores on verbal tasks were likely to have low scores on other tests.

Over the years, the idea of "one factor" that determines intellectual functioning has been frequently challenged. One such critic, Thurstone (1938), proposed the existence of not only one but rather three intellectual skills: verbal, mathematical, and spatial.

Robert Sternberg (1985, 1997) also supported a hypothesis about a multidimensional structure of intelligence and suggested the existence of three fundamental aspects of intelligence, that is, analytic, creative, and practical. According to his arguments, most intelligence tests measured only analytic skills. Analytic problems in the test are usually clearly defined, have a single correct answer, and come with all the information needed for a solution. On the contrary, practical problems are usually not clearly defined. The person has to seek additional information and can offer various "correct" solutions to the problem under consideration. To solve these problems successfully the person would need to have accumulated everyday experiences and be motivated enough to find the solution.

Studying the diversity of human behavior and achievement, Howard Gardner (1983) argued that along with logical, linguistic, or spatial intelligence measured by psychometric tests, there are other special kinds of musical, bodily kinesthetic, and personal intelligence (a person's ability to understand himself or herself, or other people). However, as you may see, the ability to plan, evaluate a particular situation, and make useful decisions about the situation is essential for human survival and well being. Then again, skills such as musical and body kinesthetic—in most cases—are not necessarily essential for human endurance and adaptation.

From the beginning of the empirical studies of intelligence, culture was claimed to be its important "contributor." For example, Jean Piaget (1972) argued that intelligence has similar cross-cultural developmental mechanisms. On one hand, children in all countries assimilate new information into existing cognitive structures. On the other hand, these cognitive structures accommodate themselves to the changing environment. Lev Vygotsky (1978) believed that intelligence could not be understood without taking into consideration the cultural environment in which the person develops.

In psychology, most attention has been given to the so-called **psychometric approach to intelligence.** This view is based on an assumption that our intelligence can "receive" a numerical value (Wechsler, 1958). This approach is also probably the most controversial one because of an ongoing debate about how accurately these values can be assigned and interpreted.

From an introductory psychology class you perhaps remember that typically, most intelligence tests contain a series of tasks. Each test contains several subtests that measure various cognitive skills. When you take the test you are asked to solve verbal and nonverbal problems, make perceptual judgments, solve puzzles, find word associations, explain pictures in your own words, memorize sequences of words or numbers, and so on. After your answers are checked, your score is converted into a special score. Then your score is compared with the average score of your peers—presumably, and in most cases, this includes people of the same nationality and age group as you are. In fact, the comparison will yield your actual intelligence quotient, or for short, IQ. Approximately 95 percent of the population have scores on IQ tests within two standard deviations of 15. That means most people's IQs—95 out of 100—will be somewhere between 70 and 130.

There has long been intense controversy about the validity of measures and interpretation of intelligence test scores and there are at least two major points in debates about intelligence testing:

1. What do intelligence tests actually measure?
2. How can it be proven that the test score was not influenced by factors such as the attitudes, motivation, or emotional sets of test takers?

Critically important for those who attempt to interpret cultural differences on intelligence scores are (1) the distinction between cognitive potential, (2) cognitive skills developed through interaction with cultural environment, and (3) scores on a particular test. The problem is that the standard tests may not provide for the direct assessment of cognitive skills shaped by a particular cultural environment. Please consider the following assumption: unless intelligence tests accommodate the activities that people perform in their day-to-day life, the tests created in one culture will continue to be biased against other cultural groups. This means that the test performance may not represent the individual's cognitive potential (Vernon, 1969). Moreover, factors such as language, test content, and motivation reportedly contribute to an individual's performance on tests (Sternberg, 1997). For example, there are many aspects of human intelligence, such as wisdom and creativity, that many tests are simply not designed to measure.

 By nature, men are nearly alike; by practice, they get to be wide apart.
CONFUCIUS (441–479 B.C.)—CHINESE PHILOSOPHER

Another major point of most discussions is how to interpret the numerical value of intelligence. If 12-year-old boys and girls in a northern part of a city scored 90 on a test, whereas boys and girls from a southern part of the city scored 105 on the same test, what does this mean? The most fired debates take place when intelligence value is assigned to ethnic or national groups. Apparently, some significant differences in body size, shape, and skin color do not evoke such heated discussions and, as a result, we have misunderstanding and blaming rather than detailed interpretations of group differences between intelligence scores.

Now for what is likely the most difficult part of the discussion on intelligence. Before we continue our analysis, let us express one concern. As we suggested earlier, there are perhaps very few issues in psychology that have become as divisive as the concept of intelligence. Around the world debates about intelligence are often motivated by a variety of political, ideological, and group interests (Neisser et al., 1996). In some cases a particular political agenda comes first and psychology serves as a provider of data. Scientific arguments are often overshadowed by emotional rhetoric. We accept, of course, that people who want to advance their particular views could use cross-cultural psychology for this purpose. Therefore, the goals of cross-cultural psychology perhaps will be better served if these views are not rejected outright but presented and critically analyzed.

Ethnic Differences in IQ Scores

Most of the questions that cross-cultural psychology attempts to address are concerned with a set of measurable similarities and differences among different cultural, ethnic, and national groups. Are ethnic groups characterized by a particular pattern of intellectual ability? For example, can one prove that Italians, in general, are more creative than Germans, but that the German mode of thinking is more "precise" than the Brazilian mode? Do some cultural groups have a "better" memory than others? Are some ethnic groups more knowledgeable than others and, if yes, in what particular areas? Do poverty and other devastating social problems influence intelligence? Is systematic formal schooling the key to human intellectual equality? Is such equality achievable in principle?

These and many other questions have intrigued cross-cultural psychologists for more than a century. In the United States early attempts to measure IQs were targeted at minorities and new immigrants arriving in this country. For example, in 1921 the National Academy of Sciences published the results of one of the first massive national studies on intelligence. The results allowed the organizers of this study to rank newly arrived immigrants according to their IQ scores. This is how the "intellectual" order of the immigrants looked: England, Holland, Denmark, Scotland, Germany, Canada, Belgium, Norway, Austria, Ireland, Turkey, Greece, Russia, Italy, Poland. In addition, the data showed the first evidence that blacks generally scored lower than whites on those tests. It was also reported that the Polish in this study did not score significantly higher than the blacks did (Kamin, 1976).

Today various tests show differences in intelligence scores among large cultural groups. For example, in the United States, Asian Americans (of East Asian origins) score the highest, followed by European Americans, Hispanics, and lastly African Americans. Thus, on the average, African American schoolchildren score 10–15 percent lower on a standardized intelligence test than white schoolchildren do. Similar results were reported for adults (Anastasi, 1988; Suzuki & Valencia, 1997). For better comprehension of the differences between some of the groups, just imagine that the average white person tests higher than about 80 percent of the population of blacks and an average black person tests higher than about 20 percent of the population of whites.

The mean intelligence test scores for Latino groups are usually between those of blacks and whites (Pennock-Roman, 1992). If we divide all of the U.S. citizens along their religions, we will find that Jews, and specifically Jews of European origin, test

CROSS-CULTURAL SENSITIVITY

Because of stereotyping (see Chapter 10 on social perception) some people may believe that all members of a group—or at least most of them—have either high or low IQ scores. However, the overall ethnic or national differences say little about diversity within particular groups. It is important to mention stereotyping because it may have an indirect impact on school performance and perhaps other activities. How? Imagine, for instance, a teacher knows that there are five Hispanic and three black children in her class. Making a stereotypical judgment, the teacher would assume that these children should have lower intelligence test scores and, therefore, are less capable of learning than other children in class. This stereotype may create an expectation and attitude that result in the teacher, having only good intentions, giving "easier" assignments to these children, and not challenging them in their educational effort. Do you think that such a situation is not possible?

CRITICAL THINKING

Test Scores: Boys and Girls

Larry Hedges and Amy Nowell from the University of Chicago analyzed six major national surveys on male and female teenagers' performance on intelligence tests (*Science*, July 1995). Seven times as many boys as girls scored in the top 5 percent on science tests, and about twice as many boys as girls scored in the top 5 percent on math tests. However, boys were more likely than girls to score near the bottom of the scale on tests of reading comprehension, memory, and perceptual speed. During a 30-year period, the fluctuations in most measured abilities were very small.

Some people use this as an argument in defense of a biological foundation of human intelligence. What is their reasoning? They argue that the differences in IQ scores between men and women could be attributed to social inequality between the sexes. They also argue that over the past 30-year period major social changes have been implemented and equality has finally been achieved. Because these changes did not significantly affect the average score difference between men and women, there must be other, nonsocial factors that influence human intelligence.

However, this logic is flawed. It is equally plausible to argue that the social efforts to change inequality have been too little! Moreover, sex bias—overt or covert treatment of a person based on his or her sex—may manifest in various subtle ways. Why, for example, do girls have higher scores on quantitative tasks in the earliest stage of school than boys? By the end of high school this tendency reverses. Perhaps, traditionally, there has been more encouragement at school for boys and young men to learn math and science while girls and young women are encouraged to excel in literature, social science, etc. In fact, women outscore men on most verbal tasks, such as reading and spelling (Stanley, 1993).

higher than any other religious group in the United States. Even though it is established that Americans, primarily those of Japanese, Chinese, and Korean ancestry, have higher scores than American whites, there is no consistency in research findings. The differences in scores that do occur are usually in the low single digits. The average difference between black and white IQ scores is established at every level of the socioeconomic ladder. In other words, upper-class blacks have lower test scores than upper-class whites, and lower-class whites have higher test scores than lower-class blacks. However, cross-generational studies of intelligence imply that the gap between black and white ethnic groups tends to narrow (Vincent, 1991). We shall get back to this issue later in the chapter.

Some groups are found to have higher scores on certain scales and lower scores on others. For instance, the verbal intelligence scores of Native Americans were found to be lower than these same scores were for other ethnic groups. However, some studies showed the existence of high visual-spatial skills in some Native American groups (McShane & Berry, 1988). East Asians score slightly higher than whites on nonverbal intelligence and equal or slightly lower on verbal intelligence. Moreover, studies suggest that the visual and spatial abilities of East Asians are superior to their verbal abilities despite substantial political and socioeconomic differences among East Asian countries (Hernstein & Murray, 1994).

There were attempts to find linkages between the frequency of cases of mental retardation (significantly subaverage intellectual functioning and serious adaptational problems) and learning disability (significantly subaverage functioning in an area of academic performance) within particular ethnic groups. However, the results were inconclusive. In some studies, African American and Hispanic students were diagnosed with mental retardation and learning disabilities at higher percentages than other groups. According to these studies, Asian American students belonged to the opposite side of the spectrum (Suzuki & Valencia, 1997). Other studies did not yield any significant difference in mental retardation between the groups (Grubb, 1992).

 It is not enough to have a good mind; the main thing is to use it well.
RENÉ DESCARTES (1596–1650)—FRENCH PHILOSOPHER AND MATHEMATICIAN

Explaining Group Differences in Test Scores: Intelligence and Intelligent Behavior

In an attempt to explain some group differences on intelligence test scores, Robert Sternberg (1997) suggested distinguishing between intelligence and intelligent behavior. Intelligence, from his standpoint, is a mental process that may or may not result in particular behavioral patterns. These patterns of intelligent behavior vary from culture to culture. Something considered intelligent among members of one culture may not be viewed as such in other cultures. If a Washingtonian knows how to negotiate the conditions of a 3-year lease with a car dealer, this skill may not be—and likely will not be—very useful at a farm market in Istanbul or Helsinki. Dealing with different cultural contexts, people develop different cognitive skills and acquire dissimilar ways of thinking and learning that are useful in their particular cultural environment. Take, for example, the way people use categories to describe their experience. Traditionally, among navigators in Southeast Asia, the word "south" is often used to refer only to "seaward," which can be any side of the horizon (Frake, 1980). This centuries-old understanding of directions is inappropriate and confusing to visiting foreigners.

However, people may share some general understandings about what intelligence is because the underlying psychological mechanisms of intelligence are expected to be quite similar in all individuals. Among these processes are abilities to understand a problem, identify its type, prepare a solution, find resources to solve the problem, manage the process of solution, and, finally, evaluate the outcome of behavior. Nevertheless—and this is a key element in the understanding of intelligent behavior—the specific content of such behavior in each of these stages is determined by the specific environment in which the individual lives. A chess master in India uses these strategies to make particular moves on a chessboard, whereas a farmer in Bosnia, using the same psychological mechanisms, secures a good deal buying a new tractor.

Reasoning that is causal, scientific, and based on empirical facts is not applicable in all cultures all the time (Shea, 1985). A ritualistic dance of a Brazilian tribesman may be considered "unintelligent" behavior for many people in London or Tokyo: "Look at him, he is dancing to stop the rain," some taunt sarcastically. These same taunting individuals, however, go every week to their temples and churches and, by doing this, commit themselves to similar ritualistic acts. Moral? People develop cognitive skills best adapted to the needs of their lifestyle (Dasen et al., 1979).

Not all the mental abilities that are displayed by an individual can be measured by psychometric procedures. Likewise, even though the person may have particular mental skills, he or she is not always able to "transfer" these abilities into behavior. For some people, there are no favorable circumstances to display their intellectual skills. Others do not want to demonstrate their intellectual skills for a specific reason: for example, some do not want to look "better" than others. This may take place because people assign different values to different activities—often determined by social-cultural experiences—and therefore strive to achieve their personal goals in a different way.

All in all, one problem that faces psychologists in most countries—and in American society in particular—is an intense focus on test scores that mainly measure formal intelligence, leaving little or no interest in intelligent behavior found in specific situations.

Do Biological Factors Contribute to Intelligence?

According to the **nativist view**, all cognitive phenomena are inborn. They unravel as a result of biological "programming," and environmental perception requires little active construction by the organism. Hypothetically, according to this view, a boy in Nepal or a girl in Venezuela are both expected to develop some elements of conceptual thinking by approximately the age of 7. No one can make these children think conceptually when they are 4 years old. This view argues that hereditary factors determine both the depth and scope of our intellectual skills.

These are not just the empty statements of a handful of researchers. In the 1980s two scientists asked more than 1000 scholars to give their opinion about IQ, in particular about the differences in IQ scores among ethnic groups. Even though only 1 percent suggested that the differences are always caused by genetic factors, almost 45 percent of the professionals reported that the differences are the product of both genetic and environmental variations (many could not or did not want to give a definitive answer). Remarkably, of all of those interviewed only one in seven said that the difference is entirely due to environmental factors (Snyderman & Rothman, 1988).

There is evidence that heredity plays an important role in human intelligence. For example, the intelligence scores of identical twins raised either together or apart correlate almost +0.90 (Bouchard et al., 1990). Twenty-five percent of cases of mental retardation are caused by known biological defects (Grossman, 1983). Moreover, the intelligence scores of adopted children strongly correlate with the scores of their biological parents, whereas there is only a weak correlation between scores of adoptive parents and adopted children (Munsinger, 1978). The correlation between the IQ scores of two biologically unrelated individuals, who were raised together, is also relatively low: +0.20 (Bouchard & McGue, 1981). It is also known that vocabulary size, or the number of words a person remembers and uses in his or her communications, may depend on genetic predispositions. However, even though various data suggest high correlations between parents and children and brothers and sisters in terms of their intellectual skills, these data tell little about what would happen to people's IQ scores if they lived in a different social context than the one in which they actually grew up. Moreover, genetic links for individual differences and similarities do not imply that group differences—on the national level, for example—are also based on genetic factors (Sternberg, 1995).

Besides genetic factors, cross-cultural psychologists examine how particular environmental conditions affect human physiology and whether such biological changes influence cognitive skills. It was found, for instance, that the presence or absence of a particular chemical in a specific geographic region might have affected the overall cognitive performance of the population living in that territory. To illustrate, iodine-deficient areas are found in some regions of Indonesia as well as in Spain. Clinicians report that substantial iodine deficiency in the human body can cause severe mental and neurological abnormalities (see Bleichrodt et al., 1980). In accordance with predictions, cognitive test scores obtained from children living in iodine-deficient areas of Spain and Indonesia were much lower than the scores obtained from children residing in neighboring areas where the water contained sufficient amounts of iodine.

We now turn to a discussion of recent studies related to cognitive processes in order to illustrate how and to what extent they are shaped by cultural and social factors.

A CASE IN POINT

Intelligence and Genetics

Biologists created "smarter" than average mice by adding a single gene to rodent embryos. This minor genetic alteration improved the mice's performance on a wide range of cognitive tasks and learning. The researchers claim that they can insert a gene that helps the brain recognize patterns of cause and effect and can help to create pets, farm animals, or other creatures with unusual intellectual capacities. Critics, however, suggest that intelligence is a complex phenomenon. They argue that intelligence is not only genetic, but that social and environmental experiences influence the way the brain assimilates and organizes information (Weiss, 1999).

Questions: Do you think that in the future, such "intelligence-enhancing" operations would actually increase IQ scores? What kinds of ethical problems could these operations cause? Who do you think would benefit the most if such medical procedures were available: mostly the wealthy or mostly the poor?

Incompatibility of Tests: Cultural Biases

Our friend Roberto, a young psychologist from Miami, designed a test to measure the decision-making skills in small-business managers. Could he use this test in Columbia, Chad, or any other country? Yes, he can try. But will his assessments of decision making in these countries be accurate? In Chapter 2 we learned about equivalency, one of the important requirements of any comparative research. If a test were designed for a particular ethnic group, the test questions or tasks may not have similar meaning for other cultural groups. Many specialists (Mishra, 1988; Irvine & Berry, 1983; Berry, 1988; Poortinga & Van der Flier, 1988) emphasize the importance of such issues as "culture fairness" and "test transfer."

Theoretically, cognitive processes are believed to be similar in virtually all healthy individuals of different groups. However, these processes are applied to various, person-specific environmental, social, psychological, and cultural circumstances (Cole et al., 1971). People develop dissimilar cognitive skills because they are shaped by different contexts. A girl who goes to a private school in Paris, stays with her 45-year-old single mother, and has her own bedroom and personal computer lives in an environment that is quite different from that of a North Korean boy who shares his room with two siblings, attends public school, does not have a personal computer, and has very young parents who work in a shoe factory. A test may adequately measure some elementary cognitive skills in these two children, but at the same time it can be of a little use in terms of measuring other, culture-specific cognitive skills.

Some specialists imply that most intelligence tests benefit specific ethnic groups because of the test vocabulary—words and items used in the test questions. For instance, tests may contain internal bias because they use words that are familiar only to some groups. As a result, members of these groups receive higher scores than those who do not belong to these groups. For example, try to solve the following problem.

Find the odd man out: Rose   Tulip   Forget-me-not   Basil

The correct answer is "basil" because all other words stand for flowers, and basil is not a flower. The critics of this type of question might argue that unless the subject knows something about different flowers and plants, it will be very difficult for him or her to find the right answer. Those of us having access to flowers will benefit in this situation. Moreover, one may assume that there are more girls who are familiar with the names of flowers than there are boys. Therefore, girls will probably give more correct answers than boys.

Let us use another example. You know that metaphors and proverbs are frequently used to help people express themselves and be better understood. A good metaphor or allegory should enhance perception. An American instructor could say, for example, a "Trojan horse" to describe an act of secret intrusion. The expression "cold war" may be used to describe a family conflict in which the spouses barely coexist but do not fight against each other. However, many international students do not easily understand many American metaphors. This misunderstanding takes place chiefly because of the students' lack of experience with these expressions and not because of a lack of intellectual skills.

Cultural experience may affect test scores and some test designs demonstrate this. For example, in one study, British children were found to solve test problems more creatively than Asian students from Hong Kong, Indonesia, and Malaysia. One explanation for this finding is that the subjects were required to give numeric verbal responses to the test items, something that is not a typical problem-solving task for Asian cultures (Wrigh et al., 1978). Another example illustrates how a test can benefit members of a particular group. A culturally oriented vocabulary test unique to the African American community called BITCH 100 was given to kids of different ethnic groups. Black kids scored around a mean of 87 out of a possible 100; however, white children's mean score was only 51 (Williams & Mitchell, 1991). In general, black youths perform better than white young people on free-word recall tasks when the categories (words) are related to African American daily experience (Hayles, 1991).

Commenting on overall differences in black–white intelligence scores, some critics imply that in intelligence tests there are many words and expressions that black kids would not understand or are likely to misinterpret. For example, how would a child who grew up in a ghetto and was deprived of many sources of information understand words such as "composer," "symphony," or "regatta"? In addition, in many black communities children do not speak standard English, but rather a nonstandard form of English, a dialect sometimes called Ebonics.

 He who does not know one thing knows another.
KENYAN PROVERB

A Word about "Cultural Literacy"

Most verbal intelligence tests contain sections on general knowledge. Obviously, our "general knowledge" is based on events that took place in a particular cultural environment. Most American kindergartners possess knowledge about George Washington. Later comes information about Benjamin Franklin, the Great Depression, Titanic, "Gone With the Wind," Liberty Bell, Watergate, Fidel Castro, Michael Jordan, Nelson Mandela, hip-hop, and Nine Inch Nails. For a young Italian man, some of these words are likely to sound unfamiliar. His cultural knowledge is based on other facts, events, and developments that are different from those one can experience in America. For example, words and names such as Mussolini, Andreotti, Fiat, Brigade Rosse, Juventus, and Adriano Celentano would be identified in Italy with almost no difficulty. Could you identify all these names? The answer is "no" unless you have lived in Italy or possess great knowledge of Italian history, politics, soccer, and music.

Our literacy is culture based. There is no doubt that $2 \times 2 = 4$ in all countries. An antonym for "death" is "life" in virtually every literate community regardless of its cultural heritage or nationality. However, beyond these universal categories—at least they sound universal for most of us—there is always culture-specific knowledge. Could you come up with your own examples of culture-specific knowledge in the United States or any other country?

CRITICAL THINKING

The Testing Game?

Williams and Mitchell (1991) bring their criticism of testing procedures to a new ground. They have suggested that they see a problem not in testing bias, but rather in its implications. What matters, in their view, is how society interprets testing and what consequences are set forth for those who undergo "the testing game," which is how they refer to intelligence testing. The authors imply that individuals play this "game" in three different settings. The first are test publishers and producers, who construct the game and make the rules. The second are game advocates, who are basically professionals at colleges and universities, including professors and counselors, who do not completely understand the implications of the rules and consequences of the game. And the third are game pawns, such as students and employees, who play the game without knowing what they are playing. There are players who accept the rules in anticipation of winning and there are those who reject the rules because they know they have little or no chance of succeeding any further into the "playoffs." The fact that certain individuals having access to power and resources set the game is the most disturbing element. For instance, using SAT test scores, these powerful individuals can determine which social and educational path a person should or should not take. The authors conclude that this huge testing industry is accountable to no one and therefore it needs some serious officiating.

Numerous attempts were made to reduce cultural bias from the tests on intellectual skills (Jensen, 1980). However, it is still a debatable issue whether contemporary intelligence and other cognitive tests are culturally "neutral." Opinion polls, for instance, suggest that views on this issue are divided. For example, 53 percent of American whites consider that standardized tests, such as SATs, give an unbiased measure of a person's qualifications; only 23 percent of blacks agree with this. Moreover, 53 percent of blacks consider these tests biased against minority individuals (*Time/CNN*, September–October 1997; *Time*, November 24, 1997).

The bias issue is very controversial. Take, for example, the word "bias" which is often understood and interpreted differently. In the social and political sense bias can be described as a tendency—often unintentional—for one group to discriminate against another. In other words, one group deprives the other of particular resources and opportunities. Because test scores become indicators of potential professional and social success, people with lower test scores have fewer opportunities to succeed in the professional world. The whole business of testing and measuring intelligence may serve a great purpose: to help people understand and develop their potentials. However, no matter how noble intentions are, in reality, the test procedures in most cases limit access to power and resources for people with lower IQ scores.

Those who disagree with the existence of bias argue that IQ scores can more or less accurately predicts future success at school—high test scores are positively correlated with high scores on intelligence tests! The specialists who believe that IQ tests contain very little bias suggest that these tests predict the academic performance of any ethnic group in the same way that they predict performance of white children and adults: high IQs predict academic success and low IQs predict low school grades (Pennock-Roman, 1992). This means that any student of any ethnic group who scores high on an IQ test is likely to have fine grades in college.

Environment and Intelligence

Compare yourself with any person in the classroom. You may find someone of the same age, height, weight, nationality, income, and even lifestyle as you are. However, we do not live in identical environments. Our diversity is determined by natural factors, such as individual, professional, educational, social, and cultural circumstances. This is a popular view in psychology—accepted by cross-cultural psychologists—that human intellectual skills can be influenced by external, environmental factors (Carroll, 1983; Sternberg, 1985). In general, these factors include the overall availability of and access to resources, variety of perceptual experiences, predominant type of family climate, educational opportunities, access to books and travel, presence or absence of cultural magical beliefs, general attitudes, and cultural practices. These and other conditions have been found to influence performance on intelligence tests (Vernon, 1969). Settings such as educational incentives, quality of teaching, and teacher–student communications may also influence test scores (Irvine, 1983; Mackie, 1983). Special training programs (Keats, 1985) and additional instructional efforts (Davis & Goodnow, 1977) can determine how well a person scores on an intelligence test as well. For example, Ogbu (1994) suggested that negative attitudes about testing in general, feelings of hopelessness, and exposure to stereotypes may lower the intelligence scores of African Americans and other minority groups in the United States.

Studies show that the acquisition of many mental functions depends on interaction with the environment (Rogan & Maddonald, 1983). Take, for instance, West African traders, who spend most of their adult life traveling and negotiating. One well-known study found that the merchants are better on cognitive tasks—including problem solving—than their fellow tailors, who spent most of their life in one place and do not have such diverse contacts as the merchants (Petitto & Ginsburg, 1982). In another example, Brazilian and Colombian street children who earn their money by selling fruit and vegetables on the street—often at age 10 and 11—are able to conduct financial operations in their "minds" without making mistakes. Similar math operations, done in paper and pencil at the request of investigators, were not successful. The children did not receive formal schooling, and, as a result, they did not learn the algorithms of adding and subtracting on paper (Aptekar, 1989). In another study, after viewing a series of pictures, European children tended to describe the pictures as a sequence of events—as if they were a comic strip that appears in children's magazines. African children who were not exposed to comics tended to report that the pictures portrayed a single instant in time, not a sequence of events (Deregowski & Munro, 1974).

Aboriginal children obtain lower verbal scores than urban Australian children do and one cause may be a lack of interaction. If Aboriginal children have a chance to live side by side with white children, their test scores on verbal classification tests are relatively similar (Lacey, 1971). In general, serious deprivation of stimulation may result in the disorganization of a number of cognitive processes (Sinha & Shkula, 1974).

Certain types of environmental influences determine the individual's experience with these influences. On the other hand, people's experiences determine their adaptive reactions. As a result, cognitive skills that play a crucial role in an individual's survival may develop earlier than other skills (Ferguson, 1956). For examples, children in hunting and gathering societies develop spatial reasoning skills earlier than their peers in agricultural communities. However, children in agricultural cultures achieve understanding of concepts such as conservation of quantity, weight, and volume— knowledge necessary in agricultural activities—more rapidly than children from nomadic (traveling) groups (Dasen, 1975).

Environmental factors may affect higher mental operations, such as planning abilities. One such factor is stability of the environment. In a stable environment most changes are predictable. People are certain about their lives and feel that they are in control of their future. When conditions are unpredictable people may lack planning strategies because of the assumption that it is impossible to control the outcome of whatever you plan. All in all, in societies and communities that are stable, people perhaps have better chances of developing their planning skills than people from unstable environments (Strohschneider & Guss, 1998).

Lack of systematic schooling may also contribute to the slow development of planning strategies. Certainly, the complexity of everyday life can provide conditions for the development of planning skills even if a person has little formal education. However, if there is no access to education and environmental conditions require simple responses, the individual would tend not to develop complex planning strategies.

A general belief system may also determine planning efficacy. According to the Protestant work ethic, for instance, people's futures depend only on their own will and effort. Therefore, individuals have to plan better because better planning will improve their chances to succeed. In those cultures in which faith plays a significant role in people's assessment of the present and future, planning may not be considered such a vital activity.

Socioeconomic Factors

Intelligence scores are, in general, positively correlated with the socioeconomic status of the individual (Neiser et al., 1996). The link between socioeconomic conditions and test performance may be revealed at an early age. It was found that a child's IQ and the socioeconomic status of the child's parents are positively correlated. The higher the child's IQ, the higher his or her parents' socioeconomic rank, and vice versa (White, 1982). Children who grow up in a privileged environment tend to show higher scores than their peers from a deprived environment. For example, Yoruba children, living in upper class, educated families, demonstrated superior mental age scores when compared to Yoruba children from nonliterate families (Lloyd & Easton, 1977). A similar trend was found among 4-year old Maori and Pakeha Aboriginal children living in New Zeland (Brooks, 1976). Accordingly, no substantial differences were found in the cognitive abilities of disadvantaged children from both Australian Aboriginal and European decent (Taylor & Lacey, 1974).

According to the U.S. Census Bureau (1996), in the mid–1990s about 22 percent of American kids lived in families below the official poverty level. Poverty could contribute to these children's lower scores on tests of intelligence and lower levels of school achievement (McLoyd 1998). The individual's socioeconomic status may have both direct and indirect impact on test performance. For instance, social environments with limited amounts of resources may stimulate the development of particular cognitive traits that are useful only for those environments. If we compare large clusters of countries, for example, Western developed and traditional societies, we will find that people in Western countries generally outscore members of traditional societies on intelligence tests (including tests that do not include culture-specific tasks, questions, and problems).

Socioeconomic factors have a more pronounced effect on intelligence test scores in developing countries than in industrialized ones (Irvine, 1983). One explanation of this phenomenon is that in developed countries the gap between the rich and the poor is not as profound as it is in developing countries. The official poverty level in the United States, which is slightly more than 4,000 dollars per person per year, exceeds the average annual income of most world countries.

Some researchers suggest that high IQ scores may predict people's high social status and income (Herrnstein & Murray, 1994). The middle-class population generally has higher IQ scores than the lower-class population. Does this mean that individual socioeconomic success is possible only when an individual has high intellectual skills? This is not necessarily true. Yes, the higher IQ scores may determine the success of the individual, in particular his or her social status and income. Nevertheless, availability and access to resources—or the lack thereof—may also affect the person's intellectual potential, which results in IQ scores. One should not forget that the individual's social status determines his or her position in the society and access to resources and power. Both middle-class and well-to-do parents establish connections and develop personal and professional relationships with people from the same social stratum, thus paving the way for their own children to reach high levels on the social ladder. In other words, psychometric intelligence alone cannot decide social outcome; there are many other variables in this equation. For example, individuals who have the same IQ scores may be quite different from one other in their income and social and professional status.

Those who believe in the crucial role of socioeconomic factors in our intellectual functioning consider them the most salient influences contributing to the difference between intelligence test scores of blacks and whites is the United States. Generally, blacks have lower incomes, occupy less prestigious positions, and receive less adequate care than other minority groups. Poverty is also linked to inconsistent parenting and persistent exposure to stress that can and does affect cognitive functioning.

The Family Factor

An affluent and educated family is likely to provide a better material environment for a child and also has more resources to develop a child's intellectual potential than a poorer family. Middle-class parents typically have enough resources to stimulate the child's learning experience at home (Gottrfried, 1984). Such parents are likely to be educated and subsequently have general understanding of the importance of education. They are able to buy developmental toys, including video games and computer software. Most of them do not have problems that would prevent them from talking to their children about various topics, exposing them to interesting events, and stimulating their imagination. On the contrary, poor families have fewer resources and perhaps fewer opportunities to stimulate a child's intellectual development (Shiraev, 1988). If the parents' prime activity is to secure food and safety for the family members, then collective survival—not necessarily the intellectual development of the child—is a prime goal of the parents' activities.

In has been found in some studies that intelligence scores decline as a function of birth order. According to one theory, this trend has little to do with biological factors (Munroe & Munroe, 1983.) Every immature member of a family develops intelligence linked to the intellectual level of the older family members. The firstborn in the family has the initial advantage of an immediate environment consisting of only himself or herself and the adult parents, who have a particular set of cognitive skills. When a second child is born, he or she enters an environment consisting of himself or herself, the parents, and an individual with an immature intellectual level, that is, the older sibling. Thus, in general, the intellectual environment encountered by the firstborn is "superior" to that of the second born, and so on.

These data, although controversial, found additional support in some other studies. For example, a continuous increase in IQ scores in the African American population is correlated with the increasingly smaller family size since the 1970s. Children

A CASE IN POINT

A Global Decline in IQ Scores?

Some specialists forecast that the overall IQ level of the American and, perhaps, world population should go down (Williams & Ceci, 1997; Loehlin, 1997). Why? There is a tendency for people with high IQ scores to have fewer children than people with lower IQ scores. This tendency, for example, was common in both black and white women (see the U.S. Bureau of the Census 1992 Current Population Reports). If this trend persists, the global situation may change: there will be more people with lower IQs entering schools and the job market, outnumbering those with higher IQ scores. However, this hypothesis is not supported by facts. On the contrary, the differences in intelligence test scores between ethnic and socioeconomic groups have decreased and keep decreasing in some measurements and apparently there is no indication of a global decline in IQ scores among the general population.

from smaller families tend to achieve higher IQ scores than their counterparts from larger families (Vincent, 1991). However, extra caution is needed in such interpretations. First, the relationship here may be reverse: higher scores on IQ tests stand for higher cognitive abilities, which, in turn, affect individual attitudes about pregnancy and unprotected sex. Another explanation for the change in IQ scores is a more significant increase in the educational level of parents in black families in the 1980s and 1990s.

Parental influence can be one of the factors contributing to the difference in IQ scores between white and some other ethnic groups—predominantly minorities—that represent the middle class. Minority parents—especially those who arrived to the United States before the 1960s—are likely to be less educated than the white population. As it was mentioned earlier, parents' educational level may affect conditions that contribute to the development of the child's cognitive skills. Moreover, some minority parents may pay less attention to educational opportunities for their children than white families do. Overall pessimism and a lack of opportunity and success can cause such attitudes. On the contrary, Chinese and Japanese Americans tend to emphasize the importance of education for their children and see it as the only opportunity for future success. Partly because of family values and partly because of their academic success, Asian Americans tend to seek and get appointments in professional, managerial, or technical occupations to a greater extent that any other ethnic group (Flynn, 1991).

"Natural Selection" and IQ Scores?

According to the bell curve principle, a normal distribution of IQ scores in any given population can be roughly divided into three large categories: people with low, average, and high IQ scores. This same principle can also be used in the distribution of peoples' heights. However, although a bell curve of IQ scores and a bell curve of peoples' heights may paint a similar picture, the meanings people assign to these pictures may be quite different. For instance, we find people of all different heights in various social circles, with various occupations, and of varying intelligence. An individual's location on the bell curve of height may place him or her next to numerous types of people that he or she may never interact with in everyday life.

The bell curve of IQ scores is another story. In the United States, for example, people with high IQ scores are disproportionally represented among doctors, scientists, lawyers, and business executives. Individuals with low intelligence scores are disproportionally represented among people on welfare, prison inmates, single mothers, drug abusers, and high school dropouts (see, for example, Jensen, 1973; Rushton, 1994, 1995).

Perhaps there is nothing unusual about people with similar interests and occupations tending to communicate with each other significantly more often than with people of other occupations and interests. For example, a high IQ score indicates that you will be more likely to (1) attend college, (2) gain employment in a setting conducive to meeting and making friends with people of similar educational levels, and perhaps intelligence, and (3) marry someone with an educational background and once again, perhaps intelligence, similar to yours. Likewise, people with lower scores will likely seek love and friendship among people of the same cognitive level. Therefore, according to an assumption formulated by Herrnstein and Murray (1994), two polls of people have been "constructed" over the years: one with relatively high and the other with relatively low intelligence scores. The former is placed in an advantageous social niche with prestigious jobs, good income, and fine living conditions. The latter group finds itself in the disadvantaged stratum of low-paying jobs, unstable social environment, and low-quality living conditions.

Unfortunately, for a variety of reasons, many representatives of ethnic minorities remain in the disadvantaged group. Low IQ scores, as was mentioned earlier, predict low academic grades and fewer opportunities for individuals to get high-income jobs. Lack of resources would contribute greatly to keeping these individuals in low-income communities. Low salaries and low cost of property produce significantly less taxes than in affluent districts. Therefore, local schools—most of which depend on local property or other taxes—are not able to provide high-quality education comparable to the quality of education in affluent communities. Poor schooling conditions, lack of qualified teachers, and the absence of modern educational equipment affect the developing child's cognitive skills. In addition, as we saw earlier, poverty is responsible for a variety of indirect impacts on the intellectual development of children and adults.

 He who knows others is learned; he who knows himself is wise.
Laotse (604–531 b.c.)—**chinese philosopher**

Cultural Values of Cognition

Let us get back to Roberto's test on cognitive skills mentioned in the beginning of the chapter (remember, he designed an inventory on problem solving). According to this test, what types of problem solving are likely to be considered most efficient for a business person? There are several, a few of which are independent judgment, creativity, and speed of decision making. Will these qualities be equally valuable in all business environments and in all countries?

Judging from an ethnocentric perspective, one might suggest that the most "valuable" features for any problem-solving process are analytical, rational skills, and quick reasoning. However, such a view—though prevailing in most contemporary societies—is not universal in all cultures. Some societies may have diverse sets of cognitive values different from the ones highly regarded, for example, in Western societies (Berry, 1988). In some societies holistic—emphasizing the importance of the whole—rather than analytic decision making is valued (Dasen, 1984; Serpell, 1993). In such cases, careful reflection rather than promptness is considered the most appropriate course of action. In these primarily agricultural societies collective discussion rather than individual consideration is generally the preferred cognitive style. Therefore, in such cultures individuals tested with a standard Western psychological instrument—such as Roberto's test—will likely display a low level of cognitive development according to criteria that measure only independence and speed of judgment!

Desire to have things done quickly prevents their being done thoroughly.
CONFUCIUS (551–479 B.C.)—CHINESE PHILOSOPHER

According to another approach to the interpretation of test scores on general intelligence, the problem is in the way people across cultures value and construe intelligence. For instance, as already mentioned, the conceptualization of intelligence as quick and analytic is not shared in all cultures. If one group's concept includes being detailed and precise in responding, but the other group does not mention these features (and mentions improvisation as an element of intelligence), then precision cannot be a used as a criterion according to which the two groups are compared (Berry, 1969).

In the United States, different ethnic groups may use different frames of reference regarding intelligence (Heath, 1983; Okagaki & Sternberg, 1993). For instance, in most cases, European Americans emphasize the importance of cognitive skills such as memorization, classification, and problem solving, whereas other groups tend to emphasize characteristics such as motivation, social, and practical skills. In light of this, Sternberg (1997) implies that the emphasis on formal mental abilities does not give a fair chance to many individuals with high creative and practical mental abilities! For example, on measures of creativity, flexibility, and originality, black children and other minority groups typically do as well, and frequently better, than the white children (Hayles, 1991).

We understand now that intellectual skills are judged according to a group's standards. For example, if a culture places an emphasis on hunting, a person's good vision and ability to make quick visual judgments will be considered extremely adaptive. In other cultures the quickness of one's response will not be as essential as a critical evaluation of a task or problem at hand. In other words, the people, as representatives of a particular culture, define intelligence! If we argue for this, we inevitably move in the fields of cultural relativism (see Chapter 1). Why? Because we would challenge the existence of universal criteria for human mental activities. However, cultural relativism can also be challenged. For example, do you think that in an era of globalization of economy and informational revolution, people can, may, and probably should develop similar perceptions of what specific mental abilities are considered to be adaptive and valuable in the global community unified by the global economy?

There have been many attempts to explain the differences between Western and African cultural values and views on healthy cognitive functioning and intelligence. Boykin (1994), for example, suggested that blacks are generally different from whites and other ethnic groups. For instance, African Americans do not accept materialistic beliefs and do accept the influence of nonmaterial forces to a greater extent than other groups. They emphasize the importance of movement, rhythm, and music. They appreciate high levels of stimulation and energy and emphasize the importance of emotions and expressiveness. Furthermore, African American culture is rooted in spirituality, harmony, and affect, as well as verbal elements of communication. These features may not fit well into the Western values of rationality, calculation, discipline, individualism, and achievement, which are embodied in IQ tests. The author even suggests that the whole idea of intelligence assessment may be foreign to the African American mentality.

Most non-African theories of behavior, according to Baldwin (1991), emphasize the critical role of the gratification of desires. The emphasis of black psychology is that the essential goal of human behavior is survival. Moreover, African theology assumes that the most direct experience of the self is one that goes through affect. Therefore IQ measures cannot measure the psychology of individuals who grew up in African or African American cultures. Intelligence, from the perspective of African psychology, is a collective moral responsibility.

Shade (1992) suggested that African Americans value a unique **cognitive style**—a way in which individuals organize and comprehend the world. In the study of 178 ninth-grade students, sampled African Americans tended to be spontaneous, flexible, open-minded, and less structured in the perception of people, events, and ideas. European Americans in the sample appeared to be self-regulated, judgmental, and less open-minded than their counterparts. In another study, African American children generally learned in ways characterized by emotional emphasis, harmony, holistic perspectives, expressive creativity, and nonverbal communication (Wills, 1992). Some explain the below average standardized test scores of African American children by referring to the tests' emphasis: the abstract, analytic thinking valued by Europeans—the features that are somewhat deemphasized by blacks (Whethrick & Deregowski, 1982).

It was also implied that Mexican American students use different cognitive styles of information processing: they are more field dependent than their European counterparts in the classroom (Kush, 1996). For example, **field-dependent** learners are more attentive to external references, contexts, and instructions in their learning tasks. **Field-independent** learners tend to be autonomous in learning, solving problems, and making decisions. It was found that in American academic settings, field-independent students are more successful than field-dependent students. However, such differences in style largely disappear if children belong to the same socioeconomic level.

Certain ideological conditions may affect what people of a certain country value most in cognitive skills. Consider this example. If authorities, whoever they are—central government or local boss—make most decisions in your life, then apparently the number of choices you have may be restricted. Given a limited amount of choice, the number of activities available to you will also be limited, which is likely to affect your creativity and problem-solving ability. For example, creative thinking and self-expression are highly regarded in Western democratic societies. The paradox is that creative thinking is not a necessary asset in authoritarian societies. Why? Because this type of thinking may put the individual "above the crowd," which is neither appreciated nor tolerated by authorities. The same logic may be applied to those societies that promote dogmatic thinking and punish individuals for free exchange of ideas.

 EXERCISE 5.1

Please analyze the following theory differentiating dichotomous variables and continuous variables. Jackson (1991) introduces the following assumptions about the cognitive skills of African Americans:

- Blacks in the United States tend to perceive events as the whole visual picture whereas whites perceive reality as broken down into parts.
- African Americans tend to prefer reasoning based on contextual and interpersonal factors, whereas white Americans prefer inductive and deductive reasoning.
- African Americans prefer to approximate space, numbers, and time. European Americans tend to prefer precision based on the concert of one-dimensional time and "objective" space between individuals.
- African Americans prefer to focus on people and their activities as opposed to Europeans, who show a propensity toward things based on a Euro-centric orientation and norms.
- African Americans prefer cooperation, preservation of life, affiliation, and collective responsibility; European Americans prefer competition, conflict, control of life, ownership, and individual rights.
- African Americans are more altruistic and concerned about the "next person," while European Americans value individualism and independence.
- African Americans prefer novelty, freedom, and personal distinction to a greater degree than European Americans.

General Cognition: What Is "Underneath" Intelligence?

Numerous facts about cultural diversity as well as empirical evidence about universal principles of cognition (see the definition of cognition in the beginning of the chapter) have contributed to the foundations of many theories exploring the links between culture and intelligence. There are several cognitive processes—recognition, categorization, thinking, and memory—the analysis of which will perhaps shed some light on differences in intellectual functioning among various ethnic groups.

Classification

Are there any differences in how people classify their environment? Humans tend to see things in highly similar fashions. One of the most universal classifications is the cognitive distinction made between plants and animals (Berlin, 1992). However, those plants and animals that are essential for the survival of individuals become most carefully distinguished and named. In general, the importance of objects and animals as well as a person's familiarity with them are the most significant factors that influence categorization. Groups that are relatively distant from each other should have some differences in classifications (Schwanenflugel & Rey, 1986). This may become a source of a potential bias in the testing of cognitive skills.

Sorting

If you ask a 7-year-old child of any nationality to sort 100 colored cards into color categories the child should be expected to perform this operation without difficulty. Now ask an elderly resident of a small Ethiopian village to sort 100 compact discs according to the musical genres they represent—rock, classical, and hip-hop—this person will likely experience serious difficulties (unless he is familiar with musical genres!).

We can sort various objects even though no instructions are given on how to do it. Generally, we choose a dimension of categorization, that is, concept or characteristic. Linguists suggest that many categories used in sorting are universal. We use synonyms, such as "quick" and "fast"; antonyms, such as "clean" versus "dirty"; subcategories, such as "skunk" and "animal"; and parts, such as "heart" and "body" (Raybeck & Herrmann, 1990).

Research suggests that cultural groups tend to categorize objects in terms of their specific cultural experiences associated with these objects (Wassmann & Dasen, 1994; Wassmann, 1993; Okonji, 1971). In other words, according to experience people know what the objects are used for and then base their categorization on this knowledge (Mishra, 1997). It has also been shown that the degree of familiarity with the environment influences classificatory behavior. For example, according to a well-known study, rural Liberians performed at a lower level, compared with American students from New Mexico, in a card-sorting task. However, the Liberians were superior at sorting bowls of rice (Irwin et al., 1974).

In light of these studies, some researchers insist that one of the biases of intelligence tests is inattention to cultural types of classificatory behavior. For example, blacks prefer to pay attention to people and events rather than to ideas and objects. As a result, African Americans are better at categorizing people than objects. Moreover, they tend to categorize objects in a more relational or holistic manner as opposed to the analytical, detail-oriented procedure practiced by most Europeans (Shade, 1992).

Memory

Many comparative tests on memory contain tasks that require the subject to remember storylike information and then recall it. Are there any cultural differences in memory? Mandler and colleagues (1980) found relatively few differences in the recollection of stories between U.S. and Liberian children and adults. Similarly, common patterns in immediate recall of information were found among such distant cultural groups as English, Polish, and Shona in Zimbabwe (Whethrick & Deregowski, 1982).

Common patterns in how people recall stories do not mean there are common patterns in what people recall or how fast they process this information. Cultural, social, and educational experiences affect what we remember. Children of higher socioeconomic status receive better scores on various memorization tests compared with other students (Ciborski & Choi, 1974). Steffensen and Calker (1982) tested U.S. and Australian Aboriginal women by asking them to recall two stories about a child getting sick. The child was treated by Western medicine in one story (a situation familiar to American women), and by native medicine in the other (a situation familiar to Australian women). The stories were recalled better when they were consistent with subjects' knowledge. Similar results have been reported by other psychologists working with different cultural populations (Harris et al., 1986). Deregowski (1974) showed that urban children in Zambia recalled more test information than did rural residents. Perhaps the better educational opportunities of urban boys and girls and emphasis on memorization in school activities influence children's test performance.

Formal and Mathematical Reasoning

Formal reasoning is a basic cognitive operation that is based on abstract analysis of given premises and deriving a conclusion from them. It is particularly sensitive to systematic schooling (Scribner & Cole, 1981). Formal reasoning is different from **empirical reasoning,** which is drawn from everyday experience. A person may develop skills of empirical reasoning but do poorly on a test that measures formal reasoning skills. Russian psychologists Alexander Luria (1976) demonstrated in one of his studies that illiterate peasants in Uzbekistan, a republic of the former Soviet Union, were able to understand empirical reasoning—when objects involved in reasoning were observable—but often failed to comprehend abstract formal reasoning that required assumptions and imagination.

Many cross-cultural studies have specifically focused on mathematical problems. This was the case not only because these studies provided a good test of reasoning ability, but also because math symbols appear to be culturally neutral. One of the important findings was that Eastern cultures—such as China and Japan—are often thought to be advanced in the development of numerical abilities in their members. Indeed, Chinese participants performed significantly better on several mathematical measures than did American students (Geary et al., 1992; Stevenson et al., 1990). Davis and Ginsburg (1993) compared Beninese (African), North American, and Korean children and found little difference in performance on informal life-related mathematical problems. However, on formal problems, the Korean children performed best. Why does this trend exist? The most common explanation is based on the assumption that there is a particular set of social norms developed in East Asian countries. In particular, parents and teachers spend more time and effort on the development of formal mathematical skills in children than their counterparts overseas typically do. The differences in educational norms and attitudes most likely cause the differences in test performance between American and East Asian children (Van de Vijver & Willemsen, 1993).

Creativity

If you write a verse in English and rhyme "forever" and "together," this cannot be called creative poetry. Why? Because **creativity** typically means originality or the ability to produce valued outcomes in a novel way. The rhyme "forever–together" has already been used in hundreds of verses and songs.

In cross-cultural psychology, studies examining the role of culture in creativity focus mainly on social factors and socialization practices (Stein, 1991; Harrington, 1990). For example, persistent parental support and positive stimulation appear to be good predictors of creativity (Simonton, 1987). In a comparative Mexican American study, children from economically advantaged families showed higher creativity scores than did disadvantaged children (Langgulung & Torrance, 1972). It was also found that Arab subjects tended to score higher on verbal creativity than on spatial creativity, which is probably due to the emphasis Islamic cultures place on achieving verbal proficiency and the religious restrictions placed on pictorial reflections of reality (Mar'i & Karayanni, 1982). The same study showed that in Arab cultures males score higher than females on creativity tests. However, those subjects who were equally exposed to television, Western education, and travel showed little evidence of sex differences in their scores of creativity.

Not every specialist considers creativity as a cognitive trait though. Some psychologists link creativity to such personality features as psychological independence and self-acceptance (Barron & Harrington, 1981).

Cognitive Skills, School Grades, and Educational Systems

It has been shown in numerous studies that IQ scores correlate with school grades. In other words, if Ali has a higher IQ than John one can anticipate that Ali's grades in math, science, literature, and social studies will be better than John's. Can one then make a suggestion that higher intelligence scores determine higher school grades? Yes, such an assumption is correct, but it may contain a logical error. Why? Because the high grades one receives at school may also be determined by one's effort, motivation, interest in learning, and individual discipline. These characteristics, in turn, may be largely influenced by one's family. Add peer influence, teacher effort and commitment, and the availability of educational resources at school and home—may all determine a particular individual's grades and test scores.

We should not forget that around the globe, national school systems are organized differently. In the United States public education is primarily based on the guidelines determined by local communities. The government in Washington cannot dictate to the U.S. states or counties what students have to study in kindergarten, middle school, or high school. In many other countries, however, schools use standard curricula and students nationwide have similar textbooks on every subject. To illustrate, children in Japan are generally more advanced than their American counterparts in math. This is not happening because of a difference in IQ—the average scores are similar—but rather because the Japanese school curriculum places a heavy emphasis on mathematics.

Again, the fact that American children are behind their peers in Japan and some other Asian countries on math tests may be explained—in addition to previously given assumptions—by differences in school requirements and curricula. Due to cultural traditions, American children are allowed more freedom in choosing school activities than their counterparts overseas. The emphasis is typically placed on individual development, enjoyable activities, and respect for the child's personality. In Asian countries, on the contrary, the active promotion of the mathematical development of children is

CRITICAL THINKING

Culture, Discipline, and Test Scores

The chapter begins with a vignette in which a suggestion was made about possible linkages between high test scores and the discipline and demanding atmosphere of Chinese schools. Are there culture-related teaching styles? Cross-cultural studies show some differences in the interaction between students and teachers—the differences that may result in different learning patterns. As an example, a comparison of Chinese and Japanese students with American counterparts shows that the former not only engage in more academic activities, but teachers also pass on more information to students than do teachers in the United States (Stevenson et al., 1986).

Authoritarian psychological climate, difficult homework, and teaching methods focused on preparing students for examinations generally characterize the learning and teaching context in many Asian countries (Murphy, 1987). This pattern of accepting and obeying teachers and authorities is deliberately taught to children (Lin, 1988). Such conditions as reward and punishment also display cross-cultural variations. In Asian cultures, praise for good performance is relatively rare, whereas punishment in the form of ridicule and shaming is quite frequent (Ho, 1981). Praise is given only for exceptional achievements or moral virtues, and then it is seldom given publicly (Salili et al., 1989).

Question: Do you think teaching style has anything to do with students' higher test scores? Explain your opinion.

crucial. From the beginning the child learns rules of discipline, perseverance, and sacrifice for the sake of educational goals (Geary 1995).

Studies also show a high correlation between total years of education and IQ scores. To put it simply, people with a higher IQ are likely to continue their education at college; people with a college degree are likely to have a higher IQ than individuals with a high-school diploma (Neiser et al., 1996). A higher IQ may predict higher grades; that, in turn, may increase a person's motivation to stay in school.

 The first mark of intelligence, to be sure, is not to start things; the second mark of intelligence is to pursue to the end what you have started.
PANCHATANTRA—THE ANONYMOUS COLLECTION OF SANSKRIT ANIMAL FABLES

Culture, Tests, and Motivation

IQ test scores may be determined not only by one's intellectual skills but also by the individual's motivation, anxiety, and attitudes toward testing. For example, why is there a gap in intelligence test scores between whites and African and Mexican Americans, wheras no such gap exists for other immigrant groups, such as Arabs, Chinese, or

Iranians? Explaining the difference, scholars sometimes refer to the so-called **low effort syndrome** (Ogbu, 1991). The low effort syndrome is an example of a coping strategy: "No matter how hard I try, I will be held back."

Why does this syndrome exist? In the United States, and perhaps in some other countries, there are at least two kinds of minorities. The first is immigrant minorities, most of which come voluntarily in search of better conditions and opportunities. These minorities make use of high academic achievement as a condition of success. Cast minorities, on the other hand, were brought to America through slavery or forceful colonization. They developed a different attitude that was based on an assumption that academic success does not lead to advancements because the society pays attention not only to your education but also to your origin or ethnic background.

Indeed, it is hard to disagree with the idea that people ought to see successful results for their hard work. Otherwise, pessimism may discourage many of us from studying, learning, and striving for a better future. Those who argue that some ethnic minorities express less motivation on intelligence tests typically suggest that such individuals do not try to excel on these tests because they believe that they will not go to college anyway, the tests are biased against them, and test results are unimportant. Perceiving themselves as minority groups and understanding that power and resources do not belong to them, some individuals believe that there is no reason for them to try to succeed because success is not achievable and effort will not be rewarded by society just because of minority status. Moreover, tests may be seen by some as another instrument by which the government tries to advance the discrimination of minorities (Williams & Mitchell, 1991).

Such negative attitudes may be passed on to younger generations and become part of value systems, which encourage people to seek alternative ways of surviving that do not include education. Moreover, some blacks stereotypically define academic achievement as "white" behavior that is inappropriate for nonwhite individuals, especially African Americans (Ogbu, 1986).

Some scholars argue that the motivational levels of blacks and whites—those who take intelligence tests—are not substantially different (Hernstein & Murray, 1994). The authors give as an example, the "digit span test." During this test the subject is instructed to repeat a sequence of numbers in the order read to him or her, for example: 11, 17, 20, 16, 9, 49. After a certain number of forward sequences or a certain number of mistakes, the tester asks the subject to repeat a sequence of numbers backward. These two parts of the test are conducted immediately one after the other and have identical content: the person has to repeat the same numbers presented to him or her.

The black–white differences on this test are about twice as great on backward digits as on forward digits. The authors argue that is impossible to suggest that lack of motivation in black subjects is responsible for such differences: how come the differences are minimal on the "forward" sequence, and substantial on the "backward" sequence?

However, if you think critically, you may find that the two halves of the test are not equal in their meaning to the participant. The first half of the test requires a relatively simple operation of memorizing and repeating. The second half of the test—when the subject is asked to repeat numbers backward—requires a substantial mental effort. This may activate psychological resistance in subjects who consider such a difficult task impossible to overcome and therefore not worth the sustained effort.

❝ *A man of humanity is one who, in seeking to establish himself, finds a foothold for others and who, desiring attainment for himself, helps others to attain.*
CONFUCIUS (551–479 B.C.)—CHINESE PHILOSOPHER

❝ *Justice is like a train that's nearly always late.*
YEUGENY YEVTUSHENKO—RUSSIAN CONTEMPORARY POET AND WRITER

IQ, Culture, and Social Justice

Is the power of the few based on their intellectual skills? Exceptions notwithstanding, in most contemporary societies the amount of education received should predict, in general, social status. Indeed, the higher your educational degree, the more prestigious and well paid the profession you can apply for and eventually receive. Moreover, as indicated earlier, individuals with a higher educational degree should ultimately earn more than those with fewer years of completed education. For example, in most societies, occupations such as doctors, lawyers, dentists, college professors, and some other professions require up to 20 years of formal schooling. In other words, a high IQ score indicates higher grades in school and may eventually lead toward a higher social status—the value of which is measured by income generated and occupational prestige.

Now use your creative imagination. Can you hypothesize that there can be societies in which certain prestigious professions do not require the person to pass a series of tests or have a high academic degree? In such cases, the relationship between IQ and earning potential will not be so evident and, therefore, IQ would probably lose its discriminatory power over people's lives! Does this mean that in contemporary societies, people are divided into "upper" and "lower" social categories according to their test scores?

Some of us can easily argue that in the contemporary democratic societies people are born to be equal and laws protect their equal rights. Therefore, it is fundamentally wrong to continue to divide people socially based on their test scores. Why does the contemporary system have to be accepted as fair if it discriminates against certain groups? For instance, some ethnic minorities, primarily blacks, Hispanics, and Native Americans, have less opportunity to go to college and fewer chances of getting better jobs than those individuals who show higher IQ scores. Looking at this situation from a slightly different perspective, one could ask a question: "Why do we live in a democratic society if we have only one system, which links societal success to test scores and indicates what jobs people should pursue and eventually how much money they can make?"

Others may reply: "So what is the problem? We are all different. Some people are tall and some other people are short. We have different skills. We want to achieve different goals. We are not entitled to perform in the same way. We have to except diversity. Diversity assumes some sort of inequality." As was mentioned, intelligence test scores predict what profession an individual is likely to obtain. In the United States and many other countries certain occupations require an applicant to earn a particular college degree and pass special qualification tests. No doubt, these professions require individuals to use their intellectual skills. For example, imagine yourself as a physician.

What do you have to do daily? Most likely, you have to examine different patients with different symptoms and problems; you have to develop your research skills and observation proficiency in order to come up with the correct diagnosis; you have to communicate with insurance companies and your supervisors; you have to understand how to write prescriptions; you have to know how to talk to patients and their relatives; you must read scientific and other professional journals. Should we continue? This job requires a high academic degree. People with lower degrees or without formal schooling should be expected to perform less complex activities (Kohn & Schooler, 1983).

Perhaps people will compete with and discriminate against each other in certain walks of life. Maybe there is no way to achieve equal performance and, therefore, equal scores on school tests. However, wherever it is possible, people living in a democratic society can reduce the impact of discrimination, whether intentional or not. For the sake of argument, suppose that two children are born in the year 2005. Should we assume that they are both entitled to have an equal opportunity to compete for a better future? Let us assume this. However, in reality, from the beginning of their lives they may join the race for happiness at different "speeds." One child will have better conditions for intellectual growth, whereas the other will not live in such a favorable environment.

Will these two children have equal chances to develop equal cognitive skills, given their unequal environments, even though they had equal potential at birth? The answer is likely to be "no." However, what can one do about this situation? Should the government force everyone to give up property and resources and be equal economically and ideologically? Such attempts were made in the twentieth century by many Communist and totalitarian governments. The attempts eventually failed.

Very few of us will demand that people be totally equal and receive the same benefits regardless of their effort, skills, and moral behavior. However, we believe that a wealthy democratic society is capable of creating better conditions for its citizens by helping the disadvantaged to compete for and pursue happiness. This debate, however, brings about not only psychological, but also many moral and political questions that are beyond the scope of the present analysis.

The situation with IQ testing and scores may be changing, however. James Flynn (1987) has shown an interesting tendency of a continuous and steady worldwide rise in intelligence test performance. Detected primarily in developed countries, this effect stands for a three-point increase in IQ scores every 10 years. From a broader perspective, one can suggest that every new generation is expected to be scoring higher than its parents and others and the difference will be from 6 to 9 points. Such a difference may be caused by an increase in the technological advancement of the population. As a simple example, in the 1980s most video games were simple and one dimensional with two or three slow-moving objects. Today's video games—mostly three dimensional and multicolored—require significant preparation and training before one can successfully play any of them. Increased access to television and the Internet also adds to the complexity of the surrounding world and perhaps stimulates the development of individual psychological skills. Technology and other resources make a difference in people's lives. For example, in recent years the gap in IQ scores between American rural and urban populations has significantly decreased (Neiser et al., 1996), which may be explained by a changing environment. In rural areas children have greater access to various sources of information, such as television and the Internet, compared to the situation 20 or 40 years ago.

 An honest heart being the first blessing, a knowing head is the second.
THOMAS JEFFERSON (1743–1826)—THIRD U.S. PRESIDENT

And in the End, Moral Values

Intelligence can be viewed as a general individual ability for adaptation to changing environmental conditions (Sternberg, 1997). All in all, the contemporary view supported by many psychologists is that the most essential elements of intelligence are so-called higher level abilities, namely: reasoning, problem solving, and decision making. Intelligence is not just a reaction to changes in environmental conditions. It is also one's global capacity to learn about this environment. Persons with higher intelligence are more capable of noticing, understanding, and explaining surrounding phenomena—in various situations and forms of activities—than are persons with lower level intelligence. One belief is that people who have higher IQs have a better chance of changing our environment (Sternberg 1997).

However, such a proposition cannot reject another assumption that a person with a high IQ score and a better potential for changing the environment may also possess little or no moral values and be lacking compassion, sympathy, or kindness!

Noam Chomsky (1976), one of the most renowned specialists in human development, criticized a very popular approach to intelligence. This approach was based on an assumption that the individual's success is based on the amount of money that person makes. In fact, income and prestige are not and should not be the only measure of social success. In many countries, social accomplishment is largely determined, not necessarily by the person's ability to score high on IQ tests, but also and most importantly, by his or her survival skills. This may include the ability to (1) carry on with a

A CASE IN POINT

Rational Calculations and Moral Values

What would you do in the following situation? Imagine you are captain of a space ship that landed with a crew of 10 people on a remote planet to conduct scientific research. You learn, however, that due to some catastrophic problems, the ship cannot be launched from the planet with all the crewmembers aboard: It is 170 lb over the carrying capacity. Now the oxygen tank is almost drained. What would you do? In a famous classical series of "Star Trek," Mr. Spock, a character with superior intellectual skills—far exceeding those of other crew members—offered a very "logical" solution: To leave the least valuable crew member on the planet (where this person would die and, by this sacrifice, save the lives of the other crew members). Apparently, "less intelligent" characters opposed this heartless reasoning and offered an alternative solution. Moral values in this case overcame logical calculations.

limited supply of food and resources, (2) adapt to the environment, and (3) change the environment despite the overwhelming pressure of lawlessness, violence, pollution, and disease. Moreover, many people do not base their individual happiness, reason for working, and success only on extrinsic rewards and material factors. There are also moral satisfaction, love, friendship, and many other elements of human experience that may not be related to scores on an IQ test.

 EXERCISE 5.2

Memory and Experience

Our familiarity with a subject or topic can affect how precisely we memorize and retrieve information. Different cultural experiences, therefore, could affect the quality of our memory in particular circumstances. Consider the following sentence: *The quarterback threw an incomplete pass and his mistake forced the team to punt the ball right before the two-minute warning.* Select five people who are familiar with American football and five people who know very little or nothing about this game. Read the sentence to people in both groups. Then ask them to write down what they remembered. What kinds of results will you expect to receive? Indeed, even though it is difficult to recall all 22 words of this sentence, people from the first group (those who know football) should correctly remember most of the words. On the other hand, those who are not familiar with football will, perhaps, make several mistakes trying to convey the meaning of the sentence. Could you test these hypotheses?

 EXERCISE 5.3

Searching for a Possible Bias in Written Tests

Three-quarters of the nation's schoolchildren (sample of 60,000 in the fourth, eighth, and twelfth grades) were unable to compose a well-organized, coherent essay, according to results of a federally sponsored writing test. Most students were able to compose short essays they were asked to write. However, their writing had neither the sophistication nor proficiency expected by a national board of educators, state officials, and business leaders (Cooper, 1999). There was also a gap in the performance of different racial and ethnic groups. White and Asian students were writing better than African Americans, Hispanics, and Native Americans were. That gap was narrower in schools located on military bases, where minority students scored higher than their counterparts elsewhere. Perhaps minority students benefited from an equitable distribution of resources at the Defense Department schools and the attitudes, education, and financial security of the schools located on military bases.

However, did anyone examine the possibility of a cultural bias of the tests? Apparently no. Below are the sample questions used by the National Assessment Governing Board to test the writing skills of students in various grades. Could you examine them and write your suggestions about whether the assignments are biased against certain ethnic groups? Explain your arguments and try to achieve both sophistication and proficiency in your analysis.

> **Fourth graders.** We all have favorite objects that we care about and would not want to give up. Think of one object that is important or valuable to you. For example, it could be a book, a piece of clothing, a game, or any object you care about. Write about your favorite object. Be sure to describe the object and explain why it is valuable or important to you.
>
> **Eighth graders.** Imagine this situation! A noise outside awakens you one night. You look out the window and see a spaceship. The door of the spaceship opens, and out walks a space creature. What does the creature look like? What does the creature do? What do you do? Write a story about what happens next.
>
> **Twelfth graders.** Your school is sponsoring a voter registration drive for 18-year-old high school students. You and three of your friends are talking about the project. Your friends say the following:
>
> Friend 1: "I'm working on the young voters' registration drive. Are you going to come to it and register? You're all 18, so you can do it. We're trying to help increase the number of young people who vote and it shouldn't be too hard—I read that the percentage of 18- to–20-year-olds who vote increased in recent years. We want that percentage to keep going up."
>
> Friend 2: "I'll be there. People should vote as soon as they turn 18. It's one of the responsibilities of living in a democracy."
>
> Friend 3: "I don't know if people should even bother to register. One vote in an election isn't going to change anything."

Do you agree with friend 2 or 3? Write a response to your friends in which you explain whether you will or will not register to vote. Be sure to explain why and support your position with examples from your reading or experience. Try to convince the friend with whom you disagree that your position is the right one.

 ## CHAPTER SUMMARY

- Most definitions of intelligence include phrases such as knowing and understanding the reality around us. Intelligence is also defined as a set of mental skills that helps individuals reach a goal. Intelligence is also seen as the ability to use knowledge and skills to overcome obstacles. And finally, intelligence is defined as helping one to adapt to a changing environment.
- Intelligence is inseparable from cognition, diversified processes by which the individual acquires and applies knowledge. It usually includes processes such as recognition, categorization, thinking, and memory. Altogether, cognitive development is neither totally culturally relative nor completely uniform everywhere.
- In psychology, most attention has been given to the so-called psychometric approach to intelligence. This view is based on the assumption that our intelligence can "receive" a numerical value.

- Today various tests show differences in intelligence scores among large cultural groups. For example, in the United States, Asian Americans (of East Asian origins) score the highest, followed by European Americans, Hispanics, and lastly African Americans. Thus, on the average, African American schoolchildren score 10–15 percent lower on a standardized intelligence test than white schoolchildren.
- In an attempt to explain some group differences on intelligence test scores, Robert Sternberg suggested distinguishing between intelligence and intelligent behavior. Intelligence, from this standpoint, is a mental process that may or may not result in particular behavioral patterns. These patterns of intelligent behavior may vary from culture to culture. Something considered to be intelligent among members of one culture may not be viewed as such in other cultures.
- According to the nativist approach to intelligence, human cognitive phenomena are inborn. They unravel as a result of biological "programming," and environmental perception requires little active construction by the organism. There is evidence that heredity plays an important role in human intelligence. However, genetic links for individual differences and similarities do not imply that group differences—on the national level, for example—are also based on genetic factors.
- Some specialists imply that most intelligence tests benefit specific ethnic groups because of the test vocabulary—words and items used in the test questions. Tests may contain internal bias because they use words that are familiar to only some groups. As a result, members of these groups receive higher scores than those who do not belong to these groups.
- Many environmental conditions have been found to influence performance on intelligence tests. Among them are availability of and access to resources, variety of perceptual experiences, predominant type of family climate, educational opportunities, access to books and travel, presence or absence of cultural magical beliefs, general attitudes, and cultural practices.
- Intelligence scores are, in general, positively correlated with the socioeconomic status of the individual and the link between socioeconomic conditions and test performance shows at an early age. A child's IQ and the socioeconomic status of the child's parents are also positively correlated. An affluent and educated family is likely to provide a better material environment for a child and also has more resources to develop a child's intellectual potential than a poorer family. Poverty is responsible for a variety of indirect impacts on the intellectual development of children and adults.
- In the United States people with high IQ scores are disproportionally represented among doctors, scientists, lawyers, and business executives. Individuals with low intelligence scores are disproportionally represented among people on welfare, prison inmates, single mothers, drug abusers, and high school dropouts.
- There is a difference in the way people across cultures value and construe intelligence. For instance, the conceptualization of intelligence as quick and analytic is not shared in all cultures. If one group's concept includes being detailed and precise in responding, but the other group does not mention these features (and mentions improvisation as an element of intelligence) then precision cannot be used as a criterion according to which the two groups are compared. Certain ideological conditions may affect what people of that country value most in cognitive skills.
- Cognitive processes have cross-cultural similarity but may also develop in different ways according to specific cultural norms and societal demands. People develop cognitive characteristics best adapted to the needs of their lifestyle. Cross-cultural findings suggest that differences in categorization, memorization, labeling, creativity, and formal reasoning may be rooted in cultural factors. Various cultural groups categorize stimuli differently in terms of their specific cultural experiences associated with these objects. Many cognitive processes can develop either in similar or in

different ways according to specific cultural norms and societal demands.

- American children, generally, are allowed more freedom in choosing school activities than their counterparts overseas. The emphasis is typically placed on individual development, enjoyable activities, and respect for the child's personality. In Asian countries, on the contrary, the active promotion of the mathematical development of children is crucial. From the beginning the child learns rules of discipline, perseverance, and sacrifice for the sake of educational goals.
- Some ethnic minorities may display the so-called low-effort syndrome, or low level of motivation on intelligence tests. This typically suggests that such individuals do not try to excel on these tests because they believe that they will not go to college anyway, the tests are biased against them, and test results are unimportant.
- Overall, in developed Western societies, high IQ scores are correlated with social success. The situation with IQ testing and scores may be changing, however. There is an interesting tendency of a continuous and steady worldwide rise in intelligence test performance. Detected primarily in developed countries, this effect stands for a three-point increase in IQ scores every 10 years and may be attributed to educational efforts and technological developments.

KEY TERMS

Cognition   A general term that stands for a series of processes by which the individual acquires and applies knowledge.

Cognitive Style   An individual way in which individuals organize and comprehend the world.

Creativity   Originality or the ability to produce valued outcomes in a novel way.

Empirical Reasoning   Experience and cognitive operations drawn from everyday activities.

Field-Dependent Style   A general cognitive ability of an individual to rely more on external visual cues and to be primarily socially oriented.

Field-Independent Style   A general cognitive ability of an individual to rely primarily on bodily cues within themselves and to be less oriented toward social engagement with others.

Formal Reasoning   Basic cognitive operations based on abstract analysis of given premises and deriving a conclusion from them.

Intelligence   Global capacity to think rationally, act purposefully, overcome obstacles, and adapt to a changing environment.

Low Effort Syndrome   Low level of motivation on intelligence tests based on the belief that the tests are biased and test results are unimportant for success in life.

Nativist View   The view that all cognitive phenomena are inborn, that they unravel as a result of biological "programming," and that environmental perception requires little active construction by the organism.

Psychometric Approach to Intelligence   A view based on an assumption that our intelligence can "receive" a numerical value.

Emotion

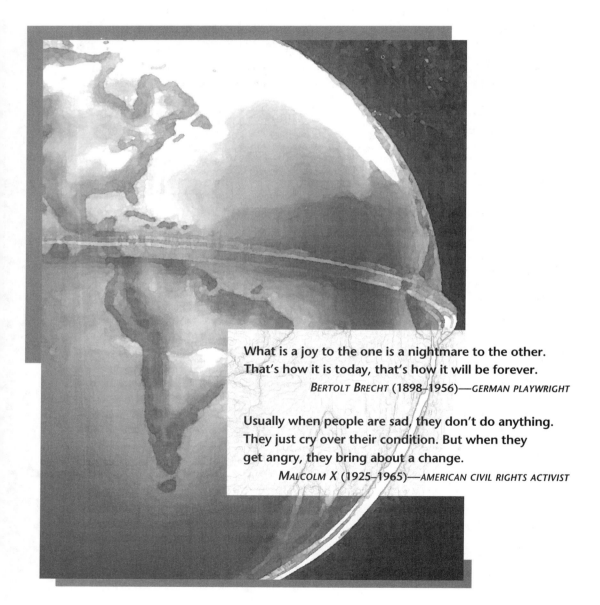

What is a joy to the one is a nightmare to the other.
That's how it is today, that's how it will be forever.
BERTOLT BRECHT (1898–1956)—*GERMAN PLAYWRIGHT*

Usually when people are sad, they don't do anything.
They just cry over their condition. But when they
get angry, they bring about a change.
MALCOLM X (1925–1965)—*AMERICAN CIVIL RIGHTS ACTIVIST*

Did you know that public kissing is not acceptable in Japan? No, this country doesn't have an antipecking law. It is simply an old and informal rule of conduct. Of course, if you travel to Japan you may recall an episode or two when young couples are kissing goodbye at a train station or airport. However, these are rare exceptions to the main rule: affection and tenderness should not be publicly displayed. Groping, kissing, hugging, and puckering are extremely rare on Japanese streets. Do not think that this cultural ban on public displays of affection is linked to the prohibition of sex. It is very much alive and prominently displayed in the Japanese media. Just watch Japanese television, especially in the late hour. Or get a racy magazine—usually sealed in plastic—from a store's top shelf. So what is so unacceptable about public kissing? Ask any person who grew up in Japan, and he or she will tell you that people in this country, from the beginning of their lives, learn how to restrain their emotions in public. It is considered a sign of weakness if an individual cannot control anxiety, fear, joy, or sadness—any form of affection—and allows others to see it. If the expression of feelings is so tightly controlled by the rules, does this mean that the emotions are suppressed in Japan to the extent that they are not felt?

Right now, at this very moment, someone in Montreal is jumping for joy because he got a job promotion. At the other end of the planet, in Jerusalem, a girl is anxiously anticipating her first batmitzvah. Stuck in traffic, an angry Moscow cab driver vents his frustration at other motorists. An army conscript in Korea is anxious before his first parachute jump. **Emotion,** or affect, is an evaluative response that typically includes some combination of physiological arousal, subjective experience (positive, negative, or ambivalent), and behavioral expression. Joy and disappointment, sadness and surprise, envy and pride, and dozens of other emotions accompany our daily lives regardless of where we live or what language we speak. We display emotions from the day we are born. We learn about them from the people around us, the books we read, and the movies we watch. Masterfully described in word, image, and sound, human emotions always draw significant interest from artists and poets. For centuries they illustrate, reflect, paint, and portray love, grief, guilt, and the excitement of human existance.

A brief educational tour through philosophy books reveals that human emotions always occupied philosophical minds. Sophisticated and fascinating observations about emotions can be found in the works of the Chinese educator and philosopher Confucius (fifth century B.C.), Epicureans and Sophists in Greece (third to fifth centuries B.C.), the Arab physician and thinker Avicenna (eleventh century), Europeans Descartes and Spinoza (seventeenth century), and many others. However, the scientific study of emotion began only recently—just over a century ago.

One of the pioneers in this field, William James (1884), offered the theory that emotion is embedded into bodily experience. The physical experience leads the person to feel aroused, and the arousal stimulates the subjective experience of anxiety, joy, and so forth. According to James, people do not jump and clap their hands because they are happy; rather they become happy because they jump and clap their hands. James even gave advice about how to feel particular emotions: *"The voluntary path to cheerfulness, if our spontaneous cheerfulness be lost, is to sit up cheerfully, and act and speak as if cheerfulness were already there. To feel brave, act as if we were brave, use all our will to that end, and courage will very likely replace fear"* (cf. Wallis, 1965, p. 156). At around the same time that James was putting forth his ideas in the United States, a Danish physiologist, Carl Lange (1885), proposed similar views on emotions. This view is now called the James–Lange theory.

Forty years later, Cannon and Bard published an alternative outlook, known as the Cannon–Bard theory of emotion. According to this approach, various life situations—such as a hairy spider crawling on your shoulder—can simultaneously elicit both an emotional experience, such as disgust or fear, and bodily responses, such as increased blood pressure or sweaty palms (Cannon, 1927). In the 1960s another theory of emotion gained popularity among psychologists. According to the theory's authors (Schachter & Singer, 1962), there are two crucial elements of emotional experience: physiological arousal and the cognitive interpretation of this arousal. In every emotion we first experience a state of physiological arousal. Then we try to explain to ourselves what the arousal means. If the situation suggests that we should experience pleasure, we call it joy. If somebody threatens us, we call this experience fear.

These theories are well established in Western psychology and are therefore called classical. However, do they explain the linkages between culture and emotional experiences? What these theories do is provide cross-cultural psychologists with at least two basic alternatives. According to one, all human emotions are universal. They have a similar underlying physiological mechanism and the specific cultural environment only applies some "make-up" on human affect. For example, in the United States a group of happy friends will "high-five" each other when their favorite team scores a goal, whereas in Europe friends are more likely to shake hands in a similar circumstance. But the joy will be felt by both groups of friends in the same way regardless of the differences in its expression. In short, sadness is sadness and elation is elation no matter where you live, in Mexico, Bosnia, Nigeria, or Vietnam.

The other alternative emphasizes both cultural origin and cultural specificity of emotion. According to this view, all human emotions may develop in specific cultural conditions and therefore can best be understood only within a particular cultural context. For example, an observer may identify a sarcastic smile on the face of a Polish worker if the observer understands both the nature of sarcasm—a form of expression in which meanings are conveyed obliquely—and the surrounding circumstances in which the sarcastic reaction was displayed.

Which one of these views received stronger empirical support? Let us consider evidence from both sides of the argument.

When We Laugh We Are Happy: Similarities of Emotional Experience

People can tell other people's emotions. Even though we do not speak someone's language, we can often understand whether this person is happy or sad. If you understand what other people feel by judging their emotional expressions, and if they can judge your emotions correctly, that means human feelings are universal. This is exactly what Charles Darwin (1872) suggested in his famous work, *Expression of the Emotions in Man and Animals.* He collected interviews from around the world and concluded that basic

A CASE IN POINT

A Dose of Laughter

It was a Thursday evening and the Jerry Seinfeld show was on television. Lyn, an exchange student, had just walked into his adviser's office. "Have you seen this show?" asked the professor, pointing to the TV set behind him. "No, this is my first week in America and I do not speak English well," said Lyn, "but I know it is a funny show." The professor raised his eyebrows. "How do you know this show is funny? You say you haven't seen it before." "Sorry," replied Lyn, "It is funny because I see people laughing on the screen."

human emotional expressions are similar because they serve an adaptive purpose. Both animals and humans signal their readiness or willingness to help, fight, or run through gestures, postures, and facial expressions. Imagine, for example, you see your friend's eyes wide open, you hear his scream, and you observe him throwing away a cup of soda. This combination of reactions might alert you to the fact that it is likely your friend is scared or disgusted by something he found in the cup. Almost immediately, you will check to see if anything—a bug?—is in your cup too. Emotions regulate social behavior and may protect people from danger. Fear and anger, for example, produce greater acceleration of heart rate than does joy. This makes sense if one thinks in evolutionary terms. Anger and fear are related to fight-or-flight responses that require the heart to pump more blood to the muscles: all in all, you have to either defend yourself or run away from a threat. In people of all cultures, fear causes a particular defensive reaction in dangerous situations. Likewise, disgust prevents us from trying potentially toxic substances such as rotten food or spoiled water (Izard, 1977).

Empirical studies demonstrate many similarities in the ways people display their feelings. A comparison of emotional facial expressions of people from Western industrialized countries and non-Western settings showed significant resemblance (Ekman, 1980). Researchers found universal patterns in the vocal expression of emotion (Bezooijen et al., 1983), and cross-cultural invariance in the behavioral expression of complex emotions such as jealousy and envy (Hupka et al., 1985).

Another interesting argument about similarities in human emotion derives from numerous studies about consistent cross-cultural similarities in the process of identification, description, and explanation of an emotional expression, for short, **emotion recognition** (Ekman, 1980; Izard, 1971). For instance, in one such study, subjects in five countries, the United States, Brazil, Chile, Argentina, and Japan, were shown photographs of people, each of whom displayed one of six emotions: happiness, sadness, anger, fear, surprise, or disgust. Most subjects correctly identified these emotions (Ekman & Friesen, 1969). People show remarkable accuracy in the interpretation of eyebrow positioning and smiling (Keating et al., 1981). For instance, smiling is universally understood as a sign of happiness, and lowered eyebrows as a sign of anger or domination. In another study, which included subjects from Estonia, Germany, Greece, Hong Kong, Italy, Japan, Scotland, Sumatra, Turkey, and the United States, Ekman and colleagues (1987) demonstrated that mixed emotional expressions, such as shame and frustration, are also visually recognizable across cultures.

Research on cross-cultural recognition of emotional intonation in the voice has yielded similar results: people typically identify the speaking person's emotion in cases in which the speaker uses a foreign tongue and the voice is recorded on tape (Albas et al., 1976; Van Bezooijen et al., 1983). In a study, subjects from Western and non-Western cultures were asked to make the face they would show when they were happy to see somebody, angry with someone, sad about bad news, and so on. These facial expressions were recorded and later analyzed. The findings suggested the existence of the same facial muscular patterns in both subject groups (Ekman & Friesen, 1978). In other words, people across cultures not only can easily recognize basic emotions, but they also use the same muscle groups to express their feelings. If so, human emotions have one common origin, that is, most likely, biological.

There is amazing similarity in the way people term emotions across different cultures and languages (Russell, 1991). In other languages there are the equivalent words for virtually every English term for emotions (Scherer et al., 1988, Scherer & Wallbott, 1994). All languages make distinctions between positive and negative affect, and this distinction is explained to young children, who begin to use words and phrases such as "nice," "mean," "good," "bad," "I like," and "I don't like" at a very early age. There are also similarities in the way in which different languages define so-called basic emotions. Although theorists may generate slightly different lists, most classifications include from five to nine emotions. Anger, fear, happiness, sadness, and disgust are present in almost every national classification. Surprise, contempt, interest, shame, joy, trust, anticipation, and guilt are present in others (Lynch, 1990; Vekker, 1977; Russell, 1991).

It is true that jealousy can hurt; however, critics argue that it is not about culture. Some men are simply more jealous than others because of their individual psychological traits and experience with women. Who is right and who is wrong in this discussion? Perhaps both sides are equally correct. On one hand we can find cultural patterns in the expression of jealousy, and on the other hand we can see tremendous individual differences in the expression and experience of it. What should you do to avoid interpersonal conflicts in such situations? At least one thing is important: willingness of both sides to negotiate and understand what is acceptable and what is not in your communication with each other.

From the evolutionary perspective, jealousy can be seen as a universal emotion that has similar roots in practically all cultures. Psychologists describe it as an indication of one's anxiety of being supplanted, or left without care or affection from another person. Nonetheless, according to one study (Buss et al., 1992), men and women experience different types of jealousy. Since a mother's primary concerns are for the care and protection of her children, many women may be looking for reliable males who have access to resources and will make them available for their children. Cross-cultural evidence illustrates that the chief selection criteria used by most women across countries are the material assets, skills, and status of a male (Schubert, 1991). In light of this reasoning, a woman's jealousy is primarily expressed about her mate's affect toward another female. Male infidelity based on emotional commitment to the other woman should be considered a threat because the man could possibly move away with his resources. On the contrary, male infidelity not accompanied by emotional attach-

CROSS-CULTURAL SENSITIVITY

M.A. is a 26-year-old legal assistant. R.R., her husband, is 35. R.R. asks his wife not to look at other men and to avoid receiving verbal compliments from her male co-workers. He argues that he follows a tradition of his home country [Egypt] where a man should be very protective of his wife. "Your wife is not a flower. You do not let others stare at her," R.R says. "My behavior is not jealousy. It is a cultural custom that many Americans do not understand."

Jealousy can have dangerous consequences. Around the world, for instance, sexual jealousy has been found to be one of the leading causes of homicides and spousal abuse (Daly & Wilson, 1988). These "crimes of passion" that are caused by jealousy attract serious attention from cross-cultural psychologists (Tsytsarev, 1997).

ment to another woman is more likely to be "forgiven." From the evolutionary view, men want to make sure that the children they rear are their own. Therefore, men in every country or culture tend to be very protective of their female partners in order to prevent them from having sexual relations with other men. Accordingly, male jealousy is likely to focus less on the female's emotions and more on whether she has "outside" sexual contacts. In this view, a man's flirting behavior is less likely to cause a negative emotion in his female partner because flirting does not indicate deep emotional commitment. Quite the opposite, a woman's flirting, which is considered a threat because in her partners' view it is associated with a possible sexual contact, would cause emotions of anxiety and anger.

All in all, supporters of the idea of the universality of human emotion argue that similar emotions exist in all cultures. We react to external events and bodily reactions with similar facial expressions, physiological changes, and subjective experiences of pleasure or displeasure. Cross-culturally, individuals are emotionally sensitive to the loss of relatives and friends, to the birth of their children, to the victories of their favorite sports team, and to criticism from others. Across cultures, sadness or grief can cause crying, anger can provoke aggression, and joy often helps people to forgive.

You Cannot Explain Pain if You Have Never Been Hurt: Differences in Emotional Experience

Many studies show that emotions may vary from culture to culture. Differences in the expression of emotional behavior, linguistic variety in the labeling of emotions, and distinct socialization practices all suggest culture-specific origins of human emotions. According to this view, people's emotions vary because they are based on different experiences that are related to the culture in which they originate.

Cultures may be at variance in the frequency and significance of common emotional reactions (Matsumoto et al., 1988). For example, some studies have pointed to cultural differences in the degree to which some groups experience positive emotions, such as joy (Markus & Kitayama, 1994b) and negative emotions, such as anger

A CASE IN POINT

A United Nations Dinner Party

Imagine you are invited to attend a New Year reception at the United Nations headquarters in New York. There you have to try many kinds of ethnic dishes prepared by the ambassadors' chefs. Among the displayed foods you find steamed beef tongue, broiled dog meat, roasted lamb brains, and a bowl of fermented horse milk. You have to try them all! Will you be disgusted by these foreign foods? Perhaps yes, if your taste for food has been developed at McDonalds or Pizza Hut. However, is it fair to suggest that your disgust, as an emotion, can be experienced only by you and not by the people who cooked these foods? The answer, of course, is: Other people can experience disgust too, but feel it in different situations. Does this mean that we all have similar emotions "within" us but that they are "activated" only in particular situations? Does this mean that our knowledge about human emotions is relative to the situation in which emotions occur?

(Solomon, 1978). Cultures also vary in linguistic descriptions of emotion. The Tahitian language, for example, has 46 different words for anger but no word for sadness. In some African languages, the same word can represent both sadness and anger. In some local Russian dialects, the phrase "I pity you" can either stand for "I love you," or indicate one's condolence.

Despite obvious similarities in the facial recognition of emotions, subjects from various cultures also vary in the degree of agreement. In one study, for example, happiness was correctly identified by 68 percent of African participants and by 97 percent of their European counterparts (Izard, 1969). The recognition rate of facial expressions on photographs was lower when subjects had little previous contact with other cultures (Izard, 1971). Schimmack (1996), after conducting a meta-analysis of the existing studies of emotion, showed that white participants were better than nonwhite participants in recognizing happiness, fear, anger, and disgust, but not surprise and sadness.

Differences in emotion recognition between representatives of two cultures may exist because some emotional expressions are cultivated in children during the socialization process and some are not. For example, in Japan, as previously mentioned, the public display of emotions is mostly discouraged because it is seen as being disruptive. This may affect the Japanese perception of people from other cultures who do display their emotions without any hesitation. For instance, a Japanese observer may see such individuals as being hyper and disruptive. Differences in the perception of emotions were found in many other countries. When Greek and British individuals observe other people in embarrassing situations, the Greeks usually overestimate the intensity of the observed emotion of embarrassment, whereas the British observers usually underestimate the intensity (Edelman et al., 1989). Such a difference may be caused by more developed norms of collectivism in Greece compared with Great Britain. Therefore, people in Greece feel more interconnected and group oriented and that makes their embarrassment more intense than it is for the British.

Now that we have learned about two distinct approaches to understanding the relationships between culture and emotion, how do we know which is correct? The first approach advocates cross-cultural universality whereas the second suggests cultural origin and specificity of human emotion (Ekman, 1994; Mead, 1975; Russell, 1994). Before we start our search for answers, consider the following case.

Emotions: Different or Universal?

Let us contemplate. Is severe pain after a stumble likely to case a negative emotion in any two individuals? Perhaps. What if one is born and raised in Puerto Rico and the other came from Iran? There is no difference: A stumble causes physical pain and pain causes a negative emotion. Should detachment from a person you love make you sad? Possibly. If you are thirsty and get a glass of water, will you experience joy? Most likely, yes. But will you necessarily feel and show your emotions exactly in the same way as others do? Not really. How we feel and how we express our feelings is based on our personality, experiences, immediate circumstances, presence or absence of people, and many other factors! For example, you may hide frustration after a clumsy fall in a public place, but scream and curse if such a fall happens in your home where no one can see you. Emotions can be seen as similar or different because we often perceive, analyze, and think about them from different points of view!

Cultural differences in emotions tend to grow larger as the level of description becomes more concrete. Here is an example. We can generally consider jealousy as sadness. Alternatively, by applying a "magnifying glass" for a more detailed analysis, jealousy may be interpreted as a blend of anger, fear, sadness, and frustration. High levels of abstraction cause us to see people from different cultures or social groups as similar in their emotions. Here we can all recall public stereotypes about "emotionless" Finns and Japanese, "hot blooded" Italians and Brazilians, and "sensuous" Arabs and French.

For a more comprehensive cross-cultural analysis of emotions, we should look "inside" the emotion. First, looking again at the definition, we should try to understand emotion as a multicomponential process (Frijda, 1986; Scherer, 1984). First, an emotion is initiated, there is an underlying physiological process for the emotion, the emotion is experienced, then it is displayed or remains hidden, it somehow affects our decisions, the emotion may cause other emotions, and it eventually fades away. Are there any cross-cultural findings that shed some light on what role culture may play in these stages? In the beginning of the chapter we indicated that emotion includes physiological arousal. Let us describe it in some detail.

Physiological Arousal

There are significant cross-cultural similarities in the underlying physiological mechanisms of emotions. Universally, we detect stimuli from our surroundings and our body. The signal then goes to the brain. The amygdala serves as the brain's "emotional computer": it assesses the affective significance of the stimulus. Therefore, irrelevant stimuli may cause no emotion. Then the hypothalamus, as a part of the limbic system,

CRITICAL THINKING

Example 1

If we limit our analysis of human emotion only to the question of whether or not an emotion is expected to occur, we will find many cross-cultural similarities among human feelings. Indeed, any starving person presumably will be happy to have a piece of bread! On the other hand, if we focus on how emotion is experienced and displayed in human activities, we are more likely to see cultural differences. Consider for example Japanese sumo wrestlers. If you have a chance to watch a sumo tournament (they are often broadcast on American television), you will discover that the wrestlers never show their emotions. Even if a wrestler experiences a tough loss, spectacular victory, excruciating pain, or the loud spectator's ovation, he remains emotionless. Not a single muscle moves on his face. After seeing these pictures one may conclude that sumo wrestlers do not experience emotions. However, it is more plausible to assume that emotions are indeed felt by the wrestlers, but they are not displayed. It takes many years of practice and education to become a professional sumo wrestler. During this time the candidates patiently learn how to hide their joy, frustration, and other feelings during the competition. In contrast to the sumo wrestler's training, South American and European soccer players are not trained to hide their emotions on the field. Instead, they may find it beneficial to exaggerate their expression of pain after a collision with an opponent because referees—observing the player's display of pain—might feel obliged to penalize the opposing team.

Other Examples

We have to pay special attention to a particular level of abstraction on which emotions are described. The very same emotion of joy, for example, may be culturally similar or cross-culturally different, depending on the level of generalization chosen for description. Perhaps many similarities in emotions are likely to be found when they are described at a high level of generality or abstraction. An emphasis in one's observations on specific emotional characteristics would perhaps highlight cultural differences. Many authors, for example, write about a *"specific"* fear that existed and still exists in people of totalitarian political cultures: these individuals are afraid of political persecution for speaking up (Smith, 1976, Gozman & Edkind, 1992, among others). However, a more *abstract* analysis may yield an interpretation of a different kind: these individuals experience a typical fear based on an absolutely adequate evaluation of a threat. As soon as the threat of persecution is eliminated, the fear may disappear as well (Shiraev & Bastrykin, 1988). Likewise, millions of undocumented aliens may experience fear of deportation from the United States. This fear is unfamiliar to American citizens if we see it as a special type of fear. Described in a more general way, this emotion loses its specificity, and fear of deportation becomes nothing more than a state of reluctant anticipation of an unpleasant event.

activates sympathetic and endocrine responses related to emotion. The brain's cortex also plays several roles with respect to emotion, particularly in the appraisal of stimuli. Moreover, the right hemisphere is believed to be responsible for the facial displays of emotion (Borod, 1992). Current research also suggests that pleasant emotions are associated with the activation of the left frontal cortex, whereas unpleasant emotions are mostly associated with the activation of the right frontal lobe (Davidson, 1992).

Cross-culturally, embarrassment has common physiological responses, and one of them is increased body temperature (Edelman et al., 1989). In a classic study researchers gave participants specific directions to contract their facial muscles in particular ways characteristic of anger, sadness, happiness, surprise, or disgust (Ekman et al., 1983). Subjects held these expressions for 10 seconds, during which particular physiological reactions were measured. The researchers found a connection between the simple act of changing facial expressions and patterns of physiological response. Different emotions produce differences in variables such as acceleration of heart rate, finger temperature, and a measure of sweat on the palms related to arousal or anxiety, also known as galvanic skin response.

African Americans in Detroit responded to frustration with sharper increases in blood pressure than did European Americans (Harburg et al., 1973). In another example, a comparison between the physiological changes reported by subjects from Southern and Northern European regions also yielded interesting results. The "hot-blooded" Southerners reported significantly more blood pressure changes while experiencing joy, sadness, and anger, whereas the "cold" northerners reported significantly more stomach sensations for joy and fear and muscle symptoms for anger (Rime & Giovannini, 1986).

But what may cause such diverse physiological reactions? Why do some stimuli cause no emotion whatsoever?

 Take away the cause, and the effect ceases; what the eye never sees, the heart never rues.
MIGUEL DE CERVANTES (1547–1616)—SPANISH NOVELIST AND POET

The Meaning of Preceding Events

Elton John, a famous British rock star, once complained about his experience in China in the middle of the 1990s. He said that in a country populated by more than a billion people, virtually no one expressed any emotion when they saw him on the street. The singer shouldn't blame himself for not being famous in China. Most people simply didn't know who he was! Indeed, the peak of his popularity came in the 1970s and early 1980s when hundreds of millions of Chinese people did not have television sets. Moreover, according to the main ideological principles reinforced by the communist government, any Western music was considered evil and was virtually prohibited. There would be, of course, a different emotional reaction if Elton John walked down the streets of London, Buenos Aires, or New York City. Surprise and excitement are typical emotions that many people experience when they suddenly meet a famous person.

There is always something that causes or initiates an emotion. A pain in your body, a lost soccer game, a meeting with a person you adore, a windy and rainy day, or an annoying flow of music streaming from a neighbor's window—many **preceding events** in our everyday lives bear particular emotional significance for us. However, do people across cultures agree that certain situations should elicit similar emotions? Do all people concede that the loss of a friend is a sad event, and that the birth of a child is a happy one? There is more than ample research data to confirm that this is the case: cross-culturally, basic emotions are generally marked by similar types of events. Let us illustrate this statement with the results of several cross-cultural studies.

Subjects from the United States, South Korea, and Samoa were asked to write stories about an event causing one of six emotions: anger, disgust, fear, happiness, sadness, or surprise (Brandt & Boucher, 1985). Then these stories were presented to other subjects for evaluation. Substantial similarities were found in the assignment of emotions related to stories among the examined cultures as well as within cultures. A year later, Wallbott and Scherer (1986) published a study that examined situations in which people experienced joy, fear, anger, sadness, disgust, shame, and guilt. Data collected in 27 countries suggested that although there were some differences among the samples, these differences were much lower than the ones within the countries! Evidence for similarity in preceding events is also shown in a study conducted by Scherer and his colleagues (1988), in which subjects were asked to describe a situation that had caused them to feel happy, sad, angry, or scared. After the task was complete, these situations were grouped into several categories. In all cultures, the most important event categories were birth and death, good and bad news, acceptance or rejection in relationships, meetings with friends, dates, temporary and permanent separation, listening to music, sexual experiences, interaction with strangers, and success or failure. In another study, both American and Malay subjects were equally accurate in their identification of emotions caused by 96 different types of events (Boucher & Brandt, 1981). Matsumoto and colleagues (1988) found a large degree of cultural agreement in how people in Japan and the United States evaluate situations that evoke particular emotions. Cross-cultural similarities were found in the perception of events that cause people to experience jealousy and envy (Hupka et al., 1985).

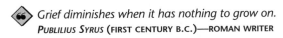 *Grief diminishes when it has nothing to grow on.*
PUBLILIUS SYRUS (FIRST CENTURY B.C.)—ROMAN WRITER

Nevertheless, the same situations can be interpreted differently across cultures, and, therefore, lead to different emotions. There is also scientific and anecdotal evidence for cultural differences in emotion-eliciting events. For example, results of a Brazilian American study suggest that stories about unusual sex and food practices are likely to elicit a reaction of disgust in the Brazilian and in less educated samples than in the American and more educated subjects, who tend not to express this emotion (Haidt et al., 1993). Most Europeans, as well as North and South Americans, for instance, consider the number 13 as unlucky and some are even afraid to live in apartment #13 or on the thirteenth floor. Kuwaiti Arabs, on the other hand, would pay little attention to this number. The living conditions in different cultures vary, resulting in the occurrence of culture-specific events that may elicit particular emotions. Fear of neighbors from a different ethnic group was one of the predominant emotions caused by the civil war in Bosnia in the 1990s. Cultural differences in antecedent events can also be related to different superstitions. People in Russia, for example, are afraid to keep an even number of flowers in a vase: an even number of flowers is typically brought to a funeral (see the Cross-Cultural Sensitivity box in Chapter 9). A Canadian student, on the other hand, is likely to be unaware of this foreign superstition and would be thrilled to receive six flowers from her fiancée.

CRITICAL THINKING

Being Alone

Have you ever had some time on your own when nobody was near you? How did you feel? Did you enjoy the time of being alone or did you long for someone to come and break the silence surrounding you? People perhaps would give different answers to these questions. "The way one feels about being alone depends on the circumstances," most of us would say. Researchers give more specific answers. In Western cultures, for example, being alone is likely to be regarded as an occasion of privacy that causes feelings of gratification or happiness (Mesquita et al., 1997, p. 271). On the contrary, for some Eskimo groups, the state of being alone is interpreted as a cause of sadness. Tahitians perceive loneliness as causing weird feelings and fear. For some Aboriginals of Australia "sitting alone" prevents one from experiencing happiness (see Briggs, 1970; Myers, 1979; Levy, 1973). Do you think that such a distinction between Western and non-Western experiences of being alone is too simplistic? Do you think that all human beings would consider any long isolation as an unpleasant event? Indeed, there are works that suggest that cross-culturally, loneliness is seen as a disturbing emotional event (Bowlby, 1982). Try to find some facts that would either confirm or disprove a hypothesis about cross-cultural similarity of emotions elicited from the condition of being alone. Most importantly, try to distinguish between conditions such as "to be alone" as a temporary situation and "loneliness" as a permanent state in one's life.

Liem (1997) analyzed the experience of shame and guilt in first- and second-generation Asian Americans and European Americans. The participants were asked to describe situations in which they felt guilty or were embarrassed. Some differences were found between the first-generation immigrants. According to this study, Europeans experienced guilt as an anticipated moral transgression: guilt indicates that a person violated an internal standard of ethical behavior even though there is no public notice of such violation. In the stories reported by first-generation Asian Americans the typical guilt-related situation is based on the feeling of failed or unfulfilled duty. For European Americans, shame centers on the presence of other people: it is shameful that other people discover your inappropriate actions. For first-generation Asian Americans shame also involves the presence of outsiders. However, another element is present that is not typical in the picture of shame among European Americans. This is a group to which the person belongs, usually his or her family. Therefore, shame is also felt as regret for letting some important people down. It is interesting that the differences in experiencing shame and guilt are insignificant between the second generation of Japanese Americans and European Americans.

 Solitude is the play field of Satan.
VLADIMIR NABOKOV—TWENTIETH-CENTURY RUSSIAN AMERICAN WRITER

As you saw, a large number of preceding events can produce similar emotional responses in most human beings, regardless of their cultural origin or current identity.

These studies suggest a high degree of similarity in human emotional sensitivity to particular life events or conditions. There is also evidence that particular emotions can be elicited by culture-specific events. People who are not familiar with various cultural norms and traditions may not recognize such emotions and may make mistakes in communications. What kinds of mistakes? Imagine, for example, a host who offers a beef sandwich to a Hindu guest at a party.

Emotion as an Evaluation

We are usually aware of our emotions, and we feel good or bad, scared, surprised, frustrated, or relieved at different times. Despite tremendous individual variations, there are some cultural norms and rules that regulate our **evaluations of emotions.** There is evidence that people may carry cultural beliefs about which emotions are most significant or suitable to particular social roles or social settings (Ellsworth, 1994; Markus & Kitayama, 1994a, White, 1994). For example, some emotions could be considered inappropriate and therefore suppressed, such as feeling envious of your brother's or sister's success. Other emotions may be absolutely legitimate and even desirable, such as feeling joy after recovering from an illness. These evaluations are attached to the situation in which an emotional response is anticipated. Pay attention, for example, to how many people react to so-called "ethnic jokes." They may laugh at a joke that ridicules members of a particular ethnic group, if the joke teller is a representative of the ethnic group about which the joke is being told. If there is no ethnic "match" between the teller and the joke, or the teller is not your good friend, you may feel disappointed or angry.

People of different cultures evaluate words that indicate particular emotions in similar ways (Frijda et al., 1995; Roseman, 1991). To illustrate, words that stand for anger are appraised similarly by Japanese, Indonesian, and Dutch subjects as indicating the experience of something unpleasant, as preventing one from reaching one's goals, or as standing for something that is unfair and for which there is something responsible.

Stipek (1998) examined how people would evaluate some hypothetical situations in a comparative Chinese American study that involved 200 students from Zhejiang Province in China and the University of California at Los Angeles. The participants were given six written stories. Half of the situations involved the participants themselves: as a person who is caught cheating, who is expecting admittance to a prestigious university, and who participates in a sports game. The other half of the cases suggested the involvement of significant others. The study showed that, in general, Americans tended to attribute pride to the cases of personal accomplishments. On the contrary, Chinese were more likely to experience pride for outcomes that benefited others. Moreover, compared with Americans, Chinese respondents reported stronger positive emotional reactions to other people's achievements. For example, Chinese participants claimed that they would feel more pride if their child was accepted into a prestigious university than if they themselves were accepted into that same university. Americans claimed that they would feel equally proud in both circumstances.

The author of this study believes these differences might best be explained by the emphasis on the collective nature of emotional experiences in China. The Chinese social orientation is based on the Confucian ideal that individuals should be mainly concerned about their place in the network of human relations. This is not a new hypothesis. As many scholars point out, Chinese tend to identify themselves in the context of significant others (Triandis, 1990). As the authors mentioned, the findings of the study examined earlier are consistent with the demands of prevailing communist ideology of the People's Republic of China. This ideology—as all other types of Communist ideologies—demands the primacy of the group over individual interests.

The results of this study can be critically evaluated, in part, from another point of view. The Chinese system of higher education is quite different from the American system because college admission is based on highly competitive written and oral examinations (some other countries have the same system of college entrance exams). Every year, a substantial number of students are not accepted and many have to wait another year to try again. In the United States, a person who is not accepted to Harvard or Stanford can apply to another school that accepts students with lower SAT scores and grade point averages. Therefore, it is expected that Chinese participants will rate these "acceptance to college" situations as more stressful than they are rated by the U.S. participants. As to sporting events, the differences in emotional experience can also be traced to public attitudes about sports in general. In socialist countries—and China is one of them—sports are considered an important human activity and winning in sports indicates societal progress. Because the government sponsors sports activities, a loss or victory becomes a public issue. If you win, you make a contribution to your group, school, province, or your entire country.

We Are Expected to Feel in a Particular Way

Emotional experiences can certainly be influenced by social norms or popular expectations. **Feeling rules** refer to particular cultural rules about how to feel in particular situations. We often consider whether our laughter (an expression of joy) or head shaking (an expression of disappointment) might evoke either positive or negative reactions from others. Emotional experiences that contradict some basic social norms could be quite different from those emotions that are in line with the existing customs. Moreover, an emotion can be felt differently considering the context in which it is displayed or observed. A Chinese father may be deeply saddened by the fact that his son is leaving home for college. However, the father's emotion may also be suppressed by his unwillingness to show his weakness in front of other family members. Joy may be experienced in a totally different way when it is accompanied by the loss of something or somebody significant. For example, recall how in Titanic, Armageddon, and Independence Day—popular American movies in the 1990s—the final celebration of survival is marked by the death of loved ones. Depending on the context, the same emotion, such as either grief or joy, can be experienced in various ways.

There is evidence suggesting that individuals feel more certain about the meaning of events and give more certain emotional responses when there are clear norms on how to interpret these events and how to respond to them (Mesquta & Frijda, 1992; Frijda & Mesquita, 1994). For example, a relationship exists between cultural and religious beliefs and anxiety related to the individual's sexual practices. For instance, women who are more orthodox (traditional) in their religious beliefs are found to complain about greater menstrual discomfort. Catholic women, for instance, show more anxiety than Protestant women do during the time of their periods (Paige, 1973).

Sometimes, however, our anticipation of what people should or should not feel leads to mistakes. In one study, Tsai and Levenson (1997) compared 22 Chinese American and 20 European American dating couples, all of whom were college aged. The participants were asked about the emotion they experienced when they tried to resolve interpersonal conflicts. The study also included physiological measurements of the participating couples. A common expectation would be that Chinese Americans would place a greater emphasis on emotional moderation (see Chapter 1) than European Americans. However, the results of the study drew a different picture. There was neither disparity in feelings nor differences in most measures of physiological responses found in the results. Perhaps the college campus environment created particular norms that reinforced certain types of feelings similar in the two ethnic groups.

How People Assess Emotional Experience

When people try to evaluate their emotional experience, they make assessments not only about the experience of the emotion along the dimensions of pleasure or displeasure, but also along several other dimensions. For example, people try to determine whether their emotions (1) are caused by a familiar or unfamiliar event, (2) suggest the existence of an obstacle, (3) create a sense of being in charge or being out of control, (4) increase or decrease self-esteem, and (5) cause praise, reproach, or mockery by one's group (Ellsworth, 1994; Matsumoto et al., 1988; Wallbott & Scherer, 1986; Frijda, 1986). Expectedly, the frequency with which these dimensions are used in emotional assessment can vary. For example, those events that may have an impact on the individual's family or social group have greater importance in collectivist than in individualistic cultures. On the contrary, the events that may affect one's self-esteem, material success, and professional achievement become the primary emotional concerns of most people in individualistic cultures (Markus & Kitayama, 1994b). Research also suggests that some of our emotions are evoked by cultural beliefs (Abu-Lughod, 1986; Rosaldo, 1980). For instance, a simple phrase such as "an independent Palestinian state" may have little significance for a welder in Michigan. The same phrase, however, will bear emotional meaning for millions of people living in the Middle East. For some it will indicate pride and honor, for others it will evoke frustration.

Socialization practices may also affect the process of appraisal. Markham and Wang (1996) compared samples of Chinese children in Beijing and Australian children in Sydney. The children were compared in terms of their ability to evaluate faces—both Chinese and white—and in their ability to express their opinions about the emotions they judged. An initial hypothesis was that the wide range of resources available to Australian children plus a diversity of social experiences that a child has in contemporary Australian society—including television and the Internet—would improve the child's ability to evaluate emotional expressions. However, the authors did not find any substantial differences in responses between the studied groups. Moreover, some Chinese children received better scores than their Australian counterparts. Why was this difference found? The authors explain this phenomenon by referring to the family norms in both societies. Typically, Chinese parents demand a higher degree of discipline from children than Australian parents. The more consistent Chinese socialization might reduce the range of evaluations applicable to emotional interpretations compared with the range of such interpretations in Australia. The authors also indicate that children from smaller families have been found to be superior in recognizing emotions. As you know, China's official demographic policy is "one family, one child" and this policy indicated the participation of smaller nuclear families in the Chinese sample.

Another study yielded comparable results. Jolley and colleagues (1998) studied how children in China and Great Britain described the mood of some picture characters. The study revealed that Chinese children were able to interpret emotions in pictures at an earlier age than the British children. The authors explain such a difference as a result of the two countries having different traditions of education. According to the Chinese art program for elementary schools—which is regulated by the central government—children are supposed to learn techniques of drawing and teachers should concentrate on how to interpret exact messages conveyed by picture characters. In Great Britain, as in most Western countries, art education curriculum may be different from school to school.

 Worry often gives a small thing a big shadow.
SWEDISH PROVERB

 Worries go down better with soup than without.
YIDDISH PROVERB

When Emotions Signal a Challenge: Cross-Cultural Research on Stress

The realization of a challenge to a person's capacity to adapt to inner and outer demands is called **stress.** This definition points to two important aspects of stress: (1) stress is a psychobiological process and (2) stress entails a transaction between people and their environments (Lazarus, 1993). If the challenge does not decrease, the organism remains constantly aroused and the body continues to divert its resources to respond to the demands (Cannon, 1932). One of the most stressful events any individual can experience is the death of a family member or close friend. Daily hassles—from the absence of food to a lack of free time—can also be sources of stress. Catastrophes and disasters such as earthquakes, floods, violence, or other traumatic events affect millions of people around the world. Cross-culturally, many survivors of such traumatic events continue to experience recurrent nightmares and difficulties in relationships, and are prone to anxiety and depression (Koopman, 1997; Nadler & Ben-Shushan, 1989; Allodi, 1991; Herman, 1992). A serious form of life stress that is increasingly confronting people throughout the world is culture shock or acculturative stress (see Chapter 12).

The actual amount of stress is difficult to measure because people have different coping strategies and evaluate stress using dissimilar criteria. The ways people evaluate stress, as well as the situations they consider stressful, are culturally determined, but also may depend on individual traits (Lin & Peterson, 1990). Poor living conditions, political instability, violence, and many other factors can also contribute to people's evaluations. Even educational systems may have an impact on how students experience stress. For example, test anxiety has repeatedly shown as lower in the United States than in other countries, such as Brazil, South Africa, and Egypt (Guida & Ludlow, 1989; El Zahhar & Hocevar, 1991).

Studying stress in African Americans, Jenkins (1995) suggested that blacks may have developed a special emotional style of behavioral response that reflects the cultural value placed on the individual's ability to manage stressful life events. In African American culture, from the author's view, emphasis is placed on the active managing of difficult situations without displaying nervous tension. Thus a difference between European Americans and African Americans may be found in their emotional assessments of reality. In blacks, their emotionality is displayed more often than it is in whites. This type of African American emotional response may be passed on from generation to generation as a cultural norm.

 EXERCISE 6.1

Imagine you conduct a Polish-American study and find that subjects in the United States and Poland have dissimilar perceptions of guilt. Will this difference indicate the existence of a psychological gap between these two nations or will it instead indicate differences in the meaning of *guilt* (English) and *vina* (Polish)?

 A human being should be aware how he laughs, for then he shows all his faults.
RALPH WALDO EMERSON (1803–1882)—AMERICAN POET AND PHILOSOPHER

Expression of Emotion

Eight-year-old Tom is looking at the scene of a car wreck with his eyes opened wide in a fixed stare. He is not hiding his fear. Anybody can read it on Tom's face. Tom's parents, who came from Taiwan, did not teach him how to express fear by turning his lips down. His American schoolteachers did not train him to lower his eyebrows in case of a threat. He expresses his fear in the same way billions of people on earth might display it through their facial expression, posture, and gestures.

The rules of emotional expression—called **display rules**—are acquired primarily during socialization (Birdwhistell, 1970). Every culture has particular sanctions that support display rules or patterns of emotional expression considered appropriate within that culture (Ekman & Friesen, 1975; Ekman et al., 1982). Throughout the history of human civilization, one way of managing an emotion has been to learn how to control its manifestation. It is interesting that such display rules are primarily concerned with the restraining of emotional expressions (Ekman, 1982). Beginning presumably with the Chinese thinker Confucius (fifth century B.C.) and the Greek philosopher Plato (fourth century B.C.), emotion has been viewed as a disruptive force in human affairs. Plato asserted that reason must restrain the passions, which otherwise distort rational thinking. Aristotle and Democritus (fourth century B.C.) had a similar view, suggesting that emotions are located in the "lower," more primitive level of the soul, whereas thinking is located on the "higher," more advanced layers. Stoicism, an ancient Greek and Roman school of philosophy, held that human beings should be free from the power of passion in order to accept both the fortunes and misfortunes of life. Most major world religions, for example, Islam, Judaism, Buddhism, and Christianity, introduced the rules by which human beings could become independent of "destructive" emotional forces, such as envy, pride, vanity, and jealousy (Smith, 1991).

There are at least two criteria for assessment of emotional expressions: frequency and intensity. For example, in the United States, many parents commonly say, "I love you" to their children and vice versa. Contrarily, in the Ukraine, Russia, or Belarus, such a verbal expression of affection is considered to be too "strong" and intrusive and may be expressed only in a few critical life situations.

If emotions are cultural and social products, the cultural norms and environmental factors should regulate the ways people express their emotions (Kitayama & Markus, 1995). Perhaps then it shouldn't be a surprise that surveys reveal a very low admission level of personal happiness and lower overall expression of one's satisfaction with life in countries going through economic and social crises. Russia and Ukraine, for instance, scored the lowest on individual expression of happiness among other European countries studied (Glad & Shiraev, 1999). Likewise, an ongoing social conflict may elicit and reinforce particular emotional responses. To illustrate, in several experimental situations, Israeli subjects responded more aggressively than their American counterparts (Margalit & Mauger, 1985). When a social situation requires an individual to be "tough," one's display of anger may become an adaptive response to stressful situations of ethnic conflict.

There are some cultural variations in the display of sadness. For instance, samurai wives in Japan smile when they are informed about their husband's death. Tahitians report feeling tired in response to losses (Levy, 1973). Crying among the Bedouins in the Egyptian desert (Abu-Lughod, 1986) is considered a sign of weakness, whereas in other Islamic cultures, such as the Turkish, it is considered an acceptable social response in particular circumstances. Display rules differ not only by culture but also by gender. Some evidence suggests that women probably express emotions more intensely and openly than do men. This is true for all emotions except anger. Women are generally more comfortable in displaying emotions such as love, happiness, shame, guilt, and sympathy, which foster affiliation and care-taking. Men, on the other hand, avoid these "soft" emotions that display, according to their opinion, male vulnerabilities (Brody & Hall, 1993). For men raised in traditional cultures, a complex emotion of honor consists of being in control of their own family and of outperforming or impressing other men. Women's honor in these cultures consists of conforming to the rules of modesty and faithfulness. Likewise, shameful events have been reported to elicit different reactions in men and women: men try to restore their honor by showing off through aggression, or by retaliation; women will react to shameful events with submissive behavior and avoidance (Abu-Lughod, 1986; Blok, 1981). During the process of anticipatory socialization (see Chapter 8) boys and girls receive different sets of instructions about the display rules for various emotions. Indeed, children as young as 3 years old recognize that females are more likely to express fear, sadness, and happiness, and males are more likely to display anger (Birnbaum, 1983).

The presence or absence of other people may also have various impacts on emotional expressions. Ekman and Friesen (1975) asked Japanese and U.S. students to watch stressful films in isolation and in the presence of an experimenter. Without the subjects' awareness the emotional expressions on their faces were recorded in both conditions. For the two samples, similar expressions were found in reaction to the same movie episodes when the subjects were alone. However, in the presence of the experimenter, the Japanese subjects showed far fewer negative expressions than did the Americans. Does this experiment partially explain why the Japanese are often seen by others as unemotional?

In another study, researchers asked American and Japanese students living in the United States to report on the frequency with which they experienced certain emotions in daily life (Markus & Kitayama, 1994b). The Americans reported an overwhelmingly greater frequency of experiencing positive than negative self-relevant feelings, but there was virtually no such effect among the Japanese. One can suggest that such differences could be caused by the Japanese subjects' unwillingness to reveal their emotions to strangers. There are also data suggesting that in Japan, for instance, the happiest people are those who experience primarily the "socially engaged emotions" of interdependence (such as friendly feelings). In the United States, on the other hand, the happiest people are generally those who experience the socially "disengaged" emotions of independence, such as pride (Matsumoto, 1994).

However, these trends in expressive behavior were not confirmed in more recent comparative Japanese American studies. In one of them, the participants from both countries were asked to rate their anticipated degree of comfort in the expression of independent and interdependent emotions (Stephan et al., 1998). The results did not reveal substantial differences between the samples. In another study, Aune and Aune (1994) studied three groups of subjects, Japanese Americans, Filipino Americans, and European Americans; each group completed self-report questionnaires in which they evaluated both positive and negative emotions experienced and expressed in romantic relationships. The participating students were asked to think about the relationship they have with their partner and the emotions they felt and expressed. The participants were also asked to rank their emotions using a special scale. The researchers did not find substantial cultural differences in how negative emotions are experienced and expressed in romantic relationships. Low scores on anger expression among the American participants were perhaps due to substantial societal pressure to suppress the expression of negative emotions in daily settings.

How can we interpret the results of these studies? Can we say then that collectivism and individualism have little impact on how people feel and communicate their emotions? We shouldn't rush to such a categorical judgment. Do not forget that the subjects in these studies were people of "mixed" cultural backgrounds: they were born in the Philippines and Japan and were studying in the United States. Perhaps in the contemporary world people learn from other cultures and begin to understand many issues and behaviors that have not been available to them prior to the new era of satellite television and the Internet. Japanese and American society are more interconnected today than they were 10 years ago. For instance, if a Japanese woman from a traditional family is shown a photograph of a nude beach, this could cause a reaction of extreme shame. However, this woman can travel abroad, to Europe or Brazil, for example, and learn more about other cultures and their practices related to nakedness. Her experience may not change her negative opinion about public nudity, however her emotional response will perhaps change.

 EXERCISE 6.2

Embarrassment is regarded as a form of social anxiety, an unpleasant emotion excited by the realization of impropriety in one's behavior. A study of five European cultures (Greece, Great Britain, Italy, Spain, and Germany) showed that blushing and increased temperature plus smiling and grinning were reported consistently across cultures (Edelman et al., 1989). There are some other observations of embarrassment, such as sticking out one's tongue, as people in the Indian Orissa culture do (Menon & Shweder, 1994). Ask at least 10 people, preferably from various cultural backgrounds, to imagine that they encounter a very embarrassing situation. How would they react in terms of facial expression and body language? Ask them to play the role of an embarrassed person. Immediately write down what you see. Will they touch their face? Will they scratch their head? Will they stick out their tongue? Will they smile and turn away? Bring your observations to class to find out whether there are some consistencies in the way people describe their embarrassment.

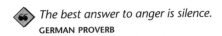 *The best answer to anger is silence.*
GERMAN PROVERB

When Emotion Hurts: Cross-Cultural Studies of Anger

Cross-culturally, **anger**—an emotion aroused by one's perception of being interfered with or threatened and/or overt or covert activities of attack or offense—is seen as an interpersonal emotion because its experience usually involves some norm violation committed by other people. There are several universal anger-evoking antecedents. They include problems in relationships, injustice, interaction with strangers, inconvenience, achievement, bad news, death, and several separation-related issues (Wallbott & Scherer, 1986; Averill, 1982; Mauro et al., 1992).

However, when a person speaking in a foreign language says, "I am angry," one should be careful not to rush to judgment because most human languages have several labels for anger (Tanaka-Matsumi, 1995; Klineberg, 1938). As an example, it is interesting to compare *anger*, as an English word, and, for instance, *song* in the Ifaluk (Pacific region) language. Both of these words refer to emotions involving appraisal of harm from another person. However, they can differ in the kind of action they bring about. *Anger* often leads to the tendency to return the other person's harm. *Song*, on the other hand, produces action that aims to alter the behavior of the offending person. Such action may include, of course, aggressive behaviors, but it may also consist of avoidant behavioral reactions, such as refusing to eat and attempted suicide (Lutz, 1988).

People get angry and interpret this emotion according to the norms of the culture in which they live. For instance, Japanese cultural traditions strongly inhibit public display of private emotions, particularly negative ones. This culture emphasizes homogeneity and conformity as necessary conditions for the maintenance of the society's interdependent network (Johnson, 1993). In collectivist cultures anger is seen as an emotion of disengagement from the society, a threat to its integrity (Markus & Kitayama, 1994b) and, therefore, is generally discouraged. In individualist societies, such as the United States, the display of anger could be judged differently because people generally recognize other people's right to independence and self-expression.

A CASE IN POINT

Different Ways of Expressing Emotions

An interesting illustration of how emotions are displayed appears in a study of the Utku Inuit culture (Briggs, 1970). The researcher found a virtual absence of anger among members of this small ethnic group. Does this observation suggest that these individuals do not experience anger at all? Not necessarily. It was found that anger can still be vented in at least two ways: against dogs and against those persons who were expelled from the community.

Please be aware that judgments about the source of anger are not necessarily caused by the norms of collectivism or individualism. In some preliterate, and apparently collectivist societies, people may believe that prolonged illness is the result of sorcery initiated by someone else (Whiting & Child, 1953). Hence, the ill person or his or her relatives may direct anger about the illness toward another person, that is, an accused sorcerer. When Chinese second graders were asked to assess several "emotional" stories, they attributed a significantly higher number of angry reactions to the stories' characters than did American second graders (Borke & Su, 1972).

 Just as courage imperils life, fear protects it.
LEONARDO DA VINCI (1452–1519)—ITALIAN ARTIST AND THINKER

Emotion and Inclination to Act

Very often, international sporting events provide an observer with excellent opportunities to make some cross-cultural comparisons. For example, when the French soccer team scored the first goal during the final 1998 World Cup championship game, one of the French-speaking radio commentators happily proclaimed that the French can win only if they score first. Positive emotions are crucial for their continuous hard work on the field. If the opposite team scored the first goal, this would be a disaster for the French players: bad news could have discouraged them from playing well. These remarks illustrate a point that has a significant meaning in our lives: emotions influence people's actions. Cross-culturally, the influence of emotions can cause us to avoid and reject some people, help and accept others, dominate or submit to some, and respect or despise others (Frijda, 1986; Frijda et al., 1995).

Some cross-cultural studies show similarities regarding action readiness evoked by certain emotions. In the extensive cross-national study cited earlier (Scherer & Wallbott, 1994), subjects were asked about whether their emotional experience had led them to move toward, move away from, or move against the object of emotion. Significant cross-cultural similarities were found. Joy caused more approach behaviors, anger elicited more aggressive behaviors, and withdrawal was the most common reaction to sadness, disgust, shame, and guilt.

There are some cultural differences in how emotions affect behavioral readiness. In a comparative study of Japanese, Dutch, and Indonesian subjects, an impulse toward a hostile behavior, as a response to anger, was more common for the Dutch group. A more "internal" impulse was common in the Indonesian and Japanese groups. The Japanese group more often reported feelings of helplessness and urges to protect themselves. They also expressed a wish to depend on someone else and a feeling of apathy at a higher level than participating Dutch and Indonesian subjects (Frijda et al., 1995). These results partly confirm findings obtained in other studies that suggest that personal dependence on intimate others as well as acceptance by others are significant components of emotional experience in Japan (Lebra, 1983; Markus & Kitayama, 1994b).

Similar emotions may produce different behavioral patterns. There is a difference, for example, in the coping styles of children in the United States and Mexico. Children from the United States tend to attempt to master stressful situations actively. This is most likely because they are encouraged to embrace an active style of coping with events by modifying their physical, social, and interpersonal environments (Diaz-Guerrero, 1979). On the contrary, Mexican children are socialized to adopt a more passive style of coping with events by modifying themselves rather than confronting obstacles in the environment. This cultural difference may be based on specific value orientations. An emphasis on the mastery of one's environment is more typical of highly technologically developed societies. Other cultures emphasize harmony and natural order. Therefore, active coping styles can be preferable in some cultures but not in others (Kluckhohn & Strodtbeck, 1961). One of the lessons we can learn is that coping with stress is relative to its cultural context. More importantly, some stress-coping therapeutic strategies that have been proven successful in one culture may not work well in other cultures.

 The tongue of a wise man lays behind his heart.
ALI IBN-ABI-TALIB (600–661)—FOURTH CALIPH OF MUSLIMS

Emotion and Judgment

In the famous classical American TV series *Star Trek*, one of the main characters, Mr. Spock, is a half-human, half-alien being who is naturally free from any emotions. His behavior is directed by pure logic. He is, of course, a fictional character, a product of creative imagination that often has little to do with real-life experiences. In reality, emotions and thought are closely linked. Emotions can influence the way people make judgments and predictions (Mayer et al., 1992). Vice versa, people's thoughts and beliefs influence their emotions. There is ample evidence that emotional states may shape cognitive processing in different ways. People who are depressed, for example, tend to underestimate the probability of their own success and overestimate the probability of bad events occurring in the future (Beck, 1991). People who experience positive affect differ from those who experience negative affect. The former have better memory and use different strategies for problem solving and categorization (Clore et al., 1994). Anger has been found to lead to more personal accusations, whereas sadness leads to a tendency to understand negative circumstances as more due to fate, chance, or unluckiness (Keltner et al.,1993).

Emotions lead to belief changes: certain emotional appraisals can cause perceptual generalizations and stereotypes. For example, an individual's negative experience with, and emotional feeling toward, a representative of a particular ethnic group can cause prejudice toward all members of that particular group. There was a significant difference found between Japanese and American subjects in their attribution of anger toward other people. Apparently, the Japanese subjects were more reluctant to identify anger as being caused by other people than were the Americans (Matsumoto et al., 1988; Scherer et al.,1988). Japan is a collectivist culture and perhaps societal interdependency is a factor that makes the inclusion of anger in cognitive attributions,

A CASE IN POINT

Victory, How Sweet It Is!

We began this chapter with a story about how rarely people in Japan expose their emotions in public. We want to add a final illustration with another vignette. This one is about the final game of the 1999 Little League World Series between Japanese children from Osaka and their American competitors from Phenix City, Alabama. When Japanese pitcher Kazuki Sumiyama threw his last fastball to strike out the American team in the last inning, he and his teammates knew that they had won the world championship! Throwing their gloves in the air, screaming and raising their arms high, 20 Japanese boys did not hide the natural eruption of their emotions. They jumped, screeched, squealed, bumped into each other, hugged each other, waved to the spectators, jumped again, laughed, and did all of those crazy things that a very happy person might do! Where was that Japanese self-restraint and self-control? What about the unwritten rule that bans public displays of emotion? We can offer many explanations for this episode. The most valuable will be that one should study human emotions in the cultural and social contexts in which they occur. Cross-culturally, people appear to have the potential to experience the same basic emotions. However, cultural differences and subsequent socialization practices encourage people to experience particular feelings, suppress others, and be emotionally involved in particular issues to which other people remain indifferent, and vice versa. Therefore, whether you are a nurse, doctor, teacher, police officer, or educated specialist, you should develop knowledge about cultural norms, display rules, and specific situations that underline the picturesque world of human feelings.

which can be a potentially destructive force, difficult. Physical violence may be interpreted in accordance with individual beliefs. Researchers have found that prisoner-activists with particularly strong political or religious convictions show the most emotional resilience to torture compared to those who do not hold such beliefs (Basoglu et al., 1994).

EXERCISE 6.3

Tietelbaum and Gieselman (1997) examined cross-race recognition for white and black faces with participants from four racial and ethnic groups: whites, blacks, Latinos, and Asians. The researchers found that same-race identifications tend to be more accurate than cross-race assessments. In other words, people from the same ethnic or racial groups have a tendency to evaluate pictorial emotions and moods more accurately than people from other social groups. The differences in accuracy were statistically significant in the range of 10 to 15 percent. It was also shown that being in the state of a pleasant mood increased accuracy of facial recognition within same ethnic groups. Another finding was that Latino and Asian participants had less difficulty recognizing emotions on white faces than on black faces.

Question: The authors believe that these results can have implications for everyday life situations, especially in cases in which the personal testimony of a witness leads to an arrest by the police. What do you think these implications are?

 EXERCISE 6.4

The following assignment was inspired by Bram Stroker's masterpiece, Dracula. *Mark or underline those segments that might evoke particular emotions in the reader. Do you expect every literate person—when he or she is reading this piece—to experience similar emotions? Do you think that there could be some cultural differences in the perception of this piece? Please explain your opinion.*

He began taking out the screws, and finally lifted off the lid, showing the casing of lead beneath. I was trying to stop him, I still believed that it was a bad dream, a nightmare. He only looked at us and said: "Now we will see it." Then he made a small hole, which was, however, big enough to admit the point of the saw. I had expected a rush of gas from the week-old corpse. We doctors, who have had to study our dangers, learned how to protect ourselves. I expected the worst and drew back. But the professor, holding up the candle into the aperture of the coffin, motioned me to look. A cold shivering wave convulsively went through my body. The coffin was empty.

In a second or two, I put myself together and said, with my voice shaking: "No, it is impossible, professor. I mean . . . some of the undertaker's people may have stolen the body. Maybe . . . it is your bad joke, professor. . . . What did you do with her body, what did you do to her?"

"Nothing, my friend; she is now beyond our control," replied the professor. "She joined the world of Un-Dead; she is a vampire, *nosferatu*. They cannot die, but they do not live as well."

Suddenly, as I turned my head, my heart grew cold. I saw something white moving between the tombs. I raised the lantern. It was she. Her lips were pink with fresh blood that had trickled over her chin. She still was moving closer to me, and with dreadful and diabolically sweet grace said: "Come to me, my friend, my lover. I need you, I want you. Trust me, I want to be with you. . . ." She was beautiful, so beautiful. . . . Screaming, the professor sprang forward, pushing me away. I saw a golden crucifix in his raised hand. Momentarily, her face changed. I swear to God I have never seen such a horrible face in my life. The color became livid, the eyebrows wrinkled in the form of a snake, and the blood-stained mouth grew to an open dark square. She was shaking in convulsions for a few seconds and then passed into the coffin through the tiny interstice. "Take this stake in your left hand, the hammer in your right hand. Point over her heart," said the professor. I did what he said. When they began the prayer for the dead, I drove the stake in. The disgusting thing in the coffin writhed with a horrifying scream. A hideous, blood-curdling screech came from the opened red lips. The sharp white teeth clamped together, the open mouth percolated crimson foam. The body twisted in wild contortions. In a minute the terrible task was over.

CHAPTER SUMMARY

- Classic theories of emotion provide little empirical evidence of cultural influences on emotional experiences. Trying to clarify the impact of the cultural factor in human emotions, cross-cultural psychologists have pursued at least two theoretical models. According to one, human emotions are universal and culture has a limited impact on them. The other view represents an assumption about the cultural origin and cultural specificity of emotion. Supporters of the universality of human emotion argue that similar emotions exist in all cultures and all emotions have similar underlying physiological mechanism.

- Compelling arguments about similarities in human emotion arrive from numerous studies about consistent cross-cultural similarities in emotion recognition and in the way people name emotions across different cultures and languages. Supporters of cultural specificity of emotion suggest that concrete emotional realities vary significantly from culture to culture. Differences in the expression of emotional behavior, linguistic variety in the labeling of emotions, and distinct socialization practices are all taken as evidence for the culture-specific origin of human emotions. According to this view, people learn how to feel and interpret other people's affects. This learning of emotional experience is related to the culture from which it originates.

- Emotions can be seen as similar or different because we often perceive, analyze, and think about them from different points of view. If we limit our analysis of human emotion to the question of whether or not an emotion is expected to occur, we will find many cross-cultural similarities among human feelings. We have to pay special attention to the particular level of abstraction on which emotions are described. Moreover, any emotion may be culturally similar or cross-culturally different, depending on the level of generalization chosen for description.

- Perhaps many similarities in emotions are likely to be found when they are described at a high level of generality or abstraction. An emphasis in one's observations on specific emotional characteristics would perhaps highlight cultural differences.

- It is useful to understand emotion as a multicomponential process. It generally includes the following components: preceding event, physiological response, assessment, expressive behavior, and change in some element of cognitive functioning. Cross-culturally, specific types of elicitors mark basic emotions. Despite tremendous individual variations, there are some cultural norms and conditions that regulate emotional experience. Some cultural differences may still be found in the different degrees to which certain emotional responses are tolerated or valued. Human emotional expression is generally acquired in the process of socialization. Cultural differences may result in differences in emotion-related cognitive processes. The prevalence of one particular emotion or of certain ways of experiencing an emotion can affect people's specific attitudes, beliefs, and even views on life.

- Human beings have the potential to experience the same basic emotions. However, our cultural differences and subsequent socialization practices encourage us to experience particular emotions, suppress others, and be emotionally involved in particular issues to which other people remain indifferent. Therefore, psychologists should gain knowledge about cultural norms, display rules, and specific and universal antecedents of various emotions and examine them within particular cultural contexts.

KEY TERMS

Anger An emotion aroused by being interfered with or threatened and overt or covert
activities of attack or offense.

Display Rules Patterns of emotional expression considered appropriate within a particular culture, age, or social group.

Emotion An evaluative response (a positive
or negative feeling) that typically includes
some combination of physiological arousal,
subjective experience, and behavioral or
emotional expression.

Emotion Recognition The process of identification, description, and explanation of an
emotional expression.

Evaluations of Emotions An individual assessment of emotions according to certain criteria or principles.

Feeling Rules Particular cultural rules about
how to feel in particular situations.

Preceding Events The environmental circumstances and individual reactions that have a
strong impact on particular emotional experiences.

Stress Perception of a challenge to a person's
capacity to adapt to inner and outer demands.

CHAPTER 7

Motivation and Behavior

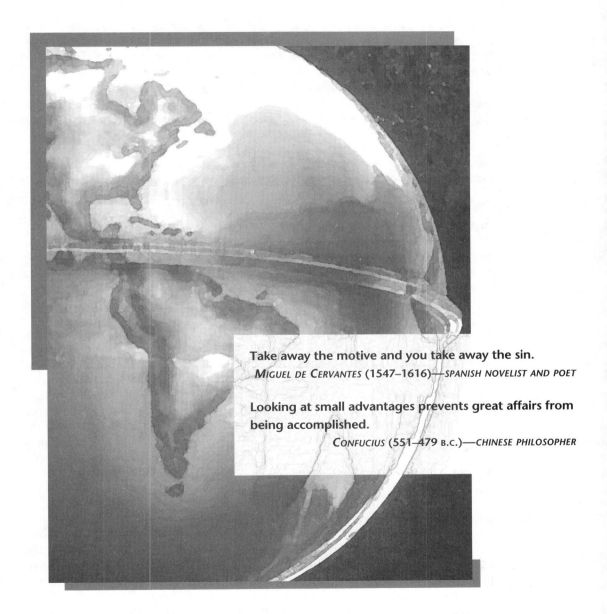

Take away the motive and you take away the sin.
MIGUEL DE CERVANTES (1547–1616)—SPANISH NOVELIST AND POET

Looking at small advantages prevents great affairs from being accomplished.

CONFUCIUS (551–479 B.C.)—CHINESE PHILOSOPHER

Daniel Crocker was a 38-year-old professional who lived peacefully in suburban Virginia, U.S.A., with his wife and two children. One day he quit his job, consulted his minister and family, and boarded a plane to Kansas, where he willingly confessed to strangling a woman 19 years ago.

Convicted for the bombing of the World Trade Center in New York, Ramzi Ahmed Yousef allegedly said in the courtroom: "I am a terrorist and I am proud of it." He received a life sentence plus 240 years for the crime.

Clementia Geraci, 3 months pregnant, made the decision of her life when doctors told her that her breast cancer had spread. She could fight the cancer aggressively and have an abortion, or she could take less hazardous cancer drugs and carry the baby to term but risk her own life. She gave birth to her son, Dylan. Four months after his birth she died.

Continuous harassment, abuse, insults, and, finally, a 16-year imprisonment did not break Nelson (Rolihlahla) Mandela. Over the years, his beliefs grew stronger, and his motivation and faith became an extraordinary symbol of black resistance against racism in South Africa. He became South Africa's first black president.

Soviet dictator Joseph Stalin refused to exchange his son—a Red Army officer and prisoner of war—for a German general captured earlier by the Soviet troops. Stalin allegedly said that one wouldn't exchange a captured soldier for a general. Stalin's son was later killed by the Nazis.

Newspaper articles reveal a lot about human behavior. However, they usually say very little about what motivates people to take extraordinary steps. What causes their determination, stamina, and will power? Where do people find resources to pursue their goals? Religion? Instincts? Rational calculations? Individual desires or collective goals? To survive we all need to breathe, eat, and avoid unnecessary pain and discomfort. But where do other needs come from? Do we learn about greed, aggression, and success? Does culture have any influence on our needs?

Motivation is a condition—usually an internal one—that initiates, activates, or maintains the individual's goal-directed behavior. The nature of human motivation is a subject of discussions and continuous attempts to find a universal theory that would explain it. Sociobiologists, for example, generally believe that biological factors best explain social behavior. Some sociological theories claim the nature of human motivation is social or economic. Classical psychologists have also contributed to the theory of motivation by determining major psychological mechanisms that underlie basic human needs. Let us briefly examine several well-established theories of motivation. A critical examination of these approaches provides cross-cultural psychologists with valuable ideas that can be used to analyze specific kinds of human motivation.

Sociobiology: A Glance into Evolution

The origin of human motivation is biological, according to sociobiology. Human beings make rational decisions, develop arts and sciences, and build up modern technologies. Still, despite obvious cultural and economic achievements, people remain a part of the larger biological universe. Above all, people need to survive. The *natural selection* principle, first described by Charles Darwin in the nineteenth century, becomes a key interpreter of human behavior in sociobiology. Due to genetic variations, some organisms are more likely to survive than others. Those who survive, pass on their "advantageous" genes to their offspring. Over many generations, genetic patterns that promote survival become dominant. For instance, hunters become successful seekers and killers of animals and gatherers become excellent finders of berries, roots, and fruit. Herbert Spencer (1954) asserted that the struggle for survival within the human species motivates people to compete for scarce resources. Individuals who are skillful competitors, who are fit for the struggle, will succeed and prosper. The unfit, or those who lack the motivation to compete, will fail. Life is unjust, but who says it should be? (Summer, 1970). Survival needs can be individual and collective. Baldwin (1991), for example, suggested that the principle of collective survival is part of the psychology of African people. Continued existence of the group—and not necessarily individual survival—is closely linked to the collective responsibility and interdependence of Africans. Perhaps this explanatory principle is applicable not only to African culture, but also to most social and ethnic groups that have been oppressed or continue to live under oppression.

The sociobiological approach to human motivation generally fails to explain the diversity of human needs and overlooks the influence of social, cultural, and religious factors. For example, personal wealth and birth rate are negatively correlated: nations that have high income per capita usually have low birth rates. According to sociobiology, the more threatened people are economically, the more children they will have, hoping that some of them will survive. On the other hand, economic security guarantees that the child will live and, therefore, people are not as motivated to have more children (Schubert, 1991b). This link has been proven in many countries around the world. However, the "wealth–birth rate" correlation is not proven in rich Arab nations of the Persian basin that continue to have high birth rates.

Theories of social instincts emphasize the universal role of basic **instincts**—relatively complex and inherited biological mechanisms, similar in humans and animals. A founder of Russian experimental psychology, V. Bekhterev (1921), wrote about the inborn "social reflexes" that determine human actions. Social reflexes are universal for all people in all cultures and cause humans to act purposefully, overthrow governments, write music, and commit crimes. A French social scientist, A. LeBon (1896), believed that "destructive instincts" possessed by all humans convert into behaviors of the big crowds: rioters, for example, are driven by their destructive impulses. Another important instinct—social contagion—makes the intentions of one person easily spread through the group. G. Tarde (1903), a prominent scientist from France, suggested that everything in human behavior—envy, vanity, friendship, hatred, and love—is the result of the natural process of imitation. According to Tarde, different social conditions, including national traditions, customs, and norms, are maintained because of people's natural instinct of imitation. All in all, these and many other theories of social instincts attempt to offer simple and attractive explanations or analogies that could be suitable for the analysis of human motivation and behavior across cultures. Yet psychological research yields little empirical evidence of the existence of human instincts as "preinstalled" software that causes human action.

In contrast to sociobiological theories, the sociological approach emphasizes the crucial role of social factors in determining individual motivation. We illustrate the sociological approach by describing two theories.

Social Science: See the Society First

Consider, for example, the views of Max Weber (1922). As we mentioned earlier in the book, he drew a line between two types of societies: preindustrial (traditional) and industrial (nontraditional). People in preindustrial societies are inseparable from traditions and customs. In these societies, people's desires and actions are viewed as appropriate and inappropriate on the basis of their links—or lack thereof—to the existing customs and rules. For example, married couples in traditional societies are not likely to pursue divorce. It is inappropriate behavior because it destroys the traditional family. Capitalist societies, on the contrary, endorse rationality as a pillar of human motivation. People deliberately assess the most efficient ways of accomplishing a particular goal. If two spouses decide that they cannot live together any longer, they could break up their marriage. Why? Because this act serves their best interest. In such cases, reason overcomes emotion, calculation replaces intuition, and scientific analysis eliminates superstition. The scarcity and value of their time often motivate people in modern societies, whereas in traditional cultures time is not viewed as a commodity (see Chapter 10).

Another prominent sociologist and economist, Karl Marx, preached that an economic condition of inequality activates human needs (Marx, 1867). Each society is divided roughly into two large and antagonistic social classes. People of the same social class, but of different ethnic groups, have much more in common than people belonging to the same ethnic or national group, but to an antagonistic social class. The oppressed want their share of resources, whereas the oppressors want to keep the status quo. Despite its attractiveness, Marxism failed to explain many other noneconomic aspects of human motivation. For example, it is easy to show that social equality, unfortunately, does not stop aggression and violence. Similarly, economic inequality does not necessarily cause hostility among people.

The next step is an overview of basic psychological theories of motivation: drive and arousal theories, as well as psychodynamic, humanistic, and cognitive approaches.

Drive and Arousal: Two Universal Mechanisms of Motivation

An internal aroused condition that directs an organism to satisfy some physiological need is called a **drive.** One of the central concepts of motivational theories is **need,** a motivated state caused by physiological or psychological deprivation (such as lack of food or water). The goal of behavior is to attain a state of stability or balance within the individual. Stimuli, such as hunger and pain, energize and initiate our behavior. Traditionally, needs are divided into two categories: *biological* and *social.* Biological needs are universal and direct human behavior toward self-preservation. Indeed, we all have to eat to survive. Social needs direct people toward establishing and maintaining relationships. The organism motivated by a need is said to be in a *drive state.* Being in a drive state, humans exhibit goal-directed behavior. The environment may press an individual to fight against an enemy, pray, and/or develop particular skills (Murray,

1938). The pressure of poverty may generate a need for financial security, causing a person to work harder and get an education. Influenced by different circumstances, another individual chooses a violent confrontation with the society that, in this person's view, caused his or her poverty.

Arousal theories of motivation suggest that people seek to maintain optimal levels of arousal by actively changing their exposure to arousing stimuli (Yerkes, 1911). Unlike hunger and thirst, the lack of sensory or other experience does not result in a physiological imbalance. But both human beings and animals always seek sensory stimulation. Ukrainian men might play chess on the park bench, an Uzbek man might stop by a tea house for a chat, and a Boston student might pay 40 dollars to see a Red Sox game. Each culture offers its own repertoire of activities, which people are motivated to seek out.

The Power of the Unconscious: Psychoanalysis

The central concept of psychoanalysis, originally developed by Sigmund Freud (1938b), is the unconscious. The unconscious is the level of consciousness that contains the thoughts, feelings, and memories that influence us without our awareness, and that we cannot become aware of at will. All humans are born with two basic drives: the life instinct and the death wish. All the tendencies that strive toward the integration of a living substance, such as loving, liking, helping, caring, building, and creating, are driven by the life instinct. The death wish represents all the tendencies toward aggression and death. To survive the individual tends to destroy alien objects and people.

The individual's personality is comprised of three major levels. The most primitive part of the personality is the Id, the component of the personality that contains inborn drives (the death wish and life instinct) and that seeks immediate gratification of its impulses according to the pleasure principle. A newborn child's behavior is guided by this principle: infants in all cultures are unaware of social rules.

Gradually, a growing child faces an increasing number of regulators of his or her behavior that systematically appear in the form of restrictions. The especially strict restrictions are usually applied to his or her developing sexual interests and aggressive impulses. This indicates the beginning development of the Superego—the level of the personality that acts as a moral guide restraining the original impulses. The Superego represents the values and the cultural standards of society, transmitted to the child through parents and other adults. Surrounded by the Id and the Superego is the Ego, a level of the personality that lets us adapt to external reality by making compromises between the Id, the Superego, and the environment.

Obviously, psychoanalysis is criticized from both theoretical and empirical points of view. Some argue that psychoanalysts overemphasize the power of unconscious motivation, inflate the meaning of the child's sexuality and aggressiveness, and lack the empirical data that would support the initial hypotheses. However, cross-cultural psychologists can use many classical psychoanalytic ideas, such as ones about the role of cultural symbols and rituals.

Humanistic Theories

These theories generate some interest among cross-cultural psychologists. They focus on human dignity, individual choice, and self-worth. Abraham Maslow (1970), a pioneer of Humanistic psychology, proposed that humans have a number of innate needs that are arranged in a hierarchy in terms of their potency (Table 7.1). Maslow grouped these needs into five categorical levels: physiological, safety, love, esteem, and self-actualization. Once an individual has satisfied the cluster of needs at a particular level, he or she is able to progress to the next hierarchical level. Thus, for example, people typically are not prompted to seek acceptance and esteem until they have met their needs for food, water, and shelter.

Maslow noted that as one ascends the hierarchy of needs, one becomes less animal-like and more humanistic. If the person has been able to satisfy adequately the needs in the first four levels, he or she is in a position to fulfill the highest order needs, namely, to actualize one's unique potential. According to Maslow, once a person enters the realm of **self-actualization**, he or she becomes qualitatively different from those who are still attempting to meet their more basic needs. The self-actualizing person's life is governed by the search for "being-values" (B-values), such as Truth, Goodness, Beauty, Wholeness, Justice, and Meaningfulness.

In contrast to most personality theorists preceding him, Maslow created his theory by studying healthy and successful people, rather than clinical cases of psychopathology. His interest in self-actualizing people began with his great admiration for Max Wertheimer (one of the founders of Gestalt psychology) and Ruth Benedict (the renowned cultural anthropologist). After discovering that these two individuals had many characteristics in common, Maslow began to search for others with the same qualities. The group that he finally isolated for more detailed study included Abraham Lincoln, Thomas Jefferson, Albert Einstein, Eleanor Roosevelt, Albert Schweitzer, Benedict Spinoza, Adlai Stevenson, and Martin Buber—all Europeans or European Americans.

Based on his informal research, Maslow developed a composite, impressionistic profile of the optimally functioning, mature, and healthy human being. Maslow concluded that self-actualizing persons exhibit a number of similar characteristics, includ-

TABLE 7.1	Abraham Maslow's Hierarchy of Needs
Level 5:	*Self-Actualization Needs*
Level 4:	*Esteem Needs*
Level 3:	*Belonging and Love Needs*
Level 2:	*Safety Needs*
Level 1:	*Physiological Needs*

Based on A. Maslow, *Motivation and Personality*, 1970.

CRITICAL THINKING

A Different Self-Actualization?

Let us explore this notion by conducting a little thought experiment. Imagine that some other theorist, with a distinctly different set of values, were to utilize Maslow's method of delineating the characteristics of self-actualization by studying his own heroes—who, for the sake of argument, happen to be Joseph Stalin of Russia, Fidel Castro of Cuba, and Mao Tse-Tung of China. Given this alternative scenario, what are some of the qualities that define the "self-actualized, optimally functioning, healthy human being?" How about authoritarian leadership traits? Egocentric orientation? Obsession with power? Need to conquer? Love of war? Paranoid ideas?

ing (1) an accurate perception of reality, (2) a continued freshness of appreciation and openness to experience, (3) spontaneity and simplicity, (4) a strong ethical awareness, (5) a philosophical (rather than hostile) sense of humor, (6) a need for privacy, (7) periodic mystical ("peak") experiences, (8) democratic leadership traits (see Chapter 11), (9) deep interpersonal relations, (10) autonomy and independence, (11) creativeness, (12) a problem-centered (rather than self-centered) orientation, (13) a resistance to enculturation, and (14) an acceptance of self, others, and nature.

A CASE IN POINT

One Need–Different Behaviors?

Would you agree that social needs are transposable? Do you think that an inability to satisfy one's needs in a particular area could motivate a person to search for a way to satisfy those needs in other areas? For example, it is suggested that not all politicians become involved in public affairs because of their need to join politics. Political careers in different cultures may have diverse origins. But in general, the political career could have provided satisfaction for the leaders' individual needs and an opportunity for further expression of their creative skills or frustration. As Betty Glad wrote, U.S. president Jimmy Carter's career was propelled by his desire for recognition "in some field," rather than a strong, overwhelming interest in a political career (Glad, 1980). Richard Nixon, former U.S. president, at the beginning of his career failed to obtain a job in a major New York law firm. Joseph Stalin, a Soviet dictator, in his youth was an ill-famed terrorist. Lech Valesa, the leader of an anticommunist movement in Poland, was a frustrated electrician. Adolf Hitler, the most notorious dictator of the twentieth century, tried first to become an artist. Vaclav Havel, the first president of the Czech republic, for many years was a dissident writer. Nelson Mandela began his career as a lawyer. Could you give other examples? Do you think that human needs are basically universal and what differs is the set of circumstances that surrounds people? In other words, different life events motivate us to pursue different goals because of dissimilar environmental circumstances that we encounter. Do you agree?

Do you think that Maslow's theory is a valid depiction of the fully functioning person, or, instead, is a reflection of Maslow's own subjective value system? Did Maslow mix ethical and moral considerations with his logic? Consider, for example, his portrayal of self-actualizing people as open, realistic, spontaneous, possessing democratic leadership traits, resistant to enculturation, and accepting of self, others, and nature. Is this an objective description of human fulfillment? Or is it a *pre*scription—masked as a *de*scription—of Maslow's own subjective ideals? As noted by M. Brewster Smith (1978), perhaps Maslow simply selected his personal heroes and offered his impressions of them.

Although the structure of needs presented by Maslow may be appropriate for individuals of all cultures, the relative strengths of the needs are culture specific. Self-preoccupation could be seen as a Western characteristic not so dominant in some other cultures. The Chinese hierarchy of values, for instance, includes the promotion of interconnectedness, in contrast to the emphasis on self-development in Maslow's version. In one study, Nevis (1983) revised Maslow's hierarchy of needs, and argued that one of the most basic needs of people in communist China is the need to belong, rather than physiological needs. Moreover, self-actualization could manifest as a devoted service to community. If a person self-actualizes by means of contributing to the group, this individual is realizing the value of collectivist self-actualization!

Maslow acknowledged that his theorizing and research on self-actualization lacked the rigor of strict empirical science. He fervently believed, however, that it was imperative to begin the process of rounding out the field of psychology by attending to "the highest capacities of the healthy and strong man as well as with the defensive maneuvers of crippled spirits" (1970, p. 33). Further, Maslow maintained that it would be misleading to believe that science is value free, since its methods and procedures are developed and utilized for human purposes.

A similar theory of motivation was formulated and empirically tested within a different cultural environment by the Soviet psychologist Arthur Petrovsky (1978), who claimed the existence of a collectivist orientation in most Soviet people. The individual is able to fulfill maximum potential when he or she accepts and internalizes the goals and values of the society. In both Chinese and Russian examples, environmental demands, socialist ideology, and traditions (like the Confucian work ethic in China, or a communist moral code of behavior in the Soviet Union) advocated harmony and cooperation, but not individualist determination, which is usually promoted in the West.

Learning and Motivation: Cognitive Theories

On October 6, 1998, Fox Television network broadcasted a new Guinness world record: In front of a shocked audience, a man swallowed several pounds of live worms. Was this behavior self-actualization or something else? Maybe greed? How about vanity?

Cognitive theories maintain that people are aware of their thought patterns and therefore can control their motivation and behavior. People learn what they want and how to achieve rewards, mastery, and affiliation. There are two types of motivation:

intrinsic and extrinsic. **Intrinsic motivation** engages people in various activities for no apparent reward except the pleasure and satisfaction of the activity itself. Edward Deci (1972) suggested that people engage in such behaviors for two reasons: to obtain cognitive stimulation and to gain a sense of accomplishment, competency, and mastery over the environment. In contrast, **extrinsic motivation** comes from the external environment. Examples of extrinsic rewards include praise, a high grade, or money given for a particular behavior. Such rewards can strengthen existing behaviors, provide people with information about their performance, and increase feelings of self-worth. In childhood, people begin to learn about both intrinsic and extrinsic rewards. For example, in one study it was found that educated American children displayed a stronger capacity for delaying their expectations for an immediate reward than less educated children, who showed the opposite trend (Doob, 1971). Differences in gender socialization may cause different motivational outcomes. A study of American, Polish, and German youth (Boehnke et al., 1989) showed that in all three samples girls preferred intrinsic motives more frequently than boys. Perhaps achievement-oriented motivation was part of the socialization of the boys in the studied nations.

Emphasizing the importance of learning and rational choice, cognitive theories can be useful in cross-cultural research. Let us now examine several specific types of human motivation. We will analyze hunger first, then move to achievement motivation, and finally we will examine sexual and aggressive motivation.

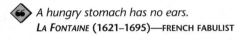

A hungry stomach has no ears.
La Fontaine (1621–1695)—**French Fabulist**

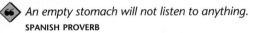

An empty stomach will not listen to anything.
SPANISH PROVERB

A Carrot and a Beef Tongue: Hunger and Food Preference

This is obvious: to live, people have to eat. There are no cultural exceptions: hunger indeed is a biological need. The body transforms food into energy for further growth and functioning. Our eagerness to eat is pushed by a physiological state (i.e., bodily chemistry and hypothalamic activity in the brain) and pulled by our learned responses to external stimuli. The biological nature of hunger explains many cross-cultural similarities in eating preferences. People in all cultures learn to salivate in anticipation of appealing foods. Our preferences for sweet and salty tastes are genetic and universal. For most children, candy is a most desirable food product. However, individual experience creates particular taste preferences. For instance, when people are continuously given highly salted foods, they develop a liking for excessive salt (Beauchamp, 1987). Thus, a person who grew up in New Orleans or Syria will be likely to consider many types of Scandinavian food tasteless.

Typically, cultural norms and traditions regulate our eating habits, determine what we consider tasty and tasteless, and establish social taboos on particular foods and food products. Arab Bedouins could eat the eye of a camel, which most Europeans would find disgusting. In some European and Asian countries, beef tongue is a deli product, whereas for most North Americans it is unacceptable. Similarly, most North Americans will refuse to eat dog meat. This type of food is acceptable in Vietnam. Moslems eat beef, but Hindus wouldn't dare touch it. On the other hand, Moslems—as well as many Jews—stay away from pork. People from other ethnic and religious groups could eat pork without hesitation. In general, people typically are cautious about trying novel meat-based products and foods (Pliner & Pelchat, 1991). However, with repeated exposure, our appreciation for the new taste typically increases. In addition, exposure to a novel food product increases our willingness to try another (Pliner, 1982; Pliner et al., 1993).

When Hunger Causes Distress: Eating Disorders

Is it true that eating disorders are more common in the West than they are in non-Western countries? That is correct. Eating disorders are more common in young white females in industrial societies (countries such as Canada, the United States, European countries, Japan, and Australia) than they are in the young females of other countries (Mumford, 1993). Two types of eating disorders, *anorexia nervosa* and *bulimia*, are both life-threatening illnesses. Being preoccupied with their body weight, people who suffer from an eating disorder—more than 90 percent of them are women—go on starvation diets and fasting, or engage in persistent food expulsion (i.e., vomiting, punishing exercises) to maintain a desirable body weight.

Cultural norms have a significant impact on whether an individual develops a preoccupation with thin-body ideals and acquires an intense fear of gaining weight (*DSM-IV*, 1994). In most cultures, certain aspects of the female anatomy became signals of how feminine and sexual a woman is. Today, in Western cultures, thinness is a major aspect of the definition of attractiveness, which increases perceived femininity. Along with some psychological factors that may predispose an individual to develop an eating disorder, social factors such as cultural models of beauty, fashion trends, and peer pressure could contribute to the formation of a self-image of being obese, fat, and unattractive (Lips, 1993). In many nontraditional cultural settings, attractiveness is associated with a smaller, thinner body shape. A larger, rounded form is associated with the "wife and mother" stereotype that many younger women desperately try to avoid (see Chapter 10).

Victory and Harmony: Achievement Motivation

When the Brazilian soccer team took second place at the 1998 World Cup in France by losing the final game, many players were crying. They were grimly upset, sad, and frustrated because of the heartbreaking loss. Throughout their lives, they dreamed of becoming world champions. Their ultimate dream did not come true. Even though most of them were millionaires playing for prestigious international soccer clubs, something was missing in their lives. And that "something" was more valuable than money. That missing element was the experience of the most important victory in soccer.

People constantly strive for achievement and excellence. Take a look at masterpieces of human creativity, the pyramids in Egypt and the Eiffel tower in Paris. Turn to a sports channel on television and see how athletes of different national, religious, and ethnic backgrounds compete for excellence. Read the poetry of Nizami, the great son of Persia, and any novel written by literary genius Gabriel Garcia Marquez of Colombia. People try to achieve what others could not. **Need for achievement** is a social need that directs people to constantly strive for excellence and success, influence and accomplishment. Activities not oriented toward these goals are not motivating and are usually performed without commitment.

Are we born with such motivation to achieve? One of the leaders in early studies of achievement motivation, David McClelland (1958), gave a categorical "no" to this question. He demonstrated that achievement motivation is rather learned during childhood. It might be acquired from parents who stress excellence and display affection and emotional rewards to their children for high levels of achievement. During the individual's life, a wide range of social and psychological factors could further influence achievement motivation. If there is no such example set for the child, he or she will not develop the need for achievement.

Particular social norms may be linked to this motivation. For example, industrial managers in Czechoslovakia (then it was a unified communist country) were found to be significantly lower on achievement motivation than their counterparts in the United States (Krus & Rysberg, 1976). It was found that American 11- to 12-year-old children already displayed more competitive and individualistic motivation than Chinese children of the same age (Domino, 1992). In another study, American mothers repeatedly chose significantly more difficult achievement goals for their children than Mexican mothers (Madsen & Kagan, 1973). In a classic research study on motivation, McClelland (1987) analyzed children's stories in 22 cultures with respect to the degree to which the stories showed themes of achievement motivation. He then related these levels of motivation to measures of economic development in the studied countries. Achievement motivation scores were highly correlated with economic growth of the children's countries! In other words, the greater the emphasis placed on achievement in the stories told to children in various nations, the more rapid the economic development in these nations as the children grew up.

Do these results suggest that people in capitalist and industrialized nations have higher achievement motivation than people living in other countries? The evidence collected by researchers yielded a positive answer to this question. For instance, in a cross-national project that involved more than 12,000 participants, Furnham et al. (1994) also showed a strong relationship between individual achievement motivation and economic growth. In particular, economic growth correlated with attitudes toward competitiveness. The stronger these attitudes, the higher the achievement motivation. The higher the achievement motivation, the greater the rate of economic growth. Using this argument, Ogbu (1986) attempted to explain lower levels of achievement motivation of black children at school. He argued that there is a specific cultural attitude that interferes with the achievement motivation. This attitude is linked to an assump-

CRITICAL THINKING

Achievement Motivation and Wealth

Let us think again about the results suggesting that achievement motivation is higher in economically advanced countries (Inkeles & Smith, 1974; McClelland, 1961). As we already know, we have to be cautious when we interpret any correlational data. Correlation does not necessarily prove that high achievement motivation *causes* economic growth. It is quite possible that a country's economic prosperity stimulates the development of achievement motivation in many successful citizens. Why? Here is the reasoning: "If I know that my effort will be rewarded, I will strive for achievement and excellence. On the other hand, if I know that because of poor economic conditions and an intrusive government, my individual effort will not be rewarded, it will be difficult to convince myself to desire achievement." Still, some psychologists suggest that studying achievement motivation could provide us with insights into why certain countries rise to economic prominence at particular times in their history (Lefton, 2000). Do you agree?

tion—proven during the years of racial segregation against blacks—that success at school does not necessarily lead to success in American society.

One of the characteristics of high achievement motivation is entrepreneurship. This is a trait that gives rise to new ideas and initiative (Miller, D. 1983). Punishment generally does not promote the generation of new ideas. In addition, in families with authoritarian parents, children develop a relatively low level of achievement motivation (Segall et al., 1990). As a nine-country study revealed, entrepreneurship is typically associated with high power distance, or tolerance for relative inequality in the workplace, high individualism, low uncertainty avoidance, and high masculinity (McGrath et al., 1992). Data obtained on an American sample (Zheng & Stimpson, 1990) proved a difference between entrepreneurs and nonentrepreneurs in four psychological characteristics of entrepreneurship, such as innovation, achievement orientation, self-esteem, and personal control.

 Where ambition ends happiness begins.
HUNGARIAN PROVERB

 Falling hurts least for those who fly low.
CHINESE PROVERB

It shouldn't take much imagination to realize that any two individuals may develop two different types of achievement motivation: low and high. One strives for excellence and success, the other is happy doing what is required and does not need recognition from others. What definitely is intriguing is the idea of cultural differences in motivation. Do the results of the studies—mentioned previously—suggest that there are high- and low-achievement-oriented nations and cultures?

This question brings the debate about cultural differences in achievement motivation to a new level. The key to the answer is that achievement or success can be under-

CROSS-CULTURAL SENSITIVITY

People often do not realize the extent to which they distort information when they stereotype. When Britain's Prince Phillip was visiting a high-tech company near Edinburgh, Scotland in 1999, he spotted a poorly wired fuse box and consequently made a remark to the company manager: "It looks as though it was put in by an Indian." The royal spokesperson apologized for the remark but you can imagine how offensive it was to millions of hardworking and high-achieving Indians and their descendants living around the world.

stood in several ways. So-called **individualist-success motivation**—the type of motivation measured in most studies cited so far—affects one's attitudes and actions and is directed to the attainment of personal goals. On the contrary, **collectivist-success motivation** directs a person to connect with other people; the individual's contribution is seen as beneficial to the members of a particular group or society in general (Parsons & Goff, 1978).

Each society chooses standards for excellence and always determines what type of goals—individual or collective—a person is expected to achieve. The individualist type prevails among people in Western cultures, such as the United States, France, and Germany. The collectivist type is more common in Eastern cultures, such as India, Korea, and Japan (Maehr & Nicholls, 1983). In Japan, for example, striving for success is motivated more often by a concern for the reaction of others than by the pursuit of personal satisfaction (Gallimore, 1974). Within Chinese culture, collective achievement orientation is regarded as most valuable (Yang, 1986). In Korea, Thailand, and China, there is a special kind of work ethic, according to which future-oriented and harmonious interpersonal networks are essential for business success (Cho & Kim, 1993). It was also found that Australian Aboriginal students placed greater emphasis on collectivist intentions, compared with non-Aboriginal students (Fogarty & White, 1994).

Discussion about collectivist and individualist achievement motivation can be found in many cross-cultural studies. Let us consider, for instance, education. Task orientation is a form of achievement motivation that involves the goal of developing one's ability to learn and grow, whereas ego orientation implies illustrating one's superiority over others (Nicholls, 1989). In a comparative study of Chinese and American elementary school students it was found that these two types of achievement orientation were present about equally in the samples studied. This result came as a surprise to researchers. China—as was suggested previously—is typically portrayed as a country with a great emphasis on the importance of interpersonal harmony, modesty, and cooperation. The sampled Chinese students, therefore, were expected to have lower ego orientation than American students. One explanation might be the Chinese educational system, which is different from the American system in that it is highly selective and competitive. To succeed, one has to be better than others, especially in terms of grades. Therefore, success in competition with other students for better grades can be the primary source of motivation for the Chinese student (Xiang et al., 1997).

Interesting results were obtained in a bicultural study of Chinese and European New Zealanders. Chinese students were found to have stronger motivation toward academic and professional achievement than their European counterparts. However, Chinese students also showed a greater sense of obligation toward fulfilling their parents' expectations, and they were more fearful of parental response to failure than Europeans students. According to Chinese cultural norms, parents demand and expect high achievement from their children at school. On the other hand, students must fulfill parental obligations, and must appreciate parental sacrifice for the sake of their children (Sue & Okazaki, 1990). Maybe this would explain the fact that by the late 1990s, Chinese immigrants in New Zealand achieved great success in educational and occupational areas, getting higher status positions in proportions larger than any other ethnic groups, including Europeans (Chi-Ying Chung et al., 1997).

There is further evidence of culture-related complexity in achievement motivation. An interview with more than 500 Anglo-Australians and Sri Lankans was conducted to compare achievement motivation in members of both groups. The individualist orientation was more prevalent in Australians than in Sri Lankans, who were predominantly family and group oriented (Niles, 1998). However, both groups were similar regarding the preferred means of achievement of their goals: they both strongly endorsed individual responsibility and the work ethic. The results did not show that one group was more motivated than the other. Most importantly, the study suggested that people are motivated to achieve different goals through different means, or different goals through the same means. It is also argued that achievement can have different meaning in different cultural settings. In short, achievement-oriented behavior is not necessarily individualistic.

CRITICAL THINKING

Collectivism or Individualism?

In 1998 Japan and other industrialized nations in Southeast Asia were going through a painful period of economic turmoil and decline. Some popular American talk-radio hosts repeatedly suggested that the economic crisis in Asian markets was caused by a cultural factor and, in particular, a collectivist approach to the management of economies. Asian governments pursuing collectivistic principles were very protective of their countries' economies and underestimated the main principle of free enterprise: economic and financial success comes only as a result of free competition. On the other hand, the rapid pursuit of individualism in achievement motivation can have negative social and psychological consequences. For example, it happened in Russia, where the "capitalization" of the society—historically built on socialist egalitarian principles—could guarantee neither economic growth nor people's satisfaction with the reforms.

Questions: Do you agree that capitalism in a society requires the acceptance of individualistic values? Or maybe you think that there *is* room for collectivist values in a capitalist society? Would you share an opinion that there are countries and cultures that have difficulties accommodating individualistic principles of free competition?

The discussion about individualist and collectivist dimensions in achievement motivation started to heat up in the 1990s, in the context of the great economic success accomplished by Japan, Singapore, Taiwan, and South Korea. The proponents of an idea about a "unique" East-Asian capitalist model suggest that these countries were able to stimulate rapid rates of industrialization while endorsing a collectivist form of motivation, quite different from Weber's famous Protestant ethic principles of Europe and America (Hu & Luk, 1997). It is likely that the discussion about individualism, achievement motivation, and economic success will continue. The debates about the "compatibility" of collectivist motivation and economic success become especially interesting in light of the devastating economic turmoil and recession that struck many Southeast Asian countries in the late 1990s.

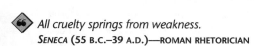

All cruelty springs from weakness.
SENECA (55 B.C.–39 A.D.)—ROMAN RHETORICIAN

Aggressive Motivation and Violence

"After each game we just wanted to beat somebody up. The best thing was to find [a person] who would challenge us. If no one dared, we would go and kick somebody's butt anyway." This was said to us by M.M., a 30-year-old father of two children, an Englishman who used to be a "soccer hooligan," as he called himself, in one of the London suburbs.

The desire to harm or injure others is called **aggressive motivation.** Physical abuse, verbal assault, angry retaliation, open hostility, and many other forms of aggressive behavior are part of our everyday life, no matter where we live. Aggressive motivation has multiple roots and causes and cannot be explained by one theory, no matter how attractive it appears. Cross-cultural psychologists compare and combine the existing data into a comprehensive view that takes into account a wide range of psychological, political, biological, socioeconomic, and cultural factors that are linked to aggressive motivation and behavior.

Biologists found, for example, that the absence of a specific chemical in the brain—nitric oxide—can transform normal mice into violent and sexually aggressive miscreants. The same mechanism might be found in humans (Brown, 1995). It is hard to believe, however, that aggression is nothing more than a biological phenomenon. Even being psychologically predisposed to violent responses, most individuals are still capable of adjusting to existing social restraints and cultural requirements. In cultures in which violent conduct is rare, people become very sensitive to any form of violence and aggression and resist it. On the other hand, in communities in which violence is a common problem-solving technique, such as in a zone in which there is ethnic conflict, people may acquire this particular behavioral pattern of violent behavior as a norm. Several cross-cultural studies bring additional support to the argument that the roots of violence may be found in society (Frey & Hoppe-Graff, 1994).

Aggression is positively reinforced when aggressive acts have utilitarian value and bolster the violent performance. The individual in such cases can gain power and control, obtain material resources, or resist provocation (Rohier, 1975). It was found, for example, that children of the same country who were raised in different social settings may display different patterns of aggressive behavior. A study of children from two Mexican regions found that those who lived in the town with a higher level of violence, performed twice as many aggressive acts as those from the other town, in which the violence level was lower (Fry, 1988). According to the report, parents who lived in high-violence areas tended to encourage their children to be aggressive and respond to violence with retaliatory actions. Moreover, aggressive behavior was higher in those families in which parents were neglecting, rejecting, lacking in affection, indifferent to the child's aggression, and abusive. This study provides an example of a bidirectional causation. On one hand, the dangerous social conditions induce parental encouragement of violence in "self-defense." On the other hand, the encouragement of aggressive behavior creates a particular social climate that permits new aggressive acts. This study, nevertheless, suggests little about why there are children and adults who do not respond to aggression with new aggression and maintain nonviolent behavior throughout their lives.

Staub (1996) investigated multiple factors of aggressive behavior in various cultural groups. Among these factors are a history of discrimination, exposure to violence, attitudes to authority, fulfillment of basic needs, lack of education, harsh treatment, abusive families, and joblessness. Violence increases in both black and white neighborhoods with a predominantly poor population. Why does it happen? Does it mean that the poor are more aggressive than other social groups? The author argues that in a society that develops materialistic values in its members, personal success is primarily determined by how much money one makes and whether this person has access to power and resources. With all possibilities for economic and social success visible, but without the capacity to make use of them, the person may experience a sense of powerlessness. This mental set, in turn, may cause frustration and aggression. In addition, if a person adopts masculine values (see Chapter 1), his frustration can be easily channeled through various violent behaviors. Unfulfilled needs may bring a person closer to a group of people—a gang, for instance—that promotes a positive identity, promises power, and offers a connection to peers. Analyzing why there are many Hispanic gangs in American cities, the author argues that because of a rapid social change in the youth's lives, the traditional attachment to the family is being rapidly destroyed. As a result, many young people are looking for affiliation and attachment elsewhere, and some of them end up being gang members.

One of the contemporary views on aggression is influenced by the frustration—aggression hypothesis (Dollard et al., 1939; Berkowitz, 1962). This theory describes aggression as the dominant unlearned response to frustration. Using this assumption, many social scientists attempted, often successfully, to explain the roots of aggressive behavior in a wide range of frustrating circumstances such as poverty, broken families, migration, urbanization, unemployment, and discrimination. There are numerous examples of studies relating aggression to unfavorable circumstances and absence of aggression to favorable conditions (Bernard, 1990). Thus, it was found that in India and the United States, positive parental affection was negatively correlated with children's aggression (Pinto et al., 1991). Parents' reaction to children's aggressive behavior is an important factor that controls and facilitates aggression. Studies show that punishment is not an effective means of aggression control (Weiss, 1992). Moreover, high levels of restriction (low permissiveness) could cause physical aggression (Schlegel & Barry, 1991).

Among psychological factors linked to aggression, specialists often mention self-esteem. Assumptions that a low level of self-esteem is related to a high frequency of delinquent behavior were taken into consideration by some researchers (Jenkins, 1995; Crain & Weissman, 1972). However, cross-cultural comparisons do not always prove this to be true. For example, three ethnic groups were examined to determine whether individual self-esteem is linked to delinquent conduct. The hypothesis was valid only for white Americans, but not for the black and Hispanic subjects (Leung & Drasgow, 1986). Aggressiveness can also be related to the child's poor social competence with peers. Without having such competency the child does not know how to negotiate conflicts, resolve difficult social situations, control emotions, or interpret the emotions of others (Asher et al., 1982).

Considerable experimental work yields evidence that aggression does not always have to be caused by underlying frustration. Violent impulses can develop as learned response patterns. Very often aggressive behavior is readily acquired through observation of aggressive models (Bandura, 1969). Major television networks, for example, often show scenes taken in various zones of conflicts, where adult fighters give interviews while brandishing their weapons. In the scenes, they are surrounded by scores of small children. Indeed, if a father is proud of his AK–47 machine gun, does he expect his son to do the same?

Aggression can become manifest early in life in various forms of children's activities, including play. In a study of 120 children from the United States, Sweden, Germany, and Indonesia, the 4-year-old children were asked to tell two stories using two toys with aggressive and neutral characteristics. The stories created by American children contained more aggressive concepts, aggressive words, and hostile characters than the narratives of other studied groups (Farver et al., 1997). It is difficult to explain such a difference. Perhaps early family experiences or children's exposure to aggression on television could have influenced the children's responses.

Are particular nations and cultures more aggressive than others? To address this question one should understand that there are no violence-free societies. Presidents and Prime ministers are assassinated in the United States and Israel, India and Sweden, Armenia and Chile. Terrorist groups attack innocent victims in Russia and in Argentina, Egypt and Peru, Tanzania and Spain. Violent acts are committed in the subways of London, Tokyo, and Moscow. There are countries in which the crime rate is declining and ones in which it is growing; there are regions with low rates of violence and areas with high rates of violence. In Norway, for example, there is less than one murder per 100,000 people. In Finland it is slightly higher than one murder per 100,000 people. In China the numbers are the same—one per 100,000; however, there is no way of knowing whether the communist government lowers the numbers deliberately. South Africa loses more than 26 people per 100,000 to homicide; that is slightly higher than the numbers in Brazil (Kovalevski, 1999). In the Philippines the situation is worse: 46 per 100,000. In the United States, a country that is typically seen by many observers as violent (Reid, 1998), the homicide rate is less than 8 per 100,000 people. The rates, however, are not the same in different states and among different groups. Homicide, for instance, is the leading cause of death for young African American men, whereas among whites automobile accidents are the number one cause of premature death. In the 1990s, a 10-year-old black boy has a 1 in 21 chance of being murdered before reaching maturity (D'Souza, 1995). However, Adelbert Jenkins (1995), a prominent black psychologist from New York University, suggests that the very question about whether one ethnic group is more violent than the other cannot be addressed without looking at it from an historic perspective. For example, speaking of American blacks, he argues that one should take into consideration a few hundred years of direct and indirect discrimination and aggression against African Americans committed primarily by white Europeans.

Societies have different thresholds of tolerance toward various acts of violence and aggression. As an illustration, in many nonindustrial societies, killing infants is not considered a crime (Minturin & Shashak, 1982). In other ethnic groups, killing is appropriate and even praised if it is committed in the name of God or retaliation. In most industrialized nations, killing in the context of war is considered to be legitimate because those who are targeted for killing belong to "outlawed" groups. Furthermore, in these societies, execution may be accepted not just because of what the convicted criminal did, or because justice is administered by constituted authority, but also because criminals put themselves outside the law and confront society.

Social norms define what types of violence are acceptable in a particular country or culture. For instance, wife-beating is not typically reported in authoritarian countries with strong traditional values. Many women feel ashamed to report their own husbands as being abusive. In many African countries, spousal abuse is even considered to be a right of men (Buckley, 1996). Authoritarian societies that do not allow the individual to express hostility would be more likely than nonrestrictive societies to create outlets of aggression, such as warfare and physical games (Worchel, 1974). If a society is tolerant toward violent aggression in general, this permissive attitude may encourage further aggression. In a survey conducted in the 1980s, two countries were compared: Poland (high level of violent crimes) and Finland (low level of violent crimes). It was found that

CRITICAL THINKING

Aggression and Testosterone

A research study found that men with testosterone levels in the top 10 percent were more likely to belong to lower socioeconomic classes (Dabbis & Morris, 1990). Does this mean that if a person has a higher testosterone level, he or she is more likely to become or stay poor? That is quite possible. Why? If an individual is aggressive and violent, he or she will not be able to succeed in a society that requires cooperation and demands compliance from its members. However, the other explanation is plausible too. We could suggest that unfavorable social conditions, abuse, and discrimination against a person may cause continuous frustration and stress that is responsible for the release of surplus amounts of testosterone in the body.

the Polish sample demonstrated a higher approval rate of more violent forms of aggression than people in the Finnish sample (Fraczek, 1985).

Marxists argued that the less violent societies were the socialist countries, where the crime rate was among the lowest in the world. They claimed that collectivist norms should keep people away from violent acts. However, socialism may restrain violence on a horizontal level (among the people) but gives a green light to violence on a vertical level (between the ruling bureaucracy and the masses.) Millions of people were executed in China, the Soviet Union, Cambodia, North Korea, and in many other socialist countries between the 1930s and 1980s. Such killings were typically justified by various ideological and political reasons and slogans. To put it simply, most totalitarian and authoritarian countries have halted street violence, but have promoted wide-scale political violence against their own people.

Numerous cross-cultural sources report that boys are more aggressive than girls (Segall et al., 1997). In virtually all cultures men and women are socialized differently: boys as fighters and problem solvers, girls as moderators and peace keepers. It is generally assumed that boys receive more inculcation of and encouragement for aggression. However, empirical research does not provide compelling evidence that encouragement is the only factor that stimulates aggression. Some psychologists argue that men are more aggressive than women because of higher testosterone levels

A CASE IN POINT

Sexual Jealousy and Aggression

Do males and females differ in aggression caused by sexual jealousy? Indeed, the incidence of husbands assaulting wives is much higher than the reverse (Daly & Wilson, 1988). The evidence that men are more likely to assault women than vice versa does not necessarily mean that males experience stronger sexual jealousy. Perhaps females experience jealousy that is just as strong, and have equally powerful motives to punish their mates, but they simply lack the strength or expertise to do so: males are generally stronger than females and have often had more experience with aggressive acts.

Despite high incidents of jealousy-based violence, sexual jealousy and subsequent aggression could decline in the future, as some researchers forecast. Why? As John Archer (1996) argues, for females, jealousy may focus primarily on the potential loss of resources (males) needed for child rearing. In this context, an unfaithful mate could threaten to leave and take resources with him. Therefore, females react very strongly to male sexual infidelity. For males, though, sexual jealousy may rest primarily on different concerns. If their mate has sexual relations with other men, the husband could end up raising other men's children. Such a socio-biological view on the nature of jealousy is challenged by contemporary societal developments. In Western societies today, women became more independent from men than they were 30 or 70 years ago. The access to resources, power, and effective contraceptives has made a difference in the lives of many women. Therefore, the significance of both biological and economic factors of jealousy are substantially reduced. What is the conclusion? Today both men and women express almost equivalent levels of jealousy and—caused by it—aggression (Lefton 2000).

in males. On the other hand, factors such as poverty, abuse, violence, lack of male role models, the glorification of war and lawlessness, and drug abuse all seem to promote deviant destructive behavior in males to a greater extent than they do in females (Eagly, 1995).

In general, members of collectivist cultures can tolerate aggression when it comes from an in-group authority more often than when it comes from a lower level in-group member or an outsider. In an experiment, two samples of Hong Kong Chinese and American citizens were compared. The Chinese were less critical of an attacker and of his or her actions as long as the attacker had a higher status than the in-group target of aggression. Americans made no consistent distinction as a function of the attacker's status or group membership. It is believed that the Chinese are high on collectivism and power distance, and that Americans are low on collectivism and relatively low on power distance (see Chapter 1). In other words, Americans tend to respond and to fight back no matter who the attacker is (Bond, 1985). Social status can also be linked to the expression of anger and aggression. In a comparative Jewish–Arab study in Israel respondents were tested on the production and appreciation of humor. Arab respondents demonstrated less aggression in humor compared to Jewish respondents (Nevo, 1984).

Sexuality is the lyricism of the masses.
CHARLES BAUDELAIRE (1821–1867)—FRENCH POET

Culture and Sexuality

Hormones and other chemicals in our body could determine the dynamics of sexual arousal and the related psychological experiences (Byrne, 1982). Thus, **sexual motivation,** or motivation to engage in sexual activity, is certainly regulated, at least in part, by human physiology. However, genes, hormones, and other biological factors just change the probability of the occurrence of certain types of sexual behavior. Societal factors including laws, customs, and norms, in fact, determine what types of sexual behavior are acceptable, under what circumstances, and with what frequency. Every culture has its own set of requirements, beliefs, symbols, and norms regarding sexuality and its expression. This set of characteristics is called **sex culture.** Sex cultures vary greatly across the world and are influenced by current religious, ideological, political, and moral values developed by society.

What we consider sexual is determined by a combination of biological, psychological, and cultural factors. Many cultures consider sexual pleasure as normal, desirable, and natural, whereas others view it as primitive, sinful, and even abnormal. For instance, in many cultures, there is a popular belief that masturbation is a sin that could cause retardation and other serious psychological problems (Kon, 1979).

Cultural beliefs about sex may affect the quality of cross-cultural research on sex. For example, the so-call refusal rate (proportion of people who do not want to participate in a study as subjects) may affect the validity of surveys on sexuality. Why? People in one country may be open to talking about sex—because of the existing cultural

A CASE IN POINT

Culture and a Sex-Related Custom

Female circumcision, is widely practiced in many African and Asian countries. Approximately 130 million African women in 28 countries are already circumcised (Walt, 1998). This procedure, often performed on women with a razor blade, includes the removal of a clitoris, and sometimes the inner and outer vaginal lips. Concerns expressed by some Western organizations have had little impact on this practice. Both men and women still believe that circumcision is good because of religious rules, and is even required for hygiene and sexual prudence. This sex-related custom—or body mutilation as some people in the United States call it—had a very unexpected political repercussion. In 1997, a woman from Togo was granted asylum in the United States as a protection from "sexual mutilation." In theory, today any woman who condemns circumcision and does not want it to be performed on her could apply for and subsequently receive asylum in the United States. Do you think that this particular asylum policy is justified? Do you think that the United States government misinterprets the sexual practices and traditions of those countries in which female circumcision is a custom? Many Western civil rights advocates, for example, do not realize that if a woman refuses to undergo circumcision in her country, she will not be able to marry and will expose herself to public ostracism.

norms of permissiveness—and agree to give interviews and answers to survey questions. People who grew up in more sexually restrictive environments are often very reluctant to give any kind of information about sex. For the reason mentioned above, it is difficult to compare cultures on criteria such as premarital and teenage sex, extramarital sex, frequency and number of sexual relationships, and sexual abuse. As we mentioned earlier, many women do not report sexual abuse against them because it is considered dishonorable for them to even mention the abuse. The shame of self-disclosure in such cases is overwhelming.

Sexual values that regulate sexual motivation can be quite different across cultures. For example, chastity (no experience with sexual intercourse) is not regarded as a particularly important value in countries such as Sweden, Denmark, Germany, or Holland. On the other hand, in countries such as China, Iran, India, and in many others chastity is essential for the woman's position in the society (Halonen & Santrock, 1995). There are marked differences in the speed of labor and indicated extreme variations in the psychological environment during labor and delivery. Faster, easier labors appear to be related to acceptance of birth as a normal phenomenon uncomplicated by shame (Newton, 1970).

Traditional sex cultures endorse restrictive rules regarding the expression of sexuality among their members. These cultures also tend to suppress the expression of sexuality. For example, in some parts of Africa and the Middle East, many people practice female circumcision (see A Case in Point box, above). It is believed that it helps keep a

TABLE 7.2	Type of Sex Culture and General Attitudes toward Sex	
Issues/Type of Sex Culture	Traditional Sex Culture	Nontraditional Sex Culture
Expression of sexuality	Heavily regulated	Somewhat regulated
Premarital sex	Prohibited and rejected	Somewhat tolerated
Extramarital sex	Prohibited and rejected	Somewhat tolerated
Homosexuality	Prohibited and rejected	Somewhat tolerated
Chastity	High value	Low value

girl chaste, clean, and free from "sinful" sexual desires. In some cultures this procedure is even considered to be religious. In the United States, before the 1900s, female circumcision was also practiced, but only by a few individuals.

In contrast, nontraditional sex cultures are generally permissive to different forms of sexual behavior. In nations such as Holland, Sweden, Russia, Australia, Denmark, and some other countries that represent the so-called nontraditional sex cultures, sex does not carry the same mystery, shame, and conflict it does in traditional cultures (see Table 7.2). Even the style of clothing represents a particular sex culture. In traditional Islamic societies, women are typically veiled and cloaked from head to foot. On the other hand, contemporary European and American fashion trends allow women to expose most parts of their bodies. Those who visit European countries know that on most public beaches many women appear topless.

 If you cannot be chaste, be cautious.
SPANISH PROVERB

Labels of "traditionalism" and "nontraditionalism" could be misleading, however. Many people who live in traditional sex cultures could express attitudes and behaviors that are more common to nontraditional sex cultures and vice versa. Family socialization, attitudes, adulthood experiences, and many other environmental factors affect an individual's sexuality—including his or her thoughts about sex, frequency of sexual acts, and type of sexual activities. For example, despite expectations, almost 70 percent of Chinese respondents (traditional sex culture) do not denounce extramarital affairs. This is a larger approval rate than is found in the United States. In fact, in the 1990s, about 50 percent of Chinese were believed to be engaged in premarital sex. About 14 percent of Chinese urban women have extramarital affairs (Rathus et al., 1993). In the "nontraditional" sex culture of the United States, many prominent figures raise their voice in support of traditional values. American politicians such as Senator Ashcroft, Governor J. Bush, former Vice President Quayle, and well-known businessman Steve Forbes all in various interviews, back premarital chastity (Edsall, 1998).

Different cultures may promote specific attitudes toward particular types of sexual lifestyles. For instance, homosexuality is tolerated in Western industrial societies. In studies conducted in the 1970s and 1980s, about 20 percent of American males reported at least one homosexual experience in their lives (Reinish, 1990). In approximately one-half of the non-European societies, homosexuality is rare (Broude & Greene, 1976). It is virtually absent in the other half of non-Western societies. However, it is difficult to prove, because people in these countries are either ashamed or afraid to talk about their sex life.

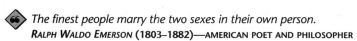

The finest people marry the two sexes in their own person.
RALPH WALDO EMERSON (1803–1882)—AMERICAN POET AND PHILOSOPHER

There are two basic understandings of causes of homosexuality. According to a genetic approach, individuals express homosexual behavior because it is motivated genetically; culture has only some impact on homosexuality. According to the environmental approach, social and cultural factors cause homosexuality more than anything else. Some authors suggest that homosexuality in ancient Greece, for example, occurred under certain political socioeconomic conditions. Among them were strong social stratification, a large poverty class, a decentralized political system, and an absence of formal education (Dickerman, 1993).

Several social and psychological conditions that may be linked to homosexuality were identified in a comprehensive ethnographic study of 70 preindustrial cultures (Barber, 1998). Despite initial predictions, homosexuality was not found to be higher in cultures with repressive attitudes toward premarital sex. Societies that practiced polygamy (multiple wives for one husband) were also low on homosexuality. Moreover, the frequency of homosexuality is very low in societies in which hunting and gathering are predominant activities. It increases in agricultural societies and goes up together with the growing complexity of modern cultures. A high density of population was also linked to homosexuality.

Male–female roles in homosexual relations are influenced by general cultural expectations of a given society. In Mexico, for example, with its strict gender-role divisions, homosexuals adhere more strictly to either male or female roles. In the United States and Canada, where gender roles are more flexible, many gay males frequently shift roles (Carrier, 1980). Homosexuality among males appears to be common in countries that highly value female virginity and separate men and women (Davenport, 1976). According to some researchers, the general public's attitudes toward homosexuality have social and cultural roots: Those countries that desire the expansion of the nation's population are less tolerant toward homosexuality (Ember & Ember, 1990). By way of illustration, 60 years ago, homosexuality was a serious crime in Nazi Germany. Before the 1990s, it was a crime in the Soviet Union. In fact, in both countries, the rapid growth of population was considered an important ideological and political goal. Homosexuals in those countries were considered criminals and mentally ill and were severely punished. For many years, even in the United States, homosexuality was considered a mental disorder. Only recently, in the early 1970s, based on the predominant opinion of American mental health specialists, was male and female homosexuality removed from diagnostic manuals (*DSM-IV*, 1994).

EXERCISE 7.1

According to a traditional view on sex, heterosexuality is normal; homosexuality is abnormal. Now consider something opposite. We decided to convert a survey (the source of which is unknown) of homosexual behavior into a questionnaire that examines heterosexuality. In the process of conversion, the words "homosexual" and "heterosexual" switch places. As a result, this change of view may explore (and challenge) one's assumptions and beliefs about human sexual orientation. Judge for yourself!

Heterosexual Questionnaire

1. What do you think caused your heterosexuality?
2. When and how did you first decide that you were heterosexual?
3. Is it possible that your heterosexuality stems from a neurotic fear of others of the same sex?
4. Is it possible that your heterosexuality is just a phase you may grow out of?
5. Isn't it possible that all you need is a good homosexual lover?
6. To whom have you disclosed your heterosexual behavior, desires, and fantasies? How did they react?
7. Why do you heterosexuals feel compelled to seduce others into your orientation?
8. Since the majority of child molesters are heterosexual, do you really consider it safe to expose your children to heterosexual teachers?
9. How can you enjoy a fully satisfactory sexual experience or deep emotional bonding with persons of the opposite sex when the obvious physical, biological, and temperamental differences between you are so vast? How can a man truly understand what pleases a woman sexually, and vice versa?
10. There seem to be very few happy heterosexuals. Techniques have been developed with which you might be able to change, if you *really* want to. Have you considered trying aversion therapy, such as receiving painful electric shocks while viewing nude photographs of the opposite sex?

Sexual and Gender Identity Disorders

Sexual dysfunctions are marked by the individual's significant disturbances in sexual desire and psychophysiological changes in the sexual response cycle, such as excitement, orgasm, and resolution. The *paraphilias* are characterized by unusual (for the individual's culture) sexual desires, urges, and fantasies. *Gender identity disorders* are characterized by persistent cross-gender identification and discomfort with one's assigned sex.

Clinical judgments about sexual dysfunctions should take into account the individual's ethnic, religious, social, educational, and cultural background. Cultural attitudes about sex and norms that regulate sexual behavior could influence sexual desire and people's expectations about sexual performance. For example, in some cultures, female sexuality is given little relevance, that is, the woman is not expected to enjoy sex. The recognition of paraphilias is complicated by the fact that there are different views on sexual deviance across countries and cultures. Different social groups could have different levels of tolerance regarding particular forms of sexual behavior.

Little is known regarding the cross-cultural prevalence of gender identity disorders. Typically, men experience more rejection and ostracism from others than women do and therefore men perhaps tend to be confused about their gender more often than women. There is some evidence that gender identity disorder is more common in nations that are more harshly rejecting of male homosexuality (Ross et al., 1981). However, the overall existing data on causal factors of gender identity disorders are generally inconclusive (Bancroft, 1989)

Sex and Sexuality: Some Cross-Cultural Similarities

Psychologists suggest, for instance, that both men and women can respond erotically to mild pain. Betzig (1989) found that cross-culturally, adultery and sterility (inability to conceive a child) were the most common reasons for divorce. There are some aspects of interpersonal male–female attractiveness that are also consistent across cultures. For example, characteristics such as kindness, understanding, intelligence, good health, emotional stability, dependability, and a pleasing disposition are considered to be cross-culturally attractive in women. Men everywhere react more negatively than women do when their partners share sexual fantasies about having sex with others. Women everywhere are more distressed than men are when their partner is kissing someone else (Rathus et al., 1993). Many aspects of nonverbal communication appear to be universal too. For instance, courting and flirtation patterns are similar across many cultures and performed for the specific purpose of mate selection and reproduction (Aune & Aune, 1994).

There are many exceptions to the general rules, however. Kissing, for example, is a cross-cultural phenomenon. However, kissing is unknown to some cultures in Africa and South America. Touching may be viewed as a normal act of communication between two strangers in Mediterranean countries, but it could be totally inappropriate in the United States. Marital fidelity appears to be virtually a cross-cultural requirement as well. However, among some Arctic peoples it is considered normal and hospitable to offer your wife to a guest. Around the world, males prefer females younger than themselves and vice versa. A study conducted in 33 countries showed similarities in preference for mate characteristics between men and women who ranked "kind and understanding" first, "intelligent" second, "exciting personality" third, "healthy" fourth, and "religious" last. Despite the overall cross-cultural gender similarity, there were some differences in preference. According to the survey, men almost universally prefer "good looks" in women, whereas women choose "good earning capacity" as the most important characteristic of the partner of the opposite sex (Buss, 1994).

There were no differences between African American and white students with respect to incidences of premarital sex (Belcastro, 1985). However, studies conducted on the general population show a different picture (National Center for Health Statistics,

A CASE IN POINT

Pop Surveys on Sex and Sexuality

According to a sex survey, 20 percent of Russians have sex daily, 50 percent of American women say they are able to tell their partner what pleases them, 71 percent of Greek women prefer sex in the daytime, and Spanish women have the most orgasms. Women in Portugal are more likely to make the first move, almost 50 percent of Japanese women who answered the survey say they may opt for sex in the middle of the night, and French women are less likely than others to have their partner use condoms. Russian women are more likely than others to explore sex with other women. Of Czech women 64 percent say sex is fabulous, compared to 57 percent in the United States and 34 percent in Italy. [*Source: Capital Times* (Madison, WI), May 16, 1998.]

Many surveys published in popular sources may be very interesting and entertaining. However, the real value of the finding remains to be established. Why? We usually know very little about the size of the studied samples, the way the participants were approached and by whom, the religion of the interviewees, their age, occupation, or ethnicity.

1995). Compared to Hispanic and white young males, ages 14–21, black youth are more sexually active. More than 35 percent of blacks report six or more sexual partners over their life. The rates for Hispanic and white youth are 12 points lower. Young African American women begin sexual life earlier than white women. However, if social class differences are taken into consideration, there were no differences between the two groups. Both groups were similarly affected by sexual abuse (Watt, 1990).

Culture seems to play a critical role in the interpretation of close relationships between men and women. For example, flirting in Yugoslavia evokes a more negative emotional response than in other European countries. In the Netherlands, sexual fantasies are less acceptable than in any other country, but kissing, dancing, and hugging arouse less jealousy in the Netherlands than in most other countries (Hupka et al., 1985).

EXERCISE 7.2

Often humor helps us to understand ourselves better. Below is an assignment that could show that sexuality is a cultural phenomenon. The way we see ourselves and other people is often based on a starting point from which we make our judgments.

Teak is 18. Teal is 18. Both are foreign college exchange students, both are juniors, and both of them will study at the City University of New York. The tuition is paid, the books are bought, and the keys to the rooms are in the young men's pockets. The new life has begun.

Teak grew up on a small Atlantic island. People on this island know nothing about kissing. Nudity is strongly prohibited. People have VCRs, however movies rated "R" are not available on the island. Premarital sex is punishable. Men and women believe that sexual experiences reduce their energy and are bad for their health. People do not even talk about sex. After a couple marries, the husband and wife are allowed to have sex once a week, at night, and as quickly as possible. Both partners should be dressed in night-clothes and cannot look at each other. Female orgasms are rare and considered to be abnormal. Sex education is prohibited by law.

Teal grew up on a small Pacific island. Children on this island, both boys and girls, are taught about sex as early as at the age of 7. Nudity is totally acceptable on the island. At the age of 13, the boys undergo a special ritual that initiates them into adult sexual life. Girls do the same at the age of 15. Every young man and woman at this age has an adult sexual partner of the opposite sex, who teaches them proficiency in sex. After a year of training, the students are allowed to have sex without supervision. Adults have sex practically every day, often in public places.

After spending a month in the United States, Teak and Teal decided to write letters to some close friends in their home countries about their experiences with sex culture in the United States. Please compose two brief letters on behalf of both young men. Compare the "letters." How could we help these young men to adjust better in the American culture? Offer specific suggestions and discuss them in class.

 ## CHAPTER SUMMARY

- Motivation is any condition—usually an internal one—that initiates, activates, or maintains the individual's goal-directed behavior. Many interesting and valuable ideas about the nature of human motivation appear in classical works of prominent social scientists. Theories of sociobiology claim that general biological laws of evolution are perfectly suitable as a fundamental explanation of human motivation. Theories *of social instincts* emphasize the crucial and universal role of basic instincts, similar in both humans and animals, as motivations of behavior. The sociological approach emphasizes the crucial role of social factors, for example, values and economic inequality, in determining the individual's behavior.

- There are several psychological theories of motivation. Drive theories pay attention to needs, motivated states caused by physiological or psychological deprivation. Arousal theories of motivation suggest that people seek to maintain optimal levels of arousal by ac-

tively changing their exposure to arousing stimuli. Psychoanalysis emphasizes the importance of unconscious processes. Humanistic theories focus on human dignity, individual choice, and self-worth. Cognitive psychologists maintain that we are aware of our thought patterns and therefore can control our motivation and overt behavior.

- In general, most of the theories emphasize the universal nature of human motivation that is influenced by various environmental factors. These factors, in turn, are products of historic, religious, political, cultural, and socioeconomic developments.

- Typically, cultural norms and traditions regulate hunger. Cultures establish culture-linked eating habits, determine what is considered tasty and tasteless, and establish social taboos on particular foods and food products. Eating disorders are more common in young white females in industrial societies than in their peers in non-Western countries.

- Achievement motivation is acquired by the individual and influenced by his or her culture. On the national level, there is a strong relationship between individual achievement motivation and economic growth. However, there are "individually" oriented and "socially" oriented achievement motives. The first type is common in Western cultures. The latter is more common in Southwest Asian countries, Korea, Japan, and perhaps in other collectivist cultures.
- There are no aggression-free countries or cultures. Aggressive motivation has many underlying factors, from chemical and physiological, to socioeconomic, psychological, and political. Cultures have different thresholds

of tolerance toward various acts of violence and aggression. Poverty, lack of opportunities, socialization experiences, history of violence, and other factors contribute to violence.
- Sexual motivation is certainly regulated, at least in part, by human physiology, but culture determines various forms of its experience and behavioral manifestation. There are traditional and nontraditional sex cultures that practice either restrictive or permissive norms of sexuality. Sexual orientation, like homosexuality, for instance, as well as various forms of sexual disorders are linked to particular social practices and values.

 ## KEY TERMS

Aggressive Motivation   The desire to harm or injure others.

Collectivist-Success Motivation   A type of achievement motivation that directs a person to connect with others; the individual's contribution is seen as beneficial to the members of a particular group or society in general.

Drive   An internal aroused condition that directs an organism to satisfy some physiological need.

Extrinsic Motivation   A type of motivation that engages people in various activities for a particular reward.

Individualist-Success Motivation   A type of achievement motivation that affects one's attitudes and actions and is directed toward the attainment of personal goals.

Instinct   A relatively complex, inherited behavior pattern characteristic of a species.

Intrinsic Motivation   A type of motivation that engages people in various activities for no

apparent reward except the pleasure and satisfaction of the activity itself.

Motivation   The psychological process that arouses, directs, and maintains behavior.

Need   A motivated state caused by physiological deprivation (such as a lack of food or water).

Need for Achievement   A social need that directs people to strive constantly for excellence and success.

Self-actualization   A final level of psychological development in which individuals strive to realize their uniquely human potential to achieve everything they are capable of achieving.

Sex Culture   A set of requirement, beliefs, symbols, and norms regarding sexuality and its expression.

Sexual Motivation   A type of motivation that engages the individual in sexual activity.

CHAPTER 8

Human Development and Socialization

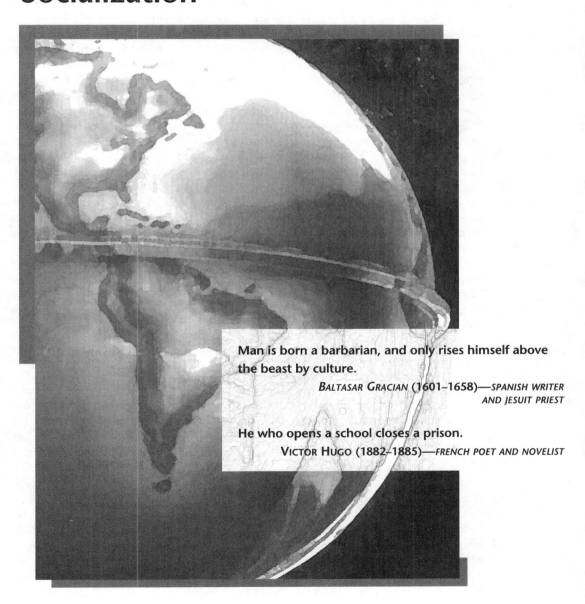

Man is born a barbarian, and only rises himself above the beast by culture.

BALTASAR GRACIAN (1601–1658)—SPANISH WRITER AND JESUIT PRIEST

He who opens a school closes a prison.

VICTOR HUGO (1882–1885)—FRENCH POET AND NOVELIST

As Lynn headed out to go shopping, she already knew her 4-year-old son was in a bad mood. All that day he had been doing all that he could to frustrate her. First he chose not to eat breakfast and then he spilled apple juice all over the carpet. He categorically refused to put on his red jacket and continuously tried to unbuckle his seatbelt in the car. Since they had arrived at the shopping mall, he had been whining continuously for 20 minutes and demanding they go to the toy store immediately. The mother's patience finally ran out when her son ran away and started picking up coins from the fountain. Lynn pulled him out of the fountain and spanked him three or four times. The son reacted first with a brief and silent pause of embarrassment and then filled the shopping mall with a high-pitched scream. A couple of crystal tears rolled down his cheeks. "This is horrible. You cannot treat your child like this," loudly said a woman passerby as she pointed at Lynn. "You shouldn't do that, Ma-am," uttered another woman. "At least not in a public place." Lynn could not understand why these strangers reacted in this way. She had arrived two years ago, as a Cambodian refugee, and thus far had had nothing critical said to her. What had she done to upset these people? Cambodian child-rearing practices allow spanking. Moreover, this type of physical punishment is a major component of the child learning process in her home country where parental authority in the family is absolute and may not be challenged. Most parental behavior is supported by the extended family, the local community, and the Buddhist religion. True, child spanking is common around the world. However, if a parent grew up in a different culture, what rule should he or she follow: traditional ethnic or contemporary American, which denounces spanking? What if the parent chooses spanking? If we tell a parent what to do, will this violate the parent's freedom of choice? We know that spanking as a custom can change. Perhaps education will stimulate such a change: Around the world, middle-class parents believe less in physical punishment than working-class parents do. Hopefully, an open competition of ideas will deem spanking the least effective method of upbringing. However, this is only a wish. The competition of ideas continues. So does spanking of children.

Development and Socialization

Psychologists distinguish between human development and socialization. **Human development** is viewed as the changes in physical, psychological, and social behavior that are experienced by individuals across the life span—from conception to death. **Socialization** is the process by which the individual becomes a member of a particular culture and takes on its values and behaviors. Neither human development nor socialization stops at age 18 or even 25. It is a life-long process with accelerations and delays, changes in direction, sudden transitions, and long-term conversions. Human development is not only growth, but also decline, and modification. In a small village in China or in a big city in South America, people change their attitudes and acquire new beliefs. They may lose skills in one area while developing expertise in other fields. A writer or an actor can become president. Presidents become writers. People go through life changes both positive and negative, migrate or stay in one place. Regardless of who you are, you may change your career and lifestyle when you are 20, 40, or 60 years old. Our socialization is virtually endless.

Human development and socialization are described by a number of theories. We begin with an overview of the impact of culture on development and socialization, and then—before describing specific life span stages—turn attention to several specific psychological theories of development.

It takes many years before the newborn baby becomes a competent member of society. Since ancient times, the world's greatest thinkers considered human development as a consequence of the interaction between environmental influences and natural individual predispositions. Attempts to describe specific mechanisms of such interaction between biological and cultural factors of human development were made by a number of psychologists throughout the twentieth century (for example, Vygotsky, 1932; Bronfenbrenner, 1979; Berry, 1995). In general, the developing child is seen as an individual with inborn dispositions and potentials that become traits within the child's environment—a part of a larger cultural system. Both the environment and the individual are commonly understood as open and interchanging systems. To put it plainly, if Said has inborn predispositions to be a great athlete, he will become one if there are particular conditions in which he can develop his potential. If he lives in Pakistan, he will become a fine cricket player. If he lives in Idaho, he will have almost no chance to play this game. Why? Cricket is not a popular game in the United States.

Quality of Life and the Child's Development

The overall quality of life—availability of food and other products, type of living conditions, quality of education and health care, presence or absence of violence in the child's life, and a number of other factors—significantly affects the child's development. Countries and cultures vary in overall density of population and number of immediate family members. A unit of two adults living with their own children is common in Western societies, such as Canada, Sweden, or the United States, whereas the large extended family in which parents, children, grandparents, cousins, and even some distant relatives live in one household is common for non-Western countries, such as Pakistan, Rwanda, or Indonesia. Technological advancements and socioeconomic improvements may affect the composition of the family. In Japan, for example, from 1955 to 1985, the number of extended families declined significantly from 44 to 15 percent (Fukada, 1991).

A study of 799 students in Greece, Cyprus, the Netherlands, Great Britain, and Germany examined the relationship of family bonds to family structure but did not find substantial differences among families in the sampled countries in terms of emotional closeness, geographic proximity to relatives, and frequency of telephone contacts (Georgas et al., 1997). However, when the extended families were analyzed, differences were found between wealthy individualist countries in the sample (Netherlands, Great Britain, and Germany) and collectivist countries (Greece and Cyprus). The extended families in the latter sample were emotionally and geographically closer to each other than the families from the individualist sample.

Not only family size but also specific aspects of family relationship can correlate with industrial and financial advancement. For instance, second- and third-generation Mexican American children show decreasing frequency of altruistic behavior compared to their first-generation Mexican American peers, who are less advanced eco-

CRITICAL THINKING

Wealth and Family Connectedness

Perhaps we shouldn't consider the relationships among family members as either dependent or independent. Interdependency is a continuous variable and is based on many factors. For instance, family members may stay together because of economic difficulties. However, emotional closeness of relatives and frequency of their communications can be determined by many other reasons. Money and other material dimensions are only part of a larger picture. Recent economic developments brought wealth, economic independence, and relative material security to millions of people in countries such as Kuwait, Singapore, and United Arab Emirates. In these and other industrialized collectivist societies, family members are more or less independent from each other financially, but continue to keep close emotional ties with their family members (Kagitcibasi, 1996). Among the most important contributing factors to such closeness are religious traditions, the size of the family, and, in part, authoritarian norms of governing that reinforce compliance and respect for authority on an interpersonal level.

nomically (Knight & Kagan, 1977). In the United States, children in families with annual incomes under $15,000 are almost five times as likely to be abused as children in middle-class families (Berger, 1995).

Access to resources and educational opportunities are likely to provide an advantageous environment for the developing child. Lev Vygotsky (1932) established that guided interaction with a more knowledgeable partner should advance the intellectual development of the child. Middle-class parents answer children's questions with more elaborate explanations than do parents of a lower social class who are generally less educated than middle-class families (Berger, 1985). It was shown in one study that Mexican mothers from low-socioeconomic status groups—contrary to mothers from other families—used tactile interaction, such as a touch and push, with their children more frequently than they used verbal means (Zepeda, 1985). In many working class communities in the United States, as well as in preindustrial communities in Africa and the Pacific, parents have a low willingness to instruct their children themselves and tend to assume that children can learn things on their own (Rogoff, 1990).

Poverty may directly affect relationships within the family. In industrial societies, relationships among siblings and between parents and their children depend primarily on their good will and other psychological factors. In preindustrial and economically underdeveloped societies, partly because of limited access to resources, close cooperation within families becomes an economic necessity (see Chapter 1).

Norms, Customs, and Child Care

The child's development and socialization depend on the people with whom the child interacts, the places where they spend time together, and the roles children play (Whiting & Whiting, 1975). Adults assign children to some roles and disallow others.

For example, cross-cultural differences in the behavior of boys and girls may be partially due to different roles assigned to them by adults. Girls are more apt to stay close to home and are more involved in child-care activities than are boys (Whiting & Edwards, 1988). Rough-and-tumble play is a common child's activity across cultures. However, in traditional Muslim countries, girls are seldom encouraged by their parents to engage in such games (Berger, 1995).

There are similarities in patterns of social support from children, spouses, relatives, and friends. Such similarities, for example, were found in North American and Indian (Asian) samples (Ventrakaman, 1995). However, comparative studies identify plenty of national and cultural differences. For example, rocking or thumb-sucking in children would be considered wrong by white South African mothers. For native African mothers such behavior is absolutely normal. American mothers respond more favorably to their babies' requests when the infants are playing with physical objects. Japanese mothers, on the other hand, are more responsive when their babies are engaged in play with them. Japanese parents, unlike American parents, rarely leave their children with baby-sitters. These children learn how to interact with other adults and

CROSS-CULTURAL SENSITIVITY

Are there any words that a teacher is not supposed to use in the multicultural classroom? Of course, profanities should be out. What about other words? Let us discuss a story in which good intentions are not always supported by the appropriate knowledge.

For example, if you were a teacher in a New York public school and all students in your class are black or Hispanic, would you choose to read them multicultural books? When Ruth Sherman, the 27-year-old teacher read a story to her class about Brenda, a little black girl from Haiti, the students liked the reading very much. They really enjoyed the teacher's funny voice and good acting. They enjoyed it so much that some students asked Ms. Sherman to make a few copies of the story so that they could read it at home. This is where the controversy begins. No, is not about the copyright law. The photocopy of the story caught some parent's eye and sparked their angry reactions (Clementson, 1998). The problem was in the title of the story: "Nappy Hair." *Nappy* is a colloquialism for curly African hair. What is wrong with it? Unfortunately this word is sometimes used as a put-down or disrespectful expression. Some parents, therefore, believed that this title should not have been used in class because it ridicules people with a certain type of hair. Others suggested that the words were not the problem. The problem was the teacher—because she was white she had no business to use such words with black children.

When we asked our colleagues to comment on this story, some of them—and they all were college professors and researchers of different backgrounds—emphasized to us that it always creates an unpleasant feeling when someone mentions anything about your body height, shape of your eyes, size of your nose, skin color, and texture of your hair in connection with your ethnicity or origin. As mentioned earlier, to be sensitive, one should develop empathy— the ability to understand and appreciate other people's feelings. The teacher in this story did nothing illegal. However, as a teacher, she touched a very sensitive string of people's identity and attached to it emotions.

this may explain why Japanese children display a higher rate of anxiety than American boys and girls do when the parents are not present (Bornstein & Tamis-LeMonda, 1989). Studies on parent–child communication show that French and Italian parents and children are more interactive than German pairs (Best et al., 1994). An exaggeration in one's gratitude is considered normal and is even expected in Arab cultures (Triandis, 1994). "Thank-you" letters are commonly sent by American boys and girls to their birthday guests. This tradition is practically unknown in Ukraine, Armenia, and many other countries.

Once a norm is established, it may be passed on from one generation to the next. In most traditional African cultures, obedience is a highly desired pattern of behavior for children, a pattern that is crucial for the child's survival in harsh living conditions (Klingelhofer, 1971). Most Western concepts of child-rearing judge obedience critically and condemn most forms of adult–child coercion. Turkish parents typically restrict their children's influence to the children's own affairs, whereas German parents are generally indulgent and accept their children as participating members with influence in the family (Schonpflug, 1990).

 The parents' age must be remembered both for joy and anxiety.
CONFUCIUS (551–479 B.C.)—CHINESE PHILOSOPHER

Parental Values and Expectations

People from different countries may develop similar views on many issues. They also may acquire culture-specific views on other people, themselves, and their children. By way of illustration, parents typically have their own developmental timetables: they expect their children to acquire particular characteristics (such as walking, talking, or reasoning) at certain ages. Research shows that despite large individual variations, there are some cultural patterns in such expectations (Super & Harkness, 1997). In one study, for example, Israeli mothers of European background expected their children to develop certain cognitive skills earlier than did mothers of non-European origin (Ninio, 1979). American mothers had earlier expectations of their children's assertiveness than Japanese mothers. On the other hand, Japanese mothers had earlier expectations about their children's ability to control their emotions and express courtesy (Hess et al., 1980). According to Levy (1996), in societies that are small, egalitarian, and with little occupational specialization, children are expected to learn "on their own," whereas in industrialized democratic societies there are explicit expectations about what, with whom, when, and how children should learn.

Parents' particular beliefs are translated into behavior that, in reverse, influences other beliefs. Japanese mothers generally view autonomy of the child as his or her ability to interact with other children. For Israeli mothers, the child's independence is the ability to perform certain instrumental tasks, such as answering the phone and setting the table (Osterweil & Nagano, 1991).

Parents from different cultural groups may hold different views on the formal education of their children and their role as parents in this process. Chao (1996) asked a sample of 48 immigrants of Chinese origin (Taiwan) and 50 European American mothers of preschool age children to indicate their views on the role of parenting in the child's school success. The Chinese mothers expressed a greater interest in education and suggested that they were willing to sacrifice for the sake of the children to a greater extent than their American counterparts. On the contrary, European American mothers stressed the importance of building their children's self-esteem, and expressed less motivation regarding their children's education. Why did these differences occur? Most of the Taiwanese immigrants to the United States who were studied came from a middle-class stratum and most of them emigrated from Taiwan for economic reasons. Therefore, one can guess that the achievement motivation in the Taiwanese subjects was perhaps higher than the motivation of the American mothers studied.

 Parents who are afraid to put their foot down usually have children who stepped on their toes.
CHINESE PROVERB

Consider another illustration. One hundred and seventy mothers from India, Japan, and England were asked to indicate the age at which they expect their child to achieve confidence in 45 different activities including education, compliance, interaction with other children, emotional control, and environmental awareness (Joshi & MacLean, 1997). It was found that competence was expected at an earlier age in Japan than it was in England. Indian mothers expected competence at a later stage than mothers in both England and Japan. Differences between Japanese expectations and English expectations were insignificant. However, the expectations of Indian mothers were considerably different from the expectations of the other two groups on all items except environmental competence, where they were "later" than Japanese but "earlier" than English mothers. Why did such differences occur? The subjects from Japan and England were taken from urban areas. Children in those regions live primarily in small

CRITICAL THINKING

Look at the Samples

The authors of the earlier mentioned three-country study suggested that the differences among the samples could not be attributed to socioeconomic factors because all the samples were taken from suburban areas and the income was approximately the same in terms of its purchasing power. However, such direct comparisons can be misleading. Even though a family in country A can purchase the same amount of food as a family in country B, the quality of purchased food could be dramatically different. If two families in two countries have access to medical care, the quality of care in country B could be significantly higher than the quality in country A. In the case studied previously, the scope and depth of the problems that India faces—overpopulation, infectious diseases, corruption, environmental problems, to name a few—can only remotely resemble the daily problems of average American and Japanese citizens.

families and the mother—who is likely to have a job—is expected to encourage her child's independence at an early age. In contrast, the Indian mothers may not be under such pressure to encourage their child's independence early. Indian children from the sample studied lived mainly in large extended families with many relatives representing two or three generations in one household. Even though one might expect that Japanese and Indian societies share similar cultural characteristics such as collectivism and the priority of family values, such similarities may be overshadowed by particular socioeconomic factors such as quality of life, availability of diversified information, and access to computers and advanced technologies.

Erikson's Stages of Psychosocial Development

Erikson (1950) theorized that all humans pass through a series of eight developmental stages that stretch from birth to death. Each stage is characterized by a developmental conflict, problem, or crisis. If the crisis has a positive resolution, the person's ego is strengthened by gaining a virtue that results in greater adaptation and a healthier personality. But, if the crisis has a negative resolution, the ego loses strength, resulting in inhibited adaptation and an unhealthier personality. For instance, if a young girl's conflict between a desire to go and play on the street (an independent decision, initiative) and fear of retribution from parents (guilt) has a positive resolution, she will emerge with the virtue of purpose; a negative outcome, however, would result in a sense of unworthiness (see Table 8.1).

TABLE 8.1	Developmental Stages According to Erikson		
Stage	Ego Crisis	Age	Positive Outcome
1	Basic trust versus mistrust	0–1	Hope
2	Autonomy versus shame and doubt	2–3	Will
3	Initiative versus guilt	3–5	Purpose
4	Industry versus inferiority	5–12	Competence
5	Ego identity versus role confusion	Adolescence	Fidelity
6	Intimacy versus isolation	Young adult	Love
7	Generativity versus stagnation	Adulthood	Care
8	Ego integrity versus despair	Maturity	Wisdom

Based on E. H. Erikson, *Childhood and Society*, 1950.

Erikson thus defined the healthy or mature personality as one that possesses the eight virtues (namely hope, will, purpose, competence, fidelity, love, care, and wisdom) that emerge from a positive resolution at each stage of development. It was Erikson's belief that the outcome of every crisis resolution is reversible. The goal in his approach to psychotherapy, therefore, was to encourage the growth of whatever virtues the person was missing to achieve happiness.

According to a comprehensive analysis (Gardiner et al., 1998), this theory could be applicable in a wide variety of cultural settings. However, as was the case with Maslow's theory (see Chapter 7), Erikson has been criticized by psychologists for mixing objective description with subjective prescription. Specifically, the virtues he uses to define the healthy individual are clearly in accordance with Western, Judeo-Christian ethics, values, and social institutions. In other words, Erikson, like many social theorists, may have been describing what he believes should be, rather than what is. We wish to emphasize that it is not our intention to impugn the value judgments implicit in the theory of Erikson; in fact, we find ourselves closely aligned with many of his beliefs. However, values and veracity are not synonymous. Further, we must remember that our perceptions of the world are inescapably colored by our own personal beliefs, and that the distinction between description and prescription frequently is a jumbled one indeed.

In Erikson's theory, the stages indicate a very general sequence that cannot always be paralleled in other countries. For most adults in economically developed societies, healthy and financially independent retirement is one of the prime areas of concern. Monetary savings and investments became a source of either elation or frustration for millions of individuals in the United States, Germany, Japan, and other countries. At the same time, billions of human beings have absolutely no money to save in the bank. Hunger, civil and ethnic wars, violence and oppression imposed by authorities, chronic ecological problems, and other cataclysms are the permanent focus of these people's daily concerns. Various unpredictable disturbances present a wide range of unpredictable problems, and the sequence of these problems is not as linear as it appears in Erikson's classification. Therefore, in many cases, more immediate strategies of survival may dominate people's lives.

In industrialized, wealthy democracies people can exercise a relative freedom of choice. They have available to them the choice of different foods, places to live, schools to attend, job opportunities, ideologies, lifestyles, and even religions. However, and this is a paradox, the process of individual development may be stressful in countries in which people are confronted with a wide variety of choices. Conversely, in many other cultures many people's identities and lifestyles are prescribed at birth. They accept a particular religion, political ideology, occupation, and place to live. People have fewer choices, and therefore their transition from one stage to another may be "smoother" than for people in the Western cultures, which have more choices. In other words, Erikson's theory could be more applicable to societies with so called **broad socialization** practices that emphasize independence and free self-expression, than in countries with **narrow socialization** that prescribes an ideology that strictly identifies both right and wrong behaviors.

It is important to note that in some cultures, social maturation is not associated with increased independence, as Erikson believed, but rather with increased interdependence. In some cases, for example, Buddhism, isolation may be rewarding and should not necessarily be avoided. Intimacy may occur at earlier life stages in some ethnic groups. Moreover, role confusion may not be typical for individuals from traditional cultures, but becomes significant for immigrants from these countries.

In general, when applying Erikson's theory to specific cultural conditions, try to analyze how each culture views each life crisis—assuming, of course, that the crisis takes place—and what is generally expected of an individual to perform, believe in, or reject to solve the crisis.

Piaget's Stages of Cognitive Development

Jean Piaget (1963) was primarily interested in how children develop the process of thinking about themselves and the world around them. According to Piaget, the child's cognitive growth is a stage-by-stage process, consisting of four stages. In stage one, the *sensorimotor* stage, infants learn about their interaction with their immediate environment. During stage two, the *preoperational* stage, children develop the foundation for language acquisition. Here children do not comprehend that other people may see things differently (*egocentrism*). At the fourth stage of *concrete operations*, children learn logic and realize that volume, amount, and weight may stay the same despite changes in the object's physical appearance (the process is called *conservation*). The fifth and final stage, *formal operations*, is when adolescents develop the ability to think abstractly.

Do children from all over the world move through these stages? Summarizing results from a handful of studies, Dasen (1994) suggested that the stage sequence—preoperational–operational–abstract thinking—appears to be universal across cultures. Children move from one stage to another as Piaget has predicted. Nevertheless, other psychologists were more cautious in their cross-cultural assessments of Piaget's findings (Gardiner et al., 1998). Most of the critical comments are related to the methodology and procedures used by Piaget and his colleagues. For instance, researchers who conducted earlier cross-cultural studies of language development using Piaget's theory had only limited knowledge of the language studied. Maybe because of this, researchers often used standardized tests that did not require the child to have language proficiency. Moreover, accurate birth dates of many children were not commonly available so that the actual age of the child studied was not always known.

Piaget's theory does a good job of explaining how children deal with conservation of volume, weight, and amount. Our everyday thinking, however, and ability to make practical decisions in a maze of daily circumstances are not explained well by this theory (Goodnow, 1990). Critics also pointed out that Piaget provoked a temptation to interpret some developmental stages as more "valuable" than others. This, in turn, leads to further categorizations. In reality, though, social success, satisfaction, or adaptation strategies, as well as certain activities and professions, do not require that the individual function on the level of formal operations. It is also questionable whether the formal operational stage is achieved by all adolescents in all societies. In both Western and non-Western settings there are many healthy, happy, and successful individuals who basically fail on formal operational tasks (Byrnes, 1988).

 A man may not transgress the bounds of major morals, but may make errors in minor morals.
CONFUCIUS (551–479 B.C.)—CHINESE PHILOSOPHER

Stages of Moral Development According to Kohlberg

Kohlberg (1981) described six stages of moral development in which children and adults are able to make several types of moral judgments. In brief, people go from lower stages of reasoning, where they prefer to avoid punishment for wrongdoing, to the higher stages, where they choose social contract and then universal principles to guide moral actions (see Table 8.2).

Snarey (1985) examined 45 empirical studies of moral judgment development conducted in 27 countries and suggested that the first four stages appear to be universal in the studied subjects of all cultures studied. However, some critics express skepticism about cross-cultural validity of this theory. Why?

The methodology used in cross-cultural studies on moral development was based on hypothetical stories about moral choices that were related well only to American subjects (Shweder et al., 1990). For example, in one such story a woman is suffering from an illness. She is prescribed an expensive drug that may save her life, however, the pharmacist in the story charges an excessive amount of money for the prescription.

TABLE 8.2	Kohlberg's Stages of Moral Development

Stage 1. Preconventional level: Judgments about what is right and what is wrong are based on fear of punishment.

Stage 2. Preconventional level: Moral conduct produces pleasure, whereas immoral conduct results in unwanted consequences.

Stage 3. Conventional level: Any behavior is good if it is approved by significant others.

Stage 4. Conventional level: The existing laws determine what is moral and immoral.

Stage 5. Postconventional level: Moral behavior is based on individual rights and underlying social circumstances.

Stage 6. Postconventional level: Moral conduct is regulated by universal ethical principles that may rise above government and laws.

The woman's husband does not have the money. The moral predicament in this vignette is whether or not it is moral to steal the drug.

It looks like a story that makes sense and the situation described is not unusual. However, in many countries, medicine is under government control and pharmacists cannot charge patients market prices. Some items are in short supply and briberies in these cases are common ways to get the prescription. Moreover, in some countries, physicians themselves—and not pharmacists—have access to medication and distribute it to their patients.

Another point of criticism is that the developmental stages are closely linked to values of Western liberalism and individualism based on moral choice. Liberal individualism, however, cannot always represent moral principles that are applicable to all cultures and peoples. In many cultures moral judgment is based mostly on existing traditions, and not necessarily on free will and choice. For certain religious groups, certain types of moral behavior are strictly prescribed in the Bible, Torah, or other religious scripture. Other studies point out that the individual's moral judgments are caused by circumstance and are not necessarily based on a certain level of the person's moral development (Matsumoto, 1994; Vassiliou & Vassiliou, 1973).

An interesting cross-cultural examination of Kohlberg's theory was conducted by Ma and Cheung (1996), who compared moral judgment of more than 1000 Hong Kong Chinese, English, and American college and high school students. The test consisted of four stories that each contained a description of a moral problem. The subjects were asked to make judgments about the possible solutions to the problem. It was found that Chinese tended to emphasize the importance of the stage 3 judgments and considered stage 4 judgments as more similar to stage 5 and 6 judgments. The English and American subjects tended to regard stage 4 judgments as more similar to stage 2 or 3 judgments.

The authors argue that moral judgments of the Chinese person are reinforced by traditional norms and regulated by conformity to primary groups. Chinese see issues, such as concerns for social order, consensus, and abiding by the law, from a collectivist perspective. A strong orientation to perform altruistic acts for the sake of close relatives and friends is part of Chinese culture. According to the authors, Chinese are also influenced by the Confucian concept of the Five Cardinal Relationships, which emphasizes the harmonious connection between sovereign and subject, father and son, husband and wife, brother and brother, and friend and friend. Social order, consensus, and law-abiding behavior are attached to the Chinese collective mentality. On the contrary, Western people are concerned primarily with individual rights and their interests being protected by the law. In the West, people easily sue each other because the law mediates interpersonal relationship. Chinese tend not to resolve their conflicts in legal institutions. They prefer instead to resolve their conflicts by using interpersonal contacts. This practice, however, can become a double-edged sword. On one hand, it may appear that interpersonal orientation is more humane and appealing than the law-based system. (Indeed, it seems healthier to settle a conflict than seek legal help.) However, an emphasis on an interpersonal system of communications may stimulate nepotism and corruption—two serious problems that Hong Kong officials themselves recognize very well.

Developmental Stages

It is widely understood that human development takes place in stages. Typically, birth and physical death—as the initial and final points of physical existence—are present in developmental classifications. Beliefs in reincarnation and immortality promote the understanding of the life span as a cycle. Views on the beginning of a child's life (i.e., when does it start, at conception or at a certain later stage?) vary cross-culturally and are based on people's educational background, religion, and other ideological values.

Birthdays, initiation rituals, weddings, graduations, job promotions, the birth of children and grandchildren, retirement, and other significant life events mark the most important points of human transition. Several biological, behavioral, and physiological changes are also recognized cross-culturally as indicators of particular life stages. Among these natural events are emergence of permanent teeth, first words, first menstruation and menopause in women, and intensive growth of facial hair in young men. Gray hair is commonly viewed as a sign of maturity despite tremendous individual variations of hair pigmentation. There are also age categorizations based on nonscientific beliefs or particular developments and life events. Such events may symbolically identify either the beginning or ending of a particular life stage. One's first intercourse could be seen as a confirmation of one's "manhood" or "womanhood." Reaching the drinking age—that is 21 in the United States and 18 in the Ukraine, for example—could also be interpreted as a sign of legal maturity.

Books on human development distinguish several common stages within the life span: prenatal period, infancy, childhood (divided into early and middle childhood), adolescence, and adulthood, which is, in turn, subdivided into three stages: early adulthood, middle adulthood, and late adulthood (see Table 8.3).

TABLE 8.3	The Periods of Human Development			
Prenatal period	**Infancy**	**Childhood**	**Adolescence**	**Adulthood**
From conception to birth: takes approximately 266 days in every ethnic, racial, or social group	From birth to 2 years: the child acquires initial motor, cognitive, and social skills	From 2 to 11–12 years: the child acquires language and learns about the most important social skills	From 11–12 to 19–20 years: the child has reached sexual maturity but has not yet taken on rights and responsibilities of the adult status	From 20 years onward: the individual has achieved adult status as prescribed by the norms and laws of a particular society

There can be slightly different categorizations of the life span, however. For example, according to Hindu tradition, infancy, early childhood, and middle childhood are not separate stages (Valsiner & Lawrence, 1997). Moreover, in more than half of the societies studied by Schlegel and Barry (1991), there was no special term for adolescence.

Life before Birth: Prenatal Period

In London and in Beijing, as well as in any other part of the planet, the typical time between conception and birth is 38 weeks. From the beginning, the developing embryo in a mother's womb can be exposed to either favorable or unfavorable conditions. For instance, the natural environment around the mother could be stable or unstable, safe or dangerous. Across the world, environmental problems and perilous conditions, such as hunger, violence, excessive radiation, exposure to chemicals, air and water pollution, to name a few, can cause various complications in pregnancy and serious birth defects. The availability or lack of professional prenatal care is also a crucial factor affecting the unborn child's development.

The fetus' life can be interrupted by a mother's decision to terminate her pregnancy. Nearly 50 million abortions are performed in the world each year. Almost 60 percent of them take place in developing countries where close to 90 percent of the over 20 million illegal and unsafe abortions are performed each year. This is despite the fact that in many cases abortion in developing countries is restricted by law and condemned by religion. The risk of death from an unsafe, or illegal, abortion in a developing country is 15 times higher than the risk in developed countries. Each year 70,000 women die as a result of such procedures (WHO Press Release WHO/28, 17 May 1999). Countries vary in terms of frequency of abortions performed. For instance, in the 1990s, there were 206 legal abortions per 100 births in Russia; in comparison, Sweden has a ratio of 30 to 100, Austria 17 to 100, and the Netherlands 10 to 100 (*Sotsiologitcheski Zhurnal*, 1, 1994).

Attitudes toward pregnancy also differ. In traditional collectivist countries, such as Malaysia, Singapore, Indonesia, Philippines, and Thailand, pregnancy is more family centered with active participation and guidance from family (Gardiner et al., 1998). In individualist societies, childbirth tends to be a rather private affair. However, one should be careful and try not to make stereotypical judgments. Many foreign exchange students, for example, mentioned to us how open many Americans are about their pregnancies: people make official statements, inform relatives and friends, and throw parties to spread the word about their condition. (An entire "episode" of a popular television series in the 1990s, *Mad About You*, was devoted to such events in the life of the show's main characters.) However, in Russia—a collectivist society—pregnancy is commonly kept secret until the changes in the woman's body become obvious. Husbands are not only absent when their wives give birth, they are prohibited from entering birth clinics and may be escorted out by the police if they dare to go inside the facility. Tradition and law often go hand in hand.

Infancy conforms to nobody; all conform to it.
RALPH WALDO EMERSON (1803–1882)—AMERICAN POET AND PHILOSOPHER

First Steps: Infancy

A newborn child needs total care. It is obvious that environmental and social conditions in which the new life begins have a crucial impact on the child's life, health, and perhaps his or her personality traits. Infant mortality, for example, varies greatly from country to country and depends on the socioeconomic and political conditions of each particular nation. For example, infant mortality in Chad is around 130 deaths per 1000 births. In Canada, the rate is 7 per 1000 (The World Factbook, 1998). Nearly 14 million children under the age of 5 die each year (WHO, 1999). Better social conditions and available health care could significantly decrease infant mortality.

The child's **temperament**, or personality traits present in infancy, presumably has a genetic basis (Buss & Plomin, 1985). Temperament may also be influenced by environmental factors. Parents respond differently when their child is crying. There are adults who easily neglect their children when they cry, and there are those who respond immediately. An immediate or delayed response to the child's crying may stimulate or inhibit certain emotions and other behavioral reactions in the infant. There are individual and cultural variations in such responses. For example, in one of the projects on cross-cultural similarities and differences in mother–infant communications, rural Kenyan and middle-class Bostonian mothers were compared. There were many similarities between the samples studied. Mothers in both locations would eagerly touch, hold, or talk to a child if he or she was crying. However, the American mothers communicated more with words and less with physical contact than did Kenyan mothers (Berger, 1995).

A variety of temperaments was found in a study of 4- to 8-month-old American, Chinese, Australian, and Greek Australian infants (Prior, 1986). Across cultures, rural infants show greater motor acceleration than urban infants. However, urban children display better adaptability to different situations in the second year of their development (Werner, 1972).

Ask a mother who has raised a healthy infant, and she will probably tell you that her son or daughter was able to recognize human faces very early. Indeed, most infants feel calm when they see familiar faces and show signs of worry when they see a stranger's face near them. A study conducted in several countries showed that most infants develop a form of attachment around their seventh month of life (Kagan et al., 1978). Such attachment patterns in a strange situation are universal and can be divided into three categories (Gardiner et al., 1998):

- anxious and avoidant [children do not pay much attention to their parent(s)];
- anxious and resistant [children tend to stay very close to their parent(s) and worry about his/her/their whereabouts];
- securely attached [children are not threatened by a stranger in the presence of the parent(s)].

Some researchers imply that the prevalence of the anxious-and-avoidant type is relatively higher in West European countries, whereas the anxious-and-resistant type

A CASE IN POINT

Customs in Parental Behavior

It is an East European custom—well maintained in the twenty-first century—not to show a newborn child to anyone except close relatives during the first month of the baby's life. Reasons? This isolation is considered to be a necessary precaution against an "evil eye." In other words, the child remains relatively deprived of other people and new experiences for some 30 days of his or her life.

Question: Do you think that this practice—that is exercised, perhaps, by millions of parents and leads to a relative isolation of the child during the first 30 days of his or her life—may somehow affect the child's psychological development?

is more prevalent in non-Western countries, such as Israel and Japan (Van Ijzendoorn & Kroonenberg, 1988).

Right-handedness appears to be prevalent in all cultures and genetic (Coren, 1992). However, different cultural practices and beliefs were found to affect the behavior of millions of children around the world. In many countries, for example, left-handedness was resisted, and both teachers and parents attempted to change this "anomaly" as they would call it, by forcing children to unlearn many of their skills that required the use of the left hand. Environmental factors also influence the ways children develop their motor activities. As an example, motor skills of African infants develop several months before they develop in white children: parents use different training strategies when they teach their children to walk (Gardiner et al., 1998).

Societal changes shape patterns of parental behavior. For example, frequency of breast-feeding and the level of a nation's industrial development are negatively correlated. In other words, breast-feeding declines the more the nation becomes industrialized and that causes further societal changes. The availability of baby formula and other foods, changes in women's occupation and social status, a general change in public attitudes, and other factors all promote freedom of choice for women who decide whether or not to breast-feed.

Technological changes may influence early socialization. Mundy-Castle (1974) noticed that Africans grow up in an environment full of people but lacking technologies. Europeans, on the contrary, tend to see fewer people and their lives are filled with technological devices. Please notice that this suggestion was made before "the computer revolution." In the new millennium, such differences between technologically advanced societies and the rest of the world are becoming perhaps more profound than were in the 1980s.

Infants are constantly surrounded by a complex system of sounds that represents a particular language. Children make important sound distinctions at a very early age and this may explain some linguistic differences that people experience when they learn a foreign language. For example, our mutual colleague from Japan has difficulties pronouncing the *L* when he speaks English (likewise, many Americans cannot pronounce the typically hard German *R*, the *KH* in Hebrew, or *GH* in the Ukrainian language).

CRITICAL THINKING

On Labeling of Dependency

It is frequently emphasized that people in Japan are more interdependent and emotionally attached to each other than people in Western societies. There are many explanations and interpretations of this assumption. Some of them refer to early socialization experiences. According to one view people in Japan possess a special instinct called *amae* that makes people interdependent (Doi, 1989). Amae is described as the tendency of the self to merge with the self of another person. This tendency becomes part of everyday life in Japan and is especially encouraged in the early mother–child relationship. How different is the Japanese *amae* from dependency, a concept known in Western psychological schools? (Dependency is a need for comfort, approval, or attention and may be described at the behavioral level as a child crying, clinging, following the mother, and other behaviors that encourage attention from caregivers.) To compare the meanings of both concepts, Vereijken et al. (1997) evaluated descriptions given by Japanese experts to *amae* and descriptions given by Western experts to dependency. The experts used a Q-sort method for the evaluation. First they were given 90 cards that each contained a written description of a particular behavior that characterizes the mother-and-child relationship. Then the experts were asked to arrange the cards in a certain order so that the cards chosen at the beginning would present the most salient behaviors, typical for amae (Japanese experts) and dependency (Western experts). The researchers found, despite predictions, a striking similarity between the behavioral definition of amae, given by Japanese experts, and the behavioral definition of dependency as provided by experts in the United States ($r. = 77$). It is quite possible that in different cultures, certain universal behavioral patterns are labeled differently. In reality, different labels may describe similar behaviors!

Japanese infants typically do not notice the difference between *L* and *R* because there is no *L* sound in the Japanese language and their parents do not use such sounds in their conversations. English-speaking infants are able to detect this difference, even if they cannot talk themselves! Perhaps our pronunciation difficulties have deep roots in our infancy when we began to recognize and memorize sounds. For example, many Russians could not distinguish the difference between sounds *i* (in *bit*) and *ee* (in *beat*). In the Russian language, there is no distinction between these two sounds. Some linguists suggest that the Danish language is especially difficult to speak because it contains so many unfamiliar sounds that non-Danish people were not exposed to as infants.

 Life's aspirations come in the guise of children.
RABINDRANATH TAGORE (1861–1941)—BENGALI POET AND NOVELIST

Discovering the World: Childhood

Mencius, an ancient Chinese philosopher, wrote that the great person is one who does not lose his childhood heart. Children are great because they are sincere and emotional. Childhood is a period of continuous growth, learning, and development. During early childhood children's thinking is wishful and fantastic. Little children are often uncertain about the difference between reality and fantasy and they often mix them together. They constantly check their thinking against the reality but still believe in the magical power of their ideas. During middle childhood, which lasts from approximately age 6 to age 12, children continue to develop thinking and social skills. Abstract thinking begins to play a greater role in their daily events. Still, the child's thinking is primarily based on observations and direct experiences. If something is tangible or observable, it is easily comprehended and interpreted. As an example, several studies involving English, Japanese, and Norwegian children suggest that they develop elaborate conceptions of war earlier than they do of peace. The conceptions of war focus primarily on aspects such as killing, fighting, and the use of weapons. Conflicts are pervasive and have concrete aspects that can be observed. Peace, on the other hand, is a less tangible and notable phenomenon. It may not register in interpersonal experience early in life to the extent that violence and aggression do (Rosenau, 1975).

Look at pictures that children draw. Some complex and colorful, some schematic and simple, they reflect what children see or wish for. Children see the reality around them and reflect it in their thoughts and fantasies. For example, 700 stories generated by 160 Chinese and American elementary-school students were analyzed. Chinese stories showed greater concern with authority, greater concern with moral rectitude, fewer instances of physical aggression, and greater salience of the role of natural forces and chance than the American sample did (Domino & Hannah, 1987). If children's drawings reflect reality, could adults make any suggestions about a child's life by discovering that themes of victimization constantly appear in drawings of Palestinian children living in Israel (Kostelny & Garbarino, 1994)? Could we explain why in American children's drawings, boys were pictured as more powerful than girls (Rubenstein, 1987)?

In practically all cultures—with the exception of regions that suffer severe food shortages—mothers try to coax their children into eating. They use various methods: from punishment to reward for good eating, from persuasion to feeding games (Dettwyler, 1989). Eating habits and food preferences of an adult person are generally linked to early-age feeding practices. Eating preferences show great variability among countries and families. Bread and many types of fruit and vegetables are common in most cultures. On the other hand, there are products that children begin to eat during childhood that are considered inappropriate for other children living in other cultures. Muslim children do not eat pork, Hindu boys and girls may never try beef, and Europeans stay away from dog's meat (see Chapter 7).

If attempts to feed children appear to be similar across different countries, cosleeping, or the practice of allowing the child to sleep in one bed with the parents, usually varies from country to country. Typically, cosleeping is resisted by American parents or at times allowed in some limited way. American and Western mothers commonly put their children in separate bedrooms. This practice is largely uncommon among Indian Mexicans (Morelli et al., 1992). Japanese mothers, on the contrary, are likely to see cosleeping as an excellent way of teaching a child to be interdependent with others (Caudill & Weinstein, 1969). One should note, however, that cosleeping is practiced in some countries, in part, because of living conditions: parents simply cannot afford a separate bedroom for each child in the family.

Many elements of social identity are formed during childhood. Children between the second and fourth grade are able to clearly identify themselves with their ethnic group, nationality, and social class (Dawson et al., 1977). At this stage, both Arab and Jewish schoolchildren in Israel were significantly different in their flag preference, clearly divided along the Arab–Jewish origins (Lawson, 1975). The arrival of television in many developing areas indicates the beginning of a new chapter in the lives of people living there. However, the impact of television can be different in every culture. In a longitudinal research conducted in northern Manitoba, it was shown that children who were already eager to explore the Western world through television, became more aggressive and out-group oriented. Children who were trying to avoid a relationship with the West became less aggressive and more in-group oriented than the other group (Granzberg, 1985).

Anyone can say without conducting research that children around the world love to play. There are some functions of play that are universal across cultures, such as teaching children about interaction patterns, cooperation, sharing, and competition. Despite these similarities, different cultural practices may develop different behavioral traits. In a study conducted in the early 1970s, playing children in North America appeared to be more competitive than children in many other societies studied (Madsen, 1971). These results, however, should be verified in contemporary conditions. Why? In the United States today, for example, a mother who signs her son or daughter up for a little league soccer team will perhaps get a note from the league explaining, very politely and cautiously, that the main purpose of the game is participation, not necessarily winning. In many contemporary children's sports leagues in the United States (i.e., baseball, football, basketball, soccer, ice hockey, and others) there are serious attempts made to emphasize a more nonachievement focus. For instance, in the fall of 1999, one of the local youth soccer leagues in Ohio prohibited parents from screaming and cheering on the sidelines because it may offend and disturb some of the children playing in the game—especially those who are losing.

Is there evidence that societal norms restricting children's behavior in many ways may cause children to become aggressive and rebel? According to the suppression–facilitation hypothesis, behaviors that are discouraged in a culture will be seen infrequently in mental health facilities. For example, if parents punish children for being

CRITICAL THINKING

Malnutrition and Development

The poor performance on verbal and intelligence tests of malnourished children appears to be a pattern across countries. Some authors suggest that these children—when parents want to prevent their crying—are often given, with very little verbal stimulation, food that contains sugar. As a result, these children have little opportunity to develop verbal and other cognitive skills (Guthrie et al., 1976). One should not forget about other factors that may contribute to the low test scores in malnourished children. Most of them are raised in poverty, with devastating living conditions and limited access to educational materials such as books, paper, and pencils (forget about developmental interactive CD ROM games!). All of these factors contribute to the deprivation of many education opportunities for these children.

violent, there should not be many violent mental patients in this country's mental facilities. The suppression–facilitation model also assumes that behaviors that are rewarded will be seen excessively. From the standpoint of another hypothesis, the adult distress threshold hypothesis, the behaviors that were discouraged in childhood will be seen in clinics more often than "acceptable" behaviors. Weisz and his colleagues (1987) tested this model in a cross-cultural study that involved Thai and American children. Buddhist traditions of Thailand are different from the American cultural norms. The former emphasizes nonaggression, politeness, modesty, and respect for others. Parents are very intolerant toward impulsive, aggressive, and "undercontrolled" behavior in their children. As the first hypothesis predicted, "overcontrolled" problems (aloofness, withdrawal) were reported more frequently for Thai children than they were for American children. Problems such as violence and disorderly behavior were reported more frequently for U.S. children. Thus the suppression—facilitation hypothesis received some empirical support.

 A boy becomes an adult three years earlier than his parents think he does, and about two years after he thinks he does.
LEWIS HERSHEY (1893–1977)—AMERICAN GENERAL

Major Rehearsal: Adolescence

John and Jorge are two 16-year-old neighbors and friends of different ethnic backgrounds. At the same time, they are so much alike. They both wear adult-size clothes, both have a shadow of a mustache on their upper lip, both play computer games for many hours a day, both contemplate getting a summer job, and both think of attending a local college in 2 years. As adolescents, they both have reached sexual maturity but have not yet taken on the rights and responsibilities of the adult status.

Adolescence is viewed not only as a developmental stage but also as a cultural phenomenon. For instance, extended schooling in many developed countries stretches the period from childhood to adulthood. On the other hand, many nonindustrialized cultures encourage their members to take on adult roles as early as possible. Thus, the adolescent stage becomes almost indistinguishable. In some countries, such as Brazil, many children begin to work full-time and take care of other family members as early as at the age of 12 and sometimes even earlier. In other societies such as India, girls can marry in their early teens and move to their husbands' homes to accept the roles of wife and mother. Cultural conditions can determine the recognition of an entire developmental stage!

The rapid changes in weight and height are important characteristics of adolescence. Cross-culturally, girls mature as much as 2 years earlier than boys. Since the beginning of observations in the 1800s in Europe and North America, girls have been maturing earlier than previously studied age groups of girls, approximately several months per every 10 years. For example, from 1850 to the 1950s, the average age of first menstruation in girls has decreased 5 years and became close to 12. This trend has significantly slowed down in the second half of the twentieth century, and was apparently not observed in less-developed non-Western countries (Frisch & Revelle, 1970). One possible explanation for this earlier maturation is the improved health care, nutrition, and living conditions of most citizens of the developed regions of the world.

Formal thinking at this developmental stage replaces concrete thinking and moral judgments are often made on the basis of the individual's values (Piaget, 1963). At the same time, adolescent thinking could be full of contradictions, unpredictable assumptions, and sudden turns. Despite their ability to make ethical judgments and their tremendous cognitive reserves, adolescents do not have the vision or wisdom often found at a more mature age. Altruism and selfishness, enthusiasm and withdrawal, tolerance and impatience may easily exist together in the same individual at the same time. Adolescence is also known for its alleged rebelliousness. Stanley Hall (1916), for instance, believed that this period of inevitable upheaval is biologically based and should be common in all adolescents in every culture. However, as observations suggest, this period is not turbulent for the majority of boys and girls (Kon, 1979, Petersen, 1988; Glad & Shiraev, 1999). Nevertheless, if the child's perception of the world is generally naïve and trustful, adolescence is often associated with the development of cynicism (Sigel, 1989). Cynicism—which is the belief that people generally and repeatedly violate prescriptive moral standards for their behavior—can become salient in adolescence because of the young person's tendencies to grow increasingly independent and critical, or because of an increasing amount of discouraging information about society that one receives in late adolescence, especially in the countries where political scandals became a common practice (Schwartz, 1975). However, we should anticipate a lack of publicly expressed cynicism in countries in which ideological and political homogeneity is strictly reinforced by the government. In such cases, an adolescent may develop cynical views without exposing them to pollsters or social scientists (Gozman & Edkind, 1992).

Social and political conditions play a significant role in individual socialization. In a study conducted in Israel, children of North American and Soviet immigrants showed significantly different patterns of behavior in the classroom. Students from North America were peer group oriented. Students from the Soviet Union were teacher oriented (Horowits & Kraus, 1984). The Soviet system of education, compared with the American system, had a very strong emphasis on student discipline and obedience. Moving into a new cultural environment, Soviet adolescent immigrants did not change their obedience-oriented behavioral pattern. In another study conducted in Israel, Soviet-educated adolescents were significantly more realistically oriented in their moral judgments than the Israelis who grew up in Israel (Ziv et al., 1975). Perhaps many years of personal humiliation and the struggle against the communist government for an opportunity to emigrate from the Soviet Union have contributed to the development of realistic and pragmatic attitudes.

Overall, social and political conditions in a particular country may affect attitudes and motivation of the young (Bronfenbrenner, 1970). For example, in the 1980s young people in Poland—a socialist country at that time—reported more aggression in their attitudes than young people in Finland (Fraczek, 1985). For several years, Poles lived under a state of emergency and violence initiated by the government and this could have triggered more violence on an interpersonal level.

In another study, 1500 high-school students from Finland and Estonia were asked to imagine themselves in three hypothetical situations (Keltikangas-Jarvinen & Terav 1996). For example, if one of your classmates is repeatedly teased by some of your other classmates, what would you do? If one of your classmates continues to be the target of a blackmailing, what would you do? If you see someone stealing money from one of your classmates, what would you do? The students then were offered several alternative solutions to these situations: aggressive, prosocial, social responsible, and avoiding. As a result, several tendencies were revealed. Estonian adolescents were more aggressive and less socially responsible in their answers than their Finnish counterparts. Moreover, avoidance was shown to be the most typical way of solving problems for Estonian students. How can one interpret the differences? The countries studied are very close geographically and share many elements of culture and history. The authors explain the results by referring to social and political factors. For more than 40 years, Estonia was a part of the Soviet Union, whereas Finland remained an independent country. Western values of individualism were persistently emphasized in child socialization in Finland. On the contrary, in Soviet Estonia, public education and socialization promoted the mantra of collectivism, obedience to authority, loyalty to the homeland, and a sense of social responsibility. Here comes some confusion in the interpretation: as far as we know, the system promotes loyalty, responsibility, and collectivism in socialists countries. Why did the actual attitudes of the young people in this study reveal the presence of aggression, avoidance, and lack of responsibility? The authors of the study suggest that despite the communist government's efforts, most young people in Estonia simply rejected the main values promoted by the authorities. However, other factors could also have contributed to the socialization of Estonian youth of the 1990s. The unprecedented political and ideological struggle in the country after it gained independence, rapid growth of crime and corruption, increasing social inequality, a virtual loss of guaranteed social security—these factors could have triggered the sense of disappointment and frustration in the population. Perhaps these negative developments of the most recent times, and not only the experiences of the early 1980s, affected attitudes of Estonian youth revealed in this study.

Collectivist and individualist norms influence individual behavior and perceptions. Elbedour et al. (1997) compared perceptions of intimacy in the relationships among Israeli Jewish and Israeli Bedouin adolescents. More than 600 students, from grades 7 to 11, completed questionnaires in which students were asked to rate statements describing same-sex adolescent friendship on a four-point scale ranging from low (1) to high (4). Statements such as, "To what extent does the following statement characterize the relationship with a close friend?" were asked. Characteristics such as emotional closeness, control, conformity, and respect for the friend were studied. Each of these characteristics was measured with the help of eight questions. The results showed that Jewish adolescents (more individualist than collectivist), as opposed to Bedouin adolescents (more collectivist than individualist), expressed less of a need to control or to conform to their friends. The Bedouin adolescents tended to emphasize both control of and conformity to friends.

Men are more like the time they live in than they are like their fathers.
ALI IBN-ABI-TALIB (600–661)—FOURTH CALIPH OF MUSLIMS

Adulthood

In all cultures, adulthood represents maturity, responsibility, and accountability. This period is typically divided into three stages: early adulthood, middle adulthood, and late adulthood (Levinson, 1978). The early adulthood stage is usually linked to formative processes, whereas the middle and late adulthood stages are associated with accomplishments of various kinds. However, the line separating these periods is unclear. Many adults have been and are able to accomplish great things at a very young age. For example, George Washington became an ambassador to France at 21. He won his first battle as a colonel at 22. Luther was 29 when he started his religious reformation of Christianity. Fidel Castro became a Cuban leader at 32. Einstein published his famous theory of relativity at 26.

Although some psychological functions decline with age, the individual's socialization during adulthood continues. Two models—the "**persistence**" or the "**openness**"—attempt to explain this process (Renshon, 1989). According to the first model, persistence, adults acquire attitudes and learn behaviors early in life and tend not to change them later. For example, if a child grows up in a religious family in Morocco, he or she will likely be religious no matter where he or she lives as an adult. The other model, openness, states the opposite: people do change their attitudes and behavior because they have to adjust to changing situations and the transformations can be substantial. In other words, early childhood and adolescent experiences do not necessarily determine who the person is today. Despite the fact that some students of socialization are intrigued by the "persistence" approach, most analysts agree that socialization does not stop at the age of 18 or 20. It was confirmed that socialization continues in the adulthood stage and many transitions in the individual's opinions and behavior take place during this developmental stage (Sigel, 1989).

Adulthood experiences vary across cultures and depend on age, gender, socioeconomic status, occupation, family structure, and a variety of life events. Violence, economic hardship, and hunger may affect the lives of an entire generation. As an example, social and political developments in Afghanistan during the last 25 years of the twentieth century were marked by a series of devastating developments. Among them were the revolution and dismissal of the king, the Soviet invasion in 1979, the war against the occupation, and the seemingly endless civil war that took tens of thousands of lives. An adult who was born in 1950, for example, during practically all stages of his adult life, was exposed to continuous stress, poverty, traumatic events, and fear for his or her own life. At the same time, a person born in 1950 in a small Norwegian town could have lived a life absolutely free of cataclysms, significant events, and unexpected turns.

In adulthood, most people develop their sense of **identity**, the view about themselves as individuals and members of society. Identity formation cannot be understood outside of its cultural context. In traditional societies, for example, people accept their identity in the systematic and coherent environment. The society is supposed to provide a sense of security for its individuals. The individual constantly refers to others for evaluation (Kagitcibasi, 1985). Individuality is especially restricted on the level of ideology or religion. People learn about their roles and acquire them while gradually moving from one life period to another. In Western industrialized societies the performance of social roles is more open to individuals, because the roles are not strongly formalized. Individuals take membership in a wide variety of diverse subgroups (Camilleri & Malewska-Peyre, 1997). Western societies, compared with non-Western ones, offer individuals a wide range of options. Individuals are not only given options, they are encouraged to choose.

I not only use all the brains I have but all I can borrow.
WOODROW WILSON (1856–1924)—TWENTY-EIGHTH U.S. PRESIDENT

In people's minds adulthood is linked to wisdom. The more mature the person is, the wiser he or she is expected to be. Societal expectations affect our perception of adult intelligence. For instance, quickness of thinking is linked to *fluid intelligence*, the ability to form concepts, think abstractly, and apply knowledge to new situations (see Chapter 5). *Crystallized intelligence* is the individual's accumulated knowledge and experience. In Western societies, speed of thinking is highly valued and fluid intelligence is interpreted as an indicator of success. In many non-Western societies, speed of operations is valued less, because experience, or crystallized intelligence, is perceived as more important that quickness (Gardiner et al., 1998). There are many mediating individual circumstances and social factors that affect crystallized intelligence. For example, a 60-year-old Iranian father can be a perfect mentor for his son, who starts a business in a small town near the Caspian Sea. The same father could be less efficient and knowledgeable after his family immigrates to another country.

In some cultures of the nonindustrialized world, the concept of middle age is indistinct. For instance, a person may be described as "young woman" or "old man," but not "a middle-aged person." Similarly, some view mid-life crisis as a stage for those who have the time and money to afford it.

The wine of life keeps oozing drop by drop, the leaves of life keep falling one by one.
OMAR KHAYYAM (TWELFTH CENTURY)—PERSIAN POET AND ASTRONOMER

Late Adulthood

When do people get old? Is aging a physical wearing and decline that takes place without a substantial change of attitudes? When do people slow down? Aging is a biological process. Although biologists haven't found conclusive explanations about universal characteristics of aging (Cox, 1988), most people of old age suffer from similar diseases (such as cancer, dementia, and arthritis), the skin becomes less elastic, and the hair loses its pigmentation. The muscles begin to atrophy, the bones become more brittle, and the cardiovascular system becomes less efficient. Most psychological functions decline too. Hearing and visual impairments are common. Memory may deteriorate while there tends to be a decrease in reaction time. However, human beings defy the "rules" of nature. Goethe, a great German poet, completed his Faust when he was 80. Lamark completed his great zoological book, *The Natural History of Invertebrates*, when he was 78. Ronald Reagan became president when he was 70. Mahatmah Gandhi reached the peak of his popularity when he was 75.

In many countries, the late adulthood period begins with retirement, when a person formally quits his or her job. If a person does not work outside the home, this period begins perhaps when the individual gives up his or her major family responsibilities. There are common national "deadlines" for formal retirement, which vary greatly. In Russia, a woman can retire at the age of 55 and men can do so 5 years later. In the United States, the common retirement age is 65. Norwegians push their retirement age up to 70. It is expected that so long as life expectancy goes up, the retirement age will go higher.

Countries vary greatly regarding their population's life expectancy. Japan and Switzerland have a life expectancy close to 80. Poverty, natural disasters, and chronic political and economic problems keep the life expectancy of some countries (Nigeria, Bangladesh, and Chad, for example) at the age of 60, 50, and even lower. This is at least 10 years or more below the average life expectancy in the developed countries (The Word Factbook, 1998).

In collectivist cultures, the elderly usually occupy a high social status. In individualist societies young people enjoy the greatest status, whereas the elderly can often be isolated and even rejected. Indeed, studies show that respect for the elderly is higher in Japan and China than it is in the United States (Yu, 1993). As in other Western countries, the parent–child relationship in the United States is more voluntary than it is, for example, in Asian countries, especially when the child reaches adulthood (Hsu, 1985). In most African and Asian societies, intergenerational families are the norm, and the younger family members customarily take care of older relatives (Gardiner et al., 1998).

Despite some cultural differences, the universal role of a grandparent can be similar. For instance, both in Japan and in the United States, elderly grandparents play a crucial role in providing support, care, and knowledge for the young people of their family (White, 1993). In both African American and European American families the relationship between a grandchild and grandfather is warmer when the latter lives near his grandchild, when the grandchild is a boy, and when the grandfather is in good health (Kivett, 1991). Unlike in collectivist countries, very few Americans live with their children and grandchildren. As the matter of fact, 80 percent of Americans prefer not to live with their grown children. One of the important causes of this attitude might be the cultural tradition of the "avoidance of dependence" in relationships. Another reason could be based on the fact that in economically developed societies, most individuals can afford to live alone, which is often very difficult to do in other, less developed countries.

French author and historian Andre Maurois wrote that growing old is no more than a bad habit that a busy man has no time to form. Age and aging are strongly related to an individual's time perspective. In turn, this time perspective may affect an individual's attitudes (Cutler, 1975). In early childhood the dominant perception is that time is virtually limitless. Early adulthood brings the realization that time is a scarce resource. Middle age and later stages lead to the perception that time becomes seriously limited. Gergen and Black (1965) pointed out that among public policy attitudes, orientations toward solutions to international problems are linked to one's per-

A CASE IN POINT

Culture and Perception of Aging

There is a trend in many Western cultures to hide signs of aging. In contemporary American society people often refrain from saying "old," and prefer to use a more neutral "senior" label. People surgically eliminate wrinkles on their faces and bodies, buy expensive cremes to keep their skin elastic, wear toupees and chignons, and try different "magic" colors to eliminate the natural gray of their aging hair. Do adults really dislike how they look when they get older? Do they believe that they become less attractive and therefore want to change their appearance to boost self-esteem? There is no evidence that this is actually true. Moreover, some studies suggest that self-esteem and personal "attractiveness" are not correlated (Kenealy et al., 1991).

Question: Do you think that the cosmetic industry and plastic surgeons—to boost their sales and get more clients—are interested in creating the "younger image" hype?

ception of personal future time: senior people have a sense of urgency and tend to settle conflicts, whereas the young may display stubbornness. Renshon (1989) argued that in the arts, the phenomenon of late-age creativity and boldness occurs often in different cultures. The last works of Shakespeare, Rembrandt, Verdi, Beethoven, and Tolstoy might suggest that the final stages of the life cycle can bring release from conventional concerns and free the artist to make major creative statements that represent a culmination of the person's vision.

Lin Yutang, a Chinese writer and journalist, wrote about the seasons of life: "I like spring, but it is too young. I like summer, but it is too proud. So I like best of all autumn, because its leaves are a little yellow, its tone mellower, its color richer, and it is tinged a little with sorrow." To agree or disagree with this assessment of the various life stages, we perhaps should live through all these seasons and compare our experiences.

EXERCISE 8.1

Develop Critical Thinking Skills Working with Original Sources

In 1983, D. Johnson and colleagues found that Mexican and U.S. children were more anxious than their Norwegian counterparts. Please find this article in *Cross-Cultural Psychology* [Johnson, D. (1983). Anxiety and social restriction. *Journal of Cross-Cultural Psychology, 14,* (4), 439–454]. Now try to analyze this paper answering the following questions. What were the samples selected for this study in three countries? Do you think that the selected samples accurately represented the entire population of children in the studied countries? List your arguments. What was the method used in this study and was it adequate? What explanations did the authors give about the established differences? Could you offer your own explanations?

CHAPTER SUMMARY

- Since ancient times, many of the world's thinkers considered human development a result of the interaction between environment and natural individual predispositions. Contemporary theories of human development emphasize the meaning of both individual and cultural factors of socialization. However, many classical developmental theories were ethnocentric and failed to take into account the richness of human diversity.

- In the interdependent families commonly found in rural traditional societies, the family structure is characterized by interdependency on both dimensions: between parents and their children and among children themselves. In independent families—the typical middle-class nuclear family in most European and North American countries—the family structure is characterized by independence on both dimensions.

- The developing child is seen as an individual with inborn dispositions and skill potential. The child's environment is a part of a larger cultural system. Both the environment and the individual are seen as open and interchanging systems. The power of the culturally regulated environment comes from the coordinated action of the three elements of the niche. They relate to each other, to outside forces, and to the developing individual.

- According to Erikson, a developing individual moves through a series of psychological crises. Each crisis, or conflict, grows primarily out of a need to adapt to the social environment and develop a sense of competence. Once a crisis is resolved, the individual moves further. This theory, with some amendments, is applicable in a wide variety of cultural settings. However, Erikson has been criticized for mixing objective description with subjective prescription. Specifically, the virtues he uses to define the healthy individual are clearly in accordance with Western, Judeo-Christian ethics, values, and social institutions.

- Studies suggest that the stage sequence (preoperational, operational, abstract thinking) and reasoning styles described by Piaget appear to be, with some limitations, universal across cultures. The limitations refer to the methodology and some procedures used by Piaget and his colleagues that are viewed as ethnocentric. Moreover, the Piaget theory explains how children deal with conservation of volume, weight, and amount. However, everyday thinking and the ability to make practical decisions in particular cultural settings are not well explained by this theory.

- According to Kohlberg, there are six stages of moral development in which children and adults are able to make several types of moral judgments. In brief, people go from lower stages of reasoning, where they prefer to avoid punishment for wrongdoing, to the higher stages, where they choose social contract and then universal principles to guide moral actions. This theory may be applied to different cultural settings. Yet, the methodology used in the cross-cultural studies on moral development was based on hypothetical stories about moral choices that were related mainly to American subjects. Another point of criticism is that the developmental stages are closely linked to values of Western liberalism and individualism based on moral choice, values which are not shared universally around the world.

- Cross-culturally, human development is understood as taking place in stages. Specialists refer to particular cultural norms and biological, behavioral, and physiological changes, which are identified cross-culturally with a particular life stage. Most books on human development distinguish several common stages within the life span: prenatal period, infancy, childhood (divided into early and middle childhood), adolescence, and adulthood, which is also divided into three stages: early adulthood, middle adulthood, and late adulthood.

- During the prenatal period, the developing embryo in the mother's womb can be exposed to either favorable or unfavorable conditions.

One's access to resources and professional prenatal care along with a stressful social and psychological environment are crucial factors affecting the unborn child's development. Attitudes about pregnancy, abortion, and childbirth vary from culture to culture and are linked to local traditions and laws.

- Each culture provides a particular set of norms regarding parent–child relationships. Cross-culturally, the child's thinking is wishful. Each child's developmental niche includes social practices, values, and demands conveyed to him or her from parents and care-givers.

- Adolescence is viewed not only as a developmental stage but also as a cultural phenomenon rooted in social and economic conditions. Many nonindustrialized cultures encourage their members to assume adult roles as quickly as possible, almost skipping the adolescence stage. Adolescence marks the beginning of sexual maturation. Despite their ability to make ethical judgments and their tremendous cognitive reserves, adolescents do not have the vision or wisdom often found at a more mature age.

- In all cultures, adulthood represents maturity, responsibility, and accountability. This period is divided into stages of early, middle, and late adulthood. Early adulthood is usually linked to formative processes and middle adulthood is associated with accomplishments. In adulthood, individuals generally form their sense of identity, which is the view of themselves as individuals and members of society.

- In many countries, the late adulthood period begins with retirement, when a person formally quits his or her job or gives up his or her major responsibilities. Late adulthood is linked to the physiological process of aging. Life expectancy, general socioeconomic conditions, individual psychological and physiological characteristics, and societal attitudes toward the elderly comprise the individual's final developmental niche.

 KEY TERMS

Adolescence The period from 11–12 to 19–20 years. The child has reached sexual maturity but has not yet taken on the rights and responsibilities of the adult status.

Adulthood The period from 20 years onward. The individual has achieved the adult status prescribed by norms and laws of a particular society.

Childhood The time from 2 to 11–12 years. The child acquires language and learns about the most important social skills.

Identity The view of oneself as an individual and a member of society.

Infancy The period from birth to 2 years when the child acquires initial motor, cognitive, and social skills.

Late Adulthood The period of physical wearing and decline.

Human Development The changes in physical, psychological, and social behavior as experienced by individuals across the life span from conception to death.

Persistence Model The theoretical view that suggests that adults acquire attitudes and behaviors early in life and tend not to change them later.

Openness Model The theoretical view that suggests that adults change their attitudes and behavior to adjust to changing situations.

Prenatal Period The time between conception and birth, which lasts approximately 38 weeks.

Socialization The process by which the individual becomes a member of a particular culture and takes on its values, beliefs, and behaviors.

CHAPTER 9

Mental Disorders

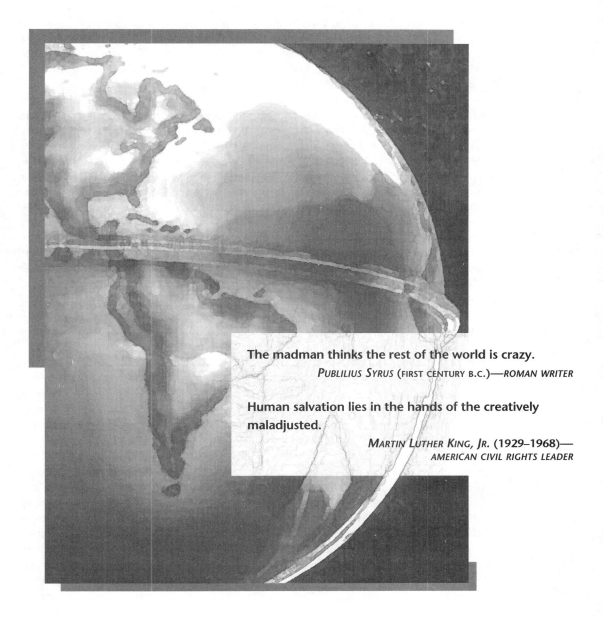

The madman thinks the rest of the world is crazy.

Publilius Syrus (first century b.c.)—*Roman writer*

Human salvation lies in the hands of the creatively maladjusted.

Martin Luther King, Jr. (1929–1968)—
American civil rights leader

The names and particular details in this story were changed in order to protect the identities of the people involved. Melissa N. was finishing her Master's degree in education at one of the southern universities. Brian W., her fiancée—they had dated since their high school graduation—decided to go back to college after several years of working and saving money. Neither had anticipated that their problems would begin at school. At the beginning of the spring semester, Brian unexpectedly received a 12-page letter handed to him by one of his classmates, a woman who appeared to be a bit older than most of the other students in the group. In the letter, filled with bizarre innuendo and a number of religious references, the woman confessed that she was in love with Brian. Moreover, she admitted that she was ready to divorce her husband and abandon her teenage children for Brian, the love of her life. Brian was shocked by this totally inexplicable confession, and showed the letter to Melissa. She suggested that Brian should talk to the woman and ask her to stop pursuing him. However, things got worse after Brian had this conversation with the woman. She started to call him on the phone. She was frequently seen waiting near the townhouse, which Brian and his fiancée were renting. The story became more complicated when the woman explained in a new letter that her soul and Brian's soul had met 300 years ago. According to the woman's religion (she was a Hindu Indian brought to the United States by her parents in the 1960s), a long time ago she and Brian were married and now she waned to restore the union of two souls that naturally belonged together. Brian and Melissa got scared. Assuming that the woman was delusional, they abruptly dropped out of school and moved to another state, thousands of miles away from their former university. Did they talk to school officials, hire a lawyer, or complain to the police? They didn't. Melissa later explained their decision: "That woman was sick. Period. She could have killed us. Thank God we escaped quickly. Neither the school nor police could have helped us. That woman was evil. That woman was ill."

Or was she? How can one judge another human being without a careful assessment of all available facts and circumstances surrounding him or her? Some people familiar with this story, including psychologists, suggest to us that the woman could be absolutely "normal." The reason she was misunderstood is that people are afraid of behaviors that do not look familiar. Some argue that eccentric or odd behaviors are not psychopathological. Behavior we do not like is not necessarily abnormal either. Maybe the woman was dangerously eccentric? One can raise serious doubts about this too. Hinduism values the idea of reincarnation and it is a "normal" belief for people who practice this religion. Besides, no one should say what beliefs we should have, right?

Wrong say other commentators, and imply that if someone displays personal, religious, or any other type of belief, he or she should understand the cultural context in which he or she lives. The woman in this story failed to understand and adjust to the cultural realities of the American society: you can have your beliefs but do not impose them on other people without their consent. Therefore, her behavior, being intrusive and harmful in the eyes of Brian and Melissa—and presumably in the eyes of millions of Americans—could be called bizarre and even abnormal. But wait a minute! Does the previous sentence indicate that if one dislikes the ideas of another person, this is a solid foundation for labeling that person's behavior pathological? What about freedom of speech, a fundamental human right? Besides, the woman in the story apparently did not do anything illegal. So, was the woman's behavior abnormal? Are the specialists able, in principle, to clearly separate psychiatric symptom or psychopathological syndrome from a cultural norm without confusing the two? We will try to answer these and many other questions related to culture and mental illness. This chapter is devoted to psychopathology, culture, and the links between them.

American Background: *DSM-IV*

According to the American Psychiatric Association's *Diagnostic and Statistical Manual of Mental Disorders*, fourth edition, or *DSM-IV*, a **mental disorder** is "a clinically significant behavioral and psychological syndrome or pattern that occurs in an individual and that is associated with present distress (a painful syndrome) or disability (impairment in one or more important areas of functioning) or with a significantly increased risk of suffering death, pain, disability, or an important loss of freedom" (*DSM-IV*, p. xxi). American clinicians usually assess the information that they have available to them about an individual from the standpoint of five axes, each of which helps professionals to examine the situation from five different viewpoints or domains of information (see Table 9.1).

 What is madness? To have erroneous perceptions and to reason correctly from them.
VOLTAIRE (1694–1778)—FRENCH PHILOSOPHER

Two Views on Culture and Psychopathology

Let us allow the subject matter to help clarify the concept of mental disorder. Psychopathology can be revealed through two types of symptoms: physical (behavioral) and psychological. Behavioral symptoms are recognizable through direct observation,

TABLE 9.1   **Multiaxial Diagnostic System**
Axis I indicates clinical syndromes and other important conditions that could be a focus of clinical attention. Axis II is for reporting Personality Disorders or Mental Retardation. Axis III is for reporting the individual's current medical conditions that are potentially relevant to the understanding or management of the individual's mental disorder. Axis IV is for reporting psychosocial and environmental problems that may affect the diagnosis, treatment, and prognosis of mental disorders. Among these problems are ones related to social environment and primary support group, educational and occupational problems, housing and economic problems, problems related to access to health care services, and legal and other social problems. Axis V is for reporting the clinician's judgment of the individual's overall level of functioning. Those professionals who prefer not to use the multiaxial system list the appropriate diagnoses for the individual.

and most of them can be empirically tested. Throughout the world, a given individual's anxiety could manifest as a set of behavioral symptoms, such as restlessness, muscle tension, or shortness of breath. On the other hand, anxiety is also reported psychologically, as a persistent worry or a state of apprehensive anticipation. But when one reports his or her symptoms, the account will inevitably contain a number of biases that originate from the person's individual experience. We have learned, for example, that people experience and explain their emotions according to cultural standards. On the other hand, the professional who evaluates the reported symptoms also places his or her judgment on the platform of a particular experience. Having these discourses in mind, could we imply that human beings that live in different cultures should understand mental disorders differently, and there is little overlap in their views on what psychopathology is? Or could we suggest that despite some cultural differences, the overall understanding of mental disorders is universal?

First, let us assume that psychological disorders are unique for each culture and cannot be understood without the context in which they develop. According to this view, psychopathology is culturally specific and should have different meanings in different societies. Religious, social, and political norms of each country should therefore determine the way mental disorders are understood and treated in a particular society. Different views on mental disorders, access to health care, and various government regulations may affect national statistics on mental-hospital admissions. For example, in the 1990s, in Panama the admission number was 121 per year per 10,000 people. The number was 100 in Finland, 94 in Sweden, 31 in the United States, 1.5 in Burma, and 1.4 in Tanzania (Triandis, 1994).

If we accept this approach to mental illness, we can no longer apply "standard" categories of mental disorders to other cultures' circumstances. Thus, it may be futile to study Major Depressive Disorder in Japan using American diagnostic methods because people in this Asian country may describe and explain bodily reactions differently than Americans do. Furthermore, what is considered psychopathological in one culture could be regarded as normal in another cultural setting and vice versa. Spirit possession syndromes are common and considered to be natural for some indigenous cultures. Just as most Americans would experience worry about the possibility of contracting a contagious disease, people in some African societies experience fear of bewitchment (Erinosho, 1978). When one claims that the alien spirits possess his or her body, this symptom, often marked by overwhelming anxiety, is likely to be diagnosed as schizophrenia in any Western culture. Dissociative Fugue, a disorder marked by sudden travel away from home or work, is known only in some cultures (*DSM-IV*, pp. 482, 485). Its prevalence could be caused by conditions such as a natural disaster or violence that targets particular ethnic or religious groups. In the former Soviet Union, homosexual behavior was considered to be both criminal and psychopathological. An admission of homosexuality could carry a penalty of up to 8 years in a prison or psychiatric facility. Moreover, in the 1990s a sizable portion of Russians believed that homosexuals were ill and should be physically exterminated (Shiraev, 1999). In the 1990s homosexuality was still considered pathological or even criminal in many countries (Iran is an example). Eating disorders are viewed as typical only for Western societies in which people have plenty of food and many individuals are preoccupied with fitness and thinness. In Puerto Rico, for instance, there is a specific behavioral syndrome called *ataques*

TABLE 9.2	**Culture-Bound Syndromes**

These are recurrent, locally specific patterns of atypical behavior and troubling experiences that may or may not be linked to a particular *DSM-IV* diagnostic category (*DSM-IV*, p. 844). **Culture-bound syndromes** are generally limited to specific societies or areas and indicate repetitive and troubling sets of experiences and observations. There is seldom equivalence of a culture-bound syndrome with a *DSM* diagnostic category. The following are examples of some culture-bound disorders:

- *Amok:* A dissociative episode characterized by a period of brooding followed by an outburst of violent, aggressive, or homicidal behavior directed at people and objects. The original reports that used this term came from Malaysia.

- *Ataque de nervios:* An idiom of distress with crying, uncontrollable shouting, trembling, and verbal and physical aggression. The syndrome is reported primarily among Latinos and Latin Mediterranean groups.

- *Bilis and colera:* This is strongly experienced anger or rage identified in Latino cultures. Symptoms include acute nervous tension, headaches, trembling, screaming, stomach disturbances, and sometimes loss of consciousness.

- *Ghost sickness:* Frequently observed among many American Indian tribes, the condition includes a preoccupation with death and the deceased, including bad dreams, loss of appetite, fainting, fear, anxiety, confusion, feelings of futility, and a sense of suffocation.

- *Rootwork:* A set of cultural interpretations that ascribes illness to hexing, witchcraft, sorcery, or the evil influence of another person. Symptoms may include anxiety, gastrointestinal symptoms (such as diarrhea, vomiting, and nausea), and fear of being poisoned or killed. The syndrome is known in the Southern United States and among some people in Caribbean societies.

- *Zar:* A general term applied in North African and Middle Eastern societies to the experience of spirits possessing an individual. People possessed by the spirit may experience apathy, withdrawal, and loss of appetite. They may be observed shouting, laughing, hitting their heads against the wall, singing, or weeping.

de nervios (see Table 9.2). This syndrome includes heart palpitations, dizziness, and brief seizure-like episodes. In Puerto Rico this behavioral pattern is considered a normal reaction to highly stressful events or misfortunes. In Seattle or Atlanta, however, these symptoms could be considered legitimate signs of an anxiety disorder.

Admitting the importance of the culture factor in principle, and agreeing today that culture has an impact on psychopathological processes (Beardsley & Pedersen, 1997), some researchers and practitioners prefer not to overemphasize the extent of cultural impact on the diagnosis and treatment of mental disorders. Moreover, some specialists maintain an opposite view on the nature of mental disorders.

According to this position, psychopathological phenomena across countries are universal in terms of their origin and expression. There are many examples that suggest such cross-cultural similarities. For instance, disorders that are rooted in basic biological functions, such as Alzheimer's disease, Parkinson's disease, substance-related disorders, and different symptoms of aphasia, have almost identical symptoms across countries. There are no reports of different incidences of Bipolar Disorder based on race or ethnicity (*DSM-IV*, p. 352). Japanese and American women, despite so many cultural disparities, did not differ in their Postpartum Depression scores (Shimizi & Kaplan, 1987). The disorder Unidentified Somatoform Disorder is commonly named "neurasthenia" in most cultures (*DSM-IV*, p. 451). Researchers have also found other illustrations of psychopathological invariance, which are not necessarily linked to human biology. Burton-Bradley (1970) described various cults in Papua and New Guinea that varied in character but had fundamental patterns common to them all. For example, in many a prophet arises and announces a millennium. His followers become active and prepare airstrips, wharves, and stores for the ancestral spirits to bring in the expected cargo. Vegetable gardens, money, and farm animals are destroyed, for in their view they will no longer be needed. When the cargo fails to arrive, the movement dies down until set off again by some new stimulus. Does this behavior resemble cases known in Western societies? Perhaps it does. Remember, for example, American cults led by David Koresh in Texas and Heavens' Gate in California in the 1990s? In both cases the cult members abandoned everything they had and followed their prophets to a promised "heavenly destiny."

Central and Peripheral Symptoms

Understanding both the cultural uniqueness and the universal nature of mental disorders, psychologists can implement a third approach to psychopathology that combines the two previously described viewpoints. Major features of mental disorder—abnormality, maladaptiveness, and distress—are universal. However, these features manifest in specific cultural conditions. Each disorder, in this context, can manifest as a set of **central symptoms** that can be observed in practically every culture and a set of **peripheral symptoms** that may be culture specific. For example, central symptoms for a case of Major Depressive Episode could be seen cross-culturally as (1) caused by biochemical factors; (2) a bodily syndrome manifested in the form of fatigue, lack of concentration, and various pains; or (3) psychological complaints such as indecisiveness, guilt, and the inability to take pleasure in previously enjoyable activities. Peripheral (culture specific) signs vary. Thus, a Canadian patient may display preoccupations with death and suicidal thoughts. On the other hand, a patient from Egypt is unlikely to express this symptom due to a strong religious opposition to suicide found in Muslim countries.

Considering this approach to mental illness, the professional should pay attention to the following areas.

1. Cultural identity of the individual, that is, his or her ethnic, religious, and other reference groups. Important facts are an individual's involvement with

both the culture of birth and the host culture, and his or her language abilities and language preferences. A simple and erroneous assumption, often present in cross-cultural literature, is that if a person is from a particular ethnic group, he or she should act and feel like that ethnic group. A person, for example, could be a refugee from Vietnam, who does not speak the English language, eats only his ethnic food, and associates only with other Vietnamese immigrants. On the other hand, an Iranian immigrant may not speak Farsi, eat exclusively fast food, and may not observe religious holidays.

2. Cultural explanations of the individual's illness. The clinician should identify how the symptoms of distress are explained in the patient's culture (misfortune, nerves, spirits, or physical symptoms), the patient's perception of the severity of his or her problem compared with cultural norms, the perceived causes of the problem or disorder, and past and current experiences with professional and other sources of care. For example, a patient from Italy might interpret her depressive symptoms as a "punishment" for not taking care of her ill father. The woman in this case may consider compulsive praying the only available way of healing. The variety of societal practices and public attitudes toward therapy can be amazing. For example, in the late 1980s and early 1990s in Russia, a country with one of the highest levels of education, millions of people were obsessed with the hypnotic subliminal "powers" of self-proclaimed healers. These "healers" would occupy hours of prime-time television, sponsored by the Russian government, during which they were "charging" people with "positive energies" in an attempt to treat the viewers' incurable diseases.

3. Psychological environment. The professional has to investigate cultural interpretations of social stressors and social supports, such as religion, family networks, and levels of functioning and disability. As an example, one could find that prejudice and hostility against a neighboring tribe or ethnic group could have significant impact on the development and treatment of Posttraumatic Stress Disorder in victims of "ethnic cleansing." Or a person with a terminal heart problem could be anxiously waiting for a heart transplantation and develop preoperational anxiety. In a similar condition, a Japanese patient could be preparing himself to die with dignity. As you might know, Japanese cultural and religious norms prohibit organ transplantation.

4. Type of relationship between the individual and the clinician, including differences in social status and culture. Here it is important to keep in mind the communication aspects of the relationship, such as language problems, an understanding of the cultural significance of the symptoms, the level of mutual disclosure, and an understanding of what is pathological. For example, gender and age stereotypes could cause mistrust and even rejection of a young female clinician in particular cultural settings, primarily in traditional cultures. On many occasions, an ethnic or religious match is also crucial in the process of communication between the patient and the therapist.

Our health is our sound relation with external objects.
RALPH WALDO EMERSON (1803–1882)—AMERICAN POET AND PHILOSOPHER

Environment, Culture, and Mental Health

What is a healthy person? Health is defined as a state of complete physical, mental, and social well-being (WHO, 1946). Some individuals, unfortunately, have genetic predispositions to particular illnesses or medical conditions. However, cultural norms, availability of resources, national standards on health, access to technology, social inequality, and many other environmental factors can affect the individual's well being.

The *psychophysiological* model, for instance, holds that health problems begin with stressors—environmental challenges, demands, and threats. Cultural conditions may affect the individual's coping responses, which could have different effects on the body's physiology and on the person's health. An individual handles stressors with his or her available psychological resources and particular ways of perceiving these stressors. In general, high levels of environmental stressors and poor coping skills could cause illness. If the individual is predisposed to a particular illness, this increases his or her chances of developing the ailment. Rapid social changes in any individual's life, especially in the family structure, may lead to uncertainty, instability, anxiety, social isolation, and, as a result, to mental illness.

There are data supporting a hypothesis that stressful events in one country will be equally stressful in another (McAndrew et al., 1998). Five-hundred and fifty-five college students in the United States, India, South Africa, and Germany were asked to rank a list of 32 life events to determine how stressful each of the events could be. The results of the study indicate a strong cross-cultural agreement as to the relative similarity of stressful major and minor life events. Researchers have found considerable evidence that environment is related to the health status of individuals. There are large national differences in life expectancy, but in general, socioeconomic conditions and life expectancy are positively correlated. For instance, African Americans are three times as likely as whites to be poor, and their life expectancy is 6 years shorter than the life expectancy of whites (U.S. national Center for Health Statistics, 1995). Illness and

A CASE IN POINT

Culture and Resistance to Certain Disorders

Social support can boost immunity and is often linked to health. In a cross-cultural Japanese American study it was shown that the more "Americanized"—in lifestyle, traditions, and values—the Japanese American becomes, the higher his or her rate of coronary disease (Japanese have a traditionally low level of heart disease). Those Japanese Americans who cannot be culturally distinguished from white Americans have the same level of heart attacks as white Americans (Marmot & Syme, 1976). Feelings of depression and isolation could suppress the immune system. In countries in which health is highly valued, individuals are more likely to seek treatment early and comply with treatment when disease is diagnosed.

poverty are linked across countries. For example, although the overall AIDS-related death rate in the United States has declined in the 1990s, the death rate for women continues to rise, particularly among ethnic minorities, who are more likely to be poor compared to other groups (Cogan, 1997).

In a report released by the Institute of Medicine and National Research Council (Branigin, 1998) it was shown that despite generally higher poverty rates, children of immigrants tend to be healthier than those of American-born parents. There are significantly lower rates of infant mortality and low-birth-weight babies among immigrant mothers compared to U.S.-born mothers, despite the fact that the latter have greater access to medical and prenatal care. Children in immigrant families have fewer long-term and short-term problems compared to children of U.S.-born parents. Adolescent children of immigrant parents have fewer mental health problems and are less likely to engage in risky behaviors or early sexual activities. However, the immigrant children's physical and mental health deteriorates the longer they remain in the United States. By the third and later generations, rates of drug abuse, teenage sex, violence, and suicide approach or exceed those of children with U.S.-born parents. How could we interpret these findings? One may contemplate that in general, on arrival in the United States, recent immigrants tend to eat more unprocessed food, such as fruits, grain, and vegetables, and have not yet joined the stream of "*hamburgerization*" of the American culture. Most importantly, recent immigrants typically have strong two-parent families, and maintain many social taboos, such as smoking and drinking, especially by women. Moreover, these families are strong, self-selected groups who are willing to take a chance and succeed in a new country. One of the reasons for decline is probably based on abandonment of discipline and protectiveness of their families by the time of arrival to the United States.

Concepts of mental illness evolve and will be evolving in the future. In today's changing world people themselves can develop various interpretations of mental health. They have certain ideas, based on common sense and some cultural knowledge, about the name of the illness, duration of the disorder, treatment, and possible consequences. They also have their own concepts about causes of mental problems. In most Western countries today, the concert of biological causes of mental illness has become popular. However, together with these scientific understandings of mental illness people maintain socioeconomic, psychological, supernatural, and other views on psychopathology.

The impact of the contemporary modernization of life also brought significant changes in how people understand mental illness. Some studies show that with modern changes that take place in the country, people change their thoughts about mental abnormality. For instance, in a study conducted in South Africa, Hindu subjects (South Africa has a large ethnic group of Hindu Indians) showed a conceptualization of mental illness in Eastern terms, with an emphasis on the spiritual nature of illness, but acceptance of Western conceptions of treatment including the use of medication (Bhana, 1986). Similarly, in the Philippines, with the increased educational level of its the population, availability of resources, and access to communications, more people change their traditional spiritual beliefs of mental illness, and often turn to medical treatment of the problems (Edman & Kameoka, 1997).

Despite similarities, there are substantial cultural differences in the way people express their attitudes toward mental disorders. Superstitions and lack of information could contribute to such differences. However, broader social and cultural norms, traditions, and beliefs may help create the individual's perception of what is considered abnormal (Secherst et al., 1973). Psychotherapists report that Asian Americans are more likely than whites to believe that mental problems are caused by physical factors and that mental health is associated with discipline and maintenance of a positive attitude. Some Hispanic Americans view mental health problems as burdens to bear or they look for religious or folk remedies. Some East European clients in America seeking psychological help view their mental problems, such as depression and anxiety disorders, as a result of the hostility of American society. There are different cultural-specific beliefs about chronic illness, for example, among the Canadian, Chinese, Indian, and Anglo-Celtic populations (Cook, 1994). In general, different forms of Conversion Disorders (symptoms of deficit affecting motor and sensory function, such as convulsion, loss of balance, paralysis, or loss of sensation) could reflect cultural ideas about distress and its expression. This disorder is more common in rural populations and individuals with lower educational levels (*DSM-IV*, p. 455). It was found that the lifetime prevalence of affective disorders, including major depressive episodes, is higher in American non-Hispanic whites compared with Mexican American immigrants. The rates for Mexican Americans born in the United States were about the same as the rates for non-Hispanics. It is hypothesized that with acculturation, Mexican Americans may learn to experience and express depression not through somatic signs but rather through cognitive and affective symptoms, which are more likely to be diagnosed by specialists as symptoms of depression (Lopez, 1994).

Many cross-cultural surveys show that men and women express mental problems in different ways. Men are more likely to have behavior-related disorders and problems (such as antisocial behavior or aggression). Women are more likely to have emotion-related dysfunctions and problems such as depression and anxiety (Castillo, 1997).

Let us explore now some specific mental disorders identified in the United States from a broader cross-cultural context.

 To be conscious is an illness—a real thorough-going illness.
FYODOR DOSTOEVSKY (1821–1881)—RUSSIAN NOVELIST

Schizophrenia

Schizophrenia is a disorder characterized by the presence of delusions, hallucinations, disorganized speech, and disorganized or catatonic behavior. Approximately 1 percent of the world's population is affected by schizophrenia, the symptoms of which appear to be universal. As an example, in a multicultural survey conducted in nine countries more than 12,000 schizophrenic patients were carefully studied. It was found that more than three-quarters of the patients were diagnosed as schizophrenic based on the results of a standard diagnostic instrument used in the survey (Berry et al., 1992). (However, it is important to notice that almost 25 percent of the examined patients could not be diagnosed with schizophrenia based on the diagnostic procedure used.)

Despite general similar occurrence rates, there are some cultural variations. For example, there is a relatively high admission rate with this diagnosis in the Republic of Ireland. In the United States, blacks have relatively higher rates of schizophrenia than whites (Levinson & Simmons, 1992). Acute and catatonic cases of schizophrenia were more prevalent in developing countries compared with developed nations (Sartorius, 1992). Delusional ideas in one culture may be nondelusional in others. Visual and auditory hallucinations could have different interpretations in various places, and speech could be mistakenly diagnosed as disorganized due to different forms of verbal presentation.

Despite the assumed biological causes, social conditions can and do affect the course of schizophrenia. Higher educational statuses of patients, for instance, were predictive of whether the illness would remain chronic, but this trend was confirmed for only non-Western countries. People may internalize their environmental influences differently, such as peer pressure, requirements, and expectations from others. Warner (1994) explained this fact by suggesting that in the Third World countries, the better educated experience higher work-related stress. Incidents of schizophrenia are higher among Irish Catholics and Irish immigrants in Canada (Murphy, 1982a). It is suggested that this could be explained by the complicated communication style of Irish people. However, national differences in schizophrenia rates could also be explained by differences in access to hospitals. As far as this assumption goes, if access to medical services and facilities is limited, a more severe case is more likely to get attention than less severe cases of illness.

Depressive Disorders

Cross-cultural studies of depression show that there are some universal symptoms. They include persistent anxiety, dysphoria, tension, lack of energy, and thoughts of guilt and insufficiency. In the United States, epidemiological surveys (that examine all people, not only patients with diagnosed mental disorders) indicate that major depressive episodes occur with equal frequency in African American, Hispanic, and European American groups (Tanaka-Matsumi & Marsella, 1976). A cross-national study of depressive symptomology conducted in countries that share many common cultural and religious traditions, such as Czechoslovakia, Sweden, Germany, Spain, England, and the United States, indicated impressive qualitative similarities (Zung, 1972).

There are some substantial ethnic variations in the expression of depression, which are also linked to various individual differences, socialization experiences, cultural definitions of disorder, and stress (Marsella et al., 1973). Marsella (1998) pointed out that the psychological representation of depression occurring in the Western cultures is often absent in non-Western societies. The low prevalence of depression in Asian countries could be explained, in part, by diagnostic practices (Tanaka-Matsumi & Draguns, 1997). As an example, persistent feelings of guilt—painful awareness about violating one's moral code or having failed to perform a duty or task—are more common in patients from Western countries than from non-Western societies (Singer, 1975). Even if guilt was also presented in some African samples of individuals with depressive disorders, it is assumed that guilt is experienced, attributed, and communicated differently in various cultural settings (Beardsley & Pedersen, 1997). In many non-Western cultures, as was mentioned, depression is interpreted in behavioral terms that include somatic, nonpsychological symptoms. For example, word associations to the word "depression" were studied in Japan and the United States. It was shown that the Japanese subjects preferred to use more external referent terms, such as "rain" and "cloud," and somatic referent terms, such as "headache" and "fatigue." In contrast, both Japanese Americans and white Americans associated predominantly internal mood state terms, such as "sad" and "lonely," with the word "depression" (Tanaka-Matsumi & Marsella, 1976). The World Health Organization (1983) found that 76 percent of people diagnosed with depression reported symptoms such as anxiety, sadness, tension, lack of energy, loss of interest, and an inability to concentrate. On the other hand, 40 percent of the examined people reported other symptoms, mostly somatic (physical) complaints. Feelings of guilt were equally common in both British and Turkish patients. However, a study by Ulusahin and colleagues (1994) showed that among British patients with depressive symptoms, there were high scores on psychological complaints (depressed mood, guilt, pessimism); the participating Turkish patients showed higher scores on somatic complaints (sleep disturbances, pains, and aches).

There are other examples of culturally specific (peripheral) symptoms of depression. For instance, headaches in Latino and Mediterranean countries, weakness, im-

CRITICAL THINKING

Social Factors in Depression?

Despite some current trends in explaining depression from a biological perspective, many specialists still turn to social factors when trying to explain major causes of depression. For example, why does depression strike so many people in Western cultures? Is it because these societies emphasize independence, individualism, and success as the main sources of happiness? Is it true that negative processes such as erosion of the family and increasing self-isolation of the people have spawned a widespread sense of hopelessness? Why is depression not so common in Asian countries? It is a common explanation today that in the East, individual success is not typically measured by one's achievements in the material sphere. Some suggest, in addition, that since depression is often linked to a grieving process, then specific mourning rituals in non-Western cultures may reduce the risk of this illness (Crittenden et al., 1992). However, we shouldn't view all East Asian countries as similar to each other. A closer look at the contemporary situation shows that Japan may be an exception among its East Asian neighbors because it has the highest rates of depression and suicide. The economic and financial crisis that struck this country in 1998 has made the situation with suicides even worse (Jordan & Sullivan, 1998).

Question: Try to guess the cause of the relatively high rates of depression in Japan. Do you think that Western standards of attaching happiness to success and obsession with hard work finally penetrated the minds of many Japanese people?

balance, and tiredness in Chinese and Asian countries, and problems of the "heart" in Middle Eastern countries could all be interpreted as depressive. There could also be experiences such as feelings of "heat" in the head, crawling sensations of insects, and experiences with dead relatives, which are reported by some patients and should not necessarily be interpreted as hallucinations (*DSM-IV*, p. 324).

Depression could be also interpreted as a learned syndrome. Using the so-called learned hopelessness model, psychologists confirm that this model has some cross-cultural validity, as it was shown on both American and Filipino subjects (Crittenden & Lamug, 1988). Available evidence indicates that depression and stress-related syndromes are commonly found in refugees. Those individuals who have higher socioeconomic status and are proficient in English appear to be better adjusted than other refugees. The learned helplessness model seems to work in explaining refugee adjustment problems and related depression (Nicassio, 1985).

Do men and women differ in their depressive symptoms? It is known that among depressive patients, women outnumber men by a ratio of 2:1. Depression is especially high in single females. In cultures in which alcohol abuse and aggression are rare, the rates of depression for women and men are almost equal (for example, in the Amish community in Pennsylvania). Other studies suggest that gender differences in depressive symptoms are substantial only among men and women of lower socioeconomic status. Across cultures, girls are particularly vulnerable to depression. As studies show, depressed girls are more dissatisfied with their bodies than girls without depression; depressed girls are also preoccupied with the way they look, and they often think of their bodies as ugly, useless, weak, etc. These concerns could also be common for some ethnic minorities, especially with distinctive physical characteristics such as skin color, color of the hair, shape of the eyes, and body height.

Culture and Suicide

Approximately every 15 minutes somebody in the United States takes his or her life. In high-pressure cultures, such as Germany, Taiwan, and the United States, suicide rates are much higher than in less achievement-oriented cultures: the ratio, for instance, between the United States and India is approximately 2:1. Japan has even higher rates of suicide than the United States, especially among the elderly. In general, rapid social transformations only sometimes produce increases in suicide rates (Desjaralis et al., 1995). There is also little support for the hypothesis of a compensatory relationship between suicide and homicide: countries with high suicide rates could also have high homicide rates (Pfeifer, 1994).

Barraclough (1988), analyzing suicide trends in adolescents and young adults, showed a relatively complicated picture of suicide rates across the world. For example, countries such as Syria, Egypt, Jordan, and Kuwait have low suicide rates. Many countries in Central and South America have low rates also, with the exception of Surinam, El Salvador, and Cuba. Scandinavian countries, as well as Central and East European states, have higher suicidal rates compared with other countries studied. Some Asian countries, such as Japan, Singapore, and Sri Lanka, have relatively higher rates. Elsewhere in the world, higher suicide rates are reported for males, with the exception of

A CASE IN POINT

Suicide in Finland: From a Conversation with a Finnish Doctor

Do you know that Finnish men are killing themselves at the highest rate among Western nations? The suicide rates in this prosperous Scandinavian country are about 30 suicides per 100,000 population (the rate for the United States is 12 per 100,000). The numbers for Finnish men are five times higher than they are for women. Remarkably, ethnic Swedes who live in Finland have lower suicide rates and ethnic Finns who live abroad still have higher suicide rates than those of native groups. How can we explain such high rates of suicide? Some would choose explanations that are easily accessible: "It's climate! It is too cold in Finland!" However, we know that people in Iceland live in a colder climate, and the suicide rates are much lower there. One may guess: "Is it alcoholism?" Indeed, Finland has high alcohol consumption rates and specialists suggest that suicides occur more frequently among the inebriated. However, there are countries with high alcohol consumption rates, such as Korea, but with lower suicide rates. "Is it societal violence? Could suicide be self-directed aggression?" The murder rates in Finland are among the highest in Europe. There are other countries that have higher rates of violence (the United States, for example) but lower rates of suicide, compared to Finland. "It is social and economic problems!" In fact, suicide rates jumped about 25 percent during the 1980s, the years of economic prosperity for Finland. However, rapid economic development is not linked to higher suicide rates in other countries. Finally, the most knowledgeable could suggest: "Is it the linguistic factor? Finns, Hungarians, and Estonians all have high suicide rates and their languages belong to the Finno-Ugric linguistic family."

Questions: Could the language alone be a cause of high suicide rates? Or maybe we should consider all of these factors together?

Cuba, Paraguay, and Thailand. The world's highest suicide rates are reported in Sri Lanka (47 per 100,000) and Hungary (39 per 100,000). Some hypothesize that ethnic violence is a cause of the high suicide rate in Sri Lanka. As to Hungary, its high suicide rates are explained by the confusion caused by rapid social developments and the country's transition from communism. However, this explanation is not correct. There are other formerly communist countries, as well as countries torn by ethnic wars, that have significantly lower suicide rates. In addition, there is no certainty about whether some national data are accurate. Some argue, for example, that in countries such as Iran, North Korea, China, and the former Soviet Union the "official" numbers of suicides did not and do not reflect the real course of events.

Suicide rates are generally lower in cultures in which religion strongly opposes "self-murder." There are relatively low levels of suicide in predominantly Catholic and Muslim countries compared with many Western and Protestant nations, where suicide is considered by some as a legitimate way of escaping physical pain, personal loss, and other misfortunes of life. However, along with religious prescriptions, there are other cultural factors that might affect people's attitudes toward suicide. As an example, suicide rates in Puerto Rico are higher than those in Mexico, both of which are Catholic countries. The difference may be explained by the coexistence among Puerto

CRITICAL THINKING

Is This a Murder Case?

Traditions and traditional ways of thinking live on and often influence our perception of events. A young Japanese American woman who lived in Los Angeles discovered that her husband was unfaithful to her. She decided to take her own life and the lives of her own children as well. Trying to commit suicide, she nevertheless survived, but she did kill both of her children. Many people in the Japanese American community, grieving over the death of the children, rallied in support of the woman, nevertheless. They argued that what she did was not a crime committed by a mentally sick person, but an act of honor, according to old Japanese beliefs and customs.

Question: What would you decide if you were a member of the jury selected for this criminal case? Explain your opinion.

Ricans of both Catholic doctrines and Indian folk beliefs (i.e., assumptions of communications between the dead and those who are alive).

In India, certain sacrificial suicides were permitted for centuries. In preindustrial Japan, suicide was traditionally approved of as a solution to certain life problems, or as an act of honor. However, there are still many cases of suicide among Japanese youngsters who, for example, fail to pass tough college entrance examinations, an educational tradition virtually unknown to Americans. Some theories of suicide suggest that there may be a relationship between societal complexity and frequency of suicide (Durkheim, 1897). A cross-cultural sample of 58 societies was selected to test this hypothesis formulated more than 100 years ago. Each selected society was rated on a scale of social development, and the number of cases of suicide in the literature for each society was recorded. There emerged a significant relationship between societal complexity (e.g., urbanization, organizational ramification, and craft specialization) and rate of suicide (Krauss, 1970).

Anxiety Disorders

There are substantial cultural variations in the expression of anxiety that range from somatic to cognitive to behavioral symptoms. Differences in diagnostic practices account in some way for cross-cultural differences in reported symptoms and could explain great cross-cultural variability for anxiety disorders (Draguns, 1980).

Take, for example, Obsessive-Compulsive Disorder, which is manifested as recurrent and persistent thoughts, impulses, or images. Could culturally prescribed ritual behavior be indicative of this disorder? Clinicians would caution against such a diagnosis. Specific repetitive behavior—praying, for example—should be judged in accordance with the norms of the individual's culture and should clearly interfere with social role functioning (*DSM-IV*, p. 420). Despite variations among countries, comparative epidemiological studies suggest that the rates of this disorder do not vary sig-

A CASE IN POINT

Witnessing Traumatic Events

Various traumatic events have direct and indirect impact on the development of various anxiety problems across countries. Dr. Cheryl Koopman (1997), a psychologist from Stanford University, conducted a cross-national examination of emotional symptoms caused by various traumatic events different in scope and intensity. She found that traumatic events such as the Holocaust, terrorism, captivity, torture, rape, political assassinations, and political violence could produce similar behavioral responses in individuals of different national, cultural, and religious backgrounds. These reactions could be described as Posttraumatic Stress Disorder, Acute Stress Disorder, or acute stress reaction (*International Classification of Diseases and Related Health Problems*, 10th ed.). Individuals who were exposed to such traumatic events, for example, political refugees, asylum seekers, and victims of ethnic "cleansing," typically have highly elevated rates of Posttraumatic Stress Disorder compared with the general population.

nificantly from country to country. Weissman and colleagues (1994) compared obsessive-compulsive disorders across the United States, Canada, Puerto Rico, Taiwan, Korea, and New Zealand, and found similar rates, with Taiwan as the exception, where the rates were much lower compared with the other countries.

Phobias, persistent and excessive fears, are also culture bound. The environment in which we live often determines the type of fear we experience. Excessive fear of magic spirits, perhaps, should be diagnosed as specific phobia in a culture where this type of fear is culturally appropriate (*DSM-IV*, p. 407). Expression of fear also depends on social demands. In Japan and Korea, for example, individuals with Social Phobia may express persistent fear of being offensive to others instead of being embarrassed. Some cultures restrict the participation of women in public life and there are strict rules applied to women's behavior in public places and regarding the clothes they wear. Therefore, a woman's reluctance to appear in public should not be automatically considered as Agoraphobia (*DSM-IV*, pp. 399, 413).

Dementia

Research has barely touched cross-cultural aspects for this organic mental illness, which is characterized by deterioration of cognitive functioning. There are a number of methodological difficulties in collecting data on dementia. It is known, for example, that white Americans might be more likely than Asian Americans, Hispanics, or blacks to institutionalize an elderly demented relative. It is not certain though whether this tendency is based on the individualistic values of white middle-class Americans, or this behavior is determined by the differences in socioeconomic conditions. The better financial status of some people allows them to keep their relatives in special retirement institutions.

CROSS-CULTURAL SENSITIVITY

When Jeff, an exchange student from Oregon was invited to a birthday party, he was thrilled. This was the first party he would attend in Russia and he knew how well Russians mastered the art of celebration. The day of the birthday, he dug out a nice souvenir from his suitcase, then caught a taxicab and decided to stop by a flower market to buy a nice bouquet—he was invited by a female student and he thought flowers would be a nice addition to the souvenir he brought from Portland. He could not anticipate that the flowers would cause so much anxiety and frustration an hour later. He bought a dozen roses—a very nice gesture according to American standards. But when he presented flowers to the host, he noticed how visibly upset she became when she put the flowers into a vase. He even saw her crying in the kitchen. A couple friends were trying to comfort her. Jeff began to wonder if his behavior had been the cause of the young woman's crying. What he learned, as he later said, was one of the strangest experiences in his life. He said that the young woman was extremely upset because he brought an even number of flowers. Coincidentally, she had recently survived a deadly illness and was extremely sensitive to the issue of death and dying. Apparently, Russians bring an even number of flowers to funerals, memorial services in church, and cemeteries. An odd number of flowers is designed for dates, weddings, and other happy celebrations. Apparently, the flowers—the number of them, in fact—that Jeff brought to the party became a disturbing signal that brought the woman's traumatic experience back to her memory. In general, Russians will not react in the same dramatic way if you bring an even number of flowers to their celebration. However, you will notice that one flower—out of the dozen or half-a-dozen you bring—disappears from the vase. Fears, phobias, and superstitions are at times rooted in folk customs and practices.

Rates of dementia among white men and women do not differ. However, institutionalized African American women have a rate of 20 percent, compared with 9 percent for black men. In those cases, the factor associated with dementia is the presence of additional medical problems. African American women have higher rates of strokes, diabetes, heart attacks, and high blood pressure than other groups in the United States. Dementia should be diagnosed cautiously and with consideration of the patient's educational and cultural background. For instance, certain tests of general knowledge may include questions about issues and items (such as people, directions, and locations) not familiar to the patient or conceptualized differently in his or her native culture (*DSM-IV*, p. 137).

Attention-Deficit/Hyperactivity Disorder (AHDH)

The essential features of this developmental disorder are persistent inattention, hyperactivity, and restlessness of the child. ADHD has been identified in many ethnic groups. There is a lower prevalence of ADHD in Great Britain, for instance, and a higher prevalence in China. However, because of the inconsistency in diagnostic procedures, it is currently impossible to make any valid cross-cultural comparisons of this phenomenon. There are different levels of tolerance in school systems around the world. It was shown that children from families of lower socioeconomic status have a higher frequency of ADHD than their counterparts from middle-class families. How can this phenomenon be explained? It seems that mothers of a lower socioeconomic class are likely to have poor care and nutrition during pregnancy. In addition, the troubled social environment of low socioeconomic status families (i.e., poverty, violence, alcoholism, or family instability) may contribute to the development of ADHD in children (Mann, 1992). One should not rule out the possibility that more educated parents might be better equipped to pay closer attention to their child's hyperactive behavior, compared with less educated parents. Such parents' concerns, often expressed as complaints, could cause overdiagnosis of ADHD by some professionals who can be persuaded by these overconcerned parents.

Personality Disorders

Personality disorders are viewed as enduring patterns of behavior and inner experience that deviate markedly from the expectations of the individual's culture. It is not just a single act. It is a persistent behavioral pattern that leads to the individual's distress and impairment in one or several important areas of functioning. As you see, the very definition of personality disorders is culture bound. Indeed, people should be diagnosed in the context of each culture's norms and thresholds of tolerance for a particular behavior. A pattern of persistent self-exposure and attention seeking, for example, could be tolerated in a big city of a Western industrial nation. The same pattern could be opposed and criticized in a rural community, especially in traditional cultural settings. Various studies conducted in Europe and North America suggest that from 6 to 9 percent of the total population display some form of personality disorder. It is also found that urban populations have higher personality disorder rates than rural groups. There are more schizoid symptoms (detachment from social relationships and restricted range of emotional expression) diagnosed in men than in women. However, more anxious and fearful symptoms are found in women than in men (Merikangas & Weissman, 1986).

Personality disorders recognized in the United States should not be confused with acculturation problems in individuals who immigrate to this country or seek political asylum only because their behavior is seen as considerably different from expectations. As an example, immigrants or individuals who move from rural environments into bigger cities show deficits in communication and could be seen as aloof, indifferent, and withdrawn (Shiraev & Danilov, 2001). Symptoms of fearful behavior and persistent suspiciousness are evident in some political refugees who go through social and cultural transitions. The symptoms include mistrust, fear of persecution, and reluctance to disclose personal information.

Some cult members may also express ideas that could be considered by outsiders as paranoid. Various circumstances, such as immigration, job relocation, and other types of unpleasant and traumatic experiences, may cause some persistent avoidant reactions, which could be easily misidentified as Avoidant Personality Disorder. Borderline Personality Disorder (instability of relationships, self-image, and emotions) has symptoms that are recognized in many countries. Histrionic Personality Disorder (excessive emotionality and attention seeking) should be diagnosed when the specialist knows enough about the diagnosed person's culture, and, in particular, its norms, limits of tolerance, patterns of style and fashion, and rules of self-exposure and personal appearance. Dependent Personality Disorder (submissive and clinging behavior) should be diagnosed only if the behavior of the person is clearly in excess of this person's cultural norms. Politeness and passivity of a Japanese spouse may be considered excessive in Italy or the United States, but might not qualify as a personality disorder in the person's own cultural context.

Antisocial Personality Disorder—a pattern of disregard for and violation of the rights of others—is commonly associated with low socioeconomic status and urban settings. In the United States, African American adults demonstrate slightly lower rates of Antisocial Personality Disorder, and Hispanic men have higher rates than non-Hispanic whites. However, typically viewed as maladaptive, an individual's aggressive strategy could be adaptive in some cases and maintained as a survival pattern. If a person is deprived of his or her basic needs, the individual's antisocial behavior is considered to be an act of rebellion against authority. However, this type of explanation does not demonstrate why there are so many individuals from lower socioeconomic classes who choose socially appropriate problem-solving means, such as education and a professional career.

There are substantial gender differences in occurrence of Antisocial Personality Disorder. First, it is more frequent in men, with a ratio of 6:1 between males and females. Second, the most common symptoms for antisocial men are frequent fistfights, arrests, sexual promiscuity, and an illegal occupation. In women, the most common symptoms are spousal abuse, marital desertion (rejection), and persistent employment difficulties (Robins, 1986).

Some psychologists argue that male aggression—frequently mentioned among the symptoms of Antisocial Personality Disorder—is a result of maternal dominance in early childhood, and thus male adult participation in child-rearing should reduce male aggression. Absence of fathers and later violent conduct of their adolescent and adult children are highly correlated. However, this thesis seems to be more appropriate for industrial than for nonindustrial societies (Irvine & Berry, 1988).

Is Substance Abuse Culturally Bound?

There are cultural and national standards for substance use and abuse. There are also wide cultural variations in attitudes toward substance consumption, patterns of substance use, accessibility of substances, and prevalence of disorders related to substance

| TABLE 9.3 | *DSM-IV* on Cultural Variations of Substance Abuse |

Caffeine consumption varies across cultures with males drinking coffee more often than females. In European and other developed countries the rates are 400 mg/day or more, whereas in the developing world the rate is approximately 50 mg/day. The cost of coffee may also be a factor contributing to consumption rates (p. 214). *Cannabis* (usually marijuana) is among the first drug of experimentation for all cultural groups in the United States (p. 219). Cocaine use affects all races, and ethnic groups and both sexes in the United States, but is most commonly found in 18–30 year olds (p. 228). Hallucinogens may be used as part of established religious practices. Inhalants are more commonly abused by the young from economically depressed areas (p. 241). The prevalence of smoking is decreasing among industrial nations, but increasing among developing countries. Prevalence of smoking is decreasing more rapidly among males than females (p. 246). Opioid dependence historically is more common in members of minority groups living in economically deprived areas in the United States. However, at the beginning of the twentieth century, opioid dependence has been seen more often among middle-class individuals (p. 254). Prescription drug abuse is more common in women, but the prevalence has many cultural variations, partly caused by different prescription practices around the world (p. 268).

(*DSM-IV*, p. 188) (Table 9.3). Marijuana is outlawed in the United States, but is legal under certain conditions in Holland. The legal drinking age in the United States is 21. In contemporary Russia, however, it is 18, and the laws against selling alcohol to minors are not heavily enforced. You can buy a bottle of wine in a student cafeteria in France, but this is impossible to do at UCLA or George Mason University. Smoking opium was legal in some Asian American communities at the turn of the century.

There is no universal criterion that would distinguish normal from abnormal drinking. Muslims and Mormons prohibit any alcohol consumption. In contrast, Spanish and Greek respondents indicate that drinking alcohol is an essential part of their culture (Bennet et al., 1993). Europeans, although only 15 percent of the world population, consume about 50 percent of the alcohol on earth. The top consumers are Portugal and France. Their residents consume seven times as much as the lowest consumer, Israel (countries in which alcohol is outlawed, such as Saudi Arabia, were not included in the analysis). The United States is in the middle of the list. In most Asian countries (except Korea), the overall prevalence of alcohol-related disorders is relatively low, and the male–female ratio is very high. Various East Asian populations have a sort of "protective mechanism" against alcohol abuse. It was found that approximately 50 percent of Korean, Japanese, and Chinese individuals lack a particular chemical in their blood, *aldehyde dehydrogenase*, that eliminates the first breakdown product of alcohol. When such individuals consume alcohol, they experience a flushed face and palpitations. Therefore, they are not as likely to consume large amounts of the substance. Cultural norms and peer

A CASE IN POINT

Some Smoking Patterns

The World Health Organization (1996) reports that more than 60 percent of Chinese men smoke—the largest national rate—with the rates for East European men being slightly lower. More than half of Asian men smoke, being ahead of Middle Eastern, Indian, and Latin American males (of whom 40 percent smoke). The lowest smoking rates (25 percent) belong to men who live in Sub-Saharan Africa. In the United States the rates are also relatively moderate: only 28 percent of men smoke. The rates for black males are higher: 31 percent of blacks smoke. Around the world, women smoke less than men. The main female smokers of tobacco are East-European women: about 30 percent of them smoke, which is 8 points above the rates for Latin American women. In the United States, 22 percent of black women smoke compared with 24 percent of white women.

pressure could change behavioral patterns though. When Asian youth immigrate to the United States, they tend to drink more than their peers who live in their home countries (Halonen & Santrock, 1995).

Some researchers refer to biological factors that cause differences in addictive behavior in certain cultural groups. For example, the *Journal of the American Medical Association* reported that cells of blacks who smoke absorb more nicotine than do cells of white or Hispanic smokers. This difference, as experts suggest, could explain why blacks tend to suffer more from tobacco-related diseases—lung cancer, for example—and have more trouble quitting the habit (Schwartz, 1998).

Is substance abuse linked to immigration? More than 35 years ago, an interesting study was published about recent immigrants' children in New York. It was found that the children were at a higher risk for developing drug problems (Valliant, 1966). How did the author explain this tendency? The families of immigrant children had sustained a traumatic loss of their native culture, language, and family ties. The families also tended to be dependent on these first-generation children for support. The children could not make up for the enormous cultural losses suffered by their parents. These data, however, contradict a more contemporary study already mentioned in this chapter. The study showed that first-generation Americans have fewer medical and psychological problems, including substance abuse, than children of U.S.-born parents. The differences between these studies' results could be explained by different factors. For instance, the second study was based on the national sample, whereas the first covered only the New York area. Moreover, the first study was conducted a long time ago and a third-of-a-century period could have changed many essential characteristics of immigrants, who are more educated and economically secure than their predecessors.

Cross-culturally, the prevalence of alcohol use is greater in men than in women. This trend is especially overwhelming in Taiwan, China, and Korea. The lifetime prevalence of alcoholism in countries that do not prohibit its consumption varies from 0.5 percent in Shanghai and 7 percent in Taiwan, to 22 percent in Korea, one of the

A CASE IN POINT

Culture, Curiosity, and Deviant Behavior

In 1845 the great French writer Alexandre Dumas wrote his famous *Le Comte de Monte Cristo*, later translated into many languages. The plot of this romantic novel is very simple. A young man betrayed by several dishonest people is wrongfully accused and sentenced for life because of treason. After many years spent in a dungeon, the man miraculously escapes, gets rich, and then settles the score with those who were responsible for his misery. While implementing the revenge, he goes through a series of adventures, and these are perhaps the main reason why so many teenagers in France and other countries, including the authors of this textbook, read this novel. We remember very well how during one such adventure, Alexandre Dumas describes his literary hero's first experience with opium. The scene was engaging; the images are charming and sexually provocative. Like an artist applying beautiful colors to a canvas, the writer keeps the reader in a state of eager anticipation, slowly moving from one fantasy-filled reflection to another, scribing and unfolding the psychological effects of opium.

Did this scene have any bearing on our life? Yes, it sparked our curiosity: if opium is so great, if the experience is so seductive, why shouldn't we try some? We did not try though. Perhaps in our minds the realization of the dangerous consequences outweighed the immediate temptation to experiment. However, across cultures, experimentation with drugs often begins as the result of such pleasure seeking, combined with peer pressure, and some persuasive images derived from books and the media.

highest in the world (Wang et al., 1992). In the United States the rate is 17 percent. On the other hand, China is among the countries with the lowest level of alcoholism. Both Korean and Chinese cultures emphasize collectivism, interdependency, and family ties. In both cultures, relatives and family networks could regulate individual behavior. However, such dramatic differences between Korean and Chinese samples could be related to the fact that Korean men often drink with friends outside the home, and drinking is more tolerated in Korea than it is in Chinese culture.

Alcohol abuse could also be significant during different stages of adjustment in some immigrant groups (Canino et al., 1992). For instance, Mexican immigrants have an incident rate of alcohol abuse that is almost twice as low as Mexican Americans who were born in the United States. American whites and blacks have similar rates of alcohol abuse and dependence. Hispanic males have higher rates, whereas Hispanic females have lower rates of alcohol abuse than other ethnic groups.

Alcohol-related disorders are associated with lower educational levels, lower socioeconomic status, and higher rates of unemployment. However, it is difficult to say what is cause and what is effect. For example, people who drop out from either high school or college have particularly high rates of alcohol-related disorders (*DSM-IV*, p. 201). Does the individual develop a substance-related problem because he or she dropped out of school or did this person drop out from school because of the substance-related problem?

Nearly 33 percent of U.S. youth have used some type of illegal drug at some point in their lives. Reported rates are generally similar among males and females. White and Hispanic males have reported higher rates of illegal drug use than black males. White females reported higher rates than both Hispanic and black females. Thirty percent of white males and females have used marijuana compared with less than 25 percent of black males and females. Use of cocaine was found to be highest among Mexican American males. White youths use drugs such as LSD, heroine, and amphetamines five times more often than black youths, with use among Hispanics somewhere in the middle (Russell, 1995).

Psychodiagnostic Biases

The cultural background of the professional can influence his or her perception of different behaviors. Psychologists are likely to have their own perceptions and attributions about the links among culture, ethnicity, and mental illness (Lopez, 1989). It is also known that doctors can misdiagnose particular diseases due to cross-cultural differences in the perception, attribution, and expression of signs of disease.

Mental health specialists should notice, for example, the importance of social distance between their patients and themselves across different cultural groupings. Even the way we observe abnormality may be affected by our own social status, and this phenomenon was noticed a long time ago. For instance, it was suggested that substantial differences in psychiatric symptoms between low- and high-status groups in the Austro-Hungarian Army in 1914 were influenced by the fact that most psychiatric observers belonged to high-status nationalities (Murphy, 1982b).

As another illustration of the diagnostic bias in the clinical setting, consider how therapist's beliefs and expectations may predispose them to "see" psychopathology wherever they look. Suppose you were to ask a therapist to explain the meaning of behaviors that clients might exhibit on arriving for their scheduled therapy session. Let us imagine further that this therapist happens to view the world through a densely filtered cultural schema of psychopathology. The therapist thus calmly and confidently offers you the following interpretations:

> *If the patient arrives early for his appointment, then he's anxious. If he arrives late, then he's hostile. And if he's on time, then he's compulsive.*

This witticism about psychoanalysis dates back to the 1930s. Although originally intended as a joke, it was far more prophetic than most people at that time could have anticipated. For it is not just a humorous illustration of "noncritical" thinking but is also a revealing and sobering parable that alerts us to the dangers inherent in maintaining schemas that allow—and even encourage—virtually any human behavior to be subsumed under one or another of pathological categories.

As we suggested earlier, some specialists are skeptical about the applicability of Western diagnostic criteria in other cultures and vice versa. They insist that distress is experienced and manifested in many culture-specific ways. Different cultures may either encourage or discourage the reporting of psychological or physiological components of the stress response (Draguns, 1996). In addition, in some cultures persistent nightmares are viewed as a spiritual and supernatural phenomenon, whereas others observe nightmares as indicators of mental or physical disturbance (*DSM-IV*, p. 581).

Some existing culture-specific disorders are difficult to interpret in terms of other national classifications. A neurological weakness, typically diagnosed in China, includes symptoms of weakness, fatigue, tiredness, headaches, and gastrointestinal complaints (Tung, 1994). The Western diagnostic assessments of patients with this disorder varied with different diagnostic procedures employed. It could be anxiety disorder, depressive disorder, or bipolar disorder (Kleinmann, 1986).

Attention-Deficit/Hyperactivity Disorder is known to occur in children of different cultures with prevalence in Western countries. This prevalence is an explanation of a trend to overdiagnose ADHD in these countries (*DSM-IV*, p. 81). Recent studies on culture-specific disorders suggest that different cultures have specific labels for behavioral disorders. Culture-bound syndromes challenge any universal categorization because of the culturally specific content of the disorders (Tanaka-Matsumi & Draguns, 1997). But no matter how you described a problem, it would manifest as a maladaptive and distressful symptom, as inability to cope with stressful situations. The key to success in diagnostic practices is to identify distress and maladaptive symptoms correctly and in their cultural context.

Much unhappiness has come into the world because of bewilderment and things left unsaid.
FYODOR DOSTOEVSKY (1821–1881)—RUSSIAN NOVELIST

The greatest happiness is to know the source of unhappiness.
FYODOR DOSTOEVSKY

Psychotherapy

If different cultural settings can affect diagnostic practices, one can assume that culture may also play a significant role in **psychotherapy,** which is the treatment of psychological disorders through psychological means, generally involving verbal interaction with a professional therapist. Research cases show, for example, that many drug rehabilitation and prevention programs designed for one particular ethnic and social category (white middle-class subjects) are applicable to other ethnic and social categories. In tolerant and supportive cultures (as well in supportive communities and families) individuals with mental disorders may function better than those in less-tolerant surroundings. In Japan, depressed patients could rely on other people to make decisions for them. In American culture, depressed patients rely more on individual decision making, and therefore are more avoidant and show lower self-esteem than Japanese patients (Radford et al., 1991). It was also shown in a World Health Organization study (1979) that patients from collectivist cultures had a better prognosis for schizophrenia, whereas patients from individualist cultures showed fewer signs of improvement (Tanaka-Matsumi & Draguns, 1997).

Different ethnic groups could have various attitudes about mental-health services. Some studies imply that Mexican Americans are significantly less likely to use outpatient mental help than other ethnic groups. Only 50 percent of Hispanics with a recent

CRITICAL THINKING

Imagine a psychotherapist tells you that "Most every ethnic minority patient I've treated has dropped out of therapy prematurely." What are some possible explanations for this correlation? Can you propose that ethnicity is the factor affecting the patients' commitment? Remember that correlation does not necessarily prove causation. Could you suggest some other factors?

1. _____
2. _____
3. _____

Suppose you read an article reporting an inverse correlation between religiosity and depression (that is, the less religious, the more depressed). What factors could account for this relationship?

1. _____
2. _____
3. _____

diagnosis of a mental disorder actually seek mental health treatment, compared with 70 percent of non-Hispanic whites. Asian Americans also seek disproportionately fewer treatment services. African Americans and Native Americans appear to use outpatient mental health services at higher rates than whites. Some studies have found that ethnic minority patients have a tendency to drop out of treatment before it can be effective more frequently than whites. Many factors can contribute to the above tendency, for example, whether those providing mental health services are themselves members of an ethnic minority group, fluent in the language of their patients, or aware of culturally specific therapeutic procedures. However, the differences in the dropout rates among various ethnic groups do not appear to be statistically significant.

Culture Match?

Many factors can affect therapists' diagnostic judgments. Among these factors is the cultural background of both the therapist and the client. We should always keep in mind that every therapist is not destined to make erroneous decisions about his or her client of a different cultural background. However, the mistakes are made and there are at least two reasons for possible misjudgments. First, some clinicians may not understand the cultural backgrounds of their clients and therefore may misinterpret their responses. Moreover, some clients express their thoughts and emotions according to the common rules in their culture. Second, knowledge of certain cultural trends may be lacking critical-thinking emphasis and thus distort diagnosis. Stereotypes and schemas create expectations about the "typical" symptoms of particular ethnic groups.

Scores of research studies have concluded that schemas greatly influence what we perceive and the manner in which we perceive it (see, for example, Bruner & Potter, 1964; Kelley, 1950; Reason & Mycielska, 1982; Vokey & Read, 1985). For instance, Diana Li-Repac (1980) investigated the effect of sociocultural differences between therapists and clients on clinical impressions, perceptions, and judgments. In her study, a sample consisting of white therapists and Chinese-American therapists assessed a series of videotaped clinical interviews. All of the therapists were told that they would be evaluating both white and Chinese clients. They were not, however, informed of the experiment's true purpose, namely, to compare therapists' clinical perceptions as a function of their own ethnicity.

Results showed that although both groups of therapists agreed in their general conceptions of psychological "normality," they differed significantly in their actual assessments of the same clients. Specifically, in comparison to the Chinese-American therapists, the white therapists viewed the Chinese clients as more depressed and inhibited and as possessing less social poise and interpersonal capacity. Conversely, Chinese-American therapists judged the white clients to be more severely disturbed than did the white therapists. These findings, notes Li-Repac, demonstrate that "cultural stereotyping is a two-way street" (p. 339).

As evidenced in this experiment, the impact of culture on diagnosis of mental disorders can be profound. In essence, each group of therapists had filtered (i.e., assimilated) the clients' behavior through their respective sociocultural schemas, and, as a consequence, arrived at strikingly different judgments. The underlying principle here again becomes manifest: More than believing what we see, we tend to see what we believe.

Ethnic match, that is, a situation where the psychotherapist and his or her client belong to the same ethnic group, may determine several developments. For instance, if the therapist and the client are "matched," it is a meaningful predictor of the duration of psychotherapy (Sue et al., 1991). African Americans with depressive symptoms tend to be misdiagnosed with schizophrenia if they are evaluated by non-black professionals. In general, matched therapists judge clients to have higher psychological functioning than do mismatched therapists. This means that ethnically matched therapists see less pathology in their clients than therapists from a different culture.

These results can be interpreted in several ways. It appears that an ethnic match between a patient and a therapist reduces diagnostic mistakes. So far, so good, but should we then always match patients and therapists? Not until we first consider the finding that ethnically matched professionals may not see some significant symptoms in their clients, thus underdiagnosing them (Russell et al., 1996).

Gender similarity has also been a reported association with a positive outcome in therapy. However, the studied effects from gender matching appear to be quite modest. What is more important is the therapist's flexibility in his or her attitudes toward sex roles and the ethnicity of the client rather than gender and ethnicity per se.

Other general psychological factors may affect the cross-cultural relationship between the professional and his or her client. For example, therapists who share an understanding of their clients' experiences are likely to make the therapy experience more significant and beneficial for the client regardless of his or her cultural background. On the other hand, unrealistic expectations about therapy on behalf of the client, who hopes to get some practical advice that will work immediately—expectations typical for clients from lower socioeconomic strata—may not be helpful for the client. Psychotherapists indicate that brief discussions, and instructional conversations with clients stimulate higher attendance, greater satisfaction, and, finally, a positive outcome. Such procedures, known as role preparation, are extremely important in cross-cultural psychotherapy.

Different countries have different laws and rules regarding the hospitalization of mental patients. In most totalitarian societies (such as Nazi Germany in the 1930s and the Soviet Union prior to 1991) it was the state's prerogative to decide whether a person should be hospitalized. In the history of the twentieth century, psychiatry has been used countless times for political and ideological purposes. In the American society today only those who show signs of imminent danger to themselves or others may be held in mental facilities against their will. In many other countries the rules required for hospitalization are not as strict as in the United States. But in general, studies indicate that mental health specialists show substantial agreement among themselves as to which patients should be considered dangerous, suicidal, or unable to testify or take care of themselves (Swenson, 1993)

All in all, the context of therapy should be consistent with the client's culture (Tanaka-Matsui, 1989). For example, Kleinmann (1978) offered a framework for successful patient–therapist interactions. At the beginning, the therapist asks clients to give their interpretation of the existing problem. Then the therapist offers his or her explanation of the problem. Then both types of explanations are compared. Finally, both therapist and client come up with a joint explanatory concept, so that they communicate in the same language and can discuss therapy and its potential outcome.

Snacken (1991) described three desirable types of therapy of between the specialist and the patient who represent different cultures. *Intercultural* therapy includes a professional who knows the language and culture of the client (he or she could belong to this cultural group). *Bicultural* therapy includes two types of healers: both the Western and the native who work together. *Polycultural* therapy involves the patient's meetings with several therapists who represent different cultures.

 EXERCISE 9.1

Here is a list of some culture-bound mental problems. Using *DSM-IV*, please find analogies in the American classification of mental disorders to each of the syndromes below. Write your answers.

- Possession (some African countries) is a belief that one's body has been taken over by a spirit, which leads to unusual and unexpected emotional and behavioral changes.
- Koro (China) is a severe anxiety based on the assumption that the penis is retracting; this fear leads to another belief of inevitable death.

- Latah is a syndrome known in some Asian and African countries that is marked by altered states of consciousness, including exaggerated obedience and impulsivity.
- Malgri is a severe abdominal pain that is believed to be caused by entering forbidden territory without purification rituals.
- Nuptial psychosis occurs among very young women in India whose lives are disrupted by arranged marriages. Sexual trauma, separation from the family, and stress contribute to symptoms of confusion, hysteria, and suicidal intentions.
- Kayak Angst is an extreme anxiety, known among the Eskimos of Western Greenland. This anxiety strikes after hours of solitary hunting in unfavorable environments.

 ## CHAPTER SUMMARY

- There are three major orientations that view and interpret the interaction between culture and psychopathology. The *universalist* approach assumes that major psychopathological phenomena are present in some form in all cultures, but that the factors that bring them out are subject to cultural influence. Within the *relativist approach*, psychologists attempt to use both culturally universal and relative understandings of psychopathology and therapeutic interventions. Supporters of the *absolutist approach* insist on invariant psychological and psychopathological phenomena across countries in terms of their origin and expression. In general, contemporary cross-cultural psychology is likely to assume that there is no culture-free psychopathology.
- Attempting to diagnose and treat an individual, the professional should know the client's reference groups and ways in which cultural context is relevant to clinical care, including psychotherapy. In particular, the specialist should pay attention to the following: (1) the cultural identity of the individual, that is, his or her ethnic, religious, and other cultural reference groups; (2) the cultural explanations of the individual's illness; (3) the cultural interpretations of social stressors and social supports, such as religion, level of functioning, and disability; and (4) the cultural elements of the relationship between the individual and the clinician.
- American clinicians use a special diagnostic manual (*DSM-IV*) to diagnose mental disorders. Clinicians usually assess information available to them about the individual from the standpoint of five axes, each of which helps professionals to examine the situation from five different viewpoints or domains of information. There are disorders that may or may not be linked to a particular *DSM-IV* diagnostic category. These are recurrent, locally specific patterns of aberrant behavior and troubling experiences that are called culture-bound syndromes. They are generally limited to specific societies or areas and indicate repetitive and troubling sets of experiences and observations.
- Cultural norms, availability of resources, national standards on health, access to technology, social inequality, and many other environmental factors could affect the individual's health and general well being.
- Despite general similar occurrence rates, there are some cultural variations in how schizophrenia is viewed, diagnosed, and

treated. There are some substantial ethnic variations in the expression of depression, which are also based on various individual differences, socialization experiences, cultural definitions of disorders, and stress. There is empirical evidence concerning the links between suicide and religiosity, age, sex, nationality, substance use, and various cultural traditions. There are substantial cultural variations in the expression of anxiety that range from somatic to cognitive to behavioral symptoms. Differences in diagnostic practices account in some way for cross-cultural differences in reported symptoms and could explain great cross-cultural variability for anxiety disorders. Although research has barely touched cross-cultural aspects for dementia, this illness should be diagnosed cautiously and with consideration of the patient's educational and cultural background. Despite cultural variations, children from families of lower socioeconomic status have a higher frequency of ADHD than their counterparts from middle class families. It is suggested that personality disorders should be viewed, diagnosed, and treated in the context of each culture's norms and thresholds of tolerance for a particular behavior. There are cultural and national standards for substance use and substance abuse. There are also wide cultural variations in attitudes toward substance consumption, patterns of substance use, accessibility of substances, and prevalence of disorders related to substance use.

• The cultural background of the professional can influence his or her perception of different behaviors. Psychologists are likely to have their own perceptions and attributions about the links of culture, ethnicity and mental illness. It is also known that doctors can misdiagnose particular diseases due to cross-cultural differences in the perception, attribution, and expression of signs of disease. Psychotherapy across countries has different historical and cultural roots and varied cultural expressions. Different countries have different laws and rules regarding the hospitalization of mental patients. General psychological and cultural factors may affect the cross-cultural relationship between the professional and his or her client. Different ethnic groups could have various attitude patterns about mental health services. In general, the context of therapy should be consistent with the client's culture to achieve the goal of cultural accommodation.

KEY TERMS

Anxiety Disorders   A category of mental disorders characterized by persistent anxiety or fears.

Attention-Deficit/Hyperactivity Disorder   A developmental disorder characterized by persistent inattention, hyperactivity, and restlessness of the child.

Central Symptoms   Symptoms of mental disorders observable in practically all cultures.

Culture-Bound Syndromes   Recurrent, locally specific patterns of aberrant behavior and troubling experience that may or may not be linked to a particular *DSM-IV* diagnostic category. Culture-bound syndromes are generally limited to specific societies or areas and indicate repetitive and troubling sets of experiences and observations.

Dementia   A deterioration of cognitive functioning, including memory loss, aphasia, or disturbed executive functioning.

Depressive Disorder   A category of mental disorders characterized by persistent anxiety, dysphoria, tension, lack of energy, and thoughts of guilt and insufficiency.

Mental Disorder   A clinically significant behavioral and psychological syndrome or pattern that occurs in an individual and that is associated with present distress (a painful syndrome) or disability (impairment in one or more important areas of functioning) or with a significantly increased risk of suffering death, pain, disability, or an important loss of freedom.

Peripheral Symptoms   Symptoms of mental disorders that are culture-specific.

Personality Disorders   Enduring patterns of behavior and inner experience that deviate markedly from the expectations of the individual's culture.

Psychotherapy   The treatment of psychological disorders through psychological means, generally involving verbal interaction with a professional therapist.

Schizophrenia   A disorder characterized by the presence of delusions, hallucinations, disorganized speech, and disorganized or catatonic behavior.

CHAPTER 10

Social Perception and Social Cognition

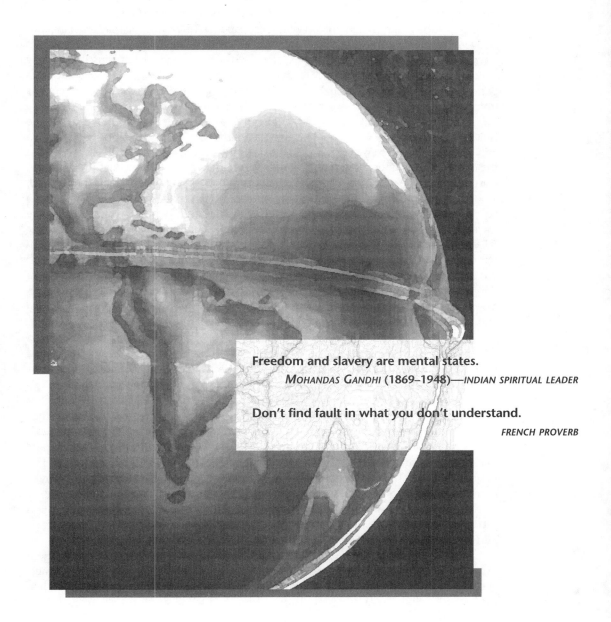

Freedom and slavery are mental states.
MOHANDAS GANDHI (1869–1948)—INDIAN SPIRITUAL LEADER

Don't find fault in what you don't understand.
FRENCH PROVERB

Famous rap artist Coolio said on the TV show *Politically Incorrect* that all people see the same things but "what people make" of that experience is different. But why are our interpretations dissimilar? Why do some of us adore what others consider disgusting? Why do some condemn what others pray for? Is it because we learn about good and evil from different cultural perspectives? For instance, if you were a Buddhist would you be mad if somebody made a lithograph of Buddha and smeared it with mud? If you were a Muslim would you be offended if somebody made a sculpture of the Prophet Mohammad with toilet paper on his head? You may think that nobody would dare to make such sordid things? Hold onto that thought while we consider some facts. In 1999, the Brooklyn Museum of Arts, the second largest museum in New York, opened an exhibition called "Sensation: Young British Artists From the Saatchi Collection." Among the many items displayed was a collage of the Virgin Mary made of cutouts from pornographic magazines with her breasts fashioned from elephant feces. If you are a Christian will you be angry? Chris Ofili, a Roman Catholic and the artist who created "The Holy Virgin Mary," said you should not be offended at all. The last thing he expected, he added, was to offend somebody. But wait! If the artist did not want to offend anybody, and the collage itself cannot cause physical injury to a human being, where does the "offense" exist? Is it in our heads? Does this mean our anger is a product of pure imagination? Indeed, a burning flag for some people is an act of disgrace; for others it is just a piece of cloth on fire. It is appropriate to call somebody "white" in America but "whitee" would be offensive to some. An extended middle finger is an obscene gesture barred from American public television. Meanwhile, a villager in Siberia would not understand this gesture at all. We interpret and explain people and events using our own emotions and values filtered through our individual and cultural experiences. People create meanings of reality in their perception and then change reality using the power of their perceptions. If you disagree, this means you see things differently than do the authors of this textbook. "There is no good and bad; our thinking makes it so," wrote Shakespeare. Was he right?

The process through which we try to understand other people and ourselves is called **social perception**. It is an established view in psychology that people acquire judgments, attitudes, and beliefs through socialization experiences from their cultural milieu. If perception is influenced by experience, then there should be commonalities and differences in social perception. People who grow up in similar environments may learn to interpret many elements of this environment in a similar way. People who were exposed to different stimuli are likely to see the world from divergent perspectives. A student from Chicago may view a car as a simple transportation device. The same car, however, could be considered a luxury for a man in a small Mongolian town. A mother spanking her child in a public place in Canada would be condemned by many bystanders. However, spanking is not treated as abuse in many countries around the world where it is commonly interpreted as a necessary and effective form of discipline (see Chapter 8)!

In short, the way we see things changes according to our experience with them (Matsumoto, 1994). The experiences of two individuals are not alike. For instance, eyewitnesses to criminal events are typically inaccurate in what they report. But when the witness belongs to a different ethnic group than the suspect, inaccuracies tend to increase (Platz & Hosch, 1988).

The process of social perception contributes to the means of thinking about the world. **Social cognition** is the process through which we interpret, remember, and then use information about the world and ourselves. In general, social cognition tends to be conservative (Aronson, 1995). We retain our past experiences and use them to make today's judgments. For instance, until recently, despite great medical advancements, organ transplantation was unavailable for patients in Japan because of particular ancient religious interpretations about the unity of the body and soul (see Chapter 12). Ethnic groups engaged in a conflict against one another see the cause of their hostility differently, each from the bias lenses of centuries-old negative stereotypes of the other.

We begin a cross-cultural analysis of social perception and cognition with an examination of attitudes and values. Then we explore how people balance their attitudes and whether consistency in attitudes is a universal trend. Next the chapter analyzes how people explain the behavior of others, and how they view justice, success, and failure. Finally, moral values, self-perception, and popular stereotypes are contemplated.

Three Spaniards, four opinions.
SPANISH PROVERB

The Nature of Attitude

Roberta does not want to make an appointment with a doctor. She says that her depressed mood is not an illness. She assures everyone that her mood is caused by her recent immigration from El Salvador. Her children, three teenagers from Arlington, say that she has been a stubborn person throughout her life. When she forms an opinion, she rarely changes it. Her family says that the mother has *an attitude*.

Attitude is a psychological representation of various features of the social or physical world. This mental depiction is based on our experiences and generates in individuals a state of readiness to respond in a particular way related to the attitude (Allport, 1935). Attitudes are not directly observable. Please do not think of attitudes as colorful marbles located in the brain. The word "attitude" is just a label that helps psychologists around the world better understand social perception and cognition.

An attitude may be analyzed along three major dimensions, or components. We want to emphasize again that these components are products of our abstract thinking, a convenient model for description, rather than the real "architectural bricks" of attitude.

- *The cognitive component.* This is our knowledge about an object or event, including facts, thoughts, and beliefs retained in memory. For example: "*I know that some parents in the United States arrange marriages for their children.*"

- *The emotional component.* This is often known as the affective component. This is our emotional evaluation of an object. The evaluation may derive from basic human emotions such as joy, fear, disgust, sadness, anger, surprise, and their various combinations. In general, the emotional component might be viewed as either a positive or negative evaluation of an object. For example: "*I vehemently oppose arranged marriages in this country as a discrimination against women's freedom of choice.*"

- **The behavioral component.** This is our behavioral predisposition to act in a certain way with respect to an object. For example: "*I not only oppose arranged marriages, but will also actively protest against this tradition.*"

Psychologists generally agree with a three-componential structure of attitude and consent that attitudes serve several universal functions (Yadov, 1978; Moghaddam, 1998). For example, attitudes help people to make sense of the world, serve an ego-defensive function, and assist individuals with self-evaluations. Finally, attitudes serve the function of allowing people to express their values.

Values

Attitudes also tend to change. For example, Rehza disliked baseball when he arrived in the United States from Iran. Above all other sports, he liked soccer, the game he played growing up in Tabriz. Things change. A few years later, Rehza became a fan of baseball and even began to attend the Dodgers games in Los Angeles. Does Rehza's opinion of baseball help us judge what type of a person he is? The likely answer is "no." An emotional attachment to the game is not typically considered a strong indicator of anything significant in a person's character. However, there are other attitudes that represent Rehza's most important views on life. Such views are called values.

Values are attitudes that reflect a principle, standard, or quality considered by the individual as the most desirable or appropriate. Values are stable and enduring views that a specific behavior (often called *instrumental value*) or goal (called *terminal value*) is preferred to another behavior or goal. Terminal values usually refer to social and personal concerns, whereas instrumental values designate morality and competency issues. Values generally hold a more central position than attitudes and therefore lead individuals to form particular views on a variety of issues (Rokeach, 1968, 1973). It is likely, for example, that an Indian woman in America would not eat a beef sandwich served to her at a friend's party because abstinence from beef (a Hindu value) is stronger than "being polite" to the host (an attitude). Likewise, an Italian autoworker strongly attached to the value of equality is likely to support (an attitude) government actions aimed at helping people from neighboring Yugoslavia (Shiraev, 2000).

Are there noticeable national or cultural differences in values? Do people around the world share the same values? If they do, what are these values? Or if there are cultural differences, do we know what values are most important? Hofstede (1980, 1991) conducted a remarkable international study of 117,000 people employed by IBM in 50 nations. To simplify the analysis, he divided the countries studied into eleven clusters: Nordic, Anglo (including the United States), Germanic, Near Eastern, developing Asian, developing Latin, developed Latin, and Japan as a separate developed Asian country. He described the following cultural dimensions that reflect four major ways

CRITICAL THINKING

Do Values Disappear?

People all over the world say that values are "disappearing" or "evaporating," that the young are "losing" the religious and moral values of previous generations. However, values do not decay or disappear. Perhaps it is more accurate to suggest that they can rise or descend in our estimation of their relative importance to us. For example, consider the recent decline in support of affirmative action in the United States. Many people have not necessarily "destroyed" their views on affirmative action, but instead, do not attach as much importance to it now as they did 15 or 20 years ago (Sears, 1996). See more about the evaluative power of language in Chapter 3.

people cope with their most important problems: (1) Individualism and Collectivism, (2) Power Distance, (3) Masculinity and Femininity, and (4) Uncertainty Avoidance (see again Chapter 1 for a description of these features).

The investigator described each of the national clusters studied. The Nordic and Anglo samples demonstrated values low on Power Distance, high on Individualism, and low on Uncertainty Avoidance. The Anglo group was high on Masculinity, but the German group was low on Masculinity. The less developed Asian countries and the Near Eastern bloc were both high in Power Distance and low in Individualism. But the most remarkable comparison was made between the Anglo and Nordic cultures on the one hand, and Near Eastern and less developed Asian countries on the other. The Anglo and Nordic groups were low on Power Distance and high on Individualism. This pattern was called *Individualist*. The opposite pattern—high Power Distance and low Individualism—common for non-Western countries, was labeled *Collectivist*.

In another study, Shalom Schwartz (Smith & Schwartz, 1997) argued about cultural differences in individual values. He suggested individual values as being connected to the way various groups cope with basic societal problems. There are three basic issues that make various social groups different from one another. These are (1) the extent to which people are independent of or dependent on groups; (2) their views on prosperity and profit, and finally (3) their views on whether it is appropriate to exploit, fit in, or submit to the outside world. An analysis of people's responses revealed their basic views distributed between two opposite ends of the spectrum of human values.

Type 1. Conservatism vs. Autonomy.   The conservative views are shared by individuals who believe in the status quo, advocate self-discipline, and care about family, social order, and tradition. Those who share values of autonomy emphasize the right of individuals to pursue their own ideals, and to enjoy the variety of life for the sake of pleasure and excitement.

Type 2. Hierarchy vs. Egalitarianism.   If a person supports the hierarchy values, he or she justifies the legitimacy of an unequal distribution of power, resources, and social roles. If a person has egalitarian values, he or she sees individuals as equals, who share basic interests and should be treated equally as human beings.

Type 3. Mastery vs. Harmony.   Mastery values encourage individuals to exercise control over society and exploit its natural resources. Ambition and high self-esteem are important individual traits that accompany mastery values. Harmony values are based on assumptions that the world should be kept as is: preserved and cherished rather than violated and exploited.

Schwartz's study included 40 countries that were divided into several groups: West European, Anglo (including the United States), East European, Islamic, East Asian, Japan (as a single country), and Latin American. East Asian nations were especially high on Hierarchy and Conservatism and low on Egalitarianism and Autonomy. West European participants showed the opposite trend. The Anglo profile fell somewhere in between the West European and East Asian samples. One interesting finding was the established correlation between the size of the household and the values of Conservatism and Hierarchy. Values such as order, discipline, and compliance were promoted more often in large families living under one roof than in smaller family units.

Western and Non-Western Values

For many years now, journalists, political scientists, sociologists, and psychologists have discussed the differences between two major cultural clusters of attitudes called Western and non-Western values. According to a philosophical tradition developed by Max Weber, the most fundamental values of Western civilization are work, achievement, striving for efficiency, and consumption of material goods. It is then argued that in non-Western civilizations, these values are somewhat important but not considered critical. The essence of non-Western values is respect of tradition, reverence to authority, and overall stability.

There are also other areas of contraposition between Western and non-Western values. Two of the most frequently mentioned are Western individualism and non-Western collectivism. The value of individualism is not as salient in the non-Western developing nations as it is in more economically developed Western countries (Hofstede, 1980). For example, individualistic values were found to be stronger in Western countries such as the United States, Germany, and Sweden than they were in Taiwan, Japan, and India (Segall et al., 1990). The value of competition was reportedly higher in urban, industrial areas than in rural regions (Munroe & Munroe, 1997).

It is commonly stated in the media that Western values are linked to economic prosperity and democratic attitudes. Therefore these values are important to all countries. An opposite view that challenges the universal importance of Western values appeared to have some supporters in the 1990s (see discussion in Chapter 7 on Motivation). It was argued that the pursuit of Western values does not produce a climate of social satisfaction. The most fundamental Western values are no longer adaptive because they have outlived their historical usefulness (Clark, 1995). In particular, assumptions such as

A CASE IN POINT

We want you to think about the opinion that Western values, including civil freedoms and individual rights, were forced on other countries by the Western world as a direct instruction of what is good and what is not. The whole idea of individual rights can be criticized because the pursuit of these rights may encourage individuals to perform completely independent actions and disregard the views of other people. Such actions may distance the person from his or her family, culture, and religion. Criticizing Western values, some political activists argue that human rights—understood from a different perspective—do not consist only of individual political and civil liberties. They suggest that rights for economic security, social protection, and preservation of tradition are just as important as individual liberties.

Questions: Do you think that there are values more attuned to Western culture than to the East? Do you think Western countries try to force those values on other countries thus interfering with their internal affairs? Should different religious and ethnic groups living in the United States or any other country accept identical values?

- the nature of human beings is selfish (Freud and Marx),
- scarcity is a primary condition of nature (Darwin), and
- progress means growth, complexity, competition, and freedom (Weber)

should be changed to "softer" non-Western concepts based on the values of harmony, inner accord, and cooperation.

Samuel Huntington (1993) predicted a deepening of the gap between Western and non-Western values. He suggested that billions of people on earth would vigorously discuss and challenge the leadership role of the West, and its materialistic Judeo-Christian values. The growth of ideological and religious fundamentalism is inevitable, in his opinion. This would further attenuate the differences between Western and non-Western values.

How do people acquire attitudes and values? How do they use them to make judgments about other people and themselves? There are theories of attitudes that have been tested cross-culturally. Let us examine some of them.

Striving for Consistency: The Cognitive Balance Theory

One theory, Heider's theory of attitude balance (Heider, 1959), states that people seek consistency among their attitudes. In general, a balance is achieved if you and a person you like agree on something or you and a person you dislike disagree about something. It is expected that we should overestimate positive traits in persons and groups we enjoy. On the other hand, we underestimate positive traits in those persons or groups we do not favor, even if the facts suggest that our adversaries are not as bad as we previously thought (Pratkanis, 1988). The theory of attitude balance examines consistency pressures within a simple, three-element, cognitive evaluation process. The first element *(A)* is a person who develops evaluations. The other two elements *(B, C)* are objects, issues, or other people who are being evaluated. For example, a young woman *(A)* adores the music of Puerto Rican singer Ricky Martin *(B)* who made a critical remark about the President of the United States *(C)*. The woman *(A)* is likely to agree with the singer *(B)* about the President of the United States *(C)*. If, however, she dislikes the criticism of the president, her attitude about Ricky Martin would probably change from very positive to somewhat positive or even negative.

Experimental research shows that the principles of cognitive balance are universal in virtually all countries studied (Triandis, 1994). It was found, however, that cognitive consistency also varies across cultures. For instance, in the United States people are more concerned about the consistency of their attitudes than individuals in Japan, where the ability to handle inconsistency is considered a sign of maturity. In the former communist countries of the Soviet bloc moral consistency required personal modesty, honesty, sacrifice on behalf of society, and public criticism of others who did not follow these standards (Gozman & Edkind, 1992; Shiraev & Bastrykin, 1988). In some Islamic societies being consistent in one's religious attitudes requires a more complex behavioral reaction than the religious behavior of many people in other societies. For instance, such consistency requires regularity of prayers, abstention from alcohol, paying of Islamic taxes, and following the proclamations of religious leaders (Moghaddam, 1998).

Avoiding Inconsistency: Cognitive Dissonance

One of the most painful human feelings is one of injustice. Every spring, Georgy, a 40-year-old former officer of the Soviet Army, goes to a cemetery in his town to spend a few minutes near the graves of five young men. They were killed during the Soviet invasion in Afghanistan in the 1980s. He knew two of them. The feeling of loss is difficult to cope with. But the most difficult undertaking, as Georgy says, is to explain and justify why these 19-year-old boys were sent to die in a foreign country. He was told by some officials that the boys were fulfilling their duty. What duty? Who were they fighting for? Was this a duty to die? This question remains unanswered, and like an invisible drill in Georgy's heart, it causes pain during long and sleepless nights. Georgy still keeps looking for answers. The pain does not go away.

People experience psychological tensions when they perceive mismatch (dissonance) between (1) attitudes and behavior, (2) two or more decisions, or (3) two or more attitudes. These tensions are known as **cognitive dissonance** (Festinger, 1957). Whenever we must decide between two or more alternatives, the final choice will be inconsistent—to some extent—with some of our beliefs or previous decisions. This inconsistency generates dissonance, an unpleasant state of emotions. As a result, we feel compelled to reduce the dissonance and avoid unnecessary discomfort. There are three techniques for reducing dissonance: (1) improving our evaluation of the chosen alternative ("This is the best dress I have ever bought."), (2) lowering our evaluation of the alternative not chosen ("The dress I didn't buy was overpriced."), and (3) not thinking or talking about the decision we made ("I bought the dress, the topic is closed.").

Why do people across cultures attempt to reduce dissonance (Camilleri & Malewska-Peyre, 1997)? One reason may be the attractive value of a harmonious, consistent, and meaningful view of the world. To avoid frustration or discomfort, we may cut off a relationship with somebody we dislike or disagree with and begin to ignore evidence inconsistent with our beliefs.

Imagine, for example, that somebody promises the world will end on a particular day and nothing actually happens on that day. Most of us would not have a positive opinion of the "prophet." However, many cases of unfulfilled prophecies in the United States have led to greater faith among the unsuccessful prophet's followers, despite evidence of the leader's failure (Sanada & Norbeck, 1975). Such people are usually called "*dogmatists.*" They typically do not change their values and beliefs even in the face of compelling facts.

Men of principle are sure to be bold, but those who are bold may not always be men of principle.
CONFUCIUS (551–479 B.C.)—CHINESE PHILOSOPHER

Psychological Dogmatism

Generally, people dislike being called "dogmatic." **Dogmatism** is a tendency to be extremely selective, rigid, and inflexible in opinions and subsequent behavior. This is a powerful alliance of attitudes and beliefs, usually organized around one central idea. This idea has absolute authority over the individual and usually causes intolerance toward other people or issues (Rokeach, 1973). The dogmatic individual has a very limited way of thinking and acting, is rigid about other people's opinions, and uncritically accepts people who represent the central dogmatic idea. The dogmatic individual typically rejects those who disagree with him or her and has difficulty assimilating new information.

What causes some groups of people to be more dogmatic than others? Ofer Feldman (1996), an Israeli-born researcher who lives and works in Japan, offered an interesting explanation. He compared dogmatism in politicians from the United States, Italy, and Japan. Japanese public officials were found to be less dogmatic than Italian politicians but more dogmatic than their American counterparts. The findings were explained in the context of differences in political systems in the countries studied. In Italy, at the time the survey was conducted, there were eight major national political parties, and each of them was advancing a different political doctrine and philosophy of life. In-group ideological pressures within each political party were high. In the United States, two major political parties were weakly organized and highly decentralized. In-group ideological pressure was not expected to be high. The author argued that the Japanese political system contained characteristics of both Italian and American political systems: high ideological solidarity and relative independence from the central party. One fact should be noted, however. The data for the American sample

A CASE IN POINT

Islamic Fundamentalism and Its Values

Islamic fundamentalism constitutes a complete way of looking at the world, a view that is different from the traditional liberal view dominant in much of the West (Monroe & Kreidie, 1997). Traditionally, from the Western standpoint, Islamic fundamentalists are often mistakenly viewed—from traditional cost–benefit positions—as rational actors. The fundamentalist perspective is best understood as a worldview, which makes little distinction between public and private. According to this view, truth is discovered by revelation, and reason is subsequent to religious doctrine. Religious values dictate and dominate all basic issues, and only within the confines of the fundamentalist identity do individuals make choices by cost–benefit calculations. Islamic fundamentalism taps into a quite different social consciousness in which religious identity determines all other options. Therefore, the individual's cognitive dissonance could be reduced by appealing to and relying on traditional religious principles and prescriptions.

were gathered on the local level: only state legislators participated in the study. Local politics is traditionally different from politics at the national level and is expected to be "pragmatic."

Social Attribution

A student came to the professor after class and asked a question about the topic discussed 10 minutes ago. Then he asked a couple of other questions and finally made a personal remark: "Sorry, I see you are divorced. Am I right?" The professor replied, "No, I am married. What made you think that I am divorced?" "Well, I saw your golden ring on your right hand—not on the left—and assumed that you are divorced," replied the student. The professor smiled, "In the country where I was born, we wear the wedding ring on the right hand. This is a tradition." Moral? The student made an assumption about the professor just by looking at his wedding ring. This episode— that really happened to one of the authors—is a demonstration of **social attribution,** the process through which we seek to explain and identify the causes of the behavior of others as well as our own actions.

Are there any common cross-cultural trends of social attribution? Across countries, we tend to evaluate more positively the persons and objects we like. On the other hand, we view negatively those who are considered to be our adversaries, even if the facts suggest that they are not as bad as we think (Pratkanis, 1988). Groups to which we belong are commonly perceived as more heterogeneous (i.e., made up of dissimilar elements) than groups to which we do not belong (Gudykunst & Bond, 1997). Across cultures, people tend to rate faces that have even a minor scar as less sociable, less attractive, and more dishonest than the same faces without the scar (Bull & David, 1986). Both Korean and American subjects see "baby-faced" adults and interpret their behavior in a similar way (McArthur & Berry, 1987).

Research on social attribution provides some evidence that people across countries, despite many similarities, express different attributions. Consider, for instance, a study in which American and Japanese subjects were asked to look at smiling or nonsmiling white and Japanese faces and rate them on how attractive, intelligent, and sociable they were. The Americans normally rated the smiling faces higher on all three dimensions. The Japanese rated the smiling faces only as more sociable, and the neutral faces as more intelligent (Matsumoto, 1994).

Attribution as Locus of Control

One of our most powerful psychological drives is our need to explain things around us. Without a sense of understanding, the world would seem unsafe, threatening, and dangerous. An important way of gaining this understanding is by seeking explanations for the causes of events in and around our lives. If we explain causations, the world may become more predictable and, therefore, controllable (Kelley, 1967). Julian Rotter (1966) showed that, theoretically, people could be placed into two large groups. One group, the "internals" (those who have an internal locus of control), prefer to explain events as influenced by controllable internal factors. The other group, the "externals" (those who have an external locus of control), prefer to explain events as influenced by uncontrollable external factors. It has been shown in numerous studies that people with an external locus of control are more easily engaged in risky enterprises—such as gambling—than are internals. The latter are also likely to become political activists. People with an internal locus of control may tend to be "difficult" patients because they may be less likely than externals to follow the doctor's recommendations. The "internals" are not easily persuaded and they tend to have stronger achievement motivation than externals.

Early publications about locus of control inspired interest in testing its cross-cultural characteristics (Semin & Zwier, 1997). Do people in a particular region or culture display a particular locus of control? Could we say, for instance, that French men are more "externally controlled" than Chinese men? Or are collectivist cultures more likely to develop an external locus of control in its members? Are we motivated to prefer one type of causal attribution to another? It would appear so. Think, for example, about Western countries. Most individuals born in Western countries are socialized to believe that people can control their destiny and are the masters of their fate. As such, society generally condones dispositional attributions and discourages situational attributions. One consequence, however, is that we frequently fool ourselves into overestimating the degree of control that we actually do have, while underestimating the impact of external factors that lie beyond our control. Put another way, we simply do not have as much control over people and events as we would like to believe that we do. Nevertheless, making dispositional attributions provides us with a comfortable illusion of control.

Despite some exceptions, individuals from Western countries are more likely to display a stronger internal locus of control than non-Western people because "Westerners" are generally suspicious of powerful governments (external forces) and possess material resources that make them less dependent on external factors. If we follow this logic are we justified in expecting every male who is a city dweller, is of a religious or ethnic majority, and has a high socioeconomic status to have an internal locus of control? Are we also making accurate predictions when we imply that every woman who is a minority from a rural area, with a low socioeconomic status will have an external locus of control? These expectations were not confirmed in comparative studies (Tobacyk, 1992; Hui, 1982). Overall, the general pattern for locus of control across the groups, countries, and cultures studied was inconsistent. A few studies, however, have yielded some differences between social groups, such as one revealing that ethnic minorities in the United States participate in lotteries more often than nonminorities (Chinoy & Babington, 1998). Persistent gambling may be a behavioral pattern typical for "externals." However, one behavioral pattern cannot stand for the individual's locus of control.

Why has cross-cultural research found little or no difference in locus of control among cultures? There could have been a methodological problem: the participants in these cross-cultural studies were getting standard, preselected questions that could have had different meanings in different countries (Munro, 1986). There is also an opinion that the locus of control scores yielded in the studies could have reflected the actual, "individualized" degree of control that people exert in the real world, not only one determined by their social status and cultural identity (Dyal, 1984; Collins, 1974). For instance, a person is expected to have an external locus of control because he is poor and lives in a rural area controlled by an authoritarian government. However, this person is a father, a husband, and older brother, and a breadwinner for his family—the roles that would actually indicate an internal locus of control!

Both external and internal factors may be viewed as contributors to an individual's sense of personal happiness. More than 200 participants from Canada (both of French and English descent), El Salvador, and the United States, all undergraduate students, were asked open-ended questions: "What makes you happy?" "What does a person

CRITICAL THINKING

Making Assumptions about Locus of Control

Compare, for instance, Sweden and the United States. In which country, in your opinion, would women be more internal? Let us assume it should be in Sweden. Why? Because women in this country appear to be in control of their lives: this Scandinavian nation enjoys high living standards, a low level of street violence, and adequate child-care and health benefits, as well as benefits of other social programs. In fact, this assumption about locus of control is wrong. Swedish women were found to be more externally oriented than were American women (Lee & Dengerink, 1992). Perhaps, in reality, in Sweden, a more egalitarian society than the United States, people feel less "in charge" of their lives than their American counterparts because the government in Sweden takes care of a wide variety of issues and problems that in the United States are left to the people to deal with on their own.

Question. This study also revealed that Swedish men and American men have a similar locus of control. What explanation can you come up with for these results?

need to be happy?" "What is a happy person?" It was found that factors contributing to happiness were perceived similarly across cultures studied (Chiasson et al., 1996). For example, the most important factors of happiness were family relationships, the ability to reach one's goals, and positive self-esteem. However, there were some differences. The participants from El Salvador referred to religious values as well as political conditions in the country as factors affecting their happiness. North Americans mentioned personal success and enjoyable life episodes.

There is no idea, no fact, which would not be vulgarized and presented in a ludicrous light.
FYODOR DOSTOEVSKY (1821–1881)—RUSSIAN NOVELIST

Explaining the Behavior of Others

A tendency to explain other's actions in terms of internal causes (such as intentions and traits), and our own behavior in terms of circumstances, environmental influences, and opportunities is called **the fundamental attribution error** (Ross, 1977; see Chapter 3 for additional analysis). Some observers, for example, would incline to explain a homeless person's difficulties in terms of his personal characteristics ("He's just a lazy bum!"). The homeless person, by contrast, is likely to explain his difficulties principally in terms of external circumstances ("No one will help me out!"). The historic war trials conducted in Germany at the conclusion of World War II provide another vivid case in point. During the Nuremberg international trial proceedings, Allied prosecutors viewed the captured Nazis as personally responsible for their actions and therefore guilty of crimes against humanity. The accused, in contrast, saw themselves as innocent victims and blamed the German political system within which they were operating with the infamous defense: "I was only following orders."

There is a tendency for members of Western and individualistic cultures to demonstrate the fundamental attribution error more often than it is displayed by people from collectivist cultures (Newman, 1993). American children and adults, for example, showed a greater fundamental attribution error than their Indian peers. This means that Americans were making more references to the personality characteristics of other people than were Indian subjects (Miller, 1984). The same result was obtained in another study, in which Dutch subjects showed more self-serving tendencies in their explanation of life events than did Japanese subjects (Semin & Zwier, 1997).

Morality is simply the attitude we adopt toward people whom we personally dislike.
OSCAR WILDE (1854–1900)—IRISH-BORN ENGLISH POET

The fundamental attribution error may be displayed when members of an ethnic group interpret actions of other rival groups. It can be easily demonstrated when one analyzes anecdotes and jokes told by one ethnic group about a neighboring ethnic group. The neighbors are usually less intelligent, clean, rational, or spiritual (Legman, 1968). In other words, the neighbor is not as good as you are because of the neighbor's inherent characteristics. Conversely, there is evidence that individuals from collectivist cultures oppose negative exposure against their own groups to a greater extent than in-

CRITICAL THINKING

On Social Attribution of Crime

Morris and Peng (1994) examined two sets of articles from Chinese and American newspapers. The articles contained comparable stories about crime. The research showed that Chinese reporters did not reveal the fundamental attribution error: they used more situation-based explanations. American reporters preferred to use more personal dispositions to explain crime. The authors also found that although Chinese and American students were not different in their interpretations of the physical world, their explanations of social events were quite different: the American students relied on internal causes and Chinese students relied on external causes. The authors explained such differences by cultural factors of collectivism and individualism.

Now give your critical opinion about the following explanation for these results. For a number of years, a totalitarian ideology was dominant in China. This ideology was based on Marxist beliefs about the crucial role of social classes and "objective" social processes that one cannot change at will. According to Marxist views, human behavior should be explained as being caused by social factors. For example, crime is a result of improper policies of local government, mistakes in parenting, or poor education. If certain social conditions are created, crime should diminish. Therefore, the communist ideology itself can be considered as a factor that contributes to a particular type of social perception.

dividualists do (Triandis, 1994). As an example, it is suggested that Germans or Americans, for instance, are more likely to tell jokes about their own people than are Pakistanis or Mexicans.

There are some cross-cultural trends in the way people describe the behavior of others. If a person's behavior confirms our expectations, people tend to explain this behavior by internal factors. If someone's behavior does not confirm our expectations, we tend to use external reasons as explanations (Ben-Ari et al., 1994). For instance, if we expect Paul, a freshman from Brazil, to be an excellent soccer player and indeed he scores three goals in a game, we are likely to say that he is a good soccer player because he *is* a Brazilian. If we find that Paul does not play well, we would try to think of the circumstances that kept him from playing well.

What causes the fundamental attribution error? When we observe somebody's behavior, our attention is focused, almost instinctively, on the person, not on his or her environment. The person's behavior so dominates our perceptions that the situation itself fades into relative obscurity, leading us to ascribe dispositional attributions of causality. In addition to behavior, physical appearance itself can produce the same outcome. As applied to entire groups of people, the salience of characteristics such as sex, age, skin color, and even manner of dress leads us to overestimate the link between what "stands out" and the actual causes of human behavior. When we observe our own behavior, our attention is focused not only on ourselves, but also on our situation. Because our environment is most salient to us, we are apt to perceive it as more causally influential. Thus, in explaining our own behavior, we are prone to arrive at situational, rather than dispositional, attributions.

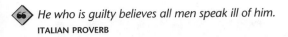 *He who is guilty believes all men speak ill of him.*
ITALIC PROVERB

Attribution of Success and Failure

The prevalence of external or internal explanations of people's behavior is measured in studies of how people explain their success or failure. It was found that cross-culturally, when people explain why individuals succeed or fail, at least three explanations are commonly used (Fletcher & Ward, 1988):

- individual ability ("I have skills" or "I do not have skills"),
- effort ("I tried hard" or "I didn't try"), and
- task difficulty ("It was not so difficult" or "It was very difficult").

If a person tends to take credit for personal success and avoid responsibility for failure, this person displays the **self-centered bias.** Imagine you take a French class but decide to drop it. If you say that your failure to learn French is caused by a lack of time (task difficulty), you are expressing a self-centered bias. Several attempts were made to examine how people in different countries use this bias in their comments about themselves. For example, a self-centered bias was found in samples studied from the United States, Yugoslavia, India, and South Africa. However, in Japanese samples, such bias was not found. Instead, researchers identified an **unassuming bias**: a tendency to explain personal success as a result of external factors, such as luck or help from others, and failure as a result of one's personal mistakes or weaknesses (Chandler et al., 1981).

Different studies suggested the existence of the unassuming bias in Asian and East Asian cultures. For example, Japanese subjects attribute failure to themselves more frequently, and success to themselves less frequently, than do their American counterparts. In addition, Japanese subjects display a group-serving bias, a tendency to explain the success of other people by internal factors and failure by external ones (Yamaguchi, 1988; Kashima & Triandis, 1986). Group-serving bias is particularly strong when individuals express their opinions in front of their group members (Bond, 1985). It was also shown that an individual's minority status typically affects his or her attribution of success. If you see yourself as a representative of a minority group that has a tense or rival relationship with the majority, you should not be expected to express a majority group-serving bias (Hunter et al., 1993).

A major change of immediate social environment—emigration from a home country as an example—can affect the way people explain their success and failure. By way of illustration, Indian women are expected to display the unassuming bias in their social perception. However, this bias did not appear in the responses of Indian female immigrants to Canada: both success and failure were attributed to internal causes (Moghaddam et al., 1990). Perhaps the influence of the norms of an individualist society influenced the women's social perception.

Different trends in interpretation of success can be found in the media. Authors of a study comparing American and Hong Kong newspapers were looking for similarities

CRITICAL THINKING

Assumptions about Individualism and Collectivism

As we already saw in Chapter 3, people's appeals to common-sense logic may lead to incorrect assumptions. Knowing about the individualistic and materialistic nature of the American society, some might assume that romantic relationships are not a great psychological value in the United States. Research provides evidence that challenges this assumption. In a survey conducted among American, Japanese, and German students, romantic love was valued higher in the United States and Germany than it was in Japan. Overall, romantic love is valued higher in nontraditional cultures than in traditional ones and in nontraditional cultures plays a more central role in people's decisions to marry. On the other hand, in collectivist cultures, family obligations often play a crucial role in marriage arrangements (Simmons et al., 1986).

Consider another example. Common sense would perhaps lead some people to the assumption that in collectivist cultures people lose their individuality and are unable to act independently because they must comply with formal rules of conduct. Following this logic, one might consider that intimacy, for instance, is not common among members of collectivist cultures. Research, however, indicates an opposite trend: intimacy is greater in collectivist societies than it is in individualist ones (Triandis, 1994).

Now think about the daily greetings exchanged between your colleagues and friends. People habitually exchange the universal: "Hello, how are you doing?—I am fine, thank you" on nearly all occasions. Rarely when we ask, "How are you?" are we genuinely interested in knowing how the person is actually doing. Similarly, by answering, "I am all right," we are revealing virtually nothing. On most occasions people exchange these phrases because this is a formal way of greeting. The intimacy barrier is not broken. Collectivists, on the other hand, are likely to feel strong obligations to know about you and take care of you if you belong to or identify yourself with their group.

and differences in the portrayal of winners and losers in various sporting events. It was found that American journalists were praising victorious athletes more often than Hong Kong reporters were. Moreover, Americans were making primarily internal attributions for their success. In Hong Kong, the reporters made mostly external attributions for losers (Hallahan et al., 1997).

 Man is so made that if he is told often enough that he is a fool he believes it.
BLAISE PASCAL (1623–1662)—FRENCH SCIENTIST AND PHILOSOPHER

Self-Perception

People can make distinctions between the world within them and the world outside. Both individual traits and environmental circumstances shape our self-perception in a variety of ways and can reflect the most prominent characteristics of an underlying culture. For centuries, as an example, the predominant form of social organization in

India was the caste system that reinforced inequality and hierarchy among all people. Expectedly, Indians view themselves and their interpersonal relationships as more hierarchically structured than Americans do (Sinha & Verma, 1983).

Another study of self-perception, conducted by Biswas and Pandey (1996), compared the self-perceptions of male members of three social groups in India. The respondents were asked to evaluate their quality of life and then each respondent's answer was matched with his socioeconomic status. The researchers found that socioeconomic upward mobility—measured as any increase in income and occupational status—did not substantially affect the respondent's self-image or perception of their social status. A respondent may earn more money than he did several years ago, have a better job, have a higher academic degree, and still perceive himself as a person of a lower status. What conclusion can be drawn from these findings? Socioeconomic changes alone do not necessarily bring about changes in the way people see themselves. Because many societies are still deeply divided along the old class, gender, ethnic, and caste lines, the "old" identities may be more salient than "new" ones despite significant changes taking place in many people's lives.

There are findings pointing to a correlation between individualism and collectivism on the one hand and self-esteem on the other. Tafarodi and Swann (1996) examined the self-esteem of more than 600 American (an individualist culture) and Chinese (a collectivist culture) college students. The study revealed that the Chinese participants were lower in perceived self-competence but higher in self-liking that were the American students. The authors argued that in collectivist cultures—which require sensitivity to the needs of others and subordination of personal goals to collective needs—it is expected that individuals develop self-liking. However, because of a relative loss of individual control often found in collectivist societies, these cultures promote restraints on feelings of self-competence. In individualist cultures, on the contrary, independence and the priority of the self are emphasized. Perhaps competence is related to material status and in the United States people feel more secure in terms of achievement than do people in China. However, it is unclear why positive feelings of self-competence in American students appear to have caused a decrease in positive feelings of self-liking. Perhaps one should be looking here for a reverse causation: a relatively low level of self-liking generates compensatory thoughts and behaviors that push individuals to achieve, produce, and accomplish.

One of the popular hypotheses derived from cross-cultural research on self-perception is an idea about the existence of a "private" and "public" self (Benedict, 1946; Triandis, 1994; Shiraev & Fillipov, 1990). Private self indicates feeling and thoughts about oneself and for oneself. Public self is a concept of self in relation to others and for others. Do you think people from collectivist cultures produce more group-centric and fewer self-centric descriptions of self than people from individualist cultures? Indeed, in collectivist, and therefore interdependent cultures (such as China, Japan, and Korea) people tend to identify their self not as an independent entity but rather as part of particular social groups (Triandis, 1994, 1989). Moreover, American subjects, when they describe themselves, tend to identify a great number of abstract traits—relatively unrelated to particular social groups. Asian subjects identify fewer of the same abstract traits (Bond & Tak-Sing, 1983). Surveys show that most Japanese subjects, for example, accept differences between their public and private self. Those who cannot accept these differences may experience social alienation and insecurity (Naito & Gielen, 1992). American respondents, on the other hand, try to eliminate the inconsistency between public and private self (Iwato & Triandis, 1993).

Do Social Norms Affect the Way We See Our Own Body Weight?

Sobal and Stunkard (1989) reviewed several anthropological studies that measured correlation between the individual's body weight and socioeconomic status. They established a remarkable tendency. In rich countries the correlation is negative: People who are thinner than others tend to be richer than others are as well! Or, if one takes a slightly different view, people who are richer tended to be thinner. In undeveloped countries the correlation is positive: Thinner people, in general, are usually poorer than others who weigh more are.

Cogan et al. (1996) examined attitudes toward obesity and fitness in university students in the United States and Ghana, in Western Africa. The participants answered questions about their weight, restrictions on eating and dieting, the degree to which their weight interferes with some social activities, perception of ideal bodies, and stereotypes of thin and heavy people. Students in Ghana rated heavier bodies more favorably than U.S. students did. American students were more likely to be dieting than were their African counterparts, and American females were the most likely to diet among the students interviewed. Moreover, U.S. females scored significantly higher on eating-restriction problems and interference of their body weight with social behavior.

In the United States, most people hold negative attitudes toward body fat. According to surveys, people attribute increased body weight to being poor or having poor health. The obese are blamed for their weight, which is assumed to be under their voluntary control. Obese women, more than men, are rated negatively by peers. These stereotypical views about one's weight do not exist in many other cultures around the world. In developing countries, for example, in which major causes of death are due to malnutrition and infection, thinness is not really desired. In countries such as India, China, the Philippines, and some Latin American countries, an increased standard of living is correlated with increasing body weight (Rothblum, 1992).

Mukai and McCloskey (1996) examined eating attitudes among Japanese and American elementary-school girls. More than 100 participants in both countries answered questions from a questionnaire designed in the United States and then translated into Japanese. Issues such as perceptions of being overweight, the number of friends on a diet, and the frequency of talking with parents about food and dieting were compared. The results of the study suggest that a preference for fitness can be considered a prevailing social value both in Japan and in the United States. In this study, significantly more American fathers than Japanese fathers were reported to be on diets to

CROSS-CULTURAL SENSITIVITY

During the 1999 MTV music awards in New York City, a popular black comedian Chris Rock—the host of the ceremony—made a controversial remark about singer Jennifer Lopez. He said that she arrived at the awards show in two limousines: one was for herself and the other was for her butt. The next morning, many commentators complained that Chris Rock's joke was extremely offensive and inappropriate. In response to the critics, the comedian remarked that he said nothing offensive. The misunderstanding was based, in his view, on some differences in cultural perception of body size. For the whites, he said, a big butt may be shameful. It is different for blacks. People were cheering this "butt" joke in Harlem, he added. After this comment was made, the commentators were divided in their opinions. Some said that Chris Rock was joking again. Others suggested that perhaps he gave a fine explanation of cultural relativity in the perception of body parts. What do you think: Was his initial remark offensive to the singer and women in general?

lose weight. It is quite possible that Japanese girls, in contrast to their American counterparts, have fewer contacts with their fathers regarding food or eating, and therefore they might have been less aware of their fathers eating attitudes. However, it is also possible that more American fathers were on diets than were Japanese fathers. Eating disorders became increasingly prevalent in Japan in the 1990s. Due to similarities found between American and Japanese samples, suggestions can be made for some effective techniques that can be used to increase awareness in Japanese adolescent girls of the dangerous consequences of eating disorders (see also the section on eating disorders in Chapter 9).

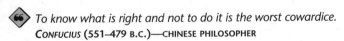

To know what is right and not to do it is the worst cowardice.
CONFUCIUS (551–479 B.C.)—CHINESE PHILOSOPHER

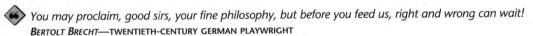

You may proclaim, good sirs, your fine philosophy, but before you feed us, right and wrong can wait!
BERTOLT BRECHT—TWENTIETH-CENTURY GERMAN PLAYWRIGHT

Duty and Fairness in Individualist and Collectivist Cultures

People say, "Do not kill, do not steal, and do not lie." Even though general moral principles of behavior may be universal, the interpretations of these principles are influenced by culture. There are two basic views on morality. The first view, a justice-based view, emphasizes the autonomy of the individual and his or her personal rights. It argues that autonomy and personal rights should be impartial and applicable to every human being. This view is supported primarily in individualist cultures. The second view, a duty-based view, is based on the belief that obligation to others is the basis of morality. This view is common in collectivist cultures. For example, in experimental situations when participants are asked to assess the behavior of other people, American subjects preferred to endorse an individual's personal choice whereas Indian subjects tended to appeal to regulations and required norms (Miller, 1994). A study of Arab teacher's attitudes found that the feeling of personal obligations to the group was the dominant factor in the teachers' work ethic (Abu-Saad, 1998).

Are there any cultural trends in people's views on the fair distribution of resources? Political psychologists suggest that there are at least two major views on fairness. The first stems from the merit standpoint, arguing people have to have access to resources according to their skills and accomplishment. A person who contributes to society can get a bigger share of the benefits from society than those who contribute less—for whatever reason. The second originates from the need standpoint, asserting that people have to receive equal shares of the benefits regardless of their "worth" to society (Sears, 1996). Children, the elderly, and the ill all may contribute little to society, however, they deserved to be treated as anybody else.

As you might anticipate, there are national differences in the way people perceive fair distribution of resources. For example, college students in the United States are more merit oriented than students in Germany, who are more need oriented (Bernman & Murphy-Bernman, 1996). Results of national surveys show that, when compared to Americans, twice as many young Germans endorse statements that (1) the government should guarantee everyone a minimum standard of living, (2) the government should place an upper limit on the amount of money anyone can make, and (3) people should help the needy even if this means getting money from those who have money. The prevailing attitudes among Americans were that individuals themselves are responsible for their material success (Cockerham et al., 1988). Even in countries that can be considered similar in terms of democratic principles of government, education, and social tradition, there could be substantial differences in how people view justice and what they consider a "fair" distribution of resources.

The differences between the United States and Germany are, in part, based on different social traditions in these countries. True, social welfare policies exist in both nations. In Germany, however, the government is involved in social welfare programs to a larger degree than it is in the United States. The situational context of the surveys could also have affected the results. The studies mentioned here were conducted in the late 1980s and early 1990s when prevailing attitudes among Germans were influenced by the necessity to provide for German unification. However, a few years later, according to opinion surveys, many Germans became skeptical of social welfare and the amount of help given to the needy (Shapiro et al., 2000).

There are cross-cultural similarities in the way people express their desire to work. Consistently from the 1950s to the present, people respond similarly to the following question: "Even if you have enough money to support yourself would you want to work?" Most of those surveyed in Japan, the United States, Israel, the Netherlands, Belgium, Germany, Great Britain, Turkey, Russia, and Cyprus indicated that they would want to continue working even if the economic necessity for working were removed (Adigun, 1997; Shiraev 1988; Yadov, 1978). One of the explanations for such cross-cultural consistency is that people consider work as a great chance to stay connected to other people. Perhaps for many human beings, their work activities also serve as a channel for self-expression, which can boost self-esteem. These assumptions, of course, should be critically interpreted because of two main reasons. One reason—these data were obtained mostly in economically advanced countries—leads to several other possible confounds: (1) respondents had better working conditions, (2) there is more likely to be a democratic atmosphere in the workplace, and (3) overall social protection could influence people's positive views about work. The second consideration is that because the questions asked in the surveys were linked to important values, some people could have given responses based not on what people felt but rather on what answers were expected of them.

Stereotypes and the Power of Generalizations

We often do not have the necessary time or psychological resources to analyze every fact as new and unique. We categorize almost everything we see, hear, and deal with. **Stereotypes** are categorical assumptions that all members of a given group have a particular trait. Stereotypes could be positive or negative, simple or differentiated, and held with or without confidence (Smith & Bond, 1993). These qualities could also vary in their degree. For example, it was found in a study that Anglo-Australians held very positive stereotypes of themselves and very negative stereotypes about Aboriginal Australians. The latter held somewhat favorable stereotypes about Anglo-Australians and only moderately positive stereotypes about themselves (Marjoribanks & Jordan, 1986).

The process of social perception often makes us simplify the incoming information and categorize it by groups. For instance, Israeli Arabs see Jews as more intellectually advanced; however, the Arabs see themselves as far superior socially—thus referring to their friendships, love, family traditions, and overall collectivism (Bizman & Amir, 1982). Stereotypical beliefs such as "most illegal immigrants are criminals," or "interracial marriages are less stable than same-race marriages," or "all Jews are wealthy," may be expressed in our daily judgments despite the fact that many times these stereotypes are incorrect. There are some undocumented aliens who commit crimes, but they represent a small proportion of all undocumented aliens in the United States. Interracial marriages are as stable as same-race matrimony. There are both rich and poor Jews.

EXERCISE 10.1

The following is a description of interpersonal communications of "typical" American, Japanese, and Arab individuals adopted from a best-selling book [Fast, J. (1970). *Body language*. New York: Pocket Books].

There are distinct differences in the way an American, Japanese, and an Arab handle their personal "territory." In Japan, crowding together is a sign of warm and pleasant intimacy. Like the Japanese, the Arabs tend to cling to one another. But while in public they are crowded together, in the privacy of their houses the Arabs have almost too much space: their houses are generally large and empty, with the people clustered together in one small area. Arabs do not like to be alone, so partitions between rooms are usually avoided. The Arab likes to touch his companion, feel him. The Japanese avoid touching and prefer to keep physical boundaries. Americans too tend to have boundaries in public places. You do not push or intrude into the space of another person. Arabs have no concept of privacy in a public place. Americans very seldom shove, push, or pinch other people in public. When two Arabs talk to each other, they look each other in the eyes with great intensity. The same intensity is rarely exhibited in the American culture.

Questions: Do you think all these statements are erroneous? What exactly is inaccurate in them? Or maybe you suggest that these judgments are somewhat accurate? Where should we draw the line between being fairly accurate and being stereotypical?

Members of an ethnic group may hold stereotypes about themselves similar to what others think about this group. For example, Walkey and Chung (1996) examined attitudes toward Chinese immigrants in New Zealand. More than 300 schoolchildren of both Chinese and European backgrounds showed that the stereotypes held by these two groups were similar. Both groups mentioned the work ethics of Chinese, especially their effort. Both interviewed groups saw Europeans as relatively less positive on work ethics and more individually than socially controlled than Chinese immigrants.

Emotions may accelerate the accessibility of stereotypes: we often use them to justify particular feelings (Zaller, 1992). There is a strong relationship between interpersonal conflict and negative stereotyping (Campbell, 1967). People in two conflicting nations often have similar negative stereotypes about each other. Do not think that the farther apart two ethnic groups live from each other, the more stereotypes they will have about each other. It is not necessarily correct. High levels of contact and proximity of two groups could also produce negative stereotypes (Marin & Salazar, 1985).

Ethnic or racial attributes appear to be more salient and notable than other characteristics, such as education, age, and social class (Gudykunst & Bond, 1997). People's "looks" are the easiest perceptions to recognize at first glance. This is why many stereotypes are produced: because we often move in our communications no further than the first glance.

In the course of evaluating similarities and differences between phenomena, we are subject to committing errors of at least two kinds: first, we allow genuine differences to be obscured by similarities, and second, we allow genuine similarities to be obscured by differences. Stereotyping is, in fact, permitting similarities between phenomena to eclipse their differences. Those who stereotype other people are prone to habitually, systematically, and automatically overestimate within-group similarities, while minimizing (or even ignoring) within-group variability (Fiske & Taylor, 1984). In other words, the individual perceives group members to be more alike than they really are and, at the same time, does not recognize many of the ways in which they are different from one another.

Moreover, groups we like and groups we do not like are seen as more different than they really are (Keen, 1986). As you can readily discern, in its most extreme form, this process is a fundamental component underlying prejudice, bigotry, chauvinism, racism, sexism, ageism, and so forth, wherein all members of the particular "out-group" are seen as essentially the same, while their individuality goes virtually unnoticed.

Let us consider, for example, cross-cultural counseling. Some therapists may fail to respect—or even recognizethe uniqueness indigenous to each individual client. Unfortunately, these therapists may perceive a client from one sociocultural group as basically the same as every other client from that group. In this way, clients are viewed *not* as distinct and varied individuals, each possessing a separate and unique constellation of life experiences, memories, feelings, perceptions, values, beliefs, hopes, fears, and dreams. Instead, they are spontaneously filtered through the therapist's own sociocultural stereotypes, from which they emerge as Koreans, Blacks, Jews, Latinos, Vietnamese, and so on. In this less-than-therapeutic environment, irrespective of individual clients' unique situations, problems, or needs, they would offer essentially the same "cookie-cutter" approach to diagnosis and treatment.

Stereotyping is making erroneous judgments. However, beware and do not reject the possibility that two or many people can have something similar in their behavior, emotion, and attitudes. How many times have you heard someone make the following pronouncement (or any derivation thereof): "You cannot compare these two people because they are totally and completely different from each other!" Here we have a vivid illustration of a person who is making the converse mistake of allowing similarities between people to be overshadowed by their differences. Thus, the individual who staunchly and adamantly maintains that "One should *never* stereotype," is effectively blinding him or herself to authentic commonalities that actually do exist within specific groups. However, by obstinately clinging to this position, such individuals practically ensure that they will remain oblivious to true similarities within (as well as between) groups of people.

A CASE IN POINT

In Search of Commonalities

The principle is to *"look for both similarities and differences"* that can be constructively applied in the cross-cultural counseling setting. Despite apparent differences two individuals can share something in common. Members of the same cultural group may be different in virtually every personality trait. Consider the following brief vignette as an example of a search for commonalities in two people.

Client: "There's no way that you can understand how I feel. After all, you're white, and I'm black. And you've never been discriminated against because of your race."

Therapist: "You are right. I can never know exactly what that feels like. We are truly different in that respect. But at the same time, I know what it's like to be discriminated against because of my religion. And I have had the experience of being persecuted out of ignorance and hatred. To that extent, we do share a common experience. We are indeed both similar and different."

Similarly, psychotherapists who tenaciously cling to their belief that "Every client should be viewed and treated as totally unique and without regard for his or her cultural background" runs the risk of allowing true—and potentially helpful—similarities between persons to be overlooked, neglected, or omitted. Unfortunately, the therapist's overemphasis on individual differences typically is realized at the expense of minimizing interpersonal commonalities. As a consequence, for instance, deeply powerful and universal life experiences that appear to be intrinsic to the human condition—such as needs for love, acceptance, empathy, esteem, or meaning—are prone to be minimized, disregarded, or even outright rejected.

Is it possible to eliminate stereotypes? Some researchers are skeptical (Devine, 1989). But it is possible to reduce the influence of stereotypes on our daily judgments. Human diversity can be greater than human sameness. There are rich and poor, educated and illiterate, happy and angry Americans, Japanese, and Arabs, who live in big cities and small towns, who either work or do not, travel or stay in one place. Above all, people have unique personal characteristics hardly placed within the narrow confines of popularly held stereotypes. What we might anticipate from an individual based on our expectations does not often match who he or she really is. Please be prepared for such inconsistencies!

 EXERCISE 10.2

Imagine that you are on a cruise where you meet the following people: (1) a man from Japan, (2) a woman from Brazil, (3) a man from France, (4) a woman from Jordan, (5) a man from Germany, and (6) a woman from Italy. You spend a great week in their company. Back home, you finally realize that your initial stereotypes about these people were confirmed. Could you match the following behaviors with the nationalities displayed above? (Complete the statements below please.) Four hundred students in Virginia and Washington D.C. have also given their assessments of popular stereotypes. You can then compare your answers with the most frequently displayed stereotypes (see Appendix 5 on the webpage).

Question: Who was this person (Japanese, Italian, French, German, Jordanian, Brazilian)?

1. This person was never late for breakfast, lunch, or dinner.
2. This person talked too much.
3. This person had three video cameras with him/her.
4. This person was the best lambada dancer in the group.
5. This person was drinking beer continuously.
6. This person was trying to date several people in your group.
7. This person was the quietest in the group.
8. This person kept smiling continuously and kept saying "yes."
9. This person said he (she) had never played poker and won't be playing.
10. This person was drinking wine continuously.

11. Military marches have been this person's favorite music
12. This person said that after marriage he (she) would love to stay home with his/her kids.
13. This person knew a lot about cheese.

EXERCISE 10.3

Both Hofstede (1980) and Smith and Schwartz (1997) found that the value of individualism and economic development of a country are strongly and positively correlated. In other words if a country is wealthy, it is more likely that its citizens will express more individualistic attitudes than citizens of a poor country will. The most convenient explanation of the link could be as follows:

- *Wealthy economies provide people with a variety of opportunities and therefore allow freedom of choice to and relative independence of individuals.*

However, a different explanation is also possible:

- *Individualistic values shared by people motivate them to work hard and develop productivity.*

Using these two types of explanations, please justify strong negative correlations between the economic wealth of a nation (evaluated on the basis of income per capita) and Power Distance and Uncertainty Avoidance. Refer to Chapter 3 if you need to refresh your memory about positive and negative statistical correlation.

CHAPTER SUMMARY

- It is an established view in psychology that social perception is culturally rooted. We acquire judgments, attitudes, and beliefs from our cultural milieu.
- One of the most fundamental elements of the process of social perception and social cognition is attitude. Cross-culturally, attitudes help us understand and make sense of the world. They serve an ego-defensive function assisting us to feel better about ourselves. Finally, attitudes serve a function that allows us to express our values.
- Cultures develop, maintain, and justify particular sets of values along the following di-

mensions: conservatism vs. autonomy, hierarchy vs. egalitarianism, and mastery vs. harmony. There could be collectivist and individualist patterns in human values. There are also debates about the existence of so-called Western and non-Western values.

- Cognitive balance and cognitive dissonance theories suggest that people seek consistency among their attitudes. Notwithstanding limitations, this trend was established among individuals in different countries. One of the forms of consistency seeking is psychological dogmatism, which has a wide range of cultural manifestations.

- Research on social attributions provides some evidence that people across countries, despite many similarities, could express different attribution styles, and these differences are deeply rooted in people's social and cultural background.
- Despite expectations about culture-bound manifestations of locus of control, its general pattern across many countries studied was highly inconsistent.
- In attempts to identify the causes of behavior and determine the source of success and failure, individuals display the fundamental attribution error, modesty bias, and egocentric bias. Culture can have an impact on various individual manifestations of the fundamental attribution error and other patterns of social attribution.
- Even though general moral principles of behavior may be universal, the interpretations of these principles can be strongly influenced

by each particular culture. There are two basic views on morality. The first view, a justice-based view of morality, is associated with beliefs that emphasize the autonomy of the individual and his or her individual rights. The second view, a duty-based view, is based on the belief that obligation to others is the basis of morality.
- Individuals make distinctions between the world within them and the world outside of them. Both individual traits and environmental circumstances shape people's self-perception in a variety of ways.
- The process of social perception often makes people simplify the incoming information and categorize it by groups. Stereotypes can lead people to think that all members of a given group have a particular trait. Research suggests that stereotypes could have a number of universal characteristics common in different cultural settings.

 ## KEY TERMS

Attitude   A psychological representation of various features of the social or physical world.

Cognitive Dissonance   Psychological tensions caused by the perceived mismatch (dissonance) between (1) attitudes and behavior, (2) two or more decisions, or (3) two or more attitudes.

Dogmatism   The tendency to be closed minded, rigid, and inflexible in one's opinions and subsequent behavior.

Fundamental Attribution Error   The tendency to explain others' actions in terms of internal causes and our own behavior in terms of circumstances, environmental influences, and opportunities.

Locus of Control   The generalized beliefs that the control of one's reinforcements rests either on controllable internal factors (internal locus of control) or on uncontrollable external factors (external locus of control).

Self-Centered Bias   The tendency to take credit for our successes and avoid responsibility for our failures.

Social Cognition   The process through which we interpret, remember, and then use information about the social world.

Social Attribution   The process through which we seek to explain and identify the causes of the behavior of others as well as our own actions.

Social Perception   The process through which we seek to know and understand other people and ourselves.

Stereotypes   Traits or characteristics generally attributed to all members of specific groups.

Unassuming Bias   The tendency to explain one's own success as a result of external factors, and one's failure as a result of personal mistakes or weaknesses.

Value   A complex belief that reflects a principle, standard, or quality considered by the individual as the most desirable or appropriate.

CHAPTER 11

Social Interaction

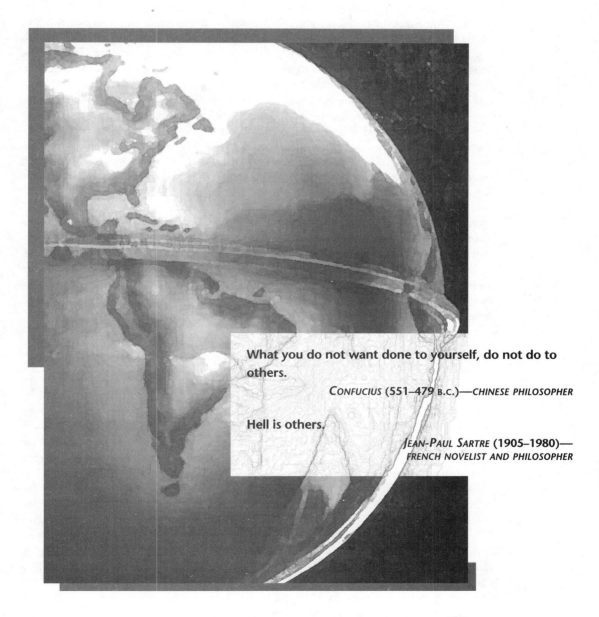

What you do not want done to yourself, do not do to others.

CONFUCIUS (551–479 B.C.)—CHINESE PHILOSOPHER

Hell is others.

*JEAN-PAUL SARTRE (1905–1980)—
FRENCH NOVELIST AND PHILOSOPHER*

Twenty-five years ago the authors of this book, two teenagers living on opposite sides of the planet, were told an anecdote. It was not particularly funny—just an amusing story about bargaining. Born in two different cultures, living under two different governments, separated by mountains of stereotypes and mistrust, we both nevertheless understood what bargaining was.

Two old friends meet in a bar in New York City. "You know," says one, "My son was a loser until I decided to give him a jump start in life." "What kind of a jump start?" the second asked. "Well, my son married a Saudi princess last week and got a job as vice president of Chase Manhattan Bank." "Married to a Saudi princess and vice president of a bank? How did you arrange this? You are a cab driver!" "Oh, I used the shuttle diplomacy method." "The shuttle diplomacy method? What is that?" "It is simple. A month ago I called the Saudi embassy and asked them if there was a princess available to marry my son. They said 'no.' I then told them that I forgot to mention that my son is vice president of Chase Manhattan Bank. They immediately said, 'That makes a difference. We would be glad to find a princess for your son.'" "But wait a minute. Your son is a drummer at a night club, not a banker!" "Well, I fixed that too. I called Chase Manhattan Bank and asked them if my son could apply for the position of vice president. They said 'no.' Then I told them that I forgot to mention that my son is married to a Saudi princess. They immediately told me, 'That makes a difference. Your son can begin work tomorrow.' So, this is what I call the shuttle diplomacy."

This anecdote is popular in many countries. The expression "shuttle diplomacy" comes from the decision-making strategies of Henry Kissinger, Secretary of State in the Nixon administration. But the political context of the anecdote is perhaps not so important. The most fascinating aspect of this story is that despite our cultural, political, and religious differences, we shared something: common rules for human behavior that were easily understood, recognized, and interpreted by us both. But are there any empirical facts to suggest that people of all cultures recognize and make use of the same rules of interaction? If no such facts exist then in what areas are we different?

Universal Interaction

It is accepted by social scientists that human beings cannot survive living in total isolation from other people. During our lives we join various groups, voluntarily or forcibly, deliberately or by chance. Anthropologists confirm that people tend to form groups in all known human societies (Coon, 1946). A **group** consists of two or more figures forming a complete unit in a composition. Groups to which we belong are called in-groups, and groups to which we do not belong are called out-groups. Initially, we might think that the members of a group come together because they live near one another. However, geographic proximity is not a necessary or sufficient condition for belonging to the same in-group. For instance, a Catholic and a Protestant may live side by side in a town in Northern Ireland but they will probably not belong to similar in-groups. Almost every group to which one of them belongs—a school, a church, or a circle of close friends—will be an out-group for the other. Alternatively, a Hindu boy from New York and a Muslim child from California may never see each other in person, but they can belong to the same fantasy-baseball league: playing against one another on the Internet.

When we join a group we attain a **status:** a relative social position within a group that can be either formal or informal. Cultures differ in the way societal norms facilitate or inhibit social mobility. For instance, status can be earned (achieved) or given at birth (ascribed). One might expect, for example, that in democratic societies individual merit serves as a foundation for social status. The old Indian system of castes, on the other hand, determined one's social position with little or no opportunity for social mobility. If one belonged to the lower caste his or her chances of becoming powerful and wealthy were slim.

Thinking critically, as opposed to solely utilizing the categorization bias, will allow us to consider three important factors in the relationship between culture and status. First, the social status of every human being in every society can be both achieved and ascribed. Second, even in the most advanced democracies there is discrimination based on gender, ethnicity, and/or religion (see Chapter 12). Third, by becoming a member of different groups, people may accept more than one social status. For example, one can be an immigrant, a mother, a daughter, a nurse, a soccer coach, and a patient—all at the same time. Having a multitude of social positions inevitably affects the way people reflect their identities, including their cultural identity.

We now know that being part of a group involves obtaining a status, but how do groups and statuses affect our behavior: through norms and social roles. **Norms** are established by a group and indicate how members of that group should and should not behave. Social **roles** are sets of behaviors that individuals occupying specific positions within a group are expected to perform. As soon as we become part of a group we encounter that group's norms and as soon as we obtain a status, we begin performing social roles. For instance, in some families, children always ask for their parents' blessing when making an important decision. In many Asian and African countries parents do not allow their children to date before marriage. These are cultural norms. In Germany, most small shops close their doors at six in the evening. This is a societal norm. Mayan children living in Guatemala learn not to give advice to an elder—a local norm of showing respect for adults (Berger, 1995). Some religious norms are very restrictive against certain foods or products.

Certain behavioral trends, such as wearing a seat belt while driving, could be seen as a norm too. There are also some cultural differences in the prevalence of such a norm among American males (see Table 11.1).

TABLE 11.1	Behavioral Trends as Norms: Safety Belt Use among Young U.S. Males Ages 18–29		
Black Males	**Asian Males**	**Hispanic Males**	**White Males**
44.1%	65.2%	65.4%	54.3%

Source: Washington Post, April 3, 1998.

A group can establish **sanctions**—certain actions reward those who follow the norms (positive sanctions) and reprove those who are deviant (negative sanctions). In most cases, norms cannot exist without sanctions attached to them. These vary from physical punishment to friendly criticism, from material rewards to verbal appreciation. As we saw in Chapter 1, many collectivist cultures (such as Russia, Pakistan, or Mexico) have stronger system sanctions and rewards than most of the individualist cultures (for example, Switzerland, the United States, or Germany). There are, of course, also cultural similarities. Both American and Japanese managers use direct and indirect forms of praise (positive sanctions) for their employees (Barnlund & Araki, 1985).

Population density can have an impact on interaction because it determines how many people a person will have direct contact with during a period of time. There are countries and regions in which people live in crowded social environments and there are regions in which large gatherings of people are rare. Compare, for example, rural Canada to Bangladesh, or central Oregon to Paris, and you will find a substantial difference in population density.

 You are a King by your own fireside, as much as any monarch on his throne.
MIGUEL DE CERVANTES (1547–1616)—SPANISH NOVELIST AND POET

As a universal cross-cultural trend, people tend to identify and protect territory on which they live. Territorial behavior includes actions that stake out or identify territory, ownership, or belongings. A fence around one's house or a bag placed on a classroom desk indicate our territorial behavior. Anthropologists suggest that territorial behavior is natural for both individuals and social groups (Schubert & Masters, 1991). Moreover, some biologists imply that territorial behavior can be instinctual. For example, some fish will defend their territory even without the presence of their natural competitors (Lorenz, 1966). Although rejecting the idea about human instincts psychologists confirm that territorial behavior is common for most social groups and in various cultural settings. The differences among groups are based on the extent of their territorial behavior. Groups that are inclusive will tend to tolerate "trespassers," whereas exclusive groups will be particularly territorial.

Together with historical and geographic circumstances that influence population density, there are also cultural factors linked to people's inclination to form small groups. Overall, it is assumed that in collectivist cultures, people more frequently join groups than do people in individualist cultures (Berkowitz, 1971). For example, in an observational study of six nations, it was found that the tendency to form groups in street settings (such as shopping, entertainment, and park areas) was quite different in the countries studied. In Turkey, people on the street formed larger groups and did it more frequently than people in Iran, Afghanistan, England, Germany, Sweden, and Italy. In the United States people displayed the lowest level of group formation.

Collectivism and individualism, as fundamental cultural attributes, may significantly influence social interaction in a wide variety of situations. We learned in Chapters 1, 7, and 8 that in individualistic cultures people usually care primarily for them-

CRITICAL THINKING

Stages of Group Development

Social psychologists imply that a group has its own life span. One group is beginning while another is ceasing to exist. This natural process includes five stages of group development. During the first stage (forming), the members get to know each other, learn about group objectives, and gather information about the situation. During the second stage (storming), the members distribute the roles within the group, and become the players of those chosen roles. During the third stage (norming), the players establish the norms or rules by which they distinguish desirable from undesirable behavior. The fourth stage (performing) is the actual functioning of the developed group. During the fifth and final stage (dissolving), the group structure is disintegrating.

   Think about different groups you have belonged to in the past or belong to now: sport teams, professional groups, a sorority or fraternity, groups of friends, and so on. Could you suggest that most of these groups went through or are going through the stages described above? If you think that there are different patterns of group development describe them.

selves and their individual family, whereas in collectivist cultures people are expected to first look after their in-groups and then themselves. In individualist cultures the importance of achievement and the individual's initiative are stressed during socialization. In collectivist societies the emphasis is placed on belonging to groups (Hofstede & Bond, 1984). Therefore, it is likely that people in collectivist cultures will interact more frequently and more intensely with in-group members than will members of individualist cultures. In most societies with collectivist norms people tend to belong to fewer groups, but such groups tend to be more stable and enduring than the groups in individualist societies. People in individualist cultures are more inclined to belong to a large variety of groups, but for shorter periods of time (Moghaddam, 1998). It is also expected that in-group favoritism and mutual influence will be stronger in collectivist cultures than in individualist ones (Gudykunst & Bond, 1996, 124). Many travelers will notice some patterns of interaction linked to individualist and collectivist norms. It is common in the United States, for example, to send written invitations to join a celebration or a party. Moreover, it is also common to request in the invitation that people respond, indicating whether they can or cannot come. This type of formal communication is considered unusual in most collectivist cultures around the world.

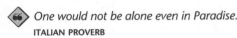

One would not be alone even in Paradise.
ITALIAN PROVERB

   No matter what our cultural background is, the presence or absence of others may significantly alter our behavior: bystanders, spectators, or even passers-by can either enhance or inhibit our performance (Zajonc, 1965). This phenomenon is called **social facilitation**. The influence of others on individual performance was studied as early as the 1900s, when the first pathbreaking experiments in social psychology demonstrated that social facilitation could be viewed as a cross-cultural phenomenon (Yaroshevski, 1975).

Another important cultural dimension that is related to individual interaction, which was discussed in Chapter 1, is *uncertainty avoidance*. Compared to individuals from cultures with low uncertainty avoidance rules, individuals who live in cultures with high uncertainty avoidance tend to be less tolerant of uncertainty and ambiguity. They tend to express culturally "approved" emotions more frequently, have a stronger desire for group consensus, are less tolerant of those who are different, and have a greater need to follow formal rules of behavior (Hofstede, 1980). Tolerance of behaviors that deviate from the expected normative patterns is a characteristic behavior in nontraditional societies. Bear in mind that tolerance and intolerance are issue specific and are better understood when studied from a comparative perspective: one should examine a specific group, under specific circumstances, and the extent to which that group experiences intolerance or tolerance for a particular issue. For example, there are many people intolerant of homosexuality; however, the scope and scale of such intolerance are different in democratic and authoritarian societies, in traditional and nontraditional cultures (see Chapter 7).

Direct Contacts

Whether in Argentina, Sweden, Australia, the Congo, or India, people have common understandings of many signs of body language: they identify belligerent gestures, recognize friendly smiles, and may panic in similar ways when feeling frightened. For example, without saying a word, almost any person can show that he or she does not know the answer to a question by using the universal body language of shrugging the shoulders. It has also been found that typically the higher the social status of an individual, the greater the vocal volume, that is, the louder he or she speaks. This is especially true in competitive interactions. People tune their vocal intensity by increasing it when interacting with those closer to them in rank and decreasing it when interacting with those further above and below in status (Schubert, 1991).

The rules of greeting and introducing oneself to other people appear to be comparable across cultures. When two or more people meet for the first time, they tend to tell something about themselves, as psychologists say, disclose themselves to each other. They say a greeting, tell their names, and usually smile. Studies show significant consistency in the rules of address across different cultures (Frager & Wood, 1992). There are also differences, of course. In some countries, as in the United States, people give each other a handshake when they meet for the first time and typically do not shake hands when they then see each other daily. In many Arab countries and in Russia, on the contrary, people shake hands with their friends and colleagues daily. Remember the effects of the naturalistic fallacy in our evaluation of observable facts? Some people in the United States may consider such attempts at daily handshaking as annoying and intrusive behavior. In the same way, an American professional traveling abroad may be perceived as "cold and detached" just because he will not shake hands with his foreign colleagues every morning. Why? Because people tend to consider things that are familiar or "typical" as normal and more acceptable than "atypical" behaviors.

Because of various individual reasons we can find people from every culture who are reluctant to disclose themselves and those who readily tell everything about who they are and what they do.

There are also cultural traditions that regulate our initial contacts. For example, situations of so-called high or low cultural contexts (Berry et al., 1992). Within high-context situations, much of the most important information is present in the context. If one says to another person, "Let us have lunch sometimes," this does not always mean that the first individual is actually going to have lunch with the other. Based on the situational context, the other person should make an evaluation and decide if it was an invitation for lunch or just a polite way to end the relationship. Within low-context situations almost all the information is in the conveyed message. Most Western countries, including the United States and Canada, are considered to be low-context cultures, whereas countries such as Japan, Korea, and Vietnam are high-context cultures. It is likely, for example, that personal self-disclosure may be more difficult for Japanese when they communicate with Americans than vice versa. Japanese inner life is often communicated more by hints and overtones than by direct interaction. Therefore, when Japanese communicate with Americans, they may look less relaxed and less flexible than their counterparts from California or Texas (Hedstrom, 1992). However, do not let your expectations create reality (please remember an element of critical thinking): when a Japanese person communicates with an American counterpart, in most cases they will speak English. In this context, who should feel more relaxed, a person who speaks English since birth or one whose foreign-language proficiency is somewhat limited?

CROSS-CULTURAL SENSITIVITY

Professional ice hockey players are tough. They shoot the puck and throw body checks. Sometimes some of them drop their gloves and fight with their bare fists. They are not joking around. The fights are for real. So are the injuries they may inflict on each other. What is the maximum penalty for fighting? Five minutes on a penalty bench. And then the player is back in the game. If you are hit, you hit back. Do not complain. Physical fighting is a part of ice hockey.

However, some words that you say on the ice rink are more painful than cuts and bruises. We are not talking about sexual profanities—if you watch any American professional game from the stands you know that these obscenities are thrown in every game and basically are left unnoticed by the sports officials and public. We are talking about ethnic and racial slurs— disparaging and extremely offensive remarks about or related to one's ethnicity, religion, or race (origin). The National Hockey League has established "zero tolerance" for racial and ethnic slurs on the ice. Moreover, the League severely punishes some players for using such slurs during the game. In 1998, for example, two players—Chris Simon and Craig Berube—were suspended and penalized financially after being charged with using racial slurs against some players from opposite teams (1998, *Associated Press*). Being sensitive with your spoken words sometimes is more important than being restrained with your fists, at least in ice hockey.

There are various social, religious, and cultural factors that regulate our direct contact with others. Eye contact plays a central role in interpersonal relations (Grumet, 1983). In most cultures people are taught not to stare at strangers. Eye contact during a conversation is a sign of sincerity and interest in most cultures; however, it is generally not the case in Korea: you have to know another person well before you start looking in this person's eyes. Pointing your finger toward a person is extremely disrespectful among Navajos and native Russians. Touching is more common in the cultures around the Mediterranean Sea and in some Slavic nations than it is in European countries such as Holland, Germany, and Finland. In Japan people follow rules that restrain them from touching friends of the opposite sex below the waist. This restriction is not considered to be important for many individuals from European and American countries (Barnlund, 1975). Latinos interact using smaller physical distances than Japanese and other East Asians. In cultures within the Mediterranean basin, it is acceptable to speak loudly. This type of communication would be considered impolite in Scandinavia. Given the many examples of what is typical and atypical in direct communication, it is not difficult to realize how helpful an understanding of cultural, ethnic, and national customs can be in cross-cultural communications.

 Success, recognition, and conformity are the bywords of the modern world where everyone seems to crave the anesthetizing security of being identified with the majority.
MARTIN LUTHER KING, JR. (1929–1968)—AMERICAN CIVIL RIGHTS LEADER

Conformity

We all sometimes do things because other people do them first. **Conformity** is a form of social influence in which individuals change their attitudes and/or behavior to adhere to a group or social norm. Experimental social psychology provides many interesting examples and explanations of human conformity. In a series of classic studies conducted by Solomon Asch in the early 1950s, subjects were put into situations in which there were no particular rewards for conformity and no explicit punishment for deviance (Asch, 1956). When faced with an absolute majority of their fellow students agreeing on the same incorrect judgments (in the series of 12 attempts), almost 75 percent of the subjects conformed at least once by responding incorrectly as the group did. In total, 35 percent of the overall responses conformed to the deliberately incorrect judgments expressed by the "actors." It was mentioned that each group applies a variety of sanctions to members who do not accept the group norms. Does this mean that we always conform to avoid negative social sanctions against us? The answer is "no." We conform not only to escape sanctions but for a variety of other reasons.

One reason, other than to escape sanctions, that we might conform is to live up to the expectations of others and therefore remain in their good graces. This is especially true when the "others" represent a majority. For example, many European women cover their heads with a scarf when they arrive in a Muslim country even though this is not required of foreigners. Decision making, especially in an unfamiliar situation, might increase conformity whereas prior commitments might reduce conformity (Deutsch & Gerard, 1955). An instance of increased conformity is seen

CRITICAL THINKING

Conformity and "Conformism"

Whether we conform or not is often based on specific circumstances. A person in unfamiliar surroundings (any newcomer, immigrant, etc.) is expected to conform in many decision-making situations. Social learning, in part, is based on conformity. But is it possible that conformity is not always caused by circumstance? Can we hypothetically suggest that there are people in every culture who are more conformity oriented, and there are others who are nonconformists? Let us assume that there is a personality trait, which we shall call *conformism*. (Note that "*conformism*," like all other psychological traits, is not something that one either "has" or does not "have"; rather, it is a matter of degree; see the discussion of "differentiating dichotomous and continuous variables" in Chapter 3 of the book). *Conformists* will be more likely to conform in many social situations. *Nonconformists* will conform in very few social situations. In many cases, you will agree with the group simply because you do not consider yourself an expert in the activity you have been asked to perform. For example, you are asked to make visual judgments. If you are nearsighted you may worry that your visual assessments are not accurate and consequently you may follow the opinions of others more readily. *Conformists*, therefore, will consider themselves as "nonexperts" in a wide range of social situations.

Questions: Do you think that *conformism* as a personality trait could be formed by particular social and political conditions in some countries that develop "nonexpert" traits in individuals by withholding a person's right to express his or her opinions and exercise freedom? For instance, could we consider most of those individuals who now live under authoritarian governments as *conformists* by force?

in a story told to us by a political science major from Venezuela. He told us that he began listening to the Howard Stern radio show because so many other students in his dorm listened to the program, not because he particularly liked what he heard. Reduced conformity may be due to a prior commitment: a person who does not drink alcohol because of her religious responsibility has fewer chances of starting to drink with her friends than those who do not have such strong commitments.

Rational actor theories explain conformity from a rational-choice perspective. According to this approach, people act as reasonable actors and choose from several alternatives available to them (Monroe, 1995). They may conform when they see benefits of an action and do not foresee negative consequences. For example, William Brustein (1998) tried to explain why Hitler's National Socialist Party in Germany had a relatively low membership before 1933 despite the party's success in local and national elections. The main reason, he suggested, was that the majority of the German population disapproved of, and even despised, Nazi members.

 Either do as your neighbors do, or move away.
MOROCCAN PROVERB

Conformity could be directly motivated by a desire to gain reward or avoid punishment. This form of behavior, often called **compliance,** may also bring people hope.

A CASE IN POINT

Sexual Harassment

"I do what others do." Is conformity a social norm? In the tradition articulated by Kurt Lewin (1951), human behavior is a function of two factors: situational and personal. Within the frame of reference of this tradition, many interesting observations can be made. For example, let us consider sexual harassment. Certain individuals, as a result of their life experience and personality traits, may possess proclivities toward sexual harassment. On the other hand, the social norms in a given society or within specific organizational settings may be tolerant of sexual harassment. To illustrate, in the Russian language, there is no exact equivalent for the phrase "sexual harassment." There are virtually no official rules or regulations that aim at preventing or even discouraging sexual harassment. There is a predominant belief among many Russians that women should take the majority of the responsibility for what happens in their sexual relationships. If a woman is acting "provocatively" then it is only she who can be blamed for any harassment or violence against her (Glad & Shiraev, 1999). If there are no words to label sexual harassment then is it easy to discount or completely deny its very existence. As a result of this cultural norm, when individuals with a proclivity for sexual harassment are placed in social situations that permit or accept this sort of behavior, tolerance of harassment is more likely to occur (Pryor et al., 1995). In short, those Russians who routinely engage in sexual harassment behavior routinely get away with it because of societal tolerance: there are so many other people who practice the same behavior. However, if these individuals were to move to the United States, it is likely there would be a substantial change in their behavior on learning how sexual harassment is viewed in the United States.

If people are poor, desperate, and depressed then the promise of a convincing solution might force them to comply with those who make such promises. Compliance, however, is not only a sign of personal weakness and desperation. Take, for example, the 1977 Jonestown suicide and the 1997 Heaven's Gate suicide: the members of these two cult groups were persuaded by the group leaders into believing that death was the only acceptable resolution for suffering and the only way to obtain spiritual salvation. Thinking critically about these and other cases of group suicide and various forms of compliance, consider that some powerful leaders who make people follow their orders may themselves have serious mental problems, such as delusions of grandeur and persecution, serious personality dysfunctions, obsession with suicide, and sadistic tendencies (Zimbardo, 1997; Osherow, 1993).

Is Conformity Universal across Cultures?

Social conformity varies across cultures. For example, there is a positive correlation between individualism and economic wealth. In countries low on individualism, conformity is popular, and autonomy is rated as less important (Berry et al., 1992). Therefore, economically wealthy countries, when compared with poorer countries, will conceivably show fewer examples of conformity. Conformity is typically lower in upper–middle class groups, and higher in lower socioeconomic class groups. It is higher in stratified and authoritarian societies as well, where parents are concerned about making their children conform to existing social norms (Kohn, 1969; Shiraev & Bastrykin, 1988). All in all, collectivist norms are likely to facilitate conformity and individualistic norms should not (Matsuda, 1985). In multicultural and diverse societies, such as the United States and Canada, the dominance of a single mainstream culture will be present to a lesser extent than the influence of a single uniform culture in less diverse societies, such as Norway or Korea. Even in ethnically diverse country such as the Soviet Union, the influence of mainstream Russian culture and single Marxist ideology was enforced by the totalitarian government, which facilitated conformity among its citizens (Gozman & Edkind, 1992).

Anticipation of negative sanctions may limit the expression of views that contradict the majority's opinion and can result in the individual's silent agreement with others. As formulated by Noelle-Neuman (1986), what individuals fear most of all with respect to their private opinions is social isolation. To avoid isolation, people try to determine what opinions other people hold. If an individual subscribes to the dominant opinion, this judgment is likely to be freely discussed and expressed. Moreover, the absence of resistance or criticism from others will strengthen the individual's opinion. On the other hand, if an individual subscribes to a perceived minority opinion, that individual will fear social isolation and will not express that opinion as freely in public. This situation results in an opinion-voicing spiral into silence, as minority opinions, being less publicly shared, appear less and less widely held. The morals? Social norms of the rejection of and intolerance to different ideas may affect not only the frequency of expression of certain ideas but also their salience among people's thoughts and attitudes. Moreover, lack of expression of such ideas leaves the existing social norms unchallenged.

Social and environmental conditions also influence individual conformity. For example, John Berry (1967) showed that conformity is higher in societies with high-food-accumulation practices (for example, the Temme of Sierra Leone) and lower in societies with low-food-accumulation practices (such as the Canadian Eskimo). In this case, low levels of conformity are perhaps conditioned by socialization practices: a young Eskimo learns very early in life how to be independent as a hunter. Studies conducted in many Asian countries indicate that people there engage in conforming behavior to a greater degree than Europeans. Specifically, Chinese were shown to be more conforming than Americans (Huang & Harris, 1973). Moreover, conformity is valued among Asians (such as Indonesians and Japanese) to a greater degree than among Europeans (Matsumoto, 1994). For example, among participants of a Rokeach Value survey, Asian subjects endorse values such as conformity and obedience, whereas West European subjects emphasize independence and personal freedom (Punetha et al., 1987). Other studies show that there are differences in conforming behavior among representatives of countries that are "similar" to each other, such as Italy and Australia (both predominantly Christian and democratic societies). Italians were found to be more conforming than British Australians (Cashmore & Goodnow, 1986).

Remember that conformity should be considered a continuous variable. One can describe both high and low levels of conformity only when contrasting two or more

CRITICAL THINKING

"We All Conform"

A European social psychologist Arthur Petrovsky (1978) believed that most of the research on conformity collected by Western psychologists contained a logical error. His main argument was that the error takes place when psychologists describe a person's act of conformity—in the face of group pressure—as a dichotomous variable: The person has only two choices, one to conform and the other not to conform. Moreover, in individualist cultures those who conform are often considered negatively in the public eye as "the led," "the followers," "people without guts," and so on. Conversely, those who do not conform are often labeled as "the leaders," "the daring," and "the independent."

Petrovsky proposed that we could avoid the availability bias (when observers pay attention to what is visible or salient) and examine conformity from a broader perspective. People, especially when they make important decisions, often take into consideration not only the factors that are influencing them in the present situation, but also their values and broader social norms. In some situations people appear to be exercising nonconforming behavior whereas, in fact, they are conforming, but to different norms. For example, a group of students decides to stop by a steak house for dinner; one of the students does not follow the group because, due to his religious views, he does not eat beef. Or a young woman, contrary to what her friends are doing, refuses to get into a car with a drunk driver behind the wheel because she believes this drink-and-drive behavior is dangerous. Should these examples, behaviors in which individuals did not side with the majority, be considered nonconforming behavior? The answer is no, but why? Recall how conformity is defined: this is a form of social influence in which individuals change their attitudes or behavior to adhere to group or social norms. In other words, when it appears to others that somebody does not yield to group pressure, this person still exercises an act of conformity. However, she or he conforms to a different set of norms. In the examples given above, the man conformed to the norms of his religion and the woman conformed to the norms of "responsible" behavior, that is, a "do not drink-and-drive" imperative.

samples. Moreover, within a single culture, there are different social sanctions applied to different groups in regard to their conforming behavior.

When comparing conformity cross-culturally one should take into consideration the social context in which the behavior occurs. With a certain degree of generalization, we can suggest that all human behavior may be viewed as acts of conformity because most healthy individuals tend to adjust their behavior to particular sets of norms. Some forms of conformity can be facilitated. For instance, we conform easily and eagerly when the conforming behavior falls into the category of socially acceptable and when there is no serious moral dilemma present. That is probably why people conform readily when they see other people engaged in socially "good" and "desirable" behavior (Aronson & O'Leary, 1982–1983; Cialdini et al., 1990).

John Weisz (Weisz et al., 1984) explains differences in conformity across cultures with the following assumption. He argues that in some situations individuals try to change the present situation and increase their rewards. These actions are called primary control. In other situations, people guarantee their rewards by adjusting to the existing conditions. This behavior is called secondary control. There is evidence that primary control is more valued in the United States than in Japan, where secondary control is more often accepted. In other words, Americans tend to pursue self-governing and independent goals whereas people in Japan are more interested in aligning themselves with others. Such differences could be explained as differences in locus of control: Americans, compared with Japanese, have a more internal attribution style (Moghaddam, 1998, p. 233).

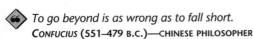

To go beyond is as wrong as to fall short.
CONFUCIUS (551–479 B.C.)—CHINESE PHILOSOPHER

If America is such a diverse and heterogeneous country, should we expect that most of its citizens are less conformist that other people, living in, for instance, Turkey, Brazil, or India? Experimental research does not provide us with impressive evidence in support of this belief. Further, some studies confirm that Americans are not less conformist than people from other cultures tested in similar experimental situations. The results of one study conducted in Japan were rather surprising. The data showed the lowest rates of conformity on the Asch experiment in Japan, lower than in the same experiment in the United States (Frager, 1970). Hypothetically, Japanese subjects, who represent a collectivist culture, were expected to conform more frequently than subjects from individualistic cultures, such as the United States. What was the cause of such unexpected results? Was it an error in experimental procedure? Apparently, in collectivist cultures, people conform toward their in-groups, and behave less cooperatively toward out-groups. In the Asch experimental procedure, the participants knew each other very little or not at all. This situation could not be termed as "in-group pressure." Studying research on conformity in Japan, Matsuda (1985) explained this phenomenon by hypothetically dividing Japanese groups into three categories. The first category—groups selected by the experimenter—does not show conformity, the second category—mutually selected friends—shows some conformity, and the third category—cohesive groups—shows maximum conformity. Fathali Moghaddam (1998) also interprets the findings about low rates of conformity in some Japanese subjects as a demonstration of how different social norms may affect experimental procedures. Most of the experiments on conformity were conducted in colleges and universities and most participants were students. For some of them, situations such as experimental interaction with "strangers" were not as significant as interaction with their families and other important groups, where conformity is apparently high. It is also interesting how uncertainty avoidance may be used to explain conformity. For example, Frager (1970) and later Gudykunst and his colleagues (1992) explained that in the United States, where uncertainty avoidance is low, people tend to have less similar "standard" rules in many social situations. In Japan, however, where uncertainty avoidance is high, people tend to have clear rules of behavior in different social contexts. Therefore, behavior with strangers could be quite different from behavior with in-group members.

Still, when we ask our students to express their opinions on how Americans compare with other national groups in regards to conformity, most say that Americans are much less conforming than people of other nationalities. Why does it appear this way to some? Those who travel can easily see that people who live in North America, Europe, and industrialized countries of the Far East have more choices in life. The choices are not only related to products and services, but also to political diversity, ideological choices, lifestyle, and religious orientations. When John has more choices in life than Mary, he can choose more possible ways to act than Mary can. In this situation, when we examine John's and Mary's behavior we would find that John's behavior is more "complex and diverse." However, this fact could not lead us to the conclusion that John is less conforming than Mary. Mary has fewer choices and opportunities in life, therefore her behavior is confined into a frame of the required behavioral models, but this does not necessarily mean she is more conforming than John.

 When you don't command obedience, don't issue orders.
ARABIC PROVERB

Following Orders

At the very moment that you are reading this, somewhere on the planet someone is giving an order to someone else. For example, someone is commanding others to rise, to move, to work, to rescue, to build, or to kill. People obey other people—parents, teachers, police officers, military commanders, husbands, wives—in every culture. **Obedience** is a form of conformity when a person simply follows orders given by others. Obedience to authority is defined as following orders given by an authority figure. This type of behavior is usually based on a belief that those with authority have the right to issue requests and give such orders.

Research on obedience in the United States and around the world is most notably associated with the name Stanley Milgram, a prominent scientist from Yale University (see Milgram, 1963). As some psychologists point out, Milgram's publications are among the most famous and widely recognized in psychology's history (Hock, 1995).

Milgram showed in his experiments that some people easily obey others and by doing that, they also readily violate their own moral standards of behavior. Moreover, he found that the circumstances under which people become obedient do not have to be extraordinary. We sometimes obey even in insignificant social situations. The Milgram experiment, and many of those that have followed, shows that obedience to authority is not only typical of the extremely weak, frustrated, or pathological, but also of many "normal" individuals when under psychological pressure. It has also been found that we tend to obey with less hesitation when somebody assumes responsibility for our actions. In these situations we may do something that we otherwise consider unthinkable.

The Milgram experiment on obedience was reproduced in many countries, apparently with similar results: people tend to obey other people who have power. Despite variations, it is more likely that in countries with high power distance, rates of obedience will be higher than in countries with low power distance. (Power distance, discussed earlier in the book, is the extent to which there is inequality between supervi-

CRITICAL THINKING

Cultural Norms and Obedience

Acts of obedience committed by other people are described and evaluated by us, the observers. When we evaluate, we often use our own standards to either disapprove of or support an individual who obeys. How can person B interpret the obedience of person A if they belong to different cultures? To think critically about an issue also means to ask additional questions about it. In the case of obedience, such a question might be why did *this* particular person follow *this* particular order? Consider, for example, an arranged marriage in India where a young woman follows her parents' suggestion to marry a man she has never seen. Might this appear to an American observer as an act of obedience (Saroop, 1999)? Perhaps it would from the standpoint that the woman simply followed a direct order coming from other people. But from the woman's point of view, her parents' decision may not be an order, but instead a suggestion based on her parents' wisdom, love, and sincere intentions. Moreover, by agreeing with her parents' choice, the young woman honors a centuries-old cultural tradition of arranged marriages. In any situation, we should not forget about the impact of external factors—such as traditions, customs, and mores—on individual behavior and obedience in particular. Please refer to the discussion of the Fundamental Attribution Error in Chapter 3.

sors and subordinates in an organization.) The power distance index is high when the members of a society accept that power in institutions is distributed unequally. Similarly, the power distance index is low when the members of a society tend to accept equality within the institutions (Hofstede, 1980).

Another factor that may affect obedience is the predominant leadership style in a studied society. An authoritarian style of leadership, for example, presumes direct communications from the leader to the led. The leader or any authority figure gives the orders, and the led must obey. Discussions and exchanges of information are significantly limited. In post-war Germany, for example, 40 percent of students who were age 12 between 1946 and 1953 reported actual participation in school discussions and debates, whereas and only 6 percent of the students who were age 12 between 1941 and 1945, during the last period of the Nazi dictatorship, reported participation in discussions (Almond & Verba, 1965). It was also found that obedience was one of the most important values cultivated by the system of German socialization during at least the past 200 years (Miller, D., 1983).

According to other studies, parents from low socioeconomic status groups value obedience more than middle-class families do (Kohn, 1969). Similar results were received in a large-scale study conducted in nine countries, in which parents were asked to say what characteristics in their children were considered to be most desirable. The answers from parents who lived in the United States and other industrialized countries, such as Korea, stressed the importance of personal independence and self-reliant behavior. Parents from less industrialized nations, such as Turkey and Indonesia, indicated the importance of obedience in their children and did not endorse independence (Kagitcibasi, 1996). Among the world's different cultural areas, African societies are rated the highest in the socialization of compliance and obedience (Munroe & Munroe, 1972). Political ideologies also seem to influence the frequency of obedient reactions. In totalitarian countries, obedient reactions were reported to be more frequent than in democratic societies (Triandis, 1994).

A thousand curses never tore a shirt.
ARABIC PROVERB

Social Influence

The capacity or ability of an individual to exercise control and/or authority is called **power**. Power can be formal or informal. Formal power is exercised mostly within activities that are defined by official regulations, laws, and institutional rules. Informal power, on the other hand, is exercised by individuals in situations without official regulations. In most traditional cultures, parents do not have formal power over their family members. But informally, most parents possess and exercise parental authority over their adult children (Shiraev & Bastrykin, 1988).

According to former UCLA professor Bertram Raven, there are six universal bases of power (Raven & Rubin, 1968). The first type is power based on *rewards*—the ability to provide positive or desirable outcomes for another person or group. The second basis is *coercion*, which could range from actual physical force or direct threats to the anticipation of punishment. The third basis of power is *expertise*. Experience, training, and special skills can be viewed as special sources of power. *Information* is the fourth basis of power. Those who have access to information, especially when other sources of information are scarce or unavailable, may also have access to power. The fifth basis of power is *referent* power. In this situation we voluntarily or involuntarily identify ourselves with a person or group because we want to be close to or similar to them. The sixth basis of power is *legitimate* power. People see some individuals as "official" leaders who have the authority to suggest to others what they should or should not do.

A CASE IN POINT

Challenging the Boss

The copilot and flight engineer of Korean Air jet Boeing 747 knew that the situation was not right: All indicators suggested a serious problem. But neither of them said anything to the captain, who failed to detect any danger. A few seconds later, the airplane slammed into the top of a hill, killing 228 passengers. Investigators confirmed that the crew—even though they knew about the problem—failed to challenge the captain. This tragedy was interpreted as an emblematic cultural issue: The pilots showed a traditional Korean deference to authority (Phillips, 1998). Would an American or Mexican pilot challenge their captain in a similar situation?

Research has shown that the way people perceive power of other individuals may affect many aspects of group behavior. Even a simple joke may be interpreted differently by people who have power and those who do not. In one survey, African American, Hispanic, and white children were presented with pairs of pictures (drawings) differing only in the ethnic identification of the victim. Children were asked to choose the funniest one of the two presented. Only white children found it funnier to see a child of another racial–ethnic group victimized than a child of their own group (McGhee & Duffey, 1983). Another illustration is sexual harassment, which is difficult to evaluate and explain without comprehending the meaning of power and inequality in male–female relationships in a culture studied.

Compared with people high in personal and social power, individuals low in **social power** and personal power are more likely to be pessimistic about their own life; the status of their country; and the past, present, and future of the world (Larsen, 1972). Members of low-power groups are expected to have more empathy for members of high-power groups than vice versa. For example, it was found that Arab Lebanese students in the United States were more successful in identifying typical "American" responses than Americans were in identifying typical "Arab" responses (Lindgren & Tebcherani, 1971).

Feeling Good about Some Views

Across the world, individuals in social groups show tendencies to adhere to their shared views so strongly that they ignore information inconsistent with those views (see discussion of "belief perseverance" in Chapter 3 of this book). This occurrence is called **groupthink.** Irving Janis, who described this amusing phenomenon, believed that groupthink is associated with concurrence seeking, and that it may often override any realistic appraisals of alternative decisions or courses of action (Brandstatter et al., 1984). The 1960s Bay of Pigs invasion, a fiasco for the Kennedy administration, is given as an illustration of groupthink in practically every psychology textbook. The cabinet members knew about the potential dangers, but nobody brought those issues to light because they apparently wanted to maintain **cohesiveness** within the inner circle of presidential advisers. Elliot Aronson proposed that the tragic failure of the space shuttle Challenger in 1986 was also the result of groupthink. The NASA engineers, in their pursuit of a common goal, ignored several warning signs of a potential disaster (Aronson, 1995).

Groupthink is a very compelling group mechanism among members of fundamentalist religious, radical political, and militant ethnic groups. When you join a group, you may be hesitant to express doubts regarding group decisions and group activities because your hesitation might be considered a sign of weakness and disloyalty (*Washington Post*, May 12, 1996, p. A9). Concurrence seeking prevented Soviet political leader Mikhail Gorbachev from being elected general secretary of the ruling Communist party in 1984, when the vast majority of the Politburo members decided not to confront a few senior leaders of the party who did not support Gorbachev. Ironically, 6 years later, his own continuous concurrence seeking among the cabinet members brought Gorbachev to the end of his political career. Preoccupations with group unity did not solve real problems (Chernyaev, 1993).

Another group phenomenon, known as **group polarization,** is almost in direct contrast to groupthink. Group polarization is the tendency of group members to shift, as a result of group discussion, toward more extreme positions than they initially held. In the case of group polarization, group cohesiveness may not be as important for the group members. In some cases, the risky shift phenomenon occurs, which means that group decisions are often riskier than individual views held by the members before discussion or decision making (Moscovici & Zavalloni, 1969). Found in various experimental situations in the United States, in many European, and some African countries, the risky shift phenomenon is also explained as being based on particular cultural norms (Brown, 1965). In other words, if a culture values risky behavior in its individuals, the risky shift is likely to occur. The risky shift phenomenon was confirmed to be present in many countries, including France, England, Canada, Israel, and New Zealand (see, for example, Rim, 1963; Vidmar, 1970). The data on risk taking across cultures are somewhat inconsistent (Foxall & Payne, 1989), but several studies place American managers in a higher risk-taking category compared with other national samples.

Is Social Loafing Universal?

Imagine you are working alone on a project. You have been asked to compare divorce rates around the world and collect statistical data through the Internet. You hope to finish the project in a few days. Unexpectedly, your professor tells you that there are two people assigned to help you finish the project. After hearing this news will you feel relief? Will you slow down your efforts, anticipating that your helpers will contribute to the work load? Indeed, many people slow down under similar circumstances thus demonstrating **social loafing**, the tendency of group members to exert less effort on a task than they would if they were working alone or when the size of the group is expanded. Is social loafing common in every social group?

The results of several cross-cultural studies show that social loafing is not a universal phenomenon. For example, research conducted in China and Japan suggests that social loafing does not occur in the group behavior studied in these countries. In some cases, the opposite phenomenon appeared. It is called "social striving," when a group enhances the individual performance of its members (Earley, 1989). It was found in some studies that Americans ("individualists") manifested social loafing, whereas Chinese ("collectivists") tended to show the opposite pattern (social striving), performing better in pairs than alone (Gabrenya et al., 1985). Perhaps in many cultures in which social loafing does not occur, the existing collectivist norms stimulate interpersonal interdependence. In other words, hypothetically, in collectivist cultures social loafing is not typical. However, this does not mean that in individualistic cultures social loafing will always be part of group relationships. Also, we should not discount the fact that the more cohesive a group becomes, the lower the occurrence of loafing (Petrovsky, 1978). Loafing is based on social circumstances and may also be increased or decreased according to psychological phenomena such as members' individual **identification** with, loyalty toward, and responsibility toward the group.

Cooperation and Competition

It doesn't take a psychologist to say that every group consists of different individuals, and each of them is unique. We all have our individual histories of achievements, failures, and aspirations. Some of us are either more or less competitive compared with others. Circumstances may change and we may also adjust our competitive patterns, becoming more cooperative or more competitive. There are circumstances that stimulate competitiveness, and there are conditions that facilitate cooperation among group members. What are those conditions?

- In competitive reward conditions, a person gains when other members lose. The worse they are, the better you are. Almost all sport competitions are based on the competitive reward principle. The same situation occurs when several companies are competing for a contract and only one can win it. Competitive elections for any public office in the United States are also based on the win–lose principle. One may win not only by improving his or her record, but also by "going negative," that is, downgrading the accomplishments of the competitors.
- In cooperative reward conditions, people's rewards are positively linked. If one does poorly, the whole group may go down. The better each member does, the more chance the whole group has to win. A group of surgeons and nurses working in an operating room, a football team on the field, or automobiles on the freeway during rush hour can all represent cooperative reward structures.
- In individualistic reward conditions the outcomes of individuals are independent of each other. If a professor gives an "A" to everyone who gains more than 100 points in the class, this system of grading is based on an individualistic reward structure. Shoppers in a food store, casino gamblers sitting side by side in front of slot machines, and patrons in a restaurant are all relatively independent of one another.

There are some cultural influences on the group reward conditions. For example, in Japanese organizations, plans are typically drafted at the lower levels of an organization. Then employees are encouraged to develop their own ideas into a draft. Then the plan gradually moves up, from lower offices to higher offices for approval (Berry et al., 1992). This type of plan drafting is not as common in the United States.

Cross-cultural studies show that Americans are among the most competitive people on earth. In business, according to the law, most government contracts to private firms must be awarded only on a competitive basis. Experiments also show that in general, children from Western technological societies are less cooperative than children from Latin American, African, and Middle Eastern countries. Additionally, there is a cross-cultural tendency for children from urban areas to be more competitive than children from rural regions, and for middle-class children to compete more often than children from lower class environments (Madsen, 1986).

There are cultural similarities too. For example, a comparative Sudanese–British study showed that in both countries people are less willing to cooperate with others when they are in the city, when the situation is not urgent, and when helping entailed high personal cost (Hedge & Yousif, 1992).

 One man with courage makes a majority.
ANDREW JACKSON (1767–1845)—SEVENTH U.S. PRESIDENT

Leaders: Born or Bred?

Leadership can be compared to the ability or capacity to lead: to guide, manage, and direct the actions and opinions of individuals. **Leadership** is the process through which some individuals (leaders) influence other group members toward attainment of specific group goals. The leader's behavior is frequently described along two dimensions. The first dimension represents performance, that is, task-related actions, such as explaining goals, distributing roles, explaining requirements, and so on. The other dimension (maintenance) is a set of psychological supports provided by the leader to his or her subordinates. This description of leadership has found support in several countries, such as Japan, India, Iran, and Russia (Hui & Luk, 1997, Schmidt & Yeh, 1992; Sventsitsy, 1988), and these characteristics seem to be universal in every culture.

There is less agreement about what makes an effective leader. The contingency theory suggests that a leader's success should be determined by his or her traits and by various features of the situation. The normative theory implies that a leader's success be based on whether he or she accepts support and participation from followers and subordinates. *Participative* leadership that allows subordinates' participation could be very effective in some conditions, especially when individuals are educated and responsible for their actions. However, it could backfire when employees are not ready to act independently whether due to lack of education or skill, or because of their unwillingness to accept responsibilities. For example, democratic freedoms available to Russians after 1991 did not increase people's political participation. Instead, pessimism, apathy, and indifference grew. One explanation is that most individuals were not ready to assume responsibilities and act independently, but rather expected a strong and "good" leader to take care of the country's problems (Glad & Shiraev, 1999).

Special attention in cross-cultural psychology can be paid to transformational leadership, often known as charismatic leadership. There is little agreement on how to define this phenomenon. However, specialists concede that charismatic leaders become personally attractive to their followers and are able to unify people to perform difficult tasks with enthusiasm and devotion. The history of human civilization gives many examples of charismatic leadership: Dr. Martin Luther King in the United States, Napoleon in France, Simon Bolivar in South America, Hitler in Germany, Indira Ghandi in India, Ayatollah Khomeini in Iran, and many others. Cultural conditions and traditions determine what traits are necessary for a successful charismatic leader.

For example, sexist attitudes prevailing among significant numbers of people could prevent a woman—even though she has outstanding leadership skills—from becoming a national leader (Starovoitova, 1998). Specialists point out that the leader's role of a benevolent father could be especially attractive in Iran (Ayman & Chemers, 1983), Germany (Koenigsberg, 1992), and Russia (Gozman & Edkind, 1992). A moral person is the best charismatic model in China, and a "nurturant" manager is more suitable for Indian conditions (Hui & Luk, 1997) than for North American circumstances.

Traditionally, psychologists recognize three major leadership styles that are described in practically all social psychology textbooks around the world. In the *authoritarian* style, the leader makes all decisions. He or she is a very controlling, directive, demanding person, who gives few explanations regarding group activities. In these cases, members are not allowed to choose their own strategies or courses of action. Roles are precisely assigned to the group members, and any deviation from group norms is punishable. Negative sanctions usually outweigh positive sanctions. In the *democratic* style, the leader makes decisions after consulting with the group members. The leader often allows group members to choose their own implementation strategies after decisions are made. The democratic leader tries to share as much information (related to the group activities) as possible with the group members. Positive and negative sanctions are equally applicable. These two styles were first described by Kurt Lewin, a prominent psychologist who immigrated to the United States as a refugee from Nazi Germany (Lewin et al., 1939). The third style is called *laissez-faire*. The leader does not try to exercise control over the group. He or she gives the group members general instructions and advice. The group members are then expected to act on their own, choosing their own methods and strategies for actions.

Which of these styles is the most effective? Initially, Lewin and his colleagues believed the democratic style to be the best and most effective one. Even the label "democratic" was most likely chosen for ideological reasons in order to emphasize the advantages of the democratic society (please refer to discussion of the "Evaluative Bias of Language" in Chapter 3). However, despite some obvious advantages, this style cannot be ranked as ideal. For example, in emergency situations, the authoritarian style may be more effective than the other styles. Moreover, in paternalistic and posttotalitarian societies the group members might not accept the democratic style. Why? Because in many difficult life situations, people need guidance with decision making because they do not have enough experience to make important life decisions for themselves. Totalitarian cultures in a process of transition are apt to present especially difficult problems along these lines. Because the authorities in such regimes make so many life choices for members and use the threat of force to prevent independent action, psychological dependency is likely to be characteristic of many members of the group. Dependency is promoted and people come to need the all-powerful leaders who feed the people's needs (Koenigsberg, 1992; Marlin, 1990).

Thinkers prepare the revolution; bandits carry it out.
MARIANO AZUELA (1873–1952)—MEXICAN NOVELIST

Over the years, social psychologists have created at least two types of explanations for the causes of leadership behavior. The first view is called "the trait approach." According to this standpoint, to become a leader one should have a set of specific predispositions or traits. These traits are universal and typical in leaders in every culture. In other words, one should expect that Saddam Hussein, Nelson Mandela, American presidents, and Turkish Prime ministers will all have a somewhat similar ensemble of personality traits related to leadership. Among the most frequently mentioned traits are abilities to accomplish group goals, intellectual skills, strong motivation, and abilities to sustain pressure.

However, not every person who has these traits has the chance to become a leader. According to the other common view, leadership is mostly situational. Leaders surface when the situation requires their presence. According to this approach dictators may emerge only in the case of a national crisis. For example, it happened in Cuba in the late 1950s when Fidel Castro came to power. If the group does not need a leader, he or she will never "appear." In a simple way, great leaders emerge only when the society is going through great difficulties. If everything is all right in a group or in a society, great leaders will not emerge. Why? Because they are not needed! Of course in reality leadership is probably a function of both "trait" and situational factors (see discussion of multiple causation in Chapter 3).

EXERCISE 11.1

Brainstorming is a group discussion technique that allows participants to generate as many different suggestions or solutions to the problem as they can in a limited period of time. The rules of brainstorming are relatively simple (Osborn, 1957). First, the group needs your ideas. The more ideas you generate the better because the quantity of ideas will influence the quality of the final decision. Second, you are free to generate any ideas you want. Perk up, do not tame down! You should not worry about being "crazy," "naïve," or "stupid." There are no naïve, crazy, or stupid suggestions in this situation! Third, criticism of other members' ideas and proposals is taboo. Be positive and generous. You will have time later to veto those ideas that you do not like. Fourth, you will help improve on the ideas and suggestions of other group members. Be constructive by showing how those ideas you support can be implemented.

Question. Do you think that brainstorming as a method of group decision making may have different effects in collectivist and individualist cultures? Which culture's norms would be most beneficial for successful brainstorming? Consider two hypotheses.

First, in individualist cultures, people are freer to express their individual opinions than in collectivist cultures. Therefore, brainstorming is naturally "fit" into any individualist culture: people do not care about criticism and express their ideas freely.

Second, in collectivist cultures, individuals are more interconnected and interdependent. Therefore, any group discussion that requires mutual support and understanding is naturally in agreement with the norms of a collectivist culture. Which of the two hypotheses would you consider to be more plausible? Explain your answer.

 ## CHAPTER SUMMARY

- Anthropologists confirm that people tend to form groups in all known human societies. By joining a group, we attain a status, a relative social, formal, or informal position, or rank within the group. As soon as we obtain a status, we begin to perform our social roles, the sets of behaviors individuals occupying specific positions within a group are expected to perform. Each group has a set of norms, or rules within a group indicating how its members should (or should not behave). Most of us identify our own in-groups, that is, groups to which we belong, and out-groups, that is, groups to which we do not belong. There are groups to which we may not belong but with which we identify ourselves: reference groups. Anthropologists suggest that territorial behavior is natural for both individuals and social groups. Groups that are inclusive will tend to tolerate "trespassers," whereas exclusive groups will be particularly territorial.

- Studies show significant consistency in the rules of address across different cultures. Despite many similarities across countries, there are various social, religious, and cultural factors that regulate our specific contacts.

- Conformity is a form of social influence in which individuals change their attitudes and/or behavior to adhere to existing group or broader group or social norms. Conformity is a universal phenomenon, which has some variations across cultures. There is a positive correlation between individualism and economic wealth. In addition, in countries low on individualism, conformity is popular, and autonomy is rated as less important. In countries with high individualism, variety is valued. In particular, studies con-

ducted in many Asian countries indicate that people of these cultures engage in conforming behavior to a greater degree than do Americans. Conformity is high in agricultural societies and low in hunting and gathering societies. It is typically lower in upper–middle-class groups, and higher in lower socioeconomic class groups. It is also higher in stratified societies.

- Obedience is a form of conformity when a person simply follows orders. People tend to obey other people who have power. Despite variations, it is more likely that in countries with high power distance, rates of obedience will be higher than in countries with low power distance.

- Groupthink is the tendency of members of groups to adhere to the shared views so strongly that they ignore information inconsistent with those views. There is evidence suggesting that groupthink is common in every culture. Group polarization is the tendency for group members to shift, as a result of group discussion, toward more extreme positions than those they initially held. In the case of group polarization, group cohesiveness may not be as important for the group members. In some cases, the risky shift phenomenon occurs, which means that group decisions are often riskier than individual views held by the members before discussion or decision making. If a culture values risky behavior in its individuals, the risky shift is likely to occur. Social loafing is the tendency of group members to exert less effort on a task than they would if working alone or when the size of the group is expanding. In many cultures in which social loafing does not occur, the existing collectivist norms stimulate interpersonal interdependence. In competitive reward structure, a person gains when other members lose. In a cooperative reward structure, people's rewards are positively linked. In an individualistic reward structure, the outcomes of individuals are independent of each other.

- Leadership is the process through which some individuals (leaders) influence other group members toward attainment of specific group goals. Goal-oriented leaders organize their activities around the group's prime goals. The group-oriented leader is concerned first with in-group relationships. The self-oriented leaders' concerns have to do with their own power. Traditionally, there are three major leadership styles recognized. In the authoritarian leadership style, the leader makes important decisions. In the democratic style, the leader makes decisions after consulting with the group members. The third is called laissez-faire, and in this style the leader does not try to exercise control over the group. He or she gives the group members general instructions and advice. The usefulness of these styles is based on particular situational or cultural conditions.

 KEY TERMS

Cohesiveness All forces acting on group members to cause them to remain part of a group, including mutual attraction, interdependence, and shared goals.

Competition A form of social interaction in which individuals or groups attempt to maximize their own outcomes, often at the expense of others.

Compliance doing or saying what others say or do.

Conformity A form of social influence in which individuals change their attitudes or/and behavior to adhere to existing social norms.

Cooperation A form of social interaction in which individuals or groups coordinate their behavior to reach a shared goal.

Group Two or more individuals forming a complete unit in a composition.

Group Polarization The tendency of group members to shift, as a result of group discussion, toward more extreme positions than those they initially held.

Groupthink The tendency of members of groups to adhere to the shared views so strongly that they ignore information inconsistent with those views.

Identification The process wherein the individual so strongly feels himself or herself a member of a group that he or she adopts its opinions, attitudes, and values.

Leadership The process through which some individuals (leaders) influence other group members toward the attainment of a specific group goal or activity.

Norms Rules within a group indicating how its members should (or should not) behave.

Obedience A form of social influence in which one person simply orders one or more others to perform some action(s).

Power The capacity or ability of an individual to exercise control and/or authority.

Roles The sets of behaviors that individuals occupying specific positions within a group are expected to perform.

Sanctions Actions that reward those who follow the norms and reprove those who are deviant.

Social Facilitation Effects on performance resulting from the presence of others.

Social Influence Efforts on the part of one person to alter the behavior or attitudes of one or more others.

Social Loafing The tendency of some group members to exert less effort on a task than they would if working alone.

Social Power The ability or capacity to exercise control, authority.

Status Relative social (formal or informal) position or rank within a group.

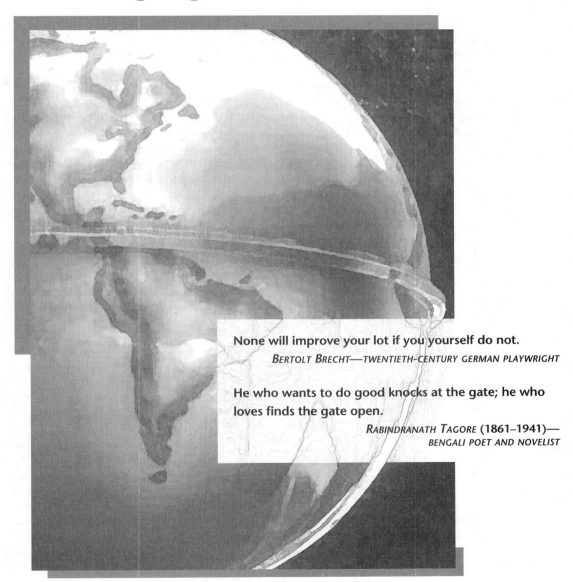

CHAPTER 12

Applied Cross-Cultural Psychology: Some Highlights

None will improve your lot if you yourself do not.

BERTOLT BRECHT—TWENTIETH-CENTURY GERMAN PLAYWRIGHT

He who wants to do good knocks at the gate; he who loves finds the gate open.

RABINDRANATH TAGORE (1861–1941)—
BENGALI POET AND NOVELIST

Psychologists are not magicians. It takes both time and significant effort to implement research data in an attempt to bring change to other people's lives. Moreover, it takes knowledge of a country and the culture in which you are working. One of our colleagues went overseas to help a country's educators improve classroom instruction for children with learning disabilities. Working on a government grant, she took with her new tests, descriptions of instruction techniques, and diagnostic inventories. Her intentions were admirable. However, implementing what she was trying to accomplish was another story. "I found that my colleagues over there struggle with a biggest monster on earth," she said. "The name of that monster is corruption. I couldn't take a step without the officials around me hinting, begging, and even openly demanding money. Not for the schools and disabled children though; [They were asking] for themselves."

Cross-cultural psychologists should know not only their research subject but also how certain policies related to this subject are exercised. It is not a secret that lack of resources and scarcity of even rudimentary democratic traditions affect the functioning of most public schools in developing countries. They are directed by central, regional, and local government bureaucracies that are extremely reluctant to give up power. Schools need money, computers, equipment, and other resources. At the same time, while looking for funds, as some specialists rightly suggest, each educational agency jealously guards the little turf it may have, suspicious of any restructuring of control that may limit its power (Holtzman, 1996). Therefore, it is crucial in the practitioner's work to discover possible sources of assistance and help, such as local religious organizations, groups of professionals, and sometimes businesses. They can—more likely than central government—initialize change. We will not mention the name of the country in which our friend was working; she asked us not to do so. In fact, it could have happened almost anywhere on the planet. The point is, although facing difficulties, psychologists should not give up trying to implement their research. Like our friend, they should not be afraid of coming back and doing what they think is morally right.

Personal curiosity—although it is a noble virtue—is not the only reason psychologists compare human behavior across cultures. As we read in Chapter 1, cross-cultural psychologists aim to examine both universal, cross-cultural, and specific, culture-related mechanisms of human activity. Psychologists want to understand cross-cultural phenomena. They also want to educate, lend a hand, make changes in people's lives, help individuals realize their potentials, and reduce their unnecessary suffering.

Psychology remains a theoretical discipline so long as it answers the questions "what?" "when?" and "why?" It becomes an applied field when it starts searching for some specific answers to the question, "How to change?" For example, how can one teach in culturally diverse classrooms, or reduce acculturative stress, advertise products to particular ethnic groups, or reduce cross-ethnic prejudice? Psychologists try to find some concrete answers to these and many other questions related to human interaction in diverse cultural settings. It is an applied field that can provide helpful information for thousands of professionals working in medicine, psychotherapy, education, community services, business, sports, and many other areas of life.

How can one teach people to be tolerant and respectful of each other? Cultural and religious tensions can be caused by simple events. In Spring 1980, the British ambassador in Riyadh was expelled after the United Kingdom's Anglia Television broadcast "Death of a Princess," a drama documentary about a Saudi princess executed for adultery (Cooper, 1996). This example is just one drop in the ocean of mistakes, miscommunications, blunders, errors, and missteps committed by people from all walks of life. Whose fault was it? Do these and other conflicts have psychological roots and therefore are they preventable?

Psychologists are not magicians—we put this Barnum statement in the opening vignette. Psychologists are not policymakers either. However, they can influence policy by creating a particular "policy climate" around almost every social issue, problem, or development. Via books, conferences, articles, public lectures, the media, and even interpersonal contacts, psychologists can disseminate their ideas, influence people's opinions, change stereotypes, and manage people's actions.

Cross-cultural psychology can provide valuable data and suggestions to psychotherapy. Psychological knowledge can be useful in international diplomacy and negotiation, advertising, and marketing. Specialists in cross-cultural psychology can help thousands of migrants adjust in a new cultural environment. We believe that as intercultural contacts increase in all parts of the world, interest in this area of cross-cultural training will almost certainly grow.

Let us examine just a few practical problems that cross-cultural psychologists may face and what kinds of solutions they may offer.

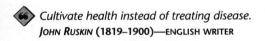

Cultivate health instead of treating disease.
JOHN RUSKIN (1819–1900)—ENGLISH WRITER

Resources and Health

Every year, the World Health Organization publishes data about major causes of illness and premature death (WHO, 1999). It will not be a surprise that environmental problems, poverty, and poverty-related issues are mentioned among prime causes of health problems around the world. For example, more than 50 million people today live in countries in which the life expectancy is less than 45 years, and these countries are the poorest in the world. Despite tremendous changes in the prevention and treatment of childhood illnesses, by 2025 there will still be 5 million deaths a year among children under 5 years of age. It is expected that 97 percent of these deaths will take place in the developing world, and most of them will be due to infectious diseases and malnutrition, which alone account for 50 percent of deaths among young children. Cases of and deaths from lung cancer and colorectal cancer will also increase, and once again the percentages will be higher among developing countries. This will largely be due to smoking and an unhealthy diet, respectively. On a positive side, stomach cancer will generally become less common, mainly because of improved food conservation and healthy dietary changes. Time and time again we see how availability and access to resources affect the overall health of the population in any country.

Human activities and human attitudes are inseparable from their ecocultural context. Overall, poverty and ecological problems significantly affect people's health-

A CASE IN POINT

Life and Death

What criteria constitute the death of the human body? Absence of all movements including breathing? Absence of heartbeat? Permanent nonattendance to stimulation? Irreversible loss of consciousness? Even though there are ongoing and heated debates about when life begins—at conception or at some point during prenatal development—there are some national standards of what is considered death of the body. In the United States, in the beginning of the 1980s, a presidential commission and state courts reached a consensus that brain death signals the end of human life. In Japan, however, there is a prominent belief that it is not only the brain that makes us human. Even a brain-dead person is alive until the last beat of his or her heart. Therefore, organ transplants, until the end of the 1990s, were banned in Japan (except cornea, kidney, and bone marrow transplants because they do not require a brain-dead donor). But despite recent changes in the government's stand on organ transplant, there are few donors because of the Japanese belief that bodies must remain intact for the trip to the afterlife. Besides, Japanese people tend to be very uncomfortable bringing part of someone else's body into their own. It is like you have part of their soul. As reported in the *Washington Post* (July 22, 1996), in the 1990s there were 200 kidney transplant operations in Japan per year. Over 20,000 people need kidney transplantation. To compare, there were 11,000 such operations conducted in the United States and thousands more in other countries.

related activities. However, are there any cultural factors, such as norms and values, that could have some effect on people's attitudes about health, and subsequently, health-related activities. Let us consider a case (see A Case in Point box, above).

 Recompense injury with justice, and recompense kindness with kindness.
CONFUCIUS (551–479 B.C.)—CHINESE PHILOSOPHER

Prejudice: Is It Inevitable?

Do psychologists believe that it is possible to diminish ethnic and religious prejudice in human beings? What is the source of prejudice? Pessimists imply that virtually all attempts to cultivate ethnic unity have failed. Neither Roman, nor Ottoman, Austro-Hungarian, British, or Soviet multiethnic empires could survive the internal pressure of people's ethnic self-determination. Optimists suggest that a multiethnic population will grow and our global society will become a union of all cultures. There will be no place for racism or ethnocentrism in this new world, because the multiethnic children cannot hate or disrespect their parents and their heritage without sacrificing their own personal integrity and peace of mind. National cultures will disappear and society will finally accept diversity.

There are many theories that attempt to explain the nature of prejudice. Let us mention several of them.

CROSS-CULTURAL SENSITIVITY

Politicians usually make statements prepared for them in advance. Speechwriters—especially when they write for a nation's leader—prepare speeches carefully and try to avoid making verbal, logical, and other psychological errors. However, when the leader ignores the written text, he or she may make embarrassing mistakes and offend people who they do not want to offend. For instance, in the late 1990s, during a speech about the conflict in Northern Ireland, President Clinton decided to improvise and said the following: "I have spent an enormous amount of time trying to help the people in the land of my forebears in Northern Ireland get over 600 years of religious fights. And every time they make an agreement to do it, they are like a couple of drunks walking out of the bar for the last time—when they get to the swinging door, they turn right around and go back in again and say, 'I just can't quite get there.' It's hard to give up these things." Although the president said he meant only to show how difficult it is for ethnic groups to settle the conflict, the metaphor was upsetting to some Irish communities because it reinforced stereotypes about the links between Irish people and alcoholism. Some suggested that it was an "offensive and insulting remark to the people of Northern Ireland" (Pearlstein, 1999). President Clinton later apologized for these impromptu comments.

- Individuals within an ethnic or national group tend to see their group as a privileged *"pseudospecies"* (Erikson, 1977). Similarly, they tend to see the enemy group as subhuman. In the distance between enemy groups emerges a psychological gap. This gap is composed of a broad spectrum of rituals— popular theories, common beliefs, social and psychological practices—that begin playfully and then become deadly (Volkan, 1988).

- In cases of real or potential conflict, people tend to believe that (1) their own lives are being threatened by the target group (by an ethnic or religious group, for example) or (2) their group is being deprived or threatened. In the latter case, which has received the label of fraternal deprivation, a person may be angry on realizing that his or her group (ethnic, religious) is not gaining as fast as some other groups are (Sears et al., 1995). According to another theory, people develop negative feelings against others when they feel entitled to a particular valued object they do not possess, and compare themselves with a group that has it (Bernstein & Crosby, 1980).

- Prejudice is learned the same way other values and behaviors are learned: as a social norm. Accepting this norm, the person who has a particular prejudice plays a social role within the individual's culture. Both norms and roles are transmitted in the process of socialization (Gielen et al., 1992).

- Prejudice is displaced aggression. The displacement occurs when the individual is not able to eliminate his or her source of frustration. Frustration causes aggression. When the individual cannot overcome obstacles to reach a goal—such incapacity is actually causing frustration—he or she chooses another object, individual, or group to become the new target of the individual's aggression (Dollard et al., 1939). This individual or group becomes a scapegoat: someone who can be blamed and abused for someone else's problems.

EXERCISE 12.1

Look at the following statements. The "Yes" viewpoints are optimistic. They show some ways and means of reducing prejudice. The "No" viewpoints are pessimistic. They tend to reject any possibility of eliminating prejudice. Choose three ("Yes" or "No" or both) viewpoints from the list below. Develop them in terms of your own understanding of prejudice and how to reduce prejudice. Support your theory with facts from empirical studies and/or opinion polls.

YES: Prejudice is an irrational attitude based on ignorance and fear. Open your mind, read, watch, listen, learn, educate yourself, get rid of your fears—and you will reduce your prejudice.

NO: Prejudice is not necessarily based on fears and ignorance. Prejudice is often a logical generalization based on facts and individual experiences. Well-educated and uneducated people could be equally prejudiced. Prejudice is a form of self-defense; if you get rid of it you disarm yourself.

YES: Social conditions direct your way of thinking. Whenever people become truly equal, whenever one group ceases to discriminate against another, the justification of prejudice will inevitably disappear. People compete for resources. If there is nothing to compete for, if nobody is left behind, then this will be the end of prejudice.

NO: Equality is a sweet myth that exists in political fairy tales. If social conditions outline the way you think, you will always be disappointed because somebody will always have more than you do, and there will always be somebody who will try to get something from you. You will always protect what you have and blame those who frighten you.

YES: We learn how to hate, we learn how to be scared, and we are told who our enemies are. Look at television, listen to radio talk show hosts, and you will be brainwashed. We have to unlearn our fears, we have to put our hatred aside. We have to change our negative attitudes toward those who think and act differently from the way we do.

NO: Prejudice is indeed an irrational fear. It is built into our psyche from the beginning of our lives. Aggression, violence, destruction, and humiliation have deep roots in our unconscious mind. We can change the direction of aggression, but not aggression itself.

YES: If our thinking is schematic, it is possible to replace one schema with another. If prejudice is a schema, it is possible to replace it with something else, with something psychologically adaptive and less destructive.

NO: Our thinking is schematic; therefore we will always perceive this world as a continuous existence and struggle between opposites. Like day and night, hot and cold, men and women, good and evil, rich and poor—we will always think of the world in these categories. That is why we will have both friends and enemies forever.

YES: Cross-cultural interaction makes people less prejudiced. Interpersonal contacts, joint projects, international exchanges, and continuous communications—all bring people closer to each other and can make people friendlier. Situations that are especially helpful are those in which people of different cultural backgrounds try to overcome obstacles by working together.

NO: Interaction is not the solution. Life often proves otherwise. Look at Bosnia, Rwanda, and all the other sites of ethnic conflict. Interaction should bring people *interdependence*; the contacts should be of *equal* status; people should *want* to eliminate tension. Only under those conditions could interaction be productive. However, those conditions are almost impossible to create.

 I distrust the incommunicable; it is the source of all violence.
JEAN-PAUL SARTRE (1905–1980)—FRENCH NOVELIST AND PHILOSOPHER

Cross-Cultural Psychology and Negotiations

Are there any differences in negotiation styles among cultures? With the tremendous increase in international trade, knowledge about cross-cultural negotiations became essential in business accords. Most of the data available in cross-cultural psychology have been accumulated in studies examining primarily American negotiators with representatives of other countries. Every business negotiation is a small play: the parties hide some facts, exaggerate others, withhold some information, and so forth. People from dissimilar cultural backgrounds may have different definitions of various aspects of the negotiation process. For example, Chinese negotiators were reportedly interested in abstract principles of business before going to discuss details of the deal (Pye, 1982). This style could be easily misinterpreted as a delay by a German or American negotiator. On the other hand, Russian businessmen traditionally would try to eat and drink alcohol with their foreign partners before starting negotiations (Theroux et al., 1991). This behavior may be seen—by a Western observer—as intrusive. Japanese negotiators are more oriented toward long-term interpersonal relationships than short-term profit, as compared with American counterparts (Graham et al., 1988). Americans in these cases would see Japanese negotiators as slow moving, hesitant to make decisions, and even introverted (March, 1989).

If two different national or ethnic groups begin a negotiation process and have to meet face to face, there are at least two areas in which both sides should arrange an early agreement or understanding. First is the distribution of talk: the rules on who speaks first, how turns should be taken, how to interrupt each other, how long to pause between assertions, etc. The second area is the exchange of information or, more specifically, how to interpret tone of voice, body language, gestures, and so on. (Yu & Bain, 1985). If there is no such preliminary understanding, individuals in low-context cultures will assume a confrontational attitude in conflicts, whereas those from high-context cultures will be more passive and tend to be nonconfrontational (Ting-Toomey, 1985).

Several negotiation strategies in different countries were studied by Graham and his associates (Graham, 1983; Graham at al., 1988, 1992). They investigated which of two strategies are used during negotiations: problem solving (consensus oriented) or competitive (winning oriented). In the United States, according to some studies, successful negotiators try to exchange information at the negotiation table and the strategies are primarily problem solving. In Japan and Korea, negotiators with a higher status have some sort of advantage and if they adopt problem-solving strategies, the other side follows. Russian and Taiwan Chinese negotiators tend to use competitive bargaining strategies. Brazilian managers prefer to use different forms of influence and persuasion to demonstrate their competitive strategies. These observations, however, were made in an experimental classroom environment and should be interpreted with caution (Hui & Luk, 1997).

It would be wrong, moreover, to refer to some experimental facts as established cultural traditions. Ask a person who has some experience with international business, and he or she would tell you that perhaps in every country there are patient and inpatient partners, those who understand humor and those who do not, people well prepared for negotiations and those who are not ready to strike a deal.

In cross-cultural psychology, conflict resolution is one of the most vital fields for research applications. Specialists on conflict resolution have to understand group dynamics, group decision-making processes, and the major characteristics of social perception. Their knowledge in psychology should help them establish strategies that, if accepted by conflicting parties, could eventually lead to successful resolutions of existing conflicts. Peter Smith and his colleagues (1997), for example, conducted a 23-nation study that examined how power distance was linked to conflict resolution procedures. In countries with high power distance, formal rules and procedures were used to handle disagreements with other groups. In countries with low power distance, sides relied primarily on informal contacts and their own experience.

Psychologists recognize several universal types of resolutions to a conflict. An imposed solution is based on an assumption that there are no win–win situations. Every solution will benefit one party—for example, an ethnic group—and harm the other. Negotiations based on the imposed solutions may take forever. That is why the moderator should take decisive measures, if, of course, the moderator has enough power and authority to take control of the situation and implement his or her decision. A distributive solution involves mutual compromises or concessions. Distributive solutions offer proposals, which are midway between the initial positions of both (or all) conflicting parties. Integrative solutions are often called win–win solutions because both sides can benefit simultaneously, without losing anything substantial (Pruitt & Rubin, 1986). See the following exercise.

EXERCISE 12.2

The Cooperation Dilemma

The class should be divided into several groups (teams). There should be at least three teams, with up to seven people in each. As a rule of the exercise, each team represents a "country." All participating countries should secretly decide what kind of foreign policy they will have toward each of the other participating countries. The participating teams have only two choices: "peace" or "war." Countries can negotiate with one another. However, they cannot know what decisions other teams are making. In other words, as in the real world, countries can negotiate and make agreements, but the actual decisions are made secretly by each team (country). As soon as all decisions are made, they must be written on a piece of paper and turned over to the professor. Here is the catch. If any two countries declare peace with each other, each gets a hypothetical reward of 1 million dollars each. If any two countries declare war on each other, each loses 2 million dollars. However, if team 1 declares peace with team 2, and team 2 declares war on team 1, the aggressor, team 2, gets 3 million dollars, and the victim, team 1, loses 1 million. The winner is the team that collects more money than the other teams. One may ask: "Where is the problem that must be solved? Each team establishes peace with one another and each team receives one million dollars for the peace with each of the participating teams!" However, in reality such a peaceful development of events does not often happen.

Note: For the period from 1991 to 2000, one the authors of this book conducted 32 such exercises in different schools around the United States. And peace was established among all the participating teams only once. In 31 other cases, there was always at least one team that declared war on one or more of its neighbors. The most common argument for declaring war was that "it is difficult to trust other teams." As one student said: "You may agree on peace, and yet, they [the other teams] can secretly declare war on you and you lose." How will you and your classmates handle such a situation? What are the strategies to prevent war and guarantee peace in this exercise?

 The body pays for a slip of the foot and gold pays for a slip of the tongue.
MALAY PROVERB

Stereotypes in Daily Life

Stereotyping is impossible to outlaw, banish, or physically expel. How can a person reduce the power of stereotypical judgments on different ethnic, national, and other groups? As we read in Chapter 10 on Social Perception, we are all prone to stereotyping. That is the nature of social perception—we help ourselves to categorize the incoming information and protect ourselves from its surplus! Professors interacting with exchange students, psychotherapists working with clients, business executives discussing marketing strategies, real estate agents helping their clients find housing, diplomats and presidents making foreign-policy decisions—they all are prone to bias in their judgments of other people and situations. Is it possible to reduce the impact of stereotypical judgments about other people? We hope that it is. There are at least two mistakes that we could make in stereotypical judgments. In the course of evaluating similarities and differences between two groups, we often

> *allow genuine differences to be obscured by similarities*
> *allow genuine similarities to be obscured by differences*

Stereotyping is, in fact, permitting similarities between phenomena to eclipse their differences. Those who stereotype other individuals and groups are prone to automatically overestimate within-group similarities while minimizing (or even ignoring) within-group differences. In other words, the individual perceives group members to be more alike than they really are (for example, "people of this ethnic group are always late for class") and, at the same time, does not recognize many of the ways in which they are different from one another (there are plenty of students in this ethnic group who are never late).

Moreover, groups we like and groups we do not like are seen as more different than they really are. In its most extreme form, this process is a fundamental component underlying prejudice, bigotry, chauvinism, and racism wherein all members of the particular "out-group" are seen as essentially the same, while their individuality goes virtually unnoticed.

Let us consider, for example, interpersonal interaction. Imagine you meet a person from an ethnic group different from yours. Unfortunately, you may perceive a man or woman from this group as basically the same as every other individual from that group. In this way, you view people *not* as distinct and varied individuals, each possessing a separate and unique constellation of life experiences, memories, feelings, perceptions, values, beliefs, hopes, fears, and dreams. Instead, these traits are spontaneously filtered through your own sociocultural stereotypes, from which they emerge as Koreans, Blacks, Jews, Latinos, Vietnamese, and so on. In this environment, then, irrespective of an individual's unique situations, problems, or needs, you would offer essentially the same "cookie-cutter" approach to their communication.

Stereotyping is making erroneous, mistaken judgments. However, beware and do not reject the possibility that two or many people can have something similar in their behavior, emotion, or attitudes. How many times have you heard someone make the following pronouncement (or any derivation thereof): "You cannot compare these two people (from two different ethnic groups, for instance) because they are totally and completely different from each other!" Here we have a vivid illustration of a person who is making the converse mistake of allowing similarities between people to be overshadowed by their differences. Thus, the individual who staunchly and adamantly maintains that "One should *never* stereotype," is effectively blinding him or herself to authentic commonalities that actually do exist within specific groups. However, by obstinately clinging to this position, such individuals practically ensure that they will remain oblivious to true similarities within (as well as between) groups of people.

Please remember, what we might anticipate from an individual based on our expectations does not often match with who he or she really is. Be prepared for such inconsistencies!

Acculturative Stress

Our first step into a new world is often accompanied by culture shock: an initial reaction of adjustment to a new culture and new life. Specialists understand acculturaltive stress as a distressful psychological reaction to any unfamiliar cultural environment. "Culture shock" or acculturative stress is typically defined as a set of complex psycho-

CRITICAL THINKING

Is This Culture Shock?

Sabir, a 23-year-old man and son of a political emigrant from the Middle East, thinks that America is not a healthy environment in which to live. For the past 5 years he has been in America, and his life has been filled with disappointment, sleepless nights, frustration, and depressive thinking. For Sabir, the new culture is seen as "unacceptable, unfriendly, and too selfish." Sabir attempted to attend two colleges, but dropped out in both cases because of, as he explained, "tremendous pressure and lack of free time." He started as a business partner in her father's consulting company, but soon quit because of a serious disagreement with his dad over their views on life. However, one of Sabir's friends said that Sabir simply wasn't motivated to work hard. Within a year, Sabir started two companies on his own, but in both cases failed to earn enough money to even return the initial investments. During the past 3 years, he dated several women but broke up with all of them. In an interview, Sabir emphasized that his culture shock has persisted over these years because of the "coldness and unfriendliness of this culture."

Comment

It is always difficult to separate symptoms of culture shock from all other individual problems that might be unrelated to culture shock. In this particular case, one shouldn't deny that some elements of culture shock are present in Sabir. However, a person who speaks nearly flawless English, who gets some reasonable financial support from his father, and has not experienced discrimination against him in this country perhaps is unhappy with the way his life is turning out. American culture and its traditions are used as easy scapegoats for his business failures and personal problems. It is difficult to condemn yourself for your own mistakes, and easier to instead place blame on something or someone else. Sabir didn't have symptoms of distress prior to his arrival in the United States. But at the same time, his emotional problems began with the start of his independent adult life. Therefore, it is always important to find out whether a culture change itself has become the major cause of distress.

logical experiences, usually unpleasant and disruptive (Furnham & Bochner, 1986, p. 3). Almost 40 years ago, in early pathbreaking studies on this subject, it was empirically confirmed that people arriving in a new culture may rapidly develop negative psychological symptoms (Oberg, 1960). It was noticed, for example, that there were increased rates of psychiatric hospitalization among foreign immigrants and their newly arrived children compared with nonimmigrants (Fried, 1964). It wasn't clear, however, whether culture shock itself had been causing higher hospitalization rates or if there were other, undetected factors, such as the health of migrants prior to their arrival in their new home. But what became apparent for psychologists was that persons and groups undergoing any social and cultural change should experience a certain amount of psychological displeasure or distress, the extent of which is based on many circumstances, both psychological and social (Berry & Annis, 1974). In general, many early definitions focused on culture shock as a syndrome, a reactive state of specific pathology or deficit: the individual moves into an unfamiliar environment and then develops negative symptoms. Assuming this approach, researchers have focused on descriptions of culture shock, its duration, and relationships between culture shock and various psychological problems (Pedersen, 1995; Persidsky & Kelly, 1992; Weinstein, 1989; Barankin et al., 1989; Kohn et al., 1989). It was shown that many emotional disorders, such as depression and anxiety, experienced by newcomers have been directly related to culture shock. It became more apparent that aliens may alternate between anger and depression, especially during the initial stages of their adjustment in a new culture (Mirsky et al., 1992). However, there is reasonable skepticism about the expected existence of psychopathology in all individuals adapting to new cultures. For example, Furnham and Bochner (1986) described culture shock as a learning experience that

CROSS-CULTURAL SENSITIVITY

Cultural adjustment is also the process of adaptation to various smells and odors. For example, J.K., an ESL college student in Virginia, says in an interview, "Koreans eat Kimchi, a traditional food with garlic and pepper. It gives you nice garlic breath. I realized how people here [in America] disliked this. I stopped eating it after being here for 2 weeks and that was very difficult for me because traditional American food was tasteless for me at that time" (cf. Shiraev & Boyd, 2001). This example demonstrates at least two important points. First, there are cultural norms regarding what odors or smells are considered appropriate and inappropriate. For example, if almost everyone eats foods with garlic, these people can hardly notice that they, or others, have garlic breath. However, if you had a dish with garlic in it for lunch, and no one else did, then people around you would certainly notice that you smelled of garlic. Second, most of us are able to adapt to particular smells and dominant odors in a new country that we live in or travel to (remember, sensory adaptation is a universal psychological process). Most travelers, for instance, say that they quickly get used to the smell of soy sauce in Japan. If the situation requires, many can adjust to unpleasant street odors in some world cities not equipped with sewer systems. Nonsmoking travelers can adapt to the smell of cigarette smoke in most countries in eastern and southern Europe, where smoking regulations are very loose compared to strict antismoking rules in the United States.

TABLE 12.1	Some Symptoms of Culture Shock and Their Descriptions

Symptoms of Culture Shock	Description of Symptoms
Culture shock as nostalgia	The person may feel longing for relatives, friends, and familiar cues and experiences.
Culture shock as disorientation and loss of control	Familiar cues about how another person is supposed to behave are missing. Disorientation creates anxiety, depressive thinking, and a sense of desperation.
Culture shock as dissatisfaction over language barriers	Lack of or difficulties in communication may create frustration and feelings of isolation.
Culture shock as loss of habits and lifestyle	The individual is not able to exercise many previously enjoyed activities; this causes anxiety and feelings of loss.
Culture shock as perceived differences	Differences between the host and home cultures are typically exaggerated and seem difficult to accept.
Culture shock as perceived value differences	Differences in values are typically exaggerated; new values seem difficult to accept.

Adapted from Shiraev and Boyd (2001).

includes the acquisition and development of the skills, the rules, and the roles required in the new cultural setting. Harry Triandis, another renowned psychologist, views culture shock as a loss of control that people experience when they interact with members of a different culture (Triandis, 1994, p. 239). Loss of control is in most cases maladaptive but does not necessarily cause marked psychological disturbances. In one of the most recently developed theories, culture shock is seen as the process of initial adjustment to an unfamiliar environment. Culture shock is associated with individual development, education, and even personal growth (Pedersen, 1995, pp. 1–2). See also Table 12.1.

Culture and Cognitive Tests

Minority children, as far as we know, show lower scores on intelligence and other cognitive-skills tests. Assuming that the test is not biased against particular cultural groups and the child has adequate proficiency in the language of testing, what can a teacher or parent do to improve the child's test performance?

Jenkins (1995), in his well-known work on the psychology of African Americans, suggests that there are several ways by which adults can improve intelligence test scores of minority children. He suggested that even though many minority children lack developmental experiences—due to poverty, overcrowded housing, and inadequate parenting—this deficit can be overcome. To achieve this, some children may need the teacher to pay special attention to their cognitive functioning. For others, it is important to give extra attention to the emotional context in which intellectual learning takes place. For example, it is beneficial to create a particular cooperative classroom environment and, in addition, include parents in the educational process. If formal intellectual problem-solving procedures involve interesting and pleasing challenges, the child is likely to appreciate such an academic situation and become engaged in such activities more frequently than he or she previously was. The problem is that many minority children begin to feel competence in nonacademic situations, basically in the street-game contexts. In other words, the street often shapes these children's intellectual skills, not the educators.

Of course, one of the most difficult tasks for the psychologist is the engagement of parents in the educational process. Overall, on the larger world scale, success has not been great. However, there are many national cases that demonstrate the possibilities of such interactions. For example, in Turkey, Kagitcibasi (1995) developed a special educational, community-based project with the local mothers. The interactive training included analyses of special cognitive tasks and biweekly group discussion sessions about children, their problems, and parent–child communications.

There is an ongoing debate about the language of test administration for bilingual children. On some concept-acquisition and reasoning-skills tests, bilingual children tend to perform at a slightly higher level if tested in their native language, that is, the language they speak at home (Takano & Noda, 1993; Keats et al., 1976). However, Stephen Wright and his colleagues (1997) found that in those cases of ethnic student diversity, the language of instruction and the teacher's ethnicity had no significant impact on student success in class. Perhaps language becomes a factor only at the early stages of the second-language acquisition.

Race and Perception of Political Candidates

Do people vote for candidates' position or for their ethnic or racial origin? What role does race play in the evaluation of political candidates? Some studies present evidence of the absence of the race factor in evaluations of political candidates. In an original experimental project (Colleau et al., 1990) researchers examined the effect of racial cues on how people attribute personality traits to black political candidates. By simply manipulating the candidate's race (the face of a "one-term Democratic Senator"), they reported black persons as being more highly regarded than either white persons or people not paired with a racial cue. The explanations of such results could be based on an assumption that we know nothing about the racial attitudes of the participants prior to the experiment. They may not have been racially prejudiced in the first place. Second, people could overcompensate in favor of the black candidate because of the favorable perception of his previous achievements.

A CASE IN POINT

Race and Attitudes

There is the widespread opinion that black Americans are politically liberal. Is it a stereotype or fact? Tuch and Sigelman (1997) measured responses of blacks and whites about their attitudes. On a seven-point scale ranging from "extremely liberal" to "extremely conservative," blacks, on average, fall just to the liberal side of the moderate, "middle-of-the-road" center point, and whites, on average, fall just to the conservative side. Overall, fewer than 40 percent of blacks consider themselves liberal, and 25 percent call themselves conservative. By comparison, about 25 percent of whites are self-proclaimed liberals, and slightly over 33 percent are conservatives. As a group, blacks are only slightly less conservative than whites. Therefore, a stereotype about the overwhelming liberalism or conservatism of particular groups is not accurate.

However, other research conducted in this field suggests that race has an impact on candidate evaluations. The influence of the race factor was demonstrated in an experimental study conducted by Moskowitz and Stroh (1994). Their manipulations included race, party affiliation, and the candidate's political record. Analyzing the results, the authors suggested that black political candidates must overcome a huge obstacle of stereotyping. The conclusion of this study is rather pessimistic. Therefore, the success of black candidates hinges not so much on their electoral strategies as on the predispositions of the electorate.

Solidarity with your own ethnic or religious group has, probably, a deeper cause than simply following one's group norms. According to the social competition theory (Tajfel, 1982) individuals identify with in-groups to promote their self-esteem, based on a belief that their group is superior to out-groups. Thus, voting for a candidate of one's own race or ethnic group may enhance self-esteem by creating a vicarious sense of empowerment. This sense of empowerment may compensate for feelings of inadequacy created by perception of personal economic and social deprivation (Bovasso, 1993).

A nation, like a tree, does not thrive well
Till it is engrafted with a foreign stock.
RALPH WALDO EMERSON (1803–1882)— AMERICAN POET AND PHILOSOPHER

Immigration and Immigrants

What attitudes does the American public hold about immigrants? Traditionally, immigrants have been stereotypically portrayed as ideal "precitizens": they are grateful to the country that gives them a new life, they are loyal, they eagerly attach themselves to political institutions, they flatter the existing system and want to understand it. However, the situation changed dramatically after the 1970s. A positive public stereotype has been replaced by a negative one. According to this stereotype, immigrants are primarily illegal, they steal jobs from honest and hard-working citizens, they live on taxpayer's money, they create criminal problems, and they pose a threat to American culture in general.

An opinion poll conducted by Princeton Survey Research Associates in 1999 reveals this "cooling" trend in attitudes about immigrants. Only 30 percent of the surveyed Americans strongly agreed that immigrants strengthen the country because of the newcomers' hard work and talents. However, 34 percent—every third American—strongly supported a view that immigrants are a burden to the United States because these people take jobs, housing, and health care.

Positive attitudes are also frequently expressed toward those immigrants who suffered in their home countries, and especially to their children. People hold negative views toward migrants when they do not assimilate and they impose the threat of a potential labor surplus. Negative attitudes toward immigrants are frequently linked to the respondents' unpleasant personal experiences, personal insecurity, and perception of the "society consensus" disruption. There is a common trend in expectations toward immigrants: hosts owe immigrants less than they owe citizens, and immigrants should fit into the dominant patterns of the society (Hoskin, 1989).

If a president runs for office, could he or she count on immigrant voters? What social attitudes do immigrants hold? Immigrants come to the United States having different social and political backgrounds. Not all of them necessarily are poor and desperate in their search for any work. They have different reasons for immigration. Generally, three factors influence the trends of immigrant's opinions. First is his or her current socioeconomic status. Second is the immigrant's view on his or her economic perspectives. The third factor is the person's ideological and political attachments. The importance of the third factor was demonstrated in a study conducted in California. Pei-te Lien (1994) found that despite a huge socioeconomic gap and cultural differences between Asian and Mexican Americans in California, both groups bear some similarities in political participation. Being more informed and having a higher sense of civic duty significantly increases the likelihood of voting or the rate of participation in campaign contributions, contacting media and public officials, and working with groups to solve community problems.

Perhaps it should not come as a surprise that despite the generally positive attitude about the hosting country, most immigrants perceive discrimination against them. This is not a contradiction but rather a realistic assessment of their situation (Portes & Bach, 1985.)

A 1995 Fannie Mae survey suggested the symbolic significance of homeownership to immigrants. The survey revealed that 71 percent of immigrants identify buying a home as a milestone in life that would make them feel "more comfortable in the U.S." and more "a part of the community." The survey found that 28 percent of immigrant renters rate buying a home as their "number-one priority." In comparison, only 10 percent of all adult renters (both native and foreign born) say that owning a home is their top priority (Pitkin et al., 1997).

Overall, 71 percent of citizens reported that they were registered to vote and 58 percent reported actually voting in the 1996 Presidential election. Native-born citizens were more likely to report that they were registered and voted (71 percent and 59 percent, respectively) than naturalized citizens (63 percent and 53 percent, respectively). Across most social, economic, and demographic factors, native-born citizens were more likely to vote than naturalized citizens. However, among Hispanics and those with incomes less than $15,000, the reverse was true: 53 percent of naturalized Hispanic citizens compared with 42 percent of native-born Hispanic citizens voted. Among those in the lowest income bracket (less than $10,000), 47 percent of naturalized citizens voted compared with only 41 percent of the native born.

Are there differences in registration and voting behavior between naturalized and native-born Americans? Research in cross-cultural political psychology gives some answers. In general, those who are more established in society are the most likely to register and vote—older individuals, homeowners, married couples, and people with more schooling, higher incomes, and good jobs. Much like the larger citizen population, naturalized and native-born citizens are more likely to register and vote the longer they have lived at their current residence. Also in both groups, people residing in the southern United States are less likely to register and to vote compared with people living in other regions (Bass & Casper, 1999).

 The real fault is to have faults and not to amend them.
Confucius (551–479 b.c.)—CHINESE PHILOSOPHER

Cross-Cultural Psychology and Human Rights

What if cultural norms of a particular country or ethnic group violate basic human rights? Who determines what rights are basic and universal? How do cross-cultural psychologists recommend choosing priorities between indigenous practices and international standards? According to basic requirements established by the United Nations, an international organization that includes virtually every country in the world, people—no matter where and under what government they live—have the right to pursue their universal moral and civil freedoms. International human rights law has been specifically designed to protect the full range of human rights required for people to "have a full, free, safe, secure and healthy life" (UN, 1966). It is stated that the right to live a dignified life can never be attained unless all basic necessities of life—work, food, housing, health care, education, and culture—are adequately and equitably available to everyone. Based squarely on this fundamental principle of the global human rights system, international human rights law has established individual and group rights relating to the civil, cultural, economic, political, and social spheres.

For example, torture—severe pain or suffering, whether physical or mental, that is intentionally inflicted on a person for political, religious, or ideological purposes or permitted "with the consent or acquiescence of a public official or other person acting in an official capacity"—is condemned and prohibited by the United Nations (UN, 1984). This rule does not instigate intense debates probably because of cross-cultural consensus against violence. However, many human rights advocates and some politicians in Europe condemn the death penalty in the United States. U.S. public opinion, on the other hand, overwhelmingly condemning torture elsewhere, still supports the death penalty in the United States.

A more complicated dilemma occurs in relation to other human rights. According to the United Nations, a child should be able to express his or her views freely, the state should respect the child's freedom of thought and religion, and children also "have the right to privacy and adults cannot unlawfully interfere in the child's privacy" (UN, 1989). Meanwhile, in many countries, according to cultural customs and religious norms, children's rights are not considered to be a subject of public debate. There is opposition from many states, for example, to the right of children to choose their own religion. Representatives from China, for instance, oppose the rights of children to form groups and exercise freedom of association. The rights of children that emphasize self-expression can be easily challenged in countries with authoritarian governments. Further, the United Nations requires that states ensure that children have access to a wide variety of resources including a standard of living that is adequate and physical, mental, spiritual, moral, and social development. These requirements are impossible to fulfill for the countries in which the amount of resources is limited.

Earlier in the book we learned that "real" socialization practices are quite different from those established by the United Nations. For example, in theory, states should guarantee the right to an education. This requirement is very difficult to implement, especially in countries such as Brazil, India, and Indonesia in which millions of children begin to work at a very early age and may quit school altogether.

In addition, the United Nations declares the priority of the child's individual rights over his or her rights within a social group, such as family. Many argue that these provisions indicate the individualistic values of Western society that are very difficult to accept for individuals living in other countries—such as Pakistan, Botswana, and Thailand—with different cultural conditions, specifically of a collectivist tradition.

Countries and governments vary in beliefs about the property distribution of power in the family, the degree to which behavior should be regulated by individuals themselves versus external rules, the importance of individual rights versus group and family loyalties, and the scope of responsibility individuals should have for themselves and their families (Murphy-Bernman et al., 1996).

CRITICAL THINKING

Cross-cultural psychologists should have the courage to ask questions about something that many people often consider "obvious" and therefore "normal" (see Chapter 3). For example, is the American view on democracy ethnocentric? Do American and West European politicians make ethnocentric judgments when they demand democracy in countries such as Cuba, China, Serbia, or Rwanda, to name a few? Some specialists imply that holding of free and open elections, which is considered democratic and therefore "good" for the West, may bring chaos and instability to some other countries (Pei, 1998, p. 69). Without asking these questions and looking for answers, one can follow an easy path of dogmatic thinking.

These examples, perhaps, suggest that culture may have a significant impact on how individuals and governments define the best interest of the child. Nevertheless, most of the existing contradictions exist and will continue to be an issue because of the tremendous economic burden suffered by billions of people and their general lack of protection against natural disasters and intrusive governments.

The United Nations also recognizes some fundamental rights of women. Any exclusion or restriction made on the basis of sex, which has the effect or purpose of discrimination against women in political, economic, social, cultural, civil, or any other fields, should be deemed unlawful and therefore condemned (UN, 1979). However, such demands directly contradict many cultural traditions and religious practices in many countries. Ms. Kasinga, of Togo, a country in Western Africa, came to the United States in 1994 seeking sanctuary from her tribe's custom of mutilating the genitals of young women (Jet, 1996). Is female circumcision a form of abuse or a cultural custom? We already discussed this topic earlier in the book. If a country—such as Afghanistan in the late 1990s—establishes a strict religious law denying equal education, employment, and medical care to women, should we judge such treatment as a cultural norm misunderstood by Western experts? There is no "correct" answer to this question because any answer will most likely carry a value judgment.

Culture, Ethnicity, and Equality

What attitude do people use to express their view on affirmative action? American law prohibits any discrimination against individuals because of their race, color, sex, religion, or national origin. Born of the civil rights movement in the 1960s, affirmative action calls for minorities to be given special consideration in employment, education, and business decisions. Why? Because overall, minorities and women are in vastly lower paying jobs and still face active discrimination in some sectors. The proponents of affirmative action say that equal opportunity can be achieved only by legal and political means (Hill, 1997). This policy is implemented to increase diversity in business, education, and social activities, and helps remedy past and present discrimination. In its modern form, affirmative action can call for an admissions officer faced with two similarly qualified applicants to choose the minority over the white, or for a manager to recruit and hire a qualified woman for a job instead of a man.

However, an increasingly assertive opposition movement argues that favoring members of one group (women, for example) over another (men, for instance) simply moves discrimination from one group and imposes it on the other. Affirmative action, they argue, provides benefits to one group of people over another group of people because of the color of their skin, their ethnic heritage, or their gender. This situation is often called "reverse discrimination." Critics blame affirmative action for robbing them of promotions and other opportunities. They argue that with free competition, the marketplace itself would promote those individuals who can contribute to community and society, without giving these people special treatment.

The United States Supreme Court has limited affirmative action and suggested that affirmative action can be used only where there is ongoing discrimination against minorities and women. Some states, California, for example, are moving to abolish affirmative action in education and job recruitment. The lawsuit against Atlanta is among dozens of similar cases filed across the country in recent years challenging government-run affirmative action programs that consider race and gender as factors. Many of the suits have proven successful and have resulted in governments either dismantling their programs or restructuring them so that they are based on class or geography rather than race or gender (Fletcher, 1999).

Statistically, both whites and blacks support compensatory programs, that is, job training and special education, which are designed to help members of disadvantaged groups compete more effectively in the marketplace (Welch & Sigelman, 1991). However, most whites reject programs that they view as implementing preferential treatment, such as quotas in college admissions and hiring of members of a particular group. A poll taken by *Parade* magazine (April 4, 1999)—three-quarters of the respondents were white and one-quarter represented other groups—showed that more than 80 percent of the respondents rejected set-aside quotas and programs for minorities.

Why is affirmative action under attack and losing its popularity among Americans? In the past 30 years Americans have changed many of their beliefs about race and racial equality. Being increasingly supportive of racial and ethnic integration during the 1970s and early 1980s, support of specific policies to bring about integration has been ambiguous (Ball-Rokeach & Loges, 1992) and even oppositional (Sidanius & Pratto, 1993; Sears, 1988). One possible explanation of this trend, which is the most fundamental component of equality, is people's adherence to the basic values of conservatism. They promote self-reliance, efficiency, and social responsibility (Sniderman et al., 1993).

According to the second view, minority middle-class groups are closely aligned with those of middle-class whites. Therefore, middle-class blacks, Hispanics, and other minorities are adopting opinions generally associated with middle-class whites rather than with lower- and working-class groups. From this perspective, minorities' assimilation into the mainstream of American society decreases racial or ethnic group identification. Therefore, occupation and education are expected to be more important than ethnicity in the formation of attitudes (Tuch & Sigelman, 1997).

The outcome of the current trends in attitudes about affirmative action will be a key in many aspects of social life and ethnic policies in the United States in the coming years.

Can some ethnic and racial disparities be explained by psychological factors? Let us consider one case. African Americans, in general, compared with other groups with similar incomes, are found to have more bad financial credit records, according to a study released by Freddie Mac. Overall, 48 percent of blacks and 27 percent of whites had bad credit ratings. The study found that in the United States, whites with an annual income of less than $25,000 had better credit records as a group than African Americans earning between $65,000 and $75,000. Almost 48 percent of African Americans with incomes between $45,000 and $65,000 had bad credit, compared with only

21.6 percent of whites. Hispanics in that bracket had a slightly worse record than whites—28 percent had credit problems. Only 15.7 percent of Asians with the same income had a bad credit rating. The study also found that even the poorest Asians—with incomes under $25,000—had credit records comparable to the wealthiest whites studied—those with incomes between $65,000 and $75,000. Only 12.5 percent of the wealthier Asians had credit problems, compared with 20.4 percent of the wealthier whites and 34.5 percent of wealthier blacks (Loose, 1999). Why is this happening? Can we—just for the sake of this analysis—use only psychological explanations? Perhaps not. Any psychological cause is interconnected with several contextual factors, among which availability of resources plays a major role.

Perhaps black Americans, in general, have fewer resources to fall back on in times of trouble than other groups. Because most middle-class blacks come from poor families, their parents and other relatives are less likely to have the resources to help them during an economic crisis. Asian families, on the contrary, may have more savings and are able to rely on relatives in case of financial trouble. Other studies have documented racial discrimination in lending, even among people with equal incomes and equally good credit ratings. Cultural attitudes may also contribute. For example, it is known that people who believe they control their lives tend to budget better and save more. However, those suggestions may be challenged by the findings of Banks and colleagues (1991) who examined 39 studies on locus of control in the African American population. Blacks have not been shown to have an external locus of control; moreover more than half of the studies reported an internal pattern of responding and almost 45 percent of the published data establish blacks as neither internal nor external (see Chapter 10 about locus of control).

 To be a poor man is hard, but to be a poor race in a land of dollars is the very bottom of hardship.
W.E.B. Du Bois (1882–1932)—AMERICAN SOCIOLOGIST, WRITER, AND TEACHER

Discrimination and Minority Status

People often talk about hidden discrimination against minorities. Are there any studies that confirm the presence of hidden discrimination? Yes, such studies exist. We give just one example. Nearly half of Washington area African Americans and Latinos seeking apartment insurance may be encountering discrimination, according to a report released by the Fair Housing Council of Greater Washington (Horwitz, 1999). Minority testers used racially identifiable names and voices, and called more than 60 insurance offices seeking information about renters insurance. In 150 cases, responses to black and Latino callers were compared with responses to white callers, and 45 percent revealed discrimination.

- Two testers—black and white—called about an estimation (a quote) of how much he should pay for an insurance policy. The white tester was asked how much coverage was needed for the building, and whether any claims had been filed in the past 3 years. Then the caller was given a verbal and written quote. The black tester was asked about the construction of the building, the number of units, distance to a fire hydrant, prior losses there, bankruptcy history, prior annulments, number of people in the household, flood zones, date of birth, and Social Security number. The black tester then did not receive a return phone call from the company.

- The white tester requested a quote by mail, and the agent agreed. The Latino tester, speaking to the same agent, requested a quote by mail and the agent said the company did not mail quotes.

We displayed just one example of discrimination based on stereotypes. We are sure that a search through academic journals, networks, newspaper and magazine articles, or any advanced search on the web would provide you with dozens of published reports on ethnicity, race, and discrimination.

Multiculturalism and Religion: A Campus Context

We learn about tolerance and respect for the customs, rules, and religious views of others. One way of learning about tolerance is information exchange. If a college student wants to tell other students about his religion, will it benefit other students? Is there evidence that free expression of religious views fosters mutual understanding among students? Almost 90 percent of Americans identify with a religion, in other words, can tell which religion they belong to (General Social Surveys, 1972–1996; see also Appendix 4). The United States is home to many world religions. As you perhaps know many Pilgrims—the first European settlers in America—came to this country with a particular religious vision. Moreover, back in Europe many of them were subject to discrimination, persecution, and quite often physical extermination. Today, like throughout all American history, those individuals who are persecuted in their home countries for their religious beliefs and practices can receive asylum in the United States.

As a free individual you have the right to choose to follow any religion or no religion. The U.S. Constitution permits private religious activity in colleges and universities. However, you have to understand some rules and regulations related to religious activity on campuses. These rules are generally the same for both public and private schools (some private institutions of higher education may have their own guidelines about religious behavior on their campuses; check, for example, the book's website. This is one of the cases in which all people, that is, students, teachers, counselors, and administrators, should follow formal rules.

All in all, in the United States, the government and religion are separated. Therefore, state-funded colleges and universities will not have courses in their curricula designed to promote any particular religion. However, you may find courses on the history of religion, comparative religion, and others that teach about the role of religion in the history of the United States and other countries.

Students have the right to pray individually or in groups and to discuss any religious views with their peers so long as these discussions are not disrupting the peace. Students can read any religious scripture, say grace before meals, and pray before tests. However, students must not forget that their school activities come first. For example, do not pray during the test for an hour and then ask the professor for extra time to finish the test.

Can students express religious beliefs in the form of projects and reports? Yes they can and no one should reject their work because of its religious content, such as quotes, symbols, and examples. However, remember that the work should be relevant to the assignment.

Anyone can talk about any religion during classroom discussion. It constitutes free speech. Similarly, people can criticize religion and promote atheistic views. Your professor may not silence you, for example, just because you make critical statements against religion. However, do not forget that other students also have the right to speak and they may criticize your views too.

Please remember that any criticism against a particular religion should not become excessive and overwhelming. In this case such criticism may be called religious harassment. Surprisingly, any intrusive attempts to promote one's religion by soliciting someone's participation are qualified as harassment too.

Religious messages on shirts, jackets, and hats may not be prohibited on campus and if you wear such printed messages, you should not be persecuted for this. Students may wear religious attire, such as crosses, yarmulkes, turbans, and headscarves. If your religious beliefs do not allow you to wear gym clothes because they are too revealing, you may not be forced to do so.

 EXERCISE 12.3

Is It a Culture War?

By the end of the 1990s France placed strict limits on the number of non-French films that could be shown in its theaters. French leaders say this is important to support their film industry and to protect French culture from American cultural imperialism. Other commentators say this rule unfairly excludes American films from the market and promotes instead French ethnocentrism and nationalism.

Questions: Do you think France—as well as any other country—should or should not be able to put limits on the showing of non-French films? Do you consider such actions a culture war that severely limits free exchange of information and ideas? Do you think that every country's culture should be protected by limiting foreign cultural influences? Please explain your answers. (*Source*: The Center on Policy Attitudes, University of Maryland, 1999.)

 Whole progress is precarious, and the solution of one problem brings us face-to-face with another problem.
Martin Luther King, Jr. (1929–1968)—AMERICAN CIVIL RIGHTS LEADER

Conclusion

Environmental problems and global climatic changes are expected to develop throughout the twenty-first century. Despite economic progress, 20 percent of the world population lives in absolute poverty. By the end of the twentieth century there were over 30 low-intensity wars in the world and more hidden ethnic conflicts. Civil hostilities and bloody coups continue to tear nations and regions apart. Cross-cultural psychology can respond to the emerging global challenges and opportunities, and become a scientific and applied field that accumulates research data from many other disciplines. Psychologists are able to offer suggestions for dissolution of both local and global problems, especially those that include ethnic, religious, and other tensions. As a result, a more intense cultural dialogue may start that would signify the beginning of the exchange of values and ideas that different cultures can offer to each other. Among these values could be materialism and spiritualism, consumption and recycling, family planning, and greater respect for the elderly (Marsella, 1998).

Cross-cultural psychology should accept diversity of ideas, values, and opinions. Indeed, there are centuries-old customs rooted in economic, religious, political, and other cultural foundations. Many human traditions should be respected. However, specialists should not support the continuation of any policies or programs that permit propaganda of war. They should denounce and reject promotion or justification of ethnic discrimination, racism, religious intolerance, physical and sexual abuse, and ideas of the inferiority of particular groups and the superiority of others.

Of course, cross-cultural psychology alone cannot offer solutions to the world's problems. However, your knowledge in this field, the skills you develop studying cross-cultural psychology, and the ideas you share with others will definitely help you become better prepared to seek out solutions. A great Chinese thinker, Laotse, said that any journey of a thousand miles begins with one step. So let us take this step together, and see what we can do to make this world a better place.

 ## CHAPTER SUMMARY

- Cultural beliefs affect people's attitudes about life and death. In the United States, in the beginning of the 1980s, a presidential commission and state courts reached a consensus that brain death signals the end of human life. In Japan, however, there is a prominent belief that it is not only the brain that makes us human. Even a brain-dead person is alive until the last beat of his or her heart.
- Pessimists say that virtually all attempts to cultivate ethnic unity have failed. No multiethnic nation can survive the internal pressure of people's ethnic self-determination. Optimists suggest that a multiethnic popu-

lation will grow and our global society will become a union of all cultures. There will be no place for racism or ethnocentrism in this new world, because the multiethnic children cannot hate or disrespect their parents and their heritage without sacrificing their own personal integrity and peace of mind.
- There are similarities and differences in negotiating styles and conflict-resolution strategies. Knowledge about the other side's cultural strategies is a key to successful negotiation.
- What we might anticipate from an individual based on our expectations about his or her

culture does not often match who he or she really is. Please be prepared for such inconsistencies.

- Migration is often accompanied by culture shock: an initial reaction of adjustment to a new culture. Specialists understand acculturative stress as a distressful psychological reaction to any unfamiliar cultural environment. Often named "culture shock," acculturative stress is typically defined as a set of complex psychological experiences, usually unpleasant and disruptive.

- Assuming that cognitive tests are not biased against particular cultural groups and the child has adequate proficiency in the language of testing, the teacher or parent can improve the child's test performance.

- Being supportive, in general, about affirmative action, most Americans reject programs that in their view are implementing preferential treatment, such as quotas in college admissions and hiring of members of a particular group.

- Race and ethnicity have some impact on peo-ple's political and social attitudes. However, their influence is rather ambiguous.

- Traditionally, immigrants have been stereotypically portrayed as ideal "precitizens." However, the situation changed after the 1970s. A positive public stereotype has been replaced by a negative one. According to this stereotype, immigrants are primarily illegal, they steal jobs from honest and hard-working citizens, they live on taxpayer's money, they create criminal problems, and they pose a threat to American culture in general.

- Discrimination against particular groups should be explained by many factors and reasons. Psychological explanations should supplement socioeconomic and sociological ones.

- Sometimes cultural norms of a particular country or ethnic group violate basic human rights and freedoms (understood from an international perspective). Determining what rights are basic and universal and choosing priorities between indigenous practices and international standards almost always requires a value judgment.

Appendix 1

The Interdependence of Values, Perceptions, and Language

Suggested responses from Lee's perspective:

Jenny	Lee	Jenny	Lee
problem	*challenge*	abnormal	*unique*
failure	*learning experience*	ethnocentrism	*ethnic pride*
terrorist	*freedom fighter*	chauvinism	*patriotism*
hostage	*detainee*	cultural impurity	*cultural diversity*
murder	*sacrifice*	discrimination	*distinction*
genocide	*ethnic cleansing*	reverse discrimination	*affirmative action*
brainwashed	*enlightened*	child abuse	*disciplined upbringing*
handicapped	*physically challenged*	child neglect	*permissive upbringing*
disabled	*differently abled*	handout	*subsidy*
primitive	*natural*	kleptomaniac	*nontraditional shopper*

Appendix 2

Answers to Identifying Dichotomous versus Continuous Variables

feminine–masculine: *(C)*
married–single: *(D)*
conscious–unconscious: *(C)*
prejudiced–unprejudiced: *(C)*
slavery–freedom: *(C)*
racist–nonracist: *(C)*
homosexual–heterosexual: *(C)*
licensed–unlicensed: *(D)*
integration–segregation: *(C)*
alcoholic beverage–nonalcoholic
    beverage: *(D)*
sexist–nonsexist: *(C)*

perfect–imperfect: *(C)*
young–old: *(C)*
present–absent: *(D)*
rich–poor: *(C)*
liberal–conservative: *(C)*
airborne–grounded: *(D)*
responsible–not responsible: *(C)*
acculturated–unacculturated: *(C)*
mailed–unmailed: *(D)*
democracy–dictatorship: *(C)*

guilty verdict–not guilty verdict: *(D)*

heterogeneous–homogeneous: *(C)*

materialistic–spiritualistic: *(C)*

traditionalist–reformist: *(C)*

addicted–not addicted: *(C)*

similar–different: *(C)*

    dead–alive: *(D)*

tolerance–intolerance: *(C)*

successful basketball shot–

    unsuccessful shot: *(D)*

power on–power off: *(D)*

subjective–objective: *(C)*

politically correct–politically

    incorrect: *(C)*

Appendix 3

The Barnum Effect and Sociocultural Groups

As you look through the following list of Barnum statements, ask yourself this question: Are there many groups about whom it could be said that these descriptions are *not* true?

- "They are a proud people."
- "They see themselves as distinct."
- "They are protective of their young."
- "They can be suspicious of strangers."
- "They value loyalty and commitment."
- "They have special customs."
- "They wish to make things better for future generations."
- "They are similar to others in some ways, but not in other ways."
- "They can be their own worst enemy."
- "They know what it's like to struggle."
- "They have been misperceived by others."
- "They have experienced discrimination."
- "They can only be pushed so far."
- "They don't want to relinquish their values and beliefs."
- "They try to cope with adversity in the best way they know how."
- "They are naturally peace loving, but will fight for the right to survive."

Notice how easily the Barnum Effect can occur in relation to a diverse array of specific sociocultural groups:

- "Men care about success."
- "Women resent being taken for granted."
- "Infants seek pleasure."
- "Children crave love and approval."
- "Teenagers want to be seen for who they are."
- "Middle-age adults wish that life were easier."

- "Senior citizens don't want to be ignored."
- "Christians try to be forgiving."
- "Jewish people have feelings of insecurity."
- "Catholics know about guilt."
- "Hispanics can be very passionate."
- "Asians respect their ancestors."
- "Europeans have had their share of troubles."
- "Americans are a diverse group of individuals."
- "Immigrants seek a better life."
- "Democrats are concerned about the needy."
- "Capitalists want more than they have."
- "Civil libertarians are opposed to excessive government."
- "The physically disabled resent being seen as inferior."
- "AIDS patients don't want to be ostracized."
- "Welfare recipients don't like being overly dependent."
- "Gang members need to feel that they belong to something."
- "Teachers value knowledge."
- "Artists want the freedom to express themselves."
- "Psychologists have their own problems."
- "Schizophrenics view the world in a unique way."

Appendix 4

EXERCISE 3.11

Exploring Compound Pathways

Suggested answers to exercise on the multiple causes of homophobia:

- religious convictions
- belief that homosexuality is immoral
- belief that homosexuality is a mental illness
- repulsed by the thought of sex with same gender
- peer approval
- compliance with community norms
- sheltered or puritanical upbringing
- past victim of homosexual molestation
- pejorative stereotypes in mass media
- need to protect children
- need to feel superior
- general intolerance of differentness

- unconscious projection of self-hatred
- reaction formation against own homoerotic desires
- unrealistic fear of AIDS

Appendix 5

Some Major U.S. Religious Bodies, 1999

Religious Body	Number of Followers
Protestant (Christian)	85,500,000
Roman Catholic Church (Christian)	61,207,914
Church of Jesus Christ of Latter-Day Saints (Mormons)	4,923,100
Orthodox Christian (Russian, Greek, Ethiopian, and others)	5,631,000
Muslim	6,000,000
Buddhist	1,864,000
Hindu	795,000
Jewish	5,602,000

Sources: *Yearbook of American & Canadian Churches*, 1999; Kendall, D. (1999). *Sociology in our times.* New York: ITP.

Appendix 6

EXERCISE 10.2

Answers to Compare

1. German man (60%), Japanese man (30%), other answers (10%).
2. Brazilian woman (30%), Italian woman (35%), French man (25%), other answers (10%).

3. Japanese man (98%), other answers (2%).
4. Brazilian woman (100%).
5. German man (80%), Japanese man (10%), other answers (10%).
6. French man (95%), German man (4%), other answers (1%).
7. Jordanian woman (60%), Japanese man (25%), other answers (15%)
8. Japanese man (85%), other answers (15%).
9. Jordanian woman (80%), other answers (10%).
10. French man (65%), Japanese man (25%), other answers (10%).
11. German man (98%), other answers (2%).
12. Jordanian woman (70%), Brazilian woman (15%), other answers (15%).
13. French man (90%), other answers (10%).

References

Abu-Lughod, L. (1986). *Veiled sentiments*. Berkeley: University of California Press.

Abu-Saad, I. (1998). Individualism and Islamic work beliefs. *Journal of Cross-Cultural Psychology*, 29(3), 377–383.

Adams, F., & Osgood, C. (1973). A cross-cultural study of the affective meaning of color. *Journal of Cross-Cultural Psychology*, 4(2), 135–156.

Adigun, I. (1997). Orientations to work: A cross-cultural approach. *Journal of Cross-Cultural Psychology*, 28, 352–355.

Adler, A. (1931). *What life should mean to you*. Boston: Little, Brown.

Adorno, T., Frenkel-Brunswik, E., Levinson, D., & Sanford, R. (1950). *The authoritarian personality*. New York: Harper & Row.

Akbar, N. (1991). The evolution of human psychology for African Americans. In R. Jones (Ed.), *Black psychology* (3rd ed., pp. 99–123). Berkeley, CA: Cobb & Henry.

Albas, D. C., McCluskey, K. W., & Albas, C. A. (1976). Perception of the emotional content of speech. *Journal of Cross-Cultural Psychology*, 7, 481–490.

Allodi, F. A. (1991). Assessment and treatment of torture victims. *The Journal of Nervous and Mental Disorders*, 179, 4–11.

Allport, G. (1935). Attitudes. In C. Murchison (Ed.), *A handbook of social psychology*. Worcester, MA: Clark University Press.

Allport, G. (1954). *The nature of prejudice*. Cambridge, MA: Addison-Wesley.

Almond, G., & Verba, S. (1965). *The civic culture*. Boston: Little, Brown.

Altman, I. (1975). *The environment and social behavior*. Monterey, CA: Brooks/Cole.

Amenomouri, M., Kono, A., Fournier, J., & Winer, G. (1997). A cross-cultural developmental study of directional asymmetries in circle drawing. *Journal of Cross-Cultural Psychology*, 28(6), 730–742.

Amir, Y., Haliva, Y., & Sagie, D. (1976). Verbal and behavioral aspects of commitment among Arabs and Jews. *Journal of Cross-Cultural Psychology*, 7(1), 37–49.

Anastasi, A. (1988). *Psychological testing* (6th ed.). New York: Macmillan.

Anderson, C. (1987). Temperature and aggression: Effects on quarterly, yearly, and city rates of violent and nonviolent crime. *Journal of Personality and Social Psychology*, 52, 1161–1173.

Andreason, N. J. C., & Canter, A. (1974). The creative writer: Psychiatric symptoms and family history. *Comprehensive Psychiatry*, 15(2), 123–131.

Andreason, N. J. C., & Powers, P. S. (1975). Creativity and psychosis: An examination of conceptual style. *Archives of General Psychiatry*, 32, 70–73.

Antrobus, J. (1991). Dreaming: Cognitive processes during cortical activation and high afferent thresholds. *Psychological Review*, 98, 96–121.

Appadurai, A. (1990). Disjuncture and difference in the global cultural economy. In M. Featherstone (Ed.), *Global culture: Nationalism, globalism, and modernity* (pp. 295–310). London: Sage.

Aptekar, L. (1989). Columbian street children: Gamines and Chupagruesos. *Adolescence*, 24, 783–794.

Archer, J. (1996). Sex differences in social behavior: Are the social role and evolutionary explanations compatible? *American Psychologist*, 51(9), 909–917.

Aronson, E. (1995). *The social animal*. New York: W. H. Freeman.

Aronson, E., & O'Leary, M. (1982–1983). The relative effectiveness of models and prompts on energy conservation: A field experiment in a shower room. *Journal of Environmental Systems*, 12, 219–224.

Asch, S. (1946). Forming impression of personality. *Journal of Abnormal and Social Psychology*, 41, 258–290.

Asch, S. (1956). Studies of independence and conformity: A minority of one against unanimous majority. *Psychological Monographs*, 9, #416.

Asher, S., Renshaw, P., & Hymel, S. (1982). Peer relations and the development of social skills. In S. Moore (Ed.), *The young child: Reviews of research*. Washington, DC: NAEYC.

Aune, R., & Aune, K. (1994). The influence of culture, gender, and relational status on appearance management. *Journal of Cross-Cultural Psychology*, 25(2), 258–272.

Averill, J. (1982). *Anger and aggression: An essay on emotion*. New York: Springer-Verlag.

Ayman, R., & Chemers, M. M. (1983). Relationship of supervisory behavior ratings to work group effectiveness and subordinate satisfaction among Iranian managers. *Journal of Applied Psychology, 68,* 338–341.

Baldwin, J. (1991). African (Black) psychology: Issues and synthesis. In R. Jones (Ed.), *Black psychology* (3rd ed., pp. 125–135). Berkeley, CA: Cobb & Henry.

Baldwin, J., Brown, R., & Hopkins, R. (1991). The black self-hatred paradigm revised: An Africentric analysis. In R. Jones (Ed.), *Black psychology* (3rd ed., pp. 141–161). Berkeley: Cobb & Henry.

Ball, G. (1962). Lawyers and diplomats. Address before the N.Y. Lawyers Association, December 13, 1962. Department of State Bulletin, December 31, 987–991.

Ball, T., & Dagger, R. (1991). *Political ideologies and the democratic ideal.* New York: Harper Collins.

Ball-Rokeach, S., & Loges, W. (1992). Choosing equality: The correspondence between attitudes about race and the value of equality. *Journal of Social Issues, 50*(4), 9–18.

Bancroft, J. (1989). *Human sexuality and its problems.* Edinburgh: Churchill Livingstone.

Banks, W. C., Ward, W., McQuater, G. V., & DeBritto, A. M. (1991). Are blacks external? On the status of locus of control in black population. In R. Jones (Ed.), *Black psychology* (3rd ed., pp. 181–192). Berkeley, CA: Cobb & Henry.

Bandura, A. (1969). *Principles of behavioral modification.* New York: Holt, Rinehart & Winston.

Bandura, A. (1977). *Social learning theory.* Englewood Cliffs, NJ: Prentice-Hall.

Barankin, T., Konstantareas, M. M., & de Bosset, F. (1989). Adaptation of recent Soviet Jewish immigrants and their children to Toronto. *Canadian Journal of Psychiatry, 34,* 512–518.

Barber, J. W. (1971). *The book of 1000 proverbs.* New York: American Heritage Press. (Original work published 1876.)

Barber, N. (1998). Ecological and psychological correlates of male homosexuality: A cross-cultural investigation. *Journal of Cross-Cultural Psychology, 29*(3), 387–401.

Bard, L. A., Carter, D. L., Cerce, D. D., Knight, R. A., Rosenberg, R., & Schneider, B. (1987). A descriptive study of rapists and child molesters: Development, clinical, and criminal characteristics. *Behavioral Sciences and the Law, 5,* 203–220.

Barkow, J. H., Cosmides, L., & Tooby, J. (Eds.). (1992). *The adapted mind: Evolutionary psychology and the generation of culture.* New York: Oxford University Press.

Barnlund, D. (1975). *Public and private self in Japan and the United States.* Tokyo: Simul Press.

Barnlund, D. C. (1989). Communicative styles of Japanese and Americans: Images and realities. Belmont, CA: Wadsworth.

Barnlund, D., & Araki, S. (1985). Intercultural encounters: The management of compliments by Japanese and Americans. *Journal of Cross-Cultural Psychology, 16*(1), 9–26.

Baron, R. (1970). Magnitude of model's apparent pain and ability to aid the model as determinants of observer reaction time. *Psychonomic Science, 21,* 196–197.

Baron, R. (1998). *Psychology.* Boston: Allyn & Bacon.

Baron, R., & Byrne, D. (1994). *Social psychology.* Boston: Allyn & Bacon.

Baron, R., & Kalsher, M. (1996). The sweet smell of . . . safety? *Proceedings of the Human Factors and Ergonomics Society, 40,* 1282.

Barraclough, B. (1988). International variations in the suicide rate of 15–24 year olds. *Social Psychiatry and Psychiatric Epidemiology, 23,* 75–84.

Barron, F., & Harrington, D. (1981). Creativity, intelligence, and personality. *Annual Review of Psychology, 32,* 439–476.

Bartlett, J. (1968). *Familiar quotations* (14th ed.). Boston: Little, Brown.

Basoglu, M., Paker, M., Paker, O., Ozmen, E., Marks, I., Sahin, D., & Sarimurat, N. (1994). Psychological effect of torture: A comparison of tortured with non-tortured political activists in Turkey. *American Journal of Psychiatry, 151,* 6–81.

Bass, L., & Casper, L. (1999). *Population division working paper No. 28.* Washington, DC: U.S. Bureau of the Census.

Bassili, J. (1995). On the psychological reality of party identification: Evidence from the accessibility of voting intentions and of partisan feelings. *Political Behavior, 17*(4), 339–359.

Baumrind, D. (1983). Rejoinder to Lewis's reinterpretation of parental firm control effects: Are authoritative families really harmonious? *Psychological Bulletin, 94,* 132–142.

Beardsley, L., & Pedersen, P. (1997). Health and culture-centered intervention. In J. Berry & C. Kagitcibasi (Eds.), *Handbook of cross-cultural psychology: Social behavior and applications* (Vol. 3, pp. 413–448). Needham Heights: Allyn & Bacon.

Beauchamp, G. (1987). The human preference for the excess salt. *American Scientist, 75,* 27–33.

Beck, A. (1991). Cognitive therapy: A 30-year retrospective. *American Psychologist, 46,* 368–375.

Bekhterev, V. (1921). *Kollektivnaya refleksologya [Collective reflexology].* Petrograd: Kolos.

Belcastro, P. (1985). Sexual behavior differences between black and white students. *Journal of Sex Research, 21,* 56–67.

Ben-Ari, R., Schwarzwald, J., & Horiner-Levi, E. (1994). The effects of prevalent social stereotypes on intergroup attribution. *Journal of Cross-Cultural Psychology, 25*(4), 489–500.

Benedict, R. (1946). *The chrysanthemum and the sword: Patterns of Japanese culture.* Boston: Houghton Mifflin.

Bengston, V., & Black, K. (1973). Intergenerational relations and continuities in socialization. In K. Schaie & P. Baltes (Eds.), *Personality and socialization* (pp. 207–234). New York: Academic Press.

Bennet, L., Janca, A., Grant, B., & Sartorius, N. (1993). Boundaries between normal and pathological drinking: A cross-cultural comparison. *Alcohol, Health, and Research World, 17,* 190–196.

Berger, K. (1995). *The developing person through the life span*. New York: Worth Publishers.

Berkowitz, W. (1971). A cross-national comparison of some social patterns of urban pedestrians. *Journal of Cross-Cultural Psychology, 2*(2), 129–144.

Berkowitz, L. (1962). *Aggression: A social psychological analysis*. New York: McGraw-Hill.

Berlin, B. (1992). *Ethnobiological classification: Principles of categorization of plants and animals in traditional societies*. Princeton: Princeton University Press.

Berlyne, D. E. (1960). *Conflict, arousal, and curiosity*. New York: McGraw-Hill.

Berlyne, D. E. (1971). *Aesthetics and psychobiology*. New York: Appleton-Century-Crofts.

Berlyne, D. E. (1974). *Studies in the new experimental aesthetics*. New York: Wiley.

Berman, A. L., & Jobes, D. A. (1992). Suicidal behavior of adolescents. In B. Bongar (Ed.), *Suicide: Guidelines for assessment, management and treatment*. New York: Oxford University Press.

Bernard, T. (1990). Angry aggression among "truly disadvantaged." *Criminology, 28*, 73–96.

Bernman, J., & Murhy-Bernman, V. (1996). Cultural differences in perceptions of allocators of resources. *Journal of Cross-Cultural Psychology, 27*(4), 494–509.

Bernstein, M., & Crosby, F. (1980). An empirical examination of relative deprivation theory. *Journal of Experimental Social Psychology, 16*, 442–456.

Berry, J. W. (1966). Temne and Eskimo perceptual skills. *International Journal of Psychology, 1*, 207–229.

Berry, J. W. (1967). Independence and conformity in subsistence level societies. *Journal of Personality and Social Psychology, 7*, 415–418.

Berry, J. W. (1968). Directory of cross-cultural psychological research. *International Journal of Psychology, 3*, 137–148.

Berry, J. W. (1969). On cross-cultural comparability. *International Journal of Psychology, 4*, 119–128.

Berry, J. W. (1971). Ecological and cultural factors in spatial perceptual development. *Canadian Journal of Behavioral Science, 3*, 324–336.

Berry, J. W. (1983). The sociogenesis of social sciences: An analysis of the cultural relativity of social psychology. In B. Bain (Ed.), *The sociogenesis of language and human conduct* (pp. 449–458). New York: Pergamon.

Berry, J. W. (1983). Textured contexts: Systems and situations in cross-cultural psychology. In S. H. Irvine & J. W. Berry (Eds.), *Human assessment and cultural factors* (pp. 117–125). New York: Plenum.

Berry, J. W. (1988). Cognitive values and cognitive competence among the bricoleurs. In J. W. Berry, S. H. Irvine, & E. B. Hunt (Eds.), *Indigenous cognition: Functioning in cultural context* (pp. 9–20). Dordrecht: Nijhoff.

Berry, J. W. (1995). The descendents of a model. *Culture and Psychology, 1*, 373–380.

Berry, J. W. (1997). Immigration, acculturation and adaptation. *Applied Psychology: An International Review, 46*, 5–68.

Berry, J. W., & Annis, R. (1974). Acculturative stress. *Journal of Cross-Cultural Psychology, 5*(4), 382–397.

Berry, J. W., & Annis, R. C. (Eds.). (1988). *Ethnic psychology: Research and practice with immigrants, refugees, native peoples, ethnic groups, and sojourners*. Lisse, The Netherlands: Swets & Zeitlinger.

Berry, J. W., & Dasen, P. R. (1974). Introduction. In J. W. Berry & P. R. Dasen (Eds.), *Culture and cognition* (pp. 1–20). London: Methuen.

Berry, J. W., & Sam, D. (1997). Acculturation and adaptation. In J. W. Berry, M. H. Segall, & C. Kagitcibasi (Eds.), *Handbook of cross-cultural psychology: Social behavior and applications* (Vol. 3, pp. 291–326). Needham Heights, MA: Allyn & Bacon.

Berry, J. W., Poortinga, Y. H., Segall, M. H., & Dasen, P. R. (1992). *Cross-cultural psychology: Research and applications*. New York: Cambridge University Press.

Berscheid, E. (1982). Attraction and emotions in interpersonal relationships. In M. S. Clark & S. T. Fiske (Eds.), *Affect and cognition: The 17th Annual Carnegie Symposium on Cognition*. Hillsdale, NJ: Erlbaum.

Best, D. (1994). Parent-child interactions in France, Germany, and Italy. *Journal of Cross-Cultural Psychology, 25*(2), 181–193.

Best, D., & Williams, J. (1997). Sex, gender, and culture. In J. W. Berry, M. H. Segall, & C. Kagitcibasi (Eds.), *Handbook of cross-cultural psychology: Social behavior and applications* (Vol. 3, pp. 163–212). Needham Heights, MA: Allyn & Bacon.

Best, D., Naylor, C., & Williams, J. (1975). Extension of color bias research to young French and Italian children. *Journal of Cross-Cultural Psychology, 6*(4), 391–400.

Betancourt, H., & Lopez, S. R. (1993). The study of culture, ethnicity, and race in American psychology. *American Psychologist, 48*, 629–637.

Betzig, L. (1989). Causes of conjugal dissolution: A cross-cultural study. *Current Anthropology, 30*(5), 654–676.

Beveridge, W. M. (1940). Some differences in racial perception. *British Journal of Psychology, 30*, 57–64.

Bhagat, R., & Landis, D. (Eds.). (1996). *Handbook of intercultural training*. Thousand Oaks, CA: Sage.

Bhana, K. (1986). Generational changes in conceptions of mental illness. *Journal of Cross-Cultural Psychology, 17*(4), 493–505.

Bickman, L. (1972). Social influence and division of responsibility in an emergency. *Journal of Experimental and Social Psychology, 8*, 438–445.

Birch, H., & Gussow, J. (1970). *Disadvantaged children: Health, nutrition, and school failure*. New York: Harcourt, Brace & World.

Birdwhistell, R. L. (1970). *Kinesics and context*. Philadelphia: University of Philadelphia Press.

Birnbaum, D. W. (1983). Preschoolers' stereotypes about sex differences in emotionality: A reaffirmation. *Journal of Genetic Psychology, 143*, 139–140.

Biswas, U. N., & Pandey, J. (1996). Mobility and perception of socioeconomic status among tribal and caste group. *Journal of Cross-Cultural Psychology, 27*(2), 200–215.

Bizman, A., & Amir, Y. (1982). Mutual perceptions of Arabs and Jews in Israel. *Journal of Cross-Cultural Psychology, 13*(4), 461–469.

Blais, A., Young, R., Fleury, C., & Lapp, M. (1995). Do people vote on the basis of minimax regret? *Political Research Quarterly, 48*(4), 827–836.

Blakemore, C., & Cooper, G. F. (1970). Development of the brain depends on the visual environment. *Nature, 228*, 477–478.

Bleichrodt, N., Drenth, P. J., & Querido, A. (1980). Effects of iodine deficiency on mental and psychomotor abilities. *American Journal of Physical Anthropology, 53*, 55–67.

Bloch, A. (1980). *Murphy's law, book two.* Los Angeles: Price/Stern/Sloan.

Blok, A. (1981). Rams and Billy-goats: A key to Mediterranean code of honor. *Man, 16*, 427–440.

Boas, F. (1911). *The mind of primitive man.* New York: Macmillan.

Bock, P. K. (1988). *Rethinking psychological anthropology: Continuity and change in the study of human action.* New York: W.H. Freeman.

Bock, P. K. (Ed.). (1994). *Psychological anthropology.* Westport, CT: Praeger.

Boehnke, K., Silberstein, R., Eisenberg, N., Reykowski, J., & Palmonari, A. (1989). Developmental patterns of pro-social motivation. *Journal of Cross-Cultural Psychology, 20*(3), 219–243.

Bond, M. (1985). How are responses to verbal insult related to cultural collectivism and power distance? *Journal of Cross-Cultural Psychology, 16*(1), 111–127.

Bond, M. (Ed.). (1986). *The psychology of the Chinese people.* Hong Kong: Oxford University Press.

Bond, M., & Tak-Sing, C. (1983). College students' spontaneous self concept: The effects of culture among respondents in Hong-Kong, Japan, and the United States. *Journal of Cross-Cultural Psychology, 14*, 153–171.

Bond, M. H., Hewstone, M., Wan, K. C., & Chui, C. K. (1985). Group-serving attributions across intergroup contexts: Cultural differences in the explanation of sex-typed behaviors. *European Journal of Social Psychology, 15*, 435–451

Borgida, E., & Nisbett, R. E. (1977). The differential impact of abstract vs. concrete information on decisions. *Journal of Applied Social Psychology, 7*, 258–271.

Borke, H., & Su, S. (1972). Perceptions of emotional responses to social interactions by Chinese and American children. *Journal of Cross-Cultural Psychology, 3*(3), 309–314.

Bornstein, M. H., & Tamis-LeMonda, C. (1989). Maternal responsiveness and cognitive development in children. In M. H. Bornstein (Ed.), *Maternal responsiveness: Characteristics and consequences* (pp. 49–61). San Francisco: Jossey-Bass

Borod, J. (1992). Interhemispheric and intrahemispheric control of emotion: A focus on unilateral brain damage. *Journal of Consulting and Clinical Psychology, 60*, 339–348.

Bouchard, T., Lykken, D., McGue, M., Segal, N. L., & Tellegen, A. (1990). Sources of human psychological differences: The Minnesota study of twins reared apart. *Science, 250*, 223–228.

Bouchard, T., & McGue, M. (1981). Familial studies of intelligence: A review. *Science, 212*, 1055–1059.

Boucher, J., & Brandt, M. (1981). Judgment of emotion: American and Malay antecedents. *Journal of Cross-Cultural Psychology, 12*(3), 272–283.

Boucher, J., & Carlson, G. (1980). Recognition of facial expressions in three cultures. *Journal of Cross-Cultural Psychology, 11*(3), 263–280.

Bourguignon, E. E. (1954). Dreams and dream interpretation. *American Anthropologist, 56*(2), 262–268.

Bourguignon, E. E. (1976). *Possession.* San Francisco: Chandler & Sharp.

Bourguignon, E. E. (1994). Trance and meditation. In P. K. Bock (Ed.), *Psychological anthropology* (pp. 297–314). Westport, CT: Praeger.

Bovasso, G. (1993). Self, group, and public interest motivating racial politics. *Political Psychology, 14*(1), 3–20.

Bowbly, J. (1982). *Attachment* (Vol. I). New York: Basic Books.

Boykin, A. (1994). Harvesting talent and culture: African-American children and educational reform. In R. Rossi (Ed.), *Schools and students at risk* (pp. 116–138). New York: Teachers College Press.

Brandstatter, H., Davis, J., & Stocker-Kreichgauer, G. (Eds.). (1984). *Group decision making.* New York: Academic Press.

Brandt, M. E., & Boucher, J. D. (1985). Judgment of emotions from antecedent situations in three cultures. In I. R. Lagunes & Y. H. Poortinga (Eds.), *From a different perspective: Studies of behavior across cultures* (pp. 348–362). Lisse, The Netherlands: Swets & Zeitlinger.

Branigin, W. (1998). Fitting in leaves children less fit. *The Washington Post*, September 10, A1.

Braude, J. (1963). *Speaker's desk book of quips, quotes, and anecdotes.* Englewood Cliffs, NJ: Prentice -Hall.

Brehm, J. W., & Self, E. A. (1989). The intensity of motivation. *Annual Review of Psychology, 40*, 109–131.

Briggs, J. L. (1970). *Never in anger: Portrait of an Eskimo family.* Cambridge, MA: Harvard University Press.

Brislin, R. (1970). Back-translation for cross-cultural research. *Journal of Cross-Cultural Psychology, 1*(3), 185–216.

Brislin, R. (1993). *Understanding culture's influence on behavior.* Fort Worth, TX: Harcourt Brace Jovanovich.

Brislin, R., & Horvath, A.-M. (1997). Cross-cultural training and multicultural education. In J. W. Berry, M. H. Segall, & C. Kagitcibasi (Eds.), *Handbook of cross-cultural psychology: Social behavior and applications* (Vol. 3, pp. 327–369). Needham Heights, MA: Allyn & Bacon.

Brody, L., & Hall, J. A. (1993). Gender and emotion. In M. Lewis & J. Haviland (Eds.), *Handbook of emotions* (pp. 447–460). New York: Guilford Press.

Bronfenbrenner, U. (1970). *Two worlds of childhood: U.S. and U.S.S.R.* New York: Russell Sage Foundation.

Bronfenbrenner, U. (1979). *The ecology of human development: Experiments by nature and design.* Cambridge, MA: Harvard University Press.

Brooks, I. (1976). Cognitive ability assessment with two New Zealand ethnic groups. *Journal of Cross-Cultural Psychology, 7*(3), 347–355.

Broude, G., & Greene, S. (1976). Cross-cultural codes on twenty sexual attitudes and practices. *Ethnology, 15,* 409–429.

Brown, D. (1995). Aggression tied to chemical. *The Washington Post,* November 23, A1.

Brown, P., & Wald, G. (1964). Visual pigments in single rods and cones in the human retina. *Science, 144,* 45–52.

Brown, R. (1965). *Social psychology.* New York: Free Press.

Bruner, J. S., & Potter, M. C. (1964). Interference in visual recognition. *Science, 144,* 424–425.

Brustein, W. (1998). The costs and benefits of joining an extremist party: Membership in the pre-1933 Nazi party. *Research in Political Sociology, 8,* 35–56.

Buckley, S. (1996). In Africa, abuse of wives viewed as a right and a rite. *The Washington Post,* May 2, A1.

Buda, R., & Elsayed-Elkhouly, S. (1998). Cultural differences between Arabs and Americans: Individualism and collectivism revisited. *Journal of Cross-Cultural Psychology, 29,* 487–492.

Bull, R., & David, I. (1986). The stigmatizing effect of facial disfigurement. *Journal of Cross-Cultural Psychology, 17*(1), 99–108.

Buri, J. R., Louiselle, P. A., Misukanis, T. M., & Mueller, R. A. (1988). Effects of parental authoritarianism and authoritativeness on self-esteem. *Personality and Social Psychology Bulletin, 14,* 271–282.

Burnstein, E., & Vinokur, A. (1975). What a person thinks upon learning he has chosen differently from others. *Journal of Experimental Social Psychology, 11,* 412–426.

Burton-Bradley, B. (1970). Transcultural psychiatry in Papua and New Guinea. *Journal of Cross-Cultural Psychology, 1*(2), 177–183.

Buss, A. H., & Plomin, R. (1985). *Temperament: Early developing personality traits.* Hillsdale, NJ: Erlbaum.

Buss, D. (1994). Sex differences in human mate preferences. *Behavioral and Brain Sciences, 12,* 1–49.

Buss, D. M., Larsen, R. J., Westen, D., & Semmelroth, J. (1992). Sex differences in jealousy: Evolution, physiology, and psychology. *Psychological Science, 3,* 251–255.

Butcher, J., Jeeyoung, L., & Nezami, E. (1998). Objective study of abnormal personality in cross-cultural settings. *Journal of Cross-Cultural Psychology, 29*(1), 189–211.

Bynum, E. B. (1993). *Families and the interpretation of dreams: Awakening the intimate web.* New York: Harrington Park Press/Haworth Press.

Byrne, D. (1982). Predicting human sexual behavior. In A. G. Kraut (Ed.), *The Stanley Hall lecture series* (Vol. 2, pp. 363–368). Washington, DC: American Psychological Association.

Byrnes, J. P. (1988). Formal operations: A systematic reformulation. *Developmental Review, 8,* 66–87.

Camilleri, C., & Malewska-Peyre, H. (1997). Socialization and identity strategies. In J. W. Berry, P. R. Dasen, & T. S. Saraswathi (Eds.), *Handbook of cross-cultural psychology: Basic processes and human development* (Vol. 2, pp. 41–67). Needham Heights, MA: Allyn & Bacon.

Campbell, D. (1967). Stereotypes and the perception of group differences. *American Psychologist, 22,* 817–829.

Canino, G. L., Burman, A., & Caetano, R. (1992). The prevalence of alcohol abuse and/or dependency in two Hispanic communities. In J. E. Helzer & G. J. Canino (Eds.), *Alcoholism in North America, Europe, and Asia* (pp. 131–158). New York: Oxford University Press.

Cann, J. (1995). Nomination politics and ideological polarization: Assessing the attitudinal effects of campaign involvement. *The Journal of Politics, 57*(1), 101–120.

Cannon, W. B. (1927). The James-Lange theory of emotions: A critical examination and an alternative theory. *American Journal of Psychiatry, 39,* 106–124.

Cannon, W. B. (1932). *The wisdom of the body.* New York: W. W. Norton.

Cantor, N., & Mischel, W. (1977). Traits as prototypes: Effects on recognition memory. *Journal of Personality and Social Psychology, 35,* 38–48.

Cantor, N., & Mischel, W. (1979). Prototypes in person perception. In L. Berkowitz (Ed.), *Advances in experimental social psychology* (Vol. 12, pp. 3–52). New York: Academic Press.

Caprio, F. (1943). A psycho-social study of primitive conceptions of death. *Criminal Psychotherapy,* 303–317.

Carmines, E., & Berkman, M. (1994). Ethos, ideology, and partisanship: Exploring the paradox of conservative democrats. *Political Behavior, 16*(2), 203–220.

Carrier, J. (1980). Homosexual behavior in cross-cultural perspective. In J. Marmor (Ed.), *Homosexual behavior: A modern reappraisal.* New York: Basic Books.

Carroll, S. (1989). The socializing impact of the women's movement. In R. Sigel (Ed.), *Political learning in adulthood: A sourcebook of theory and research.* Chicago: The University of Chicago Press.

Carroll, J. B. (1983). Studying individual differences in cognitive abilities: Implications for cross-cultural studies. In S. H. Irvine & J. W. Berry (Eds.), *Human assessment and cultural factors* (pp. 213–235). New York: Plenum.

Cartwright, R. D. (1992). "Masochism" in dreaming and its relationship to depression. *Dreaming, 1,* 147–159.

Cashmore, J., & Goodnow, J. (1986). Influences on Australian parents' values: Ethnicity vs sociometric status. *Journal of Cross-Cultural Psychology, 17,* 441–454.

Casmir, G., & Keats, D. (1996). The effects of work environment and in-group membership on the leadership preferences of Anglo-Austrians and Chinese Australians. *Journal of Cross-Cultural Psychology, 27*(4), 436–457.

Castillo, R. J. (1997). *Culture and mental illness.* Pacific Grove, CA: ITP.

Caudill, W., & Weinstein, H. (1969). Maternal care and human behavior in Japan and America. *Psychiatry, 32,* 12–43.

Center for the American Woman in Politics. (1987). *Gender gap facts sheet.* New Brunswick, NJ: Center for the American Woman in Politics.

Chandler, T. A., Shama, D. D., Wolf, F. M., & Planchard, S. K. (1981). Multi-attributional causality: A five cross-national samples study. *Journal of Cross-Cultural Psychology, 12,* 207–221.

Chao, R. K. (1996). Chinese and European American mother's beliefs about the role of parenting in children's school success. *Journal of Cross-Cultural Psychology, 27,* 403–423.

Chernyaev, A. (1993). *Shest let s Gorbachevym. [Six years with Gorbachev].* Moscow: April.

Cheung, F. M., Leung, K., Fan, R. M., Song, W. Z., Zhang, J. X., & Chang, J. P. (1996). Development of the Chinese personality assessment inventory (CPAI). *Journal of Cross-Cultural Psychology, 27,* 181–199.

Chiasson, N., Dube, L., & Blondin, J. -P. (1996). Happiness: A look into the folk psychology of four cultural groups. *Journal of Cross-Cultural Psychology, 27*(6), 673–691

Child, I. E. (1969). Esthetic. In G. Lindsey & E. Aronson (Eds.), *The handbook of social psychology* (Vol. 3, pp. 853–916). Reading, MA: Addison-Wesley.

Chinoy, I., & Babington, C. (1998). Low-income players feed lottery cash cow. *The Washington Post,* May 3, A1.

Chi-Ying Chung, R., Walkey, F., & Bemak, F. (1997). A Comparison of achievement and aspirations of New Zealand, Chinese, and European students. *Journal of Cross-Cultural Psychology, 28*(4), 481–489.

Cho, Y., & Kim, Y. (1993). The cultural roots of entrepreneurial bureaucracy: The case of Korea. *Public Administrative Quarterly, 16,* 509–524.

Chomsky, N. (1976). The fallacy of Richard Herrnstein's IQ. In N. J. Block & G. Dworkin (Eds.), *The IQ controversy* (pp. 285–298). New York: Pantheon Books.

Cialdini, R., Schaller, M., Houlihan, D., Arps, K., Fultz, J., & Beaman, A. (1975). Reciprocal confessions procedure for inducing compliance: The door-to-face technique. *Journal of Personality and Social Psychology, 31,* 206–215.

Cialdini, R., Reno, R., & Kallgren, C. (1990). A focus theory of normative conduct: Recycling the concept of norms to reduce littering in public places. *Journal of Personality and Social Psychology, 58,* 1015–1029.

Ciborski, T., & Choi, S. (1974). Nonstandard English and free recall: An exploratory study. *Journal of Cross-Cultural Psychology, 5*(3), 271–279.

Clark, H., & Clark, E. (1980). Pain response in Nepalese porters. *Science, 209,* 410–412.

Clementson, L. (1998). Caught in the cross-fire. *Newsweek,* December 14, 38–39.

Clore, G. L., Schwarz, N., & Conway, M. (1994). Affective causes and consequences of social information processing. In R. S. Wyer & T. K. Strull (Eds.), *Handbook of social cognition* (Vol. 1, pp. 323–417). Hillsdale, NJ: Erlbaum.

Cockerham, W., Kunz, G., & Lueschen, G. (1988). Social stratification and health styles in two systems of health care delivery: A comparison of the United States and West Germany. *Journal of Health and Social Behavior, 29,* 113–126.

Cogan, J. (1977). Hate crimes and women's health lead agenda. *SPSSI Newsletter,* May, 12–13.

Cogan, J., Bhalla, S., Sefa-Dedeh, A., & Rothblum, E. (1996). A comparison study of United States and African students on perceptions of obesity and thinness. *Journal of Cross-Cultural Psychology, 27*(1), 98–113.

Cohen, D., & Nisbett, R. E. (1994). Self-protection and culture of honor: Explaining southern violence. *Personality and Social Psychology Bulletin, 20,* 551–567.

Cohen, L. (Ed.). (1977). *Statistical Power Analysis for the Behavioral Sciences.* San Diego, CA: Academic Press.

Cole, M. (1996). *Cultural psychology: A once and future discipline.* Cambridge, MA: Belknap/Harvard.

Colleau, S., Glynn, K., Lybrand, S., Merelman, R., Mohan, P., & Wall, J. (1990). Symbolic racism in candidate evaluation: An experiment. *Political Behavior, 12*(4), 385–402.

Collings, G. (1989). Stress containment through meditation. *Prevention in Human Services, 6,* 141–150.

Collins, B. E. (1974). Four components of the Rotter internal-external scale: Belief in a difficult world, a just world, a predictable world, a politically responsive world. *Journal of Personality and Social Psychology, 29,* 381–391.

Connell, R. (1971). *The child's construction of politics.* Carlton, Victoria: Melbourne University Press.

Connell, R. (1972). Political socialization and the American family: The evidence re-examined. *Public Opinion Quarterly, 36,* 323–333.

Cook, P. (1994). Chronic illness beliefs and the role of social networks among Chinese, Indian, and Anglo-celtic Canadians. *Journal of Cross-Cultural Psychology, 25*(4), 452–465.

Coon, C. (1946). The universality of natural groupings in human societies. *Journal of Educational Sociology, 20,* 162–168.

Coon, D. (1998). *Introduction to psychology.* Pacific Grove, CA: Brooks/Cole.

Cooper, J. (1996). The end of the affair. *Middle East Economic Digest, 40,* 2.

Cooper, K. J. (1999). Students weak in essay skills, *The Washington Post,* September 29, A3.

Coopersmith, S. (1967). *The antecedents of self-esteem.* San Francisco: Freeman.

Coren, S. (1992). *The left-hander syndrome.* New York: Free Press.

Costa, P. T., & McCrae, R. M. (1997, May). Personality trait structure as a human universal. *American Psychologist, 52*(5), 509–516.

Cowley, G. (1996). The biology of beauty. *Newsweek,* June 3, 61–66.

Cox, H. G. (1988). *Later life: The realities of aging*. Englewood Cliffs, NJ: Prentice Hall

Crain, R., & Weissman, C. (1972). *Discrimination, personality, and achievement: A survey of northern blacks*. New York: Seminar Press.

Crittenden, K., & Lamug, C. (1988). Causal attribution and depression. *Journal of Cross-Cultural Psychology, 19*(2), 216–231.

Crittenden, K., Fugita, S., Bae, H., Laming, C., & Lin, C. (1992). A cross-cultural study of self-report depressive symptoms among college students. *Journal of Cross-Cultural Psychology, 23*(2), 163–178.

Crock, F., & Mitchison, G. (1983). The function of dream sleep. *Nature, 304*, 111–114.

Cutler, N. (1975). Toward a generational conception of political socialization. In D. Schwartz & S. Schwartz (Eds.), *New directions in political socialization*. New York: The Free Press.

Dabbis, J., & Morris, R. (1990). Testosterone, social class, and antisocial behavior in a sample of 4,462 men. *Psychological Science, 1*, 209–211.

Daly, M., & Wilson, M. (1988). Evolutionary social psychology and family homicide. *Science, 242*, 519–524.

Darley, J., & Batson, D. (1973). From Jerusalem to Jericho: A study of situational and dispositional variables in helping behavior. *Journal of Personality and Social Psychology, 27*, 100–108.

Darley, J. M., & Fazio, R. H. (1980). Expectancy confirmation processes arising in the social interaction sequence. *American Psychologist, 35*, 867–881.

Darwin, C. (1872/1979). *The expression of the emotions in man and animals*. London: John Muray/Julan Friedman; New York: Philosophical Library.

Darwin, C. (1953). *The next million years*. Garden City, NY: Doubleday.

Dasen, P. (1975). Concrete operational development in three cultures. *Journal of Cross-Cultural Psychology, 6*(2), 156–163.

Dasen, P. R. (1984). The cross-cultural study of intelligence: Piaget and the Baoule. *International Journal of Psychology, 19*, 407–434.

Dasen, P., Berry, J., & Witkin, H. (1979). The use of developmental theories cross-culturally. In L. Eckenberg, Y. Poortinga, & W. Lonner (Eds.), *Cross-cultural contributions to psychology*. Amsterdam: Swets & Zeitlinger.

Dasen, P. R. (1994). Culture and cognitive development from a Piagetian perspective. In W. J. Lonner & R. Malpass (Eds.), *Psychology and culture*. Boston: Allyn & Bacon.

Davenport, W. (1976). Sex in cross-cultural perspective. In F. A. Beach (Ed.), *Human sexuality in four perspectives* (pp. 115–163). Baltimore: Johns Hopkins University Press.

Davidoff, H. (1952). *The pocket book of quotations*. New York: Pocket Books.

Davidson, R. (1992). Emotion and affective style: Hemispheric substances. *Psychological Science, 3*, 39–43.

Davies, J. (1963). *Human nature in politics*. New York: Wiley.

Davis, D. (1995). Exploring black political intolerance. *Political Behavior, 17*(1), 1–15.

Davis, J., & Ginsburg, H. (1993). Similarities and differences in the formal and informal mathematical cognition of African, American and Asian Children: The role of schooling and social class. In J. Altarriba (Ed.), *Cognition and culture: A cross-cultural approach to cognitive psychology* (pp. 343–360). Amsterdam: Elsevier Science.

Dawes, R. M. (1994). *House of cards: Psychology and psychotherapy built on myth*. New York: Free Press.

Dawson, J. (1975). Socioeconomic differences in size judgments of discs and coins by Chinese primary VI children in Hong Kong. *Perceptual and Motor Skills, 41*, 107–110.

Dawson, R., Prewitt, K., & Dawson, K. (1977). *Political socialization*. Boston: Little, Brown.

Deci, E. L. (1972). Effects of contingent and non-contingent rewards and controls on intrinsic motivation. *Organizational Behavior and Human Performance, 8*, 217–229.

Delli Carpini, M. (1989). Age and history: Generations and sociopolitical change. In R. Sigel (Ed.), *Political learning in adulthood: A sourcebook of theory and research*. Chicago: The University of Chicago Press.

Deregowski, J. B. (1974). Teaching African children pictorial depth perception: In search of a method. *Perception, 3*, 309–312.

Deregowski, J., & Munro, D. (1974). An analysis of "Polyphasic Pictorial Perception." *Journal of Cross-Cultural Psychology, 5*(3), 329–339.

Deregowski, J. B., Muldrow, E. S., and Muldrow, W. F. (1972). Perceptual recognition in a remote Ethiopian population. *Perception, 1*, 417–425.

Desjaralis, R., Eisenberg, L., Good, B., & Kleiman, A. (1995). *World mental health: Problems and priorities*. New York: Oxford University Press.

Dettwyler, K. A. (1989). Style of infant feeding. Parental/caretaker control of food consumption in young children. *American Anthropologist, 91*, 696–703.

Deutsch, M., & Gerard, G. (1955). A study of normative and informational social influence upon individual judgment. *Journal of Abnormal and Social Psychology, 51*, 629–636.

Devine, P. G. (1989). Stereotypes and prejudice: Their automatic and controlled components. *Journal of Cross-Cultural Psychology, 9*, 259–284.

Diaz-Gueffero, R. (1975). *Psychology of the Mexican*. Austin, TX: University of Texas Press.

Diaz-Guerrero, R. (1979). The development of coping style. *Human Development, 2*, 320–331.

Dickerman, M. (1993). Reproductive strategies and gender construction: An evolutionary view of homosexuals. *Journal of Homosexuality, 24*, 55–71.

Dickson, D. H., & Kelly, I. W. (1985). The "Barnum Effect" in personality assessment: A review of the literature. *Psychological Reports, 57*, 367–382.

Dion, K. (1990). Stereotyping physical attractiveness. *Journal of Cross-Cultural Psychology, 21*(3), 378–398.

Disraeli, B. (1850). *Vivian Grey*. New York: Harvard Publishing Co.

Dogan, M. (1990). *How to compare nations: Strategies in comparative politics*. Chatham, NJ: Chatham Publishers.

Doi, T. (1989). The concept of Amae and its psychoanalytic applications. *International Review of Psychoanalysis, 16*, 349–354.

Dolan, K. (1995). Attitudes, behavior, and the influence of the family: A reexamination of the role of family structure. *Political Behavior, 17*(3), 251–265.

Dole, A. (1995). Why not drop race as a term? *American Psychologist, 50*(1), 40.

Dollard, J., Doob, L., Miller, N., Mowrer, O., & Sears, R. (1939). *Frustration and aggression*. New Haven, CT: Yale University Press.

Domino, G. (1986). Sleep in advanced age: A comparison of Mexican American and Anglo American elderly. *Hispanic Journal of Behavioral Sciences, 8*, 259–273.

Domino, G. (1992). Cooperation and competition in Chinese and American children. *Journal of Cross-Cultural Psychology, 23*(4), 456–467.

Domino, G., & Hannah, M. T. (1987). A comparative analysis of social values of Chinese and American children. *Journal of Cross-Cultural Psychology, 18*(1), 58–77.

Dong, Q., Weisfeld, G., Boardway, R., & Shen, J. (1996). Correlations of social status among Chinese adolescents. *Journal of Cross-Cultural Psychology, 27*(4), 476–493.

Doob, L. W. (1971) *Patterning of time*. New Haven, CT and London: Yale University Press.

Douglas, J., & Bloomfield, J. (1968). *Children under five*. London: Allen & Unwin.

Doyle, A. -B., & Aboud, F. (1988). Developmental patterns in the flexibility of children's ethnic attitudes. *Journal of Cross-Cultural Psychology, 19*(1), 3–18.

Draguns, J. G. (1980). Psychological disorders of clinical severity. In H. Triandis & J. G. Draguns (Eds.), *Handbook of cross-cultural psychology* (Vol. 6, pp. 99–174). Boston: Allyn & Bacon.

Draguns, J. G. (1996). Multicultural and cross-cultural assessment of psychological disorder: Dilemmas and decisions. In J. Impara & G. R. Sodowsky (Eds.), *Buros-Nebraska Symposium on Motivation and Testing* (pp. 37–84). Lincoln, NE: Buros Institute of Mental Measurements.

D'Souza, D. (1995). *The end of racism*. NY: Free Press.

Duda, J. (1986). Perceptions of sport success and failure among white, black, and Hispanic adolescents. In J. Watkins, T. Reilly, & L. Burwitz (Eds.), *Sport science* (pp. 214–222). London: E. & F. N. Spon.

Dukas, H., & Hoffman, B. (Eds.). (1979). *Albert Einstein: The human side*. Princeton, NJ: Princeton University Press.

Durkheim, E. (1924 /1974) *Sociology and Philosophy*. New York: Free Press

Durkheim, E. (1897/1964). *Suicide*. New York: Free Press

Durodoye, B. (1997). Factors of marital satisfaction among African American couples and Nigerian male/African American female couples. *Journal of Cross-Cultural Psychology, 28*(1) 71–80.

Dyal, J. (1984). Cross-cultural research with the locus of control construct. In H. Lefcourt (Ed.), *Research with the locus of control construct* (Vol. 3, pp. 209–306). New York: Academic Press.

Dziurawiec, S., & Deregowski, J. (1992). "Twisted perspective" in young children's drawings. *British Journal of Developmental Psychology, 10*, 35–49.

Eagly, A. (1995). The science and politics of comparing women and men. *American Psychologist, 50*(3), 145–158.

Earley, P. (1989). Social loafing and collectivism: A comparison of the United States and the People's Republic of China. *Administrative Science Quarterly, 34*, 565–581.

Easton, D., & Dennis, J. (1967). The child acquisition of regime norms: Political efficacy, *American Political Science Review, 6*, 25–30.

Easton, D., & Dennis, J. (1969). *Children in the political system: Origins of political legitimacy*. New York: Mc-Graw-Hill.

Eckhardt, W. (1971a). Conservatism, east and west. *Journal of Cross-Cultural Psychology, 2*(2), 109–128.

Eckhardt, W. (1971b). Eastern and western religiosity. *Journal of Cross-Cultural Psychology, 2*(3), 283–291.

Edelman, R., Asendroff, J., Contarello, A., Zammuner, V., Georgas, J., & Villanueva, C. (1989). Self-reported expression of embarrassment in five European cultures. *Journal of Cross-Cultural Psychology, 20*(4), 357–371.

Edman, J., & Kameoka, V. (1997). Cultural differences in illness schemas. *Journal of Cross-Cultural Psychology, 28*(3), 252–265.

Edsall, T. (1998). Candidates find virtue in chastity as an issue. *The Washington Post*, September 28, A11.

Ehrlich, E., & De Bruhl, M. (1996). *The international thesaurus of quotations*. New York: Harper Perennial (Harper Collins).

Ekman, P. (1980). *The face of man*. New York: Garland Press.

Ekman, P. (1982). *Emotion in the human face*. New York: Cambridge University Press.

Ekman, P. (1994). Strong evidence of universals in facial expression: A reply to Russall's mistaken critique. *Psychological Bulletin, 115*, 268–278.

Ekman, P., & Friesen, W. V. (1969). The repertoire of nonverbal behavior: Categories, origins, usage and coding. *Semiotica, 1*, 49–98.

Ekman, P., & Friesen, W. V. (1975). *Unmasking the face*. Englewood Cliffs, NJ: Prentice Hall.

Ekman, P., & Friesen, W. V. (1978). *The facial action coding system*. Palo Alto, CA: Consulting Psychologists Press.

Ekman, P., & Oster, H. (1979). Facial expressions of emotions. *Annual Review of Psychology, 30*, 527–554.

Ekman, P., Friesen, W. V., O'Sallivan, M., Diacoanni-Tarlatris, I., Krause, R., Pitcarin, T., Schrer, K., Chan, A., Heider, K., LeCompte, W., Ricc -Bitti, P., & Tomita, M. (1987). Universals and cultural differences in the judgments of facial expressions of emotion. *Journal of Personality and Social Psychology, 17*, 124–129.

Ekman, P., Levenson, R., & Friesen, W. (1983). Autonomic nervous system activity distinguishes between emotions. *Science, 221*, 1208–1210.

Elbedour, S., Shulman, S., & Kedem, P. (1997). Adolescent intimacy: A cross-cultural study. *Journal of Cross-Cultural Psychology, 28*(1), 5–22.

Ellenbogen, G. C. (Ed.). (1996). *More oral sadism and the vegetarian personality: Readings from the Journal of Polymorphous Perversity*. New York: Brunner/Mazel.

Ellsworth, P. (1994). Senses, culture, and sensibility. In S. Kitayama & H. Markus (Eds.), *Emotion and culture: Empirical studies of mutual influence* (pp. 23–50). Washington, DC: American Psychological Association.

El Zahhar, N., & Hocevar, D. (1991). Cultural and sexual differences in test anxiety, trait anxiety, and arousability: Egypt, Brazil, and the United States. *Journal of Cross-Cultural Psychology, 22* (2), 238–249.

Ember, C., & Ember, M. (1990). *Anthropology*. Englewood Cliffs, CA: Prentice Hall.

Emerson, R. W. (1866). *Essays, first series*. Boston, MA: Ticknor & Fields.

Erikson, E. H. (1950). *Childhood and society*. New York: Norton.

Erikson, E. (1968). *Identity: Youth and crisis*. New York: Norton.

Erikson, E. (1977). *Toys and reasons: Stages in the ritualization of experience*. New York: Norton.

Erinosho, O. (1978). Sociocultural antecedents of magical thinking in a modernizing African society. *Journal of Cross-Cultural Psychology, 9*(2), 201–209.

Erskine, H. (1971). The polls: Women's role. *Public Opinion Quarterly, 35*, 275–290.

Estes, C. P. (1992). *Women who run with the wolves*. New York: Ballantine Books.

Evans, G. W., Palsane, M. N., & Carrere, S. (1987). Type A behavior and occupational stress: A cross-cultural study of blue-collar workers. *Journal of Personality and Social Psychology, 52*, 1002–1007.

Farver, J. A., Welles-Nystrom, B., Frosch, D., Wimbarti, S., & Hoppe-Graff, S. (1997). Toy stories: Aggression in children's narratives in the United States, Sweden, Germany, and Indonesia. *Journal of Cross-Cultural Psychology, 28*(4), 393–420.

Feldman, K., & Newcomb, T. (1971). *The impact of college on students: An analysis of four decades of research*. San Francisco: Jossey-Bass.

Feldman, O. (1996). The political personality in Japan: An inquiry into the belief system of Diet members. *Political Psychology, 17*, 657–682.

Feldman, R. S., & Prohaska, T. (1979). The student as Pygmalion: Effect of student expectation on the teacher. *Journal of Educational Psychology, 71*, 485–493.

Feldman, R. S., & Theiss, A. J. (1982). The teacher and student as Pygmalions: Joint effects of teacher and student expectations. *Journal of Educational Psychology, 74*, 217–223.

Ferguson, G. A. (1956). On transfer and abilities of man. *Canadian Journal of Psychology, 10*, 121–131.

Fersch, E. A. (1980). *Psychology and psychiatry in courts and corrections*. New York: Wiley.

Feshbach, S., & Weiner, B. (1986). *Personality* (2nd ed.). Lexington, MA: Heath.

Festinger, L. (1957). *A theory of cognitive dissonance*. Stanford: Stanford University Press.

Fiedler, F. (1964). A contingency model of leadership effectiveness. In L. Berkowitz (Ed.), *Advances in experimental social psychology* (Vol. 1, pp. 149–190). New York: Academic Press.

Fischer, C. S., Hout, M., Jankowski, M. S., Lucas, S. R., Swidler, A., & Voss, K. (1996). *Inequality by design: Cracking the bell curve myth*. Princeton, NJ: Princeton University Press.

Fiske, S. T., & Taylor, S. E. (1984). *Social cognition*. Reading, MA: Addison-Wesley.

Fiske, S. T., & Taylor, S. E. (1991). *Social cognition* (2nd ed.). New York: McGraw-Hill.

Fletcher, G. J. O., & Ward, C. (1988). *Attribution theory and process: A cross-cultural challenge to social psychology*. Beverly Hills, CA: Sage.

Fletcher, M. (1999). Affirmative action plan challenged: Group sues Atlanta on contract policy. *The Washington Post*, August 27, A10.

Flynn, J. (1987). Massive IQ gains in fourteen nations: What IQ tests really measure. *Psychological Bulletin, 101*, 171–191.

Flynn, J. (1991). *Asian-Americans: Achievement beyond IQ*. Hillsdale, NJ: Erlbaum.

Foa, U. (1987). Interrelation of social resources. *Journal of Cross-Cultural Psychology, 18*(2), 221–233.

Fogarty, G., & White, C. (1994). Differences between values of Australian Aboriginal and non-Aboriginal students. *Journal of Cross-Cultural Psychology, 25*(3), 394–408.

Forer, B. R. (1949). The fallacy of personal validation: A classroom demonstration of gullibility. *Journal of Abnormal and Social Psychology, 44*, 118–123.

Foulkes, D. (1985). *Dreaming: A cognitive-psychological analysis*. Hillsdale, NJ: Erlbaum.

Fowers, B. J., & Richardson, F. C. (1996). Why is multiculturalism good? *American Psychologist, 51*, 609–621.

Foxall, G. R., & Payne, A. F. (1989). Adaptors and innovators in organizations: A cross-cultural study of the cognitive styles of managerial functions and subfunctions. *Human Relations, 42*, 639–649.

Fraczek, A. (1985). Moral approval of aggressive acts. *Journal of Cross-Cultural Psychology, 16*(1), 41–54.

Frager, R. (1970). Conformity and anti-conformity in Japan. *Journal of Personality and Social Psychology, 15*, 203–210.

Frager, R., & Wood, L. (1992). Are the rules of address universal? *Journal of Cross-Cultural Psychology, 23*(2), 148–162.

Frake, C. (1980). The ethnographic study of cognitive systems. In C. Frake (Ed.), *Language and cultural descriptions* (pp. 1–17). Stanford: Stanford University Press.

Fredrickson, G. (1981). *White supremacy: A comparative study of American and South African history.* Oxford: Oxford University Press.

Freeman, M. (1997). Democratic correlations of individualism and collectivism: A study of social values in Sri Lanka. *Journal of Cross-Cultural Psychology, 28*(3), 321–341.

Freud, A. (1946). *The ego and the mechanisms of defense.* New York: International Universities Press.

Freud, S. (1920). *A general introduction to psychoanalysis.* New York: Boni and Liveright.

Freud, S. (1938a). *A general introduction to psycho-analysis.* New York: Archer.

Freud, S. (1938b). *The basic writings of Sigmund Freud.* New York: Random House.

Frey, C., & Hoppe-Graff, S. (1994). Serious and playful aggression in Brazilian boys and girls. *Sex Roles, 30,* 249–268.

Friedman, M., & Rosenman, R. H. (1959). Association of specific overt behavior pattern with blood and cardiovascular findings—blood cholesterol level, blood clotting time, incidence of *arcus senilis,* and clinical coronary blood disease. *Journal of the American Medical Association 162,* 1286–1296.

Frijda, N. H. (1986). *The emotions.* Cambridge: Cambridge University Press.

Frijda, N. H., & Mesquita, B. (1994). The social roles and functions of emotions. In S. Kitayama & H. Markus (Eds.), *Emotion and culture: Empirical studies of mutual influence* (pp. 51–88). Washington, DC: American Psychological Association.

Frijda, N. H., Markam, S., Sato, K., & Wiers, R. (1995). Emotions and emotion words. In J. A. Russell, A. S. R. Manstead, J. C. W., & J. M. Fernandes-Dols (Eds.), *Everyday conceptions of emotion: An introduction to the psychology, anthropology and linguistics of emotion* (pp. 121–143). Dordrecht: Kluwer.

Frijda, N. H., Mesquita, B., Sonnemans, J., & Van Goozen, S. (1991). The duration of affective henomena or emotions, sentiments and passions. In K. Strongman (Ed.), *International review of studies of emotion* (Vol. 1, pp. 197–225). Chichester, England: Wiley and Sons.

Frisch, R. E., & Revelle, R. (1970). Height and weight at menarche and a hypothesis of critical body weights and adolescent events. *Science, 169,* 397–398.

Fry, D. (1988). Intercommunity differences in aggression among Zapotec children. *Child Development, 59,* 1008–1019.

Fujneman, Y., Willemsen, M., & Poortinga, Y. (1996). Individualism-collectivism: An empirical study of a conceptual issue. *Journal of Cross-Cultural Psychology, 27*(4), 381–402.

Furnham, A., & Bochner, S. (1986). *Culture shock.* London: Methuen

Furnham, A., Kirkcaldy, B., & Lynn, R. (1994). National attitudes to competitiveness, money, and work among young people: First, second, and third world differences. *Human Relations, 47*(1), 119–132.

Futuyma, D. J. (1979). *Evolutionary biology.* Sunderland, MA: Sinauer.

Gabrenya, W., Wang, Y., & Lataner, B. (1985). Social loafing on an optimizing task. *Journal of Cross-Cultural Psychology, 16*(2), 223–242.

Gabrieldis, C., Stephan, W., Ybarra, O., Dos Santos Pearson, V. M., & Villareal, L. (1997). Preferred styles of conflict resolution. Mexico and the United States. *Journal of Cross-Cultural Psychology, 28*(6), 661–677.

Gallimore, R. (1974). Affiliation motivation and Hawaiian-American achievement. *Journal of Cross-Cultural Psychology, 5*(4), 481–489.

Gardiner, H., Mutter, J., & Kosmitzki, C. (1998). *Lives across cultures: Cross-cultural human development.* Boston: Allyn & Bacon.

Gardner, H. (1983). *Frames of mind: The theory of multiple intelligencies.* New York: Basic Books.

Geary, D., Fan, L., & Bow-Thomas, C. (1992). Numerical cognition: Loci of ability differences comparing children from China and the United States. *Psychological Science, 3,* 180–185.

Geary, D. (1995). Reflections of evolution and culture in children's cognition: Implications for mathematical development and instruction. *American Psychologist, 50*(1), 24–37.

Georgas, J., Poortinga, Y., Angleitner, A., Goodwin, R., & Charalambous, N. (1997). The relationship of family bonds to family structure and function across cultures. *Journal of Cross-Cultural Psychology, 28*(3), 303–320.

Gergen, K., & Black, K. (1965). Aging, time perspective, and preferred solutions to international conflicts. *Journal of Conflict Resolution, 9,* 177–186.

Gergen, K. J., Guierce, A., Lock, A., & Misra, G. (1996). Psychological science in cultural context. *American Psychologist, 51,* 496–503.

Gielen, U., Adler, L., & Milgram, N. (1992). *Psychology in international perspective.* Amsterdam: Swets & Zeitlinger.

Gilbert, R., & Shiraev, E. (1992). Clinical psychology and psychotherapy in Russia. *Journal of Humanistic Psychology, 32*(3), 28–40.

Gilens, M. (1995). Racial attitudes and opposition to welfare. *The Journal of Politics, 57*(4), 994–1014.

Glad, B. (1980). *Jimmy Carter: In search of the big White House.* New York: Norton.

Glad, B., & Shiraev, E. (Eds.). (1999). *The Russian transformation.* New York: St. Martin's.

Gleick, J. (1987). *Chaos: Making a new science.* New York: Penguin Books.

Glenn, N., & Hefner, T. (1972). Further evidence of aging and party identification. *Public Opinion Quarterly, 36,* 31–47.

Glock, C. (1962). On the study of religious commitment. *Religious Education, 62*(4), 98–110.

Goertzel, T. (1994). Belief in conspiracy theories. *Political Psychology, 15*(4), 731–742.

Goodnow, J. J. (1990). The socialization of cognition: What's involved? In J. W. Stigler, R. A. Shweder, &

G. Herdt (Eds.), *Cultural psychology: Essays on comparative human behavior* (pp. 259–286). Cambridge: Cambridge University Press.

Goodnow, J. J., & Levine, R. A. (1973). The grammar of action: Direction and sequence in children's copying. *Cognitive Psychology, 4,* 82–98.

Gordon, M. (1964). *Assimilation in American life: The role of race, religion, and national origins.* New York: Oxford University Press.

Gottrfried, A. W. (Ed.). (1984). *Home environment and early cognitive development: Longitudinal research.* New York: Academic Press

Gould, S. J. (1994). The geometer of race. *Discover,* November 15, 65–81.

Gould, S. J. (1997). This view of life: Unusual unity. *Natural History, 106,* 20–23, 69–71.

Gozman, L., & Etkind, A. (1992). *The psychology of posttotalitarianism in Russia.* London: Centre for Research into Communist Economies.

Graham, J. L. (1983). Brazilian, Japanese, and American business negotiations. *Journal of International Business Studies, 14,* 47–61.

Graham, J. L., Evenko, L. I., & Rajan, M. N. (1992). An empirical comparison of Soviet and American business negotiations. *Journal of International Business Studies, 23,* 387–418

Graham, J. L., Kim, D., Lin, C., & Robinson, M. (1988). Buyer-seller negotiations around the Pacific Rim: Differences in fundamental exchange processes. *Journal of Consumer Research, 15,* 48–54.

Granvold, D. (Ed.) (1994). *Cognitive and behavioral treatment.* Pacific Grove, CA: Brooks/Cole.

Granzberg, G. (1985). Television and self-concept formation in developing areas. *Journal of Cross-Cultural Psychology, 16*(3), 313–328.

Green, D., & Palmquist, B. (1994). How stable is party identification? *Political Behavior, 16*(4), 437–452.

Greenberg, E. (1981). Industrial democracy and the democratic citizen. *Journal of Politics, 43,* 964–981.

Greenfield, P. M. (1997a). Culture as process: Empirical methods for cultural psychology. In J. W. Berry, Y. H. Poortinga, & J. Pandey (Eds.), *Handbook of cross-cultural psychology: Theory and method* (Vol. 1, pp. 301–346). Needham Heights, MA: Allyn & Bacon.

Greenfield, P. M. (1997b). You can't take it with you. Testing across cultures. *American Psychologist, 52,* 1115–1124.

Greenstein, F. (1965a). *Children and politics.* New Haven, CT: Yale University Press.

Greenstein, F. (1965b). Personality and political socialization: Theories of authoritarian and democratic character. *Annals, 361,* 81–95.

Greenwald, J. (1986). Is there cause for fear of flying? *Time,* January 13, 39–40.

Gregory, R. (1978). *Eye and brain: The psychology of seeing.* New York: McGraw-Hill.

Grey, A., & Kalsched, D. (1971). Oedipus east and west: An exploration via manifest dream content. *Journal of Cross-Cultural Psychology, 2*(4), 337–352.

Griffith, R. C., Miyagi, O., & Tago, A. (1958). The universality of typical dreams: Japanese Americans. *American Anthropologist, 60,* 1173–1179.

Gross, M. (1995). Moral judgment, organizational incentives and collective action in abortion politics. *Political Research Quarterly, 48*(4), 827–836.

Grossman, H. J. (1983). *Classification in mental retardation.* Washington, DC: American Association on Mental Deficiency.

Grubb, H. J. (1992). Intelligence at the low end of the curve: Where are the racial differences? In K. H. Burlew, W. C. Banks, H. P. McAdoo, & D. A. ya Azibo (Eds.), *African American psychology* (pp. 219–228). Newbury Park, CA: Sage.

Grumet, G. (1983). Eye contact: The core of interpersonal relatedness. *Psychiatry, 46,* 172–182.

Gudykunst, W., & Bond, M. H. (1997). Intergroup relations across cultures. In J. W. Berry, M. H. Segall, & C. Kagitcibasi (Eds.), *Handbook of cross-cultural psychology: Social behavior and applications* (Vol. 3, pp. 119–161). Needham Heights, MA: Allyn & Bacon.

Gudykunst, W. B., Nishida, T., & Morisaki, S. (1992). Cultural, relational, and personality influences on uncertainty reduction process. *Western Journal of Speech Communication, 53,* 13–29.

Guida, F., & Ludlow, L. (1989). A cross-cultural study of test anxiety. *Journal of Cross-Cultural Psychology, 20*(2), 178–190.

Gussler, J. (1973). Social change, ecology, and spirit possession among the South African Nguni. In E. Bourguignon (Ed.), *Religion, altered states of consciousness, and social change* (pp. 88–126). Columbus, OH: Ohio State University Press.

Guthrie, G., Masangakay, Z., & Guthrie, H. (1976). Behavior, malnutrition, and mental development. *Journal of Cross-Cultural Psychology, 7*(2), 169–181.

Haidt, J., Koller, S. H., & Dias, M. G. (1993). Affect, culture, and morality, or is it wrong to eat your dog? *Journal of Personality and Social Psychology, 65,* 613–628.

Hall, S. (1916). *Adolescence.* New York: Appleton-Century-Crofts.

Hall, E. T. (1959). *The silent language.* Greenwich, CT: Fawcett.

Hallahan, M., Lee, F., & Herzog, T. (1997). It's not just whether you win or lose, it's also where you play the game: A naturalistic, cross-cultural examination of the positivity bias. *Journal of Cross-Cultural Psychology, 28,* 768–778.

Halonen, J., & Santrock, J. (1995). *Psychology: Contexts of behavior.* Madison, WI: Brown & Benchmark.

Hamilton, D. L. (1979). A cognitive-attributional analysis of stereotyping. In L. Berkowitz (Ed.), *Advances in experimental social psychology* (Vol. 12, pp. 53–81). New York: Academic Press.

Hamilton, D. L. (1981). *Cognitive processes in stereotyping and intergroup behavior.* Hillsdale, NJ: Erlbaum.

Harburg, E., Erfurt, J. C., Hauenstein, L. S., Chape, C., Schull, W. J., & Schork, M. A. (1973). Socio-ecological stress, suppressed hostility, skin-color, and black-white male blood pressure: Detroit. *Psychosomatic Medicine, 35,* 276–296.

Harkness, S. (1992). Human development in psychological anthropology. In T. Schwartz, G. M. White, & C. A. Lutz (Eds.), *New directions in psychological anthropology* (pp. 102–121). New York: Cambridge University Press.

Harkness, S., & Super, C. M. (1992). The developmental niche: A theoretical framework for analyzing the household production of health. *Social Science and Medicine, 38,* 217–226.

Harrington, D. M. (1990). The ecology of human creativity: A psychological perspective. In M. A. Runco & R. S. Albert (Eds.), *Theories of creativity* (pp. 143–169). Newbury Park, CA: Sage.

Harris, B. (1979). Whatever happened to little Albert? *American Psychologist, 34,* 151–160.

Harris, R. J., Schoen, L. M., & Hensley, D. L. (1992). A cross-cultural study of story memory. *Journal of Cross-Cultural Psychology, 23,* 133–147.

Hawton, K. (1992). Suicide and attempted suicide. In E. S. Paykel (Ed.), *Handbook of affective disorders* (2nd ed.). New York: Guilford.

Hayles, R. V. (1991). African-American strength: A survey of empirical findings. In R. Jones (Ed.), *Black psychology* (3rd ed., pp. 379–400). Berkeley: Cobb & Henry.

Heath, S. B. (1983). *Ways with words.* New York: Cambridge University Press.

Hedge, A., & Yousif, Y. (1992). Effects of urban size, urgency, and cost on helpfulness. *Journal of Cross-Cultural Psychology, 23*(1), 107–115.

Hedstrom, L. (1992). Interpersonal style: Contrasting emphases on individuality and group conformity in Japan and America. In U. Gielen, et al. (Eds.), *Psychology in International Perspective.* Amsterdam: Swets & Zeitlinger.

Heider, F. (1959). *The psychology of interpersonal relations.* New York: Wiley.

Heilbroner, R. (1993). Don't let stereotypes warp your judgments. In V. Cyrus (Ed.), *Experiencing race, class, and gender in the United States.* Mountain View, CA: Mayfield.

Heiman, G. (1996). *Basic statistics for the behavioral sciences.* Boston: Houghton Mifflin

Hellas, P., & Lock, A. (1981). *Indigenous psychologies.* London: Academic Press.

Herman, J. L. (1992). *Trauma and recovery: The aftermath of violence. From domestic violence to political terror.* New York: Basic Books

Hermans, J. M., & Kempen, J. G. (1998). Moving cultures: The perilous problems of cultural dichotomies in a globalizing society. *American Psychologist, 53*(10), 1111–1120.

Herrnstein, R. J., & Murray, C. (1994). *The bell curve: Intelligence and class structure in American life.* New York: Free Press.

Herskovits, M. J. (1948). *Man and his works: The science of cultural anthropology.* New York: Knopf.

Hess, R., & Torney, J. (1967). *The development of political attitudes in children.* Chicago: Aldine.

Hess, R. D., Kashiwagi, K., Azuma, H., Price, G. G., & Dickinson, W. P. (1980). Maternal expectation for mastery of developmental tasks in Japan and the United States. *International Journal of Psychology, 15,* 259–271.

Hill, J. (1997). Affirmative action: Roots to success. *Los Angeles Times,* March 13.

Ho, D. (1981). Traditional patterns of socialization in Chinese society. *Acta Psychologica Taiwanica, 23,* 81–95.

Ho, D. (1998). Indigenous Psychologies: Asian Perspectives. *Journal of Cross-Cultural Psychology, 29*(1), 88–103.

Hobson, J. A. (1988). *The dreaming brain.* New York: Basic Books.

Hock, R. (1995). *Forty studies that changed psychology.* Englewood Cliffs, NJ: Prentice-Hall.

Hofstede, G. (1980). *Culture's consequences: International differences in work-related values.* Beverly Hills, CA: Sage.

Hofstede, G. (1991). *Cultures and organizations: Software in the mind.* London: McGraw-Hill.

Hofstede, G. (1996). Gender stereotypes and partner preferences of Asian women in masculine and feminine cultures. *Journal of Cross-Cultural Psychology, 27*(5), 533–546.

Hofstede, G., & Bond, M. H. (1984). Hofstede's cultural dimensions: An independent validation using Rokeach's value survey. *Journal of Cross-Cultural Psychology, 15,* 417–433.

Holcomb, H. R. (1996). Moving beyond just-so stories: Evolutionary psychology as protoscience. *Skeptic, 4*(1), 60–66.

Holtzman, W. (1996). Community psychology and full-service schools in different cultures. *American Psychologist, 52,* 381–389.

Horne, J. (1988). *Why we sleep.* New York: Oxford University Press.

Horowits, R., & Kraus, V. (1984). Patterns of cultural transition. *Journal of Cross-Cultural Psychology, 15*(4), 399–416.

Horwitz, L. (1983). Projective identification in dyads and groups. *International Journal of Group Psychotherapy, 33,* 254–279.

Horwitz, S. (1999). Minority renters face insurance bias. Group reports on "subtle" discrimination. *The Washington Post.* September 29, B1.

Hoskin, M. (1989). Socialization and anti–socialization: The case of immigrants. In R. Sigel (Ed.), *Political learning in adulthood: A sourcebook of theory and research.* Chicago: The University of Chicago Press.

Hovland, C., & Weiss, W. (1951). The influence of source credibility on communication effectiveness. *Public Opinion Quarterly, 15,* 635–650.

Hsu, F. L. K. (1972). *Psychological anthropology.* Cambridge, MA: Schenkman.

Hsu, F. L. K. (1985). The self in cross-cultural perspective. In A. J. Marsella, G. DeVos, & F. L. K. Hsu (Eds.), *Culture and self: Asian and western perspectives* (pp. 24–55). New York: Tavistock.

Huang, L., & Harris, M. (1973). Conformity in Chinese and Americans. *Journal of Cross-Cultural Psychology, 4*(4), 427–434.

Hudson, W. (1960). Pictorial depth perception in subcultural groups in Africa. *Journal of Social Psychology, 2*, 89–107.

Huesmann, L. R. (1982). Television violence and aggressive behavior. In D. Pearl & L. Bouthilet (Eds.), *Television and behavior: Ten years of scientific progress and implications for the 1980s.* Washington, DC: U.S. Government Printing Office.

Huesmann, L. R., Lagerspetz, K., & Eron, L. D. (1983). Intervening variables in the television violence-aggression relation: Evidence from the two countries. *Developmental Psychology, 19*, 71–77.

Hui, C. H. (1982). Locus of control: A review of cross-national research. *International Journal of Intercultural Relations, 6*, 301–323.

Hui, H., & Luk, C. L. (1997). Industrial/organizational psychology. In J. W. Berry, M. H. Segall, & C. Kagitcibasi (Eds.), *Handbook of cross-cultural psychology: Social behavior and applications* (Vol. 3, pp. 371–411). Needham Heights, MA: Allyn & Bacon.

Hunsberger, B. (1995). Religion and prejudice: The role of religious fundamentalism, quest, and right-wing authoritarianism. *Journal of Social Issues, 51*(2), 113–129.

Hunter, J. A., Stringer, M., & Coleman, J. T. (1993). Social explanations and self-esteem in Northern Ireland. *The Journal of Social Psychology, 133*, 643–650

Huntington, S. (1993). Clash of civilizations. *Foreign Affairs, 72*, 22–49.

Hupka, R. (1985). Romantic jealousy and romantic envy. *Journal of Cross-Cultural Psychology, 16*(4), 423–446.

Hupka, R., Buunk, B., Falus, G., Fulgosi, A., Ortega, E., Swain, R., & Tarabrina, N. (1985). Romantic jealousy and romantic envy: A seven-nation study. *Journal of Cross-Cultural Psychology, 16*(4), 423–446.

Hyman, H. (1959). *Political socialization.* Glencoe, IL: The Free Press.

Inkeles, A., & Smith, D. (1974). *Becoming modern: Individual changes in six developing countries.* Cambridge: Harvard University Press.

Irvine, S., & Berry, J. (Eds.). (1983). *Human abilities in cultural context.* Cambridge: Cambridge University Press.

Irvine, S. H. (1983). Testing in Africa and America: The search for routes. In S. H. Irvine & J. W. Berry (Eds.), *Human assessment and cultural factors* (pp. 45–58). New York: Plenum.

Irwin, M., Schafer, G., & Feiden, C. (1974). Emic and unfamiliar category sorting of Mano farmers and U.S. undergraduates. *Journal of Cross-Cultural Psychology, 5*, 407–423.

Iwato, S., & Triandis, H. (1993). Validity of auto- and heterostereotypes among Japanese and American students. *Journal of Cross-Cultural Psychology, 24*(4), 428–444.

Izard, C. E. (1969). The emotions and emotional constructs in personality and culture research. In R. B. Catell (Ed.), *Handbook of modern personality theory.* Chicago: Aldine.

Izard, C. E. (1971). *The face of emotion.* New York: Appleton-Century-Crofts.

Izard, C. E. (1977). *Human emotions.* New York: Plenum.

Jackson, G. (1991). The African genesis of the black perspective in helping. In R. Jones (Ed.), *Black psychology* (3rd ed., pp. 533–558). Berkeley, CA: Cobb & Henry.

Jahoda, G., & Krewer, B. (1997). History of cross-cultural and cultural psychology. In J. W. Berry, Y. H. Poortinga, & J. Pandey (Eds), *Handbook of cross-cultural psychology: Theory and method* (Vol. 1, pp. 1–42). Boston: Allyn & Bacon.

James, W. (1884). What is emotion? *Mind, 19*, 188–205.

Jamieson, D. W., Lydon, J. E., Stewart, G., & Zanna, M. P. (1984). Pygmalion revisited: New evidence for student expectancy effects in the classroom. Paper presented at the meeting of the American Psychological Association.

Jamison, K. R. (1993). *Touched with fire: Manic-depressive illness and the artistic temperament.* New York: Free Press.

Jenkins, A. (1995). *Psychology and African Americans* (2nd ed.). Needham Heights, MA: Allyn & Bacon.

Jennings, M., & Markus, G. (1986). *Yuppie politics. ISR Newsletter* (August). Ann Arbor: University of Michigan.

Jennings, M., & Niemi, R. (1974). *The political character of adolescence: The influence of families and schools.* Princeton: Princeton University Press.

Jennings, M., & Niemi, R. (1981). *Generations and politics.* Princeton: Princeton University Press.

Jensen, A. R. (1973). *Educability and group differences.* London: Methuen.

Jensen, A. R. (1980). *Bias in mental testing.* New York: Free Press.

Jet. (1996). Young woman [Fauziya Kasinga] fleeing African mutilation ritual released in U.S., May 13, v. 89 n. 26 p. 14.

Johnson, D. (1983). Anxiety and social restriction. *Journal of Cross-Cultural Psychology, 14*(4), 439–454.

Johnson, F. (1993). *Dependency in Japanese socialization.* New York: New York University Press.

Jolley, R., Zhi, Z., & Thomas, G. (1998). The development of understanding moods metaphorically expressed in pictures. *Journal of Cross-Cultural Psychology, 29*(2), 358–376.

Jones, E. E., & Nisbett, R. E. (1972). The actor and the observer: Divergent perceptions of the causes of behavior. In E. E. Jones et al. (Eds.), *Attribution: Perceiving the causes of behavior.* Morristown, NJ: General Learning Press.

Jordan, M., & Sullivan, K. (1998). Death of three salesmen—partners in suicide. *The Washington Post*, October 7, A1.

Joshi, M. S., & MacLean, M. (1997). Maternal expectations of child development in India, Japan, and England. *Journal of Cross-Cultural Psychology, 28*(2), 219–234.

Jung, C. G. (1943/1953). Two essays on analytical psychology. In H. Read (Ed.) and F. C. Hull (Trans.),

The collected works of C. G. Jung (Vol. 7, pp. 8–292). Princeton, NJ: Princeton University Press.

Jung, C. G. (1951/1959). Aion: Researches into the phenomenology of the self. In H. Read (Ed.) and F. C. Hull (Trans.), *The collected works of C. G. Jung* (Vol. 9ii, pp. 3–269). Princeton, NJ: Princeton University Press.

Jung, C. G. (1921/1971). Psychological types. In H. Read (Ed.) and F. C. Hull (Trans.), *The collected works of C. G. Jung* (Vol. 6, pp. 3–555). Princeton, NJ: Princeton University Press.

Kagan, J., Kearsley, R. B., & Zealazo, P. (1978). *Infancy: Its place in human development.* Cambridge, MA: Harvard University Press.

Kagitcibasi, C. (1985). Culture of separateness—Culture of relatedness. *Papers in Comparative Studies, 4,* 91–99.

Kagitcibasi, C. (1995). Is psychology relevant to global human development issues? Experience from Turkey. *American Psychologist, 50,* 293–300.

Kagitcibasi, C. (1996). *Family and human development across cultures: A view from the other side.* Mahwah, NJ: Erlbaum.

Kagitcibasi, C. (1997). Individualism and collectivism. In J. W. Berry, M. Segall, & C. Kagitcibasi (Eds.), *Handbook of cross-cultural psychology* (Vol. 3, pp. 1–49). Needham Heights, MA: Allyn & Bacon.

Kahneman, D., & Tversky, A. (1982). The simulation heuristic. In D. Kahneman, P. Slovic, & A. Tversky (Eds.), *Judgment under uncertainty: Heuristics and biases.* New York: Cambridge University Press.

Kalyvas, S. (1994). Hegemony breakdown: The collapse of nationalization in Britain and France. *Politics and Society, 22*(3), 316–348.

Kamin, L. (1976). Heredity, intelligence, politics, and psychology. In N. J. Block & G. Dworkin (Eds.), *The IQ controversy* (pp. 374–382). New York: Pantheon Books.

Kant, I. (1981). *Grounding for the metaphysics of moral* (J. W. Ellington, Trans.). Indianapolis, IN: Hackett Publishing Co. (Original work published 1785.)

Kashima, Y. (1987). Concepts of person: Implications in individualism/collectivism research. In C. Kagitcibsi (Ed.), *Growth and progress in cross-cultural psychology* (pp. 410–424). Lisse, The Netherlands: Swets & Zeitlenger.

Kashima, Y., & Triandis, H. (1986). The self-serving bias in attributions as a coping strategy. *Journal of Cross-Cultural Psychology, 17,* 83–97.

Kassinove, H., Sukhodolsky, D., Eckhardt, C., & Tsytsarev, S. (1997). Development of a Russian state-trait anger expression inventory. *Journal of Clinical Psychology, 53*(6), 543–557.

Kassinove, H. (Ed.). (1995). Anger disorders: Definition, diagnosis, and treatment. Washington DC: Taylor and Francis.

Keating, C. F., Mazur, A., Segall, M., Cysneiros, P. G., Divale, W. T., Kilbride, J. E., Komin, S., Leahy, P., Thurman, B., & Wirsing, R. (1981). Culture and perception of social dominance from facial expressions. *Journal of Personality and Social Psychology, 40,* 615–626.

Keats, D., Keats, J., & Rafael, W. (1976). Concept acquisition in Malaysian bilingual children. *Journal of Cross-Cultural Psychology, 7*(1), 87–99.

Keats, D. M. (1985). Strategies in formal operational thinking: Malaysia and Australia. In I. R. Lagunes & Y. H. Poortinga (Eds.), *From a different perspective: Studies of behavior across cultures* (pp. 306–318). Lisse: Swets & Zeitlinger.

Keen, S. (1986). *Faces of the enemy.* New York: Harper & Row.

Kelley, H. (1986). The process of causal attribution. *American Psychologist, 28,* 107–128.

Kelley, H. H. (1950). The warm-cold variable in first impressions of persons. *Journal of Personality, 18,* 431–439.

Kelley, H. H. (1967). Attribution theory in social psychology. In D. Levine (Ed.), *Nebraska Symposium of Motivation* (Vol. 15, pp. 192–240). Lincoln, NB: University of Nebraska Press.

Kelley, J. (1994). Frustrated Russians cool to the USA. *USA Today,* January 12, 1.

Kelly, M. (1998). Fiddling while DC implodes. *The Washington Post,* August 12, A1.

Keltikangas-Jaervinen, L., & Terav, T. (1996). Social decision-making strategies in individualist and collectivist cultures: A comparison of Finnish and Estonian adolescents. *Journal of Cross-Cultural Psychology, 27*(6), 714–732.

Keltner, D., Ellsworth, P. C., & Edwards, K. (1993). Beyond simple pessimism: Effects of sadness and anger on social perception. *Journal of Personality and Social Psychology, 64,* 740–752.

Kendall, P., & Hammen, C. (1995). *Abnormal psychology.* Boston: Houghton Mifflin.

Kenealy, P., Gleeson, K., Frude, N., & Shaw, W. (1991). The importance of the individual in the "causal" relationship between attractiveness and self-esteem. *Journal of Community and Applied Social Psychology, 1,* 45–56.

Kern, M., & Just, M. (1995). The focus group method, political advertising, campaign news, and the construction of candidate images. *Political Communication, 12,* 127–145.

Keyes, R. (1995). *The wit and wisdom of Harry Truman.* New York: Harper Collins.

Kharchev, D. (Ed.). (1994). *Mnenia o Mire i Mir Mnenii.* [*Opinions about the World and a World of Opinions*] No. 1–4.

Kilbride, J., & Yarczower, M. (1976). Recognition of happy and sad facial expressions among Baganda and U.S. children. *Journal of Cross-Cultural Psychology, 7*(2), 181–192.

Kilbride, J., & Yarczower, M. (1980). Recognition and imitation of facial expressions: A cross-cultural comparison between Zambia and the United States. *Journal of Cross-Cultural Psychology, 11*(3), 281–296.

Kim, U., & Berry, J. W. (1993). *Indigenous psychologies.* Thousand Oaks, CA: Sage

Kinder, D., & Mendelberg, T. (1995). Cracks in American apartheid: The political impact of prejudice among desegregated whites. *The Journal of Politics*, *57*(2), 402–424.

Kitayama, S., & Markus, H. (1991). Culture and the self: implications for cognition, emotion, and motivation. *Psychological Review*, *98*, 224–253.

Kitayama, S., & Markus, H. R. (1995). Culture and self: Implications for internationalizing psychology. In N. R. Goldberg & J. B. Veroff (Eds.), *The culture and psychology reader* (pp. 366–383). New York: New York University Press.

Kivett, V. R. (1991). Centrality of the grandfather role among older rural black and white men. *Journals of Gerontology*, *46*(5), 250–258.

Klein, M. (1946). Notes on some schizoid mechanisms. *International Journal of Psycho-Analysis*, *33*, 433–438.

Kleinman, A. (1978). Clinical relevance of anthropological and cross-cultural research: Concepts and strategies. *American Journal of Psychiatry*, *135*, 427–431.

Kleinman, A. (1986). *Social origins of distress and disease: Depression, neurasthenia, and pain in modern China.* New Haven, CT: Yale University Press.

Klineberg, O. (1938). Emotional expression in Chinese literature. *Journal of Abnormal and Social Psychology*, *33*, 517–520.

Klingelhofer, E. (1971). What Tanzanian secondary school students plan to teach their children. *Journal of Cross-Cultural Psychology*, *2*(2), 189–195.

Kluckhohn, F., & Strodtbeck, F. (1961). *Variations in value orientation.* Evanston, IL: Row & Peterson.

Kluckohn, C. (1951). Values and value orientation in the theory of action. In T. Parsons & E. Shils (Eds.), *Toward a general theory of action.* Cambridge, MA: Harvard University Press.

Knight, G., & Kagan, S. (1977). Acculturation of pro-social and competitive behaviors among second- and third-generation Mexican-American children. *Journal of Cross-Cultural Psychology*, *8*(3), 273–285.

Koenigsberg, R. (1992). *Hitler's ideology.* New York: Library of Social Science.

Kohlberg, L. (1981). *The philosophy of moral development: Moral states and the idea of justice.* San Francisco: Harper & Row.

Kohn, M. (1969). *Class and conformity.* Homewood, IL: Dorsey.

Kohn, M. (1980). Job complexity and adult personality. In N. Smelser & E. Erikson (Eds.), *Themes of work and love in adulthood.* Cambridge, MA: Harvard University Press.

Kohn, M., & Schooler, C. (1983). *Work and personality: An inquiry into the impact of social stratification.* Norwood, NJ: Ablex.

Kon, I. S. (1979). *Psychologya yunosheskogo vozrasta [Psychology of adolescence].* Moscow: Prosveshenie.

Koopman, C. (1997). Political psychology as a lens for viewing traumatic events. *Political Psychology*, *18*(4), 831–847.

Koren, S. (1992). *The left-hander syndrome.* New York: Free Press.

Korten, D. (1971). The life game: Survival strategies in Ethiopian folktales. *Journal of Cross-Cultural Psychology*, *2*(3), 209–224.

Kostenly, K., & Garbarino, J. (1994). Coping with consequences of living in danger: The case of Palestinian children and youth. *International Journal of Behavioral Development*, *17*, 595–611.

Kovalevski, S. (1999). Murder madness bedevils Jamaica. *The Washington Post.* July 29, A13.

Kozan, K., & Ergin, C. (1998). Preference for third party help in conflict management in the United States and Turkey. *Journal of Cross-Cultural Psychology*, *29*(4), 525–539.

Krauss, H. (1970). Social development and suicide. *Journal of Cross-Cultural Psychology*, *1*(2), 159–167.

Krippner, S. (1996). The dream models of the Mapuches in Chile. *Dream Time*, *13*(2), 14–15.

Krus, D., & Rysberg, J. (1976). Industrial managers and NACH. *Journal of Cross-Cultural Psychology*, *7*(4), 491–499.

Kush, J. (1996). Field-dependence, cognitive ability, and academic achievement in Anglo American and Mexican American students. *Journal of Cross-Cultural Psychology*, *27*(5), 561–575.

Kuwano, S., Namba, S., & Schick, A. (1986). A cross-cultural study on noise problems. In A. Schick, H. Hoge, & G. Lazarus-Mainka (Eds.), *Contribution to psychological acoustics* (pp. 371–395). Oldenburg: Universitat Oldenburg.

Lacey, P. (1971). Classificatory ability and verbal intelligence among high-contact Aboriginal and low socioeconomic white Australian children. *Journal of Cross-Cultural Psychology*, *2*(1), 39–49.

Lafferty, W. (1989). Work as a source of political learning. In R. Sigel (Ed.), *Political learning in adulthood: A sourcebook of theory and research.* Chicago: The University of Chicago Press.

Laing, D. G., Preskott, J., Bell, G. A., & Gillmore, A. (1993). A cross-cultural study of taste discrimination with Australians and Japanese. *Chemical Senses*, *18*, 161–168.

Laing, R. D. (1967). *The politics of experience.* New York: Pantheon Books.

Laing, R. D. (1969). *The politics of the family and other essays.* New York: Pantheon Books.

Langaney, A. (1988). *Les hommes, passe, present, conditionnel [The men, past, present, conditional].* Paris: Armand Colin.

Langaney, A., Van Blijenburgh, N. H., & Sanchez-Mazas, A. (1992). *Tous parents, tous differents. [All related, all different].* Paris: Chabaud.

Lange, C. G. (1885/1922). The emotions: A psycho-physiological study. In C. G. Lange & W. James (Eds.), *Psychology classics* (Vol. 1). Baltimore: Williams & Wilkins.

Langgulung, H., & Torrance, E. (1972). The development of causal thinking of children in Mexico and the United States. *Journal of Cross-Cultural Psychology*, *3*, 315–320.

Langton, K. (1969). *Political socialization.* New York: Oxford University Press.

Larsen, K. (1972). Determinants of peace agreement, pessimism-optimism, and expectation of world conflict: A cross-national study. *Journal of Cross-Cultural Psychology, 3*(3), 283–292.

Latane, B., & Nida, S. (1981). Ten years of research on group size and helping. *Psychological Bulletin, 89*(2), 308–324.

Laughlin, C., McManus, J., & d'Aquili, E. (1992). *Brain, symbol, and experience.* New York: Columbia University Press.

Lawrence, J., & Lee, R. E. (1955). *Inherit the wind.* New York: Random House.

Lawson, E. (1975). Flag preference as an indicator of patriotism in Israeli children. *Journal of Cross-Cultural Psychology, 6,* 490–499.

Lazarus, R. S. (1993). From psychological stress to the emotions: A history of changing outlooks. *Annual Review of Psychology, 44,* 1–21.

Leach, M. L. (1975). The effect of training in the pictorial depth perception of Shona children. *Journal of Cross-Cultural Psychology, 6,* 457–470.

LeBon, G. (1896). *The crowd: A Study of the popular mind.* London: Ernest Benn.

Lebra, T. S. (1983). Shame and guilt: A psychocultural view of the Japanese self. *Ethos, 11,* 192–209.

Lee, R., & Ackerman, S. (1980). The sociocultural dynamics of mass hysteria: A case study of social conflict in West Malaysia. *Journal of Cross-Cultural Psychiatry, 43,* 78–88.

Lee, V., & Dengerink, H. (1992). Locus of control in relation to sex and nationality. *Journal of Cross-Cultural Psychology, 23*(4), 488–497.

Lefton, L. (2000). *Psychology.* Boston: Allyn & Bacon.

Legman, D. (1968). *Rationale of the dirty joke.* New York: Grove Press.

Lenart, S. (1994). *Sharing political attitudes: The impact of interpersonal communication and mass media.* Thousand Oaks, CA: Sage.

Lepper, M. R., Ross, L., & Lau, R. R. (1986). Persistence of inaccurate beliefs about the self: Perseverance effects in the classroom. *Journal of Personality and Social Psychology, 50,* 482–491.

Lerner, M. J. (1970). The desire for justice and reactions to victims. In J. McCauley & L. Berkowitz (Eds.), *Altruism and helping behavior.* New York: Academic Press.

Lester, D. (1988). Youth suicide: A cross-cultural perspective. *Adolescence, 23,* 955–958.

Leung, K. (1988). Some determinants of conflict avoidance. *Journal of Cross-Cultural Psychology, 19*(1), 125–136.

Leung, K., & Drasgow, F. (1986). Relation between self-esteem and delinquent behavior. *Journal of Cross-Cultural Psychology, 17*(2), 151–167.

Levenson, R., Ekman, P., Heider, K., & Friesen, W. (1992). Emotion and autonomic nervous system activity in the Minangkabau of West Sumatra. *Journal of Personality and Social Psychology, 62,* 972–988.

Levenson, S. (1979). *You don't have to be in Who's Who to know what's what.* New York: Simon & Schuster.

LeVine, R. (1973). *Culture, behavior, and personality.* Chicago: Aldine.

LeVine, R. (1982). *Culture, behavior, and personality* (2nd ed.). Chicago: Aldine.

LeVine, R., & Bartlett, K. (1984). Pace of life, punctuality, and coronary heart disease in six countries. *Journal of Cross-Cultural Psychology, 15*(2), 233–255.

Levine, J. (1991). The role of culture in the representation of conflict in dreams: A comparison of Bedouin, Irish, and Israeli Children. *Journal of Cross-Cultural Psychology, 22*(4), 472–490.

Levine, R., & Wolff, E. (1992). Social time: The heartbeat of culture. In S. Hurscheberg (Ed.), *One world, many cultures* (pp. 518–524). New York: Macmillan.

Levin, M. (1995). Does race matter? *American Psychologist, 50*(1), 45–46.

Levinson, D. (1978). *The seasons of a man's life.* New York: Knopf.

Levinson, D. (Ed.). (1989). *Family violence in cross-cultural perspective.* Newbury Park, CA: Sage.

Levinson, D., & Simmons, G. (1992). Blacks, schizophrenia, and neuroleptic treatment. *Archives of General Psychiatry, 49,* 165.

Levy, D. A. (1985). Optimism and pessimism: Relationships to circadian rhythms. *Psychological Reports, 57*(3), 1123–1126.

Levy, D. A. (1993). Psychometric infallibility realized: The one-size-fits-all psychological profile. *Journal of Polymorphous Perversity, 10*(1), 3–6.

Levy, D. A. (1997). *Tools of critical thinking: Metathoughts for psychology.* Boston, MA: Allyn & Bacon.

Levy, D. A., Kaler, S. R., & Schall, M. (1988). An empirical investigation of role schemata: Occupations and personality characteristics. *Psychological Reports, 63,* 3–14.

Levy, R. (1996). Essential contrasts: Differences in parental ideas about learners and teaching in Tahiti and Nepal. In S. Harkness & C. M. Super (Eds.), *Parents' cultural belief systems: Their origins, expressions, and consequences* (pp. 123–142). New York: Guilford.

Levy, R. I. (1973). *Tahitians: Mind and experience in the Society Islands.* Chicago: University of Chicago Press.

Lewin, K., Lippitt, R., & White, R. (1939). Patterns of aggressive behavior in experimentally created social climates. *Journal of Social Psychology, 10,* 271–299.

Liddell, C. (1997). Every picture tells a story—or does not? Young South African children interpreting pictures. *Journal of Cross-Cultural Psychology, 28*(3), 266–283.

Liem, R. (1997). Shame and guilt among first-and-second generation Asian Americans and European Americans. *Journal of Cross-Cultural Psychology, 28*(4), 365–392.

Lin, E., & Peterson, C. (1990). Pessimistic explanatory style and response to illness. *Behavioral Therapy and Research, 28,* 243–248.

Lin, Y. N. (1988). Family socioeconomic background, parental involvement and students' academic performance by elementary school children. *Journal of Counseling, 11,* 95–141.

Lindgren, H., & Tebcherani, A. (1971). Arab and American auto- and heterostereotypes: A cross-cultural study of empathy. *Journal of Cross-Cultural Psychology, 2*(2), 173–180.

Lips, H. (1993). Gender and other stereotypes: Race, age, appearance, disability. In V. Cyrus (Ed.), *Experiencing race, class, and gender in the United States.* Mountain View, CA: Mayfield.

Li-Repac, D. (1980). Cultural influences on clinical perception: A comparison between Caucasian and Chinese-American therapists. *Journal of Cross-Cultural Psychology, 11*(3), 327–342.

Lloyd, B., & Easton, B. (1977). The intellectual development of Yoruba children. *Journal of Cross-Cultural Psychology, 8*(1), 3–11.

Lloyd-McGarvey, E., Sheldon-Keller, A., & Canterbury, R. (1999). Date rape on the college campus: Does alcohol use make it excusable? Manuscript under review.

Loehlin, J. (1997). Dysgenesis and IQ. What evidence is relevant? *American Psychologist, 52*(11), 1236–1239.

Lonner, W. J. (1980). The search for psychological universals. In H. C. Triandis & W. W. Lambert (Eds.), *Handbook of cross-cultural psychology: Perspectives* (Vol. 1, pp. 143–204). Boston: Allyn & Bacon.

Lonner, W. J. (1990). The introductory psychology text and cross-cultural psychology: Beyond Ekman, Whorf, and biased I.Q. tests. In D. Keats, D. Monro, & L. Mann (Eds.), *Heterogeneity in cross-cultural psychology: Selected papers from the ninth international conference of the International Association for Cross-Cultural Psychology* (pp. 4–22). Lisse, the Netherlands: Swets & Zeitlinger.

Lonner, W. J. (1992). Does the association need a name change? *Cross-Cultural Psychology Bulletin, 26,* 1.

Lonner, W. J., & Adamopoulos, J. (1997). Culture as antecedent to behavior. In J. W. Berry, Y. H. Poortinga, & J. Pandey (Eds), *Handbook of cross-cultural psychology* (Vol. 1, pp. 43–83). Boston: Allyn & Bacon.

Loose, C. (1999). Racial disparity found in credit rating. *The Washington Post.* September 21, A1.

Lopez, S. R. (1989). Patient variable biases in clinical judgment: Conceptual overview and methodological considerations. *Psychological Bulletin, 106,* 184–204.

Lopez, S. R. (1994). Latinos and the expression of psychopathology: A call for the direct assessment of cultural influences. In C. A. Telles & M. Karno (Eds.), *Mental disorders in Hispanic populations* (pp. 109–127). Los Angeles, CA: UCLA.

Lord, C. G., Ross, L., & Lepper, M. (1979). Biased assimilation and attitude polarization: The effects of prior theories on subsequently considered evidence. *Journal of Personality and Social Psychology, 37,* 2098–2109.

Lorenz, K. (1966). *On aggression.* New York: Harcourt, Brace & World.

Lovell, J., & Stiehm, J. (1989). Military service and political socialization. In R. Sigel (Ed.), *Political learning in adulthood: A sourcebook of theory and research.* Chicago: The University of Chicago Press.

Luria, A. R. (1976). *Cognitive development: Its cultural and social foundations.* Cambridge, MA: Harvard University Press.

Lutz, C. (1982). The domain of emotion words on Ifaluk. *American Ethologist, 9,* 113–128.

Lutz, C. (1988). *Unnatural emotions: Everyday sentiments on a Micronesian atoll and their challenge to western theory.* Chicago: University of Chicago Press.

Lynch, O. M. (1990). The social construction of emotion in India. In O. M. Lynch (Ed.), *Divine passions: The social construct of emotion in India* (pp. 3–34). Berkeley: University of California Press.

Ma, H. K., & Cheung, C. K. (1996). A cross-cultural study of moral stage structure in Hong Kong Chinese, English, and Americans. *Journal of Cross-Cultural Psychology, 27*(6), 700–713.

Maccoby, E., Mathewa, R., & Morton, A. (1954). Youth and political change. *Public Opinion Quarterly, 18,* 23–39.

Macionis, J. (1999). *Sociology.* Englewood Cliffs, NJ: Prentice Hall.

Mackie, D. (1983). The effect of social instruction on conservation of spatial relations. *Journal of Cross-Cultural Psychology, 14*(2), 131–151.

Madsen, M. (1986). Developmental and cross-cultural differences in the cooperative and competitive behavior of young children. *Journal of Cross-Cultural Psychology, 2,* 365–371.

Madsen, M., & Kagan, S. (1973). Mother-directed achievement of children in two cultures. *Journal of Cross-Cultural Psychology, 4*(2), 221–228.

Madsen, M. C. (1971). Developmental and cross-cultural differences in the cooperative and competitive behavior of young children. *Journal of Cross-Cultural Psychology, 2,* 365–371.

Maehr, M., & Nicholls, J. (1983). Culture and achievement motivation: A second look. In N. Warren (Ed.), *Studies in cross-cultural psychology* (Vol. 2, pp. 221–226). London: Academic Press.

Maher, T. (1976). "Need for resolution" ratings for harmonic musical intervals. *Journal of Cross-Cultural Psychology, 7,* 259–276.

Malpass, R. S. (1993). What will become of the association during these times of change? *Cross-Cultural Psychology Bulletin, 27,* I2.

Mandler, G. (1975). *Mind and emotion.* New York: Wiley.

Mann, J. (1992). Cross-cultural differences in rating hyperactive-disruptive behaviors in children. *American Journal of Psychiatry, 149,* 1539–1542.

March, R. M. (1989). No-nos with negotiations with Japanese. *Across the Board, 26,* 44–51.

Margalit, B., & Mauger, P. (1985). Aggressiveness and assertiveness. *Journal of Cross-Cultural Psychology, 16*(4), 497–511.

Mari, S., & Karayanni, M. (1982). Creativity in Arab culture: Two decades of research. *Journal of Creative Behaviour, 16*, 227–238.

Marin, G., & Salazar, J. M. (1985). Determinants of hetero- and autostereotypes: Distance, level of contact, and socioeconomic development in seven nations. *Journal of Cross-Cultural Psychology, 16*(4), 403–422.

Marjoribanks, K., & Jordan, D. (1986). Stereotyping among aboriginal and Anglo-Australians. *Journal of Cross-Cultural Psychology, 17*(1), 17–28.

Markham, R., & Wang, L. (1996). Recognition of emotion by Chinese and Australian children. *Journal of Cross-Cultural Psychology, 27*(5), 616–643.

Markus, H. R., & Kitayama, S. (1991). Culture and self: Implications for cognition, emotion, and motivation. *Psychological Review, 98*, 224–253.

Markus, H. R., & Kitayama, S. (1994a). The cultural shaping of emotion: A conceptual framework. In S. Kitayama & H. Markus (Eds.), *Emotion and culture: Empirical studies of mutual influence* (pp. 339–351). Washington, DC: American Psychological Association.

Markus, H. R., & Kitayama, S. (1994b). The cultural construction of self and emotion: Implications for social behavior. In S. Kitayama & H. Markus (Eds.), *Emotion and culture: Empirical studies of mutual influence* (pp. 89–130). Washington, DC: American Psychological Association.

Marmot, M., & Syme, S. (1976). Acculturation and coronary heart disease in Japanese Americans. *American Journal of Epidemiology, 104*, 225–247.

Marsella, T. (1998). Toward a "global-community psychology": Meeting the needs of a changing world. *American Psychologist, 53*(12), 1282–1291.

Marsella, A., Kinzie, D., & Gordon, P. (1973). Ethnic variations in the expression of depression. *Journal of Cross-Cultural Psychology, 4*(4), 435–458.

Marsella, A., Murray, M., & Golden, C. (1974). Ethnic variations in the phenomenology of emotions. Shame. *Journal of Cross-Cultural Psychology, 5*(3), 312–327.

Marshall, R. (1997). Variances in values of individualism and collectivism across two cultures and three social classes. *Journal of Cross-Cultural Psychology, 28*(4), 490–495.

Marx, K. (1867/1967). *Capital: A critique of political economy*. New York: International Publishers.

Marx, K. (1972). *The essential writings*. New York: Bender

Maslow, A. (1954). *Motivation and personality*. New York: Harper & Row.

Maslow, A. (1970). *Motivation and personality* (2nd ed.). New York: Harper & Row.

Matsuda, N. (1985). Strong, quasi- and weak conformity among Japanese in the modified Asch procedure. *Journal of Cross-Cultural Psychology, 16*, 83–97.

Matsumoto, D. (1992). American-Japanese cultural differences in the recognition of universal expressions. *Journal of Cross-Cultural Psychology, 23*(1), 72–85.

Matsumoto, D. (1994). *People: Psychology from a cultural perspective*. California: Brooks/Cole.

Matsumoto, D. (1996). *Culture and psychology*. Pacific Grove, CA: Brooks/Cole.

Matsumoto, D., Kudoh, T., Scherer, K., & Wallbott, H. (1988). Antecedents of and reactions to emotions in the United States and Japan. *Journal of Cross-Cultural Psychology, 19*(3), 267–286.

Matsumoto, D., Weissman, M., Preston, K., Brown, B., Kupperbush, C. (1997). Context-specific measurement of individualism-collectivism on the individual level: The individualism-collectivism interpersonal assessment inventory. *Journal of Cross-Cultural Psychology, 28* (6), 743–767.

Mauro, R., Sato, K., & Tucker, J. (1992). The role of appraisal in human emotions: A cross-cultural study. *Journal of Personality and Social Psychology, 62*, 301–317.

Mayer, J., & Holms, J. P. (Eds.). (1996). *Bite-size Einstein: Quotations on just about everything from the greatest mind of the twentieth century*. New York: St. Martin's Press.

Mayer, J., Gasche, Y., Braverman, D., & Evans, T. (1992). Mood-congruent judgment is a general effect. *Journal of Personality and Social Psychology, 63*, 119–132.

McAndrew, F., Akande, A., Turner, S., & Sharma, Y. (1998). A cross-cultural ranking of stressful life events in Germany, India, South Africa, and the United States. *Journal of Cross-Cultural Psychology, 29* (6), 717–727.

McArthur, L., & Berry, D. (1987). Cross-cultural agreement in perceptions of baby-faced adults. *Journal of Cross-Cultural Psychology, 18*(2), 165–192.

McClelland, D. C. (1958). The use of measures of human motivation in the study of society. In J. Atkinson (Ed.), *Motives in fantasy, action, and society* (pp. 518–554). Princeton: Van Nostrand,

McClelland, D. C. (1961). *The achieving society*. Princeton: Van Nostrand.

McClelland, D. C. (1987). *Human motivation*. New York: Cambridge University Press.

McCourt, K. (1977). *Working-class women and grass-roots politics*. Bloomington: Indiana University Press.

McGhee, P., & Duffey, N. (1983). Children's appreciation of humor victimizing different racial-ethnic groups. *Journal of Cross-Cultural Psychology, 14*(1), 29–40.

McGinnis, E. (1949). Emotionality and perceptual defense. *Psychological Review, 56*, 244–251.

McGrath, R., Yang, E., & Tsai, W. (1992). Does culture endure, or is it malleable? Issues for entrepreneurial economic development. *Journal of Business Venturing, 7*, 441–458.

McGuire, W. J., & Papageorgis, D. (1961). The relative efficacy of various types of prior belief defense in producing resistance against persuasion. *Journal of Abnormal and Social Psychology, 62*, 327–337.

McIntosh, J. L. (1992). Suicide in the elderly. In B. Bongar (Ed.), *Suicide: Guidelines for assessment, management and treatment*. New York: Oxford University Press.

McLellan, D. (1972). *Karl Marx: His life and thought*. Norwalk, CT: Easton Press.

McLoyd, V. (1998). Socioeconomic disadvantage and child development. *American Psychologist, 53*,(2), 185–204.

McLuhan, M. (1971). *The Gutenberg galaxy: The making of typographic man.* London: Routhledge and Kegan Paul.

McManus, J., Laughlin, C. D., & Shearer, J. S. (1993). The function of dreaming in their cycles of cognition. A biogenic structural account. In A. Moffit, M. Kramer, & R. Hoffmann (Eds.), *The function of dreaming* (pp. 21–50). Albany: SUNY Press.

McShane, D., & Berry, J. (1988). Native North Americans: Indian and Inuit abilities. In S. H. Irvine & J. W. Berry (Eds.), *Human abilities in cultural context* (pp. 385–426). New York: Cambridge University Press.

Mead, M. (1975). Review of Darwin and facial expression. *Journal of Communication, 25,* 209–213.

Meade, R. (1972). Future time perspectives of Americans and subcultures in India. *Journal of Cross-Cultural Psychology, 3*(1), 93–99.

Meehl, P. E. (1956). Wanted—A good cookbook. *American Psychologist, 11,* 262–272.

Meehl, P. E. (1973). Why I do not attend case conferences. In P. E. Meehl (Ed.), *Psychodiagnosis: Selected papers* (pp. 225–302). Minneapolis, MN: University of Minnesota Press.

Menon, U., & Shweder, R. (1994). Kali's tongue: Cultural psychology and the power of shame in Orissa, India. In S. Kitayama & H. Markus (Eds.), *Emotion and culture* (pp. 241–284). Washington, DC: APA.

Merikangas, K., & Weissman, M. (1986). Epidemiology of DSM-III Axis II Personality Disorders. In A. Frances & R. Hales (Eds.), *The American Psychiatric Association annual review.* Washington, DC: American Psychiatric Press.

Merrit, A., & Helmreich, R. (1996). Human factors on the flight deck. *Journal of Cross-Cultural Psychology, 27*(1), 5–24.

Mesquita, B., & Frijda, N. H. (1992). Cultural variations in emotion: A review. *Psychological Bulletin, 112,* 179–204.

Mesquita, B., Frijda, N., & Scherer, K. (1997). Culture and emotion. In J. W. Berry, P. R. Dasen, & T. S. Saraswathi (Eds.), *Handbook of cross-cultural psychology: Basic processes and human development* (Vol. 2, pp. 255–297). Needham Heights, MA: Allyn & Bacon.

Milgram, S. (1963). Behavioral study of obedience. *Journal of Abnormal and Social Psychology, 67,* 371–378.

Miller, A. (1983). For your own good: Hidden cruelty in child-rearing and the roots of violence. New York: Farrar, Strauss, & Giroux.

Miller, D. (1983). The correlates of entrepreneurship in three types of firms. *Management Science, 29,* 770–791.

Miller, J. (1983). *States of mind.* New York: Pantheon Books.

Miller, J. G. (1984). Culture and the development of everyday social explanation. *Journal of Personality and Social Psychology, 46,* 961–978.

Miller, J. G. (1994). Cultural diversity in the morality of caring: Individually oriented versus duty based interpersonal moral codes. *Cross-Cultural Research, 28,* 3–39.

Miller, J. G. (1997). Theoretical issues in cross-cultural psychology. In J. W. Berry, Y. H. Poortinga, & J.

Pandey (Eds.), *Handbook of Cross-Cultural Psychology* (Vol. 1, pp. 301–346). Needham Heights, MA: Allyn & Bacon.

Miner, M., & Rawson, H. (1994). *The new international dictionary of quotations* (2nd ed.). New York: Signet.

Ministry of Health and Welfare of Japan. (1998). *The Washington Post,* October 7, A28.

Minturin, L., & Shashak, J. (1982). Infanticide as a terminal abortion procedure. *Behavioral Science Research, 17,* 70–90.

Mirsky, J., Barasch, M., & Goldberg, K. (1992). Adjustment problems among Soviet immigrants at risk. Part I: Reaching out to members of the 1000 "families" organization. *Israel Journal of Psychiatry Related Sciences, 29,* 135–149.

Mishra, R. C. (1988). Learning strategies among children in the modern and traditional schools. *Indian Psychologist, 5,* 17–24.

Mishra, R. C. (1997). Cognition and cognitive development. In J. W. Berry, P. R. Dasen, & T. S. Saraswathi (Eds.), *Handbook of cross-cultural psychology: Basic processes and human development* (Vol. 2, pp. 143–176). Needham Heights, MA: Allyn & Bacon.

Misra, G., & Gergen, K. J. (1993). On the place of culture in the psychological sciences. *International Journal of Psychology, 28,* 225–243.

Moghaddam, F. (1998). *Social psychology.* New York: Freeman.

Moghaddam, F., Ditto, B., & Taylor, D. (1990). Attitudes and attributions related to psychological symptomatology in Indian immigrant women. *Journal of Cross-Cultural Psychology, 21,* 335–350.

Monroe, K., & Kreidie, L. (1997). The perspective of Islamic fundamentalists and the limits of Rational Choice Theory. *Political Psychology.* 18, 1, 19–44.

Monroe, K. (1995). Psychology and rational actor theory. *Political Psychology, 16*(1), 1–21.

Moos, R. H., & Billings, A. G. (1982). Conceptualizing and measuring coping resources and processes. In L. Goldberger & S. Breznitz (Eds.), *Handbook of stress.* New York: Macmillan.

Moos, R. H., & Schaefer, J. A. (1986). Life transitions and crises. In R. Moss & J. Schaefer (Eds.), *Coping with life crises: An integrated approach.* New York: Plenum Press.

Morelli, G. A., Rogoff, B., Oppenheim, D., & Goldsmith, D. (1992). Cultural variations in infants' sleeping arrangements: Questions of independence. *Developmental Psychology, 28,* 604–613.

Morris, A., Hatchett, S., & Brown, R. (1989). Black political socialization. In R. Sigel (Ed.), *Political learning in adulthood: A sourcebook of theory and research.* Chicago: The University of Chicago Press.

Morris, M. W., & Peng, K. (1994). Culture and cause: American and Chinese attributions for social and physical events. *Journal of Personality and Social Psychology, 67,* 949–971.

Morse, J. M., & Park, C. (1988). Differences in cultural expectations of the perceived painfulness of childbirth. In K. Michaelson (Ed.), *Childbirth in America:*

Anthropological perspectives. South Hardley, MA: Bergin & Garvey.

Moscovici, S. (1981). Foreword. In P. Hellas & A. Lock (Ed.), *Indigenous psychologies.* London: Academic Press.

Moscovici, S., & Zavalloni, M. (1969). The group as a polarizer of attitudes. *Journal of Personality and Social Psychology, 12,* 125–135.

Moskowotz, D., & Stroh, P. (1994). Psychological sources of electoral racism. *Political Psychology, 15*(2), 307–329.

Moss, R. (1996). Dreaming with the Iroquois. *Dream Time, 13*(2), 6–7.

Mukai, T., & McCloskey, L. (1996). Eating attitudes among Japanese and American elementary school girls. *Journal of Cross-Cultural Psychology, 27*(4), 424–435.

Mumford, D. B. (1993). Eating disorders in different cultures. *International Review of Psychiatry, 5,* 109–113.

Mundy-Castle, A. C. (1974). Social and technological intelligence in western and non-western cultures. *Universita, 4,* 46–52.

Munro, D. (1986). Work motivation and values: Problems and possibilities in and out of Africa. *Australian Journal of Psychology, 38,* 285–296.

Munroe, R. L., & Munroe, R. H. (1972). Obedience among children in an East African society. *Journal of Cross-Cultural Psychology, 3*(4), 395–399.

Munroe, R. L., & Munroe, R. H. (1983). Birth order and intellectual performance in East Africa. *Journal of Cross-Cultural Psychology, 14*(1), 3–16.

Munroe, R. L., & Munroe, R. H. (1997). A comparative anthropological perspective. In J. W. Berry, Y. H. Poortinga, & J. Pandey (Eds.), *Handbook of cross-cultural psychology* (Vol. 1, pp. 171–213). Boston: Allyn & Bacon.

Munroe, R. L., Munroe, R. H., & Whiting, B. B. (Eds.). (1981). *Handbook of cross-cultural human development.* New York: Garland.

Munsinger, H. A. (1978). The adopted child's IQ: A critical review. *Psychological Bulletin, 82,* 623–659.

Murphy, H. B. M. (1982a). *Comparative psychiatry: The international and intercultural distribution of mental illness.* New York: Springer-Verlag.

Murphy, H. B. M. (1982b). Culture and schizophrenia. In I. Ali-Assa (Ed.), *Culture and psychopathology* (pp. 251–250). Baltimore: University Park Press.

Murphy, D. (1987). Offshore education: A Hong Kong perspective. *Australian University Review, 30,* 43–44.

Murphy-Bernman, V., Levesque, H., & Bernman J. (1996). U. N. convention on the rights of the child. *American Psychologist, 51,* 1257–1261.

Murray, H. (1938). *Explorations in personality.* New York: Oxford University Press.

Myambo, K. (1972). Shape constancy as influenced by culture, western education, and age. *Journal of Cross-Cultural Psychology, 3*(3), 221–232.

Myers, F. (1979). Emotions and the self. *Ethos, 7,* 343–370.

Myers, D. (1995). *Psychology.* New York: Worth.

Nadler, A., & Ben-Shushan, D. (1989). Forty years later: Long-term consequences of massive traumatization as manifested by holocaust survivors from the city and the kibbutz. *Journal of Consulting and Clinical Psychology, 57,* 287–293.

Naito, T., & Gielen, U. (1992). Tatemae and Honne: A study of moral relativism in Japanese culture. In U. Gielen, L. Adler, & N. Milgram (Eds.), *Psychology in International Perspective.* Amsterdam: Swets & Zeitlinger.

Naroll, R., Benjamin, E., Fohl, F., Fried, M., Hildereth, R., & Schaefer, J. (1971). Creativity: A cross-historical pilot survey. *Journal of Cross-Cultural Psychology, 2*(1), 181–188.

Nasar, J. L. (1984). Visual preferences in urban street scenes. *Journal of Cross-Cultural Psychology, 15,* 79–93.

National Center for Health Statistics. (1995). *The Washington Post Health,* July 11, 13.

Neiser, U., Boodoo, G., Bouchard, T., Boykin, W., Brody, N., Ceci, S., Halpern, D., Loehlin, J., Perloff, R., Sternberg, R., & Urbina, S. (1996). Intelligence: Knowns and unknowns. *American Psychologist, 51*(2), 77–101.

Nevis, E. C. (1983). Cultural assumptions and productivity: The United States and China. *Sloan Management Review, 24,* 17–29.

Nevo, O. (1984). Appreciation and production of humor as an expression of aggression. *Journal of Cross-Cultural Psychology, 15*(2), 181–198.

Newcomb, T. (1943). *Personality and social change: Attitude formation in a student community.* New York: Dryden Press.

Newcomb, T. (1961). *The acquaintance process.* New York: Holt, Reinhart & Winston.

Newman, L. S. (1993). How individuals interpret behavior: Idiocentrism and spontaneous trait inference. *Social Cognition, 11,* 243–269.

Newton, N. (1970). The effect of psychological environment on childbirth: Combined cross-cultural and experimental approach. *Journal of Cross-Cultural Psychology, 1*(1), 85–90.

Nicassio, P. (1983). Psychological correlates of alienation. *Journal of Cross-Cultural Psychology, 14*(3), 337–351.

Nicassio, P. (1985). The psychological adjustment of the Southeast Asian refugee. *Journal of Cross-Cultural Psychology, 16*(2), 153–173.

Nichols, J. (1989). *The competitive ethos and demographic education.* Cambridge, MA: Harvard University Press.

Nicholson, J., Seddon, G., & Worsnop, J. (1977). Teaching understanding of pictorial special relationships to Nigerian secondary school students. *Journal of Cross-Cultural Psychology, 8,* 401–414.

Niles, S. (1998). Achievement goals and means: A cultural comparison. *Journal of Cross-Cultural Psychology, 29*(5), 656–667.

Ninio, A. (1979). The native theory of the infant and other material attitudes in two subgroups in Israel. *Child Development, 50,* 976–980.

Nobles, W. (1991). African philosophy: Foundations for black psychology. In R. Jones (Ed.), *Black psychology* (3rd ed., pp. 47– 63). Berkeley, CA: Cobb & Henry.

Noelle-Neumann, E. (1986). *The spiral of silence: Public opinion—our social skin.* Chicago: University of Chicago Press.

Oberg, K. (1960). Culture shock: adjustment to new cultural environments. *Practical Anthropology, 7,* 177–182.

Offermann, L., & Hellmann, P. (1997). Culture's consequences for leadership behavior: National values in action. *Journal of Cross-Cultural Psychology, 28*(3), 342–351.

Ogbu, J. (1986). The consequences of the American caste system. In U. Neisser (Ed.), *The school achievement of minority children: New perspectives* (pp. 19–56). Hillsdale, NJ: Erlbaum.

Ogbu, J. (1991). Minority coping responses and school experience. *Journal of Psychohistory, 18,* 434–456.

Ogbu, J. (1994). From cultural differences to differences in cultural frames of reference. In P. M. Greenfield & R. R. Cocking (Eds.), *Cross-cultural roots of minority child development* (pp. 365–391). Hillside, NJ: Erlbaum.

Okagaki, L., & Sternberg, R. (1993). Parental beliefs and children's school performance. *Child Development, 64,* 36–56.

Okano, Y., & Spilka, B. (1971). Ethnic identity, alienation, and achievement orientation in Japanese-American families. *Journal of Cross-Cultural Psychology, 2*(3), 273–282.

Okonji, O. M., (1971). A cross-cultural study of the effects of familiarity on classificatory behavior. *Journal of Cross-Cultural Psychology, 2*(1), 3–49.

O'Leary, A. (1990). Stress, emotion, and human immune function. *Psychological Bulletin, 108,* 363–382.

Opotow, S., & Clayton, S. (1994). Green justice: Conceptions of fairness and the natural world. *Journal of Social Issues, 50* (3), 1–11.

Ornstein, R. E. (1977). *The psychology of consciousness.* New York: Penguin Books.

Ortony, A., Clore, J. L., & Collins, A. (1988). *The cognitive structure of emotions.* New York: Cambride University Press.

Osborn, A. (1957). *Applied imagination.* New York: Scribners.

Osherow, N. (1993). Making sense of the nonsensical: An analysis of Jonestown. In E. Aronson (Ed.), *Readings about the social animal* (pp. 68–86). New York: W. H. Freeman.

Osterweil, Z., & Nagano, K. (1991). Maternal views on autonomy. *Journal of Cross-Cultural Psychology, 22*(3), 362–375.

Paige, K. (1973). Women learn to sing the menstrual blues. *Psychology Today,* September, 41.

Papajohn, J., & Spiegel, J. (1971). The relationship of culture value orientation change and Rorschach indices of psychological development. *Journal of Cross-Cultural Psychology, 2*(3), 257–272.

Park, K. (1988). East Asians' responses to western health items. *Journal of Cross-Cultural Psychology, 19*(1), 51–64.

Parker, D., & Deregowski, J. (1990). *Perception and artistic style.* Amsterdam: North-Holland.

Parsons, J., & Goff, S. (1978). Achievement motivation: A dual modality. *Educational Psychologist, 13,* 93–96.

Parsons, T. (1951/1964). *The Social System.* New York: Free Press.

Pascal, B. (1966). *Pensees* (A. J. Krailsheimer, Trans.). Harmondsworth, Middlesex, England: Penguin Books.

Paul, R. A. (1994). My approach to psychological anthropology. In M. M. Suarez-Orozco, G. Spindler, & L. Spindler (Eds.), *The making of psychological anthropology* II (pp. 80–102). Fort Worth, TX: Harcourt Brace.

Pearlstein, S. (1999). Clinton offers regret for "drunks" remark. *The Washington Post,* October 9, A20.

Pedersen, P. (1995). *The five stages of culture shock: Critical incidents around the world.* Connecticut: Greenwood Press.

Pei, M. (1998). Is China democratizing? *Foreign Affairs,* January/February, 68–82.

Pei-te, L. (1994). Ethnicity and political participation: A comparison between Asian and Mexican Americans. *Political Behavior, 16*(2), 237– 264.

Pela, O. (1983). American and Nigerian hospital personnel attitudes toward gerontology patients. *Journal of Cross-Cultural Psychology, 14*(1), 123–127.

Pennock-Roman, M. (1992). Interpreting test performance in selective admissions for Hispanic students. In K. F. Geisinger (Ed.), *Psychological testing of Hispanics* (pp. 95–135). Washington DC: American Psychological Association.

Persidsky, I., & Kelly, J. (1992). Adjustment of Soviet elderly in the United States: An educational approach. *Gerogogics: European Research, 1,* 129–140.

Petersen, A. C. (1988). Adolescent development. *Annual Review of Psychology, 39,* 583–607.

Petitto, A., & Ginsburg, H. (1982). Mental arithmetic in Africa and America: Strategies, principles, and explanations. *International Journal of Psychology, 17,* 81–102.

Petrovsky, A. (1978). *The psychological theory of the collective.* Moscow: Academy of Sciences.

Pfeiffer, W. (1994). *Transkulturele pschiatrie.* Stuttgart, Germany: Thieme

Phillips, D. (1998). Is a culture a factor in air crashes? *The Washington Post,* March 18, A17.

Phinney, J. (1996). When we talk about American ethnic groups, what do we mean? *American Psychologist, 51,* 918–927.

Piaget, J. (1952). *The origins of intelligence in children.* New York: International Universities Press.

Piaget, J. (1954). *The construction of reality in the child.* New York: Basic Books.

Piaget, J. (1963). *The child's conception of the world.* Paterson, NJ: Littlefield, Adams.

Piaget, J. (1970). Piaget's theory. In P. H. Mussen (Ed.), *Carmichael's manual of child psychology* (3rd ed., Vol. 1, pp. 773–847). New York: John Wiley.

Piaget, J. (1972). *The psychology of intelligence.* Totowa, NJ: Littlefield Adams.

Piaget, J., & Weil, A. (1951). The development in children of the idea of the homeland and of relations with other countries. *International Social Science Bulletin, 3,* 561–578.

Pike, K. L. (1967). *Language in relation to a unified theory of the structure of human behavior.* The Hague, the Netherlands: Mouton.

Piker, S. (1998). Contributions of psychological anthropology. *Journal of Cross-Cultural Psychology, 29*(1), 9–31.

Pinto, A., Folkers, E., & Sines, J. (1991). Dimensions of behavior and home environment in school-age children: India and the United States. *Journal of Cross-Cultural Psychology, 22,* 491–508.

Pitkin, J., Myers, D., Simmons, P., & Megbolugbe, I. (1997). *Immigration and housing in the United States: Trends and prospects.* Report of early findings from the Fannie Mae Foundation Immigration Research Project.

Platz, S. G., & Hosch, H. M. (1988). Cross-racial/ethnic eyewitness identification: A field study. *Journal of Applied Social Psychology, 13,* 972–984.

Pliner, P. (1982). The effects of mere exposure on liking for edible substances. *Appetite: Journal for Intake Research, 3,* 283–290.

Pliner, P., & Pelchat, M. (1991). Neophobia in humans and the special status of foods of animal origin. *Appetite: Journal for Intake Research, 16,* 205–218.

Pliner, P., Pelchat, M., & Grabski, M. (1993). Reduction of neophobia in humans by exposure to novel foods. *Appetite: Journal for Intake Research, 20,* 111–123.

Pollack, R. (1963). Contour detectability thresholds as a function of chronological age. *Perceptual and Motor Skills, 17,* 411–417.

Pollock, J. (1975). Early socialization and elite behavior. In D. Schwartz & S. Schwartz (Eds.), *New directions in political socialization.* New York: The Free Press.

Pontius, A. (1997). No gender difference is found in spatial representation by schoolchildren in Northwest Pakistan. *Journal of Cross-Cultural Psychology, 28*(6), 779–786.

Poortinga, Y. H. (1983). Psychometric approaches to intergroup comparison: The problem of equivalence. In S. H. Irvine & J. W. Berry (Eds.), *Human assessment and cultural factors* (pp. 237–257). New York: Plenum.

Poortinga, Y. H. (1997). Towards convergence? In J. W. Berry, Y. H. Poortinga, & J. Pandey (Eds.), *Handbook of cross-cultural psychology: Theory and method* (Vol. I, pp. 347–387). Boston: Allyn & Bacon.

Poortinga, Y. H., & van de Vijver, F. (1994). IACCP or IACP? *Cross-Cultural Psychology Bulletin, 8,* 3–4.

Poortinga, Y. H., & Van der Flier, H. (1988). The meaning of item bias in ability tests. In S. H. Irvine & J. W. Berry (Eds.), *Human abilities in cultural context* (pp. 166–183). New York: Cambridge University Press.

Poortinga, Y. H., van de Vijver, F. J. R., Joe, R. C., & Van de Koppel, J. M. H. (1987). Peeling the onion called culture: A synopsis. In C. Kagitcibasi (Ed.), *Growth and progress in cross-cultural psychology* (pp. 22–34). Lisse, the Netherlands: Swets & Zeitlinger.

Portes, A., & Bach, R. (1985). Latin journey: Cuban and Mexican immigrants in the U.S. Berkeley: University of California Press.

Pratkanis, A. (1988). The attitude heuristic and selective fact identification. *British Journal of Social Psychology, 27,* 257–263.

Price-Williams, D. (1969). *Cross-cultural studies.* Harmond & Worth, England: Penguin.

Prior, M. (1986). Temperament in Australian, American, Chinese and Greek infants. *Journal of Cross-Cultural Psychology, 17*(4), 455–474.

Pruitt, D., & Rubin, J. (1986). Social conflict: Escalation, stalemate, and settlement. New York: Random House.

Pryor, J., Giedd, J., & Williams, K. (1995). A social psychological model for predicting sexual harassment. *Journal of Social Issues, 51*(1), 69–84.

Punamaki, R. L., & Joustie, M. (1998). The role of culture, violence, and personal factors affecting dream content. *Journal of Cross-Cultural Psychology, 29*(2), 320–342.

Punetha, D., Giles, H., & Young, L. (1987). Ethnicity and immigrant values: Religion and language choice. *Journal of Language and Social Psychology, 6,* 229–241.

Pye, L. W. (1982). *Chinese commercial negotiating style.* Cambridge, MA: Oelgeschlager, Gunn & Hain.

Raden, D. (1994). Are symbolic racism and traditional prejudice part of a contemporary authoritarian attitude syndrome? *Political Behavior, 16*(3), 365–381.

Radford, M., Nakane, Y., Ohta, Y., Mann, L., & Kalucu, R. (1991). Decision making in clinically depressed patients: A transcultural social psychological study. *Journal of Nervous and Mental Disease, 179,* 711–719.

Ramirez, M., Castaneda, A., & Herold, L. (1974). The relationship of acculturation to cognitive style among Mexican Americans. *Journal of Cross-Cultural Psychology, 5*(4), 424–437.

Ramon, S. (1972). The impact of culture change on schizophrenia in Israel. *Journal of Cross-Cultural Psychology, 3*(4), 373–382.

Rathus, S., Nevid, J., & Fischer-Rathus, L. (1993). *Human sexuality in a world of diversity.* Boston: Allyn & Bacon.

Raven, B., & Rubin, J. (1968). *Social psychology.* New York: Wiley.

Ray, V. F. (1952). Techniques and problems in the study of human color perception. *South Western Journal of Anthropology, 8,* 201–219.

Raybeck, D., & Herrmann, D. (1990). A cross-cultural examination of semantic relations. *Journal of Cross-Cultural Psychology, 21*(4), 452–473.

Reason, J., & Mycielska, K. (1982). *Absent-minded? The psychology of mental lapses and everyday errors*. Englewood Cliffs, NJ: Prentice-Hall.

Reid, T. (1998). Terror in capitol no surprise to world. *The Washington Post*, July 26, A21.

Reinish, J. (1979). Prenatal influences on cognitive abilities. In M. Wittig (Ed.), *Sex related differences in cognitive functioning*. New York: Academic Press.

Reinish, J. (1990). *The Kinsey institute new report on sex: What you must know to be sexually literate*. New York: St. Martin's Press.

Renshon, S. (1975a). Birth order and political socialization. In D. Schwartz & S. Schwartz (Eds.), *New directions in political socialization*. New York: The Free Press.

Renshon, S. (1975b). The role of personality development in political socialization. In D. Schwartz & S. Schwartz (Eds.), *New directions in political socialization*. New York: The Free Press.

Renshon, S. (1989). Psychological perspectives on theories of adult development and the political socialization of leaders. In R. Sigel (Ed.), *Political learning in adulthood: A sourcebook of theory and research*. Chicago: The University of Chicago Press.

Renshon, S. (1994). The psychology of Clinton presidency: First appraisals. *Political Psychology, 15*, 375–394.

Retschitzky, J., Bossel-Lagos, M., & Dasen, P. (Eds.). (1989). La recherche interculturelle *[Intercultural research]*. Paris: Harmatta'n.

Reuning, H., & Wortley, W. (1973). Psychological studies of the Bushmen. *Psychologia Africana, Monograph Supplement* No. 7.

Reveen, P. (1987–1988). Fantasizing under hypnosis: Some experimental evidence. *The Skeptical Inquirer, 12*, 181–183.

Rim, Y. (1963). Risk-taking and need for achievement. *Acta Psychologica, 21*, 108–115.

Rime, B., & Giovannini, D. (1986). The psychological patterns of reported emotional states. In K. R. Scherer, H. G. Wallbott, & A. B. Summerfield (Eds.), *Experiencing emotion: A cross- cultural study* (pp. 84–97). Cambridge: Cambridge University Press.

Ring, K. (1992). *The omega project: near death experiences, UFO encounters, and mind at large*. New York: Morrow.

Rivers, W. H. R. (1901). Vision. In A. Haddon (Ed.), *Psychology and physiology: Reports of the Cambridge anthropoligical exhibition to Torres straits* (Vol. 2, Pt. 1). Cambridge: Cambridge University Press.

Robins, L. (1986). Epidemiology of antisocial personality. In M. Weissman, P. Applebaum, & L. Roth (Eds.), *Social, epidemiologic, and legal psychiatry*. New York: Basic Books.

Rogoff, B. (1990). *Apprenticeship in thinking: Cognitive development in social context*. New York: Oxford University Press.

Rogoff, B., & Chavajay, P. (1995). What's become of research on the cultural basis of cognitive development? *American Psychologist, 50*(10), 859–877.

Rohier, I. (1975). A social-learning approach to political socialization. In D. Schwartz & S. Schwartz (Eds.), *New directions in political socialization*. New York: The Free Press.

Rokeach, M. (1973). *The nature of human values*. New York: Free Press

Roll, S. (1987). Dreams. In T. M. Abel, R. Metraux, & S. Roll (Eds.), *Psychotherapy and culture* (pp. 176–195). Albuquerque: University of New Mexico Press.

Roll, S., & Brenneis, C. B. (1975). Chicano and Anglo dreams of death. *Journal of Cross-Cultural Psychology, 6*(3), 377–385.

Roll, S., Rabold, K., & McArdle, L. (1976). Disclaimed activity in dreams of Chicanos and Anglos. *Journal of Cross-Cultural Psychology, 7*(3), 335–342.

Rosaldo, M. Z. (1980). *Knowledge and passion: Ilongot notions of self and social life*. Cambridge: Cambridge University press.

Roseman, I., Spindel, M., & Jose, P. (1990). Appraisals of emotion-eliciting events: Testing a theory of discrete emotions. *Journal of Personality and Social Psychology, 59*, 899–915.

Roseman, I. J. (1991). Appraisal determinants of discrete emotions. *Cognition and Emotion, 5*, 161–200.

Rosenau, N. (1975). The sources of children's political concepts: An application of Piaget's theory. In D. Schwartz & S. Schwartz (Eds.), *New directions in political socialization*. New York: The Free Press.

Rosenhan, D. L., & Seligman, M. E. P. (1995). *Abnormal psychology* (3rd ed.). New York: Norton.

Rosenthal, R., & Fode, K. (1963). The effect of experimental bias on the performance of the albino rat. *Behavioral Science, 8*, 183–189.

Rosenthal, R., & Jacobson, L. (1968). *Pygmalion in the classroom: Teacher expectation and pupils' intellectual development*. New York: Holt, Rinehart, & Winston.

Rosenzweig, M., Bennett, E., & Diamond, M. (1972). Brain changes in response to experience. *Scientific American, 226*, 22–29.

Ross, L. (1977). The intuitive psychologist and his shortcomings: Distortions in the attribution process. In L. Berkowitz (Ed.), *Advances in experimental social psychology* (Vol. 10). New York: Academic Press.

Ross, L. D., & Lepper, M. R. (1980). The perseverance of beliefs: Empirical and normative considerations. In R. A. Shweder (Ed.), *New directions for methodology of behavioral science: Fallible judgment in behavioral research*. San Francisco: Jossey-Bass.

Ross, L., Lepper, M. R., & Hubbard, M. (1975). Perseverance in self-perception and social perception: Biased attribution processes in the debriefing paradigm. *Journal of Personality and Social Psychology, 32*, 880–892.

Ross, M. W., Walinder, J., Lundstroem, B., & Thuwe, I. (1991). Cross-cultural approaches to transexualism: A comparison between Sweden and Australia. *Acta Psychiatrica, 63*, 75–82.

Rothbaum, F., & Tsang, B. Y.-P. (1998). Love songs in the United States and China. *Journal of Cross-Cultural Psychology, 29*(2), 306–319.

Rothblum, E. (1992). Women and weight: An international perspective. In U. Gielen, L. Adler, & N. Milgram (Eds.), *Psychology in international perspective.* Swets & Zeitlinger: Amsterdam.

Rotheram-Borus, M. J., & Petrie, K. (1996). Patterns of social expectations among Maori and European children in New Zealand. *Journal of Cross-Cultural Psychology, 27*(5), 576–597.

Rotter, J. (1966). Generalized expectations for internal vs. external control of reinforcement. *Psychological Monographs, 80*, 1–28.

Rowes, B. (1979). *The book of quotes.* New York: Dutton.

Rubenstein, J. (1987). A cross-cultural comparison of children's drawings of same- and mixed-sex peer interaction. *Journal of Cross-Cultural Psychology, 18*(2), 234–250.

Rushton, J. P. (1994). Sex and race differences in cranial capacity from International Labour Office Data. *Intelligence, 19*, 281–294.

Rushton, J. P. (1995). *Race, evolution, and behavior.* New Brunswick, NJ: Transaction.

Russell, C. (1995). Do you know what your kids are doing? *The Washington Post Health*, July, 10–12.

Russell, G., Fujino, D., Sue, S., Cheung, M.-K., & Snowden, L. (1996). The effects of therapist-client ethnic match in the assessment of mental health functioning. *Journal of Cross-Cultural Psychology, 27*(5), 598–615.

Russell, J. (1994). Is there universal recognition of emotion from facial expression? A review of cross-cultural studies. *Psychological Bulletin, 115*, 102–141.

Russell, J. A. (1991). Culture and the categorization of emotions. *Psychological Bulletin, 110*, 426–450.

Sadie, S. (1980). *The new grove dictionary of music and musicians* (Vol. 9). London: Macmillan.

Salili, E., Hwang, C. E., & Choi, N. F. (1989). Teachers' evaluative behavior: The relationship between teachers' comments and perceived ability in Hong Kong. *Journal of Cross-Cultural Psychology, 20*, 115–132.

Sanada, T., & Norbeck, E. (1975). Prophecy continues to fail. *Journal of Cross-Cultural Psychology, 6*(3), 331–341.

Saroop, S. (1999). *Indian American attitudes regarding arranged marriages in the United States.* (Unpublished manuscript).

Sartorius, N. (1992). Prognosis for schizophrenia in the Third World: A re-evaluation of cross-cultural research. A Commentary. *Culture, Medicine, and Psychiatry, 16*, 81–84.

Schachter, S., & Singer, J. (1962). Cognitive, social, and psychological determinants of emotional state. *Psychological Review, 69*, 379–399.

Scheepers, P., Felling, A., & Peters, J. (1992). Anomie, authoritarianism and ethnocentrism. *Politics and the Individual, 2*(1), 43–59.

Scherer, K. R. (1984). Toward a concept of "modal emotions." In P. Ekman & R. J. Davidson (Eds.), *The nature of emotion: Fundamental questions* (pp. 25–31). Oxford: Oxford University Press.

Scherer, K. R., & Wallbott, H. G. (1994). Evidence for universality and cultural variation of different emotional response patterning: *Journal of Personality and Social Psychology, 66*, 310–328.

Scherer, K. R., Wallbott, H. G., Matsumoto, D., & Kudoh, T. (1988). Emotional experience in cultural context: A comparison between Europe, Japan, and the United States. In K. R. Scherer (Ed.), *Faces of emotions* (pp. 5–30). Hillsdale, NJ: Erlbaum.

Schimmack, U. (1996). Cultural influences on the recognition of emotion by facial expressions: Individualistic or Caucasian cultures? *Journal of Cross-Cultural Psychology, 27*(2), 37–50.

Schlegel, A., & Barry, H. (1991). *Adolescence: An anthropological inquiry.* New York: Free Press.

Schlinger, H. D., Jr. (1996). How the human got its spots: A critical analysis of the just so stories of evolutionary psychology. *Skeptic, 4*(1), 68–76.

Schmidt, S., & Yeh, R.-S. (1992). The structure of leader influence. *Journal of Cross-Cultural Psychology, 23*(2), 251–264.

Schneider, F. (1970). Conforming behavior of black and white children. *Journal of Personality and Social Psychology, 16*, 466–471.

Schonpflug, U. (1990). Perceived decision-making influence in Turkish migrant workers' and German workers' families. *Journal of Cross-Cultural Psychology, 21*(3), 261–282.

Schubert, G. (1991a). Human vocalizations in agonistic political encounters. In G. Shubert & R. Masters (Eds.), *Primate politics.* Carbondale: Southern Illinois University Press.

Schubert, G. (1991b). *Sexual politics and political feminism.* Greenwich, CT: JAI Press.

Schubert, G., & R. Masters (Eds.). (1991). *Primate politics.* Carbondale: Southern Illinois University Press.

Schwanenflugel, P. J., & Rey, M. (1986). The relationship between category typicality and concept familiarity: Evidence from Spanish- and English-speaking monolinguals. *Memory & Cognition, 14*, 150–163.

Schwartz, D., & Manella, C. (1975). Popular music as an agency of political socialization: A study in popular culture and politics. In D. Schwartz & S. Schwartz (Eds.), *New directions in political socialization.* New York: The Free Press.

Schwartz, D., & Schwartz, S. (1975). *New directions in political socialization.* New York: The Free Press.

Schwartz, D., Garrison, J., & Alouf, J. (1975). Health, body images and political socialization. In D. Schwartz & S. Schwartz (Eds.), *New directions in political socialization.* New York: The Free Press.

Schwartz, J. (1998). Blacks absorb more nicotine, suffer greater smoking toll, studies say. *The Washington Post*, July 8, A3.

Schwartz, S. (1975). Patterns of cynicism: Differential political socialization among adolescence. In D.

Schwartz & S. Schwartz (Eds.), *New directions in political socialization.* New York: The Free Press.

Schwartz, S. (1994). Are there universal aspects in the structure and content of human values? *Journal of Social Issues, 50,* 19–45.

Scribner, S., & Cole, M. (1981). *The psychology of literacy.* Cambridge, MA: Harvard University Press.

Sears, D. (1988). Symbolic racism. In P. Katz & D. Taylor (Eds.), *Eliminating racism: Profiles in controversy.* New York: Plenum Press.

Sears, D. (1996). Presidential address: Reflections on the politics of multiculturalism in American society. *Political Psychology, 17*(3), 409–420.

Sears, D., Taylor, S., Peplau, L. A., & Freedman, J. (1995). *Social psychology.* Englewood Cliffs, NJ: Prentice-Hall.

Secherst, L., Fay, T. L., & Hafeez Zaidi, S. M. (1972). Problems of translation in cross-cultural studies, *Journal of Cross-Cultural Psychology, 3*(1), 41–56.

Secherst, L., Fay, T., Zaidi, H., & Flores, L. (1973). Attitudes toward mental disorder among college students in the United States, Pakistan, and the Philippines. *Journal of Cross-Cultural Psychology, 4*(3), 342–360.

Segall, M. H. (1984). More than we need to know about culture, but are afraid not to ask. *Journal of Cross-Cultural Psychology, 15,* 153 –162.

Segall, M. H. (1993). Cultural psychology: Reactions to some claims and assertions of dubious validity. *Cross-Cultural Psychology Bulletin, 27*(3), 2–4.

Segall, M. H., Campbell, D. T., & Herskovits, M. J. (1966). *The influence of culture on visual perception.* Indianapolis, IN: Bobbs-Merrill.

Segall, M. H., Dasen, P. R., Berry, J. W., & Poortinga, Y. H. (1990). *Human behavior in global perspective: An introduction to cross-cultural psychology.* New York: Pergamon.

Segall, M., Dasen, P., Berry, J., & Poortinga, Y. (1999). *Human Behavior in Global Perspective.* Boston: Allyn & Bacon.

Segall, M. H., Ember, C. R., & Ember, M. (1997). Aggression, crime, and warfare. In J. W. Berry, M. H. Segall, & C. Kagitcibasi (Eds.), *Handbook of cross-cultural psychology* (Vol. 3, 3rd ed., pp. 213–254). Needham Heights, MA: Allyn & Bacon.

Selye, H. (1976). *The stress of life.* New York: McGraw-Hill.

Semin, G., & Zwier, S. (1997). Social cognition. In J. Berry, M. Segall, & C. Kagitcibasi (Eds.), *Handbook of cross-cultural psychology* (Vol. 3, pp. 51–76). Needham Heights, MA: Allyn & Bacon.

Serpell, R. (1993). *The significance of schooling: Life journeys in an African society.* Cambridge: Cambridge University Press.

Shade, B. (1991). African American patterns of cognition. In R. Jones (Ed.), *Black psychology* (3rd ed., pp. 47–63). Berkeley, CA: Cobb & Henry.

Shade, B. (1992). Is there Afro-American cognitive style? An exploratory study. In K. H. Burlew, W. C. Banks, H. P. McAdoo, & D. A. ya Azibo (Eds.), *African American psychology* (246–259). Newbury Park: Sage.

Shapiro, R., Nacos, B., & Isernia, P. (Eds.). (2000).*Decision-making in the glass house.* Boulder: Rowman & Littlefield.

Shea, J. D. (1985). Studies of cognitive development in Papua New Guinea. *International Journal of Psychology, 20,* 33–61.

Shimizi, Y., & Kaplan, B. (1987). Postpartum depression in the United States. *Journal of Cross-Cultural Psychology, 18*(1), 15–30.

Shiraev, E. (1988). I semya v otvete (The family is responsible). In A. Sventsitsky (Ed.) *The power of discipline.* Leningrad: Lenizdat.

Shiraev, E. (1999). Attitudinal changes during the transition. In B. Glad & E. Shiraev (Eds.), *The Russian transformation* (pp. 155–166). New York: St. Martin's Press.

Shiraev, E. (2000). People say, advisers advise, and officials decide. In R. Shapiro, B. Nacos, & P. Isernia (Eds.), *Decision-making in the glass house.* Boulder: Rowman & Littlefield.

Shiraev, E., & Bastrykin, A. (1988). *Fashion, idols, and the self.* St. Petersburg: Lenizdat.

Shiraev, E., & Boyd, J. (2001). *The accent of success.* Englewood Cliffs, NJ: Prentice Hall.

Shiraev, E., & Danilov, S. (1999). Pop music as a mirror of the Russian transformation. In Shiraev, E. & Glad, B. (Eds.), *The Russian Transformation* (pp. 213–226). New York: St. Martin's Press.

Shiraev, E., & Danilov, S. (2001). *Fear of deportation.* (Forthcoming). Maryland: Lexington.

Shiraev, E., & Fillipov. A. (1990). Cross-cultural social perception. *St. Petersburg University Quarterly, 13,* 53–60.

Shiraev, E., & Tsytsarev, S. (1995). *Addictive behavior in addictive societies.* Paper delivered at the Annual Meeting of the International Society of Political Psychology, Washington, DC.

Shweder, R. A., & Sullivan, M. A. (1993). Cultural psychology: Who needs it? *Annual Review of Psychology, 44,* 497–527.

Shweder, R., Mahapatra, M., & Miller, J. (1990). Culture and moral development. In J. Stigler, R. Shweder, & G. Herdt (Eds.), *Cultural psychology* (pp. 130–204). New York: Cambridge University Press.

Sidanius, J., & Pratto, F. (1993). Racism and support of free-market capitalism: A cross-cultural analysis. *Political Psychology, 14*(3), 381– 401.

Sidanius, J., Pratto, F., & Bobo, L. (1994). Social dominance orientation and the political psychology of gender: A case of invariance? *Journal of Personality and Social Psychology, 67,* 998–1011.

Sifneos, P. (1973). The prevalence of alexithymic characteristics in psychosomatic patients. *Psychotherapy and Psychosomatics, 22,* 255–262.

Sigel, R. (1970). *Learning about politics.* New York: Random House.

Sigel, R. (1989). Introduction: Persistence and change. In R. Sigel (Ed.), *Political learning in adulthood: A sourcebook of theory and research.* Chicago: University of Chicago Press.

Sigel, R., & Reynolds, J. (1979–1980). Generational differences and the women's movement. *Political Science Quarterly, 94,* 635–648.

Simmons, C., vomKolke, A., & Shimizu, H. (1986). Attitudes toward romantic love among American, German, and Japanese students. *Journal of Social Psychology, 126,* 327–336.

Simon, H. (1983). *Reason in human affairs.* Stanford: Stanford University Press.

Simonton, D. (1987). Developmental antecedents of achieved eminence. *Annals of Child Development, 5,* 131–169.

Singer, K. (1975). Depressive disorders from a transcultural perspective. *Social Science and Medicine, 9,* 289–301.

Sinha, D., & Shukla, P. (1974). Deprivation and development of skill for pictorial depth perception. *Journal of Cross-Cultural Psychology, 5*(4), 434–445.

Sinha, J., & Verma, J. (1983). Perceptual structuring of dyadic interactions. *Journal of Cross-Cultural Psychology, 14,* 187–199.

Skjele, H. (1991). The rhetoric of difference: On women's inclusion into political elites. *Politics and Society, 19*(2), 233–263.

Skrypnek, B. J., & Snyder, M. (1982). On the self-perpetuating nature of stereotypes about women and men. *Journal of Experimental Social Psychology, 18,* 277–291.

Slovic, P. (1987). Perception of risk. *Science, 236,* 280–285.

Smith, C. A., & Ellsworth, P. C. (1985). Emotions and anthropology: The logic of emotional world view. *Inquiry, 21,* 181–199.

Smith, H. (1976). *The Russians.* New York: Quadrangle.

Smith, H. (1991). *The world's religions.* San Francisco: Harper.

Smith, M. B. (1978). Psychology and values. *Journal of Social Issues, 34,* 181–199.

Smith, P., & Schwartz, S. (1997). Values. In J. Berry, M. Segall, & C. Kagitcibasi (Eds.), *Handbook of cross-cultural psychology* (Vol. 3, pp. 77–118). Needham Heights, MA: Allyn & Bacon.

Smith, P. B., & Bond, M. H. (1993). *Social psychology across cultures: Analysis and perspectives.* Hemel Hempstead, England: Harvester/ Wheatsheaf.

Snacken, J. (1991). Guide pour le pratique dans un contexte multiculturel et interdisciplinaire. In J. Leman & A. Gailly (Eds.), *Therapies interculturelles* (pp. 135–140). Bruxelles, Belgium: Editions Universitaires, De Boeck Universite.

Snarey, J. (1985). Cross-cultural universality of social-moral development: A critical review of Kohlbergian research. *Psychological Bulletin, 97,* 202–232.

Sniderman, P., Tetlock, P., & Peterson, R. (1993). Racism and liberal democracy. *Politics and the Individual, 3,* 1–28.

Snyder, C. R., Shenkel, R. J., & Lowery, C. R. (1977). Acceptance of personality interpretations: The "Barnum Effect" and beyond. *Journal of Consulting and Clinical Psychology, 45*(1), 104–114.

Snyder, M. (1984). When belief becomes reality. In L. Berkowitz (Ed.), *Advances in experimental social psychology* (Vol. 18). New York: Academic Press.

Snyder, M., & Swann, W. B., Jr. (1978). Behavioral confirmation in social interaction: From social perception to social reality. *Journal of Experimental Social Psychology, 14,* 148–162.

Snyder, M., Tanke, E. D., & Berscheid, E. (1977). Social perception and interpersonal behavior: On the self-fulfilling nature of social stereotypes. *Journal of Personality and Social Psychology, 35,* 656–666.

Snyderman, M., & Rothman, S. (1988). The IQ controversy: The media and public policy. New Brunswick, NJ: Transaction Books.

Solomon, R. S. (1978). Emotions and anthropology: The logic of emotional world views. *Inquiry, 21,* 181–199.

Spanos, N. (1987-1988). Past-life hypnotic regression: A critical view. *The Skeptical Inquirer, 12,* 174–180.

Spearman, C. E. (1927). *The abilities of man.* London: Macmillan.

Spencer, H. (1954). *Social statistics.* New York: Schalkenbach.

Spiro, M., & Swartz, L. (1994). Mother's reports of behavior problems in three groups of South African preschool children. *Journal of Cross-Cultural Psychology, 25*(3), 339–352.

Staephan, W., Stephan, C. W., & De Vargas, M. C. (1996). Emotional expression in Costa Rica and the United States. *Journal of Cross-Cultural Psychology, 27*(2), 147–160.

Stanley, L. (1993). Boys and girls who reason well mathematically. In G. N. Bock & K. Ackrill (Eds.), *The origins and development of high ability.* Chichester, England: Wiley.

Staub, E. (1996). Cultural-societal roots of violence: The examples of genocidal violence and of contemporary youth violence in the United States. *American Psychologist, 51*(2), 117–132.

Steckenrider, J., & Cutler, N. (1989). Aging and adult political socialization: The importance of roles in transitions. In R. Sigel (Ed.), *Political learning in adulthood: A sourcebook of theory and research.* Chicago: University of Chicago Press.

Steffensen, M., & Calker, L. (1982). Intercultural misunderstandings about health care: Recall of descriptions of illness and treatments. *Social Science and Medicine, 16,* 1949–1954.

Stein, M. (1991). On the socio-historical context of creativity programs. *Creativity Research Journal, 4,* 294–300.

Stemberg, R. (1995). In search of the human mind. Fort Worth, TX: Harcourt-Brace.

Stephan, C. W., Stephan, W., Saito, I., & Barnett, S. (1998). Emotional expression in Japan and the United States: The nonmonolithic nature of individualism and collectivism. *Journal of Cross-Cultural Psychology, 29*(6), 728–748.

Sternberg, R. (1985). *Beyond IQ: A triarchic theory of human intelligence.* New York: Cambridge University Press.

Sternberg, R. (1997). The concept of intelligence and its role in lifelong learning and success. *American Psychologist, 52*(10), 1030–1037.

Stevenson, H. W., Lee, S. Y., & Stigler, J. W. (1986). Mathematics achievement of Chinese, Japanese and American children. *Science, 231,* 693–699.

Stevenson, H., Lee, S. Y., Chen, C., Lummis, M., Stigler, J., Fan, L., & Ge, R. (1990). Mathematical achievement of children in China and the United States. *Child Development, 61,* 1053–1066.

Stipek, D. (1998). Differences between Americans and Chinese in the circumstances evoking pride, shame, and guilt. *Journal of Cross-Cultural Psychology, 29*(5), 616–629.

Strong, B., DeVault, C., & Sayad, B. (1998). *The marriage and family experience.* Belmont, CA: ITP.

Stronschneider, S., & Guss, D. (1998). Planning and problem solving: Differences between Brazilian and German students. *Journal of Cross-Cultural Psychology, 29*(6), 695–716.

Sue, S., & Okazaki, S. (1990). Asian American educational achievements: A phenomenon in search of an explanation. *American Psychologist, 45,* 913–920.

Sue, S., Fujino, D., Hu, L., Takeuchi, D., & Zane, N. (1991). Community mental health services for ethnic minority groups. *Journal of Counseling and Clinical Psychology, 59,* 533–540.

Sullivan, H. S. (1954). *The psychiatric interview.* New York: Norton.

Sullivan, H. S. (1962). *Schizophrenia as a human process.* New York: Norton.

Summer, W. (1970). *What social classes owe to each other.* Caldwell, ID: Caxton.

Sumner, W. (1906). *Folkways.* Boston: Ginn and Co.

Sunar, D. (1982). Female stereotypes in the United States and Turkey. *Journal of Cross-Cultural Psychology, 13*(4), 445–460.

Super, C., & Harkness, S. (1997). The cultural structuring of child development. In J. W. Berry, P. R. Dasen, & T. S. Saraswathi (Eds.), *Handbook of cross-cultural psychology: Basic processes and human development* (Vol. 2, pp. 1–41). Needham Heights, MA: Allyn & Bacon.

Suzuki, L., & Valencia, R. (1997). Race-ethnicity and measured intelligence: Educational implications. *American Psychologist, 52*(10), 1103–1114.

Sventsitsky, A. (Ed.). (1988). *Avtoritet distsipliny [The Power of discipline].* Leningrad: Lenizdat.

Swenson, L. C. (1993). *Psychology and law.* Pacific Grove, CA: Brooks/Cole.

Sycheva, V. (1994). Impoverishment of the "people's masses" of Russia. *Sotsiologitheski Zhurnal, 1,* 66–69.

Symons, D. (1979). *The evolution of human sexuality.* New York: Oxford University Press.

Tafarodi, R., & Swann, W. (1996). Individualism-collectivism and global self-esteem: Evidence for a cultural trade-off. *Journal of Cross-Cultural Psychology, 27,* 651–672.

Tajfel, H. (Ed.). (1982). *Social Identity and Intergroup Relations.* Cambridge: Cambridge University Press.

Tajfel, H. (Ed.). (1984). *The social dimension: European developments in social psychology* (Vol. 2). London: Cambridge University Press.

Takano, Y., & Noda, A. (1993). A temporary decline of thinking ability during foreign language processing. *Journal of Cross-Cultural Psychology, 24*(4), 445–462.

Tanaka-Matsui, J. (1989). The cultural difference model and applied behavior analysis in the design of early childhood intervention. In L. L. Adler (Ed.), *Cross-cultural research in human development: Lifespan perspectives* (pp. 37–46). New York: Praeger.

Tanaka-Matsumi, J. (1995). Cross-cultural perspectives on anger. In H. Kassinove (Ed.), *Anger disorders: Definition, diagnosis, and treatment.* Washington, DC: Taylor and Francis.

Tanaka-Matsumi, J., & Draguns, J. (1997). Culture and psychopathology. In J. W. Berry, M. H. Segall, & C. Kagitcibasi (Eds.), *Handbook of cross-cultural psychology.* (Vol. 3, pp. 449–491). Needham Heights, MA: Allyn & Bacon.

Tanaka-Matsumi, J., & Marsella, A. (1976). Cross-cultural variations in the phenomenological experience of depression. *Journal of Cross-Cultural Psychology, 7*(4), 379–390.

Tarde, G. (1903). *The Laws of imitation.* New York: Holt, Rinehart & Winston.

Taub, J. (1971). The sleep-wakefulness cycle in Mexican adults. *Journal of Cross-Cultural Psychology, 2*(4), 353–362.

Taylor, D., & Simard, L. (1972). The role of bilingualism in cross-cultural communication. *Journal of Cross-Cultural Psychology, 3*(1), 101–108.

Taylor, L., & deLacey, P. R. (1974). Three dimensions of intellectual functioning in Australian Aboriginal and disadvantaged European children. *Journal of Cross-Cultural Psychology, 5*(1), 49–55.

Taylor, S. E., & Crocker, J. (1981). Schematic bases of social information processing. In E. T. Higgins, C. P. Herman, & M. P. Zanna (Eds.), *Social cognition: The Ontario symposium* (Vol. 1, pp. 89–134). Hillsdale, NJ: Erlbaum.

Taylor, S. E., & Fiske, S. T. (1975). Point of view and perceptions of causality. *Journal of Personality and Social Psychology, 32,* 439–445.

Taylor, S. E., Peplau, L. A., & Sears, D. O. (1994). *Social psychology* (8th ed.). Englewood Cliffs, NJ: Prentice-Hall.

Tedlock, B. (1987). Dreaming and dreamer research. In B. Tedlock (Ed.), *Dreaming: Anthropological and psychological interpretations.* Cambridge: Cambridge University Press.

Theroux, E., Kaplan, F., Semler, E., & Speransky, H. (1991). *The Harper Collins business guide to Moscow.* New York: Harper & Row.

Thomas, A., & Chess, S. (1977). *Temperament and development.* New York: Brunner/Mazel.

Thorton, A., & Freedman, D. (1979). Changes in sex role attitudes of women, 1962–1977: Evidence from a panel study. *American Sociological Review, 44,* 831–842.

Thouless, R. H. (1932). A racial difference in perception. *Journal of Social Psychology, 4*, 330–339.

Thurstone, E. L. (1938). *Primary mental abilities.* Chicago: University of Chicago Press.

Tietelbaum, S., & Geiselman, E. (1997). Observer mood and cross-racial recognition of faces. *Journal of Cross-Cultural Psychology, 28*(1), 93–106.

Ting-Toomey, S. (1985). Toward a theory of conflict and culture. *International and Intercultural Communication Annual, 9*, 71–86.

Tobacyk, J. J. (1992). Changes in locus of control beliefs in Polish university students before and after democratization. *Journal of Cross-Cultural Psychology, 13*(2), 217–222.

Tobacyk, J., & Tobacyk, Z. (1992). Comparisons of belief-based personality constructions in Polish and American university students. *Journal of Cross-Cultural Psychology, 23*(3), 311–325.

Tomkins, S. S. (1962). *Affect, imagery, consciousness, Vol. 1, The positive affects.* New York: Springer-Verlag.

Triandis, H. (1989). The self and social behavior in different social contexts. *Psychological Review, 96*, 506–520.

Triandis, H. (1990). Cross-cultural studies of individualism-collectivism. In J. Berman (Ed.), *Nebraska Symposium on Motivation 1989.* Lincoln: Nebraska University Press.

Triandis, H. (1994). *Culture and social behavior.* New York: McGraw-Hill.

Triandis, H. C. (1995). *Individualism and collectivism.* Boulder, CO: Westview.

Triandis, H. C. (1996). The psychological measurement of cultural syndromes. *American Psychologist, 51*(4), 407–415.

Triandis, H. C., & Brislin, R. (1984). Cross-cultural psychology. *American Psychologist, 39*, 1006–1016.

Triandis, H. C., Lambert, W. W., Berry, J. W., Lonner, W. T., Heron, A., Brislin, R., & Draguns, J. (Eds.). (1980). *Handbook of cross-cultural psychology* (Vols. 1–6). Boston: Allyn & Bacon.

Tripp, R. T. (1970). *The international thesaurus of quotations.* New York: T. Crowell.

Tsai, J., & Levenson, R. (1997). Cultural influences on emotional responding: Chinese American and European American dating couples during interpersonal conflict. *Journal of Cross-Cultural Psychology, 28*(5), 600–625.

Tsytsarev, S. (1997). Pathological anger in "crimes of passion." *Security Journal, 9*, 203–204.

Tuch, S., & Sigelman, L. (1997). Race, class, and black-white differences in social policy views. In B. Norrander & C. Wilcox (Eds.), *Understanding Public Opinion.* Washington DC: CQ Press.

Tung, M. P. M. (1994). Symbolic meanings of the body in Chinese culture and "somatization." *Culture, Medicine and Psychiatry, 18*, 483–492.

Turner, F. (Ed.). (1992). *Social mobility and political attitudes: Comparative perspectives.* New Brunswick, NJ: Transaction Publishers.

Tutty, L., Rothery, M., & Grinnell, R. (1996). Qualitative research for social work. Boston: Allyn & Bacon.

Tversky, A., & Kahneman, D. (1973). Availability: A heuristic for judging frequency and probability. *Cognitive Psychology, 5*, 207–232.

Tversky, A., & Kahneman, D. (1974). Judgment under uncertainty: Heuristics and biases. *Science, 185*, 1124–1131.

Tversky, A., & Kahneman, D. (1982). Judgments of and by representativeness. In D. Kahneman, P. Slovic, & A. Tversky (Eds.), Judgment under uncertainty: Heuristics and biases. New York: Cambridge University Press.

Tylor, E. (1871). *Primitive cultures.* London: Murray.

Ullman, M., & Zimmerman N. (1979). *Working with Dreams.* New York: Delacorte Press/Eleanor Friede.

Ulusahin, A., Basoglu, M., & Paykel, E. S. (1994). A cross-cultural comparative study of depressive symptoms in British and Turkish clinical samples. *Social Psychiatry and Psychiatric Epidimeology, 29*, 31–39.

Unger, R. K. (1983). Through the looking glass: No wonderland yet! (The reciprocal relationship between methodology and models of reality). *Psychology of Women Quarterly, 8*, 9–32.

Updike, J. (1994). *Brazil.* New York: Fawcett Crest.

U.S. Bureau of the Census (1997, March). *Current population survey.* Washington, DC: U.S. Department of Commerce.

Valliant, G. (1966). Parent-child cultural disparity and drug addiction. *Journal of Nervous and Mental Diseases, 142*, 534–539.

Valsiner, J., & Lawrence, J. (1997). Human development in culture across the life span. In J. W. Berry, P. R. Dasen, & T. S. Saraswathi (Eds.), *Handbook of cross-cultural psychology: Basic processes and human development* (Vol. 2, pp. 69–106). Needham Heights, MA: Allyn & Bacon.

Van Bezooijen, C., Otto, S., & Heenan, T. (1983). Recognition of vocal expression of emotion: A three-nation study to identify universal characteristics. *Journal of Cross-Cultural Psychology, 14*(4), 387–406.

van de Vijver, F., & Willemsen, M. E. (1993). Abstract thinking. In J. Altarriba (Ed.), *Cognition and culture: A cross-cultural approach to cognitive psychology* (pp. 317–342). Amsterdam: Elsevier Science.

van de Vijver, F. J. R., & Leung, K. (1997a). *Methods and data analysis for cross-cultural research.* Thousand Oaks, CA: Sage.

van de Vijver, F. J. R., & Leung, K. (1997b). Methods and data analysis of comparative research. In J. W. Berry, Y. H. Poortinga, & J. Pandey (Eds.), *Handbook of cross-cultural psychology.* (Vol. 1, pp. 257–300). Needham Heights, MA: Allyn & Bacon.

Van den Berghe, P. (1978). *Race and racism.* New York: Wiley.

Van Ijzendoorn, M. H., & Kroonenberg, P. M. (1988). Cross-cultural patterns of attachment: A meta-analysis of the strange situation. *Child Development, 59*, 147–156.

Vassiliou, V., & Vassiliou, G. (1973). The implicative meaning of the greek concept of philomoto. *Journal of Cross-Cultural Psychology, 4*(3), 326–341.

Vekker, L. (1978). *Psikhicheskie protsessy [Psychological processes]* (Vol. 2). Leningrad: Leningrad State University Press.

Vereijken, C., Riksen-Walraven, J. M., & Van Lieshout, C. (1997). Mother-infant relationships in Japan: Attachment, dependency, and amae. *Journal of Cross-Cultural Psychology, 28*(4), 442–462.

Vernon, P. (1969). *Intelligence and cultural environment.* London: Methuen.

Vick, K. (1998). Marriage or grade school? *The Washington Post,* July 1, A1.

Vidmar, N. (1970). Group composition and the risky shift. *Journal of Experimental Social Psychology, 6,* 153–166.

Vincent, K. (1991). Black/white IQ differences: Does age make the difference? *Journal of Clinical Psychology, 47,* 266–270.

Vokey, J. R., & Read, J. D. (1985). Subliminal messages: Between the devil and the media. *American Psychologist, 40,* 1231–1239.

Volkan, V. (1988). The need to have enemies and allies. Northvale, NJ: Jason Aronson.

Vrij, A., & Winkel, F. (1994). Perceptual distortions in cross-cultural interrogations. *Journal of Cross-Cultural Psychology, 25*(2), 284–295.

Vygotsky, L. (1932/1978). *Mind and society.* Cambridge, MA: Harvard University Press.

Wade, C., & Tavris, C. (1993). *Critical and creative thinking: The case of love and war.* New York: Harper Collins.

Wade, C., & Tavris, C. (1996). *Psychology.* New York: Harper Collins.

Walker, B. (1993). *The art of the Turkish tale.* Lubbock, TX: Texas Tech University Press.

Walkey, F., & Chung, R. C.-Y. (1996). An examination of stereotypes of Chinese and Europeans held by some New Zealand secondary school pupils. *Journal of Cross-Cultural Psychology, 27*(3), 283–292.

Wallbott, H. G., & Scherer, K. R. (1986). How universal and specific is emotional experience? Evidence from 27 countries on five continents. *Social Science Information, 25,* 763–795.

Wallis, C. (1965). *The treasure chest.* New York: Harper and Row.

Walt, V. (1998). Village by village, circumcising a ritual. *The Washington Post,* June 7, C1–2.

Wang, C.-H., Liu, W., Zhang, M.-Y., Yu, E. S., Xia, Z.-Y., Fernandes, M., Lung, C.-T., Xu, C.-L., & Qu, G.-Y. (1992). Alcohol use, abuse, and dependency in Shanghai. In J. E. Helzer & G. J. Canino (Eds.), *Alcoholism in North America, Europe, and Asia* (pp. 264–288). New York: Oxford University Press.

Ward, C. (1994). Culture and altered states of consciousness. In W. Lonner & R. Malpass (Eds.), *Psychology and culture.* Boston: Allyn & Bacon.

Warner, R. (1994). *Recovery from schizophrenia: Psychiatry and political economy,* (2nd ed.). New York: Routledge.

Wasserman, D. (1966). Man of La Mancha. New York: Random House.

Wassmann, J. (1993). When actions speak louder than words: The classification of food among the Yupno of Papua-New Guinea. *Newsletter of the Laboratory of Comparative Human Cognition, 15,* 30–40.

Wassmann, J., & Dasen, R. R. (1994). "Hot" and "Cold": Classification and sorting among the Yupno of Papua-New Guinea. *International Journal of Psychology, 29,* 19–38.

Watt, G. (1990). Reexamining factors predicting Afro-American and white American women's age at first coitus. *Archives of Sexual Behavior, 18,* 271–298.

Weber, M. (1922/1968). Economy and society: An outline of interpretive sociology. New York: Bedminster Press.

Wechsler, D. (1958). *The measurement and appraisal of adult intelligence.* Baltimore: Williams & Wilkins.

Weigel, R., Loomis, J., & Soja, M. (1980). Race relations on prime time television. *Journal of Personality and Social Psychology, 30,* 724–728.

Weiner, B. (1980). A cognitive (attribution)-emotion-action model of motivated behavior: An analysis of judgment of help-giving. *Journal of Personality and Social Psychology, 39,* 186–200.

Weinstein, L. B. (1989). Transcultural relocation: Adaptation of older Americans to Israel. *Activities, Adaptation & Aging, 13,* 33–42.

Weisfeld, G. E., Muczenski, D. M., Weisfeld, C. C., & Omark, D. R. (1987). Stability of boy's social success among peers over an eleven-year period. In J. A. Meacham (Ed.), *Contributions to human development* (Vol. 18, pp. 55–80). Basel, Switzerland: Karger.

Weiss, B. (1992). Some consequences of early harsh discipline: Child aggression and a maladaptive social information processing style. *Child Development, 63,* 1321–1335.

Weiss, R. (1999). Scientists add a gene, and intelligence soars. *The Washington Post,* September 2, A1.

Weissman, M. M., Bland, R. C., Canino, G., Greenwald, S., Hwu, H., Lee, C. K., Newman, S. C., Oakley-Browne, M., Rubio-Stipec, M., Wickramaratne, P. J., Wittchen, H., & Yeh, E. (1994). The cross-national epidemiology of obsessive-compulsive disorder. *Journal of Clinical Psychiatry, 55,* 5–10.

Weissner, T. S., Gallimore, R., & Jordan, C. (1988). Unpacking cultural effects on classroom learning: Native Hawaiian peer assistance and child-generated activity. *Anthropology and Education Quarterly, 19,* 327–351.

Weisz, J., Suwanlert, S., Chaiyasit, W., & Walter, B. (1987). Over and undercontrolled referral problems among children and adolescents from Thailand and the United States. *Journal of Counseling and Clinical Psychology, 55,* 719–726.

Weisz, J. R., Rothbaum, F. M., & Blackburn, T. C. (1984). Standing out and standing in: The psychology of control in America and Japan. *American Psychologist, 39,* 955–969.

Welch, S., & Sigelman, L. (1991). Changes in public attitudes toward women in politics. *Social Science Quarterly, 31,* 312–321.

Werner, E. (1972). Infants around the world: Cross-cultural studies of psychomotor development from birth to two years. *Journal of Cross-Cultural Psychology, 3*(2), 111–134.

Westen, D. (1996). *Psychology: Mind, brain, and culture.* New York: Wiley.

Whethrick, N. E., & Deregowski, J. B. (1982). Immediate recall: Its structure in three different language communities. *Journal of Cross-Cultural Psychology, 13*(2), 210–216.

White, K. (1982). The relation between socioeconomic status and academic achievement. *Psychological Bulletin, 91,* 461–481.

White, G. M. (1994). Affecting culture: Emotion and morality in everyday life. In S. Kitayama & H. Markus (Eds.), *Emotion and culture: Empirical studies of mutual influence* (pp. 219–239). Washington, DC: American Psychological Association.

White, M. (1993). *The material child: Coming of age in Japan and America.* New York: Free Press.

Whiting, B. B., & Edwards, C. P. (1988). *Children of different worlds: The formation of social behavior.* Cambridge, MA: Harvard University Press.

Whiting, B. B., & Whiting, J. W. M. (1975). *The children of six cultures: A psycho-cultural analysis.* Cambridge, MA: Harvard University Press.

Whiting, J. W. M., & Child, I. L. (1953). *Child training and personality: A cross-cultural study.* New Haven, CT: Yale University Press.

Whittaker, J., & Whittaker, S. (1972). A cross-cultural study of geocentrism. *Journal of Cross-Cultural Psychology, 3*(4), 417–421.

WHO (1999). *World health day: Active aging makes the difference,* April 7, http://www.who.int/whday/en/pages1999/whd99_3.html

Wible, D., & Hui, C. H. (1985). Perceived language proficiency and person perception. *Journal of Cross-Cultural Psychology, 16*(2), 206–222.

Wilbanks, W. (1987). The myth of a racist criminal justice system. *Criminal Justice Research Bulletin, 3,* 5.

Wilbanks, W. (1994). The myth of a racist criminal justice system. In R. Monk (Ed.), *Taking sides. Clashing views on controversial issues in race and ethnicity.* Guitford, CT: The Dushkin Publishing Group.

Wilder, D. (1981). Perceiving persons as a group: Categorization and intergroup relations. In D. Hamilton, (Ed.), *Cognitive processes in stereotyping and intergroup behavior.* Hillsdale, NJ: Erlbaum.

Williams, J. E., & Best, D. (1982). *Measuring sex stereotypes: A thirty-nation study.* Beverly Hills, CA: Sage.

Williams, J. E., & Best, D. (1990). *Sex and psyche: Gender and self viewed cross-culturally.* London: Sage.

Williams, R., & Mitchell, H. (1991). The testing game. In R. Jones (Ed.), *Black psychology* (3rd ed., pp. 193-206). Berkeley: Cobb & Henry.

Williams, W., & Ceci, S. (1997). Are Americans becoming more or less alike? Trends in race, class, and ability differences in intelligence. *American Psychologist, 52*(11), 1226–1235.

Wills, M. G. (1992). Learning styles of African American children: A review of the literature and interventions. *African American Psychology* (pp. 260–278). Newbury Park, CA: Sage.

Wispe, L. G., & Drambarean, N. C. (1993). Physiological need, word frequency, and visual duration threshold. *Journal of Experimental Physiology, 46,* 25–31.

Wittmer, J. (1971). Perceived parent-child relationships: A comparison between Amish and non-Amish young adults. *Journal of Cross-Cultural Psychology, 2*(1), 87–94.

Wolf, F. M. (1986). *Meta-analysis: Quantitative methods for research synthesis.* Newbury Park, CA: Sage.

Worchel, S. (1974). Societal restrictiveness and the presence of outlets for the release of aggression. *Journal of Cross-Cultural Psychology, 5*(1), 109–119.

Word, C. H., Zanna, M. P., & Cooper, J. (1974). The nonverbal mediation of self-fulfilling prophecies in inter-racial interaction. *Journal of Experimental Social Psychology, 10,* 109–120.

The world fact book (1998). Washington, DC: CIA.

World Health Organization. (1946). *Constitution.* New York: World Health Organization Interim Commission.

World Health Organization. (1979). *Schizophrenia: An international follow-up study.* Geneva: WHO.

World Health Organization. (1983). *Depressive disorders in different cultures.* Geneva: WHO.

World Health Organization. (1996). Data on Smoking. *The Washington Post,* November 19. A1.

Wright, G., Phillips, L., Whalley, P., Choo, G., Tan, I., & Wishuda, A. (1978). Cultural differences in probabilistic thinking. *Journal of Cross-Cultural Psychology, 9*(3), 285–297.

Wright, R. (1994). *The moral animal: The new science of evolutionary psychology.* New York: Vintage.

Wright, S., Horn, S., & Sanders, W. (1997). Teacher and classroom context effects on student achievement: Implications for teacher evaluation. *Journal of Personnel Evaluation in Education, 11,* 57–67

Wundt, W. (1908). *Logik: Logik der Geisteswissenschaften [Logic: Logic of the Humanities]* (Vol. 3). Stuttgart, Germany: Enke.

Wundt, W. (1913). *Elemente de Völkerpsychologie.* Leipzig: Alfred Kroner Verlag.

Xiang, P., Lee, A., & Solomon, M. (1997). Achievement goals and their correlates among American and Chinese students in physical education: A cross-cultural analysis. *Journal of Cross-Cultural Psychology, 28*(6), 645–660.

Yadov, V. (1978). *K voprosy o dispozitsionnoi regulatsii socialnogo povedevia lichnosti [To the question of the dispositional regulation of the social behavior of the individual].* Leningrad: Academy of Sciences.

Yamaguchi, H. (1988). Effects of actor's and observer's roles on causal attribution by Japanese subjects for success and failure in competitive situations. *Psychological Reports, 63,* 619–626.

Yang, K. (1986). Chinese personality and its change. In M. Bond (Ed.), *The psychology of the Chinese people.* Hong Kong: Oxford University Press.

Yaroshevski, V. (1975). *Istoriya psychologii [A history of psychology].* Moscow: Prosveshenie.

Yerkes, R. (1911). *Introduction to psychology.* New York: Holt.

Yu, A., & Bain, B. (1985). *Language, social class and cognitive style: A comparative study of unilingual and bilingual education in Hong Kong and Alberta.* Hong Kong: Hong Kong Teacher's Association Press.

Yu, L. C. (1993). Intergenerational transfer of resources within policy and cultural contexts. In S. H. Zarit, L. I. Pearlin, & K. W. Schaie (Eds.), *Caregiving systems.* Hillsdale, NJ: Erlbaum.

Zajonc, R. B. (1965). Social facilitation. *Science, 149,* 269–274.

Zajonc, R. (1968). The attitudinal effect of mere exposure. *Journal of Personality and Social Psychology, Monograph Supplement, 9,* 1–27.

Zajonc, R. (1980). Feeling and thinking: Preferences need no inferences. *American Psychologist, 35,* 151–175.

Zajonc, R. B., & McIntosh, D. N. (1992). Emotion research: Some promising questions and some questionable promises. *Psychological Science, 3,* 70–74.

Zaller, J. (1992). *The nature and origins of mass opinion.* Cambridge: Cambridge University Press.

Za'rour, G. (1972). Superstitions among certain groups of Lebanese Arab students in Beirut. *Journal of Cross-Cultural Psychology, 3*(3), 273–282.

Zendal, I., Pihl, R., & Seidman, B. (1987). The effects of learning sets on torque. *Journal of Clinical Psychology, 43,* 272–275.

Zepeda, M. (1985). Mother-infant behavior in Mexican and Mexican-American women: A study of the relationship of selected prenatal, perinatal and postnatal events. *Dissertation Abstracts International, 45*(9–A), 2756.

Zhang, J., & Bond, M. H. (1998). Personality and filial piety among college students in two Chinese societies. *Journal of Cross-Cultural Psychology, 29*(3), 402–417.

Zheng, R., & Stimpson, D. (1990). A cross-cultural study of entrepreneurial attitude orientation. *Information on Psychological Sciences,* 23–25.

Zimbardo, P. (1997). What messages are behind today's cults? *APA Monitor,* May 1977, 14

Ziv, A., Shani, A., & Nebenhaus, S. (1975). Adolescents educated in Israel and in the Soviet Union. *Journal of Cross-Cultural Psychology, 6*(1), 108–121.

Zung, W. (1972). A cross-cultural survey of depressive symptomatology in normal adults. *Journal of Cross-Cultural Psychology, 3*(2), 177–183.

Author Index

Subject Index